Celebrating Life Customs around the World

Celebrating Life Customs around the World

From Baby Showers to Funerals

Volume 2

Adolescence and Early Adulthood

VICTORIA WILLIAMS

ABC-CLIO

An Imprint of ABC-CLIO, LLC
Santa Barbara, California • Denver, Colorado

Copyright © 2017 by ABC-CLIO, LLC

All rights reserved. No part of this publication may be reproduced, stored in a retrieval system, or transmitted, in any form or by any means, electronic, mechanical, photocopying, recording, or otherwise, except for the inclusion of brief quotations in a review, without prior permission in writing from the publisher.

Library of Congress Cataloging-in-Publication Data

Names: Williams, Victoria, author.
Title: Celebrating life customs around the world : from baby showers to funerals / Victoria Williams
Description: Santa Barbara, California : ABC-CLIO, 2017. | Includes bibliographical references and index.
Identifiers: LCCN 2016036558 (print) | LCCN 2016037544 (ebook) | ISBN 9781440836589 (hardback) | ISBN 9781440846519 (volume 1) | ISBN 9781440846526 (volume 2) | ISBN 9781440846533 (volume 3) | ISBN 9781440836596 (ebook)
Subjects: LCSH: Manners and customs. | Rites and ceremonies.
Classification: LCC GT76 .W54 2017 (print) | LCC GT76 (ebook) | DDC 390—dc23
LC record available at https://lccn.loc.gov/2016036558

ISBN: 978-1-4408-3658-9 (set)
ISBN: 978-1-4408-4651-9 (vol. 1)
ISBN: 978-1-4408-4652-6 (vol. 2)
ISBN: 978-1-4408-4653-3 (vol. 3)
EISBN: 978-1-4408-3659-6 (set)

21 20 19 18 17   1 2 3 4 5

This book is also available as an eBook.

ABC-CLIO
An Imprint of ABC-CLIO, LLC

ABC-CLIO, LLC
130 Cremona Drive, P.O. Box 1911
Santa Barbara, California 93116-1911
www.abc-clio.com

This book is printed on acid-free paper ∞

Manufactured in the United States of America

Contents

Preface   xxi
Introduction   xxiii
Geographical List of Entries   xxxiii

Volume 1: Birth and Childhood

Akan Baby-Naming Ceremonies, Ghana	1
Akka Goddess Customs, Saami	4
Apache Baby Ceremonies, Apache	7
Atiq Ceremony, Inuit	9
Baba Marta, Bulgaria	13
Babinden: Day of the Midwife, Bulgaria	17
Baby Gender Prediction Chart, China	20
Baby Racing, International	21
Baby Showers, International	22
Baby Welcoming, Paganism	24
Baptism and Christening, Christianity	25
Bedwetting Remedies, Traditional, International	29
Beschuit met Muisjes, *Suikerboon*, and *Dragées*, Europe	31
Birth Trees, International	33
Birthday Cakes, International	34
Birthday Candles, International	37
Birthday Cards, International	38
Birthday Torments, International	40
Birthdays, International	42
Birthstones, International	44
Bismillah Ceremony, Islam	47

CONTENTS

Blessingway Ceremony, Navajo	48
Blidworth Cradle Rocking Ceremony, England	51
Blooding, United Kingdom	53
Blue Peter Badge, United Kingdom	54
Breastfeeding, International	55
Brit Milah, Judaism	59
Bulgarian Birth Customs, Bulgaria	63
Burying the Placenta, International	67
Calabash Chalk, Nigeria, United Kingdom, United States, and Canada	71
Cardboard Box Beds, Finland	72
Cerne Abbas Giant, England	75
Changeling Beliefs, International	77
Child Beauty Pageants, International	80
Childermas, Christianity	83
Childhood Vaccinations, International	85
Children's Laureate, United Kingdom	87
Chinese Pregnancy and Birth Rituals, China (including Taiwan)	89
Christening Gown, Christianity	93
Christingle, United Kingdom	95
Related Primary Document: Christingle Service Script	97
Churching of Women, Christianity	98
Related Primary Document: Churching of Mothers Ceremony Script, Greek Orthodox	100
Couvade, International	104
Covering the Belly Button Traditions, Latin America	108
Cradleboard, Native American	109
Crying-Baby Sumo Competition, Japan	111
Cutting the Umbilical Cord Traditions, International	112
Dala Horse, Sweden	115
Devadasi System, India	116
Dream Catcher, Native American	119
Eating Human Placenta, International	123

El Bolo, Mexico	125
El Salto del Colacho Baby Jumping Festival, Spain	126
Entering the *Bashali*, Pakistan	128
Fady, Madagascar	133
Fairytales, International	134
Father's Day, International	138
Fire-Hair Shaving and *Khwan* Ceremonies, Thailand	140
First Communion, Christianity	142
Food Taboos in Pregnancy, International	144
Ghanaian Birthday Traditions, Ghana	149
Girl Guides, International	151
Government-Approved Baby Names, International	153
Related Primary Document: Government-Approved Names, Iceland	157
Grasmere Rushbearing, England	164
Groaning Cheese and Groaning Cake, United Kingdom and North America	166
"Happy Birthday" Song, International	171
Hesono-o: Wrapping Umbilical Cord as Keepsake, Japan	173
Hindu Baby Rituals, Hinduism	175
Hopi Naming Rites, Hopi	177
Jamu Medicine and Massage, Indonesia	181
Kangaroo Care, International	183
Kodomo No Hi: Children's Day, Japan	184
Korean Childbirth Customs, Korea	186
Kumari and *Deuki*, Nepal	189
Kyrgyzstani Childhood Traditions, Kyrgyzstan	193
La Cuarentena, Latin America	197
Ladybird Books, England	198
Lamaze Technique and Bradley Method, International	201
Latvian Birth Traditions, Latvia	203
Legong, Indonesia	204
Little Edith's Treat, England	207
Lohusa Şerbeti, Turkey	208

CONTENTS

Lotus Birthing, International	210
Lullabies, International	213
May Crowning Ritual, Catholicism	217
Mistletoe, International	218
"Monday's Child," England	220
Monstrous Punishments for Naughty Children, International	221
Moon-Yuet, China	226
Mother Roasting, Southeast Asia	228
Mothering Sunday, Christianity	230
Mundan Ceremony, India	232
Muslim Birth Rites, Islam	234
Muslim Male Circumcision, Islam	235
Mutterpass, Germany, and *Carnet de Santé Maternité*, France	237
Name Days, Catholic and Orthodox, and *Slava*, Serbian Orthodox	241
Nativity Play, International	244
Navjote Ceremony: Zoroastrian Initiation, Zoroastrianism	246
Nordic Napping, Europe	249
Nursery Rhymes, International	250
Nyabutan Ceremony, Indonesia	253
Obando Fertility Dance, Philippines	255
One-Child Policy, China	256
Oshichiya Meimeishiki, *Hyakunichimairi*, and *Okuizome*, Japan	259
Pantomime, United Kingdom	261
Parental Leave, International	265
Related Primary Document: Maternity Leave Guide, United Kingdom	267
Related Primary Document: Parental Leave Guide, Australia	269
Related Primary Document: Paternity Leave Guide, United Kingdom	270
Party Games, International	273
Pasni Weaning Ceremony, Nepal	275
Phallus Festivals, International	277
Pidyon Haben: Redemption of the First Born, Judaism	280
Piñata, Mexico	283

Potty Training, International	286
Pregnancy Yoga, International	289
Quccija, Malta	291
Saining, Scotland	293
Saint Nicholas, Christianity	294
Sambatra Mass Circumcision Festival, Madagascar	298
Sarung Buaian, Malaysia	300
Scouts, International	302
Scroggling the Holly, England	304
Sebou, Egypt	305
Setsubun: Children's Bean-throwing Festival, Japan	307
Shengxiao, China	310
Sikh Baby Rites and *Naam Karan* Naming Ceremony, Sikhism	311
Silver Spoon, United Kingdom	313
Slow Parenting Movement, International	314
Spitting on Babies, International	316
Sprinkling Cake, Ireland	317
Steiner Schools, International	318
Swaddling, International	320
Tibetan Pregnancy and Birth Customs, Tibet	323
Tooth Fairy and Tooth Mouse, International	324
Traditional Teething Remedies, International	327
Trokosi: Female Ritual Servitude, Ghana, Benin, and Togo	330
Tuj, Guatemala	333
Upanayana: Sacred Thread Ritual, Hinduism	337
Waldkindergärten, International	341
Warding Off the Evil Eye, International	342
Water Birth, International	346
Wedding Ring Test, United Kingdom	348
Weihnachtsmärchen and Advent Calendars, Germany	349
Wetting the Baby's Head, International	350
Whuppity Scoorie and Lanimer Day, Scotland	351

CONTENTS

Wiccaning, Wicca	353
Wik-Mungkan Naming Ceremony, Aborigine, Australia	355
Witch Ball, International	356
Worry Dolls and *Katsina* Dolls, Guatemala and Hopi	357
Zuo Yuezi, China	361
Zur-zur and *Yankan Gishiri*, Sub-Saharan Africa	362
Selected Bibliography for Volume 1	365
Comprehensive Index	369

Volume 2: Adolescence and Early Adulthood

Afghani Betrothal, Afghanistan	1
Andrzejki: St. Andrew's Eve, Poland	3
Arranged Marriage and Forced Marriage, International	5
Assyrian Betrothal and Weddings, International	9
Baccalauréat and *Matura*, Europe	15
Bachelor and Spinster Balls, Australia	16
Bar Mitzvah and *Bat Mitzvah*, Judaism	19
Beards, International	21
Bed-Courtship, Amish	23
Birthday Humiliations for Singletons, Denmark and Germany	26
Blackening the Bride, Scotland	28
Breast Ironing, Africa and Elsewhere	30
British Wedding Traditions, United Kingdom	32
Bulgarian Weddings, Bulgaria	37
Bullet Ant Initiation, Brazil	41
Burning the Ashen Faggot, England, and The Burning of the Clavie, Scotland	43
Cajun Weddings, United States	47
Chinese Coming-of-Age Ceremonies, China	49
Chisungu, Zambia	52
Chokha Thavani Viddhi: Devipujak Purification Trial, India	55
Choosing Options, England, Wales, and Northern Ireland	56
Christian Wedding Ceremony, Christianity	58

Coming of Age Day, Japan	61
Courtship Whistling, Mexico	64
Cow Jumping, Ethiopia	66
Dastaar Bandi and *Amrit Sanchar*, Sikhism	69
Dipo Womanhood Ceremony, Ghana	71
Diwali and *Kali Pooja*, India	73
Related Primary Document: Sandip Roy, "The Great Diwali Fight and Obama," 2009	76
Dunmow Flitch Trials, England	78
Dyngus Day, Eastern Europe and United States	79
Ear-Piercing Ceremonies, Myanmar and Malaysia	83
Face in Birthday Cake, Mexico	85
Fattening Room Seclusion, Nigeria	86
Female Genital Cutting, Africa, Middle East, Asia, and Elsewhere	89
Fidanzamenti, Italy	94
Filipino Debut, Philippines	95
Forehead-Cutting Initiation, Africa	98
Gap Year, International	103
Gretna Green, Scotland	104
Gwallye, South Korea	105
Hadaka Matsuri, Japan	109
Hair Removal, International	111
Hajj, Islam	113
Handfasting, Scotland, also Neo-Paganism	117
Related Primary Document: Handfasting Ceremony (Sample)	118
Handparting, Wicca	127
Hijab, Islam	128
Hijra, Indian Sub-Continent	131
Hindu Wedding Ceremony, Hinduism	133
Hmong Names, Laos, Myanmar, Vietnam, Cambodia, and Thailand	136
Hora, Eastern Europe, and *Horah*, Judaism	139
Horseshoes, International	141

Human Tooth Sharpening, Indonesia and Africa	142
Inter-Railing, Europe	147
Initiation by Semen Transferal, Papua New Guinea and Vanuatu	148
Iria Ceremony, Nigeria	153
Isanaklesh Gotal, Mescalero Apache	155
Jewish Wedding Customs, Judaism	159
Jumping Over the Broom, United Kingdom and United States, also Neo-Paganism	163
Jury Duty, International	165
Related Primary Document: Jury Duty Guide, United States	169
Related Primary Document: Jury Summons Guide, United Kingdom	170
Kumbh Mela, Hinduism	173
La Quinceañera, Latin America, the Caribbean, and the United States	177
La Soupe, France	180
Ladouvane and St. Sylvester's Day, Bulgaria	182
Land Diving, Vanuatu	183
Lazarovden, Bulgaria	186
Leap Year Proposal, International	189
Lindo, Croatia	190
Lip Plugs, Africa and South America	191
Lobola, Southern Africa	195
Log Riding, Japan	197
Looking for Fern Blossoms, Eastern Europe	199
Lovespoons, Wales	201
Maasai Warrior Initiation, Kenya and Tanzania	205
Majáles, Czech Republic	208
Marriage Banns, Christianity	210
Related Primary Document: Marriage Banns Legislation, United Kingdom	211
Matis Hunting Trials, Brazil	215
Maypoles, Europe	219
Mehndi, International	222

Menstrual Customs, International	224
Menstrual Taboos, International	228
Money Dance, International	233
Moonie Weddings, International	235
Moroccan Weddings, Morocco	237
Muslim Wedding Ceremony, Islam	241
Neck Elongation, Thailand, Myanmar, and South Africa	243
Nkumbi, Democratic Republic of Congo	245
Nyumba Ntobhu: Traditional Same-Sex Marriage, Tanzania	247
Omiai: Japanese Matchmaking, Japan	251
Pika and *Nyora*, Zimbabwe and Mozambique	253
Polterabend, Germany	254
Polyandry, International	258
Polygyny, International	261
Povitica, Eastern Europe	263
Purity Ball, United States	264
RAG Week, United Kingdom and Ireland	267
Reed Dancing Chastity Ceremony, Kingdom of Swaziland	269
Ritual Tattooing, International	272
Rumspringa, United States and Canada	277
Russefeiring, Norway, and Schoolies Week, Australia	281
Same-Sex Marriage, International	285
Related Primary Document: Same-Sex Civil Partnership Ceremony Text, United Kingdom	288
San-San-Kudo, Japan	291
Scarification, Africa and Papua New Guinea	293
Schuhplattler and *Ländler*, Germany and Austria	297
Secular Confirmation, Europe	300
Shabka, Islam and Coptic Christianity	302
Shanghai Marriage Market, China	305
Sharo: Public Flogging, Nigeria and Benin	307

CONTENTS

Shinbyu, Buddhism	310
Sikh Wedding Ceremony, Sikhism	312
Singles' Day, China, and Black Day, South Korea	315
Sisters' Meal Festival, China	317
Sock Garland, Germany, and Sock Dance, Canada	318
St. Catherine's Day, France	320
St. Dwynwen's Day, Wales	322
Sünnet, Turkey	323
Sunrise Ceremony, Apache, United States	326
Thaipusam: Extreme Ritual Flesh Modification, Hinduism	333
Tooth-Filing Ceremony, Indonesia	335
Training Bras, United States, Europe, and Australasia	338
Trobriand Ritualized Sex and Commitment, Papua New Guinea	341
Twenty-First Birthday Traditions, International	344
Urethral Subincision, Australia, Africa, and South America	347
Vinok, Ukraine	353
Virginity Testing, International	355
Vision Quest, Native American	358
Visiting-Girls Courtship Tradition, China	361
Walkabout, Australia	365
Wedding Anniversaries, International	367
Wedding Cakes, International	369
Wedding Dress and Wedding Ring, International	373
Related Primary Document: Yumi Sakugawa, "An Asian American Wedding," 2009	377
Wedding March and Bridal Chorus, International	379
White Coat Ceremony and Pinning Ceremony, International	381
Wodaabe Courtship Dance and Festival, Africa	383
Xhosa Circumcision, South Africa	387
Zou Hun: Mosuo Walking Marriages, China	391
Selected Bibliography for Volume 2	395
Comprehensive Index	399

Volume 3: Aging and Death

"Abide With Me," United Kingdom, North America, and Australasia	1
Albanian Funeral Customs, Albania	3
Alkaline Hydrolysis, United Kingdom, Australia, and United States	5
All Souls' Day, Europe and South America	6
Ankou, France and England	10
Assisted Suicide, International	11
Bees, United Kingdom	17
Buddhist Attitudes Toward Death, Buddhism	18
Cairn, International	23
Changing of the Guard Ceremony, United States	24
Chelsea Pensioners, England	26
Chinese Death Customs, China	29
Christian Death Rituals, Christianity	35
Condemned Prisoner's Last Meal, United States	37
Condolences, International	40
Cremation, International	41
Croning, Saging, and Elderling Ceremonies, Paganism	44
Crucifixion Rituals, Philippines	47
Death Dance, International	51
Delaware Indian Death Rituals, North America	53
Related Primary Document: Ray Fadden, Letter to President Harry S. Truman Regarding Burial of an Indian at Arlington National Cemetery, September 3, 1951	55
Denville Hall & Brinsworth House, England	56
Dia de los Muertos: Day of the Dead, Latin America and United States	58
Doom Metal and Funeral Doom, International	62
Easter Eggs, Christianity	65
Eating the Ashes of the Dead, Brazil and Venezuela	67
Edir, Ethiopia, and *Engozi*, Uganda	70
Eleanor Crosses, England	72
Embalming, United States	73

CONTENTS

Endocannibalism, Papua New Guinea and Brazil	76
Eulogies, International	80
Related Primary Document: President Reagan's Address to the Nation Following the Challenger *Shuttle Disaster, 1986*	81
Eyam Plague Sunday Service, England	83
Famadihana, Madagascar	85
Fantasy Coffins, Ghana	87
Finger Amputation, Papua New Guinea	90
Funeral Cakes and Funeral Candy, International	92
Funeral Plants, Europe	94
Funeral Songs, International	97
Goth Subculture, International	99
Grave Rental and Exhumation, Europe and Asia	102
The Great Passing, Romania	105
Hallowe'en and *Martinstag,* International	109
Halva, International	113
High-Platform Exposure of the Corpse, Australia	115
Hindu Death Customs, Hinduism	118
Isola di San Michele: Venice's Cemetery Island, Italy	121
Japanese Death Customs, Japan	123
Jazz Funeral, United States	127
Jewish Death Customs, Judaism	129
Koliva, International	135
Lakota Death Rituals, Lakota, North America	139
Related Primary Document: Native American Grave Protection and Repatriation Act, 1990	142
"The Last Post" and "Taps," International	152
Living with the Dead, Indonesia	155
"Lyke-Wake Dirge," England	158
Maidens' Garlands, England	161
Malagan, Papua New Guinea	162
Maundy Money, United Kingdom	164
Memento Mori and *Vanitas*, International	167

Message from the Queen, United Kingdom	171
Minute's Silence, International	173
Mirila, Croatia	175
Missing Man Formation, International	177
Mizuko Kuyo: Japanese Fetus Memorial Service, Japan	180
Mortuary Totem Poles, Haida and Tlingit	183
Mummification, International	185
Muslim Death Rituals, Islam	188
National Mourning, International	191
Ngaben, Indonesia	193
Nine-Nights, Caribbean	196
Obituary, International	199
Ossuaries, Europe	200
Passing Bells, England and Scotland	205
Passion Play, Christianity	206
Pauper's Funeral, United Kingdom	209
Personalized Hearses, United Kingdom	211
Plastination, Germany	213
Pregnancy and Infant Loss Remembrance Day, International	216
Qingming Festival, China	219
Remembrance Day and Remembrance Sunday, International	223
Related Primary Document: Remembrance Sunday Early Day Motion, United Kingdom	226
Retirement and Pensions, International	228
Related Primary Document: Social Pension/Superannuation Guide, New Zealand	232
Related Primary Document: State Pension Government Guide, United Kingdom	234
Riderless Horse, International	236
Romanian Funeral Customs, Romania	237
Royal Wootton Bassett, England	239
Sakalava Royal Death Traditions and *Fitampoha*, Madagascar	243
Sallekhanā, Jainism	245

CONTENTS

San La Muerte, South America	246
Santa Muerte, Mexico and United States	249
Saturday of Souls, Orthodox Christianity, Bulgaria, and Serbia, and *Radonitsa*, Russia	251
Senior Sporting Events, International	254
Shrunken Heads, Peru and Ecuador	255
Sikh Death Customs, Sikhism	257
Sky Burials, Autonomous Tibet and China	259
Soul Cakes and Soul Breads, Europe	263
Space Burial, Outer Space	267
Spontaneous Shrines, International	269
State Funeral, International	271
Stations of the Cross, Christianity	275
Suicide Landmarks, International	278
Tangihanga: Māori Mourning Ritual, New Zealand	281
Taxidermy, International	283
Tear Catchers and Mourning Jewelry, International	286
Tết Nguyên đan, Vietnam	288
Tomb of the Unknown Soldier, International	292
Tombstone Tourism, International	297
Tongan Funerals, Tonga	300
Traditional Mourning Colors, International	302
University of the Third Age, International	307
Vrindavan: The City of Widows, India	309
Wake, International	313
Wearing Flowers to Honor War Dead, International	314
Wiccan Funerals, Wicca	318
Related Primary Document: Wiccan Funeral for an Elderly Woman	321
Windmills, The Netherlands	323
Yew Trees, Europe	327
Yu Lan Jie: The Hungry Ghost Festival, China	329

Zaduszki, Poland	333
Zombies and Voodoo Death Traditions, Haiti	335
Zoroastrian Funerals, India	338
Selected Bibliography for Volume 3	343
Comprehensive Index	347

Preface

It is not often that an author can claim (truthfully) that all readers should find something in her book to which they can relate. That is, however, certainly true of this book, a three-volume encyclopedia of life customs around the world. While not everyone that reads this book will marry or have children, all readers are born and all will die, so there is, I hope, something in this book to interest everyone.

This multivolume encyclopedia concentrates on rites of passage, traditions, rituals, and life customs that take place around the world. While I deliberately focused on activities that may be less familiar to American readers, many of the activities detailed are American or at least occur in the United States. Some of these customs involve millions of participants, such as breastfeeding, while others are known of by only a handful of people, such as the "Blidworth Cradle Rocking Ceremony." Many of the customs included in this book are rooted in the real world—such as potty training and jury duty—while others are deeply indebted to folklore such as "Monstrous Punishments for Naughty Children" and "Akka Goddess Customs." Meanwhile, some customs, such as those surrounding fairytales and lullabies, were not customs I had really considered as being associated with childhood until I wrote them. Having written my PhD thesis on fairytales, I had rather forgotten that fairytales are, primarily, intended for children rather than as texts to study.

The scope of this book takes in North America, South America, Europe, Africa, Asia, the Middle East, Oceania, and even outer space, and covers customs experienced by men, women, children, and animals (e.g., "Taxidermy"), in groups or as individuals. Volume 1 examines customs pertaining to birth and early childhood. Volume 2 looks at the coming-of-age customs of adolescents and those in early adulthood. Volume 3 covers entries relating to aging and death. A number of the entries in the books deal with subject matter that some readers may find distressing or distasteful, particularly entries such as "Female Genital Cutting," "Breast Ironing," "Initiation by Semen Transferal," and various entries on circumcision, but I have endeavored to write these entries as sensitively as possible. The same is true with the many entries on death customs and tombs.

This book is primarily aimed at researchers though I have purposely kept the writing as jargon-free as possible so that the general reader can also read the book from cover to cover for entertainment. Keeping the researcher in mind, however, every entry can be looked at as a stand-alone item or as part of an overarching theme. Each entry details the known history and evolution of the particular custom or rite but I have also detailed the myths and legends that lie at the heart of several of the entries. Where space allows, I have also attempted to note artworks, literature, films, and television programs that depict the various activities detailed in the entries. In addition, each entry is followed by a "See also" section that enables cross-referencing plus a brief Further Reading list. A number of selected primary document excerpts are also included that support specific entries. Finally, each volume has a selected bibliography.

The writing of this book would not have been possible without the generosity and enthusiasm of Kaitlin Ciarmiello, acquisitions editor at ABC-CLIO. I would also like to thank my family and friends for listening when I mentioned random information about obscure customs or asked them if they knew anyone that had taken part in certain activities. Most especially, I would like to thank my Mum, Rosemary Williams, who has a knack for alerting me to newspaper articles on unusual traditions and the like. An interview with my Mum is included in the entry entitled "Christingle." Thank you also to Dr. Nida Suri for her input on Indian customs and for guidance when I was writing about Islamic rituals. Thank you as well to Andrew Levicki who, as a fluent Japanese speaker and former long-time resident of Japan, provided a valuable insight into Japanese culture.

Introduction

The various points in an individual's or group's life cycle are marked by a variety of rituals, traditions, customs, and rites of passage, all of which can be placed under the umbrella term "life customs." Today the most commonly experienced life customs are associated with pregnancy, childbirth, initiation or attainment of adult physical maturity, mating or betrothal, marriage, and death, with thousands of different life customs occurring each year around the world involving living (and dead) men, women, children, and animals. The term life customs can be applied to myriad events and occasions though distinctions exist between those events dubbed rites of passage, customs, and traditions. From the beginning of an individual's life to its end, life's milestones are denoted through a huge number of time-honored traditions and unique customs. These ceremonial events have occurred in all societies throughout time. The classification of these different events varies, however, with differences existing between rituals, traditions, and rites of customs.

Many life customs are religious in nature while even more are secular. Moreover, some life customs may not even be considered to be life customs by the people undergoing them. For example, pensioners in the United Kingdom receiving their so-called bus pass is an everyday occurrence that happens without fanfare, yet when individual senior citizens are sent their pass by the government it is indeed a rite of passage as it is an official confirmation that someone has reached a certain age and, therefore, is officially classified as a senior citizen. For the most part, however, communities tend to denote these life events by holding ceremonial occasions. These ceremonial occasions tend to include at least one ritual that demonstrates that the individual experiencing the rite of passage has symbolically separated from his or her former state. This is exemplified by the Korean *Gwallye* coming-of-age ceremony for males and females turning 19 years old. The ceremony sees the 19-year-olds don special ceremonial clothing that denotes that they have attained adulthood.

Special celebrations may also be held to announce to a community as a whole that an individual has entered a new state of being (or in terms of death, beyond a state of being). In the most highly evolved societies, these types of ceremonial occasions are woven into the life of society with literal interpretations of separation, death, and rebirth tending to be portrayed through symbolism. This can be seen in the example of Christian baptisms during which the person being baptized may undergo a ritual drowning and re-emergence from sacred water as a form of initiation into the Christian faith. In addition, many communities in Western society practice customs that can be traced back to earlier times, with certain practices having their basis in ancient sacred activities. For example, the Japanese Onbashira festival sees men ride logs downhill in honor of Suwa-no-Kami, the primary goddess in the pantheon of Shinto, the main religion of Japan, while the custom of dancing around the maypole that is a summer activity in many European countries is often considered to have ancient fertility rites as its basis. Another Western custom that has its roots in earlier, sacred practices is the frequently occurring custom of the baby shower. Though a seemingly recently invented secular custom, the custom of holding baby showers can be traced back to an ancient Greek ritual that saw a baby five or seven days old undergo a rite called the *Amphidromia*, or Running Round. Then, on the 10th day, the baby's mother would invite her friends and family to a ritual called *Dekate* for a celebratory meal during which the baby's mother would dedicate gifts to Eileithyia, a goddess of childbirth.

RITUALS, TRADITIONS, AND CUSTOMS

The various life customs experienced by an individual or group can be divided into different classifications. Though the terms ritual, tradition, and custom are often used interchangeably in everyday conversation, there are, technically, different parameters for each term. Rituals are religious rites or earnest secular ceremonies consisting of a number of actions performed according to a prescribed order. Rituals usually occur at important times of life such as birth, marriage, and death and often confer protection on an individual. Examples of this kind of protective occasion linked to a life event include spitting on babies to ward off the evil eye, placing a veil over a bride's face to protect her from malignant supernatural entities, or performing a vigil for a corpse, perhaps to prevent a cat from jumping over it, and thereby precluding the reanimation of the corpse after burial as a vampire-like supernatural being, as occurs in Albania. Rituals often involve special amulets or charms that ensure the individual transitions safely to another state of being. An example of this is the skin decoration known as *mehndi* that is intended to confer blessings, grace, and good luck to Indian brides and grooms as a kind of amulet worn upon the skin.

In the popular imagination, rituals are often confused with customs and traditions, yet differences exist between the types of occasion. As opposed to a ritual, a custom is a widely accepted, conventional mode of behavior that is specific to a particular society or place. Similarly, a tradition is a practice passed down within a community that holds some symbolic meaning or special significance that connects to its origins in the past. An example of a seemingly recently invented tradition occurs at British weddings for it is now traditional when newlyweds go on honeymoon for a collection of tin cans, boots, and assorted junk to be attached to the vehicle that they use as transport, often together with a sign declaring the couple to be "Just Married." Typically, the cans are attached to a car's back fender resulting in them clanging against each other and the road surface as the car drives away. This is a fairly recently instituted custom since cars were not invented until the end of the 19th century, but the tradition most likely harks back to the French custom of the *chivari* or the German *Polterabend*. Both of these noise-making traditions are associated with weddings and are intended to drive away from newlyweds evil spirits that might harm the newlyweds out of spite or jealousy. Tradition is, therefore, essentially retrospective, nostalgic, and governed by invariance, even in the case of newly invented traditions. For this reason it is common for people to refuse to change their manner of performing an action arguing that they cannot because it is traditional to perform the action in a certain way. Hence many people's Christmas celebrations are the same year after year because they feel that they must mark their celebrations in the way that they always have on account of it being traditional to do so. Therefore, whether old or new, traditions are governed by the imposition of fixed practices that are performed repetitively and do not waver. Customs on the other hand are not as backward looking as traditions for they do modify over time, though at the same time the customs must still conform in essence to what has gone before thereby allowing for continuity. In short, therefore, custom permits flexibility while tradition prefers to adhere to precedent especially through the use of symbolic actions and paraphernalia. Though there are, therefore, differences between traditions and customs the two terms do overlap, and, moreover, intertwine. Tradition may also become bound up with ritual for although a tradition may not have had any symbolic function when it originated it may acquire a sense of ritual where none was intended while, simultaneously, establishing a set of conventions and rules that are passed on to new participants. For this reason, some traditions that began as secular traditions seem increasingly like ritual.

RITES OF PASSAGE

Another type of life event marked by certain types of actions are so-called rites of passage. Rites of passage occur the world over with the universal distribution of rites of passage a matter of fascination for scholars for centuries. Perhaps the most famous and influential work on the phenomena of rites of passage is *Les Rites de Passage* (*The Rites of Passage*, 1909), written by European anthropologist, ethnographer, and folklorist Arnold van Gennep. In this work, van Gennep coined the phrase rite of passage to describe a celebration of the transition that occurs when a person leaves one group to enter another, thereby experiencing a significant change of social status. The term rite of passage is used today in cultural anthropology to describe ceremonial events in which an individual progresses through the stages of life within their society. Van Gennep suggested that rites of passage are the means by which people shift, without causing social disturbance, from one social role to another. Van Gennep also proposed that rites of passage consist of three discernible yet consecutive elements: separation, transition, and reincorporation, or, correspondingly, pre-liminal, liminal, and post-liminal stages (from the Latin word *limen* meaning threshold). According to van Gennep, the individual that is the focus of a rite of passage is severed symbolically from his or her previous status before undergoing an adjustment to a new status. This occurs during a period of transition that culminates in the initiate's reincorporation into society under the cloak of his or her new social status. Despite the fact that the most frequently observed rites of passage correspond to crises in the life cycle of an individual, van Gennep observed that the ceremonies attendant upon rites of passage are significant for the whole of a society or culture not just the individual. This is most likely due to the fact that the most oft-celebrated rites of passage are sociocultural events.

Rites of passage occur worldwide and, if archeological findings are to be believed, have most likely taken place since time immemorial. Most societies consider the key rites of passage to be childbirth, initiation or the attainment of adulthood, marriage, and death. Indeed many of the rites of passage considered most important by society, and therefore most frequently enacted, are associated with these biological milestones of life: birth, maturity, reproduction, and death. This is because these biological crises bring about changes in an individual's social status and, therefore, in the individual's relationship with society. Rites of passage that are unconnected to biology mark transformations that are cultural. This is exemplified by initiations into societies consisting of people with specific interests or concerns such as the white coat ceremony that is a rite of passage for first-year medical students that welcomes the students into the medical profession.

There is no generally accepted classification of rites of passage, though many names have been suggested to distinguish the various types and elements of such rites. For example the term "purification ceremony" can be applied to a ritual that occurs frequently as an element of rites of passage, particularly rites associated with birth and death, but also refers to other religious events. In most cases, the aim of a purification ceremony is to prepare an individual for some kind of communication with a supernatural being. However a purification ceremony can also occur as a rite of passage that signifies the symbolic erasing of an individual's old status in readiness for his or her taking on a new social rank. For example, the post-birth Christian purification ceremony called the churching of women is held for women that have recently given birth thereby assuming the social status of a mother while the Hindu *Upanayana*, or sacred thread, ritual marks the stage of a young boy's life when he enters into Vedic education. The Upanayana ceremony also signifies the end of a boy's childhood for once a boy has undergone the ritual he is expected to immerse himself in the task of acquiring knowledge and responsibility. These examples demonstrate the way in which rituals focused on social transformation and religious transformational ceremonies overlap. This is also the case with religious transformational rites such as baptism, which also involves a degree of social transformation and celebration. Certain coming-of-age rites may also cause a change of religious status, as is the case with *Shinbyu*, the obligatory period of initiation in the life of Theravada Buddhist males that boys living in some Asian countries experience between the ages of 9 and 12 years. Not only is this a religious rite but Buddhist parents also consider their son's Shinbyu as his rite of passage to manhood.

LIFE-CYCLE CEREMONIES

Life-cycle ceremonies—the ritual counterparts of the biological crises of the life cycle—exist in all societies. All societies observe some forms of ritual surrounding the major life-cycle occasions of childbirth, marriage, and death, though the degree of elaboration of the rites and the significance accorded to them varies greatly between societies even when societies are comparable. These life-cycle ceremonies include the numerous rites attendant upon childbirth, ranging from pre-birth and pregnancy rites (such as baby showers and the wedding ring test) to practices observed during the actual moment of childbirth and post-birth rituals such as the churching of women. Rites associated with pregnancy and birth tend to stipulate different roles to the mother, father, and other family members as well as the non-family members of a community with respect to the baby. Pregnancy rites may begin when a pregnancy is confirmed and may continue until the time the baby is delivered, and, possibly, for a variable period of time after birth. This ritual process is exemplified by Korean birth customs, for a Korean woman will normally believe she has fallen pregnant after she has experienced a dream of conception called a *tae-mong*. Then, when a pregnancy is confirmed, she will inform her mother-in-law first, followed by her husband, and then, finally, her own mother. While a Korean woman is pregnant she will follow a strict diet of prescribed foods and act in a certain way. Then during the birthing process the woman will be attended to by certain female relatives and perform particular actions that are intended to hasten delivery while enhancing the *qi* life force. Then, after birth the placenta is treated in a ritual manner and the new mother must abide by certain ritual rules for a period of time.

Just as there are numerous birth rites around the world, so there are also very many coming-of-age and death rituals. The holding of coming-of-age rites varies much more than the holding of other types of rites of passage. While births and deaths are marked by most communities, some societies hold coming-of-age rites for only one sex, while some hold elaborate coming-of-age rites for one sex and contrastingly simple rites for the other. Then again other countries do not hold any coming-of-age rites at all for either sex. In the West initiation and coming-of-age rites have become increasingly secular. Though all major world religions include some sort of coming-of-age rites—such as the Jewish bar mitzvah and bat mitzvah and the Sikh *Dastaar Bandi* ceremony—coming of age rites in Western societies either are not observed or are viewed as vestiges of ancient religious rituals. An example of this is the noisy, German pre-wedding custom known as the

Polterabend. This custom is most commonly thought to have evolved from ancient pagan tribal beliefs. These ancient Germanic tribes believed that evil spirits and malign forces could be banished from weddings if guests made a great deal of noise by breaking crockery, cracking whips, and banging pans together. The ancient Germans believed that once such malign supernatural entities had been banished from the wedding they could not then go on to sabotage the newly wedded couple's married life.

A great many coming-of-age rites are socially transformational as they see individuals initiated into certain sections of society that have no direct connection with biological changes. Moreover in the West coming-of-age rites tend not to be religious occasions but rather to be secular ceremonies that are not lineage-based or the result of tribal societies. Secular Western coming-of-age rites mark the individual's induction into societies based on age, social hierarchy, or common interests. An example of a purely secular coming-of-age rite is the European rite of inter-railing. This secular rite of passage sees students travel independently across the continent, and possibly beyond, thereby symbolizing their ability to act as independent, responsible adults. Other coming-of-age rites of passage are attendant upon puberty and physical maturation with many coming-of-age rites of passage being rites of initiation that coincide with puberty. For this reason such rites are sometimes referred to as puberty rites. Puberty among females is often defined as the time when a female experiences the onset of her menstrual flow, however there is no such clearly defined criteria for the sexual maturation of males. Furthermore the age at which rites pertaining to the attainment of maturity are observed varies hugely between societies thereby suggesting that maturation is as much a social or cultural concern as it is a matter of biology. Coming-of-age rites of passage connected with puberty are often marked by ordeals or tests of manhood and womanhood the experience of which qualifies an individual to assume a new social status. Common examples of this type of trial include numerous types of circumcision (male and female), the Apache Sunrise Ceremony, and the Ghanaian Dipo Womanhood Ceremony. This latter ceremony occurs when a female is aged between 12 and 16 years and it is divided into many individual stages that involve ritual cleansing, virginity testing, and education, and it culminates in the initiate returning to society as a woman. The Dipo Womanhood Ceremony exemplifies the fact that coming of age-of-age rites, more than any other type of life custom, emphasize appropriate modes of dress, demeanor, and morality. Indeed in the run-up to certain coming-of-age rites an initiate may undergo a period of instruction to teach them the correct behavior.

Another rite of passage that involves some form of prior instruction or education is marriage. Traditionally, women that are about to be married have to undergo preliminary rites providing them with instruction in how to be a wife. Such educational rites may occur informally or as a part of a prescribed ritual and tend to include instruction on a wife's role in society while communicating her economic and social duties with regard to pleasing her husband, children, and family in general as well as her community on the whole. Women may also have to undergo tests of sexual maturity and rites that promote fertility or ensure sexual faithfulness. This pre-wedding education still occurs in Morocco where it is traditional for a bride-to-be to undergo a *beberiska* ceremony. This ceremony sees the married members of a bride's entourage give the bride a sex education lesson, for, traditionally, the bride is a young virgin who is generally ignorant of such matters. Sometimes during the beberiska ceremony the bride sits behind a curtain that symbolizes the imminent change in her life.

As well as being important events in the lives of individuals, marriage ceremonies may be considered especially significant in the stressing of social bonds between the kinship groups of the newlyweds. To this end, throughout history romantic love has not been the criterion by which individuals have found spouses. According to convention, marriage normally occurred only between people belonging to certain classes or groups with mutual love and sexual attraction being considered a matter of little or no importance. Instead what really mattered was that a marriage could provide a couple with children and maintain social norms. For this reason, some societies have long-standing traditions of matchmaking and arranged marriage. Such traditions are particularly prevalent in Bulgaria, China, Japan, and India and in expatriate communities around the world.

Many factors, such as changing religious views, a lessening in the belief in the supernatural, and social change, all seem to be contributing to a decline in the frequency with which rites of passage occur, at least in the West. As a rite of passage, marriage continues to be popular in the West, and indeed around the word. However like so many other rites of passage the popularity of marriage in the West is frequently reported as being in decline. In recent years the conventions on which marriage is based have changed significantly in some locations with the legalization of same-sex marriage. The advent of same-sex marriages demonstrates that even the most long-standing and celebrated traditions are open to change and modification. Anthropologists suggest that marriage is one of the earliest socially constructed institutions, for rites of marriage have been observed in every known society since time immemorial. The form that marriage rites take varies hugely, however, from extremely elaborate rituals to simple ceremonies that view marriage as a formal agreement of unity between families. Additionally, some marriages are religious ceremonies while others are secular events. Some societies also hold pre-marriage rites such as betrothal ceremonies that consist of complex formalities governing the exchange of material goods. Customs involving the mock capture of the bride by the groom and his relatives also occur. Like coming-of-age rites, marriage ceremonies often include obvious emblems of an individual's new social status, such as wedding rings and hair adornments. There are also a huge number of courtship traditions, rituals, ceremonies, and festivals around the world, though these vary greatly in terms of propriety and solemnity. For instance bawdy events such as Bachelor and Spinster Balls occur regularly in rural Australia. These events are one of Australia's best-loved traditions though they are also notorious for being the scene of casual sexual encounters and binge drinking. Similarly, the Eastern European custom of looking for fern blossoms during the summer solstice is more or less a euphemism for looking for a sexual encounter. Other courtship practices are more chaste, such as Kickapoo Courtship Whistling and Amish bed-courtship. Then again other rituals are intended to safeguard young adults' (especially young women's) sexual virginity. For example virginity testing takes place in various locations around the world while purity balls take place in the United States.

After the rite of passage that is marriage, the next life-cycle event that is marked by ritual and considered a rite of passage is death. All societies pay ceremonial attention to death with rituals associated with death tending toward the religious and nearly always viewed as extremely important. All societies consider the dead to be significant and so they are the focus of much ritual attention both at the time of death and over periods of time after death. Since death is universally considered a supremely significant occasion, death rites tend to be elaborate and include all of the stages of separation, transition, and reincorporation, as set out by van Gennep in his model of rites of passage. Death involves a great deal of social transformation not just for the person that dies but for their family too. For example when an individual dies they take on a new social role as a spirit or ancestor that may be considered important by the community of which they were a part when they were alive. Meanwhile the deceased's surviving spouse will experience a change in his or her social status because he or she will change from being a married partner to becoming a widow or widower. The couple's children, if any, will also see their status change from that of having two parents to being without a parent. Death rites need not be governed by religion however as the practice of erecting spontaneous shrines to the dead testifies. While writing this book this author's hometown was the center of international headlines when, in August 2014, 14-year-old Alice Gross went missing in Hanwell, west London, prompting residents to tie handmade yellow ribbons around trees, lampposts, cars, monuments, and railings to keep her disappearance in the collective memory. As police searched for Alice the so-called Alice Ribbons covered the local clock tower and spread across London and beyond. Also, as the search by the police for Alice entered its fifth week, 6,000 runners in the Ealing Half Marathon chose to wear the ribbons, some inscribed with the hashtag #FindAlice pointing to the Twitter campaign that had gathered international support including help from celebrities. When the schoolgirl's murdered body was found in a local river, the Alice Ribbons transformed from objects aiming to show hope for Alice to memorial emblems of grief with accumulations of Alice Ribbons collecting at the clock tower serving as spontaneous shrines as locals gravitated toward the landmark. The ribbons were ultimately removed in October 2014 at the request of Alice's family. Though not in any way religious, the phenomenon of the Alice Ribbon highlighted the ritual nature of so many death practices. Other newly established death customs see people take to social media to express their grief.

As well as the rites of passage that are birth, initiation, marriage, and death, the term rites of passage is also sometimes applied to institutionalized, cyclic ceremonies such as agricultural festivals that are intended to ensure bountiful harvests. Though this type of ceremony does not see participants attain a new social status these occasions are viewed as rites of passage because they contain similarities in their ritual procedures. Elements of ceremonies relating to changes in the seasons also involve acts of separation and incorporation as they symbolically bid farewell to the previous season while welcoming the new.

A wealth of symbolism is normally attendant upon all kinds of elaborate rites of passage. Often this is due to the fact that such symbols represent the discarding of one social status and the adoption of another status. Typically the symbols of new status connected to rites of passage include modifications made to visible parts of the body, distinctive clothing and jewelry, and the adoption of special emblems. Examples of ritual body modification denoting a change of status include the various types of circumcision found around the world including the type experienced by boys belonging to the South African Xhosa tribe, Indonesian tooth-filing, African pika-marking, and Papua New Guinean scarification rituals. Special ceremonial clothing worn for rites of passage include the Western wedding dress that is bought especially for the wedding service and various types of kimono that can be worn to mark the attainment of adulthood or on the occasion of a death. Symbolic ritual jewelry includes the wedding ring, whose circular shape denotes eternal fidelity and mourning jewelry that may be black to denote bereavement or contain body parts such as hair taken from the dead. Meanwhile emblems related to rites of passage include the symbols of office ranging from the badges adopted by Girl Guides and the pins presented to nurses during a nurses' pinning ceremony—a ceremony dedicated to enshrining newly qualified nurses within the fold of the nursing profession.

As well as special symbolism, many rites of passage are also associated with taboos and prohibited behavior or actions during the rites. For example, some Native Americans consider it taboo for an initiate to scratch the body with the fingers during rituals. Other taboos include the various menstrual taboos that exist around the world and that may be enacted every time a female experiences her monthly menstrual bleed.

The frequency with which rites of passage such as marriage and coming-of-age customs are conducted does seem to be decreasing, at least in the West, due in part to the seeming incompatibility of such rites with modern life and also escalating costs associated with holding certain ceremonies. However the social and psychological value of such rites in making the transition to adulthood are substantial, meaning that such ceremonies are unlikely to die out completely. Moreover, such ceremonies continue to be considered extremely important in other parts of the world. Rites associated with birth and death are universally upheld, however, and even seem to be increasing in number and importance. This may well be because birth and death are two rites of passage that everyone of all nations, religions, and sexes has no choice but to experience.

Further Reading

Berns, Roberta. *Child, Family, School, Community: Socialization and Support.* Tenth edition. Stamford, CT: CENGAGE Learning, 2016.

Hobsbawm, Eric, and Terence Ranger, eds. *The Invention of Tradition.* Cambridge, UK: Cambridge University Press, 2012.

Horrox, Camilla. "Alice Gross Yellow Ribbons of Hope to Be Removed." Get West London, October 10, 2014. Accessed September 9, 2015, at http://www.getwestlondon.co.uk/news/local-news/alice-gross-yellow-ribbons-hope-7914799.

Jones, Alison. *Larousse Dictionary of World Folklore.* Edinburgh, UK: Larousse, 1996.

Laing, Jennifer, and Warwick Frost, eds. *Rituals and Traditional Events in the Modern World.* Abingdon, UK: Routledge, 2015.

van Gennep, Arnold. *The Rites of Passage.* Abingdon, UK: Routledge, 2010.

Geographical List of Entries

VOLUME 1: BIRTH AND CHILDHOOD

Africa and Middle East
Akan Baby-Naming Ceremonies (Ghana)
Fady (Madagascar)
Ghanaian Birthday Traditions (Ghana)
Sambatra Mass Circumcision Festival (Madagascar)
Sebou (Egypt)
Trokosi: Female Ritual Servitude (Ghana, Benin, and Togo)
Zur-zur and *Yankan Gishiri* (Sub-Saharan Africa)

Asia (Central and North)
Entering the *Bashali* (Pakistan)
Kyrgyzstani Childhood Traditions (Kyrgyzstan)
Kumari and *Deuki* (Nepal)
Pasni Weaning Ceremony (Nepal)
Tibetan Pregnancy and Birth Customs (Tibet)

Asia (South and Southeast)
Baby Gender Prediction Chart (China)
Chinese Pregnancy and Birth Rituals (China including Taiwan)
Crying-Baby Sumo Competition (Japan)
Fire-Hair Shaving and *Khwan* Ceremonies (Thailand)
Hesono-o: Wrapping Umbilical Cord as Keepsake (Japan)
Jamu Medicine and Massage (Indonesia)
Kodomo No Hi: Children's Day (Japan)
Korean Childbirth Customs (Korea)
Legong (Indonesia)
Moon-Yuet (China)
Mother Roasting (Southeast Asia)
Nyabutan Ceremony (Indonesia)
Obando Fertility Dance (Philippines)
One-Child Policy (China)
Oshichiya Meimeishiki, Hyakunichimairi, and *Okuizome* (Japan)
Sarung Buaian (Malaysia)
Setsubun: Children's Bean-Throwing Festival (Japan)
Shengxiao (China)
Zuo Yuezi (China)

Australia and Pacific
Wik-Mungkan Naming Ceremony (Australia)

Europe and Russia
Baba Marta (Bulgaria)
Babinden: Day of the Midwife (Bulgaria)
Beschuit met Muisjes, *Suikerboon*, and *Dragées* (Europe)
Bulgarian Birth Customs (Bulgaria)
El Salto del Colacho Baby Jumping Festival (Spain)
Latvian Birth Traditions (Latvia)
Lohusa Şerbeti (Turkey)
Mutterpass (Germany) and *Carnet de Santé Maternité* (France)
Name Days (Catholic and Orthodox) and *Slava* (Serbian Orthodox)
Nordic Napping (Europe)
Quccija (Malta)
Weihnachtsmärchen and Advent Calendars (Germany)

India
Devadasi System (India)
Hindu Baby Rituals (Hinduism)
Mundan Ceremony (India)
Sikh Baby Rites and *Naam Karan* Naming Ceremony (Sikhism)
Upanayana: Sacred Thread Ritual (Hinduism)

International
Baby Racing (International)
Baby Showers (International)
Baby Welcoming (Paganism)
Baptism and Christening (Christianity)
Birth Trees (International)
Birthday Cakes (International)
Birthday Candles (International)
Birthday Cards (International)
Birthday Torments (International)
Birthdays (International)
Birthstones (International)
Bismillah Ceremony (Islam)
Breastfeeding (International)
Brit Milah (Judaism)
Burying the Placenta (International)
Calabash Chalk (Nigeria, United Kingdom, United States, and Canada)
Changeling Beliefs (International)
Child Beauty Pageants (International)
Childermas (Christianity)
Childhood Vaccinations (International)
Christening Gown (Christianity)
Churching of Women (Christianity)
Couvade (International)
Cutting the Umbilical Cord Traditions (International)
Eating Human Placenta (International)
Fairytale (International)
Father's Day (International)
First Communion (Christianity)
Food Taboos in Pregnancy (International)
Girl Guides (International)
Government-Approved Baby Names (International)
Groaning Cheese and Groaning Cake (United Kingdom and North America)
"Happy Birthday" Song (International)

Kangaroo Care (International)
Lamaze Technique and Bradley Method (International)
Lotus Birthing (International)
Lullabies (International)
May Crowning Ritual (Catholicism)
Mistletoe (International)
Monstrous Punishments for Naughty Children (International)
Mothering Sunday (Christianity)
Muslim Birth Rites (Islam)
Muslim Male Circumcision (Islam)
Nativity Play (International)
Navjote Ceremony: Zoroastrian Initiation (Zoroastrianism)
Nursery Rhymes (International)
Parental Leave (International)
Party Games (International)
Phallus Festivals (International)
Pidyon Haben: Redemption of the First Born (Judaism)
Potty Training (International)
Pregnancy Yoga (International)
Saint Nicholas (Christianity)
Scouts (International)
Slow Parenting Movement (International)
Spitting on Babies (International)
Steiner Schools (International)
Swaddling (International)
Tooth Fairy and Tooth Mouse (International)
Traditional Bedwetting Remedies (International)
Traditional Teething Remedies (International)
Waldkindergarten (International)
Warding Off the Evil Eye (International)
Water Birth (International)
Wetting the Baby's Head (International)
Wiccaning (Wicca)
Witch Ball (International)

North America
Apache Baby Ceremonies (Apache)
Atiq Ceremony (Inuit)
Blessingway Ceremony (Navajo)
Cradleboard (Native American)
Dream Catcher (Native American)
Hopi Naming Rites (Hopi)
Worry Dolls and *Katsina* Dolls (Guatemala and Hopi)

Scandinavia
Akka Goddess Customs (Saami)
Cardboard Box Beds (Finland)
Dala Horse (Sweden)

South and Central America
Covering the Belly Button Traditions (Latin America)
El Bolo (Mexico)
La Cuarentena (Latin America)
Piñata (Mexico)
Tuj (Guatemala)
Worry Dolls and *Katsina* Dolls (Guatemala and Hopi)

United Kingdom and Ireland
Blidworth Cradle Rocking Ceremony (England)
Blooding (United Kingdom)
Blue Peter Badge (United Kingdom)

Cerne Abbas Giant (England)
Children's Laureate (United Kingdom)
Christingle (United Kingdom)
Grasmere Rushbearing (England)
Ladybird Books (England)
Little Edith's Treat (England)
"Monday's Child" (England)
Pantomime (United Kingdom)
Saining (Scotland)
Scroggling the Holly (England)
Silver Spoon (United Kingdom)
Sprinkling Cake (Ireland)
Wedding Ring Test (United Kingdom)
Whuppity Scoorie and Lanimer Day (Scotland)

VOLUME 2: ADOLESCENCE AND EARLY ADULTHOOD

Africa and Middle East

Breast Ironing (Africa and Elsewhere)
Chisungu (Zambia)
Cow Jumping (Ethiopia)
Dipo Womanhood Ceremony (Ghana)
Fattening Room Seclusion (Nigeria)
Forehead-Cutting Initiation (Africa)
Hajj (Islam)
Iria Ceremony (Nigeria)
Lobola (Southern Africa)
Maasai Warrior Initiation (Kenya and Tanzania)
Moroccan Weddings (Morocco)
Nkumbi (Democratic Republic of Congo)
Nyumba Ntobhu: Traditional Same-Sex Marriage (Tanzania)
Pika and *Nyora* (Zimbabwe and Mozambique)
Reed Dancing Chastity Ceremony (Kingdom of Swaziland)
Sharo: Public Flogging (Nigeria and Benin)
Wodaabe Courtship Dance and Festival (Africa)
Xhosa Circumcision (South Africa)

Asia (Central and North)

Afghani Betrothal (Afghanistan)

Asia (South and Southeast)

Chinese Coming-of-Age Ceremonies (China)
Coming of Age Day (Japan)
Ear-Piercing Ceremonies (Myanmar and Malaysia)
Filipino Debut (Philippines)
Gwallye (South Korea)
Hadaka Matsuri (Japan)
Hmong Names (Laos, Myanmar, Vietnam, Cambodia, and Thailand)
Log Riding (Japan)
Omiai: Japanese Matchmaking (Japan)
San-San-Kudo (Japan)
Shanghai Marriage Market (China)
Singles' Day (China) and Black Day (South Korea)
Sisters' Meal Festival (China)
Tooth-Filing Ceremony (Indonesia)
Visiting-Girls Courtship Tradition (China)
Zou Hun: Mosuo Walking Marriages (China)

Australia and Pacific

Bachelor and Spinster Balls (Australia)
Initiation by Semen Transferal (Papua New Guinea and Vanuatu)
Land Diving (Vanuatu)
Trobriand Ritualized Sex and Commitment (Papua New Guinea)
Walkabout (Australia)

Continental Europe and Russia

Andrzejki: St. Andrew's Eve (Poland)
Baccalauréat and *Matura* (Europe)
Birthday Humiliations for Singletons (Denmark and Germany)
Bulgarian Weddings (Bulgaria)
Fidanzamenti (Italy)
Hora (Eastern Europe)
Inter-Railing (Europe)
Ladouvane and St. Sylvester's Day (Bulgaria)
La Soupe (France)
Lazarovden (Bulgaria)
Lindo (Croatia)
Looking for Fern Blossoms (Eastern Europe)
Majáles (Czech Republic)
Maypoles (Europe)
Polterabend (Germany)
Povitica (Eastern Europe)
Schuhplattler (Germany) and *Ländler* (Austria)
Secular Confirmation (Europe)
Sock Garland (Germany)
St. Catherine's Day (France)
Sünnet (Turkey)
Vinok (Ukraine)

India

Chokha Thavani Viddhi: Devipujak Purification Trial (India)
Dastaar Bandi and *Amrit Sanchar* (Sikhism)
Diwali and *Kali Pooja* (India)
Hijra (Indian Sub-Continent)
Kumbh Mela (India)

International

Arranged Marriage and Forced Marriage (International)
Assyrian Betrothal and Weddings (International)
Bar Mitzvah and *Bat Mitzvah* (Judaism)
Beards (International)
Christian Wedding Ceremony (Christianity)
Dyngus Day (Eastern Europe and United States)
Female Genital Cutting (Africa, Middle East, Asia, and Elsewhere)
Gap Year (International)
Hair Removal (International)
Handfasting (Scotland, also Neo-Paganism)
Handparting (Wicca)
Hijab (Islam)
Hindu Wedding Ceremony (Hinduism)
Horah (Judaism)
Horseshoes (International)
Human Tooth Sharpening (Indonesia and Africa)
Jewish Wedding Customs (Judaism)
Jumping Over the Broom (United Kingdom and United States, also Neo-Paganism)

Jury Duty (International)
La Quinceañera (Latin America, the Caribbean, and the United States)
Leap Year Proposal (International)
Lip Plugs (Africa and South America)
Mehndi (International)
Menstrual Customs (International)
Menstrual Taboos (International)
Money Dance (International)
Moonie Weddings (International)
Muslim Wedding Ceremony (Islam)
Neck Elongation (Thailand, Myanmar, and South Africa)
Polyandry (International)
Polygyny (International)
Ritual Tattooing (International)
Russefeiring (Norway) and Schoolies Week (Australia)
Same-Sex Marriage (International)
Scarification (Africa and Papua New Guinea)
Shabka (Islam and Coptic Christianity)
Shinbyu (Buddhism)
Sikh Wedding Ceremony (Sikhism)
Thaipusam: Extreme Ritual Flesh Modification (Hinduism)
Training Bras (United States, Europe, and Australasia)
Twenty-First Birthday Traditions (International)
Urethral Subincision (Australia, Africa, and South America)
Virginity Testing (International)
Wedding Anniversaries (International)
Wedding Cakes (International)
Wedding Dress and Wedding Ring (International)
Wedding March and Bridal Chorus (International)
White Coat Ceremony and Pinning Ceremony (International)

North America
Bed-Courtship (Amish)
Cajun Weddings (United States)
Isanaklesh Gotal (Mescalero Apache)
Sock Dance (Canada)
Purity Ball (United States)
Rumspringa (United States and Canada)
Sunrise Ceremony (Apache, United States)
Vision Quest (Native American)

South and Central America
Bullet Ant Initiation (Brazil)
Courtship Whistling (Mexico)
Face in Birthday Cake (Mexico)
Matis Hunting Trials (Brazil)

United Kingdom and Ireland
Blackening the Bride (Scotland)
British Wedding Traditions (United Kingdom)
Burning the Ashen Faggot (England) and The Burning of the Clavie (Scotland)
Choosing Options (England, Wales, and Northern Ireland)
Dunmow Flitch Trials (England)
Gretna Green (Scotland)
Handfasting (Scotland, also Neo-Paganism)
Lovespoons (Wales)
Marriage Banns (Christianity)
RAG Week (United Kingdom and Ireland)
St. Dwynwen's Day (Wales)

VOLUME 3: AGING AND DEATH

Africa and Middle East
Edir (Ethiopia)
Engozi (Uganda)
Famadihana (Madagascar)
Fantasy Coffins (Ghana)
Sakalava Royal Death Traditions and *Fitampoha* (Madagascar)

Asia (Central and North)
Sky Burials (Autonomous Tibet and China)

Asia (South and Southeast)
Chinese Death Customs (China)
Crucifixion Rituals (Philippines)
Living with the Dead (Indonesia)
Ngaben (Indonesia)
Qingming Festival (China)
Tết Nguyên Dan (Vietnam)
Yu Lan Jie: The Hungry Ghost Festival (China)

Australia and Pacific
Finger Amputation (Papua New Guinea)
High-Platform Exposure of the Corpse (Australia)
Malagan (Papua New Guinea)
Tangihanga: Māori Mourning Ritual (New Zealand)
Tongan Funerals (Tonga)

Europe and Russia
Albanian Funeral Customs (Albania)
Funeral Plants (Europe)
The Great Passing (Romania)
Isola di San Michele: Venice's Cemetery Island (Italy)
Mirila (Croatia)
Ossuaries (Europe)
Plastination (Germany)
Romanian Funeral Customs (Romania)
Saturday of Souls (Orthodox Christianity, Bulgaria, and Serbia) and *Radonitsa* (Russia)
Soul Cakes and Soul Breads (Europe)
Windmills (The Netherlands)
Yew Trees (Europe)
Zaduszki (Poland)

Elsewhere
Space Burial (Outer Space)

India
Hindu Death Customs (Hinduism)
Sallekhanā (Jainism)
Sikh Death Customs (Sikhism)
Vrindavan: The City of Widows (India)
Zoroastrian Funerals (India)

International

"Abide With Me" (United Kingdom, North America, and Australasia)
All Souls' Day (Europe and South America)
Alkaline Hydrolysis (United Kingdom, Australia, and United States)
Ankou (France and England)
Assisted Suicide (International)
Buddhist Attitudes Toward Death (Buddhism)
Cairn (International)
Christian Death Rituals (Christianity)
Condolences (International)
Cremation (International)
Croning, Saging, and Elderling Ceremonies (Paganism)
Death Dance (International)
Dia de los Muertos: Day of the Dead (Latin America and United States)
Doom Metal (International)
Easter Eggs (Christianity)
Exhumation (Europe and Asia)
Endocannibalism (Papua New Guinea and Brazil)
Eulogies (International)
Funeral Cakes and Funeral Candy (International)
Funeral Doom (International)
Funeral Songs (International)
Goth Subculture (International)
Grave Rental (Europe and Asia)
Hallowe'en (International)
Halva (International)
Jewish Death Customs (Judaism)
Koliva (International)
"The Last Post" (International)
Martinstag (International)
Memento Mori (International)
Minute's Silence (International)
Missing Man Formation (International)
Mummification (International)
Muslim Death Rituals (Islam)
National Mourning (International)
Obituary (International)
Passion Play (Christianity)
Pregnancy and Infant Loss Remembrance Day (International)
Remembrance Day and Remembrance Sunday (International)
Retirement and Pensions (International)
Riderless Horse (International)
Santa Muerte (Mexico and United States)
Senior Sporting Events (International)
Spontaneous Shrines (International)
State Funeral (International)
Stations of the Cross (Christianity)
Suicide Landmarks (International)
"Taps" (International)
Taxidermy (International)
Tear Catchers and Mourning Jewelry (International)
Tomb of the Unknown Soldier (International)
Tombstone Tourism (International)
Traditional Mourning Colors (International)
University of the Third Age (International)
Vanitas (International)
Wake (International)
Wearing Flowers to Honor War Dead (International)

North America

Changing of the Guard Ceremony (United States)
Condemned Prisoner's Last Meal (United States)
Delaware Indian Death Rituals (North America)
Embalming (United States)
Jazz Funeral (United States)
Lakota Death Rituals (Lakota)
Mortuary Totem Poles (Haida and Tlingit)

South and Central America and Caribbean

Eating the Ashes of the Dead (Brazil and Venezuela)
Japanese Death Customs (Japan)
Mizuko Kuyo: Japanese Fetus Memorial Service (Japan)
Nine-Nights (Caribbean)
San La Muerte (South America)
Shrunken Heads (Peru and Ecuador)
Zombies and Voodoo Death Traditions (Haiti)

United Kingdom and Ireland

Bees (United Kingdom)
Chelsea Pensioners (England)
Denville Hall & Brinsworth House (England)
Eleanor Crosses (England)
Eyam Plague Sunday Service (England)
"Lyke-Wake Dirge" (England)
Maidens' Garlands (England)
Maundy Money (United Kingdom)
Message From the Queen (United Kingdom)
Passing Bells (England and Scotland)
Pauper's Funeral (United Kingdom)
Personalized Hearses (United Kingdom)
Royal Wootton Bassett (England)

A

AFGHANI BETROTHAL, AFGHANISTAN

When the parents of an Afghani boy and girl decide that their children should marry, they engage a family member as a go-between. The go-between is known as a *ru-yi-bar* or *wasta* and is charged with negotiating the financial matters involved in the engagement. To begin with, it is the women of the families that initiate the complex Afghani betrothal process, with male relatives generally entering into the process only when it comes to settling the financial agreements necessary for a marriage to proceed. These arrangements include the negotiating of a dowry paid by the bride's family that is written into the marriage contract. In rural areas, the dowry tends to consist of linens, clothes, and household utensils while in cities the dowry extends to include electrical goods and modern gadgets that should last a married couple for 15 years. Large sums of money, property, and livestock may also be transferred from the groom's family to the bride's family but this is not necessarily due to the greed of the bride's family but as a sign of esteem—in Afghanistan status is conferred according to the value set upon something. Therefore, if a bride and her family are given only a small amount of money then it would be an embarrassment in the eyes of their community. Additionally, while Islam, the main religion in Afghanistan, does not allow the awarding of a bride price, property and money may be given as a personal gift to the bride for her personal use in the event of a divorce, since Islam does not include the giving of alimony. One consequence of this situation is that, as exorbitant sums of money may be demanded by bride's families, many men cannot marry until they are much older and have, therefore, had enough time to accrue the finances needed to wed. Thus it has been known for older men to marry much younger girls, leading to high levels of widowhood. Normally, however, Afghanis marry in their late teens or early twenties.

Once both families agree that a marriage can go ahead a date is set for the *labsgriftan*, meaning "promise" or "to get the word." This ceremony sees many elder women from the groom's family travel to the bride's home where they are served candies and tea and accept a tray bearing more candies and a *qand*, a special conical sweet loaf that varies in height from one to two-and-a-half feet tall with a base of about six inches. Also on the tray is an embroidered handkerchief that symbolizes the intention to marry. Before a week is over the boy's family must return the tray that this time is filled with money. Once this occurs the couple's betrothal is declared.

The next ceremony to take place is the *shirin-i-griftan* (or *khwahish khwari*), which is an official betrothal ceremony that takes place either soon after the tray is returned or after several months, depending on circumstance. It is customary for only women to attend the shirin-i-griftan, which takes place at the bride's family home and sees many of the groom's female relatives bring the bride-to-be a year's supply of dresses (around four or five), jewelry, and a silver vanity set comprising a toothpick, tweezers, and an ear-cleaner. The bride-to-be may also receive a silver pendant decorated with fish, the traditional Afghani symbol of fertility, or with circles. These circles represent the sun that in turn symbolizes a couple's happiness, loyalty, and luck. The shirin-i-griftan therefore serves as both an official betrothal party and as a way for women on both sides of the soon-to-be united families to bond. During the shirin-i-griftan ceremony a close relative of the bride then breaks the qand over the bride's head using a ceremonial ax that is decorated with a bird of life, an ancient Middle Eastern symbol of good luck that is traditionally associated with weddings in Afghanistan. It is considered auspicious if the qand breaks into many pieces when hit with the ax and the bride's family keeps the base of the loaf to make *sharbat*, a sherbet drink flavored with rose petals, and *malida*, a wheat pudding, that are served at the wedding. The sharbat served at weddings, *tokhm-i-riyan* or *tokhm-i-biryan*, is usually decorated with fruit seeds that are redolent of fertility. A special type of omelet called *wiskel* may also be served to guests.

In urban areas of Afghanistan *shirin-i-griftan* is no longer fashionable and so in cities the ceremony is either ignored or combined with the wedding ceremony (*arusi* or *wadeh*). In Kabul, the capital city of Afghanistan, upper-class and wealthy families usually host *shirin-i-griftan* ceremonies as a gala event held at prestigious restaurants and hotels rather than at the bride's home while middle-class families will hold the ceremony at semi-Western style restaurants. In urban areas the ceremony may not be attended exclusively by females. In this case the groom's close male relatives will invite other men to the ceremony while the groom's female relatives will invite other women to the event. When the *shirin-i-griftan* is combined with the wedding ceremony gifts of jewelry and clothing will be delivered to the bride by the groom's female relatives. Jewelry intended to be worn by the bride during the wedding ceremony normally consists of a bracelet called a *karah*, an arm band called a *churi*, an anklet called a *halhal*, a necklace that emits a hissing sound as it moves that is called a *selselah*, a forehead decoration called a *tik,* and a locket known as a *guluband*. Also presented to the bride are earrings called *gushwarah* and rings called *angeshter*. It used to be commonplace for brides to wear a nose ring called a *halqa-yi-bini* too, but these are no longer popular in urban areas and are also falling out of fashion in other parts of Afghanistan too.

Another pre-wedding celebration held in Afghanistan includes a henna night for women called *takht e khina*. For the *takht e khina* celebration to take place henna is transported on a tray carried in a basket decorated with flowers and candles by children from the groom's house to the bride's home. The procession is accompanied by music. At the bride's home the bride sits on her sofa wearing her wedding clothes and her elder brother brings her groom to her. However the groom's female relatives pretend to prevent the bride from approaching the groom, joking that she must first "pay, then enter." Now the party begins and the bride forms her right hand into a fist and refuses to allow the groom to decorate her hand with henna unless his mother either gives her a valuable gift or if the groom manages to force open her hand. The groom does not stay at the henna party for long, as it is essentially an all-female affair. Indeed the groom departs as soon as he has placed henna on the bride's hand and tied it with a length of white fabric. Once the groom has gone henna is distributed among all the young unmarried females present at the party. According to tradition any girl that puts henna on her little finger will soon be a bride.

The next day the wedding ceremony takes place with all expenses and arrangements borne by the groom's family. The bride's family and friends gather with her in her father's house where she sits with other females waiting for her groom and his friends and relatives to arrive and take her to the groom's home where she will be married.

See also: Arranged Marriage and Forced Marriage; Assyrian Betrothal and Weddings; *Mehndi*; Muslim Wedding Ceremony; Povitica; *Shabka*; Wedding Cake; Wedding Dress and Wedding Ring

Further Reading
Dupree, Louis. *Afghanistan*. Princeton, NJ: Princeton University Press, 1980.
Gladstone, Carey. *Afghanistan Revisited*. New York: Nova Science Publishers Inc., 2001.
Muzafarry, Fazl ul Rahim. "Afghan Muslim Wedding." OnIslam.net, August 17, 2013. Accessed June 12, 2015, at http://www.onislam.net/english/culture-and-entertainment/traditions/411646-afghan-muslim-wedding.html.

ANDRZEJKI: ST. ANDREW'S EVE, POLAND

In Poland, unmarried women and girls perform various forms of love divination customs on *Andrzejki*, or St. Andrew's Eve, which takes place November 29 (St. Andrew's Eve) through November 30 (St. Andrew's Day) each year. Similar customs also take place in Germany, Romania, Slovakia, Russia, Ukraine, Greece, and the Czech Republic. Andrzejki is a light-hearted occasion that is nonetheless popular as it creates a fun, lively atmosphere. Another reason for the popularity of the occasion is that the name of the custom refers to the name Andrzej, the Polish equivalent of Andrew, which is a very common name in Poland.

The custom of celebrating St. Andrew's Eve with an evening of fortune telling began in the 16th century. At this time, bachelors had a separate love divination occasion on St. Catherine's Day (*Katarzynki*) that fell on November 2 but this is no longer celebrated. It is not known why Saint Andrew became associated with romantic fortune telling but that such love traditions occur in winter is not surprising as the nights are long during the harsh Polish winter and in years gone by this was a time when romances would be forged between young village men and women. It follows therefore that during winter the imaginations of unmarried

> ### *Katarzynki* Gingerbread
>
> *Katarzynki* is a cloud-shaped, chocolate-covered gingerbread traditionally associated with the old Katarzynki (St. Catherine's Day) festivities that were held in Poland. According to legend, six round gingerbread cookies accidently melted into one while baking when they were being made in preparation for the St. Catherine's Day celebrations, hence the bobbly shape of Katarzynki. Though Katarzynki celebrations no longer occur the gingerbread is, nonetheless, still popular. Gingerbread is an iconic element of Polish food with a museum dedicated to gingerbread located in the medieval Polish town of Toruń (birthplace of the astronomer Nicolaus Copernicus). The town also hosts a gingerbread festival each September.

women turned to love divination to see what the future held for them in regards to romance and marriage. Though Andrzejki is said to have its origins in pagan folk traditions, Poland is now an overwhelmingly Christian (specifically Catholic) country, hence a Christian name has been given to the night of fortune telling.

There are no specific ways of performing love divination during Andrzejki but the most popular techniques feature wax, shoes, and a wedding ring. The wax method, called *lanie wosku* (pouring wax), is perhaps the most popular divination technique and sees an unmarried woman pour hot wax through the handle of a key onto cold water. In the past molten lead or tin was used instead of the wax and the key used was taken from a church door. Once the wax has hardened on the surface of the water all but one light is switched off in the room in which the divination is occurring and the wax shape is lifted up to the light so that it casts a shadow upon a wall. The shape that the shadow forms is viewed from all sides as everyone gathered for the occasion tries to divine what the cast shape means for the woman's future, particularly her marriage prospects. Similarly, the names of local men might be written on scraps of paper that are then placed on the edge of a bowl of water in the center of which a lit candle sits. The first named piece of paper to burn is taken to be the name of the man whom the unmarried woman will wed.

Another Andrzejki custom involves four cups being flipped upside down over a wedding ring, a crucifix or rosary, a doll, and a leaf or flower. This tradition is called *talerzyki*, meaning little plates. Unmarried females then choose one cup, the contents of which is said to reveal their romantic future—the wedding ring signifies that the woman will marry, the crucifix or rosary suggests the woman will become a nun, the leaf or flower predicts a life of spinsterhood, and the doll foretells that the woman will bear an illegitimate child.

Another very popular Andrzejki custom involves placing unmarried women's shoes (*buty*) one behind the other along a wall and then moving them in turn toward a door. The woman that owns the shoes that crosses the doorstep first is, according to tradition, destined to be the first to marry out of all the girls whose shoes were moved.

Such romantic tomfoolery fosters an excited atmosphere that is fuelled further by the drinking of the traditional Andrzejki drink, *szarlotka*, a mix of vodka and apple juice, that is Polish women's favorite alcoholic tipple. Another old St. Andrew's Day tradition may, however, scupper the romantic hopes of unmarried females for it is customary for girls, worn out by the revelries of Andrzejki, to eat three cloves of garlic before going to bed that night.

See also: All Souls' Day (Volume 3); *Ladouvane* and St. Sylvester's Day; *Lazarovden*; Looking for Fern Blossoms; St. Catherine's Day; *Vinok*

Further Reading

Regents of the University of Michigan. "Katarzynki i Andrzejki." *Slavic Languages: Polish*. 2003. Accessed September 27, 2015, at http://www.lsa.umich.edu/slavic/dept/Web BasedLanguage/Polish/Culture/Andrzejki/Andzrejki.htm.

Urban-Klaehn, Jagoda. "St. Andrew's Night—Tradition of Fortune Telling." Polishsite. Accessed September 27, 2015, at http://culture.polishsite.us/articles/art14fr.htm.

Van Lierop, Christiaan. "Polish Culture Explored—The Tradition of Andrzejki." BBC: Where I Live—Coventry & Warwickshire, September 24, 2014. Accessed September 27, 2015, at http://www.bbc.co.uk/coventry/features/stories/polish/polish-november-tradition.shtml.

ARRANGED MARRIAGE AND FORCED MARRIAGE, INTERNATIONAL

In many countries around the world, marriages are arranged by a couple's parents, sometimes, though not always, with the bride and groom having little say in the matter. This is a so-called arranged marriage. Such marriages are most prevalent in areas of the world that exhibit an extremely hierarchical class structure, though they also occur in the West among immigrant communities. However in the West arranged marriages can prove highly contentious. For example, children from the third generation of Sikh and Hindu families in the United Kingdom that have grown up with Western ideals of romantic love and courtship may struggle with the concept of not choosing their own life partner. Areas in which arranged marriage are common include the Indian subcontinent, Central Asia, China, some African nations and, very occasionally, in parts of Eastern Europe that maintain old traditions.

Historically European aristocracy and royalty have long practiced arranged marriage in order to forge strong political alliances and amass territory. Moreover, in France during the Middle Ages a family in the aristocracy might give away a daughter in marriage to a loyal subject as a way of thanking the subject for a service they had performed. This custom is evident in many fairytales of European origin in which a princess is given to the tale's hero as a reward for achieving a great feat. Today, however, there are two main types of arranged marriage, both of which involve the couple's parents forging an alliance between their families, sometimes by using a matchmaker as a go-between during negotiations.

In the West, the concept of arranged marriage is often associated with India where the tradition of arranged marriage began as a way of uniting upper-caste families. Then, over time the system spread to the lower caste where it was employed for the same purpose. In has been estimated that in India today 90 percent of marriages are instigated and later arranged by families and that the couples involved are happy with this process. Though India is a hugely diverse country in terms of religion and language, 80 percent of Indians are Hindu, a religion that sees marriage as a social, moral, and religious obligation. Moreover, Hinduism views marriage as a milestone on the journey to adulthood with clearly defined roles for husbands and wives. From a spiritual perspective marriage is a pre-requisite for a Hindu, for without a marriage partner they will be unable to enter the life-stage of a householder, *Grishasth ashrama*, nor will they be able to have children. For a Hindu person, not to have a child, particularly a son, is a serious issue as without offspring an individual can find no release from the cycle of reincarnation that follows the pattern of birth, death, and rebirth. Thus, Hindu people feel a great pressure to marry and it is not uncommon for a Hindu couple's family to arrange their marriage before the couple is even born with the couple having little say in their marriage even as grown adults. From an Indian socio-economic viewpoint, marriage allows families to maintain their place in society and allows parents to control their children even as adults. Indian parents also favor arranged marriage because it helps to preserve ancestral lineage and strengthen kinship groups while consolidating and expanding a family's property. Therefore, in order to ensure that a marriage is beneficial in terms of wealth creation and class maintenance, Indian families spend a great deal of time and money on finding suitable marriage partners for their offspring as the bride and groom must be comparable in terms of social class, religion, and their place within the caste system. A couple's family background and horoscopes may also be scrutinized to ensure compatibility.

In order to alleviate some of the stress of finding a spouse for arranged marriage, a family may employ a traditional matchmaker called a *nayan*. This is usually a family friend or relative that acts as a neutral intermediary when families are in the process of arranging a marriage. Nayans serve two purposes—primarily as marriage scouts whose job it is to find potential matches, and secondly as negotiators that mediate between families. As a scout and negotiator, a family sends the nayan into the community to seek possible matches. Once the nayan has located a possible match, the matchmaker notifies their clients and act as a go-between for communication. Communication continues through the nayan until a marriage agreement is settled. Once an agreement is met, the nayan may continue to assist in the wedding preparations by buying jewelry and clothing, arranging the ceremony, and notifying the wider community of the upcoming nuptials. The nayan typically does not receive a fee but may be given clothes and food by both families as a thank you for their efforts.

India's recent globalization has had only a limited impact on the country's system of arranged marriages. In modern India, there are now three sub-classes of arranged marriage: the traditional, the modified traditional, and the cooperative traditional.

All three see parents making decisions about appropriate marriage partners for their children but vary in the degree of veto offered to the children involved. In traditional arranged marriages, the adult children have no say in who they wed and do not meet their marriage partner until the day of the wedding. In the modified traditional pattern children are allowed a say during the search for a prospective spouse and may meet each other before the wedding, but they do not have a right of refusal if they do not want to marry the partner that their parents have selected for them. The cooperative traditional model allows children to have a say in the spouse selection process, meet the selected individual before the wedding and maintain the right to refuse a marriage proposal from the person chosen for them. According to researchers in recent years there has be an increase in the number of cooperative traditional arranged marriages and also a small rise in the number of Indians marrying outside of their caste and religion. Even so, because Indian society is patriarchal and patrilineal (i.e., descent and authority passes down through a family's males), women are under pressure to marry at a young age as unmarried women are seen as both a social and economic burden by their families.

Modernization is also modifying the arranged marriage process in China and Africa. For instance the Tuareg people of Niger now allow their young people a say in who they marry whereas once they did not. Indeed the Tuareg were known to promise prepubescent girls in arranged marriage, force-feeding them milk in order to given them the fuller look of an older female. The girl would then be taken to the site of her betrothal where the marriage would then be consummated. Similarly in China, where arranged marriage has long been the tradition, the marriage process is now much freer. Though families still employ traditional matchmakers, the matchmakers generally just highlight a man or woman's merits to parents looking for a spouse for their child. The matchmaker may also arrange for the paying of a dowry or other financial arrangements between the two families concerned.

Forced marriage differs from arranged marriage in that in most arranged marriages children have a veto but generally choose to comply with their parents' choice of marriage partner out of a sense of duty. Contrastingly, in forced marriage children do not have free choice as to whether to accept a marriage proposal. Forced marriage is one in which one or both partners do not consent to the marriage but are coerced into the marriage by physical, psychological, economic, sexual, or emotional duress. Examples of the emotional duress applied by parents to force their children into marriage include parents insisting that rejection of a marriage proposal will bring shame upon the family. Alternatively, arrangements for the forced marriage may be made abroad and then the bride is taken to that country without her being told the purpose of her trip. Since pressure, fear, and duress are major factors in forced marriage, many people view forced marriage as a form of domestic violence. Also, as the victims of forced marriage are usually female, some organizations consider forced marriage to be a form of violence against girls and women.

No religion encourages forced marriage as the issue is a cultural tradition rather than a religious practice. While victims of the tradition tend to be Muslim, a substantial number of those entered into forced marriage come from other groups, including the Sikh, Hindu, Orthodox Jewish, and Roma communities. While forced marriages may seem to be most prevalent in the Indian sub-continent, south and central Asia, and the Middle East, the practice is also proving to be an issue in the West. For example, in 2014 it became a criminal offence to force someone into marriage in England and Wales with the crime carrying a maximum jail term of seven years under the Anti-Social Behaviour, Crime and Policing Act 2014. The government's Forced Marriage Unit (FMU) also works at eradicating forced marriage in both the United Kingdom and abroad. The FMU, which was established in 2005, is jointly administered by the United Kingdom's Foreign and Commonwealth Office and Home Office and in 2012, was involved in 1,485 cases of forced marriage in which one in eight of the females involved was under 16 years old, the legal age of consent in the United Kingdom. Indeed the youngest victim of forced marriage in the United Kingdom was two years old. In 2013, the cases investigated by FMU involved people from 74 different countries. These countries included the nations from which the victims came, and nations to which victims are in danger of being taken or have been taken already in order to be married. Of these countries, over 40 percent of the cases were connected to Pakistan, while 10 percent involved India or Bangladesh. Conflicts in various parts of the world are said to be fuelling a rise in forced marriage globally. For example, in 2014 the United Nations Children's Fund (UNICEF) reported that 20 percent of Syrian girls under 16 years of age were being entered into forced marriages with some brides aged as young as nine years old. This is compared to one in eight girls forced into marriage in 2013. Once the girls are married they have to leave their families who they may never see again. Young girls forced into marriage also tend to have more children earlier in life which is detrimental to their physical health and also means they lack opportunities to gain an education. Meanwhile, in countries such as Afghanistan, which has signed up to the United Nations' Convention on the Rights of the Child and the Convention on the Elimination of All Forms of Discrimination against Women, forced marriage continues to be a deep-rooted cultural tradition. In Afghanistan marriage is seen as way to settle debts and reinforce family status through social bonds. Needy families view a daughter as a financial liability who must wed quickly to reduce the economic strain on her family. Also in light of the ongoing political instability in Afghanistan many families try to marry off their daughters when they are young in order to safeguard the girls' futures.

While girls and women make up the overwhelming majority of the victims of forced marriage, men may also find themselves forced to marry. This is especially true of homosexual and bisexual men whose families hope to dissuade them from following their true sexual orientation by forcing them into marriage.

In 2014, world leaders, charities, and non-governmental organizations gathered in the United Kingdom for the first Girl Summit, co-hosted by UNICEF and the United Kingdom government, which aimed to rally efforts to end female genital cutting and Child, Early and Forced Marriage (CEFM), issues that affect millions of females around the world.

See also: Afghani Betrothal; Assyrian Betrothal and Weddings; Bulgarian Weddings; Fairytales (Volume 1); Hindu Wedding Ceremony; Jewish Wedding Customs; *Lobola*; Moonie Weddings; Muslim Wedding Ceremony; *Omiai*; Shanghai Marriage Market; Sikh Wedding Ceremony

Further Reading

Dugan, Emily. "Forced Marriage: How Hundreds of Terrified British Victims of the Tradition Are Being Failed Every Year by the Services They Need Most," *The Independent*, July 17, 2015. Accessed August 27, 2015, at http://www.independent.co.uk/news/uk/crime/forced-marriage-how-hundreds-of-terrified-british-victims-of-the-tradition-are-being-failed-every-year-by-the-services-they-need-most-10394985.html.

Flanigan, Santana. "Arranged Marriages, Matchmakers, and Dowries in India." Postcolonial Studies @ Emory, October 2012. Accessed August 25, 2015, at https://scholarblogs.emory.edu/postcolonialstudies/2014/06/20/arranged-marriages-matchmakers-and-dowries-in-india/.

IloveIndia.com. "Arranged Marriage." Accessed August 25, 2015, at http://www.iloveindia.com/indian-traditions/arranged-marriage.html.

Jaiswal, Tulika. *Indian Arranged Marriages: A Social Psychological Perspective*. Abingdon, UK: Routledge, 2014.

Monger, George P. *Marriage Customs of the World: From Henna to Honeymoons*. Santa Barbara, CA: ABC-CLIO, 2004.

Press Association. "Forced Marriage Outlawed as Ministers Step Up Efforts to Curb Practice," *The Guardian*, June 16, 2014. Accessed August 25, 2015, at http://www.theguardian.com/society/2014/jun/16/forced-marriage-outlawed-ministers-curb-practice.

Walther, Cornelia. "Forced and Early Marriages Still Common for Girls in Afghanistan." UNICEF: Afghanistan, March 17, 2010. Accessed August 27, 2015, at http://www.unicef.org/gender/afghanistan_53054.html.

Warnes, Sophie. "How Prevalent Is Forced Marriage in the UK?" *The Guardian*, July 22, 2014. Accessed August 27, 2015, at http://www.theguardian.com/news/datablog/2014/jul/22/how-prevalent-is-forced-marriage-in-the-uk.

Watt, Nicholas, and Patrick Wintour. "Britain to Tackle Big Rise in Syrian Refugee Girls Forced to Marry," *The Guardian*, March 15, 2014. Accessed August 27, 2015, at http://www.theguardian.com/world/2014/mar/15/britain-tackle-rise-syrian-refugee-girls-forced-marriage.

Women's Aid Federation of England. "Topic: Forced Marriage." Accessed August 25, 2015, at http://www.womensaid.org.uk/domestic_violence_topic.asp?section=0001000100220031.

ASSYRIAN BETROTHAL AND WEDDINGS, INTERNATIONAL

In the ancient region of Assyria, which covers areas of modern-day Iraq, Iran, Turkey, and Syria, long-standing traditions such as marriage customs continue despite increasing modernization. The Assyrian people take marriage customs very seriously and as a result many Assyrian marriage customs have been enacted for generations. There are thought to be around three million Assyrians worldwide. Though the people known as the Assyrians are varied in terms of location, language, politics, and religion some commonalities exist between them. Outside of the Middle East, notable Assyrian populations can be found in Sweden, Russia, Armenia, the Netherlands, and Canada as well as in the United States. Though Assyrian marriage customs among expat communities are more relaxed, the solemn nature of Assyrian marriage means that the institution of marriage is taken very seriously in Assyria. For this reason in Assyria demonstrations of affection between betrothed couples are considered improper and even couples that have been married for a long time will incur social scorn if they show affection toward each other in public.

In Assyria, marriage is considered a permanent union of not just two people but also of two families. For this reason, Assyrian parents considered it their main duty to find suitable marriage partners for their children. The chief responsibility for arranging marriages lies with the father, who is seen as head of his household and, according to Assyrian tradition, has complete authority over his wife who in turn is expected to obey and respect her husband. Until very recently tradition dictated that fathers had absolute authority over their wives and children and, though this stance has softened a little, fathers still tend to select husbands for their daughters and arrange all marriage formalities. The social rank of a potential bride is thoroughly investigated by a boy's family before any final decisions are taken about whether or not a couple should wed. Traditionally, families select wives from the same clan or tribal division as themselves and always from the same sect of the family religion as the boy. Marriage between closely related couples (e.g., first and second cousins) is forbidden however. Assyrian families tend to marry off their daughters at a fairly young age as the girls are considered to be of little worth to the family and, moreover, unmarried daughters are seen as a financial burden. Once a father has chosen a girl for his son he seeks her hand in marriage on his son's behalf. To do this the father sets out to the girl's home accompanied by elderly male relatives and calls on the girl's family to make a formal marriage proposal. The son does not accompany his father and the girl stays in her quarters during the visit from her future father-in-law. The boy's father raises the subject of a possible marriage in an indirect manner and it is traditional for the girl's father to feign surprise at the proposed marriage. The girl's father then entrusts close family members sitting nearby to decide whether he should accept the proposal. The relatives indicate their decision by nodding or shaking their heads. If the proposal is considered favorable then the boy's father kisses the hands of the bride-to-be's father as a sign of gratitude and then drinks *arak* (anise flavored alcohol) with the girl's family. Both families then decide on a date for the betrothal ceremony, usually referred to as *matetha-d dhamanta* or *dewaqthad idha*, meaning betrothal contract, which is a day of great celebration.

On the day of the official betrothal the groom's parents and his male and female older relatives walk to the bride's home where a number of guests have gathered to see the formalities. The lengthy betrothal ceremony, which is overseen by a priest, is followed by a ring ceremony during which two guests are chosen to take the engagement ring to the bride-to-be, who is secluded in a separate room with her female relatives. Once the betrothal and ring ceremonies have concluded, the boy and girl become betrothed in the eyes of the law and obliged to marry. Once the betrothal is officially binding, a bride price is set, meaning that the groom's family must pay an amount of money to the bride's father. The amount payable is determined by much bartering between intermediaries used by the families to settle the matter. When the bride price is settled the groom's family kisses the hands of the bride's father. The groom's family then brings gifts to the bride usually including a silver belt, gold earrings, a nose ornament, and a silver anklet. The groom's family also gives the bride's mother and eldest brother many gifts. Once the gift-giving has concluded, the betrothal ceremony culminates in the rice feast, during which the groom's friends and family, together with guests from the betrothal ceremony, enjoy a celebratory meal followed by entertainment and drinking arak.

It is usual for the boy and girl to wed within two months of the betrothal and the wedding celebrations last for a week. As part of the celebrations the groom's family visits each home in their village in order to invite villagers to the wedding with relatives and other important people from surrounding areas also invited to attend the nuptials. One of the most important Assyrian wedding customs in the ritual of the groom's bathing, sometimes called *kheyapta-d khitna,* which is noteworthy as it marks the start of the wedding ceremony. According to tradition, the groom must be ritually cleansed before he can marry. Therefore, on the Saturday afternoon before his wedding the groom sits on a stool in a purpose-built, outdoor booth while his best man and other friends provide him with hot water that is heated over a wood fire. Once the groom has washed, his friends present him with new, brightly colored clothes including a special wedding outfit sometimes called *julle-h-d khumala* and a white cap decorated with ostrich feathers. The groom, together with his relatives, close male friends and village children, then walks slowly to the bride's house with the procession led by a band playing a woodwind instrument called a *zurna*. On reaching the bride's home the procession fires rifles into the air and dances. In contrast, the bride's family sit stoically as tradition dictates that they should not express joy at the upcoming wedding. Meanwhile, the bride sits silently in seclusion accompanied by her bridesmaids and female friends. Next, the bride is prepared for her wedding. The bride's preparations include washing and dressing, during which the bride is assisted by her maid of honor. The bride also has her hair plaited so that it hangs in two braids and then a headdress consisting of black material decorated with gold and silver coins is placed on her head. The bride's long dress is made of brown velvet embroidered with gold and silver threads around the waist of which a silver belt is tied. The bride also wears the gold and silver jewelry that she was given by the groom's family. As a finishing touch the bride covers her face with a veil made from opaque, pink fabric. Once the bride is dressed, she sits with her head bowed as the groom's mother is invited to see her and extol her beauty. To signal her approval of the bride, the groom's mother raises the bride's veil and kisses her head.

Next, a feast is held that lasts well into the night. This is followed early the next morning by the procession of the bride and groom to the church that will be the site of their *burakha*, or marriage service. The bride, with her face re-covered, is escorted to the church by her family and bridesmaids while the groom's party walks en masse to the church. All the while church bells ring to mark the occasion. In Assyria weddings usually take place on Sundays and last for two to four hours. The burakha is lengthy as it consists of many benedictions and special prayers. To start the ceremony the priest walks from the church altar toward the soon-to-be married couple that stands solemnly with the best man and maid of honor at their side. The priest then ties a blessed red and white silk cord around the head of the bride and groom. This ritual is symbolic of the bonds of matrimony that will bind the couple together. Next the priest asks the bride and groom if they enter into the marriage of their own volition. Other rituals that commonly take place at Assyrian weddings include steps to ward off the evil eye. For this reason it is common for the groom's male relatives to guard the church against people using supernatural powers to wish the bride and groom bad luck. Meanwhile inside the church it is traditional for a female relative of the groom to stand behind the couple during the wedding ceremony opening and closing a pair of scissors as this is thought to protect against both witchcraft and the evil eye. As an extra precaution against evil it is a very common practice to stick a pair of needles fashioned into a crucifix into the back of the groom's wedding outfit. The crucifix shape is believed to repel evil and also to redirect the evil back onto the person that initiated it. Such superstitious measures are taken because it is a commonly held belief in Assyria that some people are able to use black magic to create animosity between newlyweds, to make them infertile, and even to cause the death of the bride or groom. In addition to these customs, the Baznayeh Assyrians living in Iraq, Turkey, and Syria believe that devils live in the shoulders and backs of the priest presiding over a wedding and so prick the priest's shoulders with pins and needles in order to drive out the demons.

Later during the wedding, the priest places his hand first on the head of the groom and then on the bride as he says prayers and blessings. The groom then holds the bride's right hand and the priest holds aloft a crucifix and blesses the pair. The priest next gives a sermon on the value of marriage and explains the duties of a husband and wife. The priest then asks the couple whether they agree to love and honor each other and when they consent the priest proclaims the marriage oath. The last important ritual sees the couple's wedding rings placed in a bowl of holy wine where they are blessed. The priest then retrieves the rings and gives them to the bride and groom who place the rings on each other's fingers. The couple is then invited by the priest to drink the holy wine, something that necessitates the groom removing the veil from his bride's face. This is, therefore, very often the first time that a groom sees his wife's face.

To conclude the ceremony the priest declares the couple husband and wife and prays that God bless them. The groom's mother then strides forward and throws dried figs, walnuts, and coins over the newlyweds who are quickly surrounded by children scampering to retrieve the fruit, nuts, and money from the floor. The mother then blesses and kisses the couple. Next, the newlyweds lead a procession to the bride's family home where a feast is held. The banquet is extremely lavish as it is not only a wedding reception but also a farewell party for the bride who will have to leave her home to join her husband. The bride does not join in the festivities, however, as she is required to sit quietly and watch the feasting. At the end of the feast, the bride is led in procession from her family home to the house of her groom's father. This is often a tearful occasion as the bride is sad to leave her family.

On the way to the groom's home, it is usual for the bride's relatives to stop the groom and give him presents. When he reaches his home the groom climbs on to the roof where he treads on clay tiles. The groom then escorts his new wife toward the door where she is met by her new mother-in-law who takes dried figs, raisins, and walnuts from clay pots and places them on the bride's head. The mother-in-law then flings rice, wheat, and salt at the bride too. This is not done out of unkindness but rather as a way to ensure that the newlyweds are fertile. For her part the bride smashes the pots from which the foodstuffs were taken and then from another pot she takes a handful of butter that she rubs into the door of her new home.

Once these customs have concluded the new husband leads his bride to a special bridal chamber that is decorated with a colorful blanket and a tree from which hang pomegranates, apples, and quinces. The blanket symbolizes the home while the tree of fruit denotes affluence. Also inside the bridal chamber are two thrones for the king (husband) and queen (wife). For the next four to seven days the newlyweds are not allowed to leave these thrones often as their home is filled with much feasting and celebrating. The only time that the couple may leave their thrones is at night when, together with the maid of honor and best man, they enter a bedroom and all four individuals sleep separately. In fact, tradition dictates that the newlyweds must not sleep with each other until the week of wedding celebrations has concluded. The only physical intimacy permitted between the new husband and wife occurs at the start of the second day of festivities when the wife holds the groom's hand during a folk dance.

The week of celebrations concludes when the priest performs a final ritual blessing asking that God grant the couple many children. The couple's friends and family are present for this blessing that is known colloquially as "uncovering the bride's face" because it sees the bride's veil lifted permanently. Once the bride is uncovered, guests kiss the heads of both the husband and wife and leave money on a table to signify the end of the wedding celebrations. The next Sunday the groom takes his wife to visit her family home where figs, raisins, and walnuts are again thrown over the newlyweds. That night, the bride and groom stay over with her parents and then the next day the bride leaves her family home for the last time and goes to start her new life with her husband.

See also: Afghani Betrothal; Arranged Marriage and Forced Marriage; Bulgarian Weddings; *Hijab*; Moroccan Weddings; *Shabka*; Warding Off the Evil Eye (Volume 1)

Further Reading
Benjamin, Yoab. "Assyrian Rituals of Life-Cycle Events," Assyrian International News Agency. Accessed September 19, 2015, at http://www.aina.org/articles/yoab.htm.
Edelstein, Sari. *Food, Cuisine, and Cultural Competency for Culinary, Hospitality, and Nutrition Professionals*. Sudbury, MA: Jones and Bartlett Publishers, 2011.
Shoup, John A., ed. *Ethnic Groups of Africa and the Middle East: An Encyclopedia*. Santa Barbara, CA: ABC-CLIO, 2011.

B

BACCALAURÉAT AND *MATURA*, EUROPE

The *Baccalauréat*, commonly abbreviated as *le bac*, is an academic qualification taken by French students at the end of their time at *lycée*, or high school. The Baccalauréat takes the form of a week of exams held nationwide the passing of which determines whether a student may go on to university. The Baccalauréat is the focus of all French high school curriculums, both in France and in the country's overseas territories. Students at French-curriculum lycées in Canada and the United States may also take three sections of the general Baccalauréat: Literature, Economics and Social Sciences, Science and Mathematics. In France, students in both public and private schools take the qualification and many French people consider undergoing the highly stressful week of exams an essential French rite of passage. Moreover many people in France view the Baccalauréat as an element of French national identity. The qualification is awarded by the French Ministry of National Education.

The Baccalauréat was introduced to France by Napoleon I, the Emperor of France, in 1808. At this time, the exam questions were written in Latin and only 31 students passed the Baccalauréat to become Baccalauréat holders or *bacheliers*. As recently as 1945 the Baccalauréat was still seen as the preserve of the French intelligentsia with the qualification taken by only 3 percent of students. This contrasts with the 664,709 candidates that registered to take the exam in 2013 of which 70 percent gained a qualification. There are 91 versions of the Baccalauréat. These comprise three general options concentrated on science, economics and literature, eight Baccalauréats for technical students, and 80 professional Baccalauréats for students taking vocational programs.

The *Matura* (also called the *Mature*, *Matur*, *Maturita*, *Maturità*, *Maturität*, or *Mamypa* depending on location) is a school examination taken by students usually between 17 and 20 years of age living in a number of European countries. In some of these countries, students are required to pass the Matura in order to complete their secondary education and go to university. Therefore in this instance the Matura represents not only a final exam but also the transition from secondary to tertiary education, hence the Matura can be seen as a maturity diploma. The Matura is a feature of educational systems in many European countries, particularly Albania (where the exam is called the *Matura Shtetërore*), Austria (under the official name of *Reifeprüfung*), Bosnia and Herzegovina, Bulgaria, Croatia, Czech Republic, Hungary, Italy, Kosovo, Liechtenstein, Macedonia, Montenegro, Poland, Serbia, Slovakia, Slovenia, Switzerland, and the Ukrainian diaspora. The form that the Matura takes varies in each of these countries, as does the age at which the examination is taken.

In Poland, where the Matura is considered an important milestone in the lives of youngsters and the final element of formal education, the Matura consists of written and oral exams on selected subjects including a written test on Polish language and literature and in math. The questions asked in the Polish Matura are prepared by provincial schools and are the same for all the students taking the exam in that province. After completing a written exam a student also has to pass oral exams in two subjects of his or her choosing. Just over three months before Polish students face their Matura they get to enjoy their prom, which in Poland is known as the 100-days ball (or *studniowka*). Then once all the Matura exams have been taken a school-leavers' farewell ball is held, called *komers*.

See also: Choosing Options; Gap Year; Inter-Railing; *Russefeiring* and Schoolies Week

Further Reading
Campus France. "What Is the French Baccalauréat?" Accessed August 28, 2015, http://www.canada.campusfrance.org/en/report/what-french-baccalaure.
National Examinations Centre. "General Matura." Accessed February 3, 2015, at http://www.ric.si/general_matura/general_information/.
Sayare, Scott. "Rite of Passage for French Students Receives Poor Grade," *New York Times*, June 27, 2013. Accessed August 28, 2015, at http://www.nytimes.com/2013/06/28/world/europe/a-rite-of-passage-for-french-students-receives-a-poor-grade.html?src=me&ref=general&_r=3&.
Urban-Klaehn, Jagoda. "Education System in Poland—Overview—Maturity Exam (I)." Polishsite. Accessed February 3, 2015, at http://culture.polishsite.us/articles/art13fr.htm.

BACHELOR AND SPINSTER BALLS, AUSTRALIA

Bachelor and spinster balls, sometimes referred to simply as B and S balls or as B&S's, are fairly unsophisticated, informal social events that occur regularly in rural Australia. The events are one of Australia's most beloved traditions, though they are also notorious for being the scene of casual sexual encounters and binge drinking. Indeed many Australians swear that the initials B and S stand for beer and sex or for blokes and sheilas, the colloquial Australian terms for men and women. Bachelor and spinster balls are usually held in dusty paddocks or barns located in isolated towns of the Australian Outback—the vast, arid, remote region of Australia—and offer young single men and women a rare chance to meet members of the opposite sex, as well as to meet up with friends that live far away.

The exact history of the bachelor and spinster balls is unknown but it is believed that the concept of the bachelor and spinster ball evolved from a tradition originating in the town of Lisdoonvarna, located in County Clare, Ireland, where, since

> **Lisdoonvarna Matchmaking Festival**
>
> The annual Lisdoonvarna Matchmaking Festival is a weeklong autumn festival held in County Clare, Ireland. The festival is famed for its music, dancing, and spontaneous, late-night marriage proposals. The festival is over 150 years old and attracts around 60,000 people from around the globe who come in search of love. Locals record the details of those looking for romance and use supposedly supernatural powers to perform matchmaking. The festival is open to all and in 2013 began a gay, bisexual, and transgender matchmaking weekend.

1871, a matchmaking festival has taken place at which single men and women dance, listen to music, and socialize in the hope of finding a partner. Some of the residents of Lisdoonvarna were professional matchmakers and Irish parents would go to these career-matchmakers in order to find a husband or wife for their child. It may be that when Irish people migrated to Australia they brought with them the Lisdoonvarna matchmaking tradition.

Bachelor and spinster balls are attended by single males and females 18 years old and over who don formal wear especially for the occasion. While dinner suits are obligatory for men, the formality of such an outfit is undercut by the fact that the bachelors often accessorize their suits with bow ties made from cardboard or string. Meanwhile the spinsters tend to wear cocktail dresses or ball gowns with cowboy boots and Akubra hats, the iconic felt hat worn by Australians living in the Outback. Guests begin arriving at the balls' venue in late afternoon and the party then continues until early the next morning. While at the balls, the singletons mix, flirt, listen to live country music and drink large amounts of cheap alcohol, especially beer, rum, bourbon, and other spirits. Indeed such is the heavy alcohol consumption associated with bachelor and spinster balls that many of the balls are sponsored by drinks companies and brands such as Grey Goose Vodka, Bacardi, Bombay Sapphire, Heineken, and Whistle Pig Straight Rye Whiskey. Oftentimes guests throw around food dye, even though it is quite often prohibited by the venues holding the ball, by the police, or by municipal authorities. There are several suggested ways to remove the dye from the skin after the party has finished, such as using baby wipes containing alcohol or scrubbing the skin with a nail brush. However the dye is notoriously difficult to remove whichever method is followed and natural food dye is considered the hardest to eradicate, with even acetone-based nail varnish unable to eliminate the staining. In addition to throwing food dye, wet t-shirt competitions are also often featured as entertainment at bachelor and spinster balls.

Traditionally bachelor and spinster balls were held to allow young people to meet up and form romantic attachments. However today the balls are as much about offering youngsters the chance to catch up with their friends, who may live many hours driving or flying time away, as they are about singletons finding partners. This shift of emphasis means that the atmosphere of the balls has changed somewhat with guests focusing more on having a good time than finding a mate. This also means that the dress code has become more relaxed—while guests still wear formal wear, they spend less money on their outfits and may buy them from thrifts stores or charity shops. Other attendees even wear fancy dress with women dressing as nurses, naughty schoolgirls, and men coming disguised as cricketers, lawn bowlers, and clowns. Those who have never been to a bachelor and spinster ball are sometimes made to wear a sign marked with the word "virgin," as a way of declaring that they are new to the events.

Many bachelor and spinster balls are organized by ute, or pickup truck, fans so that the balls coincide with so-called ute master events, Australian festivals celebrating the pickup truck. Sometimes to provide additional entertainment at the balls, ute owners perform ute stunts such as making flames appear from their vehicle exhausts or performing doughnuts, that is, driving so that the rear or front of the ute moves around toward the opposite set of wheels in one continuous motion, thereby creating a circular skid-mark.

Once a bachelor and spinster ball has finished, guests normally go to sleep in a traditional Australian roll-up bed called a swag, or backpack bed, that is typically used by Australian sheep shearers, miners, and itinerant Outback dwellers often referred to as swagmen. Ball organizers often provide breakfast and sometimes offer a so-called "recovery," allowing guests to transfer to a different location where they can carry on drinking and partying in general, as well as playing sports and games.

Tickets to bachelor and spinster balls tend to cost between AU$80 (roughly US$58) and AU$110 (about US$80) with ticket prices including an all-you-can-eat dinner, all alcohol, and breakfast, plus gifts such as a hat, a cup, condoms, and lubricants. A consequence of this excessive level of alcohol consumption is that police often feel the need to perform breathalyzer tests on ball guests before they drive home and there have been isolated, word-of-mouth, unsubstantiated accounts of sexual assaults occurring.

Though a much-loved Australian tradition, the future of bachelor and spinster balls looks uncertain for several reasons. For instance, young people have started to move away from the Outback, moving to towns in search of work. Stricter alcohol laws mean that the drink culture previously enjoyed at the balls has been dampened and rising insurance costs mean that the balls are more expensive to stage. That having been said, many thousands of young Australians still drive for several hours to attend bachelor and spinster balls as they do not wish to see a cherished Australian tradition die out and because profits from bachelor and spinster balls usually go to charity with many thousands of Australian dollars being raised each time a bachelor and spinster ball takes place. Indeed in 2000, a ball held in Wamboyne, in the Australian state of New South Wales, raised over AU$53,000 for charity. Charities to benefit in the past from the hosting of bachelor and spinster balls include the Red Cross and the Royal Flying Doctor Service of Australia, a not-for-profit aeromedical organization that provides primary medical care for those living in the Outback or dwelling in remote rural Australian towns who are not able to travel the vast distance of the Outback in order to find medical assistance.

See also: Filipino Debut; Purity Balls; *Russefeiring* and Schoolies Week; Shanghai Marriage Market

Further Reading

The Age Company. "Having a Ball." Theage.com, August 3, 2005. Accessed February 11, 2015, at http://www.theage.com.au/news/national/havingaball/2005/08/02/1122748636541.html.

Bachelorsandspinsters.com. Accessed February 11, 2015, at http://bachelorsandspinsters.com.

Fairfax Media. "25 Things You Need to Know About Australia's B&S Balls," *The Daily Advertiser*, December 11, 2014. Accessed February 11, 2015, at http://www.dailyadvertiser.com.au/story/2707376/25-things-you-need-to-know-about-australias-bs-balls/.

Orpheum. "Bachelor and Spinster Balls." Everything2, March 10, 2003. Accessed February 11, 2015, at http://everything2.com/title/Bachelor+and+Spinsters+Ball.

Squires, Nick. "Outback's Notorious B and S Balls Bite the Dust," *The Telegraph*, February 11, 2006. Accessed February 11, 2015, at http://www.telegraph.co.uk/news/worldnews/australiaandthepacific/australia/1510242/Outbacks-notorious-B-and-S-Balls-bite-the-dust.html.

BAR MITZVAH AND *BAT MITZVAH*, JUDAISM

The bar mitzvah (sometimes written as *bar mitzwah*) and bat mitzvah are Jewish coming-of-age ceremonies. The name bar mitzvah derives from the Aramaic *bar* (meaning son) and *mitzvah*, which in both Aramaic and Hebrew translates as commandment. Thus the name bar mitzvah can be taken to mean son of the commandment though some people translate the term as man of duty. Similarly, the word *bat* means daughter in both Hebrew and Aramaic (though the word is pronounced as bas by the Ashkenazi Jews) so a bat mitzvah translates as daughter of the commandment. Technically children undergoing their bar mitzvah and bat mitzvah should be referred to as becoming a bar or bat mitzvah though in actuality most people use the terms bar mitzvah and bat mitzvah to refer to the ceremonies themselves rather than to those undergoing the rituals. A bar mitzvah can only take place on a day on which the Torah, the first five books of the Hebrew Bible, is read in a public service—Mondays, Thursdays, Saturdays, and holidays—plus the first day of the Hebrew month during the morning service. Though the Torah is also read aloud on fast days, it is not appropriate for bar mitzvahs to occur on these days, as fast days are solemn occasions that should not be used to hold celebrations.

Under Jewish Law, children are not compelled to observe the commandments, though they are encouraged to do so in order to learn the requirements that they will need to uphold as adults. Only when a Jewish boy reaches 13 years of age or a girl turns 12 years are they obliged to observe the commandments and undergo a coming-of-age ceremony. Traditionally, the ceremony takes place one day after a child's birthday. The age 13 is significant in the Jewish tradition as this is the age mentioned in Talmudic sources as the time when a boy reaches physical maturity and is able to be responsible for himself. In traditional Jewish lore, 13 years is the age at which Abraham abandoned the worship of idols and at which Jacob and Esau left behind the authority of their father and found independence.

The bar or bat mitzvah ceremony is a formal, public demonstration that a child takes on his or her religious obligations and thereby earns the right to take part in leading religious services, read from the Torah scroll, to count in the *minyan* (i.e., the minimum number of 10 people needed to perform some religious rituals), to appear before religious courts, to be accountable for his or her actions and to marry. Both bar mitzvahs and bat mitzvahs are times of both separation and continuousness for the child leaves behind his or her childhood to become an autonomous individual, free from parental authority, but also demonstrates a willingness to continue the Jewish tradition. A Jewish boy becomes a bar mitzvah immediately upon reaching his 13th birthday while a Jewish girl becomes a bat mitzvah when she turns 12 years of age. It is not necessary to hold a ceremony to confer their rights and duties. Indeed, though bar mitzvah and bat mitzvah ceremonies are popular, they do not fulfill any commandment. Moreover the bar or bat mitzvah is a fairly recently invented tradition that is not mentioned in the Jewish holy book the Talmud. The origin of the bar mitzvah is unknown though some Jewish scholars believe that it evolved some 600 years ago when it was commonly believed that a boy became a man on his 13th birthday. In much the same way Jewish girls were thought to achieve adulthood when they reached 12 years of age and assumed the legal responsibility of performing the *mitzvot*—the commandments of God. Twelve years old was also the age at which Jewish girls were believed to be physically mature.

The bar mitzvah ceremony known today is a multi-part ritual. During the religious part of the ceremony, the boy recites from the Torah and may also read from other religious texts. (*See* Plate 1.) The boy's parents, or possibly just his father, then recite a special blessing over the Torah that calls upon God to recognize that the boy is free from parental control and is no longer the responsibility of his parents. After this, it is commonplace for the boy to make a speech referring to the section of the Torah from which he has recited a portion. A bat mitzvah is conducted in much the same way as a bar mitzvah. Once the religious aspects of the ceremony have concluded, everybody retires to enjoy a celebratory meal. In previous years, it was usual for the bar mitzvah to share a quiet meal with his family but today, in the United States in particular, it is routine for the boy's family to host a lavish party for the boy to celebrate his coming of age. Over the years, bar mitzvah parties have become the norm in the United State and in turn have initiated their own traditions such as candle lighting, bar mitzvah cakes, and the dancing of the *horah*, which is a feature of many Jewish celebrations and takes the form of a fast-paced, joyous dance that sees the person being celebrated raised high on a chair as others dance around him or her in a circle.

Bar mitzvah ceremonies are alike in most Jewish communities though there are geographical variations. For example, in Germany boys celebrating their bar mitzvah must lead a major part of the Shabbat service while in Eastern Europe a bar mitzvah is not traditionally considered all that important and sees a boy merely having to read from the Talmud on the Monday or Thursday after his birthday. It has also become the norm among some Jewish communities for boys and their families to travel to Israel to celebrate the boy's coming of age. To this end many bar mitzvahs are held against the Western Wall in Jerusalem or near the Dead Sea. Other families travel to historic synagogues in countries such as Germany.

Another trend in bar mitzvahs is for adults that did not have a bar mitzvah when they were young to undergo a ceremony in adulthood. In this case, the ceremonies usually take place en masse and are intended to symbolize the continuity of Judaism.

See also: *Brit Milah* (Volume 1); *Hora* and *Horah*; Jewish Death Customs (Volume 3); Jewish Wedding Customs; *Pidyon Haben*: Redemption of the First Born (Volume 1)

Further Reading

Isaacs, Ronald H. *Rites of Passage: A Guide to the Jewish Life Cycle*. Hoboken, NJ: KTAV Publishing House, 1992.

Jastrow, Marcus, and Kaufmann Kohler. "Bar Mitzwah." JewishEncyclopedia.com. Accessed November 25, 2015, at http://jewishencyclopedia.com/articles/2473-bar-mizwah.

Kahn, Ava F. "Bar Mitzvah," in Jacqueline S. Reinier and Priscilla Ferguson Clement, eds., *Boyhood in America: An Encyclopedia, Volume 1: A–K*, 65–69. Santa Barbara, CA: ABC-CLIO, 2001.

Rich, Tracey R. "Bar Mitzvah, Bat Mitzvah and Confirmation," Judaism 101. Accessed November 25, 2015, at http://www.jewfaq.org/barmitz.htm.

BEARDS, INTERNATIONAL

As facial hair is usually found growing on the chin, upper lip, and cheeks of adult males, beards are symbolic of manhood and are therefore regarded with great pride by many cultures around the world. The average man has 25,000 hairs on his chin and beard hairs can grow by five to six inches per year. European and Middle Eastern men tend to have more hair follicles on their faces than African men or Asian men, who have the least.

Beards have been viewed as a sign of mature masculinity since ancient times. Assyrian sculptures dating from 900–612 BCE depict men with full beards and Assyrians are known to have curled their beards and dusted them with gold on special occasions. Similarly, the kings of ancient Persia (now Iran) used to thread their beards with gold as did the Merovingian kings who ruled France from the sixth to eighth centuries. In ancient Greece, the first sign of beard growth on the chin of a young man was dedicated to the god Apollo during a religious ritual. Such ritualized behavior reveals the cultural importance of beards. Beards serve as shorthand for all the qualities associated with grown men and the real and imagined qualities of patriarchal society, particularly authority, strength, sagacity, and sexual potency. Beards are also seen as indications of social status and, by extension, as signs of royalty and divinity. By contrast smooth-faced men have often garnered derision for displaying a lack of masculinity while bearded women are regarded as freakish by most cultures. Further to this Christianity, Judaism, and Islam all view beards as a distinction bestowed upon man by God in order to separate man from the inferiority of womanhood. Thus several ancient insults directed at men involve references to beards. For example, according to 2 Samuel 10:4–5 of the Bible, Hanun of the Ammonites shaved off the beards belonging to King David's servants. On seeing their hairless faces, the outraged king told his servants to stay in Jericho until their beards regrew. The Bible also suggests in Jeremiah 48:37 that shaving (or plucking) one's own beard was an act of mourning. Modern-day Jews belonging to the Chasidic group as well as some Orthodox Jews still follow this custom.

That beards are representative of authority, power, and divinity is revealed by the way in which Christian iconography almost always portrays God as having a flowing beard. Similarly one of the most binding oaths a Muslim can make is to swear by one's own beard and that belonging to Allah. Further, in Islam it is considered *haraam*, or sinful, for a man to shave off his beard as a beardless face denotes effeminacy. Sikh men also are forbidden from shaving their beards as Sikhs view hair as a symbolic gift of love from God.

The cultural and spiritual significance of beards harks back to wider beliefs in the magical properties of detachable body parts. For example beards, like hair, fingernails, and toenails are all thought to contain part of the human soul or a person's life essence and therefore make a person vulnerable to psychical attack it they fall into the possession of an enemy who is able to use the items for nefarious purposes. This belief is the concept of the separable soul, an element of many primitive religions and folklore worldwide, including that of many North American indigenous peoples.

Despite the cultural importance of beards, they are nonetheless affected by changing tastes and fashions. At the moment, there is currently something of a beard revival in Western Europe and North America. After World War II, the clean-shaven look worn by the military became the vogue in secular society. Though beards were taken up by some cultural groups on the edge of society such as hippies, who favored long beards, and Beatniks, who opted for short goatees, the beard generally fell out of favor. However since the mid-1990s the beard has gradually returned to prominence. This is partly because the world financial crisis of the 2000s has led to men rejecting conformist corporate fashions and because the concept of the smooth-faced metrosexual man has fallen out of fashion. The term metrosexual, which was coined by an English writer in 1994 and derives from the words metropolitan and heterosexual, refers to men who appear to spend a disproportionate amount of time grooming and using beauty products specifically designed for men. The metrosexual look was epitomized by English soccer star and fashion entrepreneur David Beckham at the start of the new millennium and by Scottish international rugby union player-turned-model Thom Evans in the 2010s.

The male uptake of products and processes usually associated with women has led to the beard revival as other men reject the metrosexual ethos, reclaiming their masculinity by turning away from male grooming and growing facial hair. As a result of this trend the so-called "mountain man" full beard is a current favorite even with men in professions not normally associated with beard-wearing including acting, sports, television journalism, and banking. However how long this beard trend will last is unknown for Australian scientists have discovered that Darwinian selection guides men's beard fashions. The scientists found that the more beards there are in society the less attractive they become to women thereby giving clean-shaven men an advantage when it comes to finding a mate in a process known as negative frequency-dependent sexual selection.

See also: Ear-Piercing Ceremonies; Female Genital Cutting; Forehead Cutting Initiation; Hair Removal; Human Tooth Sharpening; Jewish Death Customs (Volume 3); Neck Elongation; Ritual Tattooing; Scarification; Subincision into the Urethra; Training Bra; Xhosa Circumcision

Further Reading

Gera, Vanessa. "Metrosexuals Be Gone: Europe Is Agog for Beards." Yahoo News, November 20, 2014. Accessed November 21, 2014, at http://news.yahoo.com/metrosexuals-gone-europe-agog-beards-081902643.html.

IslamQA. "1189: Ruling on Shaving the Beard." Accessed November 21, 2014, at http://islamqa.info/en/1189.

Jones, Alison. *Larousse Dictionary of World Folklore*. Edinburgh, UK: Larousse, 1996.

Morgan, James. "Beard Trend Is 'Guided by Evolution,'" BBC News: Science & Environment, April 16, 2014. Accessed November 21, 2014, at http://www.bbc.co.uk/news/science-environment-27023992.

RealSikhism.com. "Hair & Turban." Accessed November 21, 2014, at http://www.realsikhism.com/index.php?subaction=showfull&id=1248364871&ucat=7.

Sherrow, Victoria. *Encyclopedia of Hair: A Cultural History*. Westport, CT: Greenwood Press, 2006.

Simpson, Mark. "The Metrosexual Is Dead. Long Live the 'Spornosexual,'" *The Telegraph*, June 10, 2014. Accessed November 21, 2014, at http://www.telegraph.co.uk/men/fashion-and-style/10881682/The-metrosexual-is-dead.-Long-live-the-spornosexual.html.

BED-COURTSHIP, AMISH

Throughout the United States most teenagers mix with the opposite sex on a daily basis, both at high school and in their private lives. This provides teenagers with a large pool of potential dating candidates. The Amish do not, on the whole, enjoy such opportunities. Amish teenagers complete their schooling at the eighth grade so the source of daily boy-girl socializing offered by school ends after the age of 14 or 15. Additionally, most Amish schools only have around 35 students so this means that Amish teenagers probably attend school with their siblings and cousins, thus limiting their dating opportunities further. Additionally denting an Amish teenager's dating chances is the fact that, apart from during their *rumspringa*—a time during which teenage Amish are given freedom to interact with non-Amish—they are unable to drive to another town in search of romance. Also instead of looking for short-lived affairs of the heart, young Amish adults must find a lifelong partner while abiding by the rules of their church. Bed-courtship, also known as bundling, is a form of dating experienced by some heterosexual Amish teenagers. In ultra-conservative, highly traditional Amish communities such as the Swartzentrubers that permit the custom of bed-courtship, a boy asks a girl if he can take her home, usually after a Sunday night singing. If the girl consents, the couple drives to the girl's home in the boy's buggy and immediately on arrival goes upstairs to the girl's bedroom. Once in the bedroom, the girl removes her outer dress but keeps on her under-dress, also known as a courting dress, which is never revealing, but can be any color except white, pink, or yellow. The boy and girl then lie on the girl's bed and spend the night together talking. The pair may kiss but may not participate in any sexual activity. Thus, it could be said that bed-courtship allows tender togetherness without sexual intimacy and therefore instills sexual self-discipline.

Bed-courtship is believed to be a very old tradition though its exact roots are obscure. The tradition is not, however, Amish in origin as it was practiced by working-class couples among 19th-century Europeans. By the start of the 20th century, the custom was introduced to the United States by Pennsylvania Dutch immigrants. The immigrants took to the bundling courtship custom partly for practical reason—houses at this time were unheated, had uncomfortable wooden furniture, and their layout provided little privacy. Thus, for courting couples, lying in bed fully clothed was usually the most comfortable place to socialize and allowed the couple both to keep warm and share intimacy. The custom was particularly popular

Bonnet Rippers: Amish Romance Novels

Amish Romance is a literary subgenre of Christian fiction, featuring Amish characters but written and read mainly by evangelical Christian women. The book industry refers to Amish romance novels as "bonnet rippers" because the term is a play on the term "bodice rippers" and because the books' covers tend to feature a woman wearing a bonnet. The first commercially successful Amish romance novel was Beverly Lewis's *The Shunning*, published in 1997. Most works of Amish romance feature chaste protagonists who engage in romance in ways that are socially and religiously acceptable to the Amish.

with the Old Order Amish. However even during the 19th century bed-courtship had started to fall out of fashion for the Swiss-German Brethren Anabaptist group abandoned the practice. Though rumors that bed-courtship encouraged unrestrained sexual activity began to circulate at this time, it should be noted that rates of premarital pregnancy among colonial American Puritans who practiced bundling were significantly lower than rates for so-called colonial backwater settlers who did not practice the courtship custom.

Bed-courtship continued to fall out of favor when progressive Amish splinter groups, such as the New Order and Paoli, started to disparage the custom in the 1960s. Today, bed-courtship is an increasingly unpopular concept and it is estimated that less than 10 percent of Amish communities allow the custom to take place. The reason for this decline is thought to be due to a handful of influential elders speaking out against the custom leading others to scorn the practice. In particular, the book *Ein Risz in der Maurer* (*A Break in the Wall*) written by an Ohio New Order Amish minister in the 1970s criticized bed-courtship claiming that the custom went against the Christian teaching of avoiding temptation as it led to impure courtship behavior during which the lusts of the flesh were ever-present. The author also claimed that bed-courtship resulted in up to 50 percent of Amish women being pregnant when they married. Dozens of Amish bookshops stocked the book and it is thought to have been instrumental in changing Amish attitudes to bundling. Eventually, bed-courtship was criticized en masse so that most Amish now believe that the practice does not conform to *Ordnung*, the simple set of unwritten rules that the Amish believe God has established for them. The reputation of bed-courtship suffered further when the Amish began to realize that outsiders looked on bed-courtship as a perverse sexual practice that bordered on the kinky. Aghast and mortified at how the outside world regarded the old practice of bundling, even those Amish that were not set against the practice began to stop the custom.

That bed-courtship has fallen out of favor is evinced by the fact that the custom is rarely depicted in Amish romance novels that focus on chaste romance rather than titillation.

See also: Courtship Whistling; Purity Balls; *Rumspringa*; Visiting-Girls Courtship Tradition; Wodaabe Courtship Dance and Festival

Further Reading

Exploring-amish-country.com. "Amish Dating Customs." Accessed January 6, 2015, at http://www.exploring-amish-country.com/amish-dating.html.

Johnson-Weiner, Karen M. *New York Amish: Life in the Plain Communities of the Empire State*. Ithaca, NY: Cornell University Press, 2010.

Nolt, Steven M., and Thomas J. Meyers. *Plain Diversity: Amish Cultures and Identities*. Baltimore, MD: The Johns Hopkins University Press, 2007.

Saper, Craig J. *Artificial Mythologies: A Guide to Cultural Invention*. Minneapolis: University of Minnesota Press, 1997.

Stevick, Richard, A. *Growing Up Amish: The Teenage Years*. Baltimore, MD: The Johns Hopkins University Press, 2007.
Weaver-Zercher, Valerie. *Thrill of the Chaste: The Allure of Amish Romance Novels*. Baltimore, MD: The Johns Hopkins University Press, 2013.

BIRTHDAY HUMILIATIONS FOR SINGLETONS, DENMARK AND GERMANY

In many areas of the world it is customary for people to face some sort of fairly benign embarrassment or physical discomfort when celebrating their birthday. Most of these birthday torments are not birthday specific, meaning that they can occur on any or all birthdays. In some countries, however, birthday torments take place only on specific birthdays and then only to certain sections of society. Usually these torments are faced by unmarried people in their twenties or thirties.

This type of birthday torment is exemplified by a custom that occurs in Denmark, especially in the Jutland peninsular, where it is traditional when an unmarried person reaches his or her 25th birthday to douse the person celebrating his or her birthday with water and then cover him or her with handfuls of cinnamon. An unmarried man that is covered in cinnamon is called a *kanelsvend* (cinnamon man) while a single woman doused in the spice is known as *kanelmø* (cinnamon maid). If the person remains unmarried then on his or her 30th birthday, pepper replaces the cinnamon. A bachelor that is covered in pepper is referred to as *pebersvend* (pepper man) while a single woman is dubbed a *pebermø* (pepper maid). The tradition of covering unmarried people in pepper on the day of their 30th birthday may derive from the fact that in the 16th century spice traders tended to be single men living secluded lives. For this reason, the original, literal meaning of the word bachelor in Danish was *pebersvend*. Later, during the 18th century, unmarried women became known as pepper maids. On the day of their 30th birthday, Danish singletons can expect to wake up to find a giant pepper mill made out of oil drums in their garden. Typically the oil drum is spray painted with the number "30" plus obscene phrases reminding the person whose birthday it is that he or she is still unmarried so might die single. The oil drums also often features some sort of prominent phallus as a way to remind the singleton that he or she does not have a legally recognized partner with whom to have sex for the rest of his or her life.

Unmarried 30-year-old men living in northern Germany also face a birthday torment for it is traditional in this area of the country for men to have to clean the steps of the local city hall. This venue is chosen because it is in city halls that most Germans are married. The German location most often associated with this custom is the town of Bremen where unmarried 30-year-old men have to sweep the steps of the local cathedral, usually having drunk schnapps beforehand, and oftentimes wearing a humorous costume to which is pinned a sign printed with the number "30." Ordinarily, the birthday celebrant performs this duty using a broom though sometimes he must use a small toothbrush to clean the steps. To make the task even harder, it is customary for the man's friends to drop bottle caps or other types of litter for the man to clear up. To compound the man's humiliation, the event is normally announced in advance in the local newspaper so that everyone knows he is going to face his "punishment." Alternatively, the man's friends may paste flyers containing an embarrassing photograph of the bachelor all over town announcing the date of his birthday and the fact that he will be cleaning the cathedral steps. This is in order that lots of people turn up to watch the man perform his cleaning duty. Moreover, to call even more attention to the man's cleaning humiliation, when the man sweeps the steps it is often to the accompaniment of music played on a barrel organ. All the while his friends cheer the man on as he cleans the steps. Another version of the torment sees the bachelor have to roll a beer barrel all the way to the city hall. Once there, the bachelor's friends drink all the beer within the barrel without allowing the bachelor to drink any alcohol.

When sweeping the steps, the man must continue sweeping until a fair maiden agrees to kiss him on the cheek. The kiss frees the bachelor from his humiliating work. The tradition of making a bachelor sweep the steps stems from the once commonly held belief that people that do not produce children are doomed to labor in obscurity after they die. Unmarried women, most especially those that have never been married, also have to clean on their 30th birthdays though they must clean the handles of the cathedral doors. Alternatively, a German woman turning 30 years old must walk from her home to the nearest city hall, polishing every doorknob on the way. This custom is known as *klinken putzen*, meaning cleaning handles, but also the metaphor used to refer to a tedious, lengthy task. Though klinken putzen seems quite benign it is actually quite an arduous task because city halls are normally located in the town centers, meaning that they are surrounded by lots of houses with door handles. Furthermore the woman's friends may make the handles especially dirty by smearing them with dirt, grease, and other substances that are hard to remove. A variation of this custom sees an unmarried woman polish the door handles of her friends' homes or clean the handles of a special door featuring handles that has been made in advance by her friends.

In some areas of Germany, a rarely seen custom sees unmarried men made to ride a donkey backward on their 40th birthday. This is because the men are considered "old donkeys" that are yet to find a wife.

See also: Bachelor and Spinster Balls; Birthday Torments (Volume 1); Birthdays (Volume 1); Face in Birthday Cake; Sock Garland and Sock Dance

Further Reading

BTZ Bremer Touristik-Zentrale. "Traditions in Bremen." Accessed November 23, 2015, at http://www.bremen-tourism.de/traditions-in-bremen.

Conger, Cristen. "Single, 30, and Danish? Prepare to Get Peppered." Stuff Mom Never Told You: The Blog, September 3, 2014. Accessed November 23, 2015, at http://www.stuffmomnevertoldyou.com/blog/single-30-and-danish-prepare-to-get-peppered/.

Deutsche Kultur. "All You Ever Wanted to Know about GERMANY!" *Deutsche Kultur*, September 12, 2007. Accessed November 23, 2015, http://deutsche-kultur.livejournal.com/14924.html.

BLACKENING THE BRIDE, SCOTLAND

Blackening the bride, known as *Reschtach* in the Celtic language, is a unique Scottish pre-wedding custom that is often regarded as bizarre by non-Scots for, unlike most traditions centered on marriage, blackening the bride is not a pleasurable event. Indeed blackening the bride is a deliberately unpleasant and humiliating experience for those who are targeted. While in most locations only the bride is subjected to the custom, in the Orkney Islands it is traditional for the groom to receive a blackening, in which case the custom is called the wedding blackening or something similar. Additionally, a couple may be blackened together as a bonding experience that connects the lovers symbolically and provides them with something to talk about in later life. Like many Celtic traditions, blackening the bride is falling out of fashion and does not occur often in major Scottish cities. However blackening the bride can be witnessed in the Orkney Islands, Aberdeen, the Grampians, the Highlands, the Outer Hebrides, Angus, Dundee, and Fife where people feel it is important to keep alive old traditions as a way of honoring their ancestors.

The origins of the blackening-the-bride tradition are not known for sure, though it is thought the ritual dates from ancient times. The folkloric explanation for the custom is that ancient peoples thought that blackening the bride would ward off supernatural beings called trows that might otherwise attempt to torment or possess the bride. The noise created during the blackening is considered by some folklorists to be connected to the tradition of noise-making common not only during the playing of the "Wedding March" tune that is customary at marriage ceremonies but also at other celebrations held in remote Scottish locations such as the Orkney Islands. In these cases the noise was thought to keep the trows and fairy-folk in general at bay, in case they tried to spirit away the bride or groom. While this explanation may seem far-fetched, remote areas of Scotland hold a strong belief in trows. Similarly, it has been suggested that blackening the bride is a way of preventing bad fairies from kidnapping the bride and carrying her off to Fairyland before the wedding takes place. A historical explanation for the custom is that it is an extension of a medieval Scottish tradition in which the hair and feet of the bride and groom were washed with water into which a long-married woman had dropped her wedding ring. The washing was supposed to be the most thorough bathing the couple would ever experience so it follows that friends and family would deliberately dirty the couple—for instance, the groom would have his legs blackened with coal by friends of the bride—before the wedding so that they did indeed need washing well. Anther explanation for the blackening tradition is that it is meant to represent the toils a woman will face in her married life. There is some credence to this rather prosaic explanation for in Scotland it is said that if a woman, or a man, can come through the blackening experience with their dignity intact then she, or he, will be able to withstand all that life throws his or her way. Any Scot who does feel that the blackening custom is too extreme would do well to look to the, now defunct, Scottish pre-wedding custom of creeling the bridegroom in which the groom had a creel, or large basket, of stones tied to his back and was forced to walk with the heavy load attached to his back all the way around his town and could only stop when his betrothed agreed to kiss him.

The custom of blackening the bride denies the bride the dignity and grace that is usually attendant upon a woman who is about to be married for the tradition sees a bride-to-be ambushed by her friends and family in a sort of mock kidnapping and transported to a site where she can be attacked in a fairly benign manner—blackened—by her loved-ones. The attacks usually consist of soaking the bride in things that look, feel and, above all, smell revolting such as rotten eggs, putrefying fish heads, sour milk, sticky molasses, stinking garbage, grimy soot, dusty flour, and so on. Indeed in the case of blackening the bride the more disgusting a substance is, the better. Anybody who sees the bride is allowed to hurl foul matter at her; even people who do not know the bride and have nothing to do with her wedding may participate. Once the bride has been blackened she is placed in full public view for several hours by being paraded through streets, tied to a vehicle, locked inside a cage attached to a car or displayed in some other way. Thus everybody gets to see the bride in this humiliated state. Meanwhile the bride's friends and family stand nearby making a great deal of noise by banging pots and pans, blowing whistles, drumming and shouting announcements of the bride's forthcoming nuptials. Next, the bride's loved ones cover her in feathers that, of course, adhere to the revolting goo that has accumulated on the bride. The last stage of the blackening-the-bride tradition sees the bride-to-be taken to a body of water into which she is thrown—it is not unusual for blackenings to conclude in the sea, which in Scotland is hardly ever warm. While this too is an unpleasant experience it does mean that the worst of the fetid gunk stuck to the bride is washed off. The bride and those who have blackened her often end up at a pub after the blackening process has finished and tend to become inebriated. Therefore it is unlikely that hard feelings will develop as a result of the blackening as everyone involved is too merry to be cross. On a deeper level, Scottish brides-to-be do not take umbrage at their treatment during their blackening as they know it is done with the best of intentions. It is rare for a Scot to refuse to be blackened for blackenings are considered festive occasions, not just for the bride, but also for her friends, family, and community in general.

See also: Bachelor and Spinster Balls; British Wedding Traditions; Gretna Green; Handfasting; Jumping Over the Broom; *Polterabend*; Protecting Children from Supernatural Beings; Saining (Volume 1); Wedding March and Bridal Chorus

Further Reading

Emerson, Stephen. "Scottish Word of the Week: Blackening," *The Scotsman*, March 27, 2015. Accessed December 11, 2014, at http://www.scotsman.com/lifestyle/heritage/scottish-word-of-the-week-blackening-1-3356224.

Galvan, Javier A., ed. *They Do What? A Cultural Encyclopedia of Extraordinary and Exotic Customs from around the World.* Santa Barbara, CA: ABC-CLIO, 2014.

Lynch, Michael, ed. *The Oxford Companion to Scottish History.* Oxford, UK: Oxford University Press, 2007.

Towrie, Sigurd. "The Wedding Blackening." *Orcadian Wedding Traditions.* Accessed December 11, 2014, at http://www.orkneyjar.com/tradition/weddings/blacken.htm.

www.trossaachs.co.uk. "Ancient Scottish Traditions." Destination Loch Lomond. Accessed December 11, 2014, at http://www.trossachs.co.uk/PDF/old-customs.pdf.

BREAST IRONING, AFRICA AND ELSEWHERE

Breast ironing is a form of breast mutilation that sees the application of hot objects such as stones, pestles, coconut shells, spoons, and even hammers, to a girl's burgeoning breasts. (*See* Plate 2.) Hot fruit peels may also be applied together with chest-binding material to give the girl's bust a flat appearance. The breasts are usually massaged after the hot implements, peel, and binding have been applied. Breast ironing is a cultural tradition in Cameroon where, according to research by Germany's Association for International Co-operation (*Gesellschaft fur Technische Zusammenarbeit*, GTZ), one in four Cameroonian females has experienced the process. Despite the prevalence of breast ironing in Cameroon the custom is little talked about and takes place in private. Breast ironing also occurs, to a lesser extent, in Benin, Chad, Togo, Guinea, Côte d'Ivoire, Nigeria, and South Africa. It was long thought that breast ironing is most prevalent in rural regions of these nations. However the custom actually occurs most often in urban areas where mothers are most worried about their daughters being raped. Though breast ironing is customarily performed on adolescents, girls as young as eight years old have been known to undergo the procedure as they have shown signs of sexual development—as a result of recent improvements in Cameroonian diets girls are maturing physically at increasingly early ages. Apart from Africa, there is a belief that breast ironing is occurring in the United Kingdom where several thousand Cameroonians have settled. As a result of this, a conference organized by CAME Women's and Girl's Development Organisation (Cawogido) was held in Ealing, west London, in 2013 in the hope of tackling breast ironing in both the United Kingdom and Africa. The United Nations, which estimates 3.8 million females have undergone breast ironing, has identified the practice as a crime against women. Further, international human rights agencies consider breast ironing to fall under the category of body mutilation alongside female genital cutting.

The exact origins of breast ironing are not known though the custom is known to have existed for centuries. It has been suggested that historically African women performed the custom in the hope of increasing girls' future production of breast milk.

Breast ironing is an intergenerational custom for, initially, it is carried out by mothers and other older female relatives and later by the girl herself. The reasons behind breast ironing lie in the Cameroonian belief that breast development signals a female's sexual maturity and sexual attractiveness, and, therefore, her readiness to marry and have children. The females who perform breast ironing seek to reduce the outward visibility of a girl's advancing sexual maturity and therefore protect her from encountering sexual harassment, rape, premature sexual activity, and marriage at a young age. In short, Cameroonian women see breast ironing as a way of achieving better prospects in later life. Some women also view breast ironing as a method of protecting young girls from contracting HIV in a country in which AIDS rates are increasing.

Though many Cameroonian women think breast ironing is physically and psychologically beneficial to girls, there are many ill effects, both physiological and psychological, associated with breast ironing. Immediate consequences include pain, blistering, cysts, tissue damage, loss of sensitivity, itching, and infections such as breast abscesses. Long-term effects include disfigurement, scarring, asymmetrical breasts, and the inability to produce breast milk. The most common psychological issue associated with breast ironing is post-traumatic stress disorder. As breast ironing is so harmful to females, there have been several health education and gender empowerment initiatives focused on eradicating breast ironing in Cameroon. These campaigns focused on the dangers of breast ironing and suggested alternative ways of protecting girls from teen pregnancy and contracting HIV. In addition, several Cameroonian government agencies have tried to change the perception of breast ironing as a way of safeguarding girls. For example, Cameroon's Ministry for the Promotion of Women and Family has implemented an ambitious campaign to educate parents of young girls about the consequences of breast ironing. Cameroonian doctors have also gone to great lengths to stress that breast ironing is a futile attempt to prevent girls' physical maturation.

A local non-governmental organization called Network of Aunties Association, or the *Réseau National des Associations de Tantines* (RENATA), which consists of women who have undergone breast ironing, is spearheading a campaign against the practice. RENATA was established in 2006 and has recruited over 6,000 trained volunteers belonging to 60 regional associations spread through the country. The volunteers are commonly known as Aunties and educate Cameroonian children, both girls and boys, about sex and the ill effects of breast ironing, disseminating information via clinics, newspapers, schools, radio programs, television broadcasts, and leaflets. The Aunties also lobby for a ban on breast ironing. Cameroon ratified the Convention of the Rights of the Child in 1993, which suggests that the Cameroonian government has a legal responsibility to protect girls from the injury and abuse of breast ironing. However as girls' mothers often perform breast ironing, the large-scale reporting of breast ironing as an offense does not occur. In addition to date there is no Cameroonian law outlawing the custom.

See also: Female Genital Cutting; Training Bra

Further Reading

Dugan, Emily. "Breast Ironing: Girls 'Have Chests Flattened Out' to Disguise the Onset of Puberty," *The Independent*, September 26, 2013. Accessed December 10, 2014, at http://www.independent.co.uk/life-style/health-and-families/health-news/breast-ironing-girls-have-chests-flattened-out-to-disguise-the-onset-of-puberty-8842435.html.

Galvan, Javier A., ed. *They Do What? A Cultural Encyclopedia of Extraordinary and Exotic Customs from around the World.* Santa Barbara, CA: ABC-CLIO, 2014.

Shoda, Elizabeth. "Getting It Off Their Chests: Women in Cameroon Speak Out Against Breast Ironing," *The Guardian*, June 12, 2012. Accessed December 10, 2014, at http://www.theguardian.com/journalismcompetition/getting-it-off-their-chests.

Smith, Merril D., ed. *Cultural Encyclopedia of the Breast.* Lanham, MA: Rowman & Littlefield, 2014.

BRITISH WEDDING TRADITIONS, UNITED KINGDOM

In Britain the traditions that people enact on their wedding day have long been dependent on their social class, wealth, religion, and whereabouts they live as well as prevailing fashions. Therefore people living in Wales will have their own specific traditions, as will couples living in Scotland, England, and Northern Ireland. British weddings must, however, conform to certain legal regulations though these rules change over time.

British weddings can take place in a variety of venues because the 1994 Marriage Act permitted venues other than churches and other religious buildings and registry offices to hold marriage ceremonies. The new law meant that by 1998 there were over 2,000 venues approved to host weddings. These venues tended to be mainly hotels and stately homes but also included such locations as sports stadia and museums. In recent years, an increasing number of British people have decided to get married abroad, either because they have family living overseas or because they wish to combine their wedding with their honeymoon. While Christian wedding ceremonies are popular in Britain, the nation is home to people belonging to a variety of religions. This means that Sikh, Muslim, Hindu, and Jewish weddings all take place in Britain as do the weddings of people belonging to alternative religions such as Wiccans and Druids, as well as Celtic-style handfastings that, though not necessarily recognized by law, are true unions for those involved.

British weddings tend to be surrounded by superstitions that are heeded to varying degrees. For instance during the 19th century a variety of days of the week were considered auspicious and inauspicious to hold weddings with Wednesdays believed to be the luckiest wedding days, followed by Monday and Tuesday. Thursday was thought of as fairly unlucky but Fridays and Saturdays were most unlucky. Indeed an old rhyme explicitly deals with the unlucky nature of some wedding days:

> Monday for wealth
> Tuesday for health
> Wednesday the best day of all

> Thursday for losses
> Friday for crosses
> Saturday for no luck at all

Today, however, few people's choice of wedding day is guided by superstition with most British weddings occurring on Saturdays for this is a day on which, traditionally, few people work. Friday is the second-most popular day for weddings. Similarly, it was thought better to wed during some months than others. This belief is embodied in the rhyme that includes the lines:

> If you marry in Lent
> You will live to repent.
> Marry in May,
> Rue for aye.

Lent was thought an unsuitable time to hold a wedding, as it was a time of abstinence. May has long been considered an inauspicious month to wed for many reasons. Before Britain was Christianized the start of summer was marked by the pagan festival of Beltane, while during the Roman rule of Britain the Feast of the Dead occurred in May. Thus it was considered inappropriate to start married life during the month of May, which had long been associated with paganism and death. Indeed such was the dread of marrying in May during Victorian times that churches were often fully booked for weddings during April as couples wanted to avoided being wed in May. It is also rumored that Queen Victoria banned any of her children from marrying in May. The superstition against marrying in May is still known through the rhyme, but nowadays many people marry in May anyway as it is a month when the weather is often warm and sunny.

As well as propagating a superstition against marrying in May, many other wedding traditions and superstitions practiced throughout Britain today originated during the Victorian era. Most of these superstitions developed from the belief that a wedding was a time when a couple was susceptible to bad luck and evil spirits. For instance, many brides conform to the common belief that they should wear "something old, something new, something borrowed, something blue" and that the groom should not see his bride wearing her wedding gown before the ceremony. While blue is considered a lucky color for brides, conversely green is thought of as extremely unlucky for brides and some wedding guests have been asked to abstain from wearing green to weddings for fear of bringing newlyweds bad luck. Other traditions that seem to occur only in Britain include the belief that it is lucky for a bride to meet a black cat on her way to her wedding venue (unlike Americans, the British consider black cats to be lucky animals), and a bride may be given a black cat charm to carry with her during the marriage service. As well as black cats, lambs, doves, and spiders are also thought lucky for brides to see on their wedding day. It is also thought lucky for a chimneysweep to be present at a wedding and even today a couple may pay a nominal amount of money to a chimneysweep to ensure the chimneysweep is visible at their nuptials. Also to ensure good luck a bride will typically include a small horseshoe in her wedding bouquet or dangle it from her wrist. On the other hand it is considered unlucky for a bride to encounter a pig on her way to her wedding or to come across a funeral as this suggests that all a bride's children will be stillborn. Brides in rural locations often fear hearing a cockcrow after dawn of their wedding day. This superstition may be linked to the crowing cock that sounded during Jesus's betrayal before the Crucifixion as detailed in the Bible. It is also thought to be bad luck for a bride to see a monk or nun on her wedding day, possibly because both monks and nuns are associated with chastity and poverty.

At a traditional British white wedding the bride is often accompanied down the aisle by her father. This tradition is known as the father giving away the bride. The bride is also accompanied by her bridesmaids—British brides tend to have few bridesmaids compared with their American counterparts and, unlike at American weddings, the bridesmaids follow the bride down the aisle carrying the train of her wedding dress rather than walking or standing before her. Bridesmaids tend to be the bride's closest friends or sisters.

After the marriage ceremony, the bride and groom lead the way out of the church followed by their bridesmaids (and pageboys, if there are some), the best man with the chief bridesmaid or matron of honor (usually a bridesmaid who is already married), the mother of the bride and the groom's father, and then, finally the groom's mother leaves with the bride's father. When these individuals have exited the church all the other guests leave too. Outside the church it is traditional to throw rice over the newlyweds. This custom dates back to at least 1486 when wheat was thrown over Henry VII's wife, Elizabeth of York. Wheat, or corn, was thrown over newly married couples up until the 19th century. By then it was also usual to throw flower petals or sugared plums over a couple too but by the end of the 19th century rice was the favored item to throw over newlyweds. Nowadays people still throw rice, or possibly paper confetti, though this has fallen out of favor on the grounds that it is environmentally unfriendly. Indeed many wedding venues in Britain expressly ban the throwing of confetti (especially inside a church) and some local authorities frown upon the throwing of paper confetti. Furthermore, some wedding venues view the throwing of confetti as a messy form of littering. Instead it is currently fashionable to throw dried flower petals over newlyweds, or rice, thereby harking back to earlier times. Similarly it has long been traditional for herbs, flower petals, or rushes to be thrown on to the aisle ahead of the bride by a little girl as she walks to the altar. This custom fell out of favor for a while but has been reimported to Britain having been made popular by British brides that have seen the practice in American films and television programs. Another (fairly recently invented) tradition that takes place outside the wedding venue sees the bride stand with her back to her wedding guests just before she departs with her husband. Unmarried female, and sometimes male, guests step forward as the bride throws her floral wedding bouquet over her shoulder toward the single guests who then endeavor to catch the bouquet in the belief that the person that catches the floral arrangement will be the next person to wed. The reason the bride stands with her back to those wishing to catch the flowers is that by not seeing where the flowers fly, the bride cannot be accused of favoritism toward a certain guest. This custom was first noted in Britain in 1923 and it is still considered an Americanism by some Brits. Actually, however, the tradition harks back to a 17th- and 18th-century British custom during which the bride and groom sat on their wedding night bed and then male guests would take an item of the bride's wedding attire, most usually her stocking, from her while female guests did the same to the groom. The guests would then stand with their back to the bride and groom and throw the items they had snatched over their shoulders. Whichever guest came closest to hitting the bride or groom with the thrown object was deemed next to marry.

At a modern British wedding reception the bride and groom will often start the partying by performing a first dance. Anecdotally this tradition seems to have gained in popularity significantly in recent years most probably partly because Britons have seen such dances in American films and also because of the popularity of the BBC television program *Strictly Come Dancing* (known elsewhere as *Dancing with the Stars*). Next, the groom dances with his mother-in-law followed by his own mother. Meanwhile the bride dances with her father-in-law followed by her father, and the best man should dance with the chief bridesmaid. The rest of the bridesmaids and pageboys are then invited to dance and when their dance has ended all the reception guests are invited to join in the dancing.

The reception is also the time when the wedding cake is cut. Traditionally, the bride and groom both grip the handle of the knife as they make the first cut into the cake, which traditionally consists of three tiers of cake that decrease in size with the largest tier at the base and the smallest at the top. The shape of the traditional wedding cake is thought to derive from the shape of the steeple of St Bride's Church in the City of London that features tiers of decreasing upward size. British wedding cakes tend to be fruitcakes as fruitcakes have a very long shelf life. Indeed it is customary for newlyweds to keep the top tier of their wedding cake to eat at the party following the christening of their first child. Normally couples arrange for their wedding cake to be baked by a professional baker, but again, anecdotal evidence suggests it is now increasingly common for a friend of the couple that is a keen amateur baker to bake the couple a wedding cake in lieu of buying them a gift. Again this new tradition is partly informed by reality television as the smash hit BBC television amateur baking competition *The Great British Bake Off* has led to an increasing number of confident amateur cake bakers. Some British couples also bake their own wedding cake, partly to save money but also because doing so gives them a chance to show off their baking prowess. Another, much older wedding cake tradition tells that unmarried guests, particularly female guests, should place a morsel of wedding cake under their pillow before going to sleep as this will increase their chance of finding a spouse. Moreover bridesmaids that do likewise are said to dream of their future husbands.

When the newlyweds go on their honeymoon it is traditional for a collection of tin cans, boots, and assorted junk to be attached to the vehicle that they use as transport, often together with a sign declaring the couple to be "Just Married." Usually this tradition is applied to cars for the cans will normally be attached to the car's back fender resulting in them clanging against each other and the road surface as the car drives away. Obviously this is a fairly recently instituted custom since cars were not invented until the end of the 19th century, but it most likely harks back to the French custom of the *chivari* or the German *Polterabend*. Both these noisy customs are associated with weddings and are intended to drive away evil spirits from newlyweds.

A post-reception custom sees the groom carry his bride over the threshold of their home. The origin of this tradition is not known and it was not widely reported as occurring in Britain until the 19th century. Similar better-documented traditions include the bride warming the threshold of her family home by tipping hot water over it and the custom of a bride's neighbors placing sand in front of her former home. The meaning of the tradition of the groom carrying the bride is unknown too though it may relate to ancient fears of tripping over a doorway, something that suggested bad luck and danger lurking within a building. Alternatively, as the action of the groom carrying the bride means that both will enter their home at the same time, the tradition may be intended to ensure that neither enters the home first thereby becoming dominant.

In modern times, British weddings have become greatly influenced by American nuptials and celebrity weddings. To this end an entire British wedding industry has developed featuring wedding fairs, magazines, websites, and wedding planners.

Competitive Wife Carrying

Wife carrying is a fairly tongue-in-cheek minority endurance sport in which a male competitor carries a female teammate through an obstacle course as quickly as possible. Though often a husband and wife, the man and woman do not have to be married to compete as a couple. The Finnish word for the sport is *Eukonkanto*, which translates into English along the lines of old-hag carrying race. This translation, combined with the sport's preference for women competitors to be meek and gentle, means the sport is considered politically incorrect by some people. Wife carrying originated during the 19th century but the first wife-carrying competition was not held until 1991.

See also: Blackening the Bride; Cajun Weddings; Christian Wedding Ceremony; Gretna Green; Hindu Wedding Ceremony; Horseshoes; Jumping Over the Broom; Jewish Wedding Customs; Lovespoons; Marriage Banns; Muslim Wedding Ceremony; *Polterabend*; Same-Sex Marriage; Sikh Wedding Ceremony; Sprinkling Cake on a Baby's Head (Volume 1); Wedding Dress and Wedding Ring; Wedding March and Bridal Chorus

Further Reading

Guides for Brides. "Wedding Etiquette & Traditions." Guides for Brides: The Wedding Directory. Accessed November 29, 2015, at http://www.guidesforbrides.co.uk/wedding-ideas/wedding-etiquette-traditions.

Hedley-Dent, Ticky. "The Confetti Fields of England: As Churches Ban 'Messy' Paper, Wedding Petals Grow on a Worcestershire Farm," *Daily Mail*, August 9, 2011. Accessed November 29, 2015, at http://www.dailymail.co.uk/news/article-2023982/The-confetti-fields-England-As-churches-ban-messy-paper-wedding-petals-grow-Worcestershire-farm.html.

Lopez, Meaghan Adele. "Throwing a Perfect Wedding: How to Combine British and American Traditions," BBC America, February 14, 2014. Accessed November 29, 2015, at http://www.bbcamerica.com/mind-the-gap/2014/02/14/perfect-wedding-combine-british-american-traditions/.

Monger, George P. *Marriage Customs of the World: From Henna to Honeymoons*. Santa Barbara, CA: ABC-CLIO, 2004.

Simpson, Jacqueline, and Steve Roud. *Oxford Dictionary of English Folklore.* Oxford, UK: Oxford University Press, 2000.

University of Oxford. "Just One in Three Weddings in England and Wales Has a Religious Ceremony." *University of Oxford: News and Events*, July 21, 2015. Accessed May 27, 2016, at http://www.ox.ac.uk/news/2015-07-21-just-one-three-weddings-england-and-wales-has-religious-ceremony.

BULGARIAN WEDDINGS, BULGARIA

Modern Bulgarian weddings contain many elements of old traditions that vary between regions but are only slightly modified to suit modern society. According to tradition, Bulgarian weddings are arranged by the parents, with a mother choosing her son's bride, usually having watched girls dancing, singing, and taking part in games during the spring festival of Saint Lazarus that saw unmarried girls perform songs and dances. Young men would watch the girls and when a girl took his fancy the young man would inform his parents. Once the young man had made his selection his parents would meet with the girl's parents and after the ritualized giving of food gifts his parents would announce the reason for their visit. If both families agreed to the match, the girl was asked her opinion about a possible wedding. Today, while the majority of Bulgarian people choose who they wish to marry, families often greatly influence the decision and some Bulgarian ethnic groups, such as the Roma Gypsies, still have arranged marriages. In such cases a father asks his daughter three times whether she consents to the marriage. If the daughter consents thrice she is considered to be pre-engaged and the groom is allowed to enter her home. The engagement occurs on a Sunday or national holiday and all family members and friends are invited to a feast. During the feast details of the marriage are ratified and gifts are exchanged. In order to make the engagement legal and binding, it was traditional for the groom-to-be to present his fiancée with an ornamental belt, earrings, and either a bracelet or ring. In return the woman would give the man a gift of an embroidered handkerchief or shirts.

Once official, an engagement could last a year or longer depending on the prevailing regional custom.

Traditionally, a Bulgarian wedding takes place in the winter, or possibly the spring, when work is not as pressing and the actual ceremony could last several days. Sometime before the day of the wedding the bride and groom hold separate parties, much like America bachelor and hen parties (bachelorette parties). These parties, which are lively events full of music and dancing, signify that the man and woman are no longer single and that they must now leave behind their unmarried friends. During the party the woman's hair is plaited and the man has his head shaved. The woman is also presented with dried figs, a fruit that in several cultures is redolent of fertility. On the Thursday before the wedding the bride's mother performs the ritual kneading of the ceremonial *pitka* bread, for the rising of the dough represents the creation of a new family. In addition, the best man makes a wedding banner. To make the banner the best man must fell a fruit-bearing tree with one strike of an axe to create a six-foot-long pole. An onion, quince, or apple is stuck to the top of the pole and wrapped in decorative foil, a hand-woven scarf, ribbons, ivy, capsicums, flowers, and strings of popcorn. In times gone by, two poles were made. One was decorated with white ribbons and given to the bride and the other was ornamented with red cloth and presented to the groom. The groom's wedding party would traditionally capture the bride's wedding banner and unite it with that belonging to the groom thereby creating one banner that was carried before the couple on their way to the couple's new home. Once at the house the banner was broken up with the cloth presented to the bride and the fruit shared by the newlyweds. Before the wedding, a wedding tree used to be created by the groom's sister-in-law-to-be as she sojourned at his house. This was a branch of fir or fruit tree decorated with red ribbons, flowers, and apples wrapped in gold foil. Like the wedding banner the tree was also carried to the couple's new home. However the tradition of the wedding tree has all but disappeared as an individual custom and now only informs the design of the wedding banner by the best man.

Soon after daybreak on the morning of the wedding, the groom is sprinkled with barley by his family and friends in order to bring him good luck. Similarly, the friends and family of the groom also fire rifles into the air to ward off evil spirits. Once these acts have been performed the groom asks for his parents' blessing and next the groom's party sets off for the best man's home where the groom presents him with a baked chicken and wine to symbolize that the best man is in charge of proceedings.

The best man and maid of honor, often the best man's wife, then lead a parade to the bride's house where they present the bride with wine, a bridal veil, candles, and candies. A custom surrounds the giving of the bridal veil for once the bride and maid of honor are alone the bride must refuse the veil twice when it is proffered by the maid of honor before accepting it on the third time of asking. According to Bulgarian tradition the bride should wear something red on her veil to counter adversity in her married life. This can take the form of a small ribbon or faux pearls attached to the cloth. Also in order to ward off evil spirits and ill fortune on the wedding day the bride should wear a clove of garlic wrapped in a small handkerchief.

Once she accepts the veil the groom and best man may enter the room. Next, the bride and groom emerge from the room carrying a cloth between them and the bride throws a bowl filled with wheat, coins, and a raw egg over her head so that the dish shatters. The more pieces the dish breaks into, the greater the luck conferred on the couple. This is similar to a tradition in northern England whereby the bride must throw a plate of wedding cake overhead to earn good luck. In England if the plate does not break when it hits the floor a wedding guest must stamp on the plate to ensure the delivery of the luck. Even more luck is incurred in Bulgaria when the bride's mother spills water from a copper cauldron across the steps of the church where the wedding ceremony is to take place. The wedding parties then make their way to church making much noise as they do so to drive away evil. It is considered very bad luck for the bride and groom's parties to encounter each other on their way to church so they take great pains to avoid seeing each other on their journey. To ensure more good fortune, the bride and groom step into the church with their right foot first. To signify the end of the ceremony, the newlyweds exchange rings, kiss and complete official paperwork. They then perform a tradition called "stepping" where each tries to tread on the other's foot in order to determine which of them will have the upper hand in the marriage.

In times past, the reception would be held at the groom's home but today it normally takes place in a restaurant. The groom's mother lays a long, white handmade cloth at the door of the reception venue for the newlyweds to walk on and she scatters flowers in their path as they enter the building. This is meant to ensure health and happiness. The groom's mother also feeds the couple a honey cake and wine while wishing them a long, sweet life. Next the groom's mother holds a loaf of bread over her head and invites the bride and groom to each pull one end of the bread. According to Bulgarian custom whoever pulls the largest piece of bread will dominate the marriage. The couple then feeds bread to each other as the guests shout "*Gorchivo.*" This means bitter and signifies that the couple should sweeten the bitterness of the bread with a kiss. After this feasting, traditional folk dances are performed and alcohol is drunk before the couple receives their wedding cake.

When the couple returns to the groom's home they are again met with a white cloth. The groom's mother greets her new daughter-in-law with bread, wine, honey, butter, and dried fruits and the door is covered with butter and honey. Once inside, the bride stands by the fireplace, the centerpiece of the home, and holds a baby boy while looking up toward the chimney as an obviously symbolic wish for a child, particularly a son. A final wedding custom takes place at dawn the next day and sees the bride remove her veil using a green twig while standing beneath a fruit tree and twisting her bridal wreath. This signals that the bride has

> ### *Todorovden*—St. Theodore's Day
>
> *Todorovden* is a Bulgarian Easter tradition. On this day it is traditional for recently married Bulgarian women to wake early and bake a round loaf decorated with an image of a horse also made out of dough. The women then distribute pieces of the bread while imitating the sounds and movements of a horse. In western Bulgaria, women go to church the day before Todorovden wearing their wedding dresses and accompanied by their mothers-in-law who bring with them ring-shaped cakes and boiled corn. As the mothers-in-law enter the church their gifts are blessed by a priest who later kicks the brides as they exit the church.

now joined the community of married women. Sometimes the bride may also be walked to a well while surrounded by members of the groom's family who sprinkle her with coins and corn.

The remote Bulgarian village of Ribnovo, which has 3,500 inhabitants, is home to a unique wedding custom, *Galena*, during which the bride has her face painted white and decorated with sequins and colored make-up. (*See* Plate 3.) Ribnovo is a snow-bound mountain location where marriages take place in the winter. The people of Ribnovo identify themselves as Muslim rather than as Bulgarians and their wedding custom suffered persecution when Bulgaria was under Communist rule (1946–1989). This was also a time when poverty made village men go elsewhere in search of work, resulting in fewer marriages in the village. On the morning of the wedding, the bride's family painstakingly accumulates her dowry, which comprises items they have stockpiled since she was born—usually knitting, quilts, sheets, aprons, socks, and carpets. On the wedding day the family hangs these items on a tall, wooden scaffold, erected specially for the event and virtually everyone in the village turns out to inspect the dowry offerings. Next the bride- and groom-to-be lead the village in a traditional *hora* dance held on the village square where other youngsters join them. However the highlight of the wedding ceremony is the painting of the bride's face, which comes at the end of the second day of the ceremony. In a room exclusively frequented by females, the bride's face is covered in a thick layer of chalky white paint and decorated with colorful sequins. Next a long, red veil is placed over the bride's hair and her head is framed with tinsel. The bride is dressed in baggy trousers and a colorful bodice and then presented by her future husband, her mother, and her grandmother to the crowd waiting outside. The bride is not allowed to open her eyes wide until the couple's union has been blessed by a Muslim priest.

See also: Arranged Marriage; Bachelor and Spinster Balls; British Wedding Traditions; *Hora* and *Horah*; *Lobola*; Muslim Wedding Ceremony; *Polterabend*; Warding Off the Evil Eye (Volume 1); Wedding Cakes; Wedding Dress

Further Reading

MacDermott, Mercia. *Bulgarian Folk Customs*. London: Jessica Kingsley Publishers Ltd., 1998.

Monger, George P. *Marriage Customs of the World: From Henna to Honeymoons*. Santa Barbara, CA: ABC-CLIO, 2004.

Reilly, Jill. "Nice Day for a White Wedding: Amazing Pictures of Bride, Eyes Wide Shut and Caked in Face Paint, Marrying in Traditional Bulgarian Winter Ceremony," *Daily Mail*, January 13, 2014. Accessed January 7, 2015, at http://www.dailymail.co.uk/news/article-2538599/Nice-day-white-wedding-Amazing-pictures-bride-eyes-wide-shut-caked-face-paint-marrying-traditional-Bulgarian-winter-ceremony.html.

Rolek, Barbara. "Old Bulgarian Wedding Customs." About Food. Accessed January 7, 2015, at http://easteuropeanfood.about.com/od/weddings/p/bulgariaweddings.htm.

Villa-marciana.com. "Wedding in Bulgaria and the Superstitions." Accessed January 7, 2015, at http://villa-marciana.com/en/wedding-in-bulgaria-1.html.

BULLET ANT INITIATION, BRAZIL

Bullet ant initiation is a series of trials for males belonging to the Sateré-Mawé tribe (also known as the Andira, Arapium, and Maue peoples) that are indigenous to the Brazilian Amazon region. This painful initiation marks the participants' transition from boys to adult warriors, beginning when the boys are around 12 years old and repeated throughout young adulthood, only ending when they reach their mid-twenties. During the ritual, a boy has to place his hand inside a glove that has been made especially for the initiation process. The glove is specific to the bullet ant initiation for into the palm leaves used to fashion the glove are woven around 30 venomous ants that are placed so that their stingers face in toward the inside of the glove and therefore toward the initiate's hand. The boy then places his gloved hand inside another, ornate, ceremonial glove.

The ants used in the trial are bullet ants (*Paraponera clavata*), which the tribe calls *Tucandera* or *tucandeira*. The ants are commonly called bullet ants as the pain inflicted by their sting is said to be equivalent to experiencing a bullet wound. The boy must demonstrate that he is sufficiently brave and strong to silently withstand the pain of the venomous bullet ant stings if he is to be considered a warrior by his tribe. By passing bullet ant initiation tests, a male can attain the status of warrior.

Bullet ant initiation has been practiced for several centuries and is one of the most important Sateré-Mawé customs. The bullet ant is particularly suitable for the initiation test as its sting, which is administered via a retractable syringe on the ant's abdomen, is thought to be the most painful of any creature belonging to the *Hymenoptera* species, which also includes bees, wasps, and sawflies. According to the Schmidt Sting Pain Index, which was invented to rate the pain of insect bites and stings on a scale from one to four with one being most benign and four the most excruciating, a bullet ant sting scores in excess of four. The Schmidt Sting Pain Index is somewhat subjective as entomologist Justin Schmidt created the index by testing the stings on himself. However Schmidt calculated that the pain caused by a single bullet ant sting is equal to that of 30 wasp stings so it is clear that any encounter with bullet ant venom is agonizing. It is the bullet ant's potential to cause excruciating pain, however, that makes the species perfect for use in the Sateré-Mawé rite of passage—the severity of the bullet ant sting is important as the initiates must show their ability to withstand pain if they wish to be deemed worthy of warrior status. Not only must the initiates undergo their trials but they must do so without audibly betraying the fact that they are experiencing terrible pain.

The pain inflicted by a single bullet ant sting lasts for between three and five hours and is gone after 24 hours have passed. However several ill effects including nausea, trembling, sweating, and the inability to use a limb that has been stung accompany the pain from the sting. Indeed some initiates have been known to be unable to use their affected limb for a day after the bullet ant initiation test. The body reacts so strongly to bullet ant venom because the venom is a neurotoxin that inhibits synaptic transmissions in the central nervous system. As well as being venomous, bullet ants are also terrifying to behold as they are the world's largest ant, measuring up to one inch long.

Luckily bullet ants are naturally non-aggressive and only sting when provoked or as a defense mechanism. As the bullet ant is not normally aggressive the Sateré-Mawé have to provoke the ants so that they will sting the initiates. Before the trial begins the bullet ants are given a sedative made from local plants so that the tribe members organizing the initiation test can place the ants within the fabric of the woven glove without receiving stings themselves. As the sedative wears off the ants wake up woven into the glove and become increasingly aggressive as they try to free themselves. By the time the ants awaken the initiate has placed his hand inside the glove. Prior to placing his hand inside the glove the initiate coats his hand with a light dusting of charcoal. This is said to confuse the ants and therefore distract them from delivering too many stings. The bullet ant test usually lasts for 10 minutes and the charcoal is the only protection from the bullet ant stings that the boys are allowed. While the boys undergo their initiation, the other members of the tribe sing traditional chants and dance around the boys in an attempt to distract them from the pain they are experiencing.

Once a boy has withstood the pain of the bullet ant stings his status within the tribe changes. However his ordeal is not yet complete for he must withstand the bullet ant glove test a total of 20 times over a period of months or even years. Only after he has endured and passed all these trials will the initiate's rite of passage conclude and the boy be considered a full tribal warrior.

Though the bullet ant initiation is notoriously painful, the idea of enduring the test does not deter Sateré-Mawé boys. Rather, the boys welcome the chance to attain manhood and also think it is important to continue the tradition in order to protect the tribe's customary ways of life in the face of contact with the outside world. Ever since Jesuit missionaries established the Tupinambaranas Mission in 1669, the Sateré-Mawé have struggled to ensure the survival of their cultural identity in the face of contact with outsiders. Traditionally, the Sateré-Mawé are forest natives and originally lived throughout the Amazon rainforest. However, today the tribe lives in 42 villages close to the town of Andira and 31 villages near the town of Marau, both of which are located in Brazil's Amazon basin. Most Sateré-Mawé are fully integrated into the modern Brazilian way of life, living in urban areas such as Manuas, the largest city in the deep Amazon region. This integration has seen many Sateré-Mawé men become bilingual and able to speak both the Sateré-Mawé language as well as Portuguese (Sateré-Mawé women do not generally speak Portuguese). However despite the high level of assimilation of the Sateré-Mawé, they maintain the bullet ant initiation ritual, one of the most important rituals within the Sateré-Mawé cultural heritage.

See also: Cow Jumping; Log Riding; Maasai Warrior Initiation; Matis Hunting Trials

Further Reading

da Silva Lorenz, Sônia. "Territory and History of the Contact with the Whites—Satere-Mawe." Povos Indigenas No Brasil, January 2000. Accessed December 17, 2014, at http://pib.socioambiental.org/en/povo/satere-mawe/967.

Galvan, Javier A., ed. *They Do What? A Cultural Encyclopedia of Extraordinary and Exotic Customs from around the World.* Santa Barbara, CA: ABC-CLIO, 2014.

Riskin, Dan. *Mother Nature Is Trying to Kill You: A Lively Tour through the Dark Side of the Natural World.* New York: Touchstone, 2014.

Vivanco Jorge M., and Tiffany Weir, eds. *Chemical Biology of the Tropics: An Interdisciplinary Approach.* Berlin, Germany: Springer-Verlag, 2011.

BURNING THE ASHEN FAGGOT, ENGLAND, AND THE BURNING OF THE CLAVIE, SCOTLAND

Burning the Ashen Faggot (sometimes written as Ashton Fagot) is an English tradition that occurs every winter in the southwest of England, especially in the counties of Dorset, Devon, and Somerset that are known collectively as the West Country. The word faggot is a local term for a bundle of twigs taken from an ash tree. Though quite a localized custom, it nonetheless occurs in many West Country pubs and private homes in the area as a way of bringing about good luck and foretelling of marriage.

The tradition of Burning the Ashen Faggot is believed to date back to the Saxon period of English history (410–1066) though the custom may have originated in Scandinavia before this time for Scandinavia has a long tradition of holding a feast called *joul* during which people would burn huge bonfires to honor the god Thor. The bonfires featured wood taken from ash trees, for according to Norse mythology the ash tree was the tree of life. Over time the ash tree gained Christian associations with the use of the ash twigs in traditions becoming Christianized. The use of the ash wood in such traditions was justified by the fact that ash was said to be the wood that the Virgin Mary used to light a fire that she used to wash baby Jesus. In Roma Gypsy lore, a fire made from ash wood was thought to have warmed Jesus after he was born on the first Christmas night. Also because the holly, ivy, and fir trees used their leaves to hide the infant Jesus they were permitted to keep their leaves all year whereas the oak and ash, which were bare at the time of Jesus's birth, were condemned to always lose their leaves in winter.

The custom of Burning the Ashen Faggot sees a bundle of ash twigs (the faggot) tied together with nine lengths of green ash bark, which, preferably, should all come from the same tree. Then on Christmas Eve the faggot is placed on a fire that has been lit with the remnants of the previous year's faggot. People then gather around the fire and watch as the faggot burns. All unmarried woman that are present as the faggot burns each choose a band of green ash and, according to tradition, whichever single woman has selected the first ash band to ignite will be the first of the singletons to wed. Moreover, it is thought that any pub or home that does not burn an ashen faggot will receive a year of ill fortune.

Another West Country winter tradition performed to ensure good luck is wassailing, or apple howling. The tradition also occurs in other areas of England in which apples are grown and cider, an alcoholic drink made from fermented apple juice, is produced such as the counties of Kent, Herefordshire, and Sussex. The word wassail derives from the Anglo Saxon words *waes hal,* meaning be healthy, words used as a drinking toast by Anglo Saxons. The tradition of wassailing is thought by some folklorists to have begun as an ancient pagan fertility ritual with the first written reference to the custom appearing in the book of poems *Hesperides*, written by Devonshire poet Robert Herrick in 1647.

Wassailing usually occurs on January 5, a date known as Twelfth Night or Epiphany. Some ultra traditionalists, however, insist on holding wassailing celebrations on January 17. This date is sometimes referred to as Old Twelvey and is the date on which Twelfth Night fell before the introduction of the Gregorian calendar to Britain in 1752, an event that removed 11 days from the length of that year. Additionally, some people celebrate wassailing on Christmas Eve as the Ashen Faggot is being burned. Wassailing consists of making offerings to the spirits of the apple trees to guarantee that the following year's harvest will be bountiful. While the offerings are made to the apple trees people make as much noise of possible usually by shouting, banging pots together, or firing gun shots into the branches of the apple trees. The noise is thought to scare away any evil spirits that might want to endanger the apple crop while also awakening dormant tree spirits.

Another custom similar to Burning the Ashen Faggot, in that it involves burning a wooden object in order to ensure good luck, exists in Scotland as the annual festival of Burning of the Clavie. The word *clavie* is Gaelic for casket and each year on January 11, the Scottish fishing village of Burghead holds a unique fire festival in order to welcome the new year, during which a wooden casket is set ablaze. The Burning of the Clavie festival dates back to the 1750s and marks the replacement of the Julian calendar with the Gregorian calendar in Britain and the resulting deduction of 11 days from the length of the year. The inhabitants of Burghead

> ### Yule Logs
>
> In several European countries, a Yule log is a specially selected log that is burned on a fire hearth from Christmas Eve to January 6. The origins of this Christmas custom are unknown though scholars suggest it may derive from Germanic paganism or Scandinavian winter solstice celebrations. The tree from which the log is taken varies throughout Europe but in essence the log is burned to ensure good luck and to encourage the coming of spring. Today, Yule logs are also eaten in the form of chocolate jellyrolls shaped like a log and decorated with powdered sugar resembling snow.

decided to make the best of the new calendar by celebrating New Year twice—once on January 1, the start of the Gregorian calendar, and again on January 11, which would be the first day of the year according to the Julian calendar. For this reason, on the evening of every January 11, a burning clavie is carried around the village followed by a large crowd of spectators as a way to mark the second New Year. The clavie consists of a barrel set atop a long pole. The barrel is then filled with peat and tar-soaked staves (i.e., the pieces of wood used to make the sides of barrels) and set on fire. The clavie is then transported through the village carried on the heads of various villagers. The first person to carry the clavie is the Clavie King, and he is accompanied by 17 villagers known as the Clavie Crew; these are villagers who have attended the ceremony before and who wear clothes scorched from carrying the burning clavie in the past.

At the start of the evening, the clavie is extremely heavy but as the clavie burns, it becomes lighter. Consequently, the villagers are able to transport the clavie to the ramparts of a Pictish fort on Doorie Hill where the barrel is wedged firmly into a stone pillar, refueled, and then allowed to burn itself out. Once the fire has burned through, the ashy remains of the clavie roll down the hill-side where the glowing embers are collected enthusiastically by bystanders because owning a piece of the clavie is said to bring good luck to its owner for the coming year.

See also: Birthstones (Volume 1); Christingle (Volume 1); Dala Horse (Volume 1); Hallowe'en and *Martinstag* (Volume 3); Nativity Play (Volume 1); Pantomime (Volume 1); Scroggling the Holly (Volume 1); *Tết Nguyên đan* (Volume 3); Warding Off the Evil Eye (Volume 1); *Weihnachtsmärchen* and Advent Calendars (Volume 1); Whuppity Scoorie and Lanimer Day (Volume 1)

Further Reading

BBC. "Burning of the Clavie Event Held in Burghead." *BBC Scotland: NE Scotland, Orkney & Shetland*, January 12, 2013. Accessed November 14, 2015, at http://www.bbc.co.uk/news/uk-scotland-north-east-orkney-shetland-20971313.

Castelow, Ellen. "Wassailing." *Historic UK: History Magazine*. 2016. Accessed May 27, 2016, at http://www.historic-uk.com/CultureUK/Wassailing/.

LegendaryDartmoor. "The Ashen Faggot." Traditions and Customs, October 9, 2014. Accessed November 14, 2015, at http://www.legendarydartmoor.co.uk/christ_fagg.htm.

Morton, Lauren. "Customs of Christmas Past," *LandLove Magazine*, November/December 2014, 110–113.

Simpson, Jacqueline, and Roud, Steve. *Oxford Dictionary of English Folklore*. Oxford, UK: Oxford University Press, 2000.

Visitor Centre Burghead. "The Burning of the Clavie." Accessed November 14, 2015, http://www.burghead.com/clavie.html.

CAJUN WEDDINGS, UNITED STATES

The Cajun people living in Southwest Louisiana have many wedding traditions. Prior to the oil boom of the 1930s, poor transport links and infrastructure meant that many Cajun people lived in remote places without churches or courthouses and did not get to see a member of the clergy, judge, or justice of the peace regularly. Cajun couples wishing to wed therefore either had to travel to the town of Lafayette to obtain a marriage license, or had to wait several weeks or even months for a priest to travel to them. Many Cajuns circumvented this problem by holding their own style of wedding ceremony at which the bride and groom would jump over a broom witnessed by their friends and family. This jumping over the broom was considered a legally binding marriage until a member of the clergy could officiate at an official wedding ceremony. Couples that wished to marry had to declare their intention so that if anybody objected, they had the opportunity to air their disquiet before the marriage occurred. Today the broom continues to play an important role in Cajun weddings for at Cajun wedding receptions the newlyweds' older, unmarried siblings have to dance with a broom (or mop) decorated to resemble another human and therefore a potential marriage partner. This is considered the comic highlight of a Cajun wedding as the siblings' dancing with the broom mocks their single status. Further to this in the town of Mamou the unmarried older siblings must dance with the mop in a tub of water.

Another notable feature of Cajun weddings is the *bal de noce*, or wedding dance, which is especially associated with working-class Cajun weddings. Traditionally, the newlyweds would begin the bal de noce with a song called *"La Marche des Mariés"* ("Wedding March"), which was followed by a waltz. Traditionally, wedding marches at Cajun weddings occur at the reception when a Cajun band—normally comprising a French accordion, steel guitar, violin, drums, and a washboard—strikes up and the dance floor is cleared allowing the bride and groom to take center stage. (*See* Plate 4.) The newlyweds hold hands and walk around the dance floor slowly at least twice while the bands plays a song. The guests then partner each other and join the newlyweds in walking around the room. Next, the newlyweds perform a waltz in the middle of the dance floor watched by everybody present. The couple then dances with their parents and then everyone else joins in the dancing. If a guest wishes to dance with the bride or groom it is customary for the guest to pin paper money to either the bride's veil or the groom's suit. This not only signals a guest's desire to dance but symbolically ensures that the newly married couple begins life with some money. The wedding march is a traditional way for Cajuns to celebrate a marriage but, though they were once very popular, such dances are rapidly falling out of fashion. In times past, the owner of a dancehall where the wedding march was taking place would pay the newlyweds $10 to $15 to stage the bal de noce at his dancehall but would charge guests an entrance fee of 15 cents. However this is no longer the case. Another musical element of the traditional Cajun wedding is the singing of songs that toast the newlyweds, such as *"La Fleur de la Jeunesse"* ("The Flower of Youth"), which is a lament describing the mingled joy and sadness of getting married.

Food, like music, is another important element of Cajun weddings. Popular dishes served at Cajun wedding receptions include crawfish *étouffée* (a thick seafood stew), gumbo (a type of soup) or jambalaya (a rice dish), *boudin* (a type of pork and rice sausage) or boudin balls, crab, shrimp or crawfish dip, cold shrimp dip, Swedish meatballs, brisket, stuffed tongue or chicken salad sandwiches, and a hollowed-out red cabbage filled with dip to eat with raw vegetables. For dessert there is often a watermelon basket filled with melon, grapes, and strawberries. It is also usual for there to be a white wedding cake that will be cut by the newlyweds while the groom's godfather slices a chocolate groom's cake. The concept of the groom's cake evolved in 19th century England from where it spread to the United States. Most groom's cakes consist of dark chocolate, fruit, and alcohol though in the past they tended to be fruitcakes. Groom's cakes are not normally served at the wedding; instead, it is traditional to slice the cake beforehand and give slices to any unmarried female guests. According to legend if the unmarried female places the cake under her pillow she will dream of her future husband. Groom's cakes fell out of favor for a while but in the last few years, the groom's cake has returned to popularity. Today, the idea of the groom's cake is popular as it allows a little bit of attention to be paid the groom on a day that is more often than not centered around the bride. Another possible reason for the groom's cake's newfound trendiness is the popularity of baking as a hobby and of television shows that showcase the artistry of cake making, particularly the making of wedding cakes. However another reason for the resurgence of the groom's cake may be that brides have realized that groom's cakes make an excellent surprise, customizable gift for their new husbands that they themselves can also enjoy. It has also been suggested that the cakes act as an apology if the bride has temporarily transformed into the so-called bridezilla in the run-up to the wedding day.

Once a Cajun reception is over the newlyweds retire for the night. However this is not necessarily the end of the festivities for another old custom, the *charivari*, may occur the day after the wedding. In the past this would see the newlyweds awakened by their guests who would deliberately make loud noises in order to wake the couple who would then have to cook their guests breakfast. Nowadays, this custom only tends to be enacted if one of the newlyweds has been divorced or widowed previously. In this case people make noise outside the window of the newlyweds only stopping the racket when the bride or groom invites the noisemakers into the house for food or drink.

See also: *Hora* and *Horah*; Jazz Funeral (Volume 3); Jumping Over the Broom; *Lindo*; Money Dance; *Polterabend*; *Povitica*; Sock Garland and Sock Dance; Wedding Cake; Wedding March and Bridal Chorus

Further Reading
Brasseaux, Ryan André. *Cajun Breakdown: The Emergence of an American-Made Music*. Oxford, UK: Oxford University Press, 2009.
Early Cajun Music. "'La Marche De La Noce'—Joe Falcon & Cleoma Breaux," May 29, 2015. Accessed June 14, 2015, at http://earlycajunmusic.blogspot.co.uk/2015_05_01_archive.html.
LeMaire, Chrissy. "A Cajun Wedding: The Traditions." RealCajunRecipes.com, February 6, 2006. Accessed June 14, 2015, at http://www.realcajunrecipes.com/2005/02/a-cajun-wedding-the-traditions/.
Martha Stewart Living Omnimedia, Inc. "History of the Groom's Cake," *Martha Stewart Weddings*, 2015. Accessed June 14, 2015, at http://www.marthastewartweddings.com/226856/grooms-cake.
Sousa, Marina. "Should You Have a Groom's Cake? Classic Tradition Becomes the Trend Again," *Huff Post Weddings: The Blog*, June 29, 2012. Accessed June 14, 2015, http://www.huffingtonpost.com/marina-sousa/should-you-have-a-grooms-_b_1638283.html.
Vidrine, Jane. "Cajun Wedding Traditions." Folklife in Louisiana. Accessed June 14, 2015, at http://www.louisianafolklife.org/LT/Articles_Essays/cajun_wed.html.

CHINESE COMING-OF-AGE CEREMONIES, CHINA

In China, individuals are not considered to be independent adults until they marry despite the fact that, according to the Chinese Constitution, people may vote in political elections when they are 18 years old. The legal marriageable age is 20 years for women and 22 for men. However fewer and fewer Chinese people marry at these ages, meaning that they do not officially become adults until well into their twenties.

China officially recognizes 56 ethnic groups resulting in a diverse range of coming-of-age ceremonies. Though many of the ceremonies have fallen out of favor over time and are no longer commonly enacted they have been recently promoted online in an effort to reinstate them in Chinese culture as part of a campaign to revive near-forgotten Chinese heritage. Two of the most well-known Chinese rites of passage for adolescents on the brink of adulthood are the Guan Li and Ji Li ceremonies. These are coming-of-age ceremonies for adherents of the Chinese philosophical belief system known as Confucianism. The name Guan Li refers to the ceremony for males while Ji Li is the version held for females. Both ceremonies are associated with the Han people, the largest ethnic group living in China that is also the world's most populous ethnic group. Both Guan Li and Ji Li ceremonies are thought to be over 2,000 years old and there is evidence that the ceremonies were practiced during the Zhou Dynasty (1045–256 BCE). Guan Li, also known as capping, is a rite of passage for Han males that occurs when men are 20 years old. During a ceremony, a man's hair is coiled around and made into a bun shape. Three caps are then placed over the bun. Traditionally Guan Li ceremonies are held in February and three days before the ceremony takes place the adolescent male that is the focus of the Guan Li ceremony selects an honored guest to be the person to perform his capping ceremony. The boy also picks a capping assistant whose job it is to help the honored guest perform the capping. During his Guan Li ceremony the male is given an inner cap initially, then another cap and then a scarf. When he has been given all three caps the male's hair is combed and made into a bun. Once the caps are placed on the bun the boy in considered to have attained full maturity. Next the guest that performed the capping gives a speech congratulating the new adult who in turn bows to his mother who has been present throughout the ceremony. The honored guest then gives the now adult man a new name, a sort of honorific title that has pleasant connotations. At this point the man may also be given some sort of extra responsibility such as being asked to run the family business.

Similarly the Ji Li, or the hair-pinning ceremony (*ji* means hairpin), is a rite of passage to adulthood for Han females between 15 and 20 years old. The ceremony symbolizes the moment when a girl becomes a woman and is ready to marry thus the ceremony usually takes place between the announcement of a girl's betrothal and her wedding day. Long shiny hair is considered to be beautiful in Chinese culture and until a girl has experienced her Ji Li she wears her hair woven in braids. During a Ji Li ceremony the female's hair is loosened, washed, and gathered into a bun with her hair pinned into place using a hairpin made of gold, jade, or wood depending on her social class. The Ji Li ceremony is almost identical to the Guan Li ceremony. One difference is that a woman receives a coronet rather than caps to mark her coming of age. Also Ji Li ceremonies take place at the family home—in the main room or an inner chamber, while Guan Li ceremonies are held at a boy's ancestral temple.

Guan Li and Ji Li ceremonies are rare these days though a recent surge of interest in Confucianism means there have been calls for the ceremonies to be held regularly among the Han people who do not currently have an official coming-of-age ceremony.

Minority ethnic groups in China have their own coming-of-age ceremonies. For example, the Blang, or Bulang, that live in the Yunnan region of southwestern China (and in areas of Thailand and Myanmar) perform a coming-of-age ceremony called *baoji*. During this ceremony adolescents sit around a fire and each dyes black the teeth of the person that they are sitting next to. Once their teeth have been blackened, the youngsters are given gifts by their parents and are permitted to start romantic relationships. Meanwhile children belonging to another ethnic group found in the Yunnan region, the Pumi people (sometimes called the Primi), are considered to become adults when they reach 13 years old. To celebrate this achievement, the Pumi perform a ceremony that sees an adolescent step forward by placing their right foot on a piece of fat and their left foot on a bag of rice. Once they have stepped on the foodstuffs, the new adult performs a traditional *kowtow* (a kneeling and bowing action). Adults initially perform the move to a stove, then to their oldest relatives, and then to their elder brother.

Some minority groups perform single-sex coming-of-age ceremonies. For instance, to mark their transition to adulthood, males belonging to the Dong people roll in mud to prove their masculinity. There are nearly three million Dong living mainly on the border of Guizhou, Hunan, and Hubei provinces. Dong males undergo the mud-rolling ceremony three times during their life— first when they are five years old and then when they are 10, with each instance of mud rolling conducted under parental supervision. When Dong boys reach 15 years of age they perform the mud-rolling independent of their parents to demonstrate that they are now adult. While the Dong ceremony only involves males, the coming-of-age ceremony performed by the Yi people is exclusively female. There are almost 8 million Yi living primarily in Yunnan, Sichuan, and Guizhou provinces as well as the northwestern part of Guangxi Zhuang Autonomous Prefecture. When a Yi girl living in the Mount Liangshan and Lesser Mount Liangshan areas is 15, 16, or 17 years old, her growing maturity is denoted by an ancient skirt-changing ceremony, or *shalaluo*. Traditionally, Yi girls remove the skirt that they wear as a child and don a colorful skirt, which symbolizes that they have become a woman. Before the ceremony begins, a Yi girl is dressed in a red and white dress with a ponytail and threads are attached to her earlobes. After the skirt-changing ceremony, the girl dons a long blue-and-black skirt, her hair is braided into two, and she puts on earrings. On the day of the ceremony, the family prepares food in the early morning. Only the girl's female friends and relatives are allowed to watch the skirt-changing ceremony. However once the ceremony has taken place, a banquet takes place to which men are invited. As the girl is now considered a woman, she is now allowed to walk by herself, shop at the market, date, and get married.

The Yi living in Yunnan Province also enact an ancient wedding custom known as kidnapping of the bride. This custom sees the groom's family send engagement presents to the bride's family and also send people to the bride's house at a pre-arranged time to mock-kidnap the bride and carry her to their home on horseback. Tradition dictates that the bride should cry for help and act as though terrified despite the fact that she knows she will be "kidnapped." Meanwhile the bride's family pretends to pursue and attack the kidnappers using water, clubs, and cinders to mount an attack that will win back the bride. The pretend kidnappers arrive at the groom's home with their faces stained black from being attacked with cinders causing much amusement. The final part of the kidnapping of the bride custom sees the acting out of a pretend fight between the bride and groom on their wedding night.

See also: Coming of Age Day; Ear-Piercing Ceremonies; *Gwallye*; *Hijab*

Further Reading

China Highlights. "Yi Minority." Accessed May 4, 2015, at http://www.chinahighlights.com/travelguide/nationality/yi.htm.

Popovic, Mislav. "Coming of Age Ceremonies in China." Traditionscustoms.com. Accessed May 4, 2015, at http://traditionscustoms.com/coming-of-age/coming-of-age-ceremonies-china.

Rasi, Alena. "Ancient Coming of Age Ceremonies." Gb Times, August 29, 2011. Accessed May 4, 2015, at http://gbtimes.com/life/ancient-coming-age-ceremonies.

Zang, Xiaowei, ed. *Understanding Chinese Society*. Abingdon, UK: Routledge, 2011.

CHISUNGU, ZAMBIA

Chisungu is a lengthy initiation ceremony for girls of the Bemba tribe living in the African nation of Zambia. The name chisungu derives from the verb *ukusunguka*, meaning to be startled or overcome, and is related to the noun *chisungusho* that translates as marvelous event. A chisungu ceremony usually occurs when a girl's breasts have started to develop and she experiences her first menstruation. Thus the ceremony marks the physical transition of a girl into a woman and is, therefore, ready to marry. A chisungu ceremony teaches a girl how to act when she is married and about the traditional roles of women in Bemba society. Men are not allowed to attend chisungu ceremonies and the ceremonies were once veiled in secrecy. Indeed only recently have the details of the ceremonies become widely known, most notably through Audrey Richards's book *Chisungu: A Girl's Initiation Ceremony among the Bemba of Zambia*. A chisungu ceremony usually involves only one girl though if two or three girls begin to menstruate at the same time then a joint ceremony may be held. The ceremony involves many various rituals all of which instill the importance of female fertility and obedience as well as reaffirming gender roles. The ceremony usually consists of several parts, the locations of which vary depending on whether the initiate lives in an urban area or in the countryside. Some phases of the ceremony may also be included in a girl's wedding ceremony rather than her chisungu ceremony.

Bemba girls are expected to know nothing about womanhood or sexuality—though this may not be the case in actuality girls must at least give the impression of being completely ignorant of sex and reproduction. For this reason the chisungu ceremony invests heavily in educating girls about their bodies and sexual relations. When a Bemba girl begins to menstruate she is dressed in a cloth called *citenge* that ties around her waist and travels down between her legs so that it covers her genitals and buttocks. The girl is then taken to the bush where she undergoes rituals involving the mufungo tree by being anointed with a paste made from its bark and spitting seeds in four directions. The girl is told to stay away from children and from fire. The girl is also taught about the so-called menstrual cloth, a sanitary napkin that is treated extremely carefully because it is believed that if the cloth is damaged then the girl will become infertile. This is the start of the chisungu ceremony, which involves the female initiate, called a *Nachisungu*, living away from her people for a period of time ranging from six weeks to three months. During this time, the girl is taught how to cook, care for a garden, act as hostess, and how to be a mother. The girl is also given sex education that involves being told that oral sex is taboo as is having sex while menstruating. It is also taboo for a husband to see his wife's menstrual blood so the girl is taught to signal that she is bleeding by placing a red cloth or stone on her bed. When a girl has her second menstrual period, she is made to take off all her clothes save her skirt and has her entire body covered in a paste made from tree bark. The girl is later washed clean and sits leaning against a wall as she is presented with special foods.

The night before the girl's ceremony occurs, speeches are made in public while the girl is given pottery statuettes to hold called *mbusa*, which symbolically represent the duties expected of married couples in both domestic and public life. The mbusa statuettes provide the girl with a tangible expression of the obligations expected of her once she has officially become a woman as signified by her chisungu ceremony. Each mbusa is associated with a song that the girl must learn so that she can recite them during her ceremony the next day and if the girl reneges on an obligation later in life the appropriate mbusa song will be sung to her to remind her of the mbusa, and, therefore, of the duty she should be performing. For example, if a girl becomes a mother and decides to go out leaving her baby unattended then an older woman that knows the girl has experienced the chisungu ceremony will sing to the girl a song associated with an mbusa that tells the tale of a mother that left her baby unattended at home resulting into the baby falling into a lit fire and burning. Thus it is apparent that the mbusa and their attendant songs have both symbolic and educational properties.

The chisungu ceremony consists of several parts that vary from time to time. However chisungu ceremonies always involve much singing and dancing and in some areas, such as Copperbelt and Northern provinces, a special three-tone drumbeat is sounded throughout. The songs and dances tend to be spontaneous and are intended to convey to the girl specific cultural messages about the correct behavior for Bemba wives and mothers. To begin the ceremony the initiate may be brought into a hut and told to sit on the floor silently with her eyes downcast in a ritual called *ukuingishya abanacisungu*. This ritual used to be a compulsory part of the chisungu ceremony but is no longer mandatory. Ukuingishya abanacisungu is intended to teach the girl to respect the elder women, *Nachimbusa*, that are participating in her chisungu ceremony. Once the girl has sat on the floor of the hut the older women gather around her and sing symbolic songs while also surrounding the girl with branches and leaves. These are meant to honor and represent the Musuku tree that is symbolic of sexual reproduction and fertility. This is important as Bemba girls are expected to produce children in order to ensure the continuation of the tribe. Sometimes a tree trunk is dropped between the initiate's legs

The older women then perform sexually suggestive moves with each other that often involve a penis shaped from clay or fabric. These suggestive movements are called bed dances. Occasionally, the initiate is ordered to undress and perform bed dances with other women who will touch the girl on her vagina and breasts to ensure that the girl understands that these are the most important female parts. The initiate may also be ordered to lie on her back and wriggle her hips. This is to teach the girl how to respond when her husband instigates sexual intercourse and how to best please her husband sexually. The girl is told to always be sexually available to her husband as he has all the rights to her body and if she cannot satisfy her husband sexually he will commit infidelity. Next the girl is given a pestle and mortar and told to pound vigorously. This is mean to instill in the girl that she must never keep her husband waiting for food. The girl then has to crawl on her hands and knees in order that she should learn humility, obedience, and respect for her tribe as well as learning to be subservient to her husband. The girl now has to pour a bowl of water over the hands of the older women. This too teaches the girl to be respectful.

The next part of the ceremony is sometimes called the Beer Dance, which involves the girl being led out of the hut and into a grassy area where she must dig a hole in the ground. Once the hole has been made, an older woman fills it with beer, which the girl must drink from the hole by lapping at it while remaining on all fours. The beer represents Bemba men and drinking the beer symbolizes the girl's need to please men always.

Although chisungu is still practiced in both rural areas and cities in Zambia, the ceremony is gradually falling out of fashion. Today most Bemba girls grow up in Christian families and attend modern schools where subjects such as biology present information different from the teachings of chisungu. Additionally chisungu presents men as being in control with women subordinate, which also sets the custom at odds with African society, which is rapidly modernizing and seeing the modification of traditional gender roles. Interviews with Bemba females that have experienced the chisungu ceremony suggest that the rituals involved make girls feel inferior to men and fearful of their future husbands. Girls also claim that the ceremony leads wives to believe that it is their husbands' right to abuse them. However many Bemba people still believe that chisungu has a place in their cultural heritage and believe that the tradition should continue even if it seems somewhat outdated. Older Bemba women assert that the chisungu ceremony empowers females because it makes women take pride in their bodies' reproductive capabilities while also encouraging the Bemba community to value women. It has also been claimed that since the chisungu ceremony hails menstruation the ceremony is a celebration of womanhood that also prizes virginity and deters girls from experiencing sex before marriage.

See also: Breast Ironing; Dipo Womanhood Ceremony; Entering the *Bashali* (Volume 1); Fattening Room Seclusion; Female Genital Cutting; Menstruation Customs

Further Reading

Countries and Their Cultures. "Bemba." World Cultures. 2015. Accessed January 7, 2015, at http://www.everyculture.com/wc/Tajikistan-to-Zimbabwe/Bemba.html.

Hinfelaar, Hugo F. *Bemba Speaking Women of Zambia in a Century of Religious Change: 1892–1992*. Leiden, Netherlands: E. J. Brill, 1994.

Lancy, David F. *The Anthropology of Childhood: Cherubs, Chattel, Changelings.* Second edition. Cambridge, UK: Cambridge University Press, 2015.

Mwanamwambwa, Adaobi Tebuho. *Women and Children's Rights in Zambia: A Case Study of the Chisungu Initiation Ceremony in the Bemba Community.* MA Dissertation. University of Witwatersrand. November 9, 2005. Accessed June 7, 2015, at http://www.google.co.uk/url?sa=t&rct=j&q=&esrc=s&source=web&cd=8&ved=0CEoQFjAH&url=http%3A%2F%2Fwww.genderlinks.org.za%2Fattachment.php%3Faa_id%3D19543&ei=lzt0VZqWGMWvUYLxgKAJ&usg=AFQjCNGhSjZbe4E5i7w7ozCYCc7Zbk4RHA&sig2=aDW1UwK0u3V2fGLKQf9xog&bvm=bv.95039771,d.d24.

Niezen, Ronald. *Public Justice and the Anthropology of Law.* Cambridge, UK: Cambridge University Press, 2010.

Rasing, Thera. *The Bush Burnt, the Stones Remain: Female Initiation Rites in Urban Zambia.* Munster, Germany: Lit Verlag, 2001.

Richards, Audrey Isabel. *Chisungu: A Girl's Initiation Ceremony among the Bemba of Zambia.* London: Faber and Faber Ltd., 1956.

White, C. M. N. "Matrimonial Cases in the Local Courts of Zambia," *Journal of African Law,* 15(3), Autumn/Automne, 1971, 251–265.

CHOKHA THAVANI VIDDHI: DEVIPUJAK PURIFICATION TRIAL, INDIA

The Devipujak community is an extremely religious society living in Gujurat, India, which follows a strong caste and religious system. The community also runs its own community courts that decide on a variety of matters including infidelity and rape. In cases where a husband suspects his wife of having an extra-marital affair or when an unmarried woman is accused of entering into sexual relations, she is subjected to a purification ritual as it is thought that only through being purified can the female be freed from her wrongdoings. Community courts do not conduct purification tests for men accused of infidelity though men may be tested in some other way to see is they are lying.

In some instances the community courts arrive at their verdicts by making accused individuals take so-called purification rituals, *Chokha thavani viddhi*. These trials are conducted by a tantric, that is, a shaman-type priest who practices black magic and believes strongly in supernatural forces. The use of tantrics to deliver verdicts predates the existence of both mainstream courts and police in India. Only through undergoing the trial can a woman that claims to have been raped or is accused of infidelity prove her innocence and thereby rehabilitate the reputation of her family and prevent them from becoming outcasts.

The purification ritual sees the tantric ask an accused female a series of questions and then the tantric checks to see if the female is telling the truth by taking a pinch of barley seeds from a bag and then asking the female to say whether the number of seeds that he is holding in his hand is even-numbered or odd-numbered. Any female that answers wrongly is judged to have lied to the tantric. The next part of the purification trials sees the same process repeated in exactly the same way except that this time a stone weighing 10 kilograms (around 22 pounds) is placed on the female's head as she answers the tantric. Alternatively the female may be told to answer while holding a 40 kilogram (roughly 88 pounds) weight above her head. The female must carry the stone until the tantric is satisfied that she has told him the truth by rightly saying whether he is holding an odd- or even-numbered quantity of seeds. There is no limit as to how many times this ritual may be performed for the tantric may choose to extend the ritual for several months, or until such a time that he decides that a goddess has purified the female of what is considered her sexual transgression. It is not known whether the purification rituals are overlooked or denounced by the Indian authorities, but to date the purification rituals have not been the subject of any police investigation.

In the summer of 2015, the Devipujak community made international headlines after it was reported that a woman who had been kidnapped and gang raped repeatedly by more than five men over a period of many months, resulting in a pregnancy, was having to undergo a purification ritual to clear her name and that of her family. According to Devipujak tradition, once a female is considered purified by passing the test, members of the community must not scorn her and neither she nor her family may be banished. However if a female fails the purification ritual this is deemed a sign that the goddess judges the female to be impure meaning the female may be ostracized from the community.

See also: Churching of Women (Volume 1); *Devadasi* System (Volume 1); *Hijra*; *Kumari* and *Deuki* (Volume 1); Virginity Testing; Vrindavan: The City of Widows (Volume 3)

Further Reading

Jain, Ankur. "Indian Gang Rape Victim Faces 'Purification Ritual.'" BBC News: India, June 14, 2015,. Accessed November 5, 2015, at http://www.bbc.co.uk/news/world-asia-india-32444349.

Thifa, Dani. "Gang-Rape Victim Raped for 8 Months Ordered to Undergo 'Purification Ritual.'" MBC Times: Life & Society. Accessed November 5, 2015, at http://www.mbctimes.com/english/gang-rape-victim-raped-purification-ritual.

CHOOSING OPTIONS, ENGLAND, WALES, AND NORTHERN IRELAND

When children in the United Kingdom reach Year 9 in school, usually at 13 or 14 years old but sometimes younger, they are asked to choose optional GCSE subjects, often colloquially known as Options. The term GCSE is the acronym for the General Certificate of Secondary Education, an academic qualification awarded for individual subjects that are studied in Year 10 and Year 11 when students are generally 14 to 16 years old.

Most schools set three compulsory GCSE subjects—English, math (called maths in the United Kingdom) and science—though some schools insist that pupils also study other subjects such as languages. Schools in England and Northern Ireland following the National Curriculum (i.e., standardized educational content taught at all local authority funded schools in both countries) must also study some form of Information Communication Technology (ICT). Other subjects that school pupils study at GCSE level are chosen by the pupils after discussions with parents and teachers and are known as Options as they do not have to be studied. Many schools arrange a so-called Options Evening where pupils, parents, and teachers can discuss which Options children should take. Additionally some schools offer pupils personality profile tests to help to decipher what job pupils should steer toward when they leave school and, therefore, which Options pupils should take for their GCSEs.

The Options available to study vary from school to school. However, by law, pupils must be offered a choice of at least one subject in each of four groups of subjects that are known as "entitlement areas." These groups of subjects are Arts, comprising art and design, dance, music, media studies, and drama; Design and Technology; Modern Foreign Languages, such as Mandarin, French, German, or Spanish; and Humanities, which includes subjects such as history and geography. Some schools also offer pupils the chance to study Options in subjects such as ancient languages (particularly classical Greek and Latin), physical education, religious studies, business, textiles, and PSHE and citizenship. PSHE stands for personal, social, health, and economic education and along with citizenship this subject focuses on sex and relationship education and drug and alcohol education and provides the skills and knowledge necessary for pupils to function as full and active members of society.

GCSE results, for both Options and compulsory subjects, are graded A*, A, B, C, D, E, F, and G. The A* grade was introduced to distinguish the highest level of achievement in a subject. Most subjects have a two-tiered structure offering Higher grades A* to D and Foundation grades C to G. This grading system means that the best grade a pupil taking a subject at Foundation level can achieve is a C grade even if the pupil gets 100 percent in his or her exam. There is also some overlap between tiers as a D grade can be awarded as a Higher or Foundation grade. Whether or not a pupil should take a subject at the Higher or the Foundation level is often a matter of discussion between pupils, teachers, and parents. Pupils that narrowly miss out on a D grade may be awarded a Grade E, while pupils that fail to reach grade G may be awarded a U grade, which stands for unclassified. In 2017 the GCSE grading system will change with pupils being awarded grades of 9, 8, 7, 6, 5, 4, 3, 2, or 1; 9, 8, and 7 will be the top three grades replacing the current top two grades of A* and A.

Choosing the right Options is important as the subjects that pupils study later at A-Level (General Certificate of Education Advanced Level) are nearly always studied by pupils as Options. A-levels are a school-leaving qualification offered by schools in the United Kingdom (and British dependencies around the world), the passing of which is usually the basis for pupils being awarded places at university.

Therefore it is important that pupils choose the appropriate subjects for the courses they wish to study at university as this may well shape the career path they follow in adult life.

See also: *Baccalauréat* and *Matura*; Gap Year; *Russefeiring* and Schoolies Week

Further Reading

BBC. "Choosing Subjects for GCSE." BBC: Learning, 2014. Accessed March 24, 2015, at http://www.bbc.co.uk/schools/parents/gcse_choosing/.

Crown Copyright. "Guidance: Personal, Social, Health and Economic (PSHE) Education." Department for Education, September 11, 2013. Accessed March 24, 2015, at https://www.gov.uk/government/publications/personal-social-health-and-economic-education-pshe/personal-social-health-and-economic-pshe-education.

Guardian News and Media Limited. "A**: The New GCSE Super Grade 9," *The Guardian*, September 14, 2014. Accessed March 24, 2015, http://www.theguardian.com/education/shortcuts/2014/sep/14/new-gcse-super-grade-9.

SchoolSuccess.co.uk. "GCSEs and Key Stage 4." GCSE Maths and Science. 2016. Accessed May 28, 2016, at http://schoolsuccess.co.uk/all-about-gcses/.

Vincent, Alan. *How to Choose Your GCSEs*. Ninth edition. Richmond, UK: Trotman & Company Ltd., 2004.

CHRISTIAN WEDDING CEREMONY, CHRISTIANITY

Traditional Christian thinking deems marriage to be a gift from God that should not be entered into without a great deal of consideration. A Christian wedding is a public declaration of a couple's devotedness to each other and their commitment to form a loyal, lasting union. Guests at a Christian wedding are therefore witnesses to a ritual celebration of the couple's committed love and devotion to each other. Moreover, the couple being married reflects the loving devotion that Christians believe exists between themselves and Christ. Many Christians believe sexual relations should only take place within the context of a marriage, as a marriage is a public declaration of a couple's love and commitment to each other. Many Christians also believe that marriage is the correct state in which to establish a family. For these reasons, Christians believe that it is very important to marry in a church so that God can bless the marriage.

The Catholic Church sees God as the author of marriage and marriage as God's way of demonstrating his love for people. Because Catholics view marriage as God's work they see marriage as a divine institution that should never be undone, even if the partners divorce in the eyes of the law. Indeed the Catholic Church believes that as long as two formerly married people are still alive they remain united in the eyes of God even if they are formally separated.

Catholics are encouraged to marry other Catholics as the Catholic Church believes only in this way can a couple achieve an ideal union. That said, today many Catholics enter into so-called mixed marriages, that is, a marriage between a Catholic person and someone belonging to another faith. Indeed it is quite usual for Catholics to enter into mixed marriages in that only one of the couple is a baptized Catholic, though the couple has to find dispensation from the priest conducting their wedding. Mixed couples are allowed to marry in Catholic churches as long as they have followed Catholic principals such as promising to stay together for life, to be loyal to each other, and to produce children, if possible. Catholic priests are required to ensure that the faith of a Catholic that has opted to marry into a mixed marriage will not be jeopardized so if a Catholic opts to marry a non-Catholic or someone that is not baptized in any religion (a so-called disparity of cult) then the couple must enter into discussions with a priest and may have to be granted dispensation by a Catholic bishop. The Catechism of the Catholic Church understands that mixed marriages can experience difficulties but suggests that through a common faith in God a couple will grow even closer to each other as they face their problems. These pre-wedding discussions and preparations are known as pre-Cana and are viewed as a process of maturation and education that will help a couple in their married life together. Pre-Cana may take the form of an intensive weekend course or may take place over a six-month period. Either way, pre-Cana is compulsory for all Catholics wishing to wed. While the couple waits to marry, they should not engage in sexual intercourse as the Church views sexual activity as the preserve of married couples. The Church takes this view because Catholics see sexual intercourse as intended to create children and so should only occur within the correct framework of marriage.

There are two types of Catholic wedding ceremonies. The first type, involving a mass and celebrated with the Eucharist, lasts for about 60 minutes. The second type of Catholic marriage ceremony does not include a mass and is much shorter in duration, lasting only about 20 minutes. When a Catholic marriage ceremony includes a mass, the ceremony begins with the entrance rite. This is a procession that may include a hymn and sees the presiding priest greet the congregation, then lead the Penitential Rite, a general confession that occurs at the beginning of each mass. Opening prayers are then said. Next the Liturgy of the Word occurs. This includes readings from the Old Testament and New Testament, a psalm, Gospel readings and a homily, which is a non-theological practical sermon. Next, the rite of marriage takes place during which questions are asked about the couple's loyalty to each other and their eagerness to have children. Then the couple exchanges their marriage vows and their wedding rings. Next, the Liturgy of the Eucharist occurs during which the altar is prepared for the arrival of the Eucharist and the Eucharist prayer is spoken. The following hymns are sung too: "Sanctus Sanctus," "Memorial Acclamation," and "Great Amen." After these hymns are sung, Communion takes place, the Lord's Prayer is spoken and the nuptial blessing takes place. This is followed by the Sign of Peace (usually hand-shaking) and then the hymn "Agnus Dei" is sung, as is the "Communion Hymn." To end the ceremony, the priest makes a final blessing, the Dismissal occurs signaling the end of the service, and the newlyweds kiss each other to signal that they are now married.

A recessional hymn may then strike up to indicate that everyone should leave the church. In the case of a Catholic wedding that does not include a mass, the Liturgy of the Eucharist is omitted.

There are a number of different Protestant religious groups, including Baptists, Lutherans, Methodists, Episcopalians, Presbyterians, and the Church of England. This variety of theological viewpoints in turn creates a variety of wedding services that though they are fairly similar each does show some variations of detail. Protestant wedding ceremonies usually feature hymn singing, readings from the Bible, and congregational responses to the couple's exchange of wedding vows. Most Protestant weddings begin with a processional that, traditionally, sees the bridegroom and his best man stand at the front of the church in front of the altar where the presiding official also waits. The wedding party then enters though the order in which the wedding party enters varies according to location and other factors. For instance, in the United States the order of the wedding party is usually as follows: groomsmen, bridesmaids, maid of honor, flower girl, ring bearer, and then the bride and her father. Conversely, Protestant weddings in the United Kingdom do not usually have groomsmen, flowers girls, or ring bearers and the bride is followed by her bridesmaids, who hold up the train of her wedding dress as she walks down the aisle.

After the processional the officiant welcomes the congregation and then a friend or family member reads from the Bible. Next, the couple exchange their wedding vows and wedding rings. In the Church of England the traditional wedding vows are:

> [T]o have and to hold
> from this day forward;
> for better, for worse,
> for richer, for poorer,
> in sickness and in health,
> to love and to cherish,
> till death do us part.

Today, however, most Protestant churches allow couples to write their own wedding vows though these vows must not go against Christian values. When exchanging rings it is usual for Church of England couples to say:

> With my body I honor you,
> all that I am I give to you,
> and all that I have I share with you,
> within the love of God,
> Father, Son, and Holy Spirit

Once the couple has exchanged their vows and rings the officiant gives a final blessing and proclaims that the couple are now married. There may also be prayers asking that God bless the couple with children though this is optional. Finally, once the proclamation of marriage has been made the wedding party leaves the church as a recessional plays. Traditionally, the newlyweds are the first to leave the church. Some Protestant wedding ceremonies also include Holy Communion and at some point in the wedding the couple may be required to sign a register, though this would be a legal requirement not a religious obligation.

See also: British Wedding Traditions; Marriage Banns; Wedding Anniversaries; Wedding Cake; Wedding Dress and Wedding Ring; Wedding March and Bridal Chorus

Further Reading

BBC. "Christian Marriage." BBC: Religions: Marriage and Weddings, June 23, 2009. Accessed October 11, 2015, at http://www.bbc.co.uk/religion/religions/christianity/ritesrituals/weddings_1.shtml#h2.

Cooke, Bernard, and Gary Macy. *Christian Symbol and Ritual: An Introduction: An Introduction.* Oxford, UK: Oxford University Press, 2005.

Langford, Andy. *Christian Weddings: Resources to Make Your Ceremony Unique.* Second edition. Nashville, TN: Abingdon Press, 2008.

Wittry, Jan. "The Protestant Wedding Ceremony." Brides.com. Accessed October 11, 2015, at http://www.brides.com/wedding-ideas/wedding-ceremonies/2006/12/the-protestant-wedding-ceremony.

COMING OF AGE DAY, JAPAN

Coming of Age Day or *Seijin no Hi* is an important rite of passage for males and females in Japan that takes the form of a national holiday. The holiday is celebrated on the second Monday in January each year. Coming of Age Day celebrates and encourages all those who have reached the age of 20—the Japanese age of majority—over the past year to help them realize that they are now adults. Once a Japanese person turns 20 years old they are legally allowed to vote, to drink and to marry without parental consent. The young adults also become liable under Japanese law and are considered subject to social responsibilities. Coming of Age Day is marked by many festivities including coming-of-age ceremonies called *seijin-shiki*, which translates as "adult ceremony," and that take place in the morning at local and prefecture offices. After these coming-of-age ceremonies families and friends hold post-ceremony parties.

Coming-of-age ceremonies have been held for a very long time in Japan and at least since 714 CE, when it is said that a young prince dressed in new clothes and adopted a different hairstyle to mark his becoming a man. Japan has celebrated coming-of-age ceremonies ever since. Medieval Samurai families would hold coming-of-age ceremonies called *Gempuku* to mark that a son had become a man. During Gempuku a boy would receive an adult name and be given an adult hairpiece called an *eboshi*. Once the youth had gone through this ceremony he had to assume adult responsibilities and was allowed to marry. Samurai daughters aged between 12 and 16 years old had their own separate ceremony called *Mogi*. During the Mogi a girl was given a kimono that symbolized her transition to womanhood. At other times in Japanese history boys marked their transition to manhood when they reached 15 years old, and girls celebrated reaching adulthood when they turned 13 years of age. During the Edo period of Japanese history (1603–1868) the transition to adulthood was marked by boys having their forelocks cropped, and girls by having their teeth dyed black. The Meiji Revolution that restored imperial rule to Japan in 1868 popularized coming-of-age ceremonies among the populace in general and, in 1876, 20 years of age became the legal age of majority. However an official holiday to mark Coming of Age Day was established only as recently as 1948, when it was intended that the day be celebrated every January 15. In 2000, it was decided to hold Coming of Age Day every second Monday in January instead. Until very recently all young people attending coming-of-age ceremonies had to be exactly 20 years of age, having celebrated their 20th birthday after the previous year's Coming of Age Day but on or before the present Coming of Age Day. Today, many of those attending coming-of-age ceremonies are 19 years old for celebrants are those whose 20th birthday is between April 2 the previous year and April 1 in the current year. For example in 2015, all Japanese people that turned 20 years old between April 2, 2014, and April 1, 2015, were invited to take part in the 2015 Coming of Age Day celebrations.

All young people that fit the age criteria and who live in the vicinity are invited to attend the coming-of-age ceremonies at the local authority office. During a coming-of-age ceremony, municipal government officials give speeches and small gifts are given to the 20-year-olds to mark that they are now considered adults. It is traditional for Japanese women to celebrate their coming of age by wearing a long-sleeved, elaborately decorated kimono called a *furisode* that is traditionally reserved for unmarried women as well as flat, thonged *zōri* sandals that are usually made from rice straw, wood, leather, or synthetic fibers. Since many young Japanese women are unable to put on a kimono single-handedly due to the intricacies involved in donning the robe, many decide to visit a beauty salon where they will be dressed and have their hair styled. There is a current trend for newly adult women (and some men) to dye their hair a shade of orange-blonde for the occasion. It is very expensive to buy a full set of kimono and sandals so many women borrow the outfit from relatives or rent the clothes for the day. Indeed in Tokyo, the capital of Japan, just renting a kimono for a Coming of Age Day ceremony costs $1,000, while a kimono can cost in excess of $10,000 to buy. As renting a kimono is much cheaper than buying a robe, kimono rental reservations often start being taken in the February the previous year. Sometimes young Japanese men don traditional dress too, including a dark kimono worn over a *hakama*, a loose, deeply pleated trouser-like garment. However nowadays many Japanese men celebrating their 20th birthday Coming of Age Day do not sport traditional Japanese clothing but rather wear a formal Western-style suit.

In the past, young people celebrating their Coming of Age Day did so in respectful silence but today after the Coming of Age Day ceremonies, the young adults usually celebrate by going to parties or drinking excessively to mark the fact that they are now legally allowed to partake of alcohol. Especially popular is *sake*, Japanese rice wine. Celebrating Coming of Age Day impresses upon the young people both their new responsibilities as adult members of society and the additional rights extended to them as adults.

However, in recent years Coming of Age Day has become a painful reminder of the growing gap between the generations in Japan. Some older Japanese have expressed the concern that many 20-year-olds do not feel or act like adults pointing to the fact that many of the younger generation celebrating their 20th birthdays adopt a deliberately rough street slang while experiencing their coming-of-age celebrations, something the older Japanese find uncouth and ugly. The older generation also dislikes that many of the 20-year-olds drink sake straight from the bottle when celebrating. Many older Japanese people feel that the boorishness of the new crop of adults is exemplified by the number of coming-of-age ceremonies that have been disrupted by loutishness. For instance, in Miyazaki, several celebrants lit firecrackers during the playing of the Japanese national anthem and in Aomori, in northern Japan, two boys mounted the stage where a coming-of-age ceremony was taking place and threw mayonnaise at each other before running off. Other ceremonies have seen official speeches disrupted by hecklers and celebrants talking on cell phones throughout their ceremonies. One incident in particular that garnered international interest occurred in Naha on the southern island of Okinawa in 2002. On this occasion seven people were arrested after youths drove through police lines in an attempt to bring a barrel of sake to a coming-of-age ceremony. Fights broke out and 200 riot police were needed to quell the situation.

As Japanese culture stresses the need to show respect to other people and demonstrate patience, many older Japanese feel disappointed by the apparent immaturity of the next generation of adults. Some commentators have sided with the rowdy celebrants highlighting the fact that coming-of-age ceremonies tend to be needlessly long and boring. However attempts to enliven proceedings have only served to fuel charges of immaturity. For example, in Urayasu, outside Tokyo, new adults have chosen to mark their transition to adulthood by visiting nearby Tokyo Disney Resort and dancing with Mickey and Minnie Mouse. Part of the reason for this seemingly childish behavior may be due to the fact that most Japanese 20-year-olds live in circumstances that are far removed from traditional ideas of what constitutes adulthood. For instance, 90 percent of Japanese 20-year-olds still live in the parental home and are financially dependent upon their parents. This is mainly because Japan has been experiencing a prolonged economic recession resulting in many 20-year-olds being stuck in low-paying, part-time work that does not entail great responsibility. In addition, the average age that Japanese young people marry and have children has risen steeply in the space of a few generations so they experience a delay in experiencing marital and parental responsibilities and so stay emotionally younger and fairly carefree for longer.

Though Japan's 20th Birthday Coming of Age Day celebrations are often riotous the events held in January 2015 were poignant occasions as the year marked the 20th anniversary of the 1995 Kobe earthquake, also known as the Great Hanshin earthquake, which killed more than 6,400 people and left hundreds of thousands homeless. In Kobe nearly 10,000 new adults observed a minute's silence at their ceremony as they watched film footage of their city's near destruction. A similar tone of somberness was observed in the nearby city of Nishinomiya, where more than 1,110 people died in the disaster.

See also: Birthdays (Volume 1); Log Riding; Minute's Silence (Volume 3); Twenty-First Birthday Traditions; *Zou hun*: Mosuo Walking Marriages

Further Reading

Allen, David, and Chiyomi Sumida. "Coming of Age Day, a Big Event for Japanese Youths, Is Steeped in Tradition," *Stars and Stripes*, January 9, 2004. Accessed December 29, 2014, at http://www.stripes.com/news/coming-of-age-day-a-big-event-for-japanese-youths-is-steeped-in-tradition-1.15223.

BBC. "Japan: Kobe Earthquake Babies Mark Adulthood." BBC News: News From Elsewhere, January 13, 2015. Accessed January 13, 2015, at http://www.bbc.co.uk/news/blogs-news-from-elsewhere-30794970.

Glum, Julia. "Japan Coming of Age Day 2015: Facts about Japanese Holiday Celebrating Young People [PHOTOS]." *International Business Times*, January 11, 2015. Accessed May 28, 2016, at http://www.ibtimes.com/japan-coming-age-day-2015-facts-about-japanese-holiday-celebrating-young-people-1775200.

Joyce, Colin. "Drunken Japanese Youths Ruin Coming of Age Rituals," *The Telegraph*, January 15, 2002. Accessed December 29, 2014, at http://www.telegraph.co.uk/news/worldnews/asia/japan/1381592/Drunken-Japanese-youths-ruin-coming-of-age-rituals.html.

Melton, J. Gordon, ed. *Religious Celebrations: An Encyclopedia of Holidays, Festivals, Solemn Observances, and Spiritual Commemorations*. Volume 2. Santa Barbara, CA: ABC-CLIO, 2011.

Pelican-travel.net. "(Japan) Coming of Age Day—Jan. 14, 2013." Accessed December 29, 2014, at https://www.pelicantravel.net/en/newsPage.php?frCd=japan&seqNo=11.

Web Japan. "Coming of Age Day." Explore Japan Calendar. Accessed December 29, 2014, at http://web-japan.org/kidsweb/explore/calendar/january/seijinshiki.html.

COURTSHIP WHISTLING, MEXICO

The Kickapoo Indians living in Coahuila, Mexico, speak many languages. Foremost among these is traditional Kickapoo, which exhibits linguistic characteristics of the base Algonkian language, though an increasing number of Kickapoo Indians are also speaking Spanish and English. Those that speak English are usually younger adults. Several researchers, particularly Robert Ritzenthaler and Frederick Peterson, have noted that young Kickapoo adults, both males and females around 15 and 16 years old, also engage in *onowecikepi* or "courtship whistling." To enable courtship whistling to work as a method of communication each young courting couple shares a distinct whistle known only to themselves. Couples use this whistling to communicate when they will rendezvous in the evening. Though whistling is used as a way of communicating in many languages only the Mexican Kickapoo use whistling as a courtship tool. The Kickapoo people living in Oklahoma do employ a form of whistling as part of their courtship patterns but the Oklahoma whistling is not systemized and cannot be used to carry out conversations. Thus it can be said that the Kickapoo living in Mexico exclusively employ the system of courtship whistling.

Originally, courting couples would communicate their messages by playing a lover's flute with each flute having its own distinctive sound. A Kickapoo man would then use his individual flute to play tunes distinct to him and therefore recognizable to his girlfriend. However since 1915 courtship whistling has been employed instead of the musical instrument as young people wanted a way of communicating that their parents could not understand. The whistling is not a form of musical serenading, but, rather, a method of communication based on the pitch, accent, and rhythm of the traditional Kickapoo language.

An individual performs a courtship whistle by pressing the thumb knuckles of both their hands vertically against their lips and blows through the small hole created. The young Kickapoo then cups three fingers of their right hand so that the ends rest at the base of the index finger on the left hand while the fingers on the left hand control the opening at the back of the hand—opening and closing the aperture controls the tone made by the lips. Thus the positioning of the fingers and palms creates the sound of the Kickapoo whistle.

Courtship whistling can be heard intermittently from dusk until midnight every night except during bad weather. Usually one or more young Kickapoo tribesmen build a fire at a local meeting place. A young Kickapoo man will then whistle to his girlfriend inviting her to join him by the fire. The girl recognizes her boyfriend's whistle because every courtship whistle is unique. Most whistled messages are made up of stock phrases such as "Come on," "I'm coming," "I'm waiting for you," "No," and "Wait a minute," though entire conversations can be conducted by way of courtship whistling.

Though often it is just one couple that meets up sometimes large groups of around 12 couples congregate to drink alcohol, sing traditional songs, talk, and, of course, woo. Many older Kickapoo disapprove of courtship whistling as they feel it enables and encourages youngsters to stay out late at night. Local native police once banned the custom but parents have never been able to stop the courtship whistling from occurring and since 1940 the tradition has been reinstated and practiced enthusiastically.

See also: Bed-Courtship; Wodaabe Courtship Dance and Ceremony

Further Reading

Hurley, William M. "The Kickapoo Whistle System: A Speech Surrogate," *Plains Anthropologist, 13*(41), August 1968, 242–247.

Milwaukee Public Museum. "Mexico Kickapoo Lifeways." Accessed January 22, 2015, at http://www.mpm.edu/research-collections/anthropology/online-collections-research/mexican-kickapoo/lifeways.

Ritzenthaler, Robert E., and Frederick A. Peterson. "Courtship Whistling of the Mexican Kickapoo Indians," *American Anthropologist, 56*(6), December 1954, New Series, Part 1, 1088–1089.

COW JUMPING, ETHIOPIA

Cow jumping, also known as the bull-jumping ceremony and commonly called jumping over the bull, is a unique public initiation rite for young men belonging to the Hamar people living in the Omo River Valley in southwestern Ethiopia. Other tribes living in the lower Omo Valley also perform the ritual including the Tsamai, Aavil, Banna, and Bashada. However it is the Hamar who are most readily associated with the cow jumping initiation ritual for cow jumping is the final ritual in a series of initiation rites that Hamar males must undergo in order to be classed as an adult member or the community and allowed to wed, have children, and own cattle. Cow jumping takes place annually at the end of the harvest, usually between July and September. Strangers are permitted to view the ritual and this has led to some critics arguing that cow jumping initiation has become little more than a sideshow put on for the amusement of tourists who pay at least US$18 per person to watch the spectacle.

Cows play a major part in the lives of the Hamar people. For instance every member of the Hamar tribe is given three names—a human name, a goat name, and a cow name. The cow jumping initiation custom is an extension of this reverence for the cow and reflects the Hamar tribe's pastoral culture.

Cow jumping initiation occurs in the following way. To start with, a young Hamar man announces that he would like to marry a girl of his choosing. However before the girl's parents can consent to the union the man must pass the cow jumping test. The cow jumping initiation is preceded by another ritual. This rite sees the man's sisters and other female relatives together with the other village women become drunk and provoke the *maz*—adult males who have completed the cow jumping initiation and now live separately from the rest of the tribe traveling from cow jumping ceremony to ceremony. As the maz has been provoked to anger the village, women consent to allow the maz to beat them with sticks on their unclothed backs (young girls are usually discouraged from taking part). The beating leaves the women with open wounds that result in scarring. However the women regard the scars with great pride for the scars are seen as a sign that they have attained true Hamar womanhood. Further, the Hamar believe that if a female relative undergoes a beating prior to a cow jumping initiation the cow jumper is eternally indebted to the female for the pain he has caused her, with the scars the living proof of the beating she has endured. Therefore the sister of the cow jumper knows that her scars mean she can appeal to her brother if she ever needs help.

To begin the cow jumping initiation, the family of the girl chosen by the jumper chooses between 6 and 30 castrated bulls for the jumper to hurdle. The cattle represent the women and children of the Hamar. For the initiation rite the young man has his head partially shaved and he is rubbed with sand in a symbolic washing away of his sins. Additionally his body is smeared with dung that is thought to provide him with strength. Finally he is stripped naked except for strips of tree bark that are strapped to his body in the shape of a cross in order to afford spiritual protection. Meanwhile the cattle are also smeared with dung to make them slippery. This additional slipperiness adds an extra level of difficulty to the cow jumping ritual for during the ritual the cows are lined up by village elders and the jumper must stand on top of one cow as it moves and then jump on to another cow as it is running. (*See* Plate 5.) The jumper must cross the line of cows four times without falling or tripping for the ritual to be completed and he may call upon the maz for help if he finds the trial difficult. Throughout the ritual the maz are in charge of limiting the movement of the cattle in an attempt to stop the jumper from falling, thereby preventing injury. Any man who falls is regarded with a degree of scorn while it is regarded as an ill omen for a male to be unable to complete the ritual and so a failed jumper is denied the right to marry. Failed jumpers are, however, permitted to retry the following year. If the consensus is that a male failed the initiation because of strong winds he is allowed to try the cow jumping test later the same year. Blind and lame males are assisted across the line of cattle by other members of the tribe. At the end of the ritual the man is blessed and sent off with the maz who shave the rest of his hair. Meanwhile the other tribe members take part in a flirtatious dance at which girls are allowed to choose who they want to dance with and indicate attraction to a tribesman by kicking him on the leg.

Only when a male has completed the initiation may he marry his chosen wife or start a herd of cattle. Indeed any man who passes the cow jumping ritual is considered by the Hamar to be strong and wealthy and is allowed to wed up to four women. In exchange for a girl's hand in marriage her family receives cattle and the couple are engaged for two months before they can marry. During this time of betrothal the couple perform acts that highlight the importance of cattle to the Hamar. For instance, they consume a drink of cow's blood and milk. To make the drink, blood is drained from a cow's neck and blended with the animal's milk.

Cow jumping was once widespread throughout Africa but changing social customs and reduced oral tradition mean that today the ritual is not as prevalent as once it was.

See also: Bullet Ant Initiation; Land Diving; Maasai Warrior Initiation; Matis Hunting Trials; Scarification

Further Reading

BBC. "The Hamar," BBC Tribe, October 29, 2014. Accessed December 7, 2014, at http://www.bbc.co.uk/tribe/tribes/hamar/#further3.

Briggs, Philip. *Ethiopia*. Sixth edition. Chalfont St. Peter, UK: Bradt Travel Guides Ltd., 2012.

Galvan, Javier A., ed. *They Do What? A Cultural Encyclopedia of Extraordinary and Exotic Customs from around the World*. Santa Barbara, CA: ABC-CLIO, 2014.

D

DASTAAR BANDI AND AMRIT SANCHAR, SIKHISM

When a Sikh boy is between 11 and 16 years old, he is taken to a *gurdwara* (Sikh temple) and undergoes a *Dastaar Bandi* (also written *Dastar Bandi*) turban-tying ceremony at which the boy wears his first turban. This is a two-fold form of initiation as the ceremony inducts the boy into the Sikh community and also marks his achievement of adulthood. A Dastaar Bandi ceremony marks the moment in a Sikh boy's life when he is ready to commit to his faith. Indeed in Punjabi the word *dastaar* means crown, the symbol of the Sikh faith.

During the Dastaar Bandi ceremony, prayers are spoken and hymns are sung and then either a *granthi* (a Sikh that keeps and reads the Sikh holy scriptures) or one of the boy's elderly male relatives ties a turban around the boy's head as a symbol of his adult status. The turban is a mandatory article of faith for Sikh men, not just a cultural article. When a Sikh man, or woman, wears a turban it ceases to be a length of cloth but rather becomes one and the same with the individual's head. The turban, therefore, has an immense spiritual significance for it symbolizes loyalty, pride, bravery, devoutness, love, and obedience. Wearing a turban provides Sikhs with inner strength thus they wear them every day. At the same time, however, wearing a turban places a burden of responsibility on the wearers as they immediately become ambassadors for their religion, representing their faith and the community of Sikhs worldwide. On a more prosaic level, turbans also act as a useful head-covering for Sikh men do not traditionally cut their hair and a turban is a practical way of keeping long hair clean and free from dust.

At some point during the Dastaar Bandi ceremony the boy is also made to observe the so-called Five Ks. The Five Ks are the physical symbols of Sikhism that are worn by adherents of the faith as a sign of devotion. The Five Ks take the form of a steel sword called a *kirpan*, a wooden comb known as a *kanga*, cotton undergarments called *kaccha*, a steel bracelet called a *kara*, and uncut hair called *kesh*.

The Rise of the Female Turban Wearer

An increasing number of Sikh women living outside of India are starting to wear turbans as a symbol of their religion. The reasons for this are manifold but include a desire to display a heightened religiosity and to be visibly Sikh in the wake of attacks on Sikhs mistaken for Muslims post-9/11. As well as wearing turbans, the women are also opting to let their facial and body hair grow untrimmed in line with the Sikh belief that hair should not be cut. The women that choose to do this claim they feel empowered by placing their devotion to their religion above societal expectations.

The Sikh ceremony of initiation akin to a baptism is called *Amrit Sanchar* for which all participants must complete a ritual washing and should be wearing four of the so-called 5 Ks—their kanga, kara, kachha, and kirpan. Through this ceremony, which can take place at any age, a Sikh person becomes *khalsa* (pure one) and acquires full membership of the Sikh Order, *Khalsa Panth*. The ceremony is important as it sees a Sikh person receive an elixir called *amrit*, a blessed blend of water and sugar that has been stirred with a double-edged sword called a *khanda*. Amrit is only given to Sikhs when they are able to fully understand the obligations that accompany its drinking. During the ceremony the amrit is accompanied by a solemn oath in the presence of Sri Guru Granth Sahib and *Panj Pyare,* or the five beloved ones. Panj Pyare is a quintet of initiated Sikh men or women that act as leaders within the Sikh community. The Panj Pyare oversee the Amrit Sanchar ceremony by preparing the initiates and administering the amrit to those ready to be initiated.

Amrit is prepared for the Amrit Sanchar ceremony in a special way and the elixir can be considered the equivalent of baptismal holy water. To make the elixir, sugar cubes or sugar cakes called *patashas* are dissolved in water inside an iron bowl called a *baata*. The Panj Pyare sit encircling the bowl and all the while the sugar water is stirred with the khanda and holy verses called the *gurbani* are intoned. Once the gurbani have been said aloud the Panj Pyare stand up holding the baata and one of the Panj Pyare says the ardaas thereby transforming the sugar water into sacred amrit. Each initiate then sips the amrit and utters a formal greeting. Amrit is also sprinkled on the eyes and hair of the initiates. Next, the Panj Pyare recount the basic teachings of Sikhism, the *Mool Mantar*, five times and then the initiates repeat the same words. One of the Panj Pyare then administers the vows of the *Rahit Maryada* and the initiates are told not to break any of the rules of discipline. The ceremony then ends with a prayer, readings from the Sri Guru Granth Sahib, and the distribution of a special dessert, *karah parshad*, to everyone that has witnessed the ceremony.

See also: Beards; Sikh Baby Rites and *Naam Karan* Naming Ceremony (Volume 1); Sikh Death Customs (Volume 3); Sikh Wedding Ceremony

Further Reading

Lee, Jonathan, H. X., and Patit Paban Mishra. "Punjabi Sikh American Rites of Passage," in Jonathan H. X. Lee and Kathleen M. Nadeau, eds., *Encyclopedia of Asian American Folklore and Folklife, Volume 3*. Santa Barbara, CA: ABC-CLIO, 2011.

Rojas, Rick. "For Young Sikhs, Turban-tying Ceremony Binds Them to Their Faith," *Washington Post*, June 20, 2010. Accessed October 11, 2015, at http://www.washingtonpost.com/wp-dyn/content/article/2010/06/19/AR2010061902865.html.

The Sikh Coalition. "Sikh Theology: Why Sikhs Wear a Turban," *The Sikh Coalition*. Accessed October 11, 2015, at http://www.sikhcoalition.org/sikh-theology-why-sikhs-wear-a-turban.

Sikh Missionary Society U.K. "Sikh Ceremonies." The Sikhs and Their Way of Life. Accessed October 10, 2015, at http://www.sikhmissionarysociety.org/sms/smspublications/thesikhsandtheirwayoflife/chapter6/.

DIPO WOMANHOOD CEREMONY, GHANA

The Dipo Womanhood Ceremony, sometimes referred to as simply Dipo or as *kloyo peemi* literally meaning "making a Krobo woman," is an extremely important, if controversial, sacred female coming-of-age ceremony performed by the Krobo people, Ghana's fourth largest ethnic group who live in the fertile zone between the coastal town of Somanya and the central town of Odumasi in the east of the country. Every Krobo female is expected to go through the ceremony so that they can be classed as a woman. The ages of the females who take part in the rite varies but most are aged between 12 and 16. The Dipo rite, which takes place annually around Easter, usually in April, has many individual stages that involve ritual cleansing, virginity testing, and education and culminates in the initiate returning to society as a woman.

The origins of the Dipo Womanhood rite are disputed though the ceremony is undoubtedly many centuries old and was probably first performed in the 11th century. There are two main theories as to the origins of the rite popular today. One theory is that mothers with female children became jealous that an elaborate puberty ceremony involving circumcision and ornate dress existed for boys but not for girls and that to rectify the situation the mothers united to create a puberty rite exclusively for daughters. Another theory suggests that an ancient priestess called Nana Kloweki, the earth goddess and queen of the gods who was married to Mawu the Creator and incarnated into human form to accompany the Krobo people on their migratory journeys, started the Dipo rite.

Until the beginning of 19th century, the Dipo rite took many months to complete. Socio-economic developments and the adoption of a national academic calendar mean that today the rite lasts for, at most, one week. Despite this truncation the rite retains vitally important spiritual and social significance. The specifics of the Dipo rite vary according to location. In order to be included in the ceremony qualified girls go to the house of the chief priest and shed their clothes as these are symbolic of childhood and then don new attire. Here the girls are joined by members of their family and then by members of their community and tourists who come to watch one of Ghana's most important rituals. The priest is assisted by so-called ritual mothers, usually female relatives of the initiates who look after two to five girls, in preparing the girls for the rite. On the first day of the Dipo ceremony the girls are paraded topless in public having had all but a small amount of hair shaved from their heads. It is important that the girls' breasts are exposed as this signifies that they are becoming fully formed adult women who are physically ready to marry. A raffia ribbon is tied around the girls' necks signifying that they have each become a *Dipoyo,* or Dipo girl, and a string of carnelian beads is tied around their waists to which is attached a red loincloth. The red of the beads and the loincloth signifies the girls' menstruation and therefore their ability to procreate. It also protects against evil spirits. From now on the initiates are permitted to cover their breasts with a cloth except when they are participating in a section of the rite. This marks the start of the girls' symbolic seclusion from the rest of their community.

On the second day of the rite, all the participants are ordered not to speak and walk in procession to a stream carrying gourds called calabashes. Here they are given a ritual bath that symbolizes the spiritual cleansing of the girls' bodies and minds. The ritual washing also sometimes sees the girls' relatives give them dirty washing to clean. The girls then return to the priest's house where the ritual mothers sprinkle the girls' faces with chalky water and red camwood, also known as African sandalwood. Next maize and sugarcane are placed on the girls' lips three times before they are allowed to eat the foods as part of the *ho fufui* (Saturday's fufu), a shared meal consisting of yam, dumplings, and palm oil soup. After the ritual meal the rest of the girls' hair is shorn. The girls are then given drinks, two local ones including palm wine, and one foreign drink (e.g., Schnapps). This tri-libation is performed in order to ask the gods to bless the girls. The next part of the rite sees a castrated goat from each of the girls' parents killed. The blood of the goat is used to wash the girls' feet. Alternatively, a red hen may be slaughtered and its blood used. This symbolically transfers the girls' impurities on to the bird. Afterward, a white hen is killed and its blood used to wash the feet. This represents the removal of the bad luck and ritually purifies the girls.

On the third day of the rite, the chief priest tells the girls to sit on a white cloth placed across a stool as this is thought to prevent the girls from having babies. A clay mixture is daubed on the girls' bodies and the intestines of the slaughtered goats are wrapped around the girls' shoulders. Next, the seminal part of the rite takes place for the girls, now dressed in white loincloths redolent of purity and holiness, are taken to the shrine of Nana Kloweki where the girls are presented to the presiding priestess who pours millet wine upon the ground and prays for the protection of the girls. The girls then wash with water infused with medicinal herbs and they have white and red marks painted on their bodies. Next, the girls, carrying long white sticks, are directed to sit three times upon the Tekpete, a legendary stone transported down Krobo Mountain by the Krobo people during the 19th century. A sanctified medicinal leaf is placed upon the girls' lips to ensure they remain silent as they sit and rise. As each girl touches the stone she is scrutinized by the ritual mothers whose job it is to check that the girls are virgins. If a girl manages to sit down on the stone and rise three times then she is said to have passed the purity test. This is extremely important for any impurity of mind or body would destroy the sanctity of the ritual. After sitting on the sacred stone of virginity the girls are carried from the temple by a male family member, usually their fathers, amid much celebration and excitement. Every girl who passes the virginity test is given a *Dipo-se* hat. These cylindrical hats, which are similar in shape to those worn by priests, are symbolic of purity and honor.

The next day the ritual mothers teach the girls the skills necessary to become a good Krobo woman. These skills include arts and crafts, dancing, deportment, grooming, and seduction—particularly how to pleasurably enhance sexual relations. The girls also learn the Klama puberty dance, the movements of which are designed to highlight the girls' desirability to the men who look on as they dance during their Oudooring Ceremony—the moment when the girls are reintroduced to their community and dance in order to attract a suitor.

Having passed through all the sections of the Dipo rite the girls' hands are decorated with permanent tribal markings as nine cuts are made between the thumb and wrists of each girl to show she has undergone the Dipo ceremony. However the rite is not quite finished even when the girls are welcomed back into their community for next an elephant hide is tied around each girl's head in order to ensure her fertility. On the fifth and final day of the rite the girls show off their *akori* or *aggrey* (ancestral beads which signify prosperity, protection, affection, and spirituality) and dress in *kente*, or hand-woven silk clothes. The Outdooring Ceremony then takes place during which the girls sing and perform the Klama dance.

The Dipo rite is the subject of fierce debate in Ghana where some consider the ritual to be sexist, undignified, and outdated, particularly the exposure of the girls' breasts and the washing of their feet in blood. As a result of this criticism, many Ghanaian Christians refuse to let their daughters participate in the ceremony. As around half of all Krobo girls living in this area of Ghana are Christian, the timing of the Dipo rite has been affected. Ghanaian Christians feel that the Dipo rite should occur prior to baptism as they believe baptism is a way of removing their sins after initiation. Thus it is clear that Ghanaian Christians view the Dipo rite as sinful and necessitates the ritual cleansing of baptism to remove the sin incurred by participation in the ritual.

See also: Breast Ironing; Fattening Room Seclusion; Female Genital Cutting; Virginity Testing

Further Reading

Galvan, Javier A., ed. *They Do What? A Cultural Encyclopedia of Extraordinary and Exotic Customs from around the World.* Santa Barbara, CA: ABC-CLIO, 2014.

Idler, Ellen L., ed. *Religion as a Social Determinant of Public Health.* Oxford, UK: Oxford University Press, 2014.

Olupona, Jacob K. *African Religions: A Very Short Introduction.* Oxford, UK: Oxford University Press, 2014.

UNCG MOMO. "Celebrating Dance Ghana Style," *Celebrating Dance Ghana Style*, October 27, 2006. Accessed November 26, 2014, at http://danceinghanaglobalarts.blogspot.co.uk.

DIWALI AND *KALI POOJA*, INDIA

Diwali is an important annual autumn festival that is celebrated by Hindus, Sikhs, and Jains across India and around the world. The festival also coincides with the Hindu New Year as the festival typically falls between mid-October and mid-November, although the exact dates are determined by the Hindu lunar calendar. People celebrate Diwali for a variety of reasons but the themes that run through the festival are the triumph of good over evil, the concept of rebirth and regeneration, and the victory of knowledge over ignorance. To mark the festival people hold firework displays, light candles, feast, give gifts, pray, and do good deeds such as feeding the poor. The name Diwali translates as rows of lighted lamps because it is traditional for people to decorate houses and public spaces with lit earthenware oil lamps called *diyas* during the festival. For this reason Diwali is often referred to as the Festival of Lights.

Diwali has its roots in ancient legend though these legends vary geographically. In northern India Diwali is seen as a way to mimic the celebrations held after Lord Rama and his wife Sita returned from 14 years in exile to their kingdom in northern India after defeating Ravanna, the king of the demons, in the 15th century BCE. Similarly, in Nepal, Diwali celebrates the triumph of Lord Krishna over the Narakasura, the demon king. Meanwhile in Gujurat, India, Diwali is held in honor of a goddess rather than a god for in this area of India the festival celebrates the goddess of wealth, Lakshmi. The association of Diwali with wealth creation means that it is customary for Hindus to start new business ventures during Diwali and to pray to Lakshmi for a prosperous year. The lamps lit at Diwali are seen as a way to guide the goddess into people's homes and Hindus in India will leave the doors and windows of their houses open during Diwali to encourage Lakshmi to visit and bestow wealth.

Another goddess is also celebrated in India at this time of year for in Bengal Diwali coincides with a celebration in honor of Kali, a complex goddess who is seen as both a frightening figure of destruction and moral ambivalence, but also as a mother-figure since she is a form of the mother goddess Durga. That the goddess is fearsome is suggested by the fact that she is normally depicted holding a severed head in one hand with a sword in the other while wearing a garland of skulls. Kali is, however, revered as the destroyer of evil and champion of justice. In Bengal Kali is the main figure venerated during the Diwali period. The celebration of the goddess is known as *Kali Pooja* (or Puja) and takes place on the night, specifically at midnight, of the new moon, Kartik, which also marks Diwali.

According to legend, two demons once became so powerful that they threatened both Indra, King of the Gods, and his Kingdom of Heaven. For this reason the gods requested protection from Mahamaya Durga, the Goddess of Shakti (divine power), a move that led to the birth of Kali who was born from Durga's forehead in order to save heaven and earth from the demons. Kali is said to have killed the powerful demons and fashioned a garland of their skulls that she placed around her neck. Legend tells, however, that Kali lost control of her bloodlust and began to kill everyone that came near her and in order to cease the slaughter Lord Shiva threw himself under her feet, an action that shocked Kali who stopped the bloodshed and repented. In Bengal this occasion is celebrated as Kali Pooja with the faithful seeking Kali's protection and blessings.

It has been claimed that Kali Pooja is a time of both devotion and danger for though the goddess is often associated with destruction, Kali Pooja sees the people of Bengal seek happiness, wealth, protection, and good luck. Just as people in northern India light diyas to celebrate Lakshmi during Diwali so people in Bengal celebrate Kali Puja by lighting lamps to honor Kali. Similarly, as people in the rest of India decorate their houses with *rangoli,* folk art designs, during Diwali, Bengali homes are decorated with rangoli during Kali Pooja. Also special foods are associated with Kali Pooja, just as sweets are traditionally eaten during Diwali. In Bengal it is traditional to sacrifice a goat to Kali though nowadays some families choose to offer a red-fleshed pumpkin to the goddess along with lentils, rice, and fish. Since Kali is a frightening goddess she is seldom worshipped in the home but at Kali Puja every effort is taken to please the goddess, who is usually worshipped at night during Kali Pooja. To end the night of Kali Pooja, it is traditional for devotees of Kali to immerse clay icons of the goddess in a river before dawn.

Another famous Indian festival, Holi, also celebrates the triumph of good over evil but also hails the end of winter. Holi generally lasts for two days (16 in the region of Braj) and is a time of joy and goodwill. The festival is mainly celebrated on the Indian subcontinent as well as places with large Indian populations. The festival is an Indian national holiday and sees people from all social classes unite to enjoy a period of togetherness during which social divisions are forgotten.

Holi is an ancient springtime festival of colors that has its roots in various Indian myths in which good triumphs over evil and love proves powerful. To celebrate Holi, participants throw brightly colored powder at each other in celebration that spring has arrived and that darkness has been vanquished by light. (*See* Plate 6.) People also light bonfires to symbolize the defeat of demons. That Holi is a time of color and light is reinforced by the fact that during the festival people wear white clothing to ensure that the thrown colors are especially visible. Another aspect of Holi is the eating of special foods including *gujiya* (sweet dumplings), *puran poli* (sweet flatbread) and *dahi bada* (sweet lentil dumplings in yoghurt), and the drinking of intoxicating *bhang* (a form of cannabis used in Indian food and drink) mixed with *thandai*, a refreshing drink made from purified water, sugar, melons, spices, nuts, and roses. These celebratory foods and drink, in addition to the essentially colorful nature of Holi, mean that the festival is a time of love, unity, and celebration.

Celebrating *Holi* in Utah

The town of Spanish Fork, Utah, is the location for the largest *Holi* celebration in the United States. Indeed each March in excess of 50,000 people of all ages, races, and social groups visit the town from across the country, as the town is the site of the Sri Radha Krishna Temple, one of America's biggest Hindu temples. The people attending the celebrations wear white clothes that clearly show up the bright-colored powder used during the Holi festivities. Attendees also listen to Hindu music and abstain from drink and drugs.

See also: *Kumari* and *Deuki* (Volume 1); Hindu Wedding Ceremony; *Kumbh Mela*; *Mehndi*; *Thaipusam*: Extreme Ritual Flesh Modification; Mundan Ceremony (Volume 1)

Further Reading

BBC. "Diwali—23rd October 2014." BBC Schools: Religion, October 20, 2014. Accessed September 20, 2015, at http://www.bbc.co.uk/schools/religion/hinduism/diwali.shtml.

Foulston, Lynn, and Stuart Abbott. *Hindu Goddesses: Beliefs and Practices.* Eastbourne, UK: Sussex Academic Press, 2009.

Galvan, Javier A., ed. *They Do What? A Cultural Encyclopedia of Extraordinary and Exotic Customs from around the World.* Santa Barbara, CA: ABC-CLIO, 2014.

Kinsley, David R. *Hindu Goddesses: Visions of the Divine Feminine in the Hindu Religious Tradition.* Berkeley, CA: University of California Press, 1988.

Rush, James. "Diwali: What Is the Festival of Lights—and How Is It Celebrated around the World?" *The Independent*, October 22, 2014. Accessed September 20, 2015, at http://www.independent.co.uk/news/world/asia/diwali-2014-what-is-the-festival-of-lights-and-how-is-it-celebrated-9810212.html.

Society for the Confluence of Festivals in India (SCFI). "Kali Pooja in Bengal." SCFI: Diwali. Accessed September 20, 2015, http://www.diwalifestival.org/kali-pooja-in-bengal.html.

Related Primary Document: Sandip Roy, "The Great Diwali Fight and Obama," 2009

In the following blog essay Sandip Roy, an editor with New America Media, considers how the various ethnic groups living in the modern United States react to multiculturalism. The essay also suggests that American Hindus are making waves in mainstream American life by participating in political activism. In the essay Roy argues that President Barack Obama could give the Diwali festival official federal recognition because the celebration is observed by millions of Hindus, Sikhs, and Jains and is a national holiday in India. By discussing the proposed issuance of a United States' Diwali postage stamp Roy also posits Diwali as a touchstone for American attitudes to multiculturalism in general and questions whether the issuing of such a stamp and the celebrating of Diwali at the White House would mean redefining, or at least widening, what it means to be American in today's United States.

OK, you have to give it to President Obama. He knows how to work the symbol.

President Obama became the first US President to celebrate Diwali, the festival of lights, in the White House.

That's been a long-standing fight of Hindu Americans.

Actually all of Diwali has been the touchstone of multicultural tussles in America.

The first big Diwali fight was about street parking. New York Mayor Bloomberg didn't want to add Diwali to its list of major holidays when street cleaning would be suspended. The City Council passed the bill in 2005 and the Mayor vetoed it. In 2007 it was finally approved. Phew.

Then there was the petition for the Diwali stamp. If Muslims could get the Eid stamp, why not a Diwali stamp? Diwali is our Christmas said the Hindus. There was an online petition for signatures. According to SAJA the petition was started by an Atlanta businessman Bob Ghosh and it even got dead signatories like former Indian prime minister Jawaharlal Nehru. The US Postal Service told them respectfully that the signatures didn't count. But like the NPR funding being cut right now hoax email, the Diwali signature email would pop up in Indian-American mailboxes every year.

That fight started a long time ago. You can tell. The stamp was worth 37 cents. In 2009 the Hindu American Foundation formally asked the US Postal Service's Citizens Stamp Advisory Committee for a Diwali stamp. Earliest that can happen—2012. No one claimed this was express mail.

But the big fight was always about the Presidency.

Next year, Diwali in the White House.

They got close with George W. Bush. But it was always Diwali in the annex to the White House. And it was always with a "senior administration official", never the Big Boss himself.

One can't blame Bush. In 2007 When Rajan Zed, a Hindu priest was invited to offer the morning prayer in the Senate protesters shouted "this is an abomination" from the gallery.

The American Family Association urged its members to protest because Zed would be "seeking the invocation of a non-monotheistic god." (Note the small g). Former Navy Chaplain Gordon Klingenschmitt said Zed "committed the sin of idolatry" with the "permission" of the government.

Now that abomination has moved from the outhouse to the inner sanctum itself. The historic East Room of the White House was the site of the Diwali celebration. Hindu Americans are tickled pink. The Hindu American Foundation has issued a press release saying "Never before had a sitting US President personally celebrated the Diwali holiday, and with that one gesture, two million Hindu-Americans felt a bit more like they belonged—one more reason to feel at home."

Of course for those who think Obama is the anti-christ this is one more proof that godless heathens have taken over the White House. But the president was careful to make sure he didn't make it seem like the ten-armed goddesses were taking over the administration. (But I think a ten-armed kick ass Goddess with a lot of Second-Amendment protected weapons would not be a bad ally to have in pushing through health care reform).

Obama invited people of different faiths to the ceremony. And he talked about the larger significance of a festival of lights—a time for celebration and contemplation.

He explained what Diwali meant for Hindus, and what it meant for Jains and what it meant for Sikhs. I was startled because having grown up in India I didn't know all that myself.

I just knew Diwali as fireworks, oil lamps and platters of sweets. It needed President Obama to explain my culture back to me with professorial authority.

It was a little embarrassing.

But anyway what are the brave Diwali fighters going to do now?

I guess they could always go back to the great battle for the Diwali stamp.

Source: *Courtesy of New America Media and Sandip Roy.*

DUNMOW FLITCH TRIALS, ENGLAND

The Dunmow Flitch Trials are an English folk custom that occurs every leap year in the town of Great Dunmow in eastern England. The Dunmow Flitch Trials sees a flitch (side) of bacon awarded to married couples if they can satisfy a judge and jury comprising six maidens and six bachelors that they have not wished themselves unmarried at any point in the last year. Despite the fact that the Dunmow Flitch Trials take place as infrequently as every four years they are one of England's most famous customs. In the past both participants and onlookers took the Dunmow Flitch Trials very seriously whereas today the custom is a light-hearted event that parodies a real trial.

The exact history of the Dunmow Flitch Trials is disputed. Some historians believe the custom originated in 1104 at the Augustinian Priory of Little Dunmow when local aristocrat Lord Reginald Fitzwalter and his wife dressed as poor folk and begged a blessing from the Prior of Little Dunmow one year and a day after they married. The Prior was impressed by the couple's devotion to each other and rewarded them for their loving loyalty by bestowing upon them a side of bacon. On receiving the bacon Fitzwalter is reputed to have revealed his true identity and awarded his land to the Priory on condition that a flitch of bacon should be presented to all couples that could prove a similar level of marital devotion. Other historians however claim that the history of the Dunmow Flitch Trials stretches back to 1244 when local aristocrat Baron Robert Fitzwalter launched the event. At this inaugural holding of the Trials a couple had to kneel on two sharp-tipped stones in the churchyard of the local church and prove that for a year and a day since they married they had never wished themselves unwed. That the Dunmow Flitch Trials are a very old event is suggested by the fact that it is referenced in *The Wife of Bath's Tale* that is one of Geoffrey Chaucer's 14th-century *Canterbury Tales* and also referred to in *Piers Plowman* by William Langland, which was written circa 1360–1399. However it was not until 1445 that the winners of the Dunmow Flitch Trials were recorded officially. This win is noted in documents from the Priory of Little Dunmow that are kept by the British Museum in London.

Since the end of World War II the Dunmow Flitch Trials have taken place every leap year. The modern version of the Trials takes the form of a court supervised by a judge, with a counsel representing the married couple, known as the claimants, and an opposing counsel that represents the donors of the Flitch of Bacon. There is also a jury of 12 unmarried adults (six men and six women), a clerk of the court who records the proceedings, and an usher who maintains order. The court convenes in a marquee erected especially for the occasion and claimants married for at least one year and one day come from around the world to try and earn the Flitch of Bacon. The Dunmow Flitch Trials is not a competition because every couple could prove their devotion successfully while being defended by their counsel and thereby win a side of bacon for themselves. It is the job of the opposing counsel to interrogate each couple and to try to persuade the jury that they are not worthy of a Flitch. Those couples that prove their love successfully are carried at shoulder-height by bearers in a ceremonial sedan-type chair called the Flitch Chair, in which they are taken from the marquee where the trials now takes place to the town's marketplace. Here, the winning claimants swear an oath that is similar to ancient marriage vows while kneeling on pointed stones. Couples that cannot prove their devotion must walk behind the Flitch Chair to the marketplace where they are given a consolation prize of a piece of gammon (hind leg of cured pork).

See also: Leap Year Proposals; St. Dwynwen's Day

Further Reading
Alexander, Marc. *The Sutton Companion to British Folklore, Myths & Legends*. Stroud, UK: Sutton Publishing Limited, 2002.
Dunmow Flitch Trials Committee. "The History of the Dunmow Flitch Trials." Accessed October 21, 2015, at http://www.dunmowflitchtrials.co.uk/history/.
Simpson, Jacqueline, and Steve Roud. *Oxford Dictionary of English Folklore*. Oxford, UK: Oxford University Press, 2000.

DYNGUS DAY, EASTERN EUROPE AND UNITED STATES

Śmigus-Dyngus, also known as *lany poniedziałek*, meaning Wet Monday, is a festivity that occurs on Easter Monday in Poland, Ukraine, and among Polish communities in the United States. Similar festivities also take place in other eastern European countries: in the Czech Republic the celebration is called *Oblévačka* and in Slovakia it is known as *Oblievačka* in Slovak (both *Oblévačka* and *Oblievačka* translate as watering), while in Hungary the day is known as *Vízbevető* meaning Water Plunge Monday. The festivity is associated with water because on this day it is traditional for young men and boys to throw water over girls that take their fancy and then spank them with twigs of pussy willow. The next day, Easter Tuesday, the girls do the same to the boys. The etymology of the name Dyngus Day is unclear though the word *Śmigus* refers to the dousing of worshippers on Easter Monday.

Dyngus Day celebrates the end of the restrictions imposed during Lent while the frivolity of the festivity celebrates the joy of Easter. The exact origins of Dyngus Day

> ### Kissing Friday
>
> Kissing Friday was an English folk custom occurring in the northern county of Yorkshire two days after Ash Wednesday. The custom allowed girls to finish school before boys on one day each year so that boys could chase the girls and kiss them without fear of being slapped or chased by irate parents. According to the custom, girls were not allowed to say no to being kissed. Though very popular during the Victorian and Edwardian eras the custom died out in the mid-20th century with attempts to revive the custom in the 1970s and 1990s proving unsuccessful.

are not known. One theory is that the day is a pre-Christian custom originating from Poland's Slavic ancestors for traditionally the pouring of water is an age-old springtime rite affording spiritual purification and conferring fertility. Since 966 CE, Dyngus Day has been linked to the baptism of first king of Poland was Prince Mieszko I, for according to Polish tradition the prince along with the rest of his court was baptized on Easter Monday. For this reason, Dyngus Day is associated with sprinkling water in celebration and thanksgiving for the fact that the first king of Poland became a Christian, thereby bringing Christianity to Poland. A rather racier theory behind the Dyngus Day traditions is that during the Middle Ages men would choose this day to spank their wives as a reminder that marital sex was forbidden during the Easter period. However Dyngus Day originated it seems that during the 15th century Polish men and women took things too far for the Bishop of Poznan issued an edict called *Dingus Prohibetur* forbidding Polish people from bothering each other on the day known as Dyngus. Despite the *Dingus Prohibetur*, the traditions of Dyngus Day thrived among Polish peasants and aristocracy alike. In the past on Polish farms male farm workers would throw water over girls whose attention they wanted to attract and then smack the girls on their legs with twigs of pussy willows. Men who wanted to make an especially good impression would throw perfume over the girls rather than water. The following day the girls who had had water or perfume thrown over them would retaliate by throwing crockery at the men.

Somewhat ironically, however, Dyngus Day is celebrated more in the United States than it is in Poland. In the United States, Dyngus Day has been celebrated among Polish communities since the 1870s. However the most famous American Dyngus Day celebration, which takes place in Buffalo, New York, originated as recently as 1961, when the festivities were initiated by the Chopin Singing Society. The Dyngus Day celebrations proved a hit and led to a number of Dyngus Day dances on the East Side and at the New York Central Terminal in Buffalo. Aside from New York smaller Dyngus Day celebrations also occur in other American cities with large Polish American populations including South Bend, Indiana; Elizabeth, New Jersey; Bristol, Connecticut; Chicago, Illinois; Cleveland, Ohio;

and Pittsburgh, Pennsylvania. The celebrations include a lot of parties that begin during the mid-morning on the Monday after Easter with large buffets of foods traditionally served at Easter in Poland such as a sausage known as *kielbasa*, eggs, ham, and breads. Traditional polka music is another traditional element of Dyngus Day for it is obligatory for people to dance at least one polka during the course of the day. Indeed the parties often do not end until dawn the next day. Spanking with pussy willow is another important element of Dyngus Day revelries as men and women flirt by tapping each other playfully with the branches. Pussy willow is the plant associated with Dyngus Day because it is the first plant to bud in spring when Dyngus Day is being celebrated. Flirtation is an important part of Dyngus Day and it is said that many couples have found true love after spanking each other with pussy willows.

See also: All Souls' Day (Volume 3); *Andrzejki*: Looking for Fern Blossoms; St. Andrew's Eve; *Schuhplattler* and *Ländler*; *Zaduszki* (Volume 3)

Further Reading

Dyngus Day. "Our Story: What Is Dyngus Day?" Accessed November 20, 2015, at http://www.dyngusday.com/#!our-story/cjg9.

Polish Plate. "Everything You Should Know about Dyngus Day." Accessed November 20, 2015, at http://polishplate.com/articles/dyngus-day,1.html.

Silverman, Deborah Anders. *Polish-American Folklore*. Urbana: University of Illinois Press, 2000.

EAR-PIERCING CEREMONIES, MYANMAR AND MALAYSIA

Throughout contemporary Western culture ear piercing is the most common form of body modification. In the West, ear piercing is most frequently performed on females, but also on males, as a form of beautification allowing people to wear earrings. These earrings rarely hold any ritualistic meaning but are rather a form of personal adornment. In some countries, such as the United States, it is considered something of a secular rite of passage for a young girl (or possibly a boy) to have her ears pierced. Usually in the West people opt to have one hole pierced in each of their ear lobes though sometimes in non-mainstream cultures people will choose to have a series of holes made in their ear lobes or ear cartilage. Western non-mainstream groups that favor multiple ear piercings as a symbol of their difference from the norm include so-called neo-tribalists, also called modern primitives, punks, and people that identify with the Goth subculture.

Contrastingly, ear piercing is performed ritualistically in many countries around the world. For instance, just as Buddhist boys living in Myanmar experience a rite of passage known as *shinbyu*, so girls living in the country undergo their own rite in which their ears are pierced. This ceremony is called *nahtwin*, or ear-boring ceremony. However unlike shinbyu, the nahtwin ceremony is more of a social, secular event than a religious ritual though it is, nonetheless, an important moment on a girl's journey to womanhood. Indeed the ear-piercing ceremony is regarded as an extremely significant event, second only to a girl's marriage. This is because for Myanmar girls, having their ear lobes pierced allows them to wear earrings when they come of age and in Myanmar earrings are as much status symbols as body-adornments.

Rather than occurring as a separate ceremony, girls' ear piercing usually takes place at the same time as boys experience shinbyu, especially if a girl's brother is involved in the shinbyu ritual. If this is the case then the ear piercing will take place before the shinbyu ceremony occurs so that the girls are able to join in the shinbyu procession. Like the shinbyu ceremony, girls may experience their ceremony as part of a mass piercing ceremony or in private and dress elaborately—just as boys dress as princes for their shinbyu so girls dress as princesses for their ear-piercing ceremony. In times past older women would use a sharp golden needle to pierce girls' ears, which was, unsurprisingly, painful. Nowadays, however, it is usual for ear-piercing guns to be used instead.

Similarly, in Malaysia many Muslims view girls' ritual ear piercing as an important step to adulthood, though according to some academics the Malaysian ear-piercing ceremony originated from a time before Islam became prevalent in Malaysia.

As an important rite of passage the Malaysian Islamic ear-piercing ceremony is accompanied by many rituals and special foods. For example girls' earlobes are pierced with a thorn taken from a lemon tree or with a golden needle. Then yellow rice is cooked together with an array of side dishes and fresh saffron mixed with coconut oil. Wealthier families hold a lavish feast for their friends and relatives that lasts for many hours on the occasion of a girl's ear-piercing ceremony. At the feast the girl sits on a raised platform as would a bride at her wedding. Less affluent families will have more modest communal meals. After the meal, prayers are said. Next, the ear-piercing ceremony, which is very brief, begins during which mantras are intoned and the girl whose ear piercing it is will have the cooking ingredients used at her feast poured over her before she takes to her seat on the platform once more. The person that performs the ear piercing is paid and also rewarded with yellow rice.

See also: Hindu Baby Rituals (Volume 1); *Shinbyu*

Further Reading

Joseph, Suad, and Afsāna Naǧmābādī, eds. *Encyclopedia of Women & Islamic Cultures: Family, Body, Sexuality and Health Volume 3*. Leiden. Netherlands: Brill, 2006.

Ministry of Hotels and Tourism, Union of Myanmar. "Traditions & Lifestyles: *Shinbyu*," *Fascinating Myanmar*, 2006. Accessed May 3, 2015, http://fascinatingmyanmar.info/traditionsandlifestyle/activitiesandlifestyles/shin_byu.html.

Sheumaker, Helen, and Shirley Teresa Wajda, eds. *Material Culture in America: Understanding Everyday Life*. Santa Barbara, CA: ABC-CLIO, 2008.

Sydney Language Solutions. "Ear-piercing Ceremony." Accessed May 3, 2015, at http://sydneylanguagesolutions.com.au/blogs/ear-piercing-ceremony/.

F

FACE IN BIRTHDAY CAKE, MEXICO

A very common Mexican custom is for people celebrating their birthday to have their face pushed into their birthday cake. The practice is ubiquitous in Mexico and also occurs in Texas. The very young and the elderly may be spared the ordeal of having their face pushed into their cake but from the age of about four years old nearly all Mexicans will experience the birthday event.

Usually the person's face is pushed into the cake once the celebratory birthday song *"Las Mañanitas"* has been sung for once the song is over everybody gathered at the birthday celebrations begins to chant *"Mordita,"* meaning bribe but taken to mean little bite, and then the birthday celebrant attempts to take a small bite of his or her birthday cake without using his or her hands or any utensils as this is thought to convey good luck. The birthday celebrant then has to avoid his or her face being pushed into the cake by those gathered around him or her while trying to nibble the cake. However it is more or less inevitable that the person will succumb and so everybody gathered around knows that the birthday celebrant will be unable to avoid being pushed into the cake. Thus the onlookers ready their cameras in order to capture the moment for posterity.

On the whole the face-in-birthday-cake custom is considered a source of merriment. However some people that have experienced the tradition have reported that they felt humiliated by having their face pushed into their cake and developed a sense of mistrust toward their parents for allowing their birthday to be a source of embarrassment and dismay. Indeed some children have been known to cry when pushed into their cake leading to a lifelong distaste for the practice. This dislike of the custom has led to accusations that the tradition is little more than a form of bullying with calls for the custom to be discontinued, though those calling for an end to the custom tend not to be Mexican.

See also: Birthday Cakes (Volume 1); Birthday Candles (Volume 1); Birthday Cards (Volume 1); Birthday Humiliations for Singletons; Birthday Torments (Volume 1); "Happy Birthday" Song (Volume 1); *La Quinceañera*; Party Games (Volume 1); *Piñata* (Volume 1); Sock Garland and Sock Dance

Further Reading

Gringa-n-Mexico. "Birthday Tradition Mexico Style." Gringa-n-Mexico, December 8, 2009. Accessed June 14, 2015, at http://gringa-n-mexico.blogspot.co.uk/2009/12/birthday-tradition-mexico-style.html.

Phillips, Jeanne. "Face-in-the-Frosting Is a No-No," *Chicago Tribune*, March 9, 2006. Accessed June 14, 2015, at http://articles.chicagotribune.com/2006-03-09/features/0603080346_1_dear-abby-cake-birthday.

FATTENING ROOM SECLUSION, NIGERIA

Fattening room seclusion is a secular rite of passage experienced by girls belonging to Nigeria's Efik tribe as well the Ibibio, Okrika, and Annang, and other tribes that live in the country's southeastern Cross River region. In contrast to Western perceptions of physical attractiveness that tend to stress extreme thinness as the ideal, Nigerian culture values plump women as they are seen as the embodiment of alluring, fertile, feminine beauty. Thus it is traditional in these tribes for prospective brides and first daughters to undergo a process of deliberate fattening as preparation for marriage, sponsored by their parents or by their fiancés. The females who undergo this process are known as *mbobo*, meaning "fattening room girl." To be a mbobo, a girl should be an unmarried virgin. Girls who undergo deliberate fattening tend to be pubertal though it has been known for girls as young as seven to experience the ritual fattening. This deliberate fattening is achieved by segregating females who are to undergo the process by installing them in special fattening rooms, called *Nkuho* in the Efik language, for weeks, possibly months, at a time where they are given carbohydrate rich foods and discouraged from exercising. The specifics of fattening room seclusion vary between tribes but in the main the process follows the pattern employed by the Efik people.

Such is the cultural value of fatness in Nigeria that women who do not belong to the tribes for which fattening is customary have been known to submit themselves to the process as have nursing mothers who return to the fattening rooms in order to regain weight lost. In the early days of Nkuho, a woman could be secluded for six months to one year, depending on how long her family could afford to keep her well fed and whether or not she had a waiting suitor. However today seclusion typically lasts for around three weeks, evidence that prevailing socio-economic factors have affected Nigeria traditions.

Fattening rooms are thought to have originated many centuries ago when the Efik lived among Egyptians for the Efik adapted an existing Egyptian custom that was traditionally linked to *Mbobi*, a form of ritual female circumcision whose name means "coming of the small breasts." Traditionally females who wished to enter the Nkuho had to undergo circumcision as a preliminary as the procedure was thought to see if a female had been promiscuous, to check for whether she was a virgin, and to enhance her erotic appeal by prettifying her genitalia. In Efik society it is very important for a female to remain a virgin until she is married. Efik folklore and popular song mock women who have had sex before marriage. Thus a woman who underwent circumcision was thought to be particularly virtuous and exempt from the barrenness that was thought to blight the lives of women who had not been circumcised. Mbobi is still the first step on a woman's route to desirable rotundness as the process precedes the segregation of the woman to the fattening room. It should, however, be noted that some Nigerians view Mbobi as barbaric and skip the step. That said, Efik women who do not undergo Mbobi tend to feel a degree of public shame and so most submit to the process figuring that physical pain is preferable to social stigma.

After a female has been circumcised, she is ready to enter fattening room seclusion with the fattening room tending to be an out-of-the-way room in her father's compound. Her initiation into the process is marked by her being bathed by a group of menopausal or elderly women usually consisting of her aunts and other villagers, though not the girl's mother. If the girl has not yet reached puberty then before she enters the water she must ensure that a green insect does not occupy her bath as the insect is thought to bring bad luck and nullify the results of the Nkuho. Once the girl has entered seclusion, only her closest female friends may visit her and men, including her fiancé, are forbidden to see her until the ritual is complete. In order to alert strangers that a mbobo is present, a miniature bamboo bed, small pots, and birds' nests are placed on the road just outside the village. The bamboo bed is a reference to the deliberately uncomfortable bamboo bed on which a girl undergoing fattening room seclusion is expected to sleep—it is felt that sleeping on knotty bamboo will soften the girl's muscles as she sleeps.

Inside the fattening room a girl is fed six meals per day usually consisting of rice, yams, cassava, beans, plantains, fish, and meat plus traditional foods such as *ayan ekpan* (grated cocoyam), *ekpan kukwo* (cocoyam cooked with spinach and shellfish or meat), and *gari* (a mix of dried cassava and water). In addition to these foods, the females also eat traditional medicines made from herbs and leaves to aid digestion. The aim of the massive food consumption is to achieve a well-rounded figure so in order to ensure the end result is achieved the girls are encouraged to sleep a lot and forbidden from exercising as this would work off the calories needed to attain a fuller figure. As well as eating a great amount of food, females may have their faces painted with white chalk and palm leaf fibers, dyed red and plaited, may be strung around a girl's neck and tied around her ankles and wrists. These are adjusted as the girl grows fatter. Alternatively, a girl belonging to the Ijaw/Ijo tribe may have brass coils called *impala* placed around her legs. The impala are intended to limit the female's capacity for physical movement and to protect the girl from male water spirits who may try to carry the girl away and make her their wife.

Although social developments have led to changes in Nkuho, many parents ignore the financial cost of fattening room seclusion and put their daughters through the ritual nonetheless. It is very expensive to pay for the necessary food and cooks as well as the attendants who need to wait on the girl at all hours of the day yet parents feel socially inadequate if they do not have the funds to sponsor their daughter's seclusion. Moreover, it is a common Nigerian belief that women who do not experience fattening room seclusion will be sickly and unproductive. There is some medical basis to this belief, as it is known that estrogen is stored in fatty tissue and women with a body fat percentage of less than 18 percent will lose their ability to menstruate and thus conceive. In addition, there is some scientific research to suggest that heavier females menstruate at an earlier age than girls with low body fat levels. Therefore fattening room seclusion can be seen as a two-fold survival strategy. On the one hand, a fatter woman will have reserves of nutrients for herself and her child during times of food scarcity. Furthermore, a heavier woman can help to ensure tribal survival, as she will also be able to procreate earlier and therefore produce more children.

Today, many females liken going into seclusion as akin to staying in a spa for as well as being fed a great deal of food, females in seclusion are also treated to grooming rituals including massages using oils, herbs, and chalk that are reputed to make a woman's skin glow by improving the circulation of her blood. However unlike a spa holiday, fattening room seclusion also includes lessons and training in everyday tasks such as cooking, housework, and child care as well as education in intimate erotic massage and training in how to please a husband sexually. Females undergoing fattening room seclusion also learn how to become upstanding members of their community, how to put up with their in-laws, and how to perform traditional dances such as *Ekombi*, a wedding dance that a girl is expected to perform on the day she emerges from her seclusion. Girls belonging to the Ijaw/Ijo tribe must perform the dance in front of spectators as part of the ceremony to celebrate their leaving fattening room seclusion. However despite the alternately lonely, intimidating, and intrusive nature of fattening room seclusion, many mbobo see their time of deliberate fattening as a welcome respite from the hardships of tribal life for in everyday life they are expected to work on family farming plots, carry heavy loads on their heads to market, transport water, and do the housework.

Once a girl has completed her seclusion, her family may send out invitations to friends and family inviting them to a party to celebrate the girl's coming out of the fattening room. If a girl has a suitor waiting for her when she leaves the fattening room then this party will take the form of an extravagant wedding at which is served traditional dishes such as *ekpan kukwo*, atama leaves (an aromatic herb), and soup made from *afang* (a pungent dark green leafy vegetable). Efik men tend to like the fact that their wives have been through the fattening process as they favor curvy figures and believe fleshy hips are useful for child-bearing. For the wedding ceremony the freshly fattened woman dresses in traditional bright clothing with her hair decorated with beads and combs. As part of the service, a short procession takes place during which similarly dressed young girls escort the bride while onlookers sing, dance, and cheer loudly. The bride then settles upon an elaborately decorated wooden throne fitted with a canopy and the accompanying young girls surround the bride-to-be with the equipment she will need to be a house-proud wife including cooking pans, pots, crockery, brooms, and tablecloths. These are thought to be the items the bride will need to establish her new home successfully. In addition, the bride also changes her outfit three times. Another part of the wedding ceremony is a performance of a traditional dance called *Abang*, meaning pot, the name of which refers to the fattening rite through which the bride has passed for the woman is now round like a pot. After the wedding, a merry feast is held during which the newly weds are given presents and blessed.

Such is the popularity of fattening room seclusion in Nigeria that a reality television program based on the rite premiered on Nigerian television in 2013. The show, *Fattening Room Television*, is based in Lagos, Nigeria's most populous city and the seventh largest city in the world. The program was an instant hit on its debut attracting huge viewing figures in over 46 African countries. Part of the reason for this popularity is that the show features not just Nigerian girls going through the traditional fattening room seclusion rite but also girls from Botswana, Ghana, Kenya, South Africa, and Zambia. The varied cast suggests that fattening room seclusion is perhaps not just limited to Nigeria but also takes place across sub-Saharan Africa. Another reason for the program's success is that it offers men a rare glimpse into a ritual that usually takes place in secrecy.

Despite the popularity of *Fattening Room Television*, Nkuho faces a clouded future. Western ideas about healthy eating and the dangers of obesity mean that some Nigerians, especially those living in major cities, are starting to view fattening room seclusion unfavorably as an expensive and time-consuming experience that could lead to health problems in later life.

See also: Dipo Womanhood Ceremony; Female Genital Cutting; *Iria* ceremony; *Pika* and *Nyora*; Virginity Testing

Further Reading
de Garine, Igor, and Nancy J. Pollock, eds. *Social Aspects of Obesity*. Amsterdam, Netherlands: Overseas Publishers Association, 1995.
Galvan, Javier A., ed. *They Do What? A Cultural Encyclopedia of Extraordinary and Exotic Customs from around the World*. Santa Barbara, CA: ABC-CLIO, 2014.
Morse, Janice M. *Cross-cultural Nursing: Anthropological Approaches to Nursing Research*. Philadelphia, PA: Gordon and Breach Science Publishers S.A., 1989.
Simmons, Ann M. "Where Fat Is a Mark of Beauty," *Los Angeles Times*, September 20, 1998. Accessed November 26, 2014, at http://articles.latimes.com/1998/sep/30/news/mn-27869.
Thaker, Aruna, and Arlene Barton, eds. *Multicultural Handbook of Food, Nutrition and Dietetics*. Chichester, UK: Blackwell Publishing Ltd., 2012.
Ukpokodu, Omiunota Nelly, and Peter Ukpokodu, eds. *Contemporary Voices from the Margin: African Educators on African and American Education*. Charlotte, NC: IAP—Information Age Publishing, Inc., 2012.

FEMALE GENITAL CUTTING, AFRICA, MIDDLE EAST, ASIA, AND ELSEWHERE

Female genital cutting (FGC), also known as female circumcision, is the collective name for traditional rituals involving the partial or complete removal of a female's external genitalia. FGC is a controversial custom that is documented to take place in 28 African countries, particularly the equatorial regions of the Horn of Africa where it is thought that 80 percent of the women living in Somalia, Djibouti, Sudan, and Eritrea have undergone the procedure. However it is Egypt that has the highest incidence of FGC for 27.2 million Egyptian women, or 91 percent of Egyptian females, have experienced FGC making Egypt the country with the highest number of FGC cases of any country. FGC is also documented to occur in Yemen in the Middle East. However non-governmental organizations, women's rights groups, and Muslim associations claim FGC occurs in all Middle East countries as well as amongst the Muslim populations in Indonesia and Malaysia. In 2010, Indonesia ruled that medical professionals could legally perform FGC.

FGC is also occurring increasingly in the West, particularly in the United Kingdom, where 66,000 females have experienced FGC and where first-generation immigrants, asylum seekers, and refugees living in major towns such as England's capital, London, plus Birmingham, Manchester, and Oxford, as well as the Welsh capital Cardiff, practice the custom. It is thought 4,000 females in London have been treated for the immediate aftereffects of FGC since 2009 despite the custom being illegal throughout the United Kingdom. Indeed the United Kingdom's National Health Service (NHS) has recently drawn up guidelines for health and social care workers to spot signs that a female has undergone FGC. Under United Kingdom law it is also illegal for a child to be taken abroad for the purposes of undergoing FGC, a crime punishable by a large fine and up to 14 years in prison. In the West, FGC is often thought of as an Islamic practice. However Christians, Ethiopian Jews, and animists also perform the procedure. Indeed though FGC is referred to in the Qur'an as an honorable practice, the Qur'an does not say that women must be circumcised, which is required for Muslim men.

Critics of FGC refer to the practice as female genital mutilation or FGM. The age at which females undergo FGC varies around the world. In Yemen, baby girls undergo FGC at around two weeks old whereas in Egypt girls endure FGC between 5 and 14 years old. In most countries, girls undergo the procedure before they reach puberty.

FGC rituals pre-date the circumcision of males associated with Judaism, Islam, and Christianity for the first reference to FGC appears in a hieroglyphic text from ancient Egypt dating from around 2400 BCE in which God Uha notes his circumcision together with 120 men and 120 women. Meanwhile the famous ancient Greek historian Herodotus calls attention to FGC among fifth-century Phoenicians, Hittites, and Ethiopians while another Greek historian, Agatharchides of Cnidus, notes that FGC was a common procedure among Egyptians in the second century BCE. Early Romans and Arabs also performed FGC probably because they were influenced by the ancient Egyptians. FGC was practiced in ancient Egypt because it was a widely held belief that all men and women were endowed with both male and female souls, which were revealed through their genitalia. Thus ancient Egyptians thought that a man's feminine soul lived in his foreskin and that a woman's male soul dwelled in her clitoris. When Egyptian children reached a certain age and deemed ready to become an adult member of society, they had to rid themselves of their non-male or non-female properties through the process of circumcision. Only a female who had experienced FGC could be considered a woman capable of reproduction. It has also been suggested that FGC was practiced by the patriarchal society of ancient Egypt because the procedure limited a woman's sexuality thereby preserving the male lineage.

In the 19th century, FGC was practiced by Western doctors under the name "clitoral excision" as a method of curing lesbianism, so-called female hypersexuality, and female anxiety in general. Indeed American medical reports note clitoral excision and the removal of the inner and outer labia being performed up until the mid-1930s in an effort to curb female masturbation among asylum inmates. In the United Kingdom, clitoral excision was practiced in British mental hospitals until the 1940s. The thinking that drove Western doctors to perform such extreme surgery still exists in the parts of the world where FGC still occurs. In countries where FGC is practiced, the clitoris is considered an aggressive organ because it threatens the dominance of the penis and is potentially dangerous to the unborn child during birth. Some cultures also fear that the clitoris will continue to grow to the size of a penis or larger if it is not removed while it is also thought that the excision of the clitoris will stop a female from experiencing sexual urges, thereby saving her from sexual temptation and preserving her virginity. Indeed the resultant scars of FGC act as physical proof of a female's chastity, which is a prerequisite to marriage in many cultures. In truth, there is some basis to the thinking behind FGC for the pain suffered by women who go through the procedure, and the physical discomfort of the subsequent healing process, means a woman is less likely to want to have sex, as penetration by a penis would quite literally tear open her flesh.

The United Nations and the National Health Service of the United Kingdom recognize four classifications of FGC:

- Type 1: The excision of the clitoral hood. This is almost always accompanied by a clitoridectomy, which is the removal of all or part of the clitoris.
- Type 2: Excision of the entire clitoris together with the inner labia.
- Type 3: Infibulation, which involves the removal of all or part of the inner and outer labia, and (usually) the clitoris. The vaginal opening is narrowed and a seal created, leaving only a small hole for the passing of urine and menstrual blood. The sealed wound is re-opened during penetrative sexual intercourse and childbirth.
- Type 4: The damaging of female genitalia for non-medical reasons. These include piercing, burning, scarring, scraping, incising, and pricking. The removal of the hymen, tightening the vagina, and cutting the vaginal walls are also included in this category.

According to the World Health Organization (WHO), between 100 and 140 million females worldwide have experienced FGC while it is thought that 3 million females undergo the process annually. Most (around 85 percent) endure Types 1 and 2 while around 15 percent undergo Type 3, which is the most common form of FGC in the African nations of Somalia, Sudan, and Djibouti.

FGC is usually arranged by a girl's mother and is performed by an older woman who is a *gedda*, or traditional circumciser, who often views carrying out FGC as a way of earning a steady income. A girl's grandmother may also take part in the custom. Elsewhere wealthy families may pay for a trained medical practitioner such as a nurse, midwife, or doctor to attend the procedure and use anesthetic and sterilized equipment. Indeed according to the United Nation's Children's Fund (UNICEF), around a fifth of all FGC is now performed by healthcare professionals in hospital surroundings. Indeed according to UNICEF almost 80 percent of FGC in Egypt is carried out under hospital conditions. The presence of medical staff during an FGC procedure is not however a guarantee that the procedure will be safer. In November 2014, 13-year-old Sohair al-Bata died after a Cairo doctor performed FGC on her in the presence of her father.

However in many countries (e.g., Gambia, Burkina Faso, and Eritrea), it is still customary for FGC to be carried out without the use of anesthetic and instead of sterilized cutting equipment it is usual for a gedda to use multiple instruments including razor blades, knives, scissors, broken glass, pointed rocks, fingernails, and thorns to cut the genitalia. Occasionally corrosive substances are inserted into the vagina to scar, tighten, and narrow the orifice. Sometimes a girl is taken as she makes her way to collect water, held down by other women, and her legs forcibly held apart so that the cutting may take place. After the genitalia have been cut the circumciser may use agave or acacia thorns to stitch the wound and the wound may be covered with mud or dirt to help the healing process. In the most severe cases the vagina is stitched closed so that a girl cannot have sex. In this case a small reed or piece of wood is inserted into the girl's body so that she is able to urinate and pass blood during her monthly period. A girl who has undergone this most severe form of FGC faces the further ordeal of being unstitched to enable her to have sex and give birth at a later date. Having had sex and given birth the girl will then be sewn up again—a procedure that is thought by proponents to keep the female faithful and hygienic.

Advocates of FGC argue that it is important for females to endure pain as part of FGC as this is thought to show the female is strong and durable. However FGC is known to lead to serious medical problems, mainly related to bleeding and infection. Immediate complications arising from FGC include shock, urine retention, urinary infection, kidney problems, damage to the bowel and urethra, infection of the wound, septicemia, tetanus, and gangrene, plus blood-borne diseases including hepatitis B and C and HIV from the use of equipment that is both unsterilized and used on multiple girls. Indeed it has been suggested that the exchange of blood and other bodily fluids during FGC is one of the reasons for the spread of HIV and AIDS in Africa. A lack of data pertaining to deaths from FGC means it is not known how many females die from the procedure. However Nigerian midwife Comfort Momoh estimates that 10 percent of females die soon after undergoing FGC as a result of suffering from shock, hemorrhaging, or becoming infected.

The long-term ill effects of undergoing FGC include urinary incontinence, chronic vaginal and pelvic infections, the pregnancy disorder preeclampsia, and formation of cysts and scar tissue, as well as irregular menstruation or amenorrhea (the total absence of menstruation) and therefore infertility. Females who experience FGC are more likely than others to need a Caesarean section when giving birth and this in turn means FGC increases infant mortality rates. Though surgery can reverse some of the physical damage caused by FGC it cannot replace the sensitive flesh that is removed during the procedure. Similarly, the psychological and emotional ill effects of FGC (e.g., flashbacks to the procedure occurring, depression, low libido, general anxiety) are permanent. Indeed the mental scars suffered by women who have undergone FGC have been likened to the trauma experienced by battle-scarred soldiers.

On February 12, 2012, the 194 member nations of the United Nations General Assembly voted unanimously to ban FGC on the grounds that the ritual is a violation of the human rights of women and girls that reflects deep-rooted sexual inequality and gender discrimination. The United Nations is committed to providing help for females who have undergone the procedure and has also expressed the aim to try to make the process less socially acceptable in those areas of the world in which FGC is practiced. To this end the United Nations has designated February 6 the annual International Day of Zero Tolerance for Female Genital Mutilation and created the hashtag #endFGM for use on the social networking website Twitter. The governments of several Muslim countries in Africa have outlawed FGC, including Egypt, Eritrea, Djibouti, Kenya, Nigeria, Senegal, Uganda, and Tanzania and several Islamic scholars have issued fatwas (i.e., religious decrees announced by an Islamic leader) against the practice. Indeed in 2006 Egypt's two most senior Islamic clerics stated that FGC has no place in Islam.

Pressure groups (e.g., Daughters of Eve and the FGM National Clinical Group) have been established in the United Kingdom to highlight the prevalence of FGC, provide information on the practice and help women who have been affected by FGC. Meanwhile Somalian model, writer, and anti-FGC activist Waris Dirie has drawn attention to the practice of FGC via her best-selling autobiography *Desert Flower*, which has been adapted into an award-winning film. Dirie has also established an anti-FGC campaign charity, the Desert Flower Foundation. Similarly, while a contestant on the television reality show "America's Next Top Model," season 10, Somalia-born model Fatima Siad revealed she had undergone FGC thereby bringing the subject to the attention of viewers.

See also: Breast Ironing; *Brit Milah* (Volume 1); Fattening Room Seclusion; Finger Amputation (Volume 3); *Hijira*; Maasai Warrior Initiation; Subincision into the Urethra; Tooth-Filing Ceremony; Virginity Testing; Xhosa Circumcision

Further Reading

Abu-Dayyeh, Suad. "Is Egypt Ready to Join Growing Global Movement to End FGM?" *The Guardian*, November 20, 2014. Accessed December 10, 2014, at http://www.theguardian.com/global-development/2014/nov/30/egypt-join-global-movement-end-fgm-sohair-al-bataa.

French, Maddy. "How Supermodel Waris Dirie Saved Girl from Female Genital Mutilation," *The Guardian*, February 16, 2014. Accessed December 7, 2014, at http://www.theguardian.com/society/2014/feb/16/supermodel-waris-dirie-female-genital-mutilation-fgm.

Galvan, Javier A., ed. *They Do What? A Cultural Encyclopedia of Extraordinary and Exotic Customs from around the World*. Santa Barbara, CA: ABC-CLIO, 2014.

Gov.uk. "Female Genital Mutilation." NHS Choices. May 28, 2014. Accessed December 7, 2014, at http://www.nhs.uk/Conditions/female-genital-mutilation/Pages/Introduction.aspx.

McHugh, Molly. "Rite of Passage, or Punishment?" *Ethos*, January 20, 2010. Accessed December 7, 2014, at http://ethosmagonline.com/archives/19.

Roberts, Michelle. "Anatomy of Female Genital Mutilation." BBC News: Health. July 22, 2014. Accessed December 7, 2014, at http://www.bbc.co.uk/news/health-27188190.

United Nations. "End Female Genital Mutilation." Accessed December 7, 2014, http://www.un.org/en/events/femalegenitalmutilationday/.

FIDANZAMENTI, ITALY

Fidanzamenti is a form of lengthy betrothal that is traditional in the south of Italy and, most especially, on the Italian island of Sicily. Until the mid 1940s, the majority of Sicilian marriages were either formally arranged by a couple's parents or allowed only with parental consent unless the couple eloped in a custom known as *fuitina*. This is still the case for a few southern Italians.

During the 19th century, a formal betrothal arranged by parents began called *fidanzati in casa* that saw fathers arrange their children's marriages. Indeed up until 1860 it was a legal requirement for fathers to formally give their blessing to a marriage. To a certain degree parents still have a great deal of input into their children's future marriage plans even when a couple are in their mid-twenties and sleeping together. Once a Sicilian couple decides to marry they exchange gold bands called *fedine* that are thinner and less expensive that wedding rings, which are called *fedi* or *fede di matrimonio*. Fedine are deliberately less ornate, cheaper versions of a wedding ring to indicate that they mark an engagement rather than a wedding. The giving and receiving of fedine is gradually disappearing as the educated Sicilian women of today, who tend to become engaged in their late twenties and thirties, do not take kindly to the idea of fedine and may actually find them offensive.

As most Sicilians live within the parental home until they marry, once an engagement is announced the boy's parents visit the girl's home to meet her parents and vice versa. When they meet it is usual for the parents to give each other flowers and share a small home-cooked meal. Then, at some point, a wedding date is set and the bride's parents agree to cover the cost of the wedding and may even agree to buy the couple a marital home. Often this date is two or three, or possibly five to ten, years in the future and the long engagement is referred to as *fidanzamenti*. Once a couple are engaged they are permitted to spend more time in each other's company (including nights) and may even be allowed to go on holiday without a chaperone.

Today fidanzati in casa is mainly practiced by less-educated Sicilians, or those living in rural areas of southern Italy. It has been estimated that only around 5 to 10 percent of couples living in major Sicilian towns such as Palermo adopt the fidanzati in casa custom. That said, parental approval of a future spouse is still very important to young people living in Sicily. Though premarital sex is more or less accepted, fidanzati in casa is believed by traditionalists to lend an air of decency to sexual relationships as couples can say that they are betrothed. In the south of Italy in particular, where unemployment rates are high, lengthy betrothals are favored as they allow a man to go off in search of work before marrying, knowing that his girlfriend is, to a degree, committed to him. This arrangement is also favored by some men as it allows them to take advantage of a long-term relationship without having to take on the responsibilities of actually being married. For this reason it is not uncommon for some women to be abandoned by their fidanzati in casa partner after they have been together for as many as seven years. Indeed there is a Sicilian saying that "Nobody buys the cow when they can milk it for free," which suggests local men's attitude to romantic commitment.

When a Sicilian couple does finally marry, they do not normally have a bridal shower party but they will set up a bridal registry and ask for several wedding gifts, many of which will be expensive. Sicilian newlyweds tend to move into fully furnished homes having spent a great deal of their betrothal selecting their furniture.

See also: Arranged Marriage; Bed-Courtship

Further Reading

Best of Sicily. "Marriage Sicilian Style." Accessed June 2, 2015, at http://www.bestofsicily.com/weddings.htm#engagements.

Monger, George P. *Marriage Customs of the World: From Henna to Honeymoons.* Santa Barbara, CA: ABC-CLIO, 2004.

Romano, Maria Luisa. "Rustic Sicilian Engagements," *Best of Sicily Magazine*, 2005. Accessed June 2, 2015, at http://www.bestofsicily.com/mag/art173.htm.

FILIPINO DEBUT, PHILIPPINES

In the Philippines, a debut, sometimes referred to as the Filipino Cotillion, is a coming-of-age rite experienced by females on their 18th birthday as well as by men celebrating their 21st birthday, though Filipino men do not tend to mark the occasion in a grand manner. In contrast, Filipino women normally mark the event by holding an elaborate party for which everybody wears formal attire. Indeed the scale and level of formality seen at Filipino debuts means the parties are often likened to weddings and many Filipino families can expect to spend as much on their daughter's debut as on their wedding. As well as in the Philippines, Filipino debuts occur in countries with sizeable Filipino populations (e.g., the United States). The number of guests present at a Filipino debut may range from a handful, if the event is smaller scale and held at the girl's home, to several hundred if held in a ballroom.

A Filipino debut is an extremely ritualized occasion during which the debutante is presented to society as a beautiful and talented woman. Universal elements of a Filipino debut are the presence of 18 roses and 18 candles that are symbolic of the 18 years of life being celebrated by the debutante. Because a Filipino debut marks a female's 18th birthday, the number 18 figures largely throughout the celebration. For example the debutante's entourage may comprise 18 male-female couples, usually made up of the girl's friends and relatives, or the debutante's court may be made up of nine boys and nine girls. Members of the debutante's entourage are often given jewellery to show that they are an important factor of the occasion. A Filipino debut is in many ways a blend of elements shared with *La Quinceañera*, a celebration held in Mexico when girls reach 15 years of age, and Anglo-European debutante balls. Like La Quinceañera, the debut is held to mark the birthday of a young woman but it is also an extremely formal event in the manner of a debutante ball. A Filipino debut is not, however, simply a combination of La Quinceañera and a debutante ball for the Filipino debut, though a very ceremonial occasion, lacks the highborn overtones of a debutante ball. That said, like a debutante ball, a Filipino debut is an expensive event to host that takes a long time to plan, particularly if a specific theme has been chosen to flavor the event. Moreover, the dress worn by the debutante is of the utmost importance just as a wedding dress is often considered the highlight of a bride's wedding experience.

A Filipino debut opens, typically, with Catholic prayers and then a speech given by one of the debutante's parents or grandparents. A slideshow or video presentation detailing key moments from the debutante's life may also be shown. Next, the debutante enters the room accompanied by her escort for the night, often her boyfriend. At the most formal Filipino debuts the debutante will enter the ballroom via a grand staircase as occurs at a debutante ball. The entry of the debutante is followed by 18 females associated with the debutante lighting and presenting a candle while making observations about the debutante. The presentation of the 18 candles is followed by an opening dance that usually sees the debutante dance with her father. The father-daughter dance denotes the daughter's first steps into womanhood and her father's acceptance of his daughter's new status as a woman. The next dance, which is sometimes called the Grand Cotillion Waltz, is often considered to be the highlight of a Filipino debut. Though called the Grand Cotillion Waltz it has become acceptable recently for the debutante to dance to an up-tempo modern pop song such as Beyoncé's "Single Ladies." The Grand Cotillion Waltz is usually performed by nine male-female pairs of dancers (including the debutante and her escort) and takes the form of an elaborate dance lasting between 5 and 12 minutes in duration. The dance often takes many months of rehearsal to perfect and is usually choreographed by a professional cotillion choreographer. The third dance of the Filipino debut is the dance sometimes referred to as the Dance of the 18 Roses. This dance sees 18 men associated with the debutante present her with a rose before asking to dance with her—traditionally, they dance a waltz. The debutante normally starts the dance partnered by her father but ends partnered by her escort for the night. Since it would take a long time for the debutante to dance a full waltz with each man the debutante will often dance merely a snippet of the dance with each male. A recently developed Filipino debut tradition is the giving

> ### Le Bal des Débutantes
>
> *Le Bal des Débutantes* (*Le Bal*) is an annual fashion event/débutante ball held in Paris that brings together around 20 young women 16 to 22 years of age from around the world. Le Bal was instituted in 1992 and sees the debutantes wear haute couture dresses and designer jewelry. The débutantes tend to come from royalty or well-known families involved with the arts, politics, sport, and business. Le Bal raises money for charity—since 2009 Le Bal has supported *Enfants d'Asie*, an educational organization for girls living in Southeast Asia and in 2015 Le Bal also supported Seleni, a non-profit organization that funds research into healthcare for young mothers. Le Bal is the only débutante ball in the world that is "by invitation only."

of the 18 treasures, which sometimes occurs after the dancing. The giving of the 18 treasures tradition sees selected family and friends of the debutante each give her a gift that she will use now that she is a young woman. These gifts can range from the sentimental to the imaginative, to the downright daft. Another recently evolved Filipino debut tradition sees the debutante drink 18 shots of alcohol.

Once all the gifts have been presented a cake may be presented to the debutante (though the cake may also be served later in the evening) and then the debutante must take the stage to demonstrate a talent or skill. Usually this means that the debutante must sing a song or play a musical instrument. Finally, to conclude the night's formalities, once the debutante has demonstrated her talent she will give a speech thanking everybody for coming to celebrate her debut. The rest of the evening is spent dancing, eating, and generally having fun.

Such is the popularity of the debut tradition in the Philippines that a whole debut industry has become established there. Indeed in the Philippines it is possible to find choreographers, caterers, and invitation printers specializing in debuts as well as debut organizers who perform much the same role as wedding planners.

See also: Filipino Debut; *La Quinceañera*; Purity Ball; Twenty-First Birthday Traditions; Wedding Dress and Wedding Ring

Further Reading

Bayor, Ronald H., ed. *Multicultural America: An Encyclopedia of the Newest Americans*. Volume 4. Santa Barbara, CA: Greenwood, 2011.

Carlo, Juan. "Proud to Be Pinoy: Traditions of the Filipino Debut." Accessed November 15, 2015, at http://www.debutbyjuancarlo.com.ph/proud-pinoy-traditions-filipino-debut/.

Kirkpatrick, Mae. "The Filipino Debut," *Bamboo Telegraph*, November 21, 2014. Accessed November 15, 2015, at http://bambootelegraph.com/2014/11/21/the-filipino-debut/.

Kte'pi, Bill. "Debut," in Mary Yu Danico, ed., *Asian American Society: An Encyclopedia*, 265–266. Thousand Oaks, CA: SAGE Publications, 2014.

FOREHEAD-CUTTING INITIATION, AFRICA

Forehead-cutting is an initiation rite to celebrate the transition from boyhood to manhood. The rite is most often associated with the African Nuer and Dinka tribes. The Nuer are spread across several African countries including Ethiopia, Sudan, South Sudan, Congo, Uganda, and Kenya. In South Sudan the Nuer number around 1 million, meaning they are the second most populous people after the Dinka group. As the Nuer are so widespread they do not have a centralized authority but instead are loosely linked via autonomous villages with shared historical bonds strengthening their ties. The Nuer people follow a pastoral lifestyle that is heavily reliant on cattle, around which the economic, cultural, and social world of the Nuer revolves.

Every member of a Nuer family has his or her own specific job to fulfill in relation to cattle: men herd the cattle, women milk the animals, and children clean up after them. When a Nuer boy approaches adulthood, he must undergo an extremely painful form of scarification that represents a rite of passage that allows him to receive cattle and, consequently, rise through the social strata of his clan. The scarification of Nuer boys takes the form of a forehead-cutting ritual that occurs when a boy is between 12 and 16 years of age. The ceremony only takes place once a boy's father has agreed that his son may be initiated and the ritual sees an elder tribesman slice several (usually six) parallel lines into the initiate's forehead using a razor blade or other sharp bladed tool. These cuts result in facial scarring, known locally as *gaar,* which identifies the boy as a member of a specific tribe. In times past, as many as 100 boys would be initiated during a single ceremony. However nowadays, because of recent conflict, only 10 or so boys are initiated together.

The forehead-cutting initiation ritual is highly ceremonial and occurs at a time to coincide with harvest time. Preparations for the ritual begin the night before it takes place, for eligible boys, who at this point are referred to as *parapol,* meaning "someone who stopped milking" in the local Nuer language, congregate to have fun dancing and playing musical instruments. Boys arrive at the festivities with their heads freshly shaven as this is required for the ceremony. When Dinka boys have their heads shaved a woman who is considered qualified on account that none of her children has died performs the shaving. As the woman has never lost a child she is considered blessed by God and therefore a suitable mother figure for the initiates. The boys may stay with their substitute mother in a hut for up to a month. During this time the eldest man in the village teaches the boys the ways of manhood and their families bring them food each day. At this stage it is considered important that the boys do not touch or be near anything female, including cows. The boys may not even drink milk or clean up dung. These measures signify that the boys have broken away from the ways of childhood for only children and women may milk cows or drink milk. Once the boys have completed their stay in the hut they travel to visit relatives who celebrate the boys' approaching initiation by holding extravagant feasts and sacrifice a bull in their honor. Bulls are very significant in Nuer culture, which considers the forehead initiation ritual to be akin to the castration of a bull and likens a Nuer boy to an ox calf. Bulls owned by the Nuer are not only castrated but also have their horns slashed as this is thought to please the bull's owners. To the Nuer, the slashing of the bull's horns is comparable to the forehead-cutting experienced by Nuer boys. The pre-initiation dancing performed by Nuer boys is called *ruath*, which is the name given to a bull-calf that has been weaned from its mother and will later be castrated. During the dance the boys wear heavy metal bangles on their left arm that are said to replicate the mutilation of a bull's left horn. The Nuer associates the left-hand side with evil and femininity and since the bangles impede the movement of the left arm they imply the boy's separation from his mother and the suppression of any inherent femininity.

On the day of the ritual, the boys attend a short blessing that confers spiritual purification. Next, the boys line up and then sit on the ground, cross-legged facing west. Sitting thus the boys wait for the sun to rise behind them. The next part of the initiation process sees the initiator arrive to perform the rite—all the while the boys remain seated on the floor. When the initiator nears a boy the elder shouts out his name and also shouts out the name of his ancestors within the clan. The initiator then grabs the boy's head and cuts across his forehead with a sharp blade using steady, unwavering movements. In order to inspire awe in the boys the initiator will sometimes smear his face with the blood of the initiates.

The resultant cuts are very deep, often touching the skull bones of the forehead. The procedure is excruciatingly painful as no anesthesia is given to the boys who, despite their pain, must not show any sign of weakness or regret as blood pours down their faces, knowing that they have been scarred for life. Any flinch or movement indicating pain would be noted as cowardice by the community looking on and would bring great shame to the boy's family. In order to block out the pain of the cutting it is common for boys to stare straight ahead, chanting the names of their ancestors repeatedly. However it should be noted that it is quite common for boys to pass out while intoning the ancestral names as the pain from the cutting becomes too great to withstand.

The permanent scars resulting from the forehead-cutting ceremony follow patterns that identify the boys as belonging to specific clans or tribes. Nuer boys receive six parallel lines to their forehead while Dinka boys receive parallel lines on the forehead that follow a V-shape. (*See* Plate 7.) Sometimes Nuer women receive forehead scars too but these are normally a pattern of dots rather than lines.

The bleeding boys must remain seated while the initiator cuts all the foreheads in the line-up. Once the cutting is over the boys sit still, bleeding, while the person who performed the cutting leaves the site of the ceremony. When all the boys have been initiated and the initiator has left, the boys continue to sit but tilt their heads downward so that their blood falls to the ground. The boys' fathers then clean the blood from certain parts of their sons' faces—the mouth, eyes, and cheeks—but not the foreheads as these are covered with a leaf that is thought to aid the healing process while also helping scars to form.

When all the ritual elements of the ceremony have been completed, festivities restart with the boys enjoying their new social status. The post-cutting celebrations are joyous and include dancing, music, and feasting. These festivities can last up to three days. At this point, the newly adult males are given an ox, which given the socio-economic importance of cattle to the Nuer and Dinka, immediately becomes the men's most valuable possession. As men, the initiates no longer have to perform tedious chores that they undertook as boys. Rather they are presented with a spear and shield by their father that signifies that they are now warrior-men able to look after their own cattle and fight in battles. A Nuer boy also receives a post-initiation "ox name." This is a name taken from the name of the ox given to him by his father once his forehead has been cut.

In order to show affection for their cattle, the men spend a great deal of time with the animals, singing to them, decorating their horns, and even sleeping next to them. As they are now men, the initiates are also considered old enough to marry and so soon begin to search for a wife with which to share their cattle.

Though to Western eyes the forehead-cutting initiation ceremony may seem brutal and unnecessary, the boys who experience the rite do so willingly. The Dinka consider the ritual and the subsequent scarring to be *dheeng*, meaning beautiful, and believe the forehead-cutting initiation ceremony to be a wonderful event. Indeed so important is the rite of passage to Nuer and Dinka males that despite the volatile political conditions in Sudan and South Sudan, many young men from these tribes living in other countries often express the desire to travel back to their homeland to receive the ritual cuts. This is because the young men will not be considered to have truly reached adulthood if they cannot display the tribal marking of forehead-cutting initiation, even if they have married.

One example of an African tribe ritually cutting the foreheads of their women occurs with the Tabwa people who live in southwestern Congo and northeastern Zambia. The Tabwa call the custom *kulemba*, meaning to beautify or inscribe a blank surface. In times past Tabwa women would have their backs, shoulders, cheeks, and foreheads scarred but today Tabwa women have their foreheads, noses, and cheeks scarred instead, usually with patterns of small lines. Tabwa women who do not display forehead scarring are considered unmarriageable. The Ga'anda people of Nigeria scar their daughters at various times throughout the girls' lives. When a Ga'anda woman's marriage is arranged and her bride price negotiated, her forehead is scarred. However as is the case with many African tribes, the Ga'anda are beginning to practice forehead-cutting less and less due to the disapproval of community leaders and the decline of arranged marriages.

See also: Arranged Marriage; Female Genital Cutting; *Pika* and *Nyora*; Ritual Tattooing; Scarification

Further Reading

DeMello, Margo. *Faces Around the World: A Cultural Encyclopedia of the Human Face*. Santa Barbara, CA: ABC-CLIO, 2012.

Galvan, Javier A., ed. *They Do What? A Cultural Encyclopedia of Extraordinary and Exotic Customs from around the World*. Santa Barbara, CA: ABC-CLIO, 2014.

Holton, M. Jan. *Building the Resilient Community: Lessons from the Lost Boys of Sudan*. Eugene, OR: Cascade Books, 2011.

Ingham, John M. *Psychological Anthropology Reconsidered*. Cambridge, UK: Cambridge University Press, 1996.

G

GAP YEAR, INTERNATIONAL

A gap year is a period of time spent constructively in-between life stages, usually between ending school and starting university or between finishing university and starting full-time employment though, increasingly, the term gap year is being applied to a year taken out of employment at any life stage, for varying amounts of time. Most people on a gap year spend their time traveling, performing voluntary work, or working abroad temporarily. Gap years are particularly popular among students in the United Kingdom, Australia, New Zealand, Canada, and the Netherlands. Most of these countries, as well as others, offer working holiday visas to help people on gap years improve their cultural links with other countries. Traditionally, gap years have not proved popular in the United States because of the cost of going to university and the strong competition for the places at the best colleges. Today, however, the concept of the gap year is becoming increasingly popular in the United States with more and more people taking a sabbatical to go traveling abroad. In the United States, where the gap year is sometimes referred to as a bridge year, students are realizing the long-term benefits of taking a gap year. Indeed surveys suggest that the number of Harvard students taking a gap year has increased by more than a third since 2000.

Though taking a gap year may seem like a fun way to spend a period of time, there is a more serious element to gap years for they are frequently being seen by youngsters as a way to improve their curricula vitae or résumés. This is because many people spend their gap year not just traveling but also gaining relevant work experience that they hope will help them find employment after university. Indeed nowadays many employers actively choose people that have taken a gap year and spent it constructively by learning about the world through travel or gaining work experience and thereby developing transferable skills, including communication, leadership, time management, and decision making abilities, that will prove beneficial in the workplace. Examples of gap year activities include performing conservation work in Africa, volunteering with charities working in developing nations, running adventure travel programs or summer schools, and taking on an internship with a company that might lead to a job after graduation from university.

Potential downsides of taking a gap year can be that traveling while not employed can prove expensive and it also means that youngsters lose track of their friends and peers who may have gone on to study while they themselves went abroad. Moreover, taking a year off between school and university can result in youngsters losing the desire to study and preferring to go into employment as they have experienced the world and wish to continue to be independent adults earning a wage.

See also: *Baccalauréat* and *Matura*; Choosing Options; Inter-Railing; RAG Week; *Russefeiring* and Schoolies Week

Further Reading
Barnes, Jonathan. *The Gap-year Guidebook 2013: Everything You Need to Know about Taking a Gap*. 21st edition. Melton, UK: John Catt Educational Ltd., 2012.
Prospects. "Gap Year." Accessed November 15, 2015, at http://www.prospects.ac.uk/gap_year_should_i_take_a_gap_year.htm.
Sherifi, Macca. "US Gap Years on the Rise." GapYear.com. Accessed November 15, 2015, at https://www.gapyear.com/news/162592/us-gap-years-on-the-rise.
Sherifi, Macca. "What Is a Gap Year?" GapYear.com. Accessed November 15, 2015, https://www.gapyear.com/articles/90431/what-is-a-gap-year.
White, Kristin M. *The Complete Guide to the Gap Year: The Best Things to Do between High School and College*. San Francisco, CA: Jossey-Bass, 2009.

GRETNA GREEN, SCOTLAND

Gretna Green is a small Scottish town just north of Scotland's border with England that is synonymous with weddings, particularly elopements. The town has a population of 2,700 people but hosts 5,000 weddings per year. To put this into perspective, the neighboring English county of Cumbria has a population of 500,000 people but in 2011 only 3,000 weddings took place across the whole of the county.

The geographical location of Gretna Green is important when trying to understand the town's history as a marriage hub. In 1754, a law passed in England preventing people under 21 years of age from marrying without parental consent. However the law did not apply to Scotland, where it was legal for girls over 12 years old and boys of 14 years or more to wed. Also in Scotland anybody could marry a couple by declaration. Therefore star-crossed English lovers would elope to Scotland and Gretna Green, at just two miles over the England-Scotland border, was the first town that the lovers would reach and where they would wed. Enterprising Gretna Green blacksmiths soon realized this could provide a lucrative income and established themselves as so-called anvil priests, carrying out marriages by declaration for a small monetary charge of a few guineas. Indeed such was the popularity of the anvil priests that in 1843 a blacksmith told *The Times* (London) newspaper that in 25 years he had personally performed 3,500 weddings. Today, the Blacksmith's Shop houses a museum dedicated to Gretna Green's romantic history and has a display featuring the blacksmith's anvil that has become the symbol of Gretna Green weddings. It is said that touching the anvil ensures the person who touches the anvil will be lucky in love.

Over time, several efforts were made to try and end the phenomenon of the Gretna Green marriage. For instance, in 1855 the member of Parliament for Newcastle suggested the town was leading to the moral decay of northern England. The following year a parliamentary act was passed that required couples to reside in the county in which they wished to marry for 21 days, thereby giving lovers caught up in the excitement of elopement a cooling-off period. In 1940, the Scottish tradition of marriage by declaration was made illegal. In 1977, it became legal for English couples 18 years old and over to marry without parental consent. Despite this change, a discrepancy still exists for in Scotland the age for marriage without parental permission is 16 but remains at 18 for couples in England and Wales.

Today, couples in Scotland are required to give 15 days notice of their intention to marry but there is no residency requirement so couples can still get married in Gretna Green at short notice. Despite the gradual reduction in the factors that make Gretna Green the capital of hasty marriages, the town retains its romantic allure. Indeed it is a common English phrase to refer to a hastily married couple as having "Run away to Gretna" and the town has built up a thriving marriage-based micro-economy for, despite the fact that the town is too small to have a supermarket, Gretna Green is home to several wedding planners, hotels, hairdressers, gift shops, and photographers. The town's romantic history also means that Gretna Green is also something of a tourist attraction and won the award for the United Kingdom's Most Coach Friendly Shopping Attraction in 2012.

See also: British Wedding Traditions; Christian Wedding Ceremony; Marriage Banns

Further Reading

GretnaGreen.com. "Gretna Green." Accessed December 15, 2014, at http://www.gretnagreen.com.

Visit Scotland.com. "Gretna Green Famous Blacksmiths Shop." Accessed December 15, 2014, at http://www.visitscotland.com/info/see-do/gretna-green-famous-blacksmiths-shop-p253221.

Webber, Esther. "Gretna Green: The Bit of Scotland Where English People Go to Get Married." BBC News Magazine, August 19, 2014. Accessed December 15, 2014, at http://www.bbc.co.uk/news/magazine-28679430.

GWALLYE, SOUTH KOREA

Gwallye is an annual coming-of-age ceremony for males and females held on the third Monday in May in Korea. The ceremony is performed for males and females turning 19 years old in that year. Some areas of the country also hold award ceremonies on this day that reward model young adults with gifts of roses, champagne, and perfume. The day is also supposed to be the occasion of a young adult's first kiss. Indeed traditionally it was requisite for a young adult to go through gwallye if they wished to wed.

Gwallye is a very old custom dating as far back as the Goryeo Dynasty (918–1392 CE). The first written record of the ceremony dates from 965. This document was written during the reign of King Gwangjong, a time when young princes were presented with adult clothing to wear as a sign that they had come of age. This royal tradition gradually became popular with the upper classes and by the time of the Joseon Dynasty (1392–1910) gwallye was performed as a family ritual during which young men were given a crown to wear by a person of high moral standing, often a friend of their grandfathers. The man was also given an adult name by which he was known henceforth. The female equivalent of gwallye is the gyerye ceremony. During the ceremony girls comb their hair into a bun that is fastened with a decorative hairpin called a *binyeo*. Girls also wear a traditional South Korean dress called a *Hanbok*, usually with a green colored top called a *jeogori* and a blue *chima*, or skirt. According to Korean custom, Gyerye ceremonies are held in the year that a girl turns 15 years old. The aim of the ceremony is to instill in young women the virtues of womanhood. Once they have gone through the ceremony the young women will traditionally visit their ancestral shrines to tell the heavens that they have become adults. However today men and women both experience gwallye. Gwallye has not, however, always been as popular as it is today. In the latter half of the 20th century, Western culture became dominant in South Korea and Western ideas of how to mark the transition to adulthood overtook indigenous traditions in popularity. For this reason in 1999, the South Korean Ministry of Culture, Sports, and Tourism, decided to resurrect the gwallye custom standardizing the coming-of-age customs for males and females with ceremonies to be performed in schools, universities, and town halls. The ceremonies were intended to reinforce young people's pride in Korean traditional culture and instill in them the true meaning of responsible adulthood.

Traditionally, gwallye is divided into three parts with youngsters being blessed by watching adults at each stage. For the first part, *sigarye*, the adolescent male wears a traditional full-length Korean jacket called *durumagi*. The second part of the ceremony, *jaegarye*, sees the boy wear a robe called a *simui* with a matching hat called a *yugeon*. Then for the final part of the ceremony, *samgarye*, the male wears a *gat*, a cylindrical hat made from woven horsehair, and his hair is pulled into a topknot. The male also wears a ceremonial outfit called a *dopo*, which comprises a coat with matching belt.

After the changes of clothes have been completed, the *chorye* occurs during which the young man bows to the guests to show his gratitude for their presence. The man also takes his first alcoholic drink. Next, during the jagwanjarye stage a young man is given a new name called a *ja*, by which he will be known. The bestowing of this name acknowledges the man's initiation to adulthood. Finally, during the *goyuje* stage a young man visits his ancestral shrine where he bows to his to older relatives.

Modern gwallye ceremonies are held en masse with events such as that held at Seoul City Hall initiating 200 adolescents made up of both native Koreans and foreign students. (*See* Plate 8.) Gwallye ceremonies held in Busan hark back to traditional gwallye ceremonies involving the three changes of clothing. Young people attending ceremonies in Busan are also taught how to wear a Hanbok, how to perform a bow properly and how to conduct a tea ceremony. Korean universities hold their own versions of gwallye ceremonies that see students wear a Hanbok, have tranquil tea parties, and receive certificates of excellence. Music concerts featuring a 12-stringed zither called a *gayageum* and performances of traditional plays are also ways to celebrate the young people's attainment of adulthood.

See also: Chinese Coming-of-Age Ceremonies; Coming of Age Day; Ear-Piercing Ceremonies

Further Reading

Ewha Voice. "An Ideal Coming-of-Age Day for Contemporary Young Adults." Ewha Voice, May 1, 2007. Accessed May 4, 2015, at http://evoice.ewha.ac.kr/news/articleView.html?idxno=1205.

Korea.net. "Time to Grow Up: Coming of Age Ceremony." May 19, 2008. Accessed May 4, 2015, at http://www.korea.net/NewsFocus/Culture/view?articleId=72765.

Yi, I-Hwa. *Korea's Pastimes and Customs: A Social History*. Paramus, NJ: Homa & Sekey Books, 2001.

HADAKA MATSURI, JAPAN

Hadaka Matsuri, meaning naked festival, is a Japanese Shinto *matsuri* (festival) that is so-called as participants wear very little clothing. The festival sees thousands of nude or near-naked men compete for a symbolic prize as a test of their manliness and endurance. Moreover, the festival is also designed to confer good luck, ward off calamity, and dispel evil spirits as participating men strive to touch a naked man that has been selected to play the role of the *Shin-otoko,* or man of God. Since those that take part in Hadaka Matsuri are said to divest themselves of misfortune the men that take part in the ritual tend to be aged 23 and 42 years of age as these are reputed to be *yaku-doshi* or bad luck years in Japan during which a person can expect to suffer misfortune. Therefore many men aged 23 and 42 years old like to participate in Hadaka Matsuri in order to touch the Shin-otoko and rid themselves of their misfortune. Hadaka Matsuri takes place in January and February at a variety of locations throughout Japan including Saidaiji Temple in Okayama where some 10,000 men compete en masse. (*See* Plate 9.) The oldest, and largest, Hadaka Matsuri occurs at Konomiya Shrine in the city of Inazawa on the island of Honshu on January 13. To take part in Hadaka Matsuri the exclusively male competitors either take part naked or wear only traditional Japanese loincloths, *fundoshi* or *yukata*, and wooden sandals. As the events of Hadaka Matsuri can be quite hazardous participants usually insert a paper into their loincloth bearing their name, blood type, and an emergency contact number in case they are injured.

There are two main theories to the origin of Hadaka Matsuri. One suggestion is that the custom dates back 500 years to a time when worshippers vied to receive paper talismans called *Go-o* that were thrown by a priest. The Go-o were tokens to mark the completion of austere New Year training performed by the priests. The worshippers that managed to win a paper talisman were said to become imbued with good luck and could look forward to happy times. As those people that received the Go-o could expect happiness and luck the number of people competing for the Go-o increased each year. Over time, the paper Go-o, which were easily damaged, were replaced with wooden *ofuda*, or inscribed long strips that are used within the Shinto religion as charms, amulets, or talismans to confer purification and protection. The second theory as to the origin of Hadaka Matsuri is that in 767 CE Emperor Shotoku ordered that all regional temples throughout Japan should cast invocations to ward off plagues. The festival is thought able to ward off disaster and sickness because the *Shin-otoko* around which the ritual revolves is thought to possess the power to absorb and disperse all the sin and misfortune

> ### Fundoshi
>
> *Fundoshi* is the traditional form of underwear for adult Japanese males. Fundoshi is made from a length of cotton fabric and although it has been superseded by Western-style undergarments fundoshi are still worn at festivals and sometimes as swimwear. There are many different types of fundoshi but the most comfortable type consists of a strip of cloth that is wound around the hips, then knotted or twisted at the small of the back with the excess fabric brought forward between the wearer's legs and tucked through a cloth belt in front so that the loose cloth hangs as an apron. It has recently been suggested that fundoshi are making a comeback among young Japanese men.

residing within the men that seek to touch him. It is a great honor for a man to be chosen to play the Shin-otoko even though to take on the role the selected man must undergo a strenuous purification process that includes removing all his body hair except his eyebrows. Meanwhile the men that strive to touch the Shin-otoko prepare themselves for competition by drinking a great deal of Japanese rice wine, *sake*, and stripping until they are dressed in just a loincloth or are completely naked. At the Hadaka Matsuri at Konomiya Shrine the Shin-otoko walks the streets of the city as other men strive to touch him in order that their sins and misfortune pass on to the Shin-otoko and can then be dispelled. As the participants approach the Shin-otoko other men acting in the role of the Shin-otoko's body guards (often former Shin-otokos) splash freezing water over the competing men. As the water is freezing cold the participating men are forced to jump up and down and generally move around in order to keep warm throughout the competition. As the naked or near-naked men seek him, the Shin-otoko makes his way to the shrine where he makes offerings to the deities. Once the Shin-otoko has prayed to the gods, he re-dresses and goes home believing himself to be carrying the competitor's sin and bad luck with him.

The event culminates at midnight in a mass gathering of the thousands of participants within the small shrine. Here, from a window some 13 feet above, a priest drops two lucky, sacred wooden sticks measuring around eight inches in length called *shingi* into the crowd. All the men then try to get hold of the shingi and the good luck that the sticks embody. The two men that are lucky enough to gain possession of the sticks must then thrust the sticks upright into a wooden box known as a *masu* that contains rice. Once the men complete this feat they are considered to have won a year's worth of happiness and good fortune. Meanwhile other men try to catch one of around 100 lucky strips of willow that are also thrown into the crowd.

A similar festival is that which occurs at Teppozu Inari Shrine in Tokyo known as the Kanchu Misogi. This is an age-old Shinto festival of winter ritual purification that is reputed to cleanse male competitors' bodies and souls while also conferring upon them good luck. The ritual is also thought to bring the men closer to the *kame* (spirits) that competitors believe will look favorably upon them for their endeavors. The festival sees men wearing just loincloths and headbands hug giant blocks of ice while submerging themselves in a pool of freezing water. After this the men then lay flat on blocks of ice, all the while praying for the good health and well-being of their families over the next 12 months. In other parts of Japan, very similar rituals take place in which men must perform tasks involving snow rather than freezing water and ice.

See also: Coming of Age Day; Hair Removal; Log Riding; *Sharo*: Public Flogging; Warding Off the Evil Eye (Volume 1)

Further Reading

Japan National Tourism. "Saidai-ji Eyo Hadaka Matsuri." *Japan: The Official Guide*. Accessed November 30, 2015, at http://www.jnto.go.jp/eng/location/spot/festival/saidaijieyohadaka.html.

Kikuko-nagoya.com. "Konomiya Naked Festival." Accessed November 30, 2015, at http://kikuko-nagoya.com/html/naked-festival.html.

Melton, J. Gordon. *Religious Celebrations: An Encyclopedia of Holidays, Festivals, Solemn Observances, and Spiritual Commemorations*. Volume 1. Santa Barbara, CA: ABC-CLIO, 2011.

Pleasance, Chris. "Ice, Ice Baby: Japanese Men Wearing Only Pants and Bandanas Hug Giant Blocks of Ice in a Freezing Pool to Cleanse Their Souls," *Daily Mail*, January 12, 2014. Accessed November 30, 2015, at http://www.dailymail.co.uk/news/article-2538063/Ice-ice-baby-Men-Japan-wearing-nappy-like-pants-bandanas-hug-giant-blocks-ice-freezing-pool-bid-cleanse-souls.html.

Plutschow, Herbert E. *Matsuri: The Festivals of Japan*. Richmond, UK: Japan Library, 1996.

Taylor, Alan. "Okayama's Naked Festival," *The Atlantic: Photo*, February 21, 2015. Accessed November 30, 2015, at http://www.theatlantic.com/photo/2015/02/okayamas-naked-festival/385724/.

HAIR REMOVAL, INTERNATIONAL

Hair removal, also referred to as epilation or depilation, is the deliberate removal of the body's androgenic hair, that is, the hair that develops on the human body during and after puberty. Hair may be removed for aesthetic, cultural, religious, sexual, hygienic, or medical reasons. The hair removed by epilation and depilation is usually located in the pubic area, under the arms, legs, face, back, and chest. Women tend to practice hair removal more often than men because many cultures consider hair growing on the legs, underarms, and pubic regions of women to be unattractive and unhygienic once females have reached puberty. There are many forms of hair removal including waxing, shaving, tweezing, using depilatory creams, sugaring, threading, and laser therapy. The method of hair removal chosen by an individual may be influenced by culture, tradition, and finances. Today in the West, shaving and waxing are the most popular methods of hair removal.

The history of hair removal is very long, dating back to prehistoric times when people held two seashells together so that they formed a rudimentary tweezer-type implement or used the sharpened edge of a rock as a razor. The ancient Egyptians developed sugaring for Egyptian men and women would apply a mixture of oil and honey to the skin that was then ripped from the body thereby removing unwanted hair. Meanwhile the first depilatory cream is believed to have been invented by the ancient Turks as early as 4000 BCE for Turkish women used a concoction called *rhusma* that they made from arsenic trisulfide, quicklime, and starch to remove their hair. Meanwhile in ancient Turkey, India, the Middle East, and China, women began to use threading as a method of hair removal. Threading involves twisting a length of cotton around individual hairs to pluck away unwanted hairs. Hindus living in ancient India also shaved their faces and pubic areas. Ancient Sumerians and ancient Romans used tweezer-like tools to remove hairs and the Romans also removed body hair using a metal implement called a *strigil* to scrape over their lubricated skin or applying a depilatory paste made from pitch, she-goat gall, donkey fat, bat blood, and powdered viper. Ancient Greek women meanwhile performed waxing and used pumice stones to abrade their skin thereby removing their pubic hair. In ancient South America, Mayans and Aztecs sharpened obsidian to function as a razor, and in North America Native Americans used seashells to scrape hair from the skin. This method was also favored by people living on islands in the Pacific Ocean, such as Samoa. In the seventh century the Islamic holy book, the Qur'an, stipulated that a man's moustache and nails should be clipped at least every 40 days and pubic and underarm hair removed. By the turn of the 16th century it had become the norm in Europe for women, and some men, to remove their pubic hair, with some people opting to wear a pubic wig called a merkin that was often made from goat hair.

Today, many cultures around the world consider varying degrees of androgenic hair removal to be the norm. Areas of the world where hair removal is the norm, particularly for women, include North America, Western Europe, Australasia, India, the Trobriand Islands, and areas where Islam is prevalent. In many Middle Eastern countries, it is traditional for bride's attendants to remove all the bride's body hair, except that on her head and her eyebrows, on the eve of a wedding. Several tribes living in central Africa perform a similar custom during which the bride's underarms and legs are shaved and her pubic hair is plucked. Meanwhile, in Brazil and Venezuela hair removal traditionally involves the sap of the coco de mono tree (*Lecythis ollaria*) being applied to the skin as a wax. This practice has evolved into the well-known beauty treatment known as the Brazilian wax in which (on women) pubic hair is removed from around the vulva, perineum, and anus. The Padilha sisters at their Manhattan beauty salon invented the Brazilian wax in 1987. Since then this method of hair removal has been championed by celebrities including pop star turned fashion designer Victoria Beckham and actress Eva Longoria and by television programs such as "Sex and the City." Such celebrity endorsements led to a surge of interest in the Brazilian wax and during the 2000s it was estimated that one in five American women under 25 years old regularly underwent Brazilian waxing while a 2010 survey found that 25 percent of American women 18 to 65 years old favored the bald look of the Brazilian wax. There is also anecdotal evidence that a growing number of American men are opting for Brazilian wax treatments known as so-called Brozilians, or sack, crack, and back waxes. The popularity of these beauty treatments has resulted in some people wondering whether pubic hair will eventually become obsolete. A number of feminist critics have also raised concerns that Brazilian wax treatments encourage the infantilization of women as waxing leaves women's vulvas hairless and therefore reminiscent of the pubic region of girls that have not reached puberty. Other feminists meanwhile have questioned whether the popularity of the Brazilian wax is another way in which patriarchal society oppresses women by compelling them to undergo painful beauty treatments in order to conform to social norms.

See also: Beards; Breast Ironing; Menstrual Taboos; Training Bra; Trobriand Ritualized Sex and Commitment

Further Reading
Accord. "A Brief History of Hair Removal." Hygiene for Health. Accessed August 11 2015, at http://www.hygieneforhealth.org.au/hair_removal.php.
Fetters, Ashley. "The New Full-Frontal: Has Pubic Hair in America Gone Extinct?" *The Atlantic*, December 13, 2011. Accessed August 12, 2015, at http://www.theatlantic.com/health/archive/2011/12/the-new-full-frontal-has-pubic-hair-in-america-gone-extinct/249798/.
Herzig, Rebecca M. *Plucked: A History of Hair Removal*. New York: New York University Press, 2015.
Sherrow, Victoria. *Encyclopedia of Hair: A Cultural History*. Westport, CT: Greenwood Press, 2006.
Toerien, Merran, Sue Wilkinson, and Precilla Y. L. Choi. "Body Hair Removal: The 'Mundane' Production of Normative Femininity," *Sex Roles*, 52(5/6), March 2005, 399–406. Accessed August 11, 2015, at http://eprints.whiterose.ac.uk/48849/1/Toerien_et_al_Mundane_production_of_normative_femininity.pdf.

HAJJ, ISLAM

Hajj, meaning pilgrimage, is an annual journey to Mecca, Saudi Arabia, that is a mandatory undertaking for all Muslims that are financially and physically able to do so. Performing the Hajj is the fifth pillar of Islam and the most meaningful demonstration of Islamic belief and unity. Though a Muslim can undertake a lesser pilgrimage, called *Umrah*, at any time, Hajj is the most important religious act in a Muslim person's life. Each year about 2 million Muslims perform Hajj, which lasts for five days and occurs only from the 9th to 13th of Dhu Al-Hijah, which is the 12th month of the Islamic lunar calendar. Those that undertake Hajj do so because they believe they will be rewarded with entry into Paradise after they die. Performing the Hajj is the religious highpoint of any Muslim's life for the pilgrimage cements their understanding of their relationship with Allah. By performing Hajj,

Muslims know that they have followed in the footsteps of the Prophet, and have also acted as part of the united Muslim *ummah*, or nation.

The exact history of Hajj is unknown but many Muslims believe that the ritual began many thousands of years ago during the time of Ibrahim (Abraham). Up until the start of the 20th century the journey to Mecca was extremely difficult and expensive to undertake. Indeed so arduous was the journey that some pilgrims would take in excess of a year to reach the city. The pilgrimage is still demanding even today and it is usual for a pilgrim to name a trusted friend or relative as executor of their will in case they die while performing Hajj. Though precautions are taken to make the pilgrimage as bearable as possible, some pilgrims still need to be taken to the hospital by helicopter as they become stricken with heat exhaustion while making their pilgrimage.

All Muslims must undertake the journey once in their lifetime if they are fit enough and also able to support their family financially while absent. The emphasis on finances is intended to ensure that Muslims put their family first, while the fitness of would-be pilgrims is stressed to exempt Muslims that are too frail to endure the arduous journey. There are some other exemptions from performing Hajj. For example if the route to Hajj is unsafe then it is not obligatory for a Muslim to perform the pilgrimage. Also a female pilgrim must take with her a relative that she cannot marry (e.g., a brother) to act as her *muhrim*, similar to a chaperone. If a woman cannot find a muhrim to accompany her then she is exempt from performing Hajj. Meanwhile, Hajj is not obligatory for children. If, however, a child does perform Hajj then he or she will have to perform the pilgrimage again as an adult.

Whatever the weather, male pilgrims performing Hajj wear a special outfit called *ihram*, which consists of two simple, unsewn white garments. Female pilgrims tend to wear normal, plain white clothes together with a headscarf. The deliberate simplicity of the garments is intended to remove all distinctions of wealth, social status, and culture so that all pilgrims stand together as equals before Allah. Only when they put on this white clothing can pilgrims venture to stations called *miqat* from where they begin their pilgrimage. It is at the miqat that pilgrims put on the ihram and recite the *talbiya*—a prayer announcing to God that pilgrims have arrived to perform pilgrimage.

During Hajj pilgrims perform many rites over five or six days. The Hajj commences with the same rituals as those of Umra. The first ritual is the *tawaf*, or circumambulation, of a cube-shaped building called the Ka'bah (or Kaaba) that is located within the Holy Mosque. During tawaf pilgrims walk en masse seven times around the Ka'bah in a counter-clockwise direction, as this is the direction of prayer for Muslims. Pilgrims begin their circumambulation from the eastern corner of the building, as this is where the Black Stone is embedded. The history of tawaf dates back to the time of Ibrahim and his son Isma'il (Ishmael) who are said to have walked around the Ka'bah seven times when they had rebuilt the structure. Therefore when pilgrims undertake tawaf they are, quite literally, following in the footsteps of the prophets Ibrahim, Isma'il, and Muhammad. Tawaf is also the concluding ritual of Hajj as the *tawaf al-wada,* or the farewell tawaf, is the last rite of the Hajj to be performed. Other rituals of the Hajj include the *sa'i* that sees pilgrims run and walk seven times between the two hills of Safa and Marwa, where male pilgrims are expected to shave their heads, or at least cut a lock of hair, as well as praying behind the Station or Maqam of Abraham and drinking the Zamzam water.

The rite of sa'i remembers the search for water by Hagar (wife of Ibrahim), after Ibrahim abandoned her in the desert as a test of faith. Having run out of supplies, Hagar ran in desperation seven times between the mountains of Safa and Marwa looking for help. On returning to her son Isma'il, Hagar found that a spring of water had sprung from the ground. This spring is now known as the Well of Zamzam. During their seven times passing between Safa and Marwa pilgrims run along a passage. Pilgrims perform this strenuous exercise to demonstrate their commitment to Islam.

These rituals take only a matter of hours to perform and can be completed in one day. Over subsequent days pilgrims continue on to visit the holy sites of Arafat, Muzdalifa, and Mina on subsequent days. At Arafat pilgrims perform a vigil (*wuquf*) that takes place from noon until sunset on the ninth of Dhu al-Hijja. Wuquf is the most important element of Hajj for the vigil sees Muslims dedicate themselves to the codes of Islam that are the basis of the Five Pillars of Islam, that is, the five mandatory acts of Islam that are the foundation of the faith. If any pilgrim fails to perform the *wuquf*, then their Hajj is considered invalid and must be undertaken again another year. Then at Muzdalifa pilgrims collect 49 stones that they will throw over several days at the three *jamrat* (pillars) in the valley of Mina near Mecca. Once at Mina, pilgrims rest in tents for three days and three nights. According to Islamic lore, Mina is the site where Ibrahim took his son Isma'il with the intention of sacrificing the boy in order to demonstrate his obedience to Allah and refusal of Satan. The story of Ibrahim tells that in order to repel temptation Ibrahim threw stones at Satan, an act that Allah rewarded by sending a sacrificial ram to Ibrahim. For this reason at Mina Muslims throw pebbles at three pillars representing both Satan and inner temptation: the largest pillar called *Jamrat al-'Aqaba* (at the narrow pass of al-'Aqaba), *Jamrat al-Wusta* (the middle one), and *Jamrat al-Sughra* (the little one). The three pillars are not stoned on the same day. Traditionally, Jamrat al-'Aqaba is stoned on day three of the Hajj, which is also the day of the important Islamic celebration known as Eid. Then on days four to six of the Hajj, all three pillars are stoned as pilgrims return to Mecca for tawaf al-wada.

Animal sacrifice also takes place on the Hajj with the resulting meat donated to the poor living in 30 countries. In total some 60,000 animals are sacrificed each year over the three days of celebration known as Eid Al-Adha that occurs during Hajj. Eid Al-Adha concludes the Hajj, the end of which is signaled by pilgrims cutting their hair and removing their ihram clothing to mark the end of their sacred state. The pilgrims then re-dress in regular clothes. Indeed two of the essential items a pilgrim will use on Hajj are scissors and a razor for twice they are obliged to perform the ritual of *taqsir* or *halq* (cutting or shaving) of their hair. The Saudi Arabian government even provides licensed barbers with a new blade for each male pilgrim—female pilgrims need only snip off a lock of their hair. By cutting their hair, pilgrims perform a symbolic shedding of worldly accessories. Also at the end of Hajj pilgrims also exchange festive wishes and gifts, as do Muslims across the world.

Because Hajj is so important to Muslims the Islamic nation of Saudi Arabia considers it a great honor to receive Hajj pilgrims and therefore dedicates substantial financial resources to the event. Over the past 40 years or so the country has spent billions of dollars to enlarge Mecca's Holy Mosque and the Prophet's Mosque in Medina, as well as to provide the modern transport infrastructure, lodgings, and other amenities pilgrims need. Indeed planning for each annual Hajj begins at the end of the previous one. However despite Saudi Arabia's good intentions tragedy can occur at the Hajj. The most recent incident saw between 769 and 1,500 pilgrims crushed in a stampede (figures vary) in September 2015 when large crowds congregated in a narrow street in Mina. Thousands of pilgrims passing down the narrow Mina streets met another large crowd, which resulted in people tripping over each another, falling, and suffocating in an hour-long crush. The tragedy has led to calls for the Hajj to be organized by a coalition of Muslim states rather than Saudi Arabia alone. However Saudi Arabia is reported to be against the idea as the country gains great respect and legitimacy from overseeing the Hajj and acting as custodians to Islam's holiest sites.

See also: Hair Removal; *Hijab*; *Kumbh Mela*; *Thaipusam*: Extreme Ritual Flesh Modification

Further Reading

Associated Press and Agencies. "Saudi Prince Says Kingdom Will Remain in Charge of Hajj after Deadly Stampede," *The Guardian*, October 12, 2015. Accessed October 12, 2015, at http://www.theguardian.com/world/2015/oct/12/saudi-prince-says-kingdom-will-remain-in-charge-of-hajj-after-deadly-stampede.

Information Office of the Royal Embassy of Saudi Arabia in Washington, D.C. "Hajj." Issues. Accessed September 2, 2015, at https://www.saudiembassy.net/issues/hajj/.

Khan, Saniyasnain, ed. *Hajj Made Simple*. New Delhi, India: Goodword Books, 2014.

PerformHajj.com. "Hajj—Pilgrimage to Mecca." *What Is Hajj?* Accessed September 2, 2015, at http://www.performhajj.com/what_is_hajj.php.

Peters, F. E. *The Hajj: The Muslim Pilgrimage to Mecca and the Holy Places*. Princeton, NJ: Princeton University Press, 1994.

Trustees of the British Museum. "The Rituals of the Hajj." The British Museum. Accessed October 12, 2015, at https://www.britishmuseum.org/explore/themes/hajj/the_rituals_of_the_hajj.aspx.

HANDFASTING, SCOTLAND, ALSO NEO-PAGANISM

The term handfasting (sometimes written as hand-fasting) is both a historic term for a betrothal or type of wedding and a modern neo-pagan term for a ceremony marking marital union. Originally handfasting referred to a betrothal but then came to mean a type of temporary marriage popular in Scotland. In the 16th century handfasting referred to betrothal and was, therefore, considered the first stage in a marriage ceremony. The handfasting saw the payment of bride prices, or the public promise to pay a dowry and could take place when the couple who would eventually wed were very young. A handfasting ceremony, which was presided over by the bride's father, took place in public and would see a couple exchange vows as binding as any marriage vows while standing under a church porch. Alternatively, as sometimes occurred in Scotland and northern England, the couple would join hands to exchange vows at a local site designated for the ceremony, usually called a plighting stone, bridal stone, or betrothal stone. The stone would feature a hole through which the couple would hold hands. In some instances the couple's hands were tied together hence entering into marriage came to be known as "tying the knot." Some historians argue that handfasting was suppressed in Scotland during the mid-16th century and only survived in the Highlands but there is ample evidence that the custom continued into the 17th century in other remote locations in the lowlands too. Indeed Scottish and northern English peasants started to use handfasting as a sort of substitute temporary trial marriage that allowed them to cohabit instead of having to wed in church—in Scotland a handfasting ceremony allowed a couple to live together for a year while in England's Lake District it was a year and a day. A similar arrangement also existed in Wales. After the period of trial marriage was up the couple could either marry each other or separate. Any child resulting from the temporary marriage was considered legitimate. Such was the popularity of handfasting that church authorities ordered that all couples entered into a handfasting must marry immediately. However most couples ignored this decree, especially in remote areas as they could not be bothered with the fuss or expense of a church wedding and considered a public handfasting vow as binding as any wedding vow. Handfasting was still popular in Scotland during the 19th century for Highland chiefs would use a type of handfasting to ensure their lineal descent by betrothing their son to the daughter of another clan chief. The couple would live as man and wife for one year and if the girl became pregnant during the year the handfasting was considered a binding marriage.

Today, handfasting is a popular form of commitment ceremony for heterosexual and same-sex couples belonging to neo-pagan religions, especially Wicca. Couples who may or may not be neo-pagan also take part in modern handfasting ceremonies to demonstrate their Celtic, specifically Scottish, heritage. This is particularly true of Americans and Canadians who travel to the Scottish Highlands to undergo a handfasting. This type of handfasting is thought to have evolved from a combination of Scandinavian Christian and pre-Christian customs introduced to Scotland around 1000 and medieval handfasting.

The binding vow taken by couples during a handfasting often expresses the wish that they will be to be together "for a year and a day," "for a lifetime," "for as long as love shall last," or something similar. However, as with many neo-pagan rites some groups may opt for a historical, traditional form of the ceremony while others may use the basic concept of the ceremony as the basis for their own version of the ceremony. In some neo-pagan handfasting ceremonies, couples may jump over a broom while others may jump over a fire and many neo-pagan handfastings take place inside a circle. Some Wiccans also undergo a three-stage handfasting rite—one as a betrothal, one as a marriage, and one as a deathbed promise to continue loving in death or as a handparting—to symbolize the three states in all things, that is, a beginning, a middle, and an end. A neo-pagan handfasting may be called a Subtle Wedding if the ceremony is modified and conducted in such a way as to allow non-pagans to understand the ceremony. However if everyone present is pagan then a handfasting may be officiated by a high priest and high priestess.

There are several customs associated with neo-pagan, particularly Wiccan, handfasting ceremonies. Foremost among these is the binding of the couple's hands using ribbon. Often guests at a handfasting tie knots of ribbon round the couple's clasped hands to symbolize their union—a literal interpretation of the term handfasting that harks back to medieval practices. This custom became popular in Wiccan communities during the 2000s and has also started to be offered by mainstream commercial wedding organizers hoping to capitalize on the increased popularity of the custom following the success of the film *Braveheart* (1995) in which the bride and groom's hands are tied with ribbon rather than exchanging rings.

See also: British Wedding Traditions; Gretna Green; Handfasting Ceremony (Sample); Handparting; Jumping Over the Broom

Further Reading

AnSgeulaiche, Scot. "Hand-fasting Ceremony in the Scottish Tradition." Scottish-master-of-wedding-ceremonies.co.uk. Accessed December 29, 2014, at http://www.scottish-master-of-wedding-ceremonies.co.uk/handfasting.php.

Drew, A. J. *A Wiccan Bible: Exploring the Mysteries of the Craft from Birth to Summerland*. Franklin Lakes, NJ: The Career Press Inc., 2003.

Law, Laura. "Handfasting Rituals." Handfasting.org. Accessed December 29, 2014, at http://handfasting.org/rituals/.

Monger, George P. *Marriage Customs of the World: From Henna to Honeymoons*. Santa Barbara, CA: ABC-CLIO, 2004.

Related Primary Document: Handfasting Ceremony (Sample)

The word handfasting (sometimes written as hand-fasting) can be used to refer to both a historic term for a type of betrothal or wedding and to a modern, neo-pagan ceremony

marking marital union. Some couples (who may or may not be neo-pagan) also participate in handfasting ceremonies in order to demonstrate their Celtic (specifically Scottish) heritage. Handfastings are a popular form of commitment ceremony for heterosexual and same-sex couples belonging to neo-pagan religions, especially followers of Wicca. The binding vow taken by couples during a handfasting may be to be together "for a year and a day," "for a lifetime," or "for as long as love shall last." However, as with many neo-pagan rites, some groups may opt for a historical, traditional form of the ceremony while others may use the basic concept of the ceremony as the basis for their own version of the ceremony. Neo-pagan handfastings are held within a circle and are usually officiated by a High Priest and High Priestess. There is no one set model of a handfasting ceremony though several customs are associated with neo-pagan, particularly Wiccan, handfastings. The most common feature of handfasting ceremonies is the binding of the couple's hands using ribbon. Sometimes the ribbon is tied in knots of ribbon round the marrying couple's clasped hands in order to symbolize the couple's union. This is a literal interpretation of the term handfasting that recalls medieval marriage customs.

The following is the text of a neo-pagan handfasting ceremony consisting of various sections: a Preamble; Welcoming of the Guests; Elemental Blessing; Drawing Down of the God and Goddess; Blessing of the Rings; Sword, Chalice and Ring Exchange; Cakes and Ale; the Handfasting itself; and, lastly, The Broom and Sword section. This section also includes the act of Jumping Over the Broom as a symbolic way of sweeping away the couple's old lives.

Ceremony sample

Adapted from a handfasting ceremony by Reverend April Gismondi of the Church of Ancient Ways

Preamble*

* This preamble, if not spoken, may go in a program.

"Good afternoon and welcome! As we will be beginning shortly I would ask that those of you with telecommunications devices, Cell phones, beepers and such, if you will please turn them off or switch them to vibrate at this time.

As this may be the first time that some of you are attending a handfasting our Bride and Groom thought you might be interested in the symbolism of what you will see today. Much of which are familiar in all but their context.

(over the top for some) The circle in which you all stand is symbolic of the cycles of life, the womb of the Great Mother, a sacred place created for mortal and divine interaction, in which any negativity from the mundane world can be left outside and all the love and joy we feel for <<BRIDE>> and <<GROOM>> contained within.

(toned down for others) The circle in which you all stand is a sacred space for a sacred event to take place. Much of the symbolism of the chuppa and the wedding band hold true in the circle, the sacred womb from which the two are born again as one and the symbol of eternity.

Although for many the sacred and the mundane meet and coexist as often as is humanly possible, marriage is very much a sacred union, for it is a union of souls in which the bride and groom pledge unto one another their higher selves and all that is divine within them selves. In the earth-based traditions it is considered the marriage of the God and Goddess within.

You will also hear an elemental blessing. All the worlds religions still parallel the agricultural calendar, because the natural world speaks its lessons softly and constantly. In the blessing we simply ask to understand and be able to see the how the attributes of each element can help us on our journey.

Almost all cultures and faiths have a sacred meal of communion with the divine. During a wedding it has the added meaning of feeding on and drinking in of the promises that a couple has made.

Those of you who have been to a Greek Orthodox ceremony will undoubtedly recognize the symbolic binding of the hands at the end of the service that inspired the terms "Bonds of Holy Matrimony" and to "Tie the knot" This custom has also been known the world over, through many different periods in history. During the Middle Ages to be seen in public holding hands was a sing that a couple were exclusive to one another. And while rings were for the very rich, love knows no bounds and a simple cord would do just fine.

Those of you who are fans of the Renaissance period will be happy to see the jumping of broom at the closing of the ceremony which symbolically sweeps clean the past reminding our Bride and Groom that the power to create the future ahead and the quality of life that they both so richly deserve is their own.

<<GROOM>>, if you will now join me your beautiful Bride awaits!"

Welcoming of the Guests

<<BRIDE>> and <<GROOM>> would like to take a moment to thank you all for being here with them today. They know that making the journey took considerable effort for a good many of you and for this they are deeply grateful. All of you are the most important people in their lives. All of the time and conversations that you have had with <<BRIDE>> and <<GROOM>> before they even met helped to make them who they needed to be to find first themselves and then each other. You have shared in their best and their worst days, and you are an irreplaceable part of their yesterdays, their today and all of their tomorrows. So as you can see although many of you don't live right around the corner you are never far from their hearts.

I look out at you now and I see a rich and diverse weave of differing beliefs, life styles, ages and viewpoints. Yet you are all here celebrating your love for <<BRIDE>> and <<GROOM>>, wishing for them all that they would want for themselves, rather than what our own hopes many have been. It sounds more like an ideal but it isn't, and it is in part what makes their life together a thing of such great beauty.

There are many reasons that we share in life's celebrations with those we love. Ritual itself is designed to cause a change in our lives. The promises that a couple makes must be practical promises that when lived by will actually help them to safeguard their future. Another important aspect of ritual is that in being here we somehow feel closer to the couple by being allowed a peek into their inner most thoughts and feelings at this intensely personal moment of their lives. It reminds the couples here of when it was their special day and the promises they once made, and allows us all to somehow feel closer to one another as the community of family and friends that we truly are.

There is a term that we hear often at events such as this with very little explanation. The term is "Perfect Love and Perfect Trust" or "Unconditional Love." In the case of a marriage, and in the case of all loving, caring, committed relationships the ideal that this speaks of is not about perfection, but of expecting and accepting imperfection and human frailty. It means that a couple must say to one another: I accept and I expect that on occasion you will anger me as I will anger you, and that you will hurt me as I will hurt you; But I know in my heart that between us there is love and affection and friendship that is stronger; And I trust that no pain is caused out ill will, or malice, or pettiness, just as I trust that we are together for a reason and that we will never throw each other away. I trust that at our best we will live together in love and joy and harmony and at our worst we will fight, with and for and beside each other, for the greater good without fear of abandonment. For the divinely inspired desire to be together for a lifetime in indeed something well worthy of fighting for. And these dear friends are the promises that you have been invited to bear witness to this day.

Elemental Blessing

"Since ancient times, people have communed with nature to learn more about themselves by example. Since it is within nature that we all do abide, we ask for <<BRIDE>> and <<GROOM>> the blessings of Nature's Elements, Air, Fire, Water and Earth. We do this that they may fully come to understand the lessons each element has to offer. The attributes of which are examples of those aspects they mirror not only within divinity but within ourselves as well."

"We ask the spirits of Air to keep open the lines of communication between this couple. May their future be as bright as the dawn on the horizon. As Air flows freely to and from and through us all, may their hearts and minds and souls come to know the world and each other in this manner. Seeing not only with their eyes, may they together grow wise with wisdom."

"Spirits of Fire, we ask that <<BRIDE>> and <<GROOM>>'s passion for each other and for life itself remain ever strong and vital, fortifying each day with a vibrancy rooted in boldness, and courage. As Fire clears the way for new growth, may they know that this power is theirs: to create change and bring about the richness and quality that comes with a true love of life."

"We ask the Spirits of Water, that their love for each other and the comfort of loved ones, like the serenity of the deep blue ocean, be the oasis that forever surrounds our Bride and Groom. May they be well loved, and love well, letting the surety with which Water makes its journey to the sea, flowing over rocks or around trees, even turning into vapor and riding a cloud, ever serve as a reminder that with love all is well and will endure."

"Spirits of Earth, we ask that you give unto those you see standing before you this day, the rock solid place to stand and fulfill his destiny. May their journey mirror the vast planes and fertile fields, expansive and alive. May they find the right seeds to sow to ensure a bountiful harvest. And when they look up at the Northern Star, may they know that it is as bright and constant as their love for each other as well as the love of the divine is for them."

"Father, Mother, Divine Spirit whose presence is felt in all things and at all times we ask your continued blessings upon this couple, upon their union and upon their family and friends who have gathered here to celebrate this joyous event with them. May they become one in truth and forever revel in the magik that is love."

Drawing Down the God and Goddess

"In the drawing down of the God and Goddess into <<BRIDE>> and <<GROOM>>, it connects them with the divinity within themselves, reminding us that in marriage it is our higher selves and the best that we have to give, that we offer to one another. As a sacred spiritual union to become the embodiment of the God and Goddess serves as a reminder that as above, so below, honoring the God and Goddess within themselves and their mate."

Bride bows head

<<BRIDE>>

Lady <<BRIDE>>, I ask you to call upon

all that is divine within you,

Let it come forth and shine.

In you dwells the essence of the Great Mother

and the divine feminine principle of the Universe

You are She who has been worshiped and adored

for centuries and throughout the ages

You are wife, mother, lover, friend,

prophet, and confidant

In you is everything that any one

could ever aspire to be and more.

In you is strength and wisdom, perfection and peace.

Shine dear one and show your true nature as Goddess.

Groom bows head

<<GROOM>>

Lord <<GROOM>>, I ask you to call upon

all that is divine within you,

Let it come forth and shine.

In you lives the essence of the Gods

The active force that has sparked and powered all life

You are He who has been worshiped and adored

for centuries and throughout the ages

You are husband, healer, protector,

visionary, friend, and confidant

In you is everything that any one

could ever aspire to be and more.

In you is strength and wisdom, perfection and peace.

Shine mighty one and show to all the God within.

<<BRIDE>>

"Queen most Secret, touch with your grace and fill this woman with your beauty and strength in the unending cycles of growth and change that are the years and seasons of lives spent together in love and wonder. Share with her your fertile nature from which all abundance flows.

<<GROOM>>

"Lord of light and life, touch with your power and fill this man with your knowledge and wisdom to guide him in this divine alchemy which is the union of two souls. Share with him the secret union of heart and mind upon which this union known as marriage must be based."

Blessing of the Rings

"<<Best Man>> and <<Maid of Honor>> will you now hold out the rings entrusted to you by <<BRIDE>> and <<GROOM>>? Your hands beneath serve as a symbol of how <<BRIDE>> and <<GROOM>> and their marriage are supported upon this earth by the love of their friends and family as blessed from above."

<<Best Man>> and <<Maid of Honor>> hold out the wedding bands in the palm of their hands Celebrant continues:

"Lord and Lady, guardians of all that is seen and unseen,

Bless these rings and this couple who shall wear them.

Keep them safe through adversity forever supported

by your eternal blessing."

Celebrant takes rings

"The ring finger of the left hand, the side of the body that holds the heart, has been used for the wedding band because for centuries people believed that there was a vein that ran directly from that finger to the heart. They also believed that the words that were spoken during the placing of the ring would resonate over and over, like the circumference of the band itself, through to the heart and soul of both giver and receiver of the most monumental promise of all, the promise of a lifetime as husband and wife."

Sword, Chalice and Ring Exchange*

*Adapted from Ed Fitch's "Rights from the Crystal Well"

"Lord <<GROOM>>, if it is truly thy desire to become one with this with this woman: Then present unto her a symbol of thy pledge, and a token of thy love."

Groom drops to one knee, and presents Sword with ring on it

"Lady <<BRIDE>>, you are the most gracious and lovely one that <<GROOM>> has ever seen, for he understands the essence of thy true self. The beauty which radiates around thee can only be rivaled by the beauty which radiates from within thee. The pledge of his sword is as the pledge of his soul. It is his prowess, his fire, his passion, his strength & courage, His ability to protect, defend and care for thee. With the strength of his blade and the endurance of its steel to represent what is in his heart, take from him now, as his beloved, the ring that rests upon it, and choose him to be your own."

Bride takes ring from Sword

<<BRIDE>>: "I accept the pledge of thy blade and the eternal promise of this wedding band."

Bride takes sword from Groom and places the blade from left shoulder to right shoulder to the top of his head. The motion, as in bestowing knighthood upon him while saying:

<<BRIDE>>: "For the boy thou were,

For the man thee art,

And for the Husband thou shall be to me,

I do choose you to be mine own."

Bride returns sword

<<BRIDE>>: "If thou wilt now place this ring upon mine finger,

I shall from this day forth,

'till beyond the end of time,

Take thee to be mine own."

Bride opens hand presenting Groom with the ring

which he then places upon her finger

<<GROOM>>: "With this ring I thee wed. I take you as my friend, my lover, my wife from this day forth and into the fullness of time where we will meet and remember and love again."

"Lady <<BRIDE>>, if it is truly your desire to become one with this man: Then present unto him a symbol of thy pledge and a token of thy love."

Bride bows before Groom and presents Chalice with ring inside

"Lord <<GROOM>>, in the eyes of this woman thou art the only man in the world. Yours is the voice of sound reason and unwavering support. You the spark to the bonfire of her passions and yours are the arms in which she would have lay down to rest. The pledge of her chalice is the pledge of all that is within her, Her felicity and devotion. The place in her heart where two souls can be sheltered and nourished, that they may grow together, ever closer, and flourish as the leaves on the trees and the fruits of the vine. As the depth and bounty of her chalice foretell the richness of your future together, take from her now the band that lies there within, and do choose her as thy own."

Groom takes ring from chalice, Bride still holding chalice

<<GROOM>>: "I accept the pledge of your chalice and the eternal promise of this wedding band."

Groom pours wine into chalice then takes it from his Bride

<<GROOM>>: "For the girl thou were,

For the woman thou art

And for the wife that thee shall be to me,

I toast and drink to thee!

And do choose you to be mine own"

Groom makes toasting gesture, drinks and returns chalice to Bride

<<GROOM>>: "If thou will now place this ring upon my finger,

I shall from this day forth,

'till beyond the end of time,

Take you to be mine own."

Groom opens hand presenting Bride with the ring

which she then places upon his finger

<<BRIDE>>: "With this ring I thee wed. I take you as my friend, my lover, my husband from this day forth and into the fullness of time where we will meet and remember and love again."

Cakes and Ale

"As the Lord and Lady are separate yet one, so have your pledges made you. Drink now of one another's love and know that you will never again thirst in your heart or in mind, for what each of you lacks the other has to give and the well spring of love flows eternally for those who drink often of its waters."

Bride and Groom sip from chalice

"As food and drink nourish the body, so does love feed the soul of marriage. Feed now one another, feed forevermore the spirit of your union and be filled always."

Bride and Groom feed one another of the cake

Handfasting

"Is it also your wish today that your hands be fasted in the ways of old?"

<<BRIDE>> and <<GROOM>>: "It is."

"Remember then as your hands are fasted, these are not the ties that bind."

Cords are held aloft

"The role already taken by the song your hearts share shall be now be strengthened by the vows you take. All things of the material world eventually return to the Earth unlike the bond and the connection your spirits share which is destined to ascend to the heavens.

"May you be forever as one in the passion and fire of you

Bride and Groom's hands are bound

"You are now as your hearts have always known you to be, Husband and Wife. You may kiss the bride!"

The Broom and Sword

"Brooms are used for cleaning and sweeping. Therefore that they are used to symbolize the sweeping away the remnants of the past which no longer serve us is appropriate. The sword symbolizes the wielding of power and personal responsibility. As the Bride and Groom jump they are reminded that remaining vigilant over these aspects of the day to day shall help them to achieve the quality of life that they aspire to. <<Maid of Honor>> and <<Best Man>> will you now lay down the Sword and Broom."

Maid of Honor lays down Broom

Best Man crosses it with the sword

"Now putting the past behind you, and remembering always that the power to create the future ahead of you is your own, jump together into your common future!"

The couple jumps, kisses again, and exits to greet their guests as the circle is quietly broken down.

Source: *Adapted from a handfasting ceremony by Reverend April Gismondi of the Church of Ancient Ways. Available at http://www.handfastings.org/ceremonysuggestions.htm. Reprinted with permission.*

HANDPARTING, WICCA

Handparting, also written as hand-parting, is a Wiccan ritual that functions as a retraction of marriage vows and a public declaration that a marriage is ending. The ceremony is, therefore, akin to divorce. Prior to the rite taking place, the couple that wishes to separate may gather together with their high priest and priestess to reach a fair division of their assets plus any financial support for children resulting from their union. However it is not necessary for both partners to be present at the ritual with many ceremonies performed with only one half of a pairing being present. The details of the division will be recorded and signed by all concerned, though if either the husband or wife is unable to attend the rite then a believer of the appropriate sex may be substituted for the absent partner. Few handparting rituals encourage participants to forgive each other, as this is not a keystone of Wiccan beliefs. Indeed Wiccans believe that forgiveness is transactional and should only be proffered when it is requested.

Most pagans that end their marriages do not participate in a handparting ritual and those that do take part in such a ceremony create their own version of the ritual. Thus, there is no set procedure for a Wiccan handparting and so ceremonies vary. One idea for a handparting ritual involving both parties sees two lengths of thread tied around the hands of the husband and wife that wish to separate. These threads are then severed while someone states that the couple is released from their marriage vows. A moment of silence then follows before the threads are gathered together and released into the wind so that they may blow away. Releasing the threads is a symbolic way of showing that the universe has reclaimed the threads, has absorbed them and in turn has also absorbed the couple's marriage bonds. These bonds are then thought to transform into a different form of energy that will see the threads put to some other use, such as being collected by birds that will use the threads to help build their nests.

Handparting is often seen as an act of release, cleansing, and healing, but that is not to say that the ritual is not also associated with regret. Handpartings are also times for contemplation as the newly separated examine the reasons for the end of their marriage and the breaking of the vows that they took when marrying. This may be true particularly for couples that spoke vows that included the line "from this life to the next, including all lives to come." Couples must also ponder their legal obligations since all legal considerations should be fulfilled before any handparting ritual takes place. While handparting has no consequence in the eyes of the law, the rite does provide a framework for Wiccans looking to divorce legally.

See also: Handfasting; Jumping Over the Broom

Further Reading

Cove Witch. "Divorce/Hand-parting Ritual." Wiccan Together, November 20, 2009. Accessed June 13, 2015, at http://www.wiccantogether.com/group/circleofeclecticwiccans/forum/topics/divorce-handparting-ritual?xg_source=activity.

Llewellyn's 2005 Wicca Almanac. St. Paul, MN: Llewellyn Publications, 2005.

Rajchel, Diana. *Divorcing a Real Witch: For Pagans and the People that Used to Love Them.* Alresford, UK: Moon Books, 2014.

HIJAB, ISLAM

Hijab, the Arabic word for barrier or partition, is the Islamic principal of modesty governing both behavior and dress codes for Muslim men and women, the most obvious form of which is the head covering worn by many Muslim females that are, somewhat erroneously, often grouped together under the umbrella term hijab. Muslim women beyond the age of puberty are required to observe the rules of hijab in front of any man that they might, in theory, marry. This means that the rules of hijab do not extend to Muslim women when in the company of their close male relatives or young children. Muslim women are not expected to wear a covering when with other Muslim women though there is some debate as whether a Muslim woman should wear the garment when in company with a non-Muslim female—some Muslims fear that if a Muslim woman is uncovered in front of non-Muslim women who are ignorant of the concept of hijab then the non-Muslims may be able to describe the uncovered Muslim's appearance, thereby allowing others to imagine what the Muslim woman looks like. By describing the Muslim woman's appearance to others the non-Muslim women would infringe the modesty inherent in hijab. The rules of hijab are relaxed for women considered to be past marrying age. Muslim women observe hijab to varying degrees; those living in especially conservative areas of the world may cover their entire body, other Muslim women believe only their hair, ears, neck, and cleavage must be covered, while others do not practice any dress code at all.

As well as an ethos of modesty and a sartorial item, the word hijab can also be used to refer to a curtain or screen hung up between a group of Muslim men and women that allows the two parties to talk to each other without changing their attire. However this practice was more common in the earliest days of Islam.

The Islamic holy book, the Qur'an, does not refer to any specific rules pertaining to modest dress and does not employ the word hijab to describe any kind of head covering. Rather the book sets out general rules of modesty, saying in 24:30 that both Muslim men and women should "lower their gaze and guard their modesty," while 24:31 states that Muslim women should not "display their beauty and ornaments" and should "draw their veils over their bosoms and not display their beauty except to their husbands." These passages from the Qur'an are open to a variety of interpretations. In the most basic terms the phrase "guard their modesty" is taken to mean that Muslim men and women should conceal their genitals and that Muslim women should also conceal their chests hence the line instructing women to "draw their veils over their bosoms." However, some Islamic authorities interpret this command in a more detailed way and employ *Hadith,* the recorded sayings of the Prophet Muhammad, to support their analyses. Similarly, the use of the word "ornaments" is also open to a range of interpretations with some Islamic scholars taking it to mean body parts while others believe the word is meant to refer to fine clothes and ornamental jewelry. Elsewhere in the Qur'an, a verse directed at all Muslim women (33:59), states "O Prophet! Tell thy wives and daughters, and the believing women, that they should cast their outer garments over their persons (when abroad)." However this too is open to interpretation as there is no definitive consensus on what the phrase "outer garments" refers to.

There are several different styles of covering worn by Muslim women, which tend, in the West to be referred to under the catchall term hijab, though in the West the word hijab is also taken to mean the headscarf worn by some Muslim women. However this scarf is more precisely called a *khimaar* or *khimar*, which, unlike hijab, is referred to in the Qur'an. A khimaar is worn when a Muslim woman is outside of her home and consists of one or two pieces of fabric that allows the woman to cover her neck, ears, and hair. Muslim women wore the khimaar during the time of Muhammad (around the sixth century) though during this time the garment was worn tied behind thereby leaving exposed women's necks and upper torso. The majority of Muslim scholars agree that the khimaar is compulsory dress for Muslim women. Another type of covering favored by particularly conservative Muslim authorities is the *muhaajaba*, a long, loose, densely woven garment that extends to cover completely everything except a woman's hands, face, and feet. Other Muslim women wear a layer that conceals all of their body except for their eyes, which may be covered by a detachable mesh veil. This body and face-covering garment is called a *niqab*. An even more comprehensively concealing garment that covers the entire body and face including the eyes, which are concealed by a mesh screen, is called a *burqa* or *burka*. Some Muslims strongly oppose the wearing of burqas arguing that if Allah had wanted women to cover their entire body then the Qur'an would not have needed to instruct males to lower their gaze. Some Muslims also question whether such all-covering garments have a place in modern society and whether the garments are actually a symbol of female oppression rather than modesty. Several European countries have attempted to ban women from wearing the niqab and burqa. For instance, in 2010 the French parliament approved a controversial bill prohibiting the wearing of the burqa and niqab in public with a similar ban introduced in Belgium in 2011. Additionally, in 2016, a number of French towns also temporarily banned Islamic women's swimwear—the so-called "burkini"—from public beaches amid much controversy. Other garments often grouped together under the term hijab are the *jilbab*, a tailored garment resembling a long-line jacket with buttons up the front, and the *al-amira*, a two-piece veil consisting of a close-fitting cap made from polyester or cotton, and a tubular scarf.

Some types of Muslim women's coverings are regional. For instance, the *abaya*, which, like the jilbab, is an outer-garment akin to a long, flowing dress, is particularly worn in the Najd region of central Saudi Arabia, and does not have any buttons but rather is tied at the side. Both the abaya and the jilbab styles come in a variety of colorways and can be quite elaborately decorated though many Muslims feel jilbabs and abayas should be black in color as a sign of piety and modesty. In addition, the *shayla*, which is predominantly worn in the Gulf region, is a long oblong scarf that is wrapped around the head and then pinned to the shoulders while in Iran and parts of Turkey many women wear a full-body cloak called the *chador* that is worn with a headscarf underneath. Additionally the burqa, though Pakistani in origin, is now especially associated with Afghanistan. Similar to the burqa are the *paranja* and the *chadari*, which, like the burqa, originate in Central Asia and entirely cover their wearers. Coverings worn in Malaysia and Indonesia include the Malaysian *selendang*, a wrap that can be draped around the shoulders or over the head, and the *kerudung*, a headscarf worn in both Malaysia and Indonesia. The *batula*, a face covering worn by women usually aged over 50 years in Qatar, the United Arab Emirates, and Oman is worn very rarely and has all but died out among younger generations.

Wearing any kind of covering is often, though not always, a matter of choice for Muslim women, especially for those living in the West. Some Muslim women wear the hijab out of religious or cultural obligations for they feel that wearing a covering allows them to demonstrate their commitment to their faith, as a way of deepening their spirituality, or as a way to express their ethnicity to the wider world. In addition many Muslim women feel comfortable wearing some sort of covering as they feel such attire prevents men from viewing them as sexual objects and allows them to be evaluated on their personality and intelligence rather than their physical appearance. Many Muslim women living in the West are trying to find a balance between adhering to their religious commitments and integrating into society at large. Such integration is seen in the manufacture of headscarves patterned with Barbie doll images or leopard prints as well as artisan hijab pins for sale on websites such as Etsy. Hijabs designed specifically for use during sporting activity are also available to buy though there are continuing controversies over whether it is suitable for women to wear any type of hijab while playing sports.

See also: *Shabka*; Training Bra

Further Reading

Arabs in America. "What Is the Hijab and Why Do Women Wear It?" Accessed April 3, 2015, at http://arabsinamerica.unc.edu/identity/veiling/hijab/.

BBC. "Hijab," BBC: Religion. September 3, 2009. Accessed April 3, 2015, at http://www.bbc.co.uk/religion/religions/islam/beliefs/hijab_1.shtml.

BBC. "In Graphics: Muslim Veils." BBC News. Accessed April 3, 2015, at http://news.bbc.co.uk/1/shared/spl/hi/pop_ups/05/europe_muslim_veils/html/1.stm.

Mitchell, Claudia A., and Jacqueline Reid-Walsh. *Girl Culture: An Encyclopedia*. Volume 1. Westport, CT: Greenwood Press, 2007.

Willsher, Kim. "France's Burqa Ban Upheld by Human Rights Court," *The Guardian*, July 1, 2014. Accessed April 3, 2015, at http://www.theguardian.com/world/2014/jul/01/france-burqa-ban-upheld-human-rights-court.

HIJRA, INDIAN SUB-CONTINENT

The hijra population living on the Indian sub-continent is a group of people that are classed as neither male nor female but as both a third gender and third sex. While some members of the hijra population are born hermaphrodite, most are not. By Western standards it is difficult to categorize the hijra. Western academics have equated them to homosexuals, transsexuals, and heterosexual cross-dressers while the Indian National AIDS Control Organization (NACO) proposes four different types of hijra: transsexuals, transvestites, hermaphrodites, and *Satia Kothi*, or drag queens. In the West, however, hijras are considered cross-dressers mainly because they tend to be biological males that dress as females. However linguistic distinctions can be made between hijra that have the body of a male and are known as *hijras* and those that have a female body and are known as *hijrin*. Hijra tend to be located in India (especially the north of the country), Pakistan, Nepal, and Bangladesh. In India hijras live together in marginalized communities called *hijra gharanas* in major cities such as Mumbai and Bombay. Here, the inhabitants are divided into separate types: those waiting to be voluntarily castrated are known as *akwa* while those that have already been voluntarily castrated are called *nirwaan*. Community members abide by their own rules, regulations, and customs. People belonging to the hijra population face social ostracism, police harassment, and discrimination. There is no official census data on the number of hijra so it is difficult to say just how many hijra exist. However wide-ranging estimates put the number at between 500,000 and 5 million.

The languages of India allow the possibility of a third gender. For example the ancient language Sanskrit includes the word *napunsaka* while Urdu contains the word *namard*. Both words cover groups of people that in English might be termed transgender, though the Indian words are also applied to homosexuals, transsexuals, and transvestites. Traditionally, the hijra population is associated with Hinduism and most particularly with the goddess Bahuchara Mata who according to folklore cut off her breasts and those of her sisters and forced a male bandit to dress and act as a woman in order to break the curse of impotency. Bahuchara Mata has a temple in Gujurat that is considered a site of pilgrimage by many hijras. However hijras have a place in Muslim tradition too for hijras traditionally served as eunuchs to Muslim rulers. As a result of this close association between hijras and Islam, many hijras have converted to Islam and many hijras are buried after death rather than cremated, which is in keeping with Islamic tradition. However many within the hijra community claim that religious figures have refused to complete funerals on learning that the dead person was a hijra. For this reason many families try to conceal the fact that the deceased was a hijra, though this is difficult if the hijra had undergone castration or breast enlargement because the deception will be discovered during the ritual washing of the corpse. However today many Hindus and Muslims still believe that hijras are blessed with the power to give good or bad luck. For this reason hijras are often asked to bless celebratory occasions such as marriages and births. Indeed it is considered unlucky to refuse a hijra money or a gift. To a certain extent hijras are still seen as conduits of the feminine divine but this reverence does not normally outweigh the discrimination and prejudice that hijras tend to experience.

To become a hijra, a man may choose to undergo a *nirwaan* or *nirvan* castration ceremony after which he will be irreversibly third gendered. However not all hijras are castrated and the procedure is entirely voluntary. When a male wishes to become a hijra he leaves his family and joins a hijra community where he is tutored by a spiritual master called a *guru* alongside five other *chelas*, or disciples, in the traditions of the hijra. In particular the chelas are taught how to earn money by performing risqué song-and-dance routines called *badhai*, which they are hired to perform at weddings and births. Such bawdy, sexually suggestive entertainment is believed to confer fertility on newlyweds, though the routines are rapidly falling out of fashion and are often now considered lewd and offensive. The tradition continues however, partly because families fear being "cursed" by the hijras if they turn down their performances, and the hijras often receive gifts of money, clothes, and food as rewards for their performances.

Once a man decides he wishes to become a hijra, he undergoes an initiation ceremony, called a *reet*, which has been likened to the Hindu sacred thread ceremony, and is performed by the guru. During the reet the initiate is told the rules and regulations of his community. These include how the hijra must walk so that his *pallu* (the loose end of a sari) does not touch anybody else as he moves and how to serve a glass of water to a visitor by carrying the glass balanced on palms that are joined together.

Once part of the hijra community, the male assumes a female name, wears feminine attire including brightly colored saris and make-up, adopts stereotypically feminine body-language, and is referred to by other hijras using feminine pronouns. (*See* Plate 10.) Many hijras opt for breast augmentation to look more like a woman and some also undergo hormone treatment. A new hijra may also participate in sexual activity with other males, usually by being the passive recipient of anal penetration. Though this anal intercourse is often driven by personal desire it can also act as training for acts of male prostitution that new hijras may perform to earn money for their new community. There have also been reports of newly initiated hijras being forced to have sex with men that have paid money to the hijra's guru. As a result of prostitution and limited access to healthcare (some hijras have reported that doctors have refused to treat them), the HIV rate for hijras living in Mumbai runs at 18 percent, which is much higher than the rate for the Mumbai population in general which is 0.3 percent. Similarly, hijras living in Dhaka, the capital of Bangladesh, have the highest rate of active syphilis (10.4 percent) among all of the populations considered most at risk of catching the disease.

To counter such issues, some hijras have established support groups aimed at fighting for hijra rights and helping hijras find alternative employment and housing. Hijra rights groups have also called for an end to Section 337 of India's Penal Code, which makes homosexual acts illegal, and have campaigned for hijras that are anatomically male to be classed as women. In recent years things have changed positively for some hijras. For instance in the Indian state of Tamil Nadu, hijras have been re-homed and in the state of Madhya Pradesh hijras have run for political office and won. Additionally, in 2014 the Indian Supreme Court ruled that hijras should be recognized on official documents under a separate classification of "third gender." This was in line with changes in the law in other countries, notably Nepal, Pakistan, and Bangladesh. India's re-categorization of hijras means that there are now quotas of government jobs for hijras as well as college places.

See also: *Devadasi* System (Volume 1); Female Genital Cutting; Initiation by Semen Transferal; Phallus Festivals (Volume 1); *Upanayana*: Sacred Thread Rite (Volume 1); Urethral Subincision

Further Reading

Bolich, G. G. *Conversing on Gender*. Raleigh, NC: Psyche's Press, 2007.
Bolich, G. G. *Transgender Realities: An Introduction to Gender Variant People and the Judgments About Them*. Raleigh, NC: Psyche's Press, 2008.
Debjani11. *Bahuchara Mata and the Hijras*. Accessed May 31, 2015, at https://debjani11.wordpress.com/bahuchara-mata-and-the-hijras/.
Khaleeli, Homa. "Hijra: India's Third Gender Claims Its Place in Law," *The Guardian*, April 16, 2014. Accessed May 31, 2015, at http://www.theguardian.com/society/2014/apr/16/india-third-gender-claims-place-in-law.
Khan, Sharful Islam, Mohammed Iftekher Hussain, Shaila Parveen, Mahbubul Bhuiyan, Gourab Islam, Sarker Gorkey, Arafat Golam Faruk, Mahmud Shohael, and Sikder Joya. "Living on the Extreme Margin: Social Exclusion of the Transgender Population (Hijra) in Bangladesh," *Journal of Health, Population and Nutrition, Special Issue: Social Exclusion: Inaugural Issue of the Gender Health and Human Rights Section*, 27(4), August 2009, 441–451.
Raode, Vaishali. "Lakshmi's Story." Words Without Borders. Accessed May 31, 2015, at http://wordswithoutborders.org/article/lakshmis-story.

HINDU WEDDING CEREMONY, HINDUISM

Marriage is one of the most important *sanskaras*, or rites of passage, in Hindu culture. The rites performed at a Hindu wedding are known as *Vivah Sanskar*. Marriage is important to Hindus as it marks the transition from the first stage of life, which is focused on education and learning, to the second stage of life, *Grihistha Ashrama*, when all attention is focused on establishing a home and family. Hindus consider marriage to be of the utmost moral and ethical importance as the sacrament is thought to join the husband and wife to the extent that their souls conjoin. The Hindu wedding ceremony is based on the marriage of Surya, the daughter of Savita (The Sun) to Ashwinikumar, for according to the Hindu scripture the *Rig-Veda*, Savita gave Surya to Ashwinikumar after he won a chariot race. A Hindu wedding ceremony sees two people that are felt to be compatible create a lifelong relationship having had the obligations and responsibilities of marriage explained to them.

Hindu wedding ceremonies may take many hours to complete and details of the ceremony vary depending on where the wedding is taking place. However there are several chief stages to the ceremony. On the day of the wedding a ceremony called *Mangal Snan*, meaning auspicious bath, takes place. This sees the bride and groom receive markings on their skin made from sandalwood and turmeric and the bride may also have *mehndi* applied to her skin. Sometimes the bride's maternal uncle will also give his niece a set of bangles that represent the best wishes of her maternal relations. Traditionally these are made from ivory but now plastic bangles are usually given instead. It is the custom that the bride will wear the bangles for several months after she marries and then distribute them among her unmarried friends so that they too will soon wed.

The wedding ceremony begins with entreaties to Lord Ganesh to bless the occasion and make the ceremony run smoothly. Blessings are also sought from the couple's elders and ancestors and prayers are said for the day to be a lucky day for a wedding ceremony to take place. The first stage of the ceremony is the *Jayamaala*, meaning garlands, which sees the bride's parents greet the bridegroom and his family at the boundary of the wedding venue. The groom, his *Barat* (the groom's singing and dancing procession) and the groom's family arrive at the wedding venue and are welcomed by the bride's family. As a welcoming gesture the bride's family presents everyone with sweets symbolizing joys to come and red powder called *kum-kum* is then daubed on the foreheads of the groom's party. Next, the families are introduced to each other officially. This is taken to be the beginning of the families' relationship with each other. The next part of the Jayamalla stage sees the bride and bridegroom exchange the garlands that give the stage its name. Once the garlands have been swapped the couple assert that they accept each other willingly and are united like water. The next stage of the ceremony, *Madhu-parka*, sees the bridegroom led to an altar called the *mandap*, where he is seated and offered a drink of yoghurt, honey, and sugar mixed with ghee and milk. Meanwhile, the bride is brought to the mandap by her maternal uncle, along with her bridesmaids. A lucky cloth called an *antarpat* separates the bride and groom symbolizing that the couple live as separate entities before the marriage. The next stages of the wedding are the *Gau Daan* and *Kanya Pratigrahan*. Gau Daan (from *gau* meaning cow and *daan* meaning donate) involves the exchange of gifts such as ornaments and clothes, while the bridegroom's mother (or sometimes the groom) gives the bride a gold, beaded necklace called a *mangala sootra* (or *mangalsutra*) that is traditionally worn by married Hindu women. The necklace is symbolic of luck, friendship, and love and takes the form of a red thread decorated with black and gold beads. The name *mangala sootra* means auspicious thread— *mangal* means auspicious and *sootra* means thread. A Hindu wife will only take off her mangal sootra on the death of her husband.

The Kanya Pratigrahan sees the father of the bride declare that his daughter accepts the groom as her husband and asks that the groom's family to accept his daughter in return. The name Kanya Pratigrahan derives from *Kanya*, which translates as the daughter, and *Pratigrahan*, which means a swap with responsiveness on both sides. Hindu parents view the giving away of their daughter as the noblest act they can perform as parents. In some Hindu wedding ceremonies the bride's mother will pour sacred water on to the hands of the bride's father. This water then flows on to the groom's hands and then on the bride's hands in order to symbolize the continuous nature of life, the debt that is owed to ancestors, and the need to establish future generations.

Next, a holy fire is lit and the priest, known as a *Purohit*, exclaims the sacred mantras of Hinduism in Sanskrit. This stage of the ceremony, which is called *Vivaha-homa*, also sees the repeated chanting of the phrase "*Id na mama*," which means "it is not for me," as offerings are made. The repeated saying of this mantra is intended to instill the virtue of selflessness that Hindus consider essential to the successful rearing of a family. Following Vivaha-homa is the *Paanigrahan*, which is the ceremony of the vows. During this stage the groom holds his bride's hand and attests that he clasps her hand in the spirit of Dharma, the religious and moral law of Hinduism, and that they are, therefore, now husband and wife. (*See* Plate 11.) The bride and groom may then tie each other's wrists with a *Sutrabandhanam*, or sacred thread.

The next stage of the wedding is called *Shilarohan*, which refers to the bride climbing over a rock. This stage demonstrates the steadfastness of the bride and her willingness to conquer all obstacles in order that her marriage is successful. During this stage the bride and groom walk around the holy fire four times. The bride leads three of these walks and the groom leads the bride on the fourth occasion. This is to show that he too must also be determined to see his marriage work. Walking around the fire fulfills the religious aspect of the wedding ceremony. The bride and groom then hold hands on to which the bride's brother, or brothers, pours barley, which is also offered to the sacred fire. The barley represents the couple's willingness to unite in order to benefit their community. The groom then parts his wife's hair and marks her parting with *sindoor*, a vermillion cosmetic made from cinnabar, a naturally occurring form of mercury sulfide, together with turmeric and lime. The sindoor is the identifying mark of Hindu wives. This ritual marking of the sindoor, called *sumangali kriya*, meaning auspicious ceremony, is very important as the sindoor marks the bride out as a married woman and is also though to protect the bride from evil. The bride then prays for her husband's longevity and applies *chandan tilak* to his forehead. This is a mark made from ash from a sacred fire, sandalwood paste, turmeric, cow dung, clay, charcoal, or red lead and usually seen as a good luck symbol.

The legal part of a Hindu wedding is called the *Sapta-Padi* or *Saptpadi*. This stage involves the bride and groom taking seven steps together while reciting a prayer with each pace. These steps represent the seven vows that the couple exchanges: the first step symbolizes that the couple will support and provide for each other, the second represents physical and mental strength, the third wealth, the fourth wisdom, the fifth offspring, the sixth wellbeing, and the seventh friendship. Sometimes, instead of the couple walking together, the bride will touch seven nuts or stones with her right toe. After the couple has taken the seven steps the bride stands or sits on the groom's left-hand side to demonstrate that she is now part of the groom's family. In her future life the bride will always sit on her husband's left.

The completion of the seven steps also sees the bride's sister or mother tie a symbolic knot in a length of material, such as a sari or shawl, to symbolize the permanent union of the two individuals. This tying of the knot is known as *gathbandhan* and is followed by the couple's exchange of wedding rings. Next, the newlyweds look at the Sun and ask that it bless them with the gift of creativity then they look toward the Pole Star and ask that they be as unfaltering as the star. The next stage, *Ashirvada*, meaning blessings, sees the couple receive blessings from their elders and from the priest that their marriage should be lengthy and successful. Having been declared husband and wife, the couple bows to all their guests and moves away from the mandap while the guests shower them with flower petals.

Two common misconceptions about Hindu marriage are that Hindus allow forced marriages and that Hinduism condones child marriage. While it is true that many Hindu marriages are arranged, Hindu scriptures forbid force or coercion in marriage. To this end, any arranged Hindu marriages must be based on the agreement of all concerned, most especially the bride and groom. In the past, Hinduism forbade child marriages but then as a result of socio-economic and political changes child marriages and the associated tradition of giving a dowry were introduced. However, reformists continually seek to stamp out this custom, and child marriages are now outlawed in India, though there continue to be reports of child marriages occurring.

See also: *Devadasi* System (Volume 1); Diwali and Kali Pooja; *Hijra*; *Kumari* and *Deuki* (Volume 1); *Mehndi*; Mundan Ceremony (Volume 1); Muslim Wedding Ceremony; Vrindavan: The City of Widows (Volume 3)

Further Reading

Bhalla, Prem P. *Hindu Rites, Rituals, Customs and Traditions*. New Delhi, India: Hindoology Books, 2009.

Hare Krishna Temple Portal. "Tilak-Tilaka: Symbol on Forehead or Between Eyebrows." Accessed June 18, 2015, at http://www.harekrsna.de/Tilak.htm

Hindu Wedding Information. Accessed June 18, 2015, at http://www.hinduwedding.info/marriage-ceremony.html.

Prinja, Nawal K. "Weddings." BBC: Religion. August 24, 2009. Accessed June 18, 2015, at http://www.bbc.co.uk/religion/religions/hinduism/ritesrituals/weddings.shtml.

HMONG NAMES, LAOS, MYANMAR, VIETNAM, CAMBODIA, AND THAILAND

The Hmong (pronounced with a silent "H"), also known as the Miao, are a cultural group originating in China and spread throughout Laos, Vietnam, Cambodia, Thailand, and Myanmar (formerly Burma). After the Vietnam War ended in 1975, a significant number of Hmong people settled in the United States. According to the 2010 census, there were 245,807 Hmong people residing in the United States with most living in California and Minnesota. There are also Hmong immigrant populations in France, Germany, and Australia.

The Hmong are divided into 18 clans determined by ancestry and they have large, extended families. The Hmong place great importance on customs and traditional cultural values and keep alive a range of traditional ceremonies in order to remember their ancestors. The group is usually thought to have originated in southwest China around 2500 BCE but left there after undergoing persecution by the Qing dynasty (1644–1912). In the face of such oppression the Hmong fled China and settled across Southeast Asia—this was particularly the case during the early 19th century. However it was while living in China that the Hmong developed a culture based upon concepts of family and ancestor worship that is extremely child-centric. The focus on children and birth occurs as a result of the Hmong belief that every child born is a reincarnated soul, hence when a baby is born he or she is referred to as *Mus Thawj thiab*, meaning, "go become again." Further, if a baby dies within three days of birth he or she does not receive funeral rites, as the baby is not thought to have lived long enough to gain a soul of its own. Once a baby reaches three days old a shaman calls upon a soul to be reincarnated within the child and the baby's dead ancestors are evoked to unite with the child's living family in blessing and protecting the new baby. In addition, the baby is given a gift of a silver necklace that is said to be imbued with the power to prevent the baby's soul from drifting. Another facet of the Hmong's family-orientated culture includes the belief that women should be known by her husband's name after marriage, which usually occurs when a female is between 14 and 18 years of age. The Hmong view this loss of name as signifying that the woman has been absorbed into her husband's family as a potential mother who will help ensure the continuance of her husband's clan. Because the Hmong are a patrilineal society that sees lineage traced through the male line, they do not see the loss of a woman's name as a loss of identity but rather as a beneficial act that reinforces the idea of the family and stresses the importance of family, ancestry, and spirituality.

Each Hmong person has a last name that reveals the clan to which he or she belongs. A married Hmong woman keeps her own clan name, but neither her clan name nor the woman's first name is used once she is married. This is because married Hmong women are considered to belong to their husband's household, so they are referred to only by their husbands' names once they are wed. The Hmong do not refer to each other by their first name but rather they address one another by their kinship title, such as aunt, brother, uncle, sister. When a woman goes through a major life event such as marriage or childbirth her name alters to reflect her new position within the family (a woman's name can also change to signify upsetting events in her life). Therefore over her lifetime a Hmong woman can expect to change names on at least three occasions until, eventually, her original name is lost to history. In Hmong society, female first names are considered

> ### China's Dead Hair Wigs
>
> Girls and young women belonging to China's Long-Horn Miao minority group wear headdresses made from the hair of their ancestors. Instead of discarding their hair when it is combed, women save the resultant loose strands and add it to collections of their spent hair. This hair is then used to make spectacular horn-shaped headdresses that are woven around special frames. The headdresses are then worn on special occasions. The wigs are passed down from mothers to daughters meaning that the headdresses ultimately include the hair from generations of female ancestors dating back hundreds of years. The wigs are dyed and cared for to keep them shiny and healthy-looking.

insignificant, as they do not help maintain the family unit. Thus replacing a female's first name with a kinship term substantiates her role within her family and reveals the part she has played in family-forming events.

This naming convention reveals the importance that the Hmong place on social structure and reveals a woman's lowly place in Hmong society, which is extremely patriarchal. That Hmong society is a patriarchal hierarchy, meaning that males hold all the highest social positions, is further revealed by the fact that daughters are not truly considered to be members of the clan into which they were born. Instead daughters are trained to be wives and mothers by their husband's clan. For Hmong women the three most important stages of life are birth, marriage, and childbirth. As each of these is an event that impacts her husband's family and are, therefore, occasions worthy of celebration, the woman is given of a new name by way of marking her role in the event. The fact that all major family events are marked by changes of name reveals the great importance the Hmong place upon kinship. The system of name modification begins at birth for when a female is born she is given the name of her family's clan as well as her own first name. Then, when the female marries she is considered to have joined her husband's clan, a change that is reflected in the name used to refer to the woman. This all helps to show that she has become part of another clan. Some family members may also refer to the new wife by kinship terms such as daughter-in-law or sister-in-law, in order to show the woman's role within her new family. When a Hmong woman has a baby her name changes to reflect her relationship with her child. Therefore the woman now takes on the name of her child in a process called teknonymy. This renaming is considered a prestigious event and solidifies the mother's place within her family. Over the course of time the name that had been given to a woman when she was born is forgotten—if the woman becomes a grandmother, for example, many decades will have passed during which her name will have changed several times. This makes it unlikely that family members will remember the woman's birth name.

Today, an increasing number of Hmong immigrants outside of Southeast Asia are abandoning the animist beliefs of their ancestors and are turning to Christianity. This is partly because as immigrants the Hmong felt it incumbent upon them to adapt to Western ways of life. However such cultural modification has led to the formation of a split between generations. While older Hmong migrants tend to try and preserve their traditions, including customs associated with marriage and childbirth, younger members of the Hmong are more assimilated into Western culture and even change their names to seem more in tune with non-Hmong society. Thus it could be that in the near future that the custom of Hmong women losing their names will die out among the Hmong living in the West. However the custom is not in danger in Southeast Asia as the practice of name modification continues to spread across China and the other Asian countries that are home to Hmong populations.

See also: Government-Approved Names (Volume 1); Name Days and *Slava* (Volume 1); Wik-Mungkan Naming Ritual (Volume 1)

Further Reading

Bankston III, Carl L. "Hmong Americans." Countries and Their Cultures. Accessed December 14, 2014, at http://www.everyculture.com/multi/Ha-La/Hmong-Americans.html.

Galvan, Javier A., ed. *They Do What? A Cultural Encyclopedia of Extraordinary and Exotic Customs from around the World*. Santa Barbara, CA: ABC-CLIO, 2014.

Stratis Health. "Hmong in Minnesota." Accessed December 14, 2014, at http://www.culturecareconnection.org/matters/diversity/hmong.html.

Wilson Owens, Christine. "Hmong Cultural Profile." EthnoMed, May 1, 2007. Accessed May 28, 2016, at https://ethnomed.org/culture/hmong/hmong-cultural-profile.

HORA, EASTERN EUROPE, AND *HORAH,* JUDAISM

The *horah* (or *hora*) is a folk dance symbolizing happiness that is traditionally danced at Jewish weddings and other celebrations such as bar mitzvahs. The dance is normally danced to the tune "Hava Nagila" and is considered the first Israeli folk dance.

The horah was introduced to Israel by Romanian Jewish dancer Baruch Agadati in 1924 when he choreograph a show performed by the Ohel Theater Company that toured settlements in the Jezreel Valley. The dance was at that time known as Hora Agadati and was an instant success, finding favor with *halutz* (pioneer) settlers. Halutz settlers liked the horah mainly because the social, circular dance symbolized equality and solidarity and also because the dance did not need men to be partnered by women. This was good as there was a shortage of women. The Hora Agadati was inspired by the hora, also referred to as horo, kola, oro or other variations, a type of circle dance that originated in the Balkan region of Eastern Europe but that is most closely associated with Romania. Today the Jewish horah is performed in Israel and among the Jewish diaspora worldwide, particularly in North America and Europe.

To dance the horah everybody present forms a circle and steps forward toward the right with their left foot. Next everybody steps forward with the right foot to match the previous action. Dancers then bring their left foot backward followed by the right foot. As these steps are being performed the dancers circle together to the right. When the dance is being performed by a lot of people it is necessary for the dancers to create several concentric circles rather than one extremely large circle. The song "Hora," performed by Avi Toledano, was the Israeli entry in the 1982 Eurovision Song Contest, an annual televised international singing competition, that was based on the horah. The song placed second overall.

The hora, which inspired the Jewish horah, is also a circle dance. In Romania, the dance is traditionally performed at weddings and other ceremonial events such as funerals. In the Romanian hora, of which there are many variations, dancers' hands are generally joined at shoulder height and kept slightly forward. The dancers then form a closed circle that moves counterclockwise, except in some parts of Banat and north Oltenia, where the dance is performed in an open circle with the dance leader leading the dancers in the formation of a spiral. To dance the hora, each dancer follows a series of three steps forward and then one step backward. The hora is typically accompanied by musicians playing instruments including the cimbalom, accordion, violin, viola, double bass, saxophone, trumpet, and pan pipes.

In Bulgaria, the term horo is used generically to describe a number of dances in which performers join together through linked hands. It is traditional to dance one of the many different types of horo at Bulgarian weddings, either in a circle or in a curving line formation. The steps performed in the horo vary greatly and do not necessarily follow the pattern of three steps forward and one step backward rather dancers may take eight steps forward and six steps backward depending on the type of horo being performed. Such is the variation in horo dances that it has been estimated that there are around one hundred different types of horo in Bulgaria. Though the younger generation of Bulgarians are on the whole more interested in Western European and American pop music, it is the case that virtually all Bulgarians can dance some sort of horo.

In Macedonia, the hora is known by the name oro. The oro is danced at all types of celebrations, including weddings, baptisms, saints' name days, national holidays, religious feast days, graduations, and birthdays. During the oro everybody present holds hands and as with other hora-type dances, performers take a number of steps forward and then one step backward. The dancers move in a circle in a counterclockwise direction as they step with the speed of dance gradually increasing all the while.

See also: Bulgarian Weddings; Cajun Weddings; Jewish Wedding Customs; *Lindo*; Money Dance; Name Days and *Slava* (Volume 1); *Schuhplattler* and *Ländler*

Further Reading

Eliznik. "Romanian Hora." Accessed November 25, 2015, at http://www.eliznik.org.uk/RomaniaDance/hora.htm.

Evans, Thammy, and Rudolf Abraham. *Macedonia*. Fifth edition. Chalfont St. Peter, UK: Bradt Travel Guides Ltd., 2015.

MacDermott, Mercia. *Bulgarian Folk Customs*. London: Jessica Kingsley Publishers Ltd., 1998.
Roginsky, Dina. "The 1910s and 1920s: Dances of the Jewish Pioneers," in Raphael Patai and Bar-Itzhak, eds., *Encyclopedia of Jewish Folklore and Traditions*. Volumes 1–2, 164. London: Routledge, 2013.
Sabra Entertainment. "Hora Dance." The Sabras—Hora Band—Israeli Jewish Wedding Band. Accessed November 25, 2015, at http://www.horaband.com/Hora_Dance.html.

HORSESHOES, INTERNATIONAL

Horseshoes are often regarded as good luck talismans and are also thought to deter evil. For this reason horseshoes are frequently depicted on greetings cards and used as decoration on festive occasions, particularly weddings. The belief that horseshoes are lucky exists internationally from Britain and North America, where they are associated with marriages, to Assyria, where they can be found carved into entrances to tombs. In Turkey and Greece, horseshoes are thought to ward off the evil eye.

The reason for the belief in horseshoes as good luck amulets is not known for sure. One theory is that they are considered lucky because they resemble the crescent shape that was worshipped by people that worshipped the moon while another suggestion is that horseshoes are lucky because they are made from iron, a metal that many people consider to be magical and to be able to protect against evil. According to Christian folklore, Saint Dunstan (circa 909–988) used a horseshoe to repel the devil, and in Britain during medieval times horseshoes were nailed to the beds of ill people in order to drive out sickness. During this time in England, horseshoes were also believed to counteract witchcraft. For this reason horseshoes were often attached to the inner doors of houses and inns as secret protectors against evil and also to make sure that the luck stayed inside the building. Today in England, horseshoes are usually nailed to the outside of buildings or above doors as open deterrents against evil. It is also traditional for British sailors to nail horseshoes to the masts of their ships to avert disaster. As late as the start of

---

Saint Dunstan and the Devil

Saint Dunstan was an abbot, bishop, and archbishop who worked to restore monastic life in England. Saint Dunstan was also described as an artist, writer, and key minister of state to several English kings. Over time, Saint Dunstan became famous for using cunning to defeat the devil. One story tells how the saint, then working as a blacksmith, nailed a horseshoe to the devil's hoof when he was asked to re-shoe the devil's horse. Having the horseshoe nailed to his hoof caused the devil much pain so Dunstan agreed to remove the horseshoe and, thereby, relieve the devil's pain only on condition that the devil promised never to enter a place where a horseshoe hung above the door.

the 20th century, horseshoes would be wrapped in red cloth and nailed above beds to prevent sleepers from having nightmares.

There is some disagreement as to how a horseshoe should be displayed as a lucky object. Some people believe that the U-shaped objects should be hung with the opening nearest the ground as this is said to allow good fortune to flow around. This positioning also means that the horseshoe looks like magnet and therefore is able to attract good luck. However nowadays most people display horseshoes so that the opening of the shoe is uppermost. This position is said to ensure that the luck does not fall out of the shoe via the opening and also means that the devil is contained within the shoe. A third variation sees the horseshoe placed on its side so that it resembles the letter C. This is considered lucky as the letter C represents Christ and is said to confer Christ's blessings on a building and those within.

Many British and North American brides choose to carry some form of horseshoe on their wedding day, often attached to their bridal bouquet, while Irish brides sometimes have a small horseshoe sewn into the hem of their wedding dress. Meanwhile wedding cakes often display a horseshoe motif in their decoration and the confetti thrown over the bride and groom when they leave their wedding venue is often tissue paper cut to resemble mini horseshoes.

See also: Birthday Cards (Volume 1); British Wedding Traditions; Dream Catcher (Volume 1); Warding Off the Evil Eye (Volume 1); Wedding Cake; Wedding Dress and Wedding Ring

Further Reading
Monger, George P. *Marriage Customs of the World: From Henna to Honeymoons*. Santa Barbara, CA: ABC-CLIO, 2004.
Simpson, Jacqueline, and Steve Roud. *Oxford Dictionary of English Folklore*. Oxford, UK: Oxford University Press, 2000.
Webster, Richard. *The Encyclopedia of Superstitions*. Woodbury, MN: Llewellyn Publications, 2008.

HUMAN TOOTH SHARPENING, INDONESIA AND AFRICA

Tooth sharpening is the practice of deliberately changing the shape of human teeth so that they become more pointy. This practice is performed for various reasons in Africa and Indonesia as well as elsewhere. For instance tooth sharpening is a traditional beautification ritual experienced by women belonging to the Mentawai tribe living on the Indonesian island of Sumatra as well as young boys belonging to the Kiv people of northeastern Nigeria. However elsewhere in Nigeria the Ibo people use tooth sharpening as a way to show that a female has sexually matured as young Ibo women are forbidden from having children until their teeth have been sharpened. Other African peoples that practice tooth sharpening include the Dinka tribe of Sudan, the Efe and Mbuti living in the Democratic Republic of Congo, and the Dogon in Mali. Tribes living in the hills of Vietnam also practice tooth sharpening.

The reasons behind tooth sharpening are not fully understood. Early anthropologists suggested that tooth sharpening was performed to assist in the cannibalistic eating of human flesh. However this hypothesis has been largely discredited. Today it is believed that tooth sharpening is performed for purely aesthetic reasons either because a tribe finds pointy teeth attractive or because men with sharp teeth are thought to be fiercer warriors. Even those who undergo the painful procedure are not especially sure why they do so, though it has been proposed that those who experience tooth sharpening understand that the pain they feel during the sharpening is enjoyed by spectators. Tribal members that watch as tooth sharpening occurs see that the person is experiencing great pain and feel flattered that someone would undergo such agony in order to become more aesthetically pleasing for their benefit.

In Africa, tooth sharpening is carried out for a number of reasons. For instance, the Dogon living in Mali shape their front teeth into sharp points in order that their teeth look like the teeth of a comb suggestive of a weaving loom. This is important as the Dogon see the sharpened teeth as a visual metaphor for a tool with which to weave the world. Meanwhile, the Makonde people of Tanzania deliberately chip their teeth so that each front tooth is level in the middle with pointed ends to demonstrate that someone has gone through the tribe's initiation ritual thereby gaining the status of an adult member of the tribe. However Christianity, education, and social change mean that the Makonde custom of tooth modification is much less common than once it was.

Tooth sharpening was once widespread throughout the Malay Peninsula, particularly among the Iban on the island of Borneo and the Batak living in northern Sumatra, tribes which saw tooth sharpening as symbolic of adulthood. However once Indonesia gained independence the practice was outlawed and rapidly fell out of favor. Today tooth sharpening in Indonesia is most associated with the Mentawai tribe. The Mentawai call tooth sharpening *pasi piat* and the practice is both an aesthetic treatment and a holistic operation for on the one hand the Mentawai feel that women become more beautiful when their teeth are fashioned into sharp points and also feel that the procedure helps a woman maintain the correct balance between her body and soul. There is no set age at which Mentawai females must undergo tooth sharpening and the procedure is considered to be voluntary. However wives often feel compelled to undergo tooth sharpening in order to please their husbands who take pride in having a wife that is willing to go through pain in order to become more beautiful. Mentawai tooth sharpening is performed using rudimentary dental instruments and without any anesthetic. In order to dull the pain of the operation women bite on green bananas.

One aftereffect of tooth sharpening is that the process removes tooth enamel. This is important to the Mentawai as the tribe also carries out tooth dyeing and the lack of tooth enamel makes it easier for the dye to stain the teeth. Indonesian adolescents living on islands in the Alor Archipelago also dye their teeth. Each July and August unwed boys and girls have their teeth blackened by a village man of around 20 years old who uses soil mixed with fruit juice as a paint. The resultant paste is smeared on a banana leaf cut to fit each individual child's mouth and for the next seven to ten days the children sleep with the paste in connection with their teeth so that eventually the paste stains their teeth black. The children are housed together in a field house and sleep and eat communally. When the children eat they are very careful to push their food deep into their mouths so as not to disturb the paste-covered leaves touching their teeth. Similarly, the children use a piece of bamboo as a drinking straw so as not to disturb the teeth staining. On the final day of their sequestration some of the children have their teeth sharpened with the procedure performed by the same person that dyed their teeth. The Iban of Borneo also dye their teeth black as well as sharpening them into points so that they resemble the teeth of a dog. A third tooth modification practice experienced by the Iban sees a hole drilled through the middle of each front tooth with a brass stud fitted through the hole. To drill the hole, the local dentist entreats the person undergoing the procedure to clamp their teeth down on a piece of soft wood and then begins to drill. The procedure is said to be excruciatingly painful.

Tooth dyeing is an established practice among other Southeast Asian communities. For instance, women of the Si La living in Laos dye their teeth black while the men dye theirs red. Meanwhile several tribes of the Philippines dye their teeth after marriage. Indeed the custom used to be so prevalent in the area that the Chinese called the region black teeth country. In Thailand tribes such as the Karen dye their teeth black with blackened teeth so highly regarded that love poems would compare women's deliberately blackened teeth to highly prized wood such as ebony. People living on the Pacific island of Palau also dye their teeth black as do tribes living on the Pacific archipelagos that make up the Caroline Islands and the Mariana Islands.

See also: Breast Ironing; Ear-Piercing Ceremonies; Female Genital Cutting; Forehead Cutting Initiation; Ritual Tattooing; Scarification; *Thaipusam*: Extreme Ritual Flesh Modification; Tooth-Filing Ceremony

Further Reading

DeMello, Margo. *Faces around the World: A Cultural Encyclopedia of the Human Face*. Santa Barbara, CA: ABC-CLIO, 2012.

The Huffington Post. "Teeth Chiseling, Indonesian Tribal Custom, Thought to Maintain Women's Beauty (VIDEO)," *The World Post*, April 29, 2011. Accessed April 29, 2015, at http://www.huffingtonpost.com/2011/04/29/indonesia-teeth-chiseling-_n_855472.html.

Sherrow, Victoria. *For Appearance' Sake: The Historical Encyclopedia of Good Looks, Beauty, and Grooming*. Westport, CT: The Oryx Press, 2001.

The Pitt Rivers Museum. "Shaped Teeth: Mozambique, Malawi and Tanzania, before 1910." Pitt Rivers Virtual Collections: Body Arts. Accessed April 29, 2015, at http://web.prm.ox.ac.uk/bodyarts/index.php/permanent-body-arts/reshaping-and-piercing/164-shaped-teeth.html.

Pitts-Taylor, Victoria. *Cultural Encyclopedia of the Body: Volumes 1 and 2*. Westport, CT: Greenwood Press, 2008.

Scott, G. Richard, and Christy G. Turner II, eds. *The Anthropology of Modern Human Teeth: Dental Morphology and Its Variation in Recent Human Populations*. Cambridge, UK: Cambridge University Press, 1997.

INTER-RAILING, EUROPE

Inter-railing, also written as interrailing, is a pan-European train journey taken by many European teenagers and young adults, particularly British youngsters, when they leave school, college, or university. Many youngsters consider the journey a rite of passage as it provides a taste of freedom and international adventure. Inter-railing is, traditionally, part of the so-called gap year—the period of time spent not in study or employment during which young adults "find" themselves, achieve a degree of independence, and learn to take responsibility for themselves.

Most youngsters that go inter-railing do so having bought a so-called InterRail pass that allows the owner to use the trains of 28 European countries as well as the rail networks of some countries outside of Europe (e.g., Morocco). The first InterRail pass launched in 1972 as a Europe train ticket for people under 21 years old. The ticket covered 21 European countries and proved an instant success with 85,000 young Europeans, most of them British, buying the pass to use the railways. By the mid-1980s, the age limit of people permitted to purchase the InterRail pass had risen to 26 years resulting in over 250,000 passes being issued annually. Today, InterRail passes are available for people of all age groups, though people applying for passes must have lived in a European country for a minimum of six months.

Nowadays, the route taken by inter-railers is dictated by the length of the journey that travelers wish to undertake as well as the number of cities or countries that they want to visit. There is also a proliferation of various types of inter-railing passes allowing different degrees of travel flexibility. Moreover, the different types of pass mean that travelers can bypass expensive travel regions such as France, Italy, and Germany and head to cheaper, less frequently visited destinations.

Most inter-railers travel in groups, though some people prefer to travel alone. The advent of the Internet means that today's inter-rail travelers tend to be much more organized than people that went inter-railing in the 1980s and 1990s for the Internet allows travelers to find accommodation in advance meaning that they no longer have to sleep at train stations or on trains as once was the case. That said, the best places to stay are often booked-up months in advance as people have booked ahead. Alternatively, travelers can take night trains. Night trains often run on the same routes as daytime trains but at faster speeds (this is true of routes such as those between Paris and Barcelona) and allow passengers to sleep on the train. From a practical point of view, this is advantageous as sleeping on the train saves on accommodation costs and, more romantically, means that a traveler goes to sleep in one country and awakes in another.

See also: Gap Year; Walkabout

Further Reading

Barnes, Jonathan. *The Gap-year Guidebook 2013: Everything You Need to Know about Taking a Gap.* 21st edition. Melton, UK: John Catt Educational Ltd., 2012.

Sawyer, Miranda. "Is Interrailing Still a Rite of Passage?" *BBC News Magazine*, August 20, 2011. Accessed June 1, 2015, at http://www.bbc.co.uk/news/magazine-14496308.

The Student Room. "The Student's Room to Inter-railing." Accessed November 15, 2015, at http://www.thestudentroom.co.uk/content.php?r=15917-The-Student-s-Guide-to-Inter-railing.

INITIATION BY SEMEN TRANSFERAL, PAPUA NEW GUINEA AND VANUATU

The transfer of semen is a compulsory part of the initiation rites for boys belonging to certain tribes in Papua New Guinea and Vanuatu. The practice is often cited as part of a code of behavior referred to by some anthropologists as ritualized homosexuality (RHS), though this term is somewhat controversial, because although the males take part in ritual semen transferal participate in sexual acts with other males, they do not identify as homosexual and soon after their initiation by semen is over the initiates will enter into heterosexual marriages. In order to avoid issues attendant on using terms such as ritualized homosexuality (RHS) some academics prefer to use a de-eroticised term to describe the activity, such as semen practices, which removes sexual overtones and elements of homoeroticism.

Semen ingestion as initiation was first documented in a study in 1922–1925 and has been well documented ever since most notably perhaps by Gilbert Herdt, who made an in-depth study of ritual semen ingestion among males belonging to the pseudonymous Sambia tribe of Papua New Guinea. Sambia society consisted of 2,000 people whose true identity Herdt obscured despite detailing vernacular words used by the tribe that could, theoretically, identify the group.

In Papua New Guinea and Vanuatu participants always view ritualized semen transferal as a rite of passage for boys to gain the strength and reproductive capacity of adult men. As part of this transformation to adulthood, emphasis is placed on a boy's biological maturation with special attention paid to how much a boy's penis enlarges as he ages. As a result of this interest in penis length ornamental gourds or other concealing items are placed over the penis. Meanwhile boys take in the semen of older tribesmen as this is seen as a way for boys to acquire the ability to procreate and become strong. Ritualized semen transferal nearly always involves a young initiate taking in the semen of an older male that has already undergone the same rite of passage, most often the boy's maternal uncle or another older male relative from their mother's side of the family.

There are various forms of ritual semen transferal. For example for such tribes as the Keraki living in the Trans-Fly region of Papua New Guinea semen transferal is usually through anal sex. A male cousin that has undergone the same initiation usually introduces a Keraki boy into anal sex at the age of 13 years during a bull-roarer ceremony. After the boy has experienced this act he is regarded as available to both other villagers and visitors to the village that wish to penetrate him. During the early part of the boy's initiation he lives with other males that have also recently been initiated in a secluded hut. The boys are expected to take part in as much same-sex sexual activity as possible in order that they may develop physically through semen transferal. When a boy leaves the hut he is regarded as a *setiriva*, or bachelor, and allowed to hunt more often and associate with tribal elders, though he must also remain a passive recipient of anal penetration. Once it is decided that the bachelor is mature enough to be classed as an adult he experiences the lime-eating ceremony during which lime is poured down his throat in order to neutralize the supposed effects of taking part in the semen transferal, mainly to ensure that the bachelor cannot become pregnant. As a man, the bachelor is now freed from the role of passive semen recipient and takes on the role of initiator to the next generation of boys. Similarly, boys of the Marind-anim tribe must experience anal intercourse for six years, starting when they are between 7 and 14 years of age. When a Marind-anim boy's hair is long enough to be braided, the boy is referred to as a girl and takes a passive role in anal sex instigated by his male elders.

Elsewhere, ritual semen transferal is through other means. For example, the Sambia tribe boys perform fellatio on older tribesmen while among other Papua New Guinean tribes, particularly the Etoro and Onabasulu, it is usual for boys to masturbate older males causing them to ejaculate. The boys then collect the resultant semen and rub it onto their skin in order to transfer the adult males' powers and abilities to their own bodies. An Etoro boy will also fellate older tribesmen, such as his sister's husband, from the age of 10 until they grow a beard and are regarded as adults.

Along with the ritualized semen ingestion boys belonging to certain tribes in Papua New Guinea and Vanuatu also have to perform other rites in order to be viewed as adults. For instance, in Papua New Guinea boys of the Sambia and Anga tribes also have to perform a cleansing ritual in the form of bloodletting before they experience semen ingestion. Meanwhile, boys belonging to the Big Nambas people of Vanuatu undergo circumincision (i.e., the slitting of their foreskin, which is then cut laterally and removed) once they have ingested semen from older males. The circumincision is performed on the boys in order to expose the glans, or head of the penis, which are seen as the locus of male potency. When the decision is taken to circumcise a boy, his father will seek a male sponsor or guardian for his son. This man has exclusive sexual rites to the boy and their relationship is very close. Indeed the boy is regarded as the man's husband and if one of the two dies the survivor is expected to grieve deeply. A Big Nambas boy may also enter into a monogamous relationship as the fellator of an adult male that continues until the time that the boy is deemed to have earned a belt made of bark that is the sign of manhood. Once the boy has earned this, his relationship with the older man ends and he himself takes a young boy as his own personal fellator.

In both cases the blood loss experienced by the boys casts the initiates in the role of menstruating females, that is females with the potential to have children, and they are also seen as feminized as they passively and deferentially take in the semen offered by the older tribesmen as wives of the tribe are expected to behave for their husbands during marital sex. Meanwhile the men from whom the boys ingest the semen are seen as mother figures as they provide the boys with nourishment through a bodily fluid as mothers do via breastfeeding. The older men are also seen as allowing the boys to be reborn as men. That society sees the older men as maternal figures is heightened by the fact that they are related to the initiates through their mothers. Indeed the Sambia people equate the oral ingestion of semen through fellatio with a baby's swallowing of breast milk.

The initiation of Sambia boys is perhaps the most oft-documented example of initiation through semen ingestion. This rite of passage begins when Sambia boys are between 7 and 10 years of age and lasts for six stages over a course of between 10 and 15 years, culminating in marriage to at least one woman and the production of offspring. The main purpose of the multi-stage initiation is to separate boys from the tribe's womenfolk, particularly their mothers. Sambia initiation rites involve large groups of boys taken from neighboring villages so that the boys form a connection from undergoing the ritual together. The first stage of the initiation sees the boys taken from their mothers and younger siblings and inducted into the company of Sambia men with whom the boys will live for many years. The boys' induction into male society, *moku*, consists of several ritualistic ordeals over the course of one week that are intended to begin the boys' transformation into adult warrior men. On the first day of the induction the boys are taken from their mothers and made to walk for several hours to an open space in another village. Next, the boys are taken to a pool of water where a tribal elder selects a sharp cane and uses it to penetrate deep into each boys' nostrils so that their blood pours into the water. All the while the boys are watched by a crowd of older tribesmen that emit war cries as the boys bleed. During this part of the initiation any boy that shows discomfort or tries to flee is treated more brutally than a boy that receives the pain passively. Next, the men that have been watching the nostril piercing announce that the boys will have to perform fellatio on bachelors belonging to the tribe in order that the boys may become adults. Meanwhile tribal elders attest that the boys must ingest the bachelors' semen if they wish to become men. Once ceremonial duties have concluded the bachelors advance toward the boys and fellatio occurs in the open space to which the boys were brought after their long walk. Though the boys understand that ingesting the semen of older males will help them grow strong it is recorded that many boys feel scared, revolted, and at the least uncomfortable at the idea of performing fellatio. Over the course of the next five days however the boys will generally perform ritualized oral sex on the bachelors many times. The fellatio is performed in the open and boys that have a favorite bachelor (i.e., one whose semen they prefer the taste of) will be taught to initiate sexual activity with their favorite by directly stimulating the bachelor's genitals. Boys that are in the first or second stage of their initiation may only perform fellatio—they are forbidden from being fellated by older boys. Further to this, older boys are forbidden from performing fellatio on first- and second-stage initiates and must only act as inseminators. Thus over the course of his initiation a Sambia boy will take on the roles of both fellator and inseminator.

The second stage of the boys initiation, *imbutu*, occurs when the boys are around 12 years old and continues the first stage for the boys try to ingest as much semen as possible so that they may become fierce warriors imbued with the power and masculinity inherent in the older tribesmen's bodily fluid. As a reward for the boys' endeavors they are treated to communal feasts. The boys also continue to be separated from females who may cause the boys to become emasculated.

While the second stage does not see any change in the boys' status within the tribe, the third stage, *ipmangwi*, results in a very important change in the boys' rank and marks the turning point from the boys being children to their being adolescents. This stage occurs when boys are between 14 and 16 years old. During the third stage the boys are now regarded as bachelors and so move from ingesting semen to inseminating other boys. To mark this change in status the boys are tied to trees, whipped, and have their noses bled again in order that they may be purified of any enfeebling female contamination that could have occurred. The whipping and bloodletting experienced by the boys is intended to make the boys feel both strengthened and angered at their treatment. However the boys do not complain, as they understand that in time they will be able to do to younger initiates what has been done to them as a form of payback.

The fourth stage, *nuposha*, occurs at any stage after the third stage when a male that has undergone the first three phases marries. Indeed the word nuposha can also be taken to mean "newlywed" and refer to a marriage ceremony. However a Sambia male will not cohabit with his bride until around the time of her first menstrual period. Even when the male does start to live with his wife he is warned to protect himself from the smell of her genitals and also told that when he eventually has vaginal intercourse with his wife he must be careful not to penetrate her too deeply lest he should enter her urethra—an act that would cause him harm. Next, a ritual occurs that connects the male's development into a man with that of a certain tree. It is in front of this tree that the male must expose himself to his wife once he has been warned of how a woman can endanger him. The fifth stage of the male's initiation, *taiketnyi*, takes place around the time of his wife's first period that is also the time when his wife is inducted into the menstrual hut to which men are forbidden entry. For this stage the male causes his nose to bleed himself and he is told in great detail how to shield himself from the polluting influence of his wife. For example the male is told to put mint leaves inside his nostrils when having marital sex, as this will prevent him from smelling his wife's genital odor. The male is also advised that once the sex act is complete he should bathe in a mud bath and also bleed his nose every month when his wife menstruates.

As the initiate has been in exclusively male society for around 12 years, he is wary of women and as he has practiced only fellatio he readily believes his tribal elder when they warn him of the dangers inherent in vaginal sex. Indeed Sambia men are told to space out their experiences of vaginal intercourse so as not to become too depleted and thereby avoid early death. Meanwhile, the male's wife is instructed in the best ways to practice fellatio so that she may please her husband and quell his fear of her and her body. This is one of the reasons that the young couple's sex life involves the wife performing fellatio on her husband before the couple has vaginal intercourse. Another reason for the fellatio is that the Sambia believe the wife must ingest her husband's semen so that she will be able to provide a similarly white fluid for her future children—breast milk that will allow her child to grow up healthily. Indeed the Sambia believe that breast milk is semen that has been transformed into a health-giving substance and that it is, therefore, fathers rather than mothers that nourish babies.

The sixth stage of the male's initiation, *moondangu*, confers upon him the full rights of manhood. This stage takes place on the birth of the male's first child the production of which is taken to prove that the male has reached adult masculinity. If the male has two children then he is thought to have attained the utmost level of adult manhood, or *aatmwunu*. Up until this point the male is allowed to continue inseminating younger boys but on the birth of his children the now adult male must stop being fellated by initiates. If a Sambia man enters into a semen transfer with another Sambia man he will be denounced as unmanly and if he is fellated by a boy he will be viewed as morally corrupt.

When the man's wife has given birth the male is told to keep away from any interaction with his wife and child until the child is weaned. This period of isolation away from the family may last for a maximum of two and a half years and during this time the male need not bleed his nose unless he has a second wife. The male is also told that he must never divulge what he has undergone during his initiation or he will be castrated and executed.

See also: Beards; Bullet Ant Initiation; Cow Jumping; Forehead-Cutting Initiation; Land Diving; Log Riding; Matis Hunting Trials; Menstrual Taboos; *Sharo*: Public Flogging; Trobriand Ritualized Sex and Commitment; Urethral Subincision

Further Reading

Allen, Michael. "Male Cults Revisited: The Politics of Blood versus Semen," *Oceania*, 68(3), March 1998, 189–199.

Creed, Gerald W. "Sexual Subordination: Institutionalized Homosexuality and Social Control in Melanesia," *Ethnology*, 23(3), July 1984, 157–176.

Elliston, Deborah A. "Erotic Anthropology: 'Ritualized Homosexuality' in Melanesia and Beyond," *American Ethnologist*, 22(4), November 1995, 848–867.

Herdt, Gilbert. *The Sambia: Ritual, Sexuality, and Change in Papua New Guinea.* Second edition. Belmont, CA: Wadsworth Cengage Learning, 2006.

Herdt, Gilbert H., ed. *Ritualized Homosexuality in Melanesia.* Berkeley, CA: University of California Press, 1984.

Herdt, Gilbert H., ed. *Rituals of Manhood: Male Initiation in Papua New Guinea.* Piscataway, NJ: Transaction Publishers, 1997.

Meyer, Melissa L. *Thicker Than Water: The Origins of Blood as Symbol and Ritual.* New York: Routledge, 2005.

Neill, James. *The Origins and Role of Same-Sex Relations in Human Societies.* Jefferson, NC: McFarland & Company Inc. Publishers, 2009.

Tripod. "The Sambia Tribe." Accessed April 26, 2015, at http://lrivera0327.tripod.com.

IRIA CEREMONY, NIGERIA

The Iria ceremony is a coming-of-age ritual for girls performed by some tribes living in Nigeria including the Waikiriki, the Iriabo, and the Okrika. The girls involved in the Iria ceremony, known as *iriapu*, are usually between 14 and 16 years of age, and are, therefore, girls that are considered marriageable. The ceremony is often regarded as a celebration of the biological maturity of female adolescents and usually consists of four elements: isolation, instruction, transition, and celebration, though the order in which the elements occur, and specific details of the ceremony vary.

According to Okrika mythology, the Iria ceremony harks back to a time when the tribe was widely dispersed and girls had to be ritually washed of the taint of incest in order for them to be able to marry their own brothers. Gradually this myth was replaced with a more elaborate one in which girls were said to form enchanted romances with water sprites from whom, during the Iria ceremony, they must be separated in order to marry mortal men. Many of the songs that the iriapu learn during Iria focus on finding love with a water-borne lover. The songs deliberately call to mind the water spirits because the Okrika believe that in order for the girls to separate from their water spirit lovers, they must first summon them by name.

Some tribes, particularly the Waikiriki, start the ritual by making girls bare their breast for the scrutiny of a watching crowd. The purpose of this appearance in front of their community is to ensure that the girl's virginity is intact—if a girl refuses to reveal her virgin breasts she will be deemed to have failed her inspection and will experience public scorn. However most women enjoy this ritual and see it as an honor. The next stage of the Iria ceremony begins immediately after the first. This stage sees girls confined to fattening rooms where they are made to gorge on rich local foods and their movement is restricted by heavy metal weights attached to their legs that chafe when they move. The physical burden of the weights is to give girls an idea of the physical discomfort of the pregnancies they are expected to bear in future. The combination of enforced gluttony and restricted movement is also a deliberate attempt to cause girls to put on weight, something that is regarded as attractive by Nigerian ideals of beauty. While staying in the fattening rooms girls also learn to sing songs about their water lovers. Many Nigerian tribes, such as the Iriabo, believe that young women must end their supposed romantic attachments to water spirits if they are to marry and bear children. During their time in the fattening room young women make many journeys to the village river at sunrise, a practice that leads to the girls' songs being called Dawn Songs. One song in particular calls attention to another facet of the Iria ceremony for the lyrics are as follows:

> Son of Okoro, waterspirit lover,
> Tell me, why are you peering into my face?
> Do you see traces of burumo painting?

(Gleason and Ibubuya, 141)

Burumo painting is an intimate form of body painting performed on women by women using *burumo*, a blue dye extracted from pulverized camwood. Local women apply the dye to the girls' bodies for the paint is thought to be attractive to the water spirits. The designs painted on to the girls' skin makes them look otherworldly, which is considered fitting as it shows that they possess a liminal position—both hovering between childhood and adulthood and also able to call upon supernatural forces as lovers. The burumo paint gradually fades during the period of the Iria ceremony representing the vanishing of the girls' romantic attachment to the water spirits.

During the women's time at the riverside, the young women practice the songs they have learned in the fattening rooms and on their last day in the fattening rooms the girls all go down to the river's edge together and unite in singing the songs. This last day of fattening is also the day when the water spirits are believe to come and try to kidnap the girls who have entered into fattening room seclusion. In order to ensure both the girls' safety and their fertility the iriapu must once and for all discard any ideal of romance embodied by their water spirit lovers. During daylight hours the girls polish the heavy metal weights placed around their legs while standing by the side of the river, all the while risking kidnap by their water spirit lovers, for according to myth the water spirits will rise to the surface and seize the girls as brides. According to tribal lore, only a male warrior spirit-personage, the *Osokolo* (who is played by a tribal elder during the Iria ceremony) can prevent the girls from being snatched by driving the spirits back from their watery dwelling into the real world of the village. The Osokolo, who is endowed with the power of the sea, acts to ensure the girls' fertility by hitting them with wooden sticks. As the girls flee the Osokolo continues to strike at them. However, although the girls are scared of being hurt they ultimately submit to being hit as they fear that if the Osokolo's stick does not hit them they will not bear healthy children. As this part of Nigeria has high rates of infant mortality it unsurprising that females will do all they can to try and safeguard their future children. The way in which this part of the ritual is carried out varies from the tribe to tribe. In some tribes the spirits are hit out of the women before they enter the fattening rooms while in other tribes, rather than the Osokolo hitting the women, village men will congregate and whack the women with the stick. The amount of clothing that the women wear during this part of the ceremony varies too for the women may or may not be bare breasted while they are hit.

See also: Fattening Room Seclusion; Virginity Testing

Further Reading

Arnett, Jeffrey Jensen, ed. *International Encyclopedia of Adolescence: A–J, index, Volume 1.* New York: Routledge, 2007.

Crespo, Abel, Emily Duque, and Diana Zuhlsdor. "Iria Ritual; A Celebration of Feminism or Femininity?" EmilyDuque9. Accessed January 6, 2015, at https://emilyduque9.wordpress.com/2013/09/25/iria-ritual-a-celebration-of-feminism-or-femininity/.

Gleason, Judith, and Allison Ibubuya. "My Year Reached, We Heard Ourselves Singing: Dawn Songs of Girls Becoming Women in Ogbogbo, Okrika, Rivers State, Nigeria, January 1990," *Research in African Literatures*, 22(3), Autumn 1991, 135–148.

Hartel, Insa, and Sigrid Schade, eds. *The Body and Representation.* Wiesbaden, Germany: Springer Fachmedien, 2002.

ISANAKLESH GOTAL, MESCALERO APACHE

Isanaklesh Gotal, commonly called The Feast, is an eight-day initiation ceremony for Mescalero Apache girls living in New Mexico when they experience their first menstrual period. The ceremony, which can be held on an individual basis or feature several girls initiated at once, is named after Isanaklesh, the Mescalero Apache Earth Mother goddess. Isanaklesh Gotal means Ceremonial (Isanaklesh) Sing (Gotal). The word Gotal therefore suggests both the celebratory aspect of the ritual and also the need to bring to the fore the supernatural power, or *diye*, needed to literally transform a pubertal girl into the goddess Isanaklesh. Isanaklesh Gotal ceremonies may take place away from public gaze or as part of an annual public feast on ceremonial land at the Mescalero Apache headquarters during the weekend that falls closest to July 4. Whether or not a girl's ceremony is private or public the girl's friends and family will gather together with supplies and assemble temporary tepees and cooking equipment. Meanwhile, the girl undergoes rituals in her own private tepee that is constructed by the girl's male relatives and the *gutaal*, or singer, that is for the purposes of the ceremony considered the ceremonial home of Isanaklesh. The tepee is referred to as the Big Tepee and the goddess is only thought to reside within the tepee once all four poles of the tepee are sung into position.

Mescalero Apaches believe that during the ceremony the girl becomes the goddess temporarily and so she is treated as such for the duration of the ceremony. For example the girl is dressed in the manner of the goddess who is often depicted as wearing moccasins decorated with crystals and turquoise, beaded jewelry, and a fringed deerskin dress that is covered in intricate beadwork, hence the girl is dressed in a deerskin dress featuring tiny metal cones at the end of the fringing to represent deer hooves.

According to Mescalero Apache mythology, Isanaklesh created the ceremony when she came into the world. However there is no single moment when the girl that is the focus of the ceremony becomes Isanaklesh. Instead, it is the elements of the ceremony, especially the ritual singing, taken as a whole that result in the girl's transformation into both goddess and woman. For the entire eight days of the ceremony the girl is attended by other females and treated as the goddess. However not only does the ceremony see the girl transform temporarily into the goddess but, by the conclusion of the ceremony, the girl is also considered to have transformed permanently into a mature Apache woman that has entered adulthood, or *'isdzaa dzili*. For both transformations to take place it is necessary for the girl to be made fully aware of her environment, to understand all the ritualistic elements of the ceremony, and to be divested of her childish ways. To this end, the Mescalero Apache see the Isanaklesh Gotal ceremony as a way to usher the girl on her way to maturity at a time when she is malleable and capable of being molded by other females, particularly her female relatives. The girl is also thought to be under the influence of the male singer that performs the sacred songs and her sponsor, a godparent-type figure, both of whom are charged with making sure the girl comprehends all that goes on during her ceremony. The singer and sponsor are both chosen in a ritualistic manner with the girl's family giving each four gifts and saying traditional entreaties to them to take on their roles.

The first four days of the ceremony are notable for their wealth of rituals and activities, including the singing of songs, the saying of sacred tales, and the showing of illustrations that are intended to stress to both the girl and the girl's family and friends the importance of the ceremony. Before dawn on the first day of the ceremony, the girl is installed in her private tepee where she is attended to by her female relatives and her sponsor. The sponsor then blesses the girl with *tadadine*, sacred cattail pollen, which Isanaklesh employed in the Creation story, and gives the girl a ceremonial bath during which her hair is washed in yucca suds, or *Ishee*. Such pampering is intended to remind the girl how nice it is to be indulged. The girl is also given leggings and moccasins to wear and she is fed traditional Apache ritual foods. During the dining experience the girl is given an *uka*, which is a special straw, through which she must drink water since water must not come into contact with her lips lest floods should ensue. Similarly, the girl is given a scratching stick, or *tsibeeichii*, to use should she wish to scratch an itch for the girl is not allowed to scratch herself for fear that where she touches her skin will become unduly wrinkled and her hair will turn gray. The scratching stick, which is normally carved by the girl's father from oak, sycamore, or cottonwood, is roughly 10 inches long with a hole at one end resembling the eye of a needle and is attached to the right-hand side of the girl's blouse. This means that the stick is in easy reach though the girl must use the stick only when necessary.

Once the girl is washed and dressed she leaves her tepee with her female attendants and carries a blanket and white deerskin that she unfurls and places on the ground in front of the tepee. The girl, who is now considered to be Isanaklesh, blesses anyone that wishes it with sacred cattail pollen that she applies across the bridge of their noses and elsewhere in order to ensure they live a long and happy life. In return, those blessed by the girl confer blessings on her and the girl then motions to the four directions of north, east, south, and west in the traditional Apache manner. Next, the girl is molded, that is, she undergoes a ritual massage that is believed to both further shape the girl into Isanaklesh and also guarantees that the girl's life will be long and fruitful. Meanwhile, the singer traces four footprints on the white deerskin using tadadine. A sacred basket is positioned east of the tepee and the girl treads on the pollen footprints while being pushed off them and made to run around the basket four times, with the basket placed nearer to the tepee with each run. Meanwhile songs are sung before the girl returns to the tepee. This ritual is also intended to give the girl a long and healthy life. In the meantime, the girl's sponsor makes the so-called ritual marker, a long, high-pitched noise that is intended to draw the attention of supernatural forces toward the girl since as she runs around the basket the girl is thought to encounter Isanaklesh and guide the goddess to her people.

After these rituals have taken place the girl may not have any casual social interaction, except for seeing see her closest relatives and friends and those that wish to be blessed by her, and appears in public only over the course of the next four nights. On the first night the girl is blessed by ritual male dancers that are believed to be transformed into supernatural beings called *hastchin* that live inside the mountains located on Mescalero land. Over the next few days various other rituals take place. For instance, over the course of the third night the girl is made to run all night long accompanied by music from the singer and then on the fourth morning she runs to the east to welcome the dawn. The singer then draws an image of the sun on his palm using galena (a shining mineral form of lead sulfide), clay, and pollen. As the sun rises, the singer raises his palms so that the sun's rays reflect off the shining illustration on his hand, and then places his palms on the girl's chest, shoulders, and head all the while blessing her. The singer then paints the girl with white clay while her tepee is uncovered and turned into a skeleton structure. Next the singer blesses watching elderly and infirm people as well as children with red clay. The last ritual of the Isanaklesh Gotal ceremony sees the girl led out of her tepee by an eagle feather so that she walks on fresh pollen footsteps drawn on deerskin. The sacred basket is then placed east of the tepee once again at the same distance as it was positioned for the last run of the first morning. The girl then runs around the basket with the basket moved further away from the tepee each time she runs. For the last run the basket is placed far to the east. When the girl reaches the basket she plucks an eagle feather from it and runs as far eastward as possible before rotating and daubing her face with white clay. The girl then returns to her tepee where she remains with her sponsor and the singer for the next four days all the while contemplating the significance of the Isanaklesh Gotal ceremony. At this point Isanaklesh is considered to have departed for the east and the girl is now a woman. Meanwhile the singer chants as the poles of a ceremonial tepee are loosened and crash to the ground and all spectators move to the feasting area where trucks have arrived laden with fruits and candies that are thrown to onlookers as gifts from the family sponsoring the feast. The noise and commotion of pulling down the tepee and throwing around foods is deliberately intended to disperse the sacred air of the ceremony.

Some Mescalero Apache girls are reluctant to undergo an Isanaklesh Gotal because they do not wish to be the focus of such an elaborate ceremony with all eyes upon them. For this reason, many girls are prepared for the ceremony emotionally and spiritually by their older female relatives, especially their mothers and grandmothers, long before their periods begin. These older family members instill in the girls that the ceremony will change their life for the better and will make their lives long and happy. Sometimes in order to alleviate girls' fears of the ceremony girls will be allowed to watch the Isanaklesh Gotal rituals of others so that they have an idea of what to expect during their own ceremony. Also, far in advance of a girl's Isanaklesh Gotal ceremony her family will start to amass the items needed for the ceremony to occur. These items include eagle feathers and the sacred pollen that can be collected only when cattails are fully ripened. On a more prosaic level it is important for families to accrue sufficient finances to cover the cost of the ceremony, which can be expensive.

Once the girl has become a woman she becomes a repository of Mescalero Apache ways and is charged with continuing the people's traditions. In this way, the girl again takes on the mantle of Isanaklesh, who like the new woman, also sought to teach future generations and ensure the continuance of her nation.

See also: Apache Baby Ceremonies (Volume 1); Cradleboards (Volume 1); Entering the *Bashali* (Volume 1); Menstrual Customs; Sunrise Ceremony

Further Reading

Carr, Nuala. "The Return of God the Mother—How to Become the Goddess/God," *Making Waves: FIU Women's Studies Journal*, 2, 2004, 31–33. Accessed May 28, 2015, at http://womenstudies.fiu.edu/students/making-waves-journal/mw_vol2.pdf.

Crawford, Suzanne J., and Dennis F. Kelley, eds. *American Indian Religious Traditions: An Encyclopedia*. Santa Barbara, CA: ABC-CLIO, 2005.

"Girl's Puberty Ceremony." The Apache Life Cycle. University of California, Santa Barbara. Accessed May 29, 2016, at http://archserve.id.ucsb.edu/courses/rs/natlink/apache/apa_life6.htm.

Hernandez-Avila, Ines, ed. *Reading Native American Women: Critical/Creative Representations*. Lanham, MD: AltaMira Press, 2005.

Rojas, Mary Virginia. "She Bathes in a Sacred Place: Rites of Reciprocity, Power, and Prestige in Alta California," *Wicazo Sa Review*, 18(1), Spring 2003, 129–156.

J

JEWISH WEDDING CUSTOMS, JUDAISM

Marriage is one of the keystones of Jewish life and as with most religions, a wedding is seen as a cause for celebration. There are many laws, rules, and customs associated with Jewish weddings as well as rituals that are enacted in the weeks leading up to the ceremony. The specifics of Jewish wedding ceremonies vary but there are some common features such as the signing of a contract, the presence of a wedding canopy, and the breaking of a glass.

In earlier times it was usual for Jewish marriages to be arranged by youngsters' parents, who would be assisted by a matchmaker called a *yenta*. Indeed some ultra-Orthodox Jewish communities still arrange marriages in this way. When a marriage is arranged the prospective groom would still be expected to ask the bride-to-be's father for permission to wed his daughter and in order to seal the engagement the groom-to-be would pay a dowry.

As soon as a Jewish couple becomes engaged, they start to take part in a variety of rituals. The first ritual is called *tena'im* (or *tenaim*) and sees the smashing of a plate or piece of crockery. The meaning of this ritual is not known for sure but the most commonly accepted reasons for the plate smashing is that it symbolizes the destruction of the Temples in Jerusalem and also shows that once an engagement is broken it cannot be repaired just as a smashed plate cannot be put back together. It is also suggested that the smashing of the crockery reminds people that even in times of happiness Jews still feel sadness.

A Jewish wedding may take place on any day of the week apart from on the Jewish Sabbath, which starts at sunset on Friday and lasts until sunset on Saturday. A Jewish wedding may also not be held on important days in the Jewish calendar, such as on the Day of Atonement or at Jewish New Year. In the United Kingdom, most Jewish weddings take place on Sundays while in the United States many Jewish weddings are held on Saturdays once the Sabbath has ended—this is particularly the case in winter when Sabbath ends earlier in the day. Ultra-Orthodox Jewish couples also hold weddings on weekdays. Jewish weddings, particularly Orthodox Jewish weddings, may occur throughout the year though the period between Pesach, or Passover, and Shavuot (a sad time of reflection) is usually avoided.

The build-up to a wedding is a time of great excitement though it is traditional for the bride and groom to not see each other during this period. One week before the wedding, a ceremony is held for the groom known as an *Aufruf* (or *Ufruf*), which means the calling up in Yiddish. The ceremony sees the groom visit the synagogue and actively participate in the service and proclaim his forthcoming marriage. During the service it is traditional for the congregation to shower the groom with candies as he takes part in the service. Children like this part of the tradition especially as they enjoy throwing the candy hard at the groom. The Aufruf is often followed by refreshments for the congregation as well as a private lunch for the couple's families. The bride must also take part in a ritual one week before the wedding for she experiences a ritual bath called a *mikveh*. This bath provides the bride with a symbolic cleansing that means she enters into marriage in a state of spiritual and physical purity. The process of mikveh varies greatly with some brides using the custom as a chance to enjoy a spa treatment. However in order for the mikveh to be fulfilled the bride must remove all her jewelry and make-up before entering the bath. The bride must then immerse herself fully in water while reciting a prayer.

Before a Jewish wedding ceremony begins, an important ceremony known as the signing of the *Ketubah* occurs. The *Ketubah* is the Jewish marriage contract that establishes the legal terms of the marriage. The Ketubah is very old, dating back to the Jewish Supreme Court—the Sanhedrin—which existed in Jerusalem in the Holy Land millennnia ago. The Ketubah is important as it protects the bride by setting out the terms of her dowry. The signing of the Ketubah takes place before the main ceremony in the presence of four witnesses plus the ceremony's officiator. During the signing, an agreement will be signed by men that states they will not contest a Jewish divorce (a *Get*) if the couple separate. This is especially meaningful for Jewish women—if their husbands deny them a Get, it leaves them unable to marry again. The signing of the Ketubah is accompanied by a ceremony called the *Bedecken*, meaning veiling. This involves the groom placing a veil over the bride's face and symbolizes the groom's determination to ensure that his wife will always be clothed and safe. The Bedecken ceremony dates from the time of the Old Testament for Isaac is said to have covered Rebekah's face when they married.

It is customary for the bride and groom to fast on their wedding day. This is a symbolic act intended to cleanse the couple of sin and to ensure that they enter into marriage in a state of spiritual cleanliness. There are no set rules for how a Jewish couple should dress for their wedding; grooms tend to wear a tuxedo or morning suit and brides favor white wedding dresses. Orthodox brides may opt for very modest attire. Similarly, there are no rules stating what music may be played during a wedding, though many Jewish couples feel uncomfortable playing "The Wedding March" by Richard Wagner because the composer is said to have held anti-Semitic views and was popular in Nazi Germany during the 1930s and 1940s when Jews were persecuted. Most couples choose traditional Jewish music for their wedding ceremony, with music usually played as the bride enters and after the ceremony.

A Jewish marriage ceremony usually happens beneath a special canopy called a *chupa* (or *huppah*), which symbolizes the couple's future home together. According to Jewish law, a marriage ceremony consists of two separate parts, the *erusin* (or *kiddushin*, meaning dedication or sanctification), and *nissu'in*, which is the actual ceremony of marriage. It is only when the bride reaches the chupa that the erusin is understood to be underway. The erusin is a simple betrothal blessing ceremony that sees the groom give his soon-to-be wife a gift of value such as a ring to signal his intent to wed her. Traditionally, Jewish weddings would take place outdoors in a field but today ceremonies are held indoors, usually in a synagogue, but there is no rule saying that they must be held in a synagogue. As long as a ceremony takes place beneath a chupa and under the supervision of a rabbi, a Jewish wedding may be held anywhere. That said, a rabbi need not perform the wedding ceremony—a rabbi merely has to be present during the service. Indeed a relative or friend may perform the ceremony if they have gained the permission of a rabbi before the ceremony takes place.

In a Jewish marriage ceremony, the bride is usually the last person to enter. The bride is often accompanied to the chupa by her father—though there is no set rule about who should accompany the bride, sometimes both parents escort the bride. Brides may also be attended by bridesmaids. Once the bride reaches the chupa she walks around the groom a number of times. The number of times that the bride walks round the groom varies with some brides opting for one walk and Orthodox brides walking around their groom seven times. Seven is a very important number at Jewish weddings. For instance, seven cups of wine are drunk during the wedding ceremony and at the celebrations after the service. The number is significant because, according to Jewish teachings, God created the world in seven days. The first of the seven cups of wine is drunk by the bride and groom during the ceremony. The couple's drinking from the cup is initiated by the rabbi or other officiate who gives the cup to the groom who then drinks from the vessel. The groom then presents it to the bride who also drinks from the cup. That bride and groom drink from the same cup symbolizes their unity and commitment to each other.

Prayers are said too as these are thought to bind the couple together. However one of the most important parts of the ceremony is the giving of the wedding ring. The wedding ring must be owned by the groom and must be in the shape of a complete, unbroken circle, unadorned with stones or embellishments. The shape of a circle is significant as it represents the couple's desire for a happy marriage.

During a Jewish ceremony, the person overseeing the service makes a speech about the couple and blesses them. The ceremony also features a prayer about the sadness felt by Jewish people at the destruction of the Temples in Jerusalem. Traditionally, a cantor sings this prayer that demonstrates that as in the engagement ceremony, even amid the joy of a happy marriage Jews remember times of pain and unhappy events in Jewish history. This is a way for Jewish people to pay their respects to Jews that have suffered in the past.

The ceremony concludes with the groom breaking a glass by stamping on it and saying "*Mazel Tov!*"—a congratulatory expression conferring good luck. The breaking of the glass symbolizes the destruction of the Temples in Jerusalem just as a plate was broken in the lead-up to the wedding. Once the glass is shattered everybody at the ceremony congratulates the newlyweds. Once the wedding ceremony has ended it is customary to allow the newlyweds a little time alone together in a separate room before returning to greet their guests as husband and wife. Jewish wedding receptions often take place in hotels or function halls. The format of the reception varies depending on how religious the newlyweds are. For instance, Orthodox receptions will see men and women dance separately whereas other receptions will permit men and women to dance together. Food served at Jewish receptions is kosher though couples that are not Orthodox may use caterers from non-kosher firms. Jewish people fall into two ethnic groups—Ashkenazi (Jews of European origin) and Sephardic (Jews with Middle Eastern, Spanish, or Portuguese heritage)—and these ethnic backgrounds will normally influence the style of a couple's wedding and the dishes served at their reception. For instance, Ashkenazi Jews tend to serve staple foods such as roast chicken, potatoes, and vegetables, while Sephardic Jews may opt for lamb or spicy chicken with couscous. One of the religious rituals enacted at the reception is a blessing over challah bread that is customarily baked before a meal. Another religious aspect of the reception is the seven blessings that are conferred upon the bride and groom.

Speeches are often made at the reception and presents are given to members of the wedding party including mothers-of-the-bride, the groom, and the bridesmaids. Music is a major part of Jewish wedding receptions and is provided by either a DJ or a band. It is traditional for traditional Jewish music to be played at the reception and a *horah* is danced too. Orthodox Jews may play exclusively Jewish music and Jewish-themed music though other Jews may choose a mix of music including traditional Jewish music. Once the reception is over, the newlyweds go on their honeymoon and begin life as husband and wife.

See also: *Hora* and *Horah*; Jewish Birth Customs (Volume 1); Jewish Death Customs (Volume 3); *Povitica*; Wedding Dress and Wedding Ring; Wedding March and Bridal Chorus; Yumi Sakugawa, "An Asian American Wedding," 2009

Further Reading

Foley, Michael P., with Alexander E. Lessard, Angela Lessard, and Alexandra Foley. *Wedding Rites: The Complete Guide to Traditional Vows, Music, Ceremonies, Blessings, and Interfaith Services*. Grand Rapids, MI: William B. Eerdmans Publishing Company, 2008.

Gordis, Daniel. "Erusin: The First of the Two Ceremonies." My Jewish Learning. Accessed July 24, 2015, at http://www.myjewishlearning.com/article/erusin-the-first-of-the-two-ceremonies/.

Greenberg, Steven. "Contemplating a Jewish Ritual of Same-Sex Union: An Inquiry into the Meanings of Marriage," in Mark D. Jordan, ed., with Meghan T. Sweeney and David M. Mellott, *Authorizing Marriage?: Canon, Tradition, and Critique in the Blessing of Same-Sex Unions*, 81–101. Princeton, NJ: Princeton University Press, 2006.

Moss, Aaron. "Why Break a Glass at a Jewish Wedding?" Chabad.org. Accessed July 24, 2015, at http://www.chabad.org/library/article_cdo/aid/542288/jewish/Why-Break-a-Glass-at-a-Wedding.htm.

Westbrook, Caroline. "Jewish Wedding Rites." BBC: Religions, July 24, 2009. Accessed July 24, 2015, at http://www.bbc.co.uk/religion/religions/judaism/rites/weddings_1.shtml.

JUMPING OVER THE BROOM, UNITED KINGDOM AND UNITED STATES, ALSO NEO-PAGANISM

Jumping over the broom, also known as jumping the broom or as a besom wedding, is a wedding ritual that sees a newly married couple jump over a broom. The custom is associated with the United Kingdom and the United States and is also part of pagan weddings. (*See* Plate 12.)

Some historians claim that the custom of jumping the broom originated in Africa as the custom is associated with the antebellum marriages of slaves in the United States. However other academics highlight a lack of evidence to this assertion and instead highlight that there is evidence that the custom took place in Europe before the slave trade began. Indeed many folklorists believe that jumping the broom originated in the United Kingdom, most probably in Wales, during the 18th century, though British gypsies (Roma) that settled in Wales during the 17th century may also have performed the custom. In Wales, the jumping over the broom custom went as follows: A broom made of birch or oak was placed diagonally in the open doorway of a home with the end of the broom's handle resting on the door post. Witnesses would then watch as the groom jumped over the broom and into the home followed by the bride. However if either of the couple touched the broom as they jumped or the broom was dislodged, the marriage would not be recognized. This form of marriage was not acknowledged by church authorities but was, nonetheless, widespread throughout Wales and was commonly practiced up until the end of the 19th century. For this reason a common expression used in the United Kingdom to describe a co-habiting, unmarried couple is that they are "married over the broomstick" or "living over the brush."

At the start of the 20th century, writers noted that jumping over the broom was still regularly practiced by Roma living in England and Scotland as late as 1909. A gypsy couple would jump over a broom and/or tongs during their wedding for two reasons. First, the broomstick and tongs symbolized the unbreakable union of marriage and second, because the broomstick represented evil witchcraft jumping over the broom symbolized that wedded love would always overcome sorcery. For this reason jumping over the broomstick was also practiced in the South Tyrol in northern Italy during the 19th and early 20th centuries. Some historians also suggest that the broomstick holds phallic properties and interpret the tradition of jumping over the broom as symbolic of sexual intercourse since it was a widely held belief that a woman that jumped over a broom would bear children. Meanwhile an old adage in the north of England holds that if a girl steps over a broomstick she will bear children out of wedlock.

In the United States, southern slave owners would often provide perfunctory wedding services for their slaves by having the slaves jump over a broomstick. This form of wedding service acted as a compromise for slaves that were not sufficiently favored by their masters to be given a more elaborate wedding ceremony and those that were not happy to live together as husband and wife without some form of formal expression of their commitment to each other. There were many variations to this ritual. For instance, sometimes the broom would be placed on the floor and other times it would be held above the ground. Similarly, sometimes a couple would jump over the broom simultaneously while other couples would jump one after the other. There are also reports of couples having to jump backward over the broom, which the slave owner held about one foot from the floor, one after the other, and whichever of the couple jumped over the broom without touching it was destined to be the boss in the relationship. If neither touched the broomstick then the marriage would be peaceful.

In recent years, jumping over the broom has become a cherished marriage custom among some African Americans that consider the custom not only a preferred nuptial ritual but also an essential element of African American tradition. To that end, a jumping-over-the-broom cottage industry has evolved that includes a proliferation of books on the subject such as *Jumping the Broom: The African American Wedding Planner* by Harriet Cole (1993), as well as specially manufactured highly ornate wedding brooms that either incorporate elements that hark back to the era of the slave trade or include some form of family keepsake. That said, African Americans that do not wish to dwell on the slave trade feel that there is a stigma attached to jumping over the broom. When the slave trade ended, many African Americans did not wish to entertain any custom associated with slavery and the tradition of jumping over the broom was, in the main, discarded. The practice survived, however, and was reinvigorated after the publication of Alex Haley's novel *Roots: The Saga of an American Family* in 1976 and the subsequent adaptation of the book into a television miniseries the following year. In Haley's book, the lead character, Kunta Kinte, jumps high over a broom when he weds his wife, Bell.

Jumping over the broom is also an element of some contemporary neo-pagan wedding ceremonies. Neo-pagan couples have adopted the custom as part of their Pan-Celtic wedding rituals along with handfasting—despite jumping the broom being Welsh in origin and handfasting being traditionally associated with Scotland. This is because neo-pagans see jumping over the broom as an expression of their Celtic heritage while at the same time viewing the broomstick as a sweeping away of both the past and evil since a superstition holds that brooms are able to sweep away all negative energies and attract good luck. Jumping over the broom is often the concluding act of a neo-pagan wedding as neo-pagans see the broom as a symbol of the sexual union of male and female for the physical shape of the broom is akin to God's sacred phallus uniting with the Goddess. The broom is therefore used by some neo-pagans in acts of "fertility magick" and is generally seen by some neo-pagans as a symbol of fertility hence it is included in some neo-pagan weddings in order to confer fertility on the newly wedded couple. In January 2015, the first gay pagan marriage took place in Edinburgh, capital of Scotland, in which the two grooms (both hedge witches) jumped over a broom wearing black robes after having undergone a handfasting ceremony. The ceremony had to take place in Scotland, as this is the only country of the United Kingdom to allow pagans to solemnize legal weddings. The marriage was presided over by the Pagan Federation

(Scotland), which has conducted similar ceremonies for hundreds of mixed sex couples since 2005.

See also: British Wedding Traditions; Handfasting; Lovespoons

Further Reading

BBC. "Same-sex Couple Married in Pagan First." BBC News: Scotland, January 19, 2015. Accessed May 29, 2015, at http://www.bbc.co.uk/news/uk-scotland-edinburgh-east-fife-30885393.

Becker, Audrey L., and Kristin Noone, eds. *Welsh Mythology and Folklore in Popular Culture: Essays on Adaptations in Popular Culture: Essays on Adaptations in Literature, Film, Television and Digital Media. Critical Explorations in Science Fiction and Fantasy*, Volume 33. Jefferson, NC: McFarland & Company Inc. Publishers, 2011.

California African American Museum. "Origin." Accessed May 29, 2015, at https://www.caamuseum.org/documents/TEMPIE%20AND%20EXTER%20(2).pdf.

Dundes, Alan. "'Jumping the Broom': On the Origin and Meaning of an African American Wedding Custom," *The Journal of American Folklore*, 109(433), Summer 1996, 324–329.

McCoy, Edain. *Magick & Rituals of the Moon*. Second edition. St. Paul, MN: Llewellyn Publications, 2001.

Monger, George P. *Marriage Customs of the World: From Henna to Honeymoons*. Santa Barbara, CA: ABC-CLIO, 2004.

Scafidi, Susan. *Who Owns Culture? Appropriation and Authenticity in American Law*. New Brunswick, NJ: Rutgers University Press, 2005.

Sullivan III, C. W. "'Jumping the Broom': A Further Consideration of the Origins of an African American Wedding Custom," *The Journal of American Folklore,* 110(436), Spring 1997, 203–204.

JURY DUTY, INTERNATIONAL

Jury duty, also known as jury service, is the act of sitting on a jury during a legal proceeding. Jury duty occurs in many countries where it is considered one of life's civic obligations. This is despite the fact that being called for jury duty is often a matter of chance and can inconvenience individuals. The number of jurors used in trials varies around the world. For example, in the United Kingdom juries consist of 12 jurors, while in Brazil 7 are used and in Norway 10 are needed. Various countries employ different legal systems so the way in which people have to act as jurors varies from country to country.

In many countries, being a juror can be a great responsibility as juries can determine guilt or innocence in criminal cases and civil cases. Criminal cases are cases in which a county, state, or national government takes legal action because it is believed that the accused person committed one or more acts deemed illegal by the government. These acts include murder and robbery and jurors may have to decide whether to send a defendant to prison or even to death if they believe that the accused is guilty. Civil cases are cases in which an individual or organization takes action against another. In such cases a jury may have to decide disputes over property or contracts. A juror performing jury duty will have to listen to evidence from both the prosecution and the defense and then decide the facts. Sometimes jurors are given specific rules known as jury instructions by the judge, which aim to help the jurors make their decisions. Jurors also take notes during the trial and use these as well as the jury instructions to decided the verdict after having discussed the case with each other. Discussions by jurors are referred to as jury deliberations and are presided over by the leader of the jury, who is known by the title of jury foreman. Once all deliberations are over the jury returns its verdict to the judge. In some areas, a verdict must be unanimous, by which is meant all jurors agree on the jury's decision. In other places, however, a decision must simply reflect the view of the majority of jurors. When a jury cannot reach a verdict, this is known as a hung jury, something that may lead the judge to announce a mistrial.

Some countries, such as Britain and Commonwealth countries, have very old jury systems while others countries have more recently developed legal systems that have evolved during the last hundred years following political or legal changes. One recent change experienced by the legal systems of many countries is the proportion of verdicts determined by juries has declined greatly. This decrease in the number of trials heard by juries, the decrease in the number of people serving jury duty, is mainly due to the imposition of a growing number of legal restrictions, increasing litigation costs, plea-bargaining, and other forms of dispute resolution. Recently, a number of countries have also considered new ways of integrating individuals into their legal systems in the role of decision makers. In the recent past Argentina, Japan, Korea, Russia, Spain, and Venezuela have all modified their legal systems to include citizens that do not belong to the legal profession, either as part of traditional juries composed solely of people that are not professionally part of the legal system or as part of mixed juries in which people that are not legal professionals sit alongside professional judges to determine verdicts.

The issue of citizen participation in trials is becoming more and more complex but legal systems worldwide suggest there is continuing support for having citizens sit on juries. Advocates of citizen participation maintain that the custom is vital to sound fact-finding as it reduces the potential for incompetence and corruption and offsets the views of judges who may hold dated or out-of-touch opinions. Proponents of jury duty maintain that juries consisting of people that do not belong to the legal profession mean that the community and society in general are represented in the courtroom thereby helping to guarantee that verdicts are consistent with prevailing local ideals concerning justice and impartiality. Juries consisting of citizens also create a buffer between a judge and potential negative community reaction when unpopular verdicts are reached. It has also been claimed that the practice of having laypeople sit on juries is beneficial to a country on the whole as it means that the country's population will be educated about the law, creates a sense of justice and legitimizes the justice system. Despite these arguments, however, the use of citizens as jurors also attracts criticism. The main charge against jury duty is that individual verdicts that seem inconsistent with publicized evidence can cause public outcry. Additionally, in the United States civil juries have been accused of being overly generous to plaintiffs. The mixed jury system that sees citizens determine the outcome of a case in consultation with professional judges has also attracted criticism, however. Critics of this system consider this approach to be ineffectual since laypeople tend to simply agree with the professional judges as they assume that the judges know or understand more than they do. Collaborative legal systems exist in Germany and France. In Germany the *Schöffen* collaborative court system sees a professional judge sit alongside two laypeople, though the specific number and composition of those assessing a case varies depending on how serious the case is and how severe the punishment, if any, will be. In France the collaborative court system also sees professional judges determine a verdict in conjunction with citizens. In France, however, the ratio of laypeople to professional judges is greater than in Germany. The French *cour d'assises* (assize court) handles serious criminal cases and sees three professional judges work with nine jurors to decide the guilt or innocence of the accused individual. In recent years a French jury court of appeal, *cour d'assises d'appel*, featuring 12 jurors and 3 professional judges, has been introduced. The cour d'assises d'appel conducts fresh examinations of case evidence and runs on the basis of majority rule. The jury models in Germany and France, although both collaborative in nature, differ in the way that lay jurors are selected and treated. In Germany, laypeople are engaged as members of the court and sit at the front of the courtroom with the professional judge. In France, however, lay jurors are selected at random from all members of the country's population that are eligible to sit as jurors. In addition, French lay jurors do not serve as members of the court as do the laypeople acting as part of the German *Schöffen*. Instead, during their time as jurors, French jurors sit apart from the judges with the jurors and judges coming together only when it is time to deliberate and reach a verdict. Another type of mixed collaborative court is the so-called expert assessor collaborative court model. This system sees members of a community that are expert in a particular area deemed relevant to a case sit with one or more judges to reach a verdict. For example this system exists in Croatia, where citizens that are teachers, lecturers, or other individuals with relevant experience of juvenile education, help to decide the outcome of cases involving juvenile defendants.

Many countries that once belonged to the British Empire inherited the English legal system, including jury service. After gaining independence from Britain, some former British colonies such as South Africa and Singapore abandoned the jury system because it was association with the British, while others, such as Hong Kong, kept the system and cemented it as a permanent element of their legal systems. In the former British colonies that kept the jury service system, there continues to be strong public support for the practice. In Great Britain, despite a recent decline in the number of jury trials, most demographic groups support the concept of individuals being tried by a jury of their peers. Indeed, when people living in England and Wales are asked their preference for verdicts being reached by a judge or a jury most people claim a preference for verdicts being reached by a jury rather than a judge or a magistrate. Similar support for the jury service system occurs elsewhere in the Commonwealth, though Canadians tend to feel that both judge and jury are as likely as each other to arrive at fair verdicts. It should be noted, however, that Canadians that have served as jurors or know others who have been jurors tend to recommend juries rather than judges as the fairest decision makers. Similarly recent research in New Zealand found that most people rated the jury system as being an excellent or good way of reaching a verdict. Meanwhile, research in Australia has found that Australians that have served as jurors are significantly more supportive of the jury system than Australians that have no experience of serving on a jury.

In the United States, a person's jury duty is initiated by a call for jury duty, usually a letter sent through the post telling an individual to be at a court on a certain date at a certain time. To be eligible for jury duty, the person must be a legal citizen of the United States, be at least 18 years of age, never been charged with a felony crime, be able to speak fluent English, and have lived in the jurisdiction in which the jury is called for at least one year. Most U.S. citizens are called for jury duty at least once and they must comply if asked as jury duty is not optional. That said, the process of jury selection usually eliminates most potential jurors with jurors questioned by attorneys and then either selected or rejected. Additionally, potential jurors considered to have a conflict of interest with the case in question—such as when somebody has prior knowledge of the case (e.g., knowing someone involved in it)—are not permitted to be on the jury of that case. This is because a conflict of interest may affect a juror's decision-making abilities. In states where the death penalty is a possibility, jurors must also be death-qualified, meaning they must not be opposed to the death penalty. There are two main types of juries in the United States: the grand jury and the trial jury. A grand jury, which occurs in about half of all American states, consists of 12 to 23 people who determine if there is sufficient evidence to proceed to full trial. Grand juries do not, however, determine a defendant's guilt or innocence. A trial jury meanwhile uses jurors in cases such as murders and robberies. In the United States, the public is strongly supportive of trial by jury. However both Britons and Americans tend to resist the idea of juries determining the outcome of cases involving terrorism charges.

See also: Dunmow Flitch Trials; Jury Duty Guide, United States; Jury Summons Guide, United Kingdom; *Trokosi*: Female Ritual Servitude (Volume 1); White Coat Ceremony and Pinning Ceremony

Further Reading

Conrad, Clay S. "Are You 'Death Qualified'?" CATO Institute, August 10, 2000. Accessed November 30, 2015, at http://www.cato.org/publications/commentary/are-you-death-qualified.

Ferguson, Andrew Guthrie. *Why Jury Duty Matters: A Citizen's Guide to Constitutional Action.* New York: New York University Press, 2013.

Hans, Valerie P. "Jury Systems around the World," *Cornell Law Faculty Publications*. Paper 305. January 1, 2008. Accessed November 30, 2015, at http://scholarship.law.cornell.edu/facpub/305.

Judiciary of the Hong Kong Special Administrative Region of the People's Republic of China. "Jury." February 1, 2012. Accessed May 29, 2016, at http://www.judiciary.gov.hk/en/crt_services/pphlt/html/jury.htm#1.

Karlsgodt, Paul G., ed. *World Class Actions: A Guide to Group and Representative Actions around the Globe*. Oxford, UK: Oxford University Press, 2012.

National Geographic. "Jury." *National Geographic: Education: Encyclopedic Entry A*. Accessed November 30, 2015, at http://education.nationalgeographic.org/encyclopedia/jury/.

Related Primary Document: Jury Duty Guide, United States

Jury duty is considered by many people to be one of the most important civic duties a person can perform. This is because by acting as a juror a person helps to protect rights and liberties within the court system. In the United States each district or county court selects at random the names of citizens from lists of registered voters and those people that hold drivers licenses and live within the district. Any person chosen at random must fill out a questionnaire that helps to establish whether or not they are fit to perform jury duty. People that are deemed qualified for jury duty are then selected at random to appear for jury duty. This process aims to ensure that jurors are representative of their community regardless of their ethnicity, gender, age, country of origin, or political persuasion.

The following is taken from the United States Courts website and details which individuals are eligible for federal jury duty in America, those people that are exempt from performing federal jury duty, and possible reasons for individuals to be excused from carrying out federal jury duty.

Juror Qualifications

To be legally qualified for jury service, an individual must:

- be a United States citizen;
- be at least 18 years of age;
- reside primarily in the judicial district for one year;
- be adequately proficient in English to satisfactorily complete the juror qualification form;
- have no disqualifying mental or physical condition;
- not currently be subject to felony charges punishable by imprisonment for more than one year; and
- never have been convicted of a felony (unless civil rights have been legally restored)

There are three groups that are exempt from federal jury service:

- members of the armed forces on active duty;
- members of professional fire and police departments; and
- "public officers" of federal, state or local governments, who are actively engaged full-time in the performance of public duties.

Persons employed on a full-time basis in any of these categories are barred from serving on federal juries, even if they desire to do so.

Excuses from Jury Service

Each of the 94 federal district courts maintains its own jury procedures and policies regarding excuses from jury service. Many courts offer excuses from service, on individual request, to designated groups of persons or occupational classes. Such groups may include persons over age 70; persons who have, within the past two years, served on a federal jury; and persons who serve as volunteer fire fighters or members of a rescue squad or ambulance crew.

The Jury Act also allows courts to excuse a juror from service at the time he or she is summoned on the grounds of "undue hardship or extreme inconvenience." The juror should write a letter to the clerk of court requesting an excuse with an explanation of hardship.

Excuses for jurors are granted at the discretion of the court and cannot be reviewed or appealed to Congress or any other entity.

Source: *Juror Qualifications, United States Courts, Federal Judiciary.* Available at http://www.uscourts.gov/services-forms/jury-service/juror-qualifications.

Related Primary Document: Jury Summons Guide, United Kingdom

In the United Kingdom, where jury duty is known as jury service, the jury system has existed since it was imported into England after the Norman conquest of the 11th century. The jury is regarded as a vital part of the English and Welsh legal system though, today, not every case is tried by jury. In England and Wales, however, the presence of a jury is considered essential to creating a sense that the criminal justice system works for the benefit of the public and cannot be abused. Though the number of jurors remains the same (at 12 jurors), the qualifications for an individual to serve on a jury have changed in the last few decades. The age limit has been reduced to 18 years of age and the eligibility to serve as a juror now includes anyone registered on the electoral register and who is not excluded from jury service for some other reason. The basic qualifications for jury service are that an individual must be between 18 and 70 years of age and have been a resident in the United Kingdom for at least 5 years since the age of 13 years. Schedule 1, part 1 of the Juries Act 1974, as amended by the Juries Disqualifications Act 1984, lists four categories of individuals considered ineligible for jury service: members of the judiciary, members of the legal profession and other persons connected with the administration of justice, members of the clergy, and the mentally ill. In addition Schedule 1, part II (as amended) disqualifies any person who has been sentenced to more than 5 years imprisonment in the United Kingdom as well as individuals who have served any part of a sentence in the past 10 years, have been on probation in the last 5 years or who are currently on bail.

The following is an excerpt from the Introduction to the United Kingdom government's online Guide to Jury Summons outlining the importance of an individual serving as a juror.

You are one of many people who have been chosen for jury service. As a juror, you will play a vital part in the legal system. Jury service is one of the most important civic duties that anyone can be asked to perform. The experiences and knowledge of each person summoned to serve will differ, yet each individual juror will be asked to consider the evidence presented and then apply their common sense in order to determine whether or not the defendant is guilty. Jurors usually try the more serious criminal cases such as burglary, fraud, or murder. These trials take place in the Crown Court. When a jury reaches a verdict, they are not only making a decision that affects the individual defendant, they are also making a decision that affects the communities in which they live. Few decisions made by members of the public have such an impact upon society as a jury's verdict. This booklet contains guidance notes to help you complete the form 'Reply to the Jury Summons'.

Source: *Guide to Jury Summons. Available at http://hmctsformfinder.justice.gov.uk /courtfinder/forms/jury-summons-guide-eng.pdf.*

K

KUMBH MELA, HINDUISM

Kumbh Mela is an annual Hindu pilgrimage held in northern India that brings together Hindu people, including saints, gurus, and monks, who wish to cleanse themselves of sin by bathing in a holy river and praying for redemption. Many Hindus also travel for Kumbh Mela in the hope of receiving spiritual guidance and blessing. For most Hindus participating in Kumbh Mela is a transformative and once-in-a-lifetime experience. Kumbh Mela is the biggest religious gathering in the world as demonstrated by the fact that in 2013 over 80 million people attended Kumbh Mela when the festival was held in Allahabad. The exact location of Kumbh Mela varies on a rotational basis between four of the holiest Hindu sites in India—the banks of the Godavari River in Nashik, the Shipra River in Ujjain, the Ganges River in Haridwar, and the confluence of the Ganges, Yamuna, and mythical Saraswati rivers in Allahabad (also called Prayag) that is referred to as the Triveni Sangam. The fabled Saraswati River is said to be invisible and flow underground to where it joins the other two rivers. The point of confluence of all three rivers is sacred to Hindus. The location and timing of each year's festival are determined astrologically by the position of the Sun in relation to the moon and Jupiter. The rotational location system of Kumbh Mela means that the festival is held in each location once every 12 years, except for the Great Kumbh Mela at Allahabad that takes place once every 144 years. Kumbh Mela normally takes place in January or February despite the fact that at this time of year the water temperature of the rivers is low. However because the timing of Kumbh Mela is determined in such a way as to ensure that the dates of the festival are auspicious, those attending the event are willing to brave the cold water. Kumbh Mela lasts for up to two months during which time eating meat and drinking alcohol are forbidden. Such is the belief in lucky dates and times that in the past pilgrims have been crushed in stampedes as they try to reach the river at the time determined by astronomers to be the most auspicious.

The exact history of Kumbh Mela is not known, though a Chinese monk called Xuangzang referred to the festival when writing about his travels in India in 629. American writer Mark Twain also mentioned his visit to Kumbh Mela when detailing his travels in Asia in 1895. The origins of Kumbh Mela lie in a well-known Hindu legend that tells of a cosmic battle between gods and demons for possession of a pitcher of *amrit* (divine nectar) that endows immortality. According to legend, the gods and demons fought each other for 12 days and nights (comparable to 12 human years) and during the quarrel four drops of the sacred nectar fell to earth and landed in the four locations that are the sites of Kumbh Mela. For this reason the name *Kumbh* (meaning pitcher or pot) and *Mela* (festival or fair) translates as Festival of the Pitcher or the Pot Fair.

The main reason for Hindus attending Kumbh Mela is to experience a ritual bath on the banks of one of these holy rivers. However not all Hindus experience Kumbh Mela in the same way with different Hindu groups participating in their own particular customs. Pilgrims start the festival by taking a ritual bath on the banks of the river that is the location for that year's festival. Next singing, religious teaching, and chanting occur, and the poor are fed. One of the most famous Hindu groups to attend Kumbh Mela is the sect of religious ascetics known as the *sadhus* (meaning holy men) who wear sheets colored saffron-yellow to demonstrate their renunciation of materiality and decorate their skin with ashes. (*See* Plate 13.) The arrival of the sadhus to the location of the festival is known as the Peshwai Procession. In 2013, this procession saw senior sadhus sit on chariots as fireworks were lit, bands played, and *Naga* (naked) sadhus performed acrobatics.

The Naga sadhus bathe naked (or only wearing a garlands of marigolds) in the river even though the water is extremely cold. The Naga sadhus forego clothing because they are devotees of Lord Shiva and emulate the god by sporting ashes rather than clothes. The nakedness of the Naga sadhus also demonstrates their rejection of worldly goods. Though the sadhus and Naga sadhus are the most eye-catching festival attendees and receive the most media coverage, the majority of festival participants are ordinary Hindus, who, for the most part, have made arduous journeys from rural areas to take part in the event. Hindus living outside of India also participate in the festival.

Though Kumbh Mela is generally regarded as a peaceful gathering, violence, including crimes such as rape and murder, does occur at the festival, something that pilgrims take to mean that the gods and demons of legend are still at war. As well as stampedes and crime there is also the danger of contracting disease caused by millions of people gathering around the naturally unsanitary location of a river. Due to this risk of disease, health authorities in Allahabad issued warnings against drinking the river water in 2013. Another safety concern for authorities is the rise in the number of families bringing elderly relatives, particularly elderly widowed family members (most especially widows), to the pilgrimage site and then abandoning them so that they stop being a financial burden to their families. Indeed, such is the recent prevalence of this practice that Kumbh Mela organizers now anticipate elderly widows being left behind and have plans in place to deal with the situation. Indian authorities do, however, go to great lengths to try and ensure the health and security of pilgrims. In 2013, a temporary city was established on the banks of the Ganges, providing 40,000 lavatories, drinking water facilities, 14 basic hospitals, 30,000 police, and 243 doctors as well as extra train services and other forms of transportation to help pilgrims reach the river. Kumbh Mela hosts also provide thousands of volunteers to help pilgrims, especially the ill, infirm, and elderly, to participate in the ritual bathing while other volunteers concentrate on ushering pilgrims that have bathed away from the river to allow others access to the water. In addition, in the high-tech era, there is also an app that allows smart-phone owning Hindus to navigate their way to the festival location.

See also: *Diwali* and *Kali Pooja*; *Hajj*; *Kumari* and *Deuki* (Volume 1); *Samskaras*; Vrindavan: The City of Widows (Volume 3)

Further Reading

Brockman, Norbert C. *Encyclopedia of Sacred Places, Volume 1*. Second edition. Santa Barbara, CA: ABC-CLIO, 2011.

Dikshit, Rajeev. "Peshwai Procession of Juna Akhada Attracts Devotees," *The Times of India*, February 28, 2013. Accessed September 13, 2015, at http://timesofindia.indiatimes.com/city/varanasi/Peshwai-procession-of-Juna-Akhada-attracts-devotees/articleshow/18737314.cms.

Dutt, Nabanita, ed. *To North India with Love: A Travel Guide for the Connoisseur*. San Francisco, CA: ThingsAsian Press, 2011.

Galvan, Javier A., ed. *They Do What? A Cultural Encyclopedia of Extraordinary and Exotic Customs from around the World*. Santa Barbara, CA: ABC-CLIO, 2014.

Pandey, Geeta. "India's Hindu Kumbh Mela Festival Begins in Allahabad." BBC News: India, January 14, 2013. Accessed September 13, 2015, at http://www.bbc.co.uk/news/world-asia-india-21006259.

Walk Through India. "The 7 Most Sacred Rivers of India." Walk Through India. Accessed September 13, 2015, at http://www.walkthroughindia.com/attraction/the-7-most-sacred-rivers-of-india/.

LA QUINCEAÑERA, LATIN AMERICA, THE CARIBBEAN, AND THE UNITED STATES

La Quinceañera, or 15th Birthday, is a celebration held in Latin America, areas of the Caribbean, and among Latin communities in the United States, particularly in Texas, to mark a girl's transition to womanhood. La Quinceañera is similar to a Sweet Sixteen party or debutante ball as it acknowledges that a girl, known as the quinceañera, has reached sexual maturity and also, therefore, a marriageable age. La Quinceañera is also referred to as *la fiesta de quince años, la fiesta de quinceañera, la quince años*, or simply as *quince*. In Portuguese-speaking Brazil, the celebration is known as *festa de debutantes, baile de debutantes*, or *festa de quinze anos*, while in the French Caribbean and French Guiana, it is called *fête des quinze ans*. Theologians point out that though La Quinceañera is closely associated with the Catholic faith it is also enjoyed by other religions, namely Anglicans, Baptists, and Lutherans and is, therefore, an important way to assist cultural assimilation in countries that are not always welcoming to immigrants and other outsiders.

The exact history of La Quinceañera is unknown and is the subject of much debate among both theologians and those who study Mexican history and culture. Some academics believe that the rite of La Quinceañera may have originated with the Aztecs who would formally mark a female's transition to womanhood by lecturing her on her adult responsibilities or alternatively harks back to the customs of the Mayans and Toltecas of the fourth century who would present male and female 15-year-olds to tribal communities during religious feasts while highlighting the teenage female's capacity for childbearing. Others suggest La Quinceañera is Aztec in origin since the Aztecs would send 12- or 13-year-old girls to one of two types of school: the *calmacac* for those who would be devoted to religious service and the *telpucucali* for girls destined for marriage. By the age of 15, the second group of Aztec girls would be ready to enter adulthood as wives and mothers. Other theories suggest that La Quinceañera derives from 17th-century French customs since the ritual includes the creation of a quasi-royal court. It is only recently that La Quinceañera has been celebrated by all strata of Latin American society. Until the Mexican Revolution of 1910, Mexican lower classes would assist the upper classes with their La Quinceañera celebrations but would not hold their own. Meanwhile, in Cuba La Quinceañera was not celebrated by the lower and middle classes until the 1940s.

Originally La Quinceañera consisted of nothing more than saying a rosary, theological meditation, and saying the Lord's Prayer and Hail Mary. Today there is no set way of celebrating La Quinceañera and many La Quinceañera celebrations now follow a theme (e.g., Cinderella's ball). Though the Catholic Church has never officially sanctioned La Quinceañera, many Latinas nonetheless view the coming-of-age rite as a religious tradition. In Mexico if the quinceañera is a Catholic then the most important element of La Quinceañera is her thanksgiving mass called *La misa de acción de gracias* during which the girl, who will have been baptized as a baby, also retakes her baptismal vows to show that she makes her commitment to God of her own adult free will. The quinceañera arrives at church for the mass wearing special occasion wear, usually an elaborately frilly, feminine dress (*el vestido*) in soft pastel colors as well as a hat or headdress. The dress that the girl wears to mass is usually her first formal adult gown, which, like a wedding dress, reveals that her status within the community has changed. The girl is accompanied by her parents and *padrinos* and *madrinas* (godfathers and godmothers) plus a court of honor consisting of maids of honor known as *damas* and *chambelanes* (chamberlains or male escorts) selected from her friends and family. During the mass, the girl's godparents give her a necklace or a locket depicting a religious figure or a prayer book and rosary set called the *libro y rosario*. This gift consists of a prayer book and rosary that are bigger than those given to a child completing their Catholic sacraments and so demonstrate that the girl is now viewed as an adult member of the Catholic community. The girl may be presented with a religious medal too. This gift is proffered by her *madrina de medella*, or sponsor of the medal, and usually depicts the most popular Mexican Catholic saint, *Virgen de Guadalupe* (the Virgin of Guadalupe). The madrina de medella is normally an older relative, such as aunt or sister, and by accepting her gift the quinceañera signals that she is now an adult woman sharing a bond with the other adult females of her community. Another older female known as the *madrina de anillo* gives the girl a ring displaying her appropriate birthstone. This ring is intended to symbolize the girl's commitment to both God and her community, though it is often pointed out that the ring is viewed by both the girl and her family as a precursor to the ring that will signal the girl's next stage in life, the wedding ring. The girl is also presented with a tiara reflecting the sentiment that in the eyes of her friends and family the girl will always be regarded as a princess. The tiara is also used to replace the hat or headdress that the girl wore when entering the church. This crowning may be performed by her godparents and accompanied by the presentation of a sceptre that symbolizes both the quinceañera's new adult authority and the fact that by experiencing La Quinceañera she must also assume the responsibilities of adulthood. The mass also sees the quinceañera recite "A Prayer for the Dedication of the Girl" in which she implores God to guide her thoughts and actions and she may be presented with a kneeling pillow specially decorated with the girl's name that is placed in position for her to kneel on during the mass. At the conclusion of the mass, the girl's younger sisters, cousins, and friends hand out commemorative favors called *bolos* to all the guests while the girl places a bouquet of flowers on the church altar or by a statue of the Virgin Mary.

La Quinceañera is not exclusively focused on the girl's relationship with God however, but also on her bond with the parents, whom she must continue to honor despite attaining adulthood. An important tradition associated with La Quinceañera, the Changing of the Shoes custom, sees the quinceañera's father or other male relative ceremoniously remove her flat shoes and replace them with high heels denoting womanhood thereby marking that her father now accepts his daughter is a woman.

Traditionally, the girl must make a choice of how she continues her special day—she can either opt for a *viaje* (a journey) or a *fiesta* (a party). Though it was once fashionable for girls to select the journey, today girls from all sections of society tend to choose a party complete with a live band that will play loud *banda*, *cumbia*, and *salsa* music. The finances of the girl's parents and padrinos directly determine the level of lavishness displayed by the fiesta. La Quinceañera celebrations held in cities usually take place in a hired banqueting hall whereas those held in villages take place in a girl's home or among folding tables in orchards or corrals. To help cover the cost of the fiesta, godparents may sometimes ask members of the quinceañera's community to sponsor her dress, the hiring of the fiesta's venue, the band, drinks, and celebration cake. During the party, a toast is held to honor the girl who also gets to cut a multi-tiered cake. A La Quinceañera cake tends to be covered in frosting that is pastel colored to match the girl's dress and so large that the doors of the party venue may need to be removed to allow the cake to enter the venue.

The culmination of La Quinceañera sees the girl perform a highly choreographed waltz routine with her father who then passes her to her favorite male escort so that they can perform another dance. After this, the quinceañera and her female friends may change their outfits to perform another even more complicated dance routine that shows off their dancing skills.

At some point during La Quinceañera the girl may be presented with *entrega de la ultima muneca*, or a Last Doll. This is a decorative figurine representing the last childish things the quinceañera will own as now she must focus on adult life. The doll also, perhaps, signifies that the girl is capable of caring for a real child rather than a pretend one. Often printed ribbons called *cápias* that bear the quinceañera's name and the date are pinned to the doll. When the quinceañera goes among her guests thanking them for attending her party, it is customary for her to clutch the Last Doll in her hand while doing so. In addition the quinceañera will sometimes pass her doll on to her younger sibling.

Though many see La Quinceañera as an avowal of a girl's religiosity others view the ritual as the time from which a young woman can indulge in adult fashions and make-up, as well as dating. A high proportion of Mexican parents do not allow their daughters to date or dress in an adult manner until they have experienced La Quinceañera. This has led some Roman Catholic leaders to criticize the custom of La Quinceañera as they feel the rite gives the impression that 15-year-old girls are sexually mature adult women since they wear dresses similar to wedding gowns and have a court of attendants resembling a wedding party.

Though La Quinceañera is extremely popular, the rite attracts criticism from feminists who point out that Latino boys are not expected to go through such a ceremony to prove their obedience to the Catholic faith and their family.

The custom of La Quinceañera is well represented in popular culture. Released in 2006, the popular film *Quinceañera* looked at the travails of a pregnant 15-year-old Mexican who finds she is expecting a child during the run-up to her La Quinceañera and despite being a virgin. Meanwhile, the award-winning feature length documentary *La Quinceañera* (2007) follows preparations for the ceremony in Tijuana, Mexico. Recently La Quinceañera has been the focus of a genre of novels aimed at young adults. These include the 2006 novel *Estrella's Quinceañera* by Malin Alegria, and *Quinceañera Means Sweet 15* (2001) by Veronica Chalmers, a humorous first-person narrative looking at a girl's preparations for her coming-of-age celebration in the face of financial difficulties and troubles associated with adolescence.

In recent years another ritual inspired by, La Quinceañera has begun—there is a growing trend for women turning 50 years of age to celebrate their *La Cincuentañera* (50th birthday). This rite draws on elements of La Quinceañera but celebrates the woman's adult life, her personal accomplishments, and her professional achievements. *La Cincuentañera* is not always totally serious, however, for instead of a madrina de medulla or madrina de anillo, a *madrina de AARP* (formerly American Association of Retired Persons) may be present at a La Cincuentañera celebration thereby highlighting the woman's advancing years.

See also: Baptism and Christening (Volume 1); Birthday Cakes (Volume 1); Birthdays (Volume 1); Birthstones (Volume 1); Face in Birthday Cake; Fairytales (Volume 1); Filipino Debut; Retirement and Pension (Volume 3)

Further Reading

Candelaria, Cordelia, Peter J. García, and Arturo J. Aldama, eds. *Encyclopedia of Latino Popular Culture, Volume 1 A–L*. Westport, CT: Greenwood Press, 2004.

Hoyt Palfrey, Dale. "La Quinceañera: A Celebration of Budding Womanhood." Mexconnect. Accessed January 3, 2015, at http://www.mexconnect.com/articles/3192-la-quinceañera-a-celebration-of-budding-womanhood.

Mitchell, Claudia A., and Jacqueline Reid-Walsh. *Girl Culture: An Encyclopedia*. Volume 1. Westport, CT: Greenwood Press, 2007.

Quinceanera-Boutique.com. "Quinceañera Tradition." Accessed January 3, 2015, at http://www.quinceanera-boutique.com/quinceaneratradition.htm.

LA SOUPE, FRANCE

France has long been thought of as a country of romance, good food, and even better wine. However a fairly revolting French wedding custom called *la soupe* (also known as *la rôtie*, *la saucée*, or *saucya*) presses the limits of the image of France as a land of love and fine dining.

La soupe is a French wedding tradition that occurs after a wedding reception when the newlyweds wish to leave the party. La soupe sees all the young people at the reception endeavor to keep the new husband and wife at the reception venue for as long as possible. Eventually the newlyweds manage to escape from those guests trying to detain them and the guests gather together and concoct a liquid mixture in a chamber pot referred to as la soupe. The liquid concoction is normally made from leftover elements from the wedding reception—wine, champagne, cake (actually a French pastry known as *croquembouche* or *croque-en-bouche*), cheese, vegetables, fruit, and cookies—and once it is mixed together the guests gang together, find the newlyweds, and force them to drink la soupe. Traditionally la soupe was viewed as a way for the bridal party to clear up the mess resulting from hosting the wedding reception and also as fuel to give the newlyweds the energy to have sex after becoming exhausted over the course of their wedding day.

This rather unpleasant custom has links to an old English tradition that was prevalent many centuries ago when England was a Catholic country. The English custom, which was very popular among the aristocracy, saw the matrimonial bed blessed by a priest and then all the wedding guests would accompany the newlyweds to their bedchamber. Here the couple would go to bed, watched by the guests, and then the priest would hand them a goblet filled with sweetened, spicy wine known as Benedictine posset. In the 17th century, the posset was made of wine, milk, egg yolks, cinnamon, nutmeg, and sugar. Once the posset was blessed everybody inside the bedchamber would drink the posset from the cup. Then, when the last of the posset had been imbibed, everybody except the newlyweds would leave the bedchamber, allowing the husband and wife privacy to enjoy the night. Sometimes, however, the guests might be in mischievous mood and decide to annoy the newlyweds by banging on the bedchamber door, singing songs with lewd lyrics, and generally irritating the couple by making a lot of noise.

Another French wedding custom involving drinking is much more pleasant than la soupe but occurs only at very traditional French weddings. This custom sees the new husband and wife drink from an ornate two-handled cup called *la coupe de marriage*. It is traditional for the goblet to be passed down from one generation to the next as a cherished family heirloom.

See also: British Wedding Traditions; *Polterabend*; Wedding Cakes

Further Reading

Monger, George P. *Marriage Customs of the World: From Henna to Honeymoons*. Santa Barbara, CA: ABC-CLIO, 2004.

World Wedding Traditions. "France: French Wedding Traditions." Accessed November 29, 2015, at http://www.worldweddingtraditions.net/french-wedding-traditions/.

LADOUVANE AND ST. SYLVESTER'S DAY, BULGARIA

Bulgaria is a land of many folk customs and traditions, a number of which focus on love, marriage, and fertility. For example *Ladouvane*, sometimes called *koumichene* and occasionally referred to as the singing of the rings, is an annual festival of love and marriage held for unmarried young girls and women of marriageable age. The name of the custom honors Lada, often considered the Slavic goddess of love, who also features in songs sung at Bulgarian weddings. In western Bulgaria, the Central Balkan region and areas located along the River Danube, the festival takes place on New Year's Eve but in other areas of the country Ladouvane takes place on Midsummer's Day, June 24. When Ladouvane takes place on Midsummer's Day it is sometimes referred to as Enyovden, meaning Enyo's Day, in honor of the folktale of the ill-fated lovers Enyo and Stana. According to folklore the lovers were set to wed when Stana lifted up her wedding veil and jumped into a river from a high bridge. Enyo became gravely ill at the news of his bride-to-be's demise and took to his bed for many years, during which time no rain fell and the river dried up. On the 10th anniversary of Stana's death, her sister dressed a rolling-pin as a bride wearing a veil. This caused Enyo to rise from his bed but the shock of moving was too great for him and Enyo died, smiling as he believed he had seen his beloved once more. On Enyo's death the land became fertile again and young women sang songs of love. Ever since young Bulgarian women have sung of marriage, weddings, and good fortune on Ladouvane/Enyovden.

Preparations for Ladouvane start early on the morning of the day before the festival when all eligible females living in villages drop their rings into a cauldron of spring water along with oats and barley, both of which are symbolic of fertility. The spring water is known as *mulchana voda*, meaning silent water, because tradition dictates that the girl who draws the water from the spring must remain silent on her way back to the village. The rings of the unmarried females are tied together on a length of red thread that is attached to a bunch of perennial herbs and other plants, including basil, crane's bill geranium, and ivy. In recent years, some men have also started to take part in Ladouvane by placing their penknives in the cauldron of spring water, but this practice is not, as yet, widespread. The cauldron full of objects is then left overnight outside under the night skies. Then the next day the woman that organized the cauldron of objects is blind-folded and pulls the rings out of the water one at a time, each time making a prediction about who the owner of the ring will marry. This part of Ladouvane, which is known as singing over the rings or singing on the rings, is always a source of great amusement for the watching females as they wait eagerly anticipating which of the local men her ring suggests she will wed.

Next, the females that placed their rings in the cauldron perform a ritual dance and sing about their hopes of finding a husband and producing healthy children. However none of the songs reveal their meanings explicitly; rather, any meanings are covertly hidden in the lyrics of the folk songs. For example, some songs contain riddles or include such oblique references to desires as asking for a husband who "rides a horse and holds a falcon," which means a rich husband of high social standing. Other songs refer to "golden bracelets jingling on the bedsheet" meaning a girl wishes to marry a blacksmith. This ritual singing is then followed by *Vassilitza*, a fortune-telling tradition in which the girls and women that sung of their romantic hopes have their fortunes told by the village wise woman. Once Ladouvane is over, on St. Sylvester's Day, January 2, the unmarried women that took part in the Ladouvane events participate in further festivities that allow the unwed females to show which males actually take their fancy rather than singing of fantasy lovers. Before sunrise on St. Sylvester's Day, unmarried village men enter and clean the barns and other outbuildings belonging to the families of the unmarried girls that take their romantic fancy. The unmarried females then dance in the village square and give gifts to the boys and men that they are interested in. In some parts of Bulgaria, if the attraction proves mutual then the girl's family asks the boy to lunch to signal that they approve of the match.

See also: Bulgarian Weddings; Looking for Fern Blossoms; Maypoles; St. Catherine's Day; St. Dwynwen's Day

Further Reading
OMDA Ltd. "Bulgarian Folk Tradition: Festivals." Accessed April 4, 2015, at http://www.omda.bg/public/engl/ethnography/festivals.html.
Plovdiv Guide. "Enyovden/Enyo's Day (Midsummer's Day)—June 24." Traditions and Name Days. Accessed April 4, 201, at http://www.plovdivguide.com/_m1703/Traditions-Namedays/ENYOVDEN--Enyos-Day--Midsummer-Day----June-24--540.
Quest Bulgaria. "New Year Celebrations in Bulgaria." Accessed April 4, 2015, at http://www.questbg.com/lifestyle/life/1788-new-year-celebrations-in-bulgaria.html.

LAND DIVING, VANUATU

Land-diving competitions, known regionally as *Gol* in Sa language, and as *Nanggol*, *Nagol* or *N'gol* in the Bislama language, are annual sporting rituals that takes place in April or May in eight villages in the southern part of Pentecost Island, one of the 83 islands that makes up the South Pacific republic of Vanuatu. There are between four and eight land diving events per year.

As well as being a sporting ritual, land diving is also a rite of passage for the event sees boys over seven years old and young men leap head first from tall wooden structures that are built especially for the land diving ritual and feature many platforms ranging from 66 feet to 100 feet high. Though when they jump the men encounter speeds of up to 45 miles per hour, they do not wear any safety equipment except for two thin, supple vines called *lianas*, which are at their most elastic in April and May hence the timing of land-diving events. The lianas are tied around their ankles in the manner of the equipment worn during bungee jumping. (*See* Plate 14.) Indeed the *Guinness World Records* book asserts that land diving is the forerunner of bungee jumping. Island men jump for many reasons most commonly to enjoy the thrill, to honor old traditions, and to impress women.

Land-diving competitors dive straight down toward the hard ground—there is no mattress, water, or nets placed beneath the men to cushion their fall—the only concession to safety is that islanders use long sticks to ruck up the soil beneath the jumping tower, softening it a little. To afford a degree of personal protection, competitors cross their arms over their chests and tilt their heads before diving so that they gently graze the ground with their shoulders. Islanders believe that the diver's touching of the ground confers a blessing of guaranteed soil fertility that will produce a plentiful yam harvest. Indeed islanders think that the higher the platform from which the divers jump, the more bountiful will be the next year's harvest. Unsurprisingly, the ritual has seen competitors suffer injuries including dislocated ankles, concussion, broken arms, ruptured spleens, and crushed vertebrae. Considering that there is no hospital on the island any injury is worrying. Land diving has also caused the death of participants. Island men know that taking part in the land-diving competition could lead to their death so participants tend to settle any disputes prior to jumping, just in case something goes wrong during their dive resulting in their death. In 1974, British royal Queen Elizabeth II watched as a competitor jumped to his death—islanders believe the man died because he wore a lucky amulet as he jumped, which is contrary to land-diving traditions. Such is the inherent danger of land diving that island officials always ignore the pleas of tourists to take part in the ritual as they fear they will be liable in the case of injury or death to a foreign visitor.

Land diving is not simply an extreme sporting event however. Rather, for the people of Vanuatu the custom reveals much of their historical and cultural relationship with the land. For much of the 20th century, Vanuatu was an Anglo-French territory, obtaining its independence as recently as 1980. However the land-diving custom existed on Vanuatu for centuries prior to colonization by European settlers, though the exact history and origins of the ritual are unclear. One theory is that land diving began as a rite of passage for young men, while another suggestion is that the competition was a ritual associated with the harvest.

However the ritual began, it has always been regarded as a coming-of-age event for young males seeking to prove that they were worthy of being considered adult members of society. When a boy makes his first jump his mother stands beneath the wooden jumping tower holding one of the boy's favorite childhood items. Once he has made the dive his mother throws away the childhood object to signify that her son has become a man.

Island folklore tells of Tamalie, a man who abused his wife so frequently that she left him. When Tamalie went looking for his wife he discovered her hiding at the top of a lofty banyan tree so Tamalie climbed the tree to reclaim his wife. However Tamalie's wife, fearing her life was endangered, tied lianas to her ankles and leapt from the tree. Tamalie mistakenly believed that his wife had killed herself and became so sad about this that he too jumped from a banyan. However Tamalie did not tie vines around his ankles so when he jumped from the tree he hit the ground and died. According to legend, the rest of the island men feared that the fact that a woman had outwitted a man undermined the island's patriarchal society and immediately set about training to jump from heights without injury. Thus, land diving was born with the men learning to leap with vines attached to their ankles, gradually coming to learn what length and tension of vine was optimal for diving. The men also perfected their land-diving skills by gradually jumping from increasingly lofty heights. At some point island elders decided that women should not take part in land diving, which is ironic considering that according to legend it was a woman who invented the sport. Today women are banned from watching any pre-diving rituals though they are allowed to choreograph dances to accompany the contest that provide the divers with emotional and spiritual support. During the competition, island women wear traditional dress as do island men who eschew Western dress and instead wear traditional attire of penis sheaths and grass skirts.

The focus of Vanuatu's land-diving contest is the wooden tower (the *nagol*) from which the divers leap. It takes around 20 men up to a month to construct the tower out of tree trunks and strong branches. The tower is used only once for the platforms are designed to disintegrate once the divers have jumped from it, making an audible cracking noise as they give way. During the building of the nagol, men live in seclusion and refrain from any sexual activity. The eve of the competition sees the men sleep at the base of the tower in order to ward off evil spirits. On the morning of the competition between 10 and 15 of the men ritually wash their bodies and anoint themselves with oil. The participants may also don necklaces made of animal teeth.

On the morning of the competition a drum is beaten and a drama is performed such as one in which a good spirit is seen to overcome a mud-covered devil. After the play a lavish communal meal is served and music is played on drums and stringed instruments. The competition begins at around 2 p.m. with the youngest divers leaping from the lowest platforms. This allows the youngsters to show their bravery and counts as training for when they attempt to jump from higher platforms when they are older. Later in the day the highlight of the competition occurs when the most experienced divers ascend the nagol, make a short oration, and then jump from the highest platforms. As the young men jump, island elders chant and crowds numbering around 300 people look on.

Despite the fact that foreigners may not take part in land diving, the sport provides the island with a valuable income from tourism. Land-diving competitions were originally held at Bunlap village on the southeast coast of Pentecost Island but the sport has relocated recently and now takes place at Wali, near Lonorore airstrip, so that tourists do not have to complete a four-hour hike across the island to view the spectacle. Such is the importance of land diving to the local economy that in the 1980s the South Pentecost Tourism Council was established by local chiefs to ensure the economic benefits of land-diving tourism were maximized. The council oversaw the preparation of land-diving events and decided which men would jump. The council also set entrance fees for visitors, decided how many tourists would be allowed to watch, and established charges for filming the event. Marketing for land-diving events was overseen by a government agency called Tour Vanuatu that charged a commission rate of 3 percent as well as the Vanuatu National Tourism Office. The villages that host land-diving competitions use the income provided by the sporting events to fund community projects and purchase items that will be used by the village as a whole such as outboard motor boats. Individual islanders received an income too, with rates varying according to their role in the event, their sex, and status. In the 1990s men earned between $10 and $20. This figure was considerably more than the pay of women, who received between $2 and $5.

See also: Cow Jumping; Log Riding

Further Reading
Galvan, Javier A., ed. *They Do What? A Cultural Encyclopedia of Extraordinary and Exotic Customs from around the World.* Santa Barbara, CA: ABC-CLIO, 2014.
Istvan, Zoltan. "Reporter's Notebook: S. Pacific Ritual Bungee Jumping." National Geographic News, November 26, 2002. Accessed December 16, 2014, at http://news.nationalgeographic.com/news/2002/11/1125_021126_TVVanuatu.html.
Stanley, David. *South Pacific.* Eighth edition. Emeryville, CA: Moon Handbooks South Pacific, 2004.
Thornhill, Ted. "Head for Heights: Tribal Daredevils Are Just Inches from Death during Bizarre Bungee-Jumping Ritual." *Daily Mail*, May 4, 2012. Accessed December 16, 2014, at http://www.dailymail.co.uk/news/article-2138837/Land-Diving-ritual-sees-tribesman-bungee-just-inches-ground.html.
Zeppel, Heather. *Indigenous Ecotourism: Sustainable Development and Management.* Wallingford, UK: CAB International, 2006.

LAZAROVDEN, BULGARIA

Lazarovden, also often referred to as *Lazarouvane*, meaning St. Lazarus's Day or Saturday of Lazarus, is a Bulgarian fertility custom of Slav origin that takes place annually eight days before Easter Sunday. The day is considered the "coming out" of eligible girls under 12 years old into society and so also marks a girl's entry into womanhood. The day has various names across Bulgaria. For instance, the festival is known as *Lazaritsi* or *Buenek* in Thrace and as *Danets* in Dobrud. However in all areas of Bulgaria the festival is celebrated as a celebration of fertility, love, and marriage for according to folk tradition if a girl does not take part in the Lazarovden celebrations she will never marry. Also, since the day is located within the Easter period, Lazarovden is not only redolent of springtime fertility rituals but also of birth and rebirth in general.

The girls that take part in Lazarovden are known as *lazarki*, meaning young Lazarus girls. However apart from qualifying a girl for marriage Lazarovden has a secondary meaning for taking part in the day also means that a girl has achieved a symbolic adulthood as the day marks the first time a girl wears an adult woman's clothing in public. A girl's participation in Lazarovden is usually the first time that she dances the *horo*, a communal dance performed at public gatherings, in public too, which, like wearing adult clothing, marks her transition to maturity. Indeed it is said that when a girl takes part in Lazarovden she changes officially from a *momiché* or *momichentsé*, meaning little girl, into a *moma*—a maiden eligible to marry.

Lazardovden is marked by much singing and dancing. Girls learn the so-called Lazaritsa ritual dances performed on the day through attending previous years' celebrations. Depending on the religion of the event organizer the leader of the dance is variously called the *Lazarki, Bouyenets*, or *Buenica*. This dance leader is a woman who leads a chain of 5 to 15 dancers, both boys and girls, from house to house paying a brief visit to each family in the village. At each house, the female dancers are given undecorated eggs as a symbol of fertility and birth. The chain of dancers performs special dances such as the *horo* and folk songs, many of which pertain to finding romance and also celebrate the beauty and purity of maidens and praise maternal love. Another of the songs sung during the festivities tells how a young bride is told to dress her young daughter in red with green flowers in her hair and then send her to the Lazarovden dance leader who will teach the girl to dance. According to tradition this song should be performed unaccompanied by a trio of sisters. A cycle of pre-wedding songs is also often sung during Lazarovden. Moreover, when the chain of dancers has stopped at every house in a village the girls in the chain sing lyrics that translate as "Go away, Lazarus, but come again next year and then you will find me as a bride already." All the various songs and dances performed by the human chain are intended to bring health, wealth, and fertility to all those that live in the houses that are visited during Lazarovden, including cattle.

Costumes are central to celebrating Lazarovden with the little girls that take part in the celebrations dressed like brides in heavily embroidered dresses, silver-buckled belts, coin necklaces, and headdresses made of grass, flowers, and ribbons. The leader of the chain of dancers wears a particularly elaborate costume though this varies between regions. For instance, in Sandanski, a town in southwestern Bulgaria, the costume comprises a white *saya*, an outer garment worn over a tunic-like shirt over an embroidered blouse. The dance leader also wears an apron into the pocket of which are tucked many differently colored handkerchiefs. In the Bulgarian capital Sofia, the dance leader wears a floral headdress to which is attached a metal ornament that dangles over the leader's forehead, while in the cities of Sliven and Yambol the headdress takes the form of a cylinder of flowers.

Lazarovden is a very important tradition in Bulgaria for once a girl has come out into society she is, according to tradition, eligible for marriage and, after participating in the various Lazaritsa dances, is also qualified to start planning her wedding. In times past, Bulgarian people believed that the more elaborate a ritual the more powerful it would be. Thus Lazarovden features elaborate clothing and singing and dancing in order to express just how central marriage is to the Bulgarian people and culture.

The day after Lazarovden is Palm Sunday, which in Bulgaria is also known as the Day of Flowers. On this day it is tradition that all the girls that took part in the Lazarovden festivities also take part in an exciting event called *kumichane*. This celebration was once widely practiced in Bulgaria and although it has fallen out of fashion somewhat, many of the customs associated with the day still occur in a several regions of the country. Kumichane sees all the Lazarki girls dress in the costumes that they wore for Lazarovden and go together to the nearest river where they look for the section of the river with the calmest water. As they travel to the river the girls sing the songs they sung during Lazarovden and pick flowers as a sign of the arrival of spring as well as carrying willow twigs and baskets of eggs. In Bulgaria, willow twigs are strongly associated with Palm Sunday for the day is also known as *Vrubnitsa*, or the Feast of the Willow Branches. This tradition dates back to pagan times for in Slav folklore willow is thought to protect people from evil and black magic and also to keep people, animals, and crops safe from diseases and bad luck.

When the girls have found the smoothest section of the river, they place pieces of ritual bread on rafts made out of the willow twigs and flowers, and float them down the river. The girl whose raft floats the furthest along the river is awarded the title of *kumitsa*, which means that she will lead the dances at the next year's Lazarovden celebrations. On becoming the kumitsa, the girl invites all the other Lazarki girls back to her home where all the girls enjoy a feast of celebratory food prepared by the kumitsa's mother. These foods include traditional breads, a hominy dish called *kachamak*, and puréed nettles.

See also: Bulgarian Weddings; Filipino Debut; *Hora* and *Horah*; *Lindo*; Reed Dancing Chastity Ceremony; Obando Fertility Dance (Volume 1); *Vinok*

Further Reading

Eliznik.org. "Bulgarian Customs." Eliznik Web Pages. Accessed April 4, 2015, at http://www.eliznik.org.uk/Bulgaria/history/bulgaria_customs.htm.

MacDermott, Mercia. *Bulgarian Folk Customs*. London: Jessica Kingsley Publishers Ltd., 1998.

OMDA Ltd. "Bulgarian Folk Tradition: Festivals." Accessed April 4, 2015, at http://www.omda.bg/public/engl/ethnography/festivals.html.

Plovdiv Guide. "Tsvetnitsa—Vrubnitsa (Palm Sunday)." Current News, April 20, 2008. Accessed April 4, 2015, at http://www.plovdivguide.com/Current-News/TSVETNITSA---VRUBNITSA-Palm-Sunday-3104.

Radio Bulgaria. "Saint Lazarus Saturday and Palm Sunday in Bulgarian Folklore." Radio Bulgaria, April 6, 2012. Accessed April 4, 2015, at http://bnr.bg/en/post/100148556/saint-lazarus-saturday-and-palm-sunday-in-bulgarian-folklore.

Sanders, Irwin T. *Balkan Village*. Lexington: The University of Kentucky Press, 2014.

LEAP YEAR PROPOSAL, INTERNATIONAL

The Gregorian calendar is divided into 365 days. However every fourth year an extra day, February 29, is added to the length of the year so that the calendar matches the length of the solar year, which is roughly 365.25 days long. In many Western countries, February 29 is considered a special date as it is on this day that women are traditionally allowed to propose to men. This is not to say that women in these countries cannot propose to men on other days of the year, just that February 29 is the day singled out for this custom. However leap years are not thought of as romantic all over the world. For instance, in Greece it is felt to be bad luck for anybody to marry during a leap year and that all leap year marriages will end in divorce.

The origins of leap year proposals are disputed though the custom is often thought to be Irish or Celtic, hence the 2010 romantic-comedy film *Leap Year* follows the travails of an American woman as she travels to Ireland to propose to her beloved. According to legend, Saint Brigid of Kildare, a nun living in Ireland during the fifth century, established the tradition of the leap year proposal by beseeching Saint Patrick, the patron saint of Ireland, to allow women to propose to their lovers after learning that many men were too nervous to ask for their beloveds' hands in marriage. Saint Patrick is said to have granted women dispensation to propose to men every seven years but this was not enough for Saint Brigid, who then persuaded Saint Patrick to let women propose every four years instead. Once Saint Patrick agreed to Saint Brigid's idea she is said to have knelt down and proposed to Saint Patrick, who refused her proposal but kissed her on the cheek and gave her a silk gown to show his esteem for her. For this reason, it is traditional in Ireland that if a man refuses a woman's proposal he must buy her a dress made of silk. However historians dispute the validity of the Saint Brigid story pointing out that the saint would have been around 10 years old when Saint Patrick died in 461, so it is unlikely that Saint Brigid proposed to Saint Patrick. Similarly, it has been suggested that the leap year proposal custom began in Scotland in 1288 when unwed Queen Margaret is said to have legislated that a woman could propose on February 29 as long as the woman bent on proposing wore a red petticoat to signal her intention to everyone with whom she came into contact. However historians believe it is unlikely that Queen Margaret did enact this rule as she would have been five years old in 1288 and probably not interested in the plight of unmarried women. Also, there is no documented record of any such law.

Other European nations also link leap years with women's permission to propose. For example, in Finland it is considered to be auspicious for women to propose to men on February 29 so Finnish women tend to only propose on this date. Moreover, if a Finnish man refuses a woman's proposal then he is required to pay the woman a penalty of enough fabric to create a skirt.

In recent years, the concept of the leap year proposal has attracted criticism from some feminists who argue that the day's special dispensation for women to propose should be abolished. It has been asserted that up until the 1960s a woman in the United States faced ridicule and scorn if she proposed to a man for she would be seen as aggressive and desperate to wed. Indeed one view during this time was that if a woman were not attractive or clever enough to have received a proposal from a man then she would probably not be able to keep a husband anyway. Some feminists view leap year proposals as a throwback to this era and stress that it is retrograde to suggest that women need a special day giving them permission to instigate marriage. However a counter-argument is that leap year proposals actually empower women by allowing them to take the lead in romance.

See also: British Weddings Traditions; Courtship Whistling; Dunmow Flitch Trials; St. Catherine's Day; St. Dwynwen's Day

Further Reading

Hallett, Stephanie. "Leap Year Proposal: What's the Story Behind It?" *Huff Post Weddings*. February 29, 2012. Accessed June 6, 2015, at http://www.huffingtonpost.com/2012/02/27/leap-year-proposal-tradition_n_1305525.html.

Monger, George P. *Marriage Customs of the World: From Henna to Honeymoons*. Santa Barbara, CA: ABC-CLIO, 2004.

The Science News-Letter. "Would the World Be Better if the Women Proposed?" *The Science News-Letter*, 37(7), Feb. 17, 1940, 102–103.

LINDO, CROATIA

The *Lindo* is a high energy, theatrical courtship folk dance originating near the capital city of Croatia, Dubrovnik. The most important musical instrument in a Lindo is the *lijerica*, a triple-stringed instrument invented in the eastern Mediterranean or Greece during the 18th century that became popular along the Adriatic coast during the 19th century. Some Croatians believe that the name of the Lindo derives from the local name for the lijerica while others think the Lindo is named after Nikola Lale Lindo, a legendary dance master. The dance has been performed for over 200 years and is the most popular traditional dance along Croatia's Dalmatian coast in areas such as Dubrovnik, as well as in Konavle, a small region southeast of Dubrovnik, the Pelješac peninsula in southern Dalmatia, and on the Adriatic islands of Lastovo and Mljet.

During a performance of the Lindo, the lijerica is played by the dance master who is seated and places the instrument on his left knee while stamping his right foot on the ground in order to dictate the rhythm for those performing the dance. To perform the Lindo the dancers travel in a circle around the dance master who shouts out instructions and humorous asides laced with sexually suggestive *double entendres* while keeping time. The dance master can also order the dancers to make shapes other than circles as they dance. As well as dictating the rhythm and shape of the dance, the dance master also chooses which couples will dance together and can instruct dancers to dance against each other in a form of improvised competitive performance.

The Lindo is performed during Croatia's main cultural event, the Summer Festival; the most renowned Lindo performers are, perhaps, the folkdance ensemble called simply Lindo. This dance troop formed in 1964 in order to spread traditional Croatian songs and dances and has since performed around the world in countries across Europe as well as in South America, Australia, Japan, and the United States. In October 2013, Dubrovnik hosted the World Conference of the International Network of Cities and Custodians of Intangible Heritage. To celebrate the occasion, 274 Lindo folk dancers performed the dance in order to achieve a Guinness world record.

Another Croatian dance, the *Sokacko Kolo* or Sokac Round Line Dance, is also associated with courtship and romance and originates from Slavonia, a historical region of Croatia. The Sokacs are an ethnographic group of Croats that migrated from Bosnia to Croatia during the 19th century. The Sokacs have a specific culture and their own traditions, including the Sokacko Kolo, which is most often performed at weddings and other celebratory occasions. The Sokacko Kolo is performed in Slavonija, Baranja, and Backa, with variations danced in Baranja, which is situated between the Dunav and Drava rivers in the Pannonian plains of Croatia. This dance begins with a fast tempo called *drmes*. Singing interrupts this fast rhythm and dancers then walk in a circle in time with the singing. This pattern is repeated until the musician in the center of the circle of dancers, called the *gajde*, who plays a bagpipe type instrument, stops playing.

See also: *Hora* and *Horah*; Obando Fertility Dance (Volume 1); *Schuhplattler* and *Ländler*; Wodaabe Courtship Dance and Festival

Further Reading

Absolute Croatia. "Lindo Folklore Ensemble." Accessed May 25 2015, at http://www.absolute-croatia.com/dubrovnik-region/dubrovnik/on-stage/item/folklore-ensemble-lindo-dubrovnik.

Croatia Week. "Ancient Croatian Folk Dance Guinness Record Attempt in Dubrovnik," *Croatia Week*, October 3, 2013. Accessed May 25, 2015, at http://www.croatiaweek.com/ancient-croatian-folk-dance-guinness-record-attempt-in-dubrovnik/.

Espinosa Chauvin, Fernando. *Dubrovnik*. Second edition. Quito, Ecuador: Trama Ediciones, 2014.

Jergan, Zeljko. "Sokacko Kolo." Croatian Dances with Zeljko Jergan. Accessed May 25, 2015, at http://archives.mvfolkdancers.com/0_Other%20Items%20of%20Interest/0_Dance%20Instructions/sokacko%20kolo.pdf.

Talam, Jasmina. *Folk Musical Instruments in Bosnia and Herzegovina*. Newcastle Upon Tyne, UK: Cambridge Scholars Publishing, 2013.

LIP PLUGS, AFRICA AND SOUTH AMERICA

Lip plugs, also written as lip-plugs and referred to as lip plates or lip discs, are a type of body modification applied to the lip of a human face. Lip plugs are usually made from wood, stone, clay, pottery, bone, or metal and tend to be just over one inch in diameter though women living in southern Chad sport lip plugs up to 12 inches in width. To insert a lip plug a hole is sliced into an individual's lower, or possibly upper, lip into which a small ornament is inserted. Once the hole has healed around the ornament, it is extracted and replaced by a larger ornament. Through this process, the hole is stretched gradually thereby allowing larger objects to be inserted into the lip.

Many different peoples, both male and female, around the world wear lip ornaments such as rings, plugs, or plates inserted into their bottom lips, including men from the Brazilian Kaiapo (or Kayapo) tribe who wear saucer-like plates in their lower lips. Similarly, the isolated Zo'e people living in the Amazonian rainforest of northern Brazil wear long wooden lip plugs, known as *m'berpót* (or *poturo*) beginning in childhood. According to Zo'e folklore, the tribe's ancestor, Sihié'abyr, taught the Zo'e how to apply the lip plugs and receiving the body adornment is one of the most important rituals in a Zo'e person's life. Zo'e girls receive their first m'berpót when they are seven years old while boys have their lip split when they are nine years of age. Once the child has had his or her lip slit, a spider monkey leg bone is inserted into the cut and then as the children age they have increasingly large lip plugs inserted into their lips. Eventually, a Zo'e person will acquire a wooden lip plug that is around three inches in diameter and eight inches in length.

Today, however, lip plugs are synonymous with certain Africa tribes. The exact purpose of African lip plugs is not known. Some researchers speculate that lip plugs evolved as a means of deterring slave traders by making women look unnatural and thereby reducing the women's value at the slave market. This has been suggested as the reason for women of the Kichepo of southern Sudan, who are thought to have started wearing lip plugs as a form of self-protection to discourage Arab slave traders. The women of the Sara-Kaba living in Chad and Central African Republic may also have started wearing lip plugs in both their lips for this reason. However the lip plugs traditionally sported by the Sara-Kaba women weigh up to 30 grams and are around 12 inches in circumference making it difficult for the women to talk, eat, or keep saliva within their mouths. Traditionally, Sara-Kaba women have their lips pierced by their fiancés shortly before their wedding. A fiancé uses a pointed object to make a slit in the lips of his bride-to-be and inserts a small object into the cut. Over time the hole stretches to allow for the insertion of larger objects such as bits of polished wood or gourds known as calabashes. Since the Sara-Kaba lip plugs inhibit everyday actions, however, fewer women are wearing them these days, meaning that the custom is gradually becoming defunct among the Sara-Kaba except for women living in the Moyen-Chari region of Chad. Sara-Kaba women that have moved to major cities have had to remove their lip plugs at the behest of employers.

Another reason for the wearing of lip plugs is that they are considered to enhance female beauty. In the 19th century, the famous explorer David Livingstone is said to have asked a Malawian chief why the women of his tribe wore lip plugs and was surprised to be told that the ornamentations were a means of beautification that were worn by women to make up for their lack of beard. Today, Makololo women living in southern Africa, including Malawi, wear lip plugs known as *pelele* to sexually arouse men. Other African women, such as the Lobi women living in Ghana and Côte d'Ivoire and the Kirdi women of Cameroon, wear lip plugs to protect against evil spirits for they believe that malevolent spirits enter the body through the mouth. Other possible reasons for women wearing lip plugs are that they are a status symbol with the size of the plug denoting a woman's social rank or level of affluence, or that when worn in both top and bottom lips the human mouth resembles the beak of sacred birds such as the spoonbill.

For the Tanzanian Makonde people lip plugs are thought of as essential personal decoration for married women. Contrastingly, among the Surma people of Ethiopia, the Djinja of Chad, and the Tlingit indigenous people living on the Pacific Northwest of North America, lip plugs are used to show that a woman is ready to marry. The lip plugs worn by Djinja women measure up to nine and a half inches in width leaving them unable to feed themselves or speak. Lip plugs are inserted into a Djinja woman by the man to whom she is betrothed because by submitting herself to pain at his hands the pattern of dominance that will be a feature of their marriage is established. Ethiopian women of the Surma tribe meanwhile have their lips slit around six months before they wed. When Surma women are in exclusively female company or by themselves they may remove their lip plugs but when they are in mixed-sex company they must wear their lip plugs. The size of their lip plugs denotes a woman's social status and how many cattle she is worth when a man wishes to marry her. Tlingit women traditionally have their lips slit by a female relative and a lip plug inserted when they enter into a period of isolation to mark their first menstruation. When a Tlingit woman married this small lip plug is replaced with a larger lip plug to indicate her status as a married woman and over time the woman will wear a succession of increasingly larger lip plugs.

Today, one of the most well-known wearers of lip plugs are the Mursi women living in Ethiopia's Omo Valley. (*See* Plate 15.) Indeed Mursi women have become something of a tourist attraction for their wearing of clay (*dhebinya*) and wood (*kiyo*) lip plugs that they also sell to visitors. However Mursi women do not wear lip plugs purely for ornamentation but rather as a way of demonstrating that females have achieved adulthood, are fertile, and, therefore, are eligible for marriage. Mursi girls receive their first lip plug when they reach puberty; a small slit is made in her lip and a small piece of wood inserted into the cut. This process symbolizes that the girl has transitioned to adulthood and become a member of the *bansanai*, the age-set to which girls that have become women belong. The lip plug signals that the girl can now be considered a sexually mature woman that is ready to wed. For this reason lip plugs are usually worn by unwed or newly married women rather than by women that are married with children. Once a Mursi girl has received her initial lip plug, over the course of a year she will receive further wooden lip plugs of increasing size followed by increasingly larger lip plugs made from clay (or wood). The size of the largest lip plug worn by a Mursi woman is determined partly by personal choice but also by how much physical strain a woman's lip can withstand. For fear for ripping her lip a Mursi woman may opt to ultimately have only a fairly small lip plug, or even not to wear a lip plug at all though a woman without a lip plug will be deemed liable to have cattle prone to disease. Additionally a Mursi woman that chooses not to have a lip plug is thought of as lazy, or *karkarre*. This may result in her having a lower value as a bride, meaning that her family may lose some of the cattle settled upon with her fiancé as part of a pre-marriage agreement.

There is much variation in the size and design of Mursi lip plugs. The four main types of clay lip plugs are colored red (*dhebi a golonya*), red-brown (*dhebi a luluma*), black (*dhebi a korra*), and/or a pale natural clay color (*dhebi a holla*). Lip plugs are colored red by placing them among hot coals and covering them with tree bark while black lip plugs are achieved by rubbing them with burned *loamy*—a medicinal plant that is applied to women's lips when they are cut. Wooden lip plugs (*burgui*) are worn exclusively by unwed females and are made only by men. Burgui are traditionally considered by the Mursi to be the most beautiful kind of lip plug though they are increasingly thought of as old-fashioned by modern Mursi tastes. Nowadays, clay lip plugs seem to be in fashion.

Mursi women normally wear lip plugs when they serve food to men, on important occasions such as weddings and harvest celebrations, at *donga* (stick fighting) competitions, and while dancing. Unwed women may also wear lip plugs when fetching water or seeing friends. It is usual for a Mursi bride to live with her mother for the first year of her marriage as this allows her lip time to heal before she shares a bed with her husband. For the first few years of marriage a Mursi bride will wear her lip plug frequently but over time the regularity diminishes so that she will wear it only when serving food to her husband and his friends or when attending public events. Thus older married Mursi women tend to hardly ever wear their lip plug. Similarly, if a Mursi woman's husband dies then she will usually discard her lip plug and never wear one again unless she is young with children and therefore needs to find another husband.

When lip plugs are removed they may leave little more than a slight scar or, if the plug was large, the lip may dangle as though deflated, giving the face a deformed appearance.

See also: Beards; Breast Ironing; Ear-Piercing Ceremonies; Forehead-Cutting Initiation; Human Tooth Sharpening; Menstrual Taboos; Neck Elongation; *Pika* and *Nyora*; Scarification; *Thaipusam*: Extreme Ritual Flesh Modification; Tooth-Filing Ceremony

Further Reading

DeMello, Margo. *Encyclopedia of Body Adornment*. Westport, CT: Greenwood Publishing Group Inc., 2007.

DeMello, Margo. *Faces around the World: A Cultural Encyclopedia of the Human Face*. Santa Barbara, CA: ABC-CLIO, 2012.

Dice.missouri.edu. "Zo'e." Hunter-Gatherers Data Sheet. Accessed October 8, 2015, at http://dice.missouri.edu/docs/tupi/Zoe.pdf.

LaTosky, Shauna. "Reflections on the Lip-plates of Mursi Women as a Source of Stigma and Self-Esteem." Mursi.org. Accessed October 8, 2015, at http://www.mursi.org/pdf/latosky.pdf.

Pitt Rivers Museum. "African Lip Plugs." Pitt Rivers Museum Body Arts. Accessed October 8, 2015, at http://web.prm.ox.ac.uk/bodyarts/index.php/permanent-body-arts/reshaping-and-piercing/158-african-lip-plugs.html.

Ross Russell, Rebecca. *Gender and Jewelry: A Feminist Analysis.* N.p.: Createspace Independent Publishing Platform, 2010.

Shell-Duncan, Bettina, and Ylva Hernlund, eds. *Female "Circumcision" in Africa: Culture, Controversy, and Change.* Boulder, CO: Lynne Rienner Publishers, 2002.

Survival International. "The Zo'e." Accessed October 8, 2015, http://www.survivalinternational.org/tribes/zoe.

LOBOLA, SOUTHERN AFRICA

Lobola, which translates as bride-price or bride-wealth and is known as *roora* in the Shona language and as *mahadi* in Sesotho, is a controversial old southern African custom still practiced today in the African nations of Lesotho and Zimbabwe. The tradition is comparable to the Western concept of dowry, though lobola places the emphasis on uniting two families through a gift of riches, rather than on bringing together two individuals in marriage with the financial onus upon the family of the future bride. In the case of lobola the groom pays his bride-to-be's family a pre-arranged price in order to wed his fiancée. The tradition is most prevalent in poor rural areas of southern Africa where high poverty rates, unemployment, and landlessness mean lobola is seen as a way of gaining assets. There are two types of marriage in rural southern Africa: civil and customary. Civil marriage is monogamous and has a legal minimum age requirement of 16 years for brides and 18 for grooms. In contrast, there is no age limit for customary marriage, which may be polygamous and requires the fathers of both the bride and groom to sign a contract and arrange lobola.

Traditionally, there were a number of ways of paying lobola. Usually lobola was calculated using cattle, as cattle were the principal sign of capital in African culture. However the Shona people living in the Hwedza Mountains of Zimbabwe would pay lobola with tools and weapons fashioned from smelted iron for centuries ago the tribe traded in iron ore, gold, and copper. Thus the lobola transactions of the Shona featured equipment such as hoes, spears, and axes made of smelted metal. If a man was unable to pay with a hoe or other tool, he would agree to *kutema ugariri* and thereby work for this bride's father until he was satisfied that his son-in-law had repaid his debt through labor. However, today city-dwelling grooms tend to pay cash to their fiancée's family.

According to lobola tradition, a groom must pay in order to marry a woman. Lobola is therefore very important in Africa as it helps to redistribute wealth, establishes relationships, creates social identity, and maintains cultural traditions. Lobola is arranged through a complicated and confusing formal system of negotiation that must be adhered to and which varies between cultures across the whole of southern Africa. The process of organizing lobola involves written contracts and a traditional ceremony—even if the families of the bride and groom know each other well or are neighbors they must complete the formal lobola process. To start the lobola process the families involved choose negotiators, usually family members such as uncles of the groom. The two families then arrange a meeting at which a bottle of brandy is placed on the meeting table as an emblematic way of dissipating any strain between the families. The families do not open the bottle of brandy, as its function is purely symbolic. This first formal meeting is called *mvulamlomo*, which translates as "mouth-opener," and can take several days to complete, only ending when the negotiators have established the amount of cattle or cash that must be paid. After this meeting the next stage of lobola begins during which the betrothed couple must follow a set of rules that usually assert that the couple must not meet again until the day of their wedding. These rules are important because they symbolize the mutual understanding and trust between the couple's families.

Controversy has always been attendant on lobola, especially since the first European colonists to settle in Africa condemned the tradition as akin to selling daughters for cattle. At this time, women were considered as chattels and marriage was viewed as a commercial transaction allowing families to procure property. At its worst, lobola meant that some women were regarded as commodities to be bought and saw women subjected to abuse by their new husbands and their husbands' families. Today, low-income families particularly uphold the custom of lobola. Many young couples wanting to wed see lobola as an avaricious attempt by unscrupulous relatives to profit from their desire to get married rather than as a bond to unify their families. Some youngsters also resent lobola as an unacceptable extravagance for people who barely earn a living wage to be expected to pay. As a result, young southern Africans are increasingly resentful of lobola, especially as an inability to pay lobola could be an impediment to their marriage. As a consequence of this, youngsters are increasingly opting to live together without marrying. Another modern consequence of lobola is that southern African women are marrying later in life as they wait to find a suitably wealthy husband.

Lobola also attracts anger from African feminists that assert that the custom encourages the social control of women and reinforces sexual roles, casting women as passive and powerless, and signifying the loss of women's individuality and freedom. One aspect of lobola that particularly irks women's rights campaigners is that lobola payments are often graded according to a female's sexual experience with the most money paid for a virgin, though men are not compelled to wed a girl whose virginity he has taken. Though exact customs vary between peoples, all southern African tribes value female virginity and in the Xhosa and Venda tribes, for example, girls are inspected regularly to check that they remain virgins. Most tribes allow external sexual intercourse to occur, that is, sex without penetration, but if a girl does become pregnant before marriage her family will try to conceal the matter as much as possible. However once her pregnancy becomes public knowledge the girl will be ridiculed and kept away from other young females lest her waywardness should contaminate them. Another controversial element of lobola is that once a man has paid lobola any children produced by his wife become his belongings and he retains guardianship of them if his wife leaves him, whatever the reason for the couple's split. However it should be noted that if a man mistreats his wife she is permitted to leave him and he should forfeit his lobola, losing the wealth he has given to his wife's family. If, on the other hand, the woman is regarded as being at fault, her family must return the lobola payment. This has lead to claims that lobola has a stabilizing effect on marriage as it is in the best interests of both the man and woman that a marriage survive.

African feminists also point out that lobola has no place in modern urban life for today African women have their own financial power—owning their own homes, having bank accounts and jobs, and buying cars—so it is outmoded to expect a groom to pay lobola of around R200,000 (roughly US$12,724) which many of them simply cannot afford without resorting to loan sharks.

Lobola is at the heart of the 2013 cross-cultural comedy film *Fanie Fourie's Lobola*, which depicts the complications that ensue when an Afrikaans man and a Zulu girl fall in love and have to navigate their way through the traditional lobola process. The film is based on the 2007 novel of the same name by Nape'a Motana.

See also: Arranged Marriage and Forced Marriage; Moroccan Weddings; Virginity Testing

Further Reading

Galvan, Javier A., ed. *They Do What? A Cultural Encyclopedia of Extraordinary and Exotic Customs from around the World*. Santa Barbara, CA: ABC-CLIO, 2014.
Indigenous Film Distribution. "Synopsis." Accessed December 19, 2014, at http://www.indigenousfilm.co.za/movie-archive/fanie-fouries-lobola-movie/.
Jacobs, Susie, Ruth Jacobson, and Jennifer Marchbank, eds. *States of Conflict: Gender, Violence and Resistance*. London: Zed Books Ltd., 2000.
Lupri, Eugen, ed. *The Changing Position of Women in Family and Society: A Cross-National Comparison*. Leiden, Netherlands: E. J. Brill, 1983.
Sekai, Nzenza. "Lobola and the Meaning of Marriage," *The Herald*, November 6, 2013. Accessed December 19, 2014, at http://www.herald.co.zw/lobola-and-the-meaning-of-marriage/.
Tshingilane, Sidwell. "Lobola Is Outdated," *City Press*, August 10, 2014. Accessed December 19, 2014, at http://www.citypress.co.za/you-say/lobola-outdated/.

LOG RIDING, JAPAN

The *Onbashira* festival is held at Lake Suwa on the Japanese island of Honshu every seven years in April and May. The word onbashira translates as "the honored pillars" and refers to the felling of 16 giant trees that are then chopped into logs for a special sporting event: log riding. Young men ride these massive logs down a mountainside in a macho show of bravado and sporting prowess despite the risk of being crushed by one of the heavy logs.

The Onbashira festival is thought to have occurred every six or seven years, depending on whether one uses the traditional local way of counting that includes the current year when counting a length of time, without interruption for the last 1,200 to 1,400 years. The festival honors Suwa-no-Kami, the primary goddess in the pantheon of Shinto, the main religion of Japan. The main temple of the Suwa-no-Kami, Suwa Taisha, is one of the oldest Shinto shrines. This temple, like others in the area, has a unique architectural feature—four wooden posts of varying heights and sizes always surround it. These poles are called *onbashira*, which translates as honored poles, and according to local custom the poles must be replaced every six years in either the Year of the Tiger or the Year of the Monkey as denoted by the Chinese zodiac. However the exact history of the Onbashira festival is unclear. While the Onbashira festival is believed to be as old as the Suwa Taisha, which is 1,200 years old, and is believed to have originated as a ritual renewal of the Suwa Grand Shrine, the first mention of the Onbashira festival appears in the *Kojiki*, a book giving accounts of Shinto mythology that is thought to be 1,400 years old.

The log-riding element of the festival is divided into three main parts. The first log-riding event, *Yamadashi*, meaning coming out of the mountains, is held in April. To allow this event to occur some of the largest trees from the forest covering a nearby mountain are felled. The felling of the trees is performed ceremoniously using axes specially made for the occasion. Once they are chopped down the trees are festooned with decorations in the traditional Shinto colors of red and white. The logs are about 52 feet long, 3 feet in diameter, and weigh up to 12 tons.

The first, and most identifiable, event of Yamadashi traditionally sees volunteers riding (and sometimes dropping) the logs down the mountainside and across fast-flowing rivers. When a log nears a muddy slope, teams of men are elected to sit atop the log and ride it downhill. This has been likened to a deadly version of the log ride found at some theme parks.

This part of the festival is called *kiotoshi* (meaning tree-drops) and is preceded by a ritual spiritual purification of each participant. Yamadashi is a very hazardous event, particularly for the men who sit at the very front of each log. Each year, several men are injured riding a log, and deaths have occurred too, which over the festival's 1,200-year history equates to a great many injuries and deaths. However these deaths are regarded as honorable and in line with Japanese culture that takes pride in facing death unafraid. Nowadays, Japanese local authorities have instituted policies to limit the number of future casualties. The next part of the festival is *Satobiki*, which is held in May. This involves placing 16 logs at each corner of the four parts of Suwa Taisha: the upper shrine (Kamisha), the lower shrine (Shimosha), the spring shrine (Harumiya), and the autumn shrine (Akimiya). Each log is put in place ritualistically and once it is erected successfully a team of people

Plate 1 A boy is called to the Torah at the Lubavitch Headquarters in Brooklyn, New York, as part of his *bar mitzvah*. (Ira Berger/Alamy Stock Photo)

Plate 2 Breast ironing is a form of body modification that sees the application of hot objects to a girl's developing breasts in an attempt to hide the outward signs of her physical maturation. Here a Cameroonian girl has her breast ironed through the application of a hot stone. (Aurora Photos/Alamy Stock Photo)

Plate 3 In Chepinsko, a village near Velingrad, Bulgaria, a Muslim bride sports traditional thick, white makeup. Once blessed by an imam, the bride will be escorted from the family home by her relatives and taken to her groom's house, where the groom will remove her makeup. (Tihov Studio/Alamy Stock Photo)

Plate 4 A woman in traditional dress plays music during a wedding at the 18th-century reproduction village Acadian Village in Lafayette, Louisiana. Music is an important part of traditional Cajun weddings with newlyweds expected to take part in special dances to celebrate their marriage. (Hemis/Alamy Stock Photo)

Plate 5 A young man belonging to the Bashada tribe participates in a cow jumping initiation ceremony held in Dimeka, Omo Valley, Ethiopia. (Eric Lafforgue/Alamy Stock Photo)

Plate 6 Men and women in Barsana, Uttar Pradesh, India, enjoying Holi, the ancient Indian festival of colors. During Holi, people wear white clothing so that the colored powder thrown during Holi festivities show up brightly. Barsana is famous for being the village associated with Radha, the beloved cowherd of the Hindu god Lord Krishna. (Idris Ahmed/Alamy Stock Photo)

Plate 7 A Nuer man displays his forehead scars. The Nuer ethnic group sees bodily scarring as both a form of beautification and a method of identification among the other ethnic communities of South Sudan. (Boaz Rottem/Alamy Stock Photo)

Plate 8 A *Gwallye* coming-of-age ceremony taking place in Seoul, South Korea, on May 18, 2015. Clothes are an important element of Gwallye ceremonies. Here participants wear traditional Korean outfits that are characterized by their bright colors, clean lines, and lack of pockets. (Aflo Co. Ltd./Alamy Stock Photo)

Plate 9 Thousands of naked men cram into Saidaiji Temple in Okayama, Japan, on February 21, 2015, as part of the *Hadaka Matsuri*, or Naked Festival. Hadaka Matsuri allows participants to test their manliness and stamina while also earning good luck. (Trevor Williams/Getty Images)

Plate 10 *Hijra* on a train in Bihar State, India, in 2009. The hijra population living on the Indian subcontinent are a group of people that are classified as neither male nor female, but as both a third gender and a third sex. (DB Images/Alamy Stock Photo)

Plate 11 A groom holds his bride's hand during a Hindu wedding held in 2009. The bride's hands have been decorated with *mehndi* (henna) patterns prior to the ceremony. (SIBSA Digital Pvt. Ltd./Alamy Stock Photo)

Plate 12 A couple prepares to jump over a broom as part of their wedding celebrations on top of Calton Hill in Edinburgh, Scotland, on July 13, 2013. (Lynne Sutherland/Alamy Stock Photo)

Plate 13 Sadhus bathe in the Godavari River on the auspicious day of *Mauni Amavasya* during the *Kumbh Mela* at Trimbakeshwar in Nashik, India. Pilgrims believe that bathing in the river will cleanse their souls in preparation for salvation. (Anshuman Poyrekar/Hindustan Times via Getty Images)

Plate 14 In Vanuatu, land diving is a rite of passage from boyhood to manhood that sees young men jump from tall towers with creepers attached to their ankles. (Hemis/Alamy Stock Photo)

Plate 15 A woman belonging to the Mursi tribe of the Omo Valley, Ethiopia, displays her lip plug in October 2007. Mursi women wear lip plugs to demonstrate that they have achieved adulthood and are eligible for marriage. (infocusphotos.com/ Alamy Stock Photo)

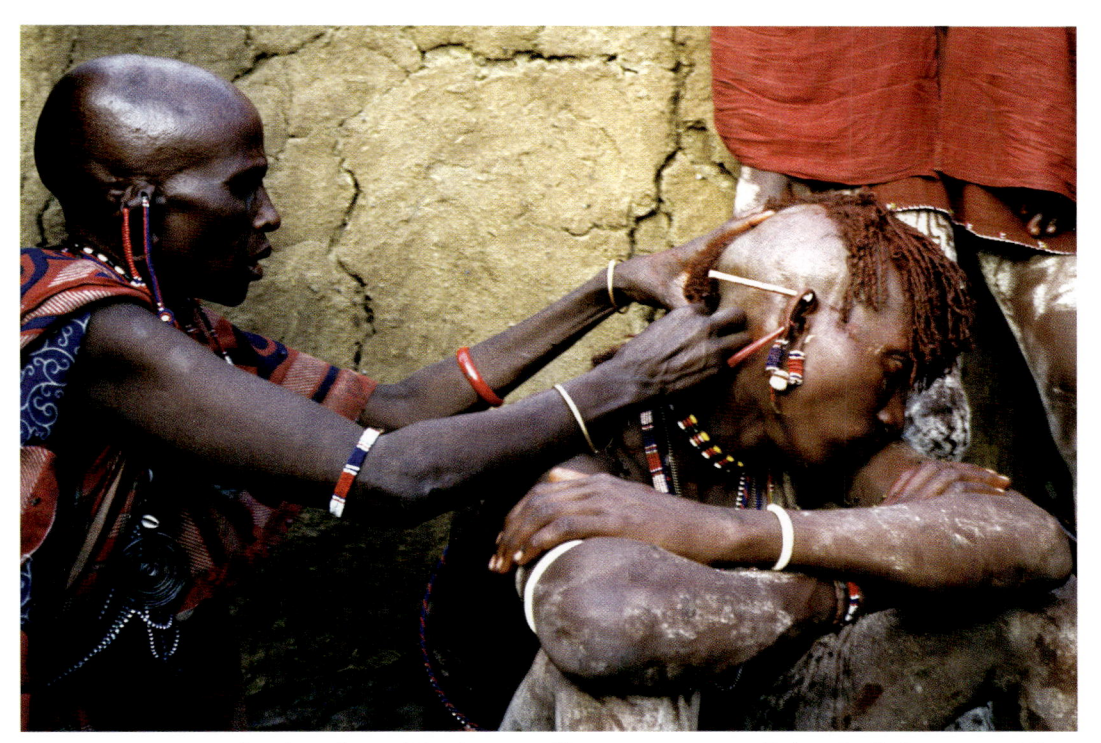

Plate 16 A Maasai mother shaves her son's head as part of his *Eunoto* ceremony. (Robert Estall Photo Agency/Alamy Stock Photo)

Plate 17 Children dance around a maypole as part of the Ickwell May Day Festival, in Ickwell, Bedfordshire, England, in 2010. Traditionally, maypoles are erected on May 1 throughout Europe, especially in England, Eastern Europe, and Scandinavia. (Greg Balfour Evans/Alamy Stock Photo)

Plate 18 A wedding reception held in Morocco on September 12, 2013. Moroccan weddings are famous for being lavishly expensive occasions that can last as long as a week. (Desislava Panteva/Getty Images)

Plate 19 A Western Samoan islander displays ritual tattoos. It is customary for young Samoan adults to receive tattoos in order to signal both their social rank and family heritage. (Patrick Mesner/Gamma-Rapho via Getty Images)

Plate 20 Novices wearing ornate clothing ride to their *shinbyu* in Bagan, Myanmar. (Eric Lafforgue/Alamy StockPhoto)

Plate 21 A Crown Dancer paints an Apache girl with sacred white clay and corn meal during her Sunrise Dance rite held at the San Carlos Indian Reservation in Arizona. (Anders Ryman/Alamy Stock Photo)

Plate 22 A Hindu devotee displays a metal skewer piercing his face as part of the annual *Thaipusam* procession in the Batu Caves, Malaysia. (Guillaume Payen/LightRocket via Getty)

Plate 23 A woman wearing a *vinok* is ready to take part in the annual Vyshyvanka March. The march sees hundreds of Ukrainians based in the United Kingdom demonstrate their Ukrainian national identity through the wearing of traditional Ukrainian national dress. (Guy Corbishley/Alamy Stock Photo)

Plate 24 A traditional *croquembouche* consisting of cream-filled choux pastry buns covered in set caramel is the eye-catching French equivalent to the wedding cake. (WeddingSnapper.com.au/Alamy Stock Photo)

Plate 25 A bride from Nordland, Northern Norway, poses in her wedding outfit. Norwegian brides typically wear traditional national dress on their wedding day. (Leslie Garland Picture Library/Alamy Stock Photo)

Plate 26 Men ready to take part in the annual Wodaabe courtship dance and festival. In preparation for the festival, men paint their faces, shave their hairline, and braid their hair. (Age Fotostock/Alamy Stock Photo)

climb on top of the log and sing a song. The third, final, and least well-known element of Satobiki is known as the Building of Hoden.

The Onbashira festival is considered an essential part of Japan's cultural history that in recent years has attracted millions of onlookers. The rise in the number of spectators is partly due to the fact that a log-raising ceremony similar to Satobiki was included in the opening ceremony of the Nagano Winter Olympic Games in 1998 thereby bringing the activity to the attention of Western spectators. As a result, the Onbashira festival has brought increasing numbers of tourists to the area around Lake Suwa. However so great is the likelihood of participants incurring injury or even dying during the festival that non-Japanese are not permitted to take part. In 2004 emergency medical care was provided at the event for the first time. However during the next festival in 2010, two men died and two more were injured after falling from a 30-foot-tall log that had been raised during the Satobiki ceremony.

The Onbashira festival continues to exhibit a dual significance for the Japanese. On the one hand, the log-riding event represents a celebration of purely masculine bravery that underlines Japanese culture, suffused as it is with inherent peril and risk of death. On the other, the festival is a symbol of Shinto tradition and cultural continuity.

See also: Cow Jumping; Crying-Baby Sumo Competition (Volume 1); *Hadaka Matsuri*; Land Diving; Maypoles

Further Reading

Galvan, Javier A., ed. *They Do What? A Cultural Encyclopedia of Extraordinary and Exotic Customs from around the World.* Santa Barbara, CA: ABC-CLIO, 2014.

Koichi. "Onbashira: The Japanese Festival Where You Ride Down Mountains on 20,000lb Logs for Some Reason." Tofugu.com, February 28, 2012. Accessed January 6, 2015, at http://www.tofugu.com/2012/02/28/onbashira-japanese-log-riding-festival/.

Melton, J. Gordon, ed. *Religious Celebrations: An Encyclopedia of Holidays, Festivals, Solemn Observances, and Spiritual Commemorations.* Volume 2. Santa Barbara, CA: ABC-CLIO, 2011.

Yoda, Hiroko. "Onbashira-sai Festival: The Log Surfers of Lake Suwa." CNN International, May 5, 2010. Accessed January 6, 2015, at http://travel.cnn.com/tokyo/play/onbashirasai-festival-holy-log-rollers-023914.

LOOKING FOR FERN BLOSSOMS, EASTERN EUROPE

The summer solstice is one of the most important days of the year in the Baltic countries of Eastern Europe, particularly Latvia and Lithuania, for on this day lively folk festivals harking back to pagan days are held. The day is also celebrated by people from Eastern Europe living in other parts of the world. The summer solstice is traditionally celebrated on different dates throughout the region, for example it is celebrated on June 22 in some areas, June 23 in other regions, and

June 24 in Latvia. Similarly, the celebrations held to mark the day are known by various names throughout the region. However in each area the day is traditionally seen as a day of merriment, and, in particular, courtship. This is symbolized by the fact that on this day people look for the mystical fern blossoms (known in Latvia as *Papardes zieds*) of legend, an ancient fertility symbol that binds together romantic couples. According to Baltic legends, the fern blossom appears only once per year, on the night of the summer solstice, and the flower's magic has the ability to bind together courting couples who spend the night of the solstice searching for the legendary flower in dark forests.

The day is celebrated in different ways in various parts of the Baltic. In Lithuania the summer solstice is called Joninės, meaning St. John's Day, with men called Jonas and women named Jenina decorated with oak-leaf garlands. As Lithuania is located far to the north in the northern hemisphere the night of Joninės is very short—as soon as the sunset disappears below the western horizon the eastern skies are filled with the first rays of dawn. For this reason this night of the year is considered to be an extra special time of magic and enchantment. Therefore it is on this night that couples venture into the forests to look for the enchanted fern blossoms of legend. Those that are lucky enough to find the legendary flowers are said to be rewarded with special powers, particularly the ability to talk to animals and birds, the power of prophesy, and the ability to locate buried treasure. Meanwhile, in Latvia the celebration is known as Ligo or Jāņi Day—the actual summer solstice is a few days before Ligo but when Christianity became prevalent in the Baltic during the 12th century the festival was moved to coincide with the feast day of Saint John the Baptist. Jāņi is an ancient festival originally celebrated in honor of Jānis, a Latvian pagan deity that appears frequently in Latvian folksongs. Jani celebrations are quite simple for people aim to travel to the countryside to build bonfires over which they jump in the hope that they will receive wealth, luck, or love. People also stay up all night drinking beer as they wait for the sunrise to arrive. Those that cannot journey to the countryside celebrate in city centers where they wander the streets wearing medieval-style national dress. As people wait for the sunrise, women pick flowers that they fashion into floral wreaths that they wear on their heads and which variously symbolize that the women are virgins or are looking for a lover. Meanwhile, the men take off their clothes and swim naked in nearby rivers and lakes. Everybody present sings medieval Latvian folksongs and then couples wander into the woods to look for the legendary fern blossom. Therefore it is apparent that the unifying factor of summer solstice celebrations held on this day across the Baltic region is a heightened sense of sensuality that sees people engage in sexual activity.

According to many folklore scholars, the legendary fern flower is a metaphor for sex. Moreover, in many areas of the Baltic there is an old saying that someone is "looking for fern blossoms," which is a euphemistic way of saying someone is on the lookout for a sexual encounter. Furthermore, Baltic children conceived around June 22 are referred to as "fern flowers," while in Latvia it is commonly accepted that a mini baby boom occurs each year roughly nine months after their parents have looked for fern blossoms on the night of the summer solstice.

See also: Bachelor and Spinster Balls; Bed-Courtship; Bulgarian Weddings; Courtship Whistling; *Lazarovden*; Maypoles; St. Catherine's Day; *Vinok*

Further Reading

Lica-Butler, Mihaela. "Latvia Searching for the Legendary Fern Blossom," *Argophilia Travel News*, June 9, 2011. Accessed May 24, 2015, at http://www.argophilia.com/news/jani/22759/.

Lithaz.org. "Lithuanian Legends: St John's Night." Accessed May 24, 2015, at http://www.lithaz.org/legends/fern_blossom.html.

McGuiness, Damien. "Latvia Midsummer: Songs, Flowers and Running around Naked," *BBC News Magazine*, June 30, 2012. Accessed May 24, 2015, at http://www.bbc.co.uk/news/magazine-18614119.

Tapon, Francis. *The Hidden Europe: What Eastern Europeans Can Teach Us*. N.p.: Sonic Trek Inc., 2012.

LOVESPOONS, WALES

A lovespoon is a carved wooden spoon traditionally given as a courting gift to signal romantic interest. Lovespoons are usually made from a single piece of a strong wood, such as sycamore, cherry, holly, walnut, or maple, and often feature intricately carved symbols of love that demonstrate the skill of the spoon's maker. Indeed, as the designs are so intricate lovespoons are not used as functioning spoons with which to eat but rather are considered purely decorative items. Lovespoons are closely associated with Wales, where they are known in the Welsh language as *llwyau caru*.

Though it has been suggested that the Vikings may have invented lovespoons, it is usually agreed that lovespoons evolved in Wales during the 16th century. The earliest known Welsh lovespoon, dating from 1667, is housed in St. Fagans National History Museum, located near Cardiff, the Welsh capital city. Originally, a man would present a lovespoon to a girl that he wished to woo—if she accepted his spoon then the romance could proceed. The artistry with which a man carved the lovespoon was important as it enabled him to demonstrate the adoration he felt for his beloved and also allowed the man to show his aptitude at carving. This ability was a practical skill that signaled the man possessed the ability to work with his hands—a necessary skill in a time when most people earned their living from manual work. As the man was able to demonstrate his dexterity a woman could assume he would be able to bring home an income if they married. The deep bowl of the lovespoon was also symbolic of a man's belief that he could provide for his wife. However the deep bowl also had a practical purpose for the earliest lovespoons were also functional items as poor women could use the utensil to eat *cawl*, a traditional Welsh broth. The deep bowl is traditionally fashioned using a special knife called a *twca cam*, which means bent knife in Welsh. The blade of this knife is curved, allowing wood to be hollowed out and produce a scooped-out bowl shape. Other common symbolic features of lovespoons include a wooden key, which symbolizes that the giver presents the keys of his home to the recipient of the spoon, and a loose wooden ball inside a wooden cage. This is symbolic of female fertility as the ball represents an embryo inside a womb. Meanwhile, a chain might be carved into the handle of a lovespoon with the number of links in the chain signaling how many children the carver wished to sire. Other symbols often carved on lovespoons include a vine, meaning growing affection; a horseshoe for good luck; a knot, representing togetherness; and a dragon, the symbol of Wales.

Over the years, however, lovespoons became increasingly decorative and came to be viewed as ornamental rather than utilitarian. While the earliest lovespoons were crudely carved using knives, later lovespoons were more refined and began to exhibit intricate carvings of pagan and Christian symbols. Some lovespoons also had a chain attached to represent that accepting a lovespoon was a symbolic way of forming a romantic attachment. During the 19th century, the Victorians began to give each other greetings cards to express affection and lovespoons became a way of showing love for family and friends rather than romantic love. Today, lovespoons are not normally presented as courting gifts but rather are given as tokens of affection to celebrate weddings, birthdays, friendships, St. Valentine's Day, and St. Dwynwyn's Day, the Welsh equivalent of St. Valentine's Day.

Other countries also produce spoons as love tokens. For example, in Norway it is traditional to give a wedding spoon, which is a carved wooden articulated chain with a spoon at each end of the chain. According to folk history these spoons originated when young courting couples were allowed to sit together, without a chaperone, in an unheated room and the boy would be expected to keep his hands busy, and therefore warm, by carving the spoon rather than touching his beloved. To ensure that this protocol was followed, the boy would have his hands inspected by his prospective father-in-law for signs that the boy had been busy carving rather than canoodling. When the couple was eventually married, they would feed each other wedding cake using the spoon carved during these visits. Then, after the wedding, the couple would hang the spoon above the door of their house and when the husband was away from home the wife would wear the spoon around her neck.

A man also customarily gave a type of lovespoon to his potential lover in the Netherlands. This lovespoon was designed to serve candy so it follows that the spoons became known as bon bon spoons. This type of lovespoon was made in the Netherlands from around 1870 to approximately 1900 and tended to be carved with illustrations featuring romantic courting couples engaged in playing music, with entwined lovebirds, or intertwined dolphins, the latter being considered a symbol of eternal love.

See also: Birthday Cards (Volume 1); British Wedding Traditions; Horseshoes; Jumping Over the Broom; *Shabka*; St. Dwynwen's Day; Wedding Cake

Further Reading

Lovespoons.co.uk. "Meanings." The Lovespoon Gallery. Accessed May 27, 2015, at, http://www.lovespoons.co.uk/meanings.htm.

Monger, George P. *Marriage Customs of the World: From Henna to Honeymoons*. Santa Barbara, CA: ABC-CLIO, 2004.

Quinn, Tom, Sian Ellis, and Paul Felix. *Book of Forgotten Crafts*. Newton Abbot, UK: David & Charles, 2011.

Spoonplanet.com. "Dutch Bon Bon Love Spoons." Accessed May 27, 2015, at http://spoonplanet.com/dutchbonlove.html.

Walters, Trish. "Love-spoons: Carvings from the Heart," *American Woodworker,* February 1996, 62–63.

M

MAASAI WARRIOR INITIATION, KENYA AND TANZANIA

The Massai are semi-nomadic ethnic people living in northern Tanzania and southern Kenya. Maasai society is steeped in ceremony and ritual, many of which revolve around the transition of a boy into a warrior. These ceremonies include *Enkipaata* (pre-circumcision ceremony inducting boys into warriorhood), *Emuratta* or *Emuratare* (circumcision), *Enkiama* (marriage), *Eunoto* (warrior-shaving ceremony), *Eokoto e-kule* (milk-drinking ceremony), *Enkang oo-nkiri* (meat-eating ceremony), and *Orngesherr* (junior elder ceremony), as well as rites of passage for both boys and girls such as *Eudoto/Enkigerunoto oo-inkiyiaa* (earlobe ceremony), and *Ilkipirat* (leg fire marks). Traditionally, boys and girls must undergo many of these initiation ceremonies before they are circumcised or before a marriage ceremony takes place. Every ceremony is important and Maasai children look forward to each ceremony in turn as they understand that the ceremonies are essential stages of life. Boys are initiated into adulthood and the warrior lifestyle in age-sets so that boys of similar ages experience initiations en masse. This means that there are always groups of initiated males ready to act as warriors.

The first stage of a boy's initiation to adulthood and warrior status is the pre-circumcision ceremony called Enkipaata. This is organized by boys' fathers and sees 14- to 16-year-old boys journey across their land for around four months accompanied by a group of elders. The boys construct up to 40 houses in a separate camp known as a *kraal*, which is where they will undergo the rest of the initiation's rituals. Before the remainder of the initiation ceremonies occurs a chief boy known as the *Olopolosi olkiteng*, is selected. The role of Olopolosi olkiteng is

---

Maasai Blood Drinking

Maasai culture places great value on cattle and cow products are an important part of the Maasai diet. The traditional Maasai diet includes milk drunk raw or soured, or in tea, and also turned into butter that is then fed to Maasai babies. Milk is also part of virtually every meal eaten by Maasai herders. The Maasai also eat raw beef but the most startling aspect of the Maasai's diet is, perhaps, the fact that they drink raw cattle blood as well as eating cooked blood. The Maasai also consume blood-milk mixtures on special occasions or when they are ill. To obtain the cattle blood the Maasai cut a cow's jugular in such a way that blood is let but the animal does not die.

not one that any boy desires as the Olopolosi olkiteng must bear the burden of all the sins of his age-set. On the eve of their initiation ceremony the boys must sleep outdoors in the forest, then, when dawn approaches, the boys run to the kraal, entering with a violent attitude. The next stage of the Enkipaata rituals sees the boys dress in loose-fitting clothing and perform dances throughout the day. Once the rituals of Enkipaata have been completed the boys are considered to be ready for their most important initiation ceremony, the circumcision ceremony known as *Emuratare*.

Emuratare is the most important part of Maasai children's initiation into adult society and is experienced by both boys and girls shortly after puberty. In recent years, however, fewer Maasai girls have been circumcised than were in earlier times. The circumcision of Maasai boys demonstrates that the boys are able to assume the adult responsibility of caring for their land. The boys' attainment of adulthood is also denoted by their carrying heavy spears and herding animals. Therefore several days before a boy is circumcised he must herd livestock for a week without a break. Then on the day of his circumcision a boy must stand out in the cold and clean himself under a cold shower of water. The circumcision ceremony takes place just before dawn and as the boy walks toward the site of the circumcision his family and friends shout at him words of encouragement mingled with threats. During the circumcision, which is performed by a man considered an experienced circumciser, the boy must not betray the pain that he feels even though he does not receive any pain-relief medication. Once the operation is over the boy receives livestock from his family and friends as he is now considered to be a brave adult capable of caring for cattle. However it takes boys three to four months to heal after their circumcision and to mark this healing period boys wear black clothes for a period of four to eight months. Once their wounds have healed boys are viewed as a new person and as a warrior.

The next stage of a boy's initiation is the formation of the *emanyatta* (also written as *manyatta*). An emanyatta is a warrior camp consisting of 20 to 40 dwellings where initiated boys spend the next 10 to 15 years of their lives eating and socializing with other Maasai warriors (referred to as *morrans*) and herding cattle. Two morran chiefs lead the initiates during their stay in the emanyatta.

At the center of the emanyatta is a flagpole bearing the Maasai national flag. This flag flies for as long as the warriors inhabit the camp. While living in the emanyatta an initiate wears a red cloak and carries a spear and shield, the emblems of warriorhood. The initiate also grows his hair long and smears his face and hair with red paint and oil. The initiates also braid their hair and adorn their bodies with beaded jewelry made by Maasai women. Though life in the emanyatta is fairly relaxed, once the initiates leave the camp they will face dangerous ordeals in their everyday life for as warriors they will be expected to perform such hazardous duties as defending their cattle from lions.

When the initiates' time at the emayatta is over they undergo the Eunoto ceremony, or elder warriors' initiation. This usually happens 10 years after men become warriors and marks the transition of men from warriors to senior warriors. Once a warrior has transitioned to the status of senior warrior through participation in the ceremony he is allowed to wed and have children. The Eunoto ceremony occurs in another camp consisting of 49 houses. The last of these houses is a large mud hut called the *Osinkira* that is built especially for the Oloiboni, a Maasai spiritual leader or prophet that oversees ceremonies and rituals and who is entertained by a different warrior on each day of the Eunoto ceremony.

During the Eunoto ceremony warriors are banned from carrying weapons and they have their heads shaved by their mothers. (*See* Plate 16.) In addition to the head shaving a ritual takes place during which an animal horn is set on fire and warriors are made to snatch a piece of the horn from the flames before the horn is reduced to ashes. Warriors do not really want to grab the horn from the fire because it is painful to do so and also because whomever claims the horn is said earn a lifetime of bad luck. However if no warrior claims a piece of the horn before the horn disintegrates the entire age-set of warriors will considered to be damned. Therefore warriors take the attitude that it is better for one of their number to be cursed than the entire age-set. On graduation from the Eunoto ceremony the warriors must distribute eight bulls that they have raised especially for the occasion among their elders. In preparation for the graduation ceremony three important age-set leaders are chosen by the warriors. These are the Olaiguanani lenkashe, the Oloboru enkeene, and the Olotuno. Although it might seem a good thing to be elected to these roles no warrior wishes to be given any of these titles, especially the title of Olotuno, as this person takes the blame for all the bad deeds for his age-set. During the graduation ceremony the warrior chosen as the Olaiguanani lenkashe is given a specially selected cow while the Oloboru enkeene is presented with a knotted leather strap that symbolizes his age-set.

A couple of months after the Eunoto ceremony, the warriors establish a small camp for the Enkang e-kule ceremony, or milk ceremony. Before the Eunoto ceremony, warriors are forbidden from eating alone, even if they are sick and do not wish for company. This tradition has been established over the years to instill in Massai men a need for self-reliance rather than dependence on women, most particularly mothers, who tend to make food for their husbands and children. Another reason for the tradition is that it teaches warriors to cope with famine. During the Enkang e-kule ceremony the entire age-set of warriors have their ochre-stained hair shaved by their mothers as a sign that they have graduated to become senior warriors.

The warriors' next initiation is Enkang oo-nkiri or meat ceremony that takes place in a special camp consisting of 10 to 20 houses. Once warriors have experienced this ceremony they are allowed to both dine alone and to eat meat prepared by women. To mark the ceremony a specially selected bull is slaughtered. Then, during a custom known as the bull skin ritual, warriors wrestle with each over the bull skin. This wrestling is significant as it is used as a means to determine whether or not a warrior's wife has been unfaithful by having sex with a younger warrior.

Wives are permitted to have affairs with warriors from the same age-set as them but not with younger warriors. If a wife is deemed guilty of this transgression then she will be scorned by her husband and by every person from her age-set. At the conclusion of the *Enkang oo-nkiri* ceremony, men and women fight against one another for the roasted meat of the bull.

The age-set's final initiation ceremony is the *Orngesherr*, or junior's elder initiation, which marks the warriors' transition to the rank of a junior elder. This ceremony, which occurs when a warrior is around 35 years of age, is performed in a camp consisting of in excess of 20 houses. During this ceremony, each warrior is honored with an elder's chair. At dawn on the day of the ceremony a warrior will sit in his chair and have his head shaved by his wife—if a warrior has multiple wives then it is the oldest wife's duty to perform the shaving. The chair presented to the warrior becomes his most prized possession and when the warrior dies it is passed down to his eldest son. After a warrior has experienced the *Orngesherr* ceremony he is considered an elder and assumes full responsibility for his family. The warrior is also now permitted to stop living with his father and establish his own independent estate.

In recent years, the multi-part Maasai warrior initiation ceremonies have become threatened by a variety of factors. For example the increasing cultural influence of Western lifestyles and religions, encroaching modernism, and environmental change all endanger the continuation of the Maasai's ceremonies.

See also: Bullet Ant Initiation; Cow Jumping; Initiation by Semen Transferal; Matis Hunting Trials; Xhosa Circumcision

Further Reading

Maasai Association. "Maasai Ceremonies and Rituals." Accessed July 16, 2015, at http://www.maasai-association.org/ceremonies.html.

McQuail, Lisa. *The Masai of Africa*. Minneapolis, MN: Lerner Publications Company, 2002.

Oldoinyo Lengai. "Local Attractions." The Mountain of God. Accessed July 23, 2015, at http://www.oldoinyo-lengai.org/local-attractions/.

MAJÁLES, CZECH REPUBLIC

Majáles is a well-established annual month-long student festival held in towns throughout the Czech Republic including the Czech capital, Prague, and Brno and Hradec Králové. The festival is viewed as both a celebration of student life and a presentation of the skills learned by students during their time at university. The festival is usually held in April and May. Majáles traditionally begins with the ceremonial building of the Májka maypole and culminates with the festival's main highlights, the Majáles Parade and the Majáles open-air festival at which leading Czech and Slovak bands play popular music. Though Majáles is a major Czech festival students from around the world attend the event. For instance, in 2014 students from the United States, Azerbaijan, Croatia, Georgia, Poland, Mexico, Slovenia, India, Afghanistan, South Africa, Moldova, Montenegro, and Syria all took part, with some 30,000 people in total visiting Majáles events that year.

Majáles was permitted to take place on May Day under the Communist rule of Czechoslovakia (which later split into the Czech Republic and Slovakia) that began in 1945 because Communists had used May Day for large-scale labor parades. However during the 1960s a climate of counter-culture began to sweep through Czechoslovakia resulting in student protests that clashed with police. This in turn led Czech authorities to rethink the Majáles formula in 1965 in an attempt to placate the students. Part of this rethinking included the election of a King of the Majáles, also known as the May King or *Kral Majáles*. This is an honorific title given to someone chosen to rule over the next year's Majáles festivities. During the 1960s as a result of this counter-culture attitude Czech students elected Beat poet Alan Ginsberg to the position of Kral Majáles in 1965. However Ginsberg was expelled from Czechoslovakia and wrote the poem *"Kral Majáles"* ("King of May") while he was on his flight out of the country. The poem is ambivalent leaving the reader to decide what to make of both the poem and the state of Czechoslovakia's politics during the 1960s.

Since 2005, all Majáles events have been overseen by Student Zone, the Czech Republic's largest student organization, an umbrella organization concerned with the well-being of all students studying at universities in the Czech Republic. Prior to 2013, Majáles was open to Czech students only. However since 2013 students from outside the Czech Republic have been allowed to take part in the festivities with a separate section called International Island given over to foreign students. Here, foreign students are permitted to give presentations about the student bodies in their homeland. The foreign students also talk about their own countries, wear national dress, give out tasters of national foods, present art works, and hand out leaflets, books, and magazines extolling the virtues of their home nations.

See also: *Baccalauréat* and *Matura*; Inter-Railing; RAG Week; *Russefeiring* and Schoolies Week

Further Reading

AbcPrague.com. "Big Student Festival Majales Is Coming Soon." April 13, 2007. Accessed May 26, 2015, at http://www.abcprague.com/2007/04/13/big-student-festival-majales-is-coming-soon.

The Alan Ginsberg Project. "Kral Majáles." April 30, 2010. Accessed May 27, 2015, at http://ginsbergblog.blogspot.co.uk/2010/04/kral-majales.html.

ASN. "ASN participated in Majales—the Largest Student Festival in Czech Republic." May 6, 2014. Accessed May 26, 2015, at http://azerbaijan-student.net/asn-participated-in-majales-the-largest-student-festival-in-czech-republic/.

Ulmanova, Hana. "The Reception of American Literature in Czechoslovakia under Communism: 1945–1989," *American Studies International*, 33(2), October 1995, 32–40.

MARRIAGE BANNS, CHRISTIANITY

Marriage banns are a series of public declarations of a couple's intention to marry. The word banns simply means proclamation. In England it is a legal requirement that banns be declared before any Church of England wedding, usually by calling the banns on three not necessarily consecutive Sundays during the three-month run-up to a wedding. Banns are normally read out by a vicar at a couple's local parish church as well as in the church that will be the location for the wedding.

Exactly when banns became an accepted custom is not known though they were already well established in medieval times when proclamations were customary among the English and among European settlers in America. In England, banns were ratified by the Synod of Westminster as early as 1200 and by the Lateran Council in 1215. The procedure for banns or proclaiming marriage has appeared in the Book of Common Prayer from the 16th century onward and in 1754 a law was instituted making it illegal for a marriage in England to proceed that had not been proclaimed through the reading of banns. This law was mainly intended to prevent elopements but actually led to the popularity of marriages in Gretna Green, the first town in Scotland that an eloping couple would reach once they left England.

In the United States it is customary for banns to be issued by a member of the clergy, or sometimes by a layperson, over three consecutive Sundays. In the past, civil officials would occasionally post or proclaim banns in courthouses or civic halls. The involvement of civil authorities in the reading of banns highlight the fact that in some American communities marriage was foremost a civil procedure rather than a religious ritual.

By publicly proclaiming a couple's intention to marry, banns allow people to come forward and declare any objection they may have to the wedding. Anyone that objects to the forthcoming marriage is said to forbid the banns. In America, some religious groups discontinued the reading of marriage banns during the 19th and 20th centuries but other religious groups have kept the tradition alive by making banns compulsory. Nowadays, all couples getting married in the United States require a license that states there is no legal impediment preventing heir marriage, a requirement that in some way harks back to the old English tradition of proclaiming marriage banns.

Today, in the United Kingdom an application for the calling of marriage banns should be made to the minister of each parish church where banns need to be called. This application should be made one week before the Sunday when it is hoped the reading of the banns will begin. Once the banns have been called, the engaged couple should obtain a certificate of publication. The marriage then must be held within three months of the last calling of the banns. If either of the couple lives abroad or is a non-British national, or there is a pressing need for the couple to wed in church before the completion of the calling of the banns, then a Common Marriage License may be necessary. Common Licenses are granted at the discretion of the church legal official to whom the application for the license is made, so an application for a license is not a guaranteed fast-track to a church wedding that will bypass the need for banns to be called. The process of applying for a Common License also demands that the couple swear an oath in person in England in front of a legal official.

In November 2015, it was announced at a Church of England synod that the Church of England might consider scrapping the long-held tradition of reading marriage banns prior to a wedding because, according to proponents of the reform, the business of reading marriage banns is too much of a burden upon vicars. Those clergymen that advocate a change to the marriage banns system propose replacing the centuries-old legal requirement of reading marriage banns with some sort of civil process.

See also: British Wedding Traditions; Christian Wedding Ceremony; Gretna Green; Marriage Banns Legislation, United Kingdom

Further Reading

The Faculty Office. "Preliminaries to Marriage: Banns and Common Marriage Licences." Accessed October 11, 2015, at, http://www.facultyoffice.org.uk/special-licences/general-information-about-marriage-law/preliminaries-to-marriagebanns-and-common-marriage-licences/.

Monger, George P. *Marriage Customs of the World: From Henna to Honeymoons*. Santa Barbara, CA: ABC-CLIO, 2004.

Sherwood, Harriet. "Church of England Could Scrap Reading of Marriage Banns." *The Guardian*, November 24, 2015. Accessed November 30, 2015, at http://www.theguardian.com/world/2015/nov/24/church-of-england-could-scrap-reading-of-marriage-banns.

Van Keuren, Luise. "Banns," in Hawes, Joseph M., ed. *The Family in America: An Encyclopedia, Volume 1 A–G*. Santa Barbara, CA: ABC-CLIO, 2001.

Related Primary Document: Marriage Banns Legislation, United Kingdom

Marriage banns are a series of public proclamations that a couple plans to marry. In England it is a legal requirement that banns be declared before any Church of England wedding, usually by calling the banns on three (not necessarily consecutive) Sundays during the three-month run-up to the marriage ceremony. Typically banns are read out by a vicar at the couple's local parish church as well as in the church that will serve as the location for the wedding. The chief law concerning marriage in parish churches belonging to the Church of England is contained in the Marriage Act 1949. This act requires that before a wedding ceremony can take place in a church, one of the following legal requirements must be fulfilled: the calling of banns, the issue of a Common Licence by the Bishop of the Diocese, the issue of a Special Licence by the Archbishop, or the issue of a Superintendent Registrar's Certificate. The Marriage Act 1949 (as well as the Marriage Measure 2008) provides certain rights to people to have their banns read but this does not extend to applications for banns using dishonest information or where the proposed marriage is sham. The following is text from legislation covered by the Marriage Act 1949.

Marriage by banns

6 Place of publication of banns.

(1) Subject to the provisions of this Act, where a marriage is intended to be solemnized after the publication of banns of matrimony, the banns shall be published—

>(a) if the persons to be married reside in the same parish, in the parish church of that parish;

>(b) if the persons to be married do not reside in the same parish, in the parish church of each parish in which one of them resides:

Provided that if either of the persons to be married resides in a chapelry or in a district specified in a licence granted under section twenty of this Act, the banns may be published in an authorised chapel of that chapelry or district instead of in the parish church of the parish in which that person resides.

(2) In relation to a person who resides in an extra-parochial place, the last foregoing subsection shall have effect as if for references to a parish there were substituted references to that extra-parochial place, and as if for references to a parish church there were substituted references to an authorised chapel of that place.

(3) For the purposes of this section, any parish in which there is no parish church or chapel belonging thereto or no church or chapel in which divine service is usually solemnized every Sunday, and any extra-parochial place which has no authorised chapel, shall be deemed to belong to any adjoining parish or chapelry.

(4) Banns of matrimony may be published in any parish church or authorised chapel which is the usual place of worship of the persons to be married or of one of them although neither of those persons resides in the parish or chapelry to which the church or chapel belongs:

Provided that the publication of banns by virtue of this subsection shall be in addition to and not in substitution for the publication of banns required by subsection (1) of this section.

7 Time and manner of publication of banns.

(1) Subject to the provisions of section nine of this Act, banns of matrimony shall be published on three Sundays preceding the solemnization of the marriage during morning service or, if there is no morning service on a Sunday on which the banns are to be published, during evening service.

(2) Banns of matrimony shall be published in an audible manner and in accordance with the form of words prescribed by the rubric prefixed to the office of matrimony in the Book of Common Prayer, and all the other rules prescribed by the said rubric concerning the publication of banns and the solemnization of matrimony shall, so far as they are consistent with the provisions of this Part of this Act, be duly observed.

(3) The parochial church council of a parish shall provide for every church and chapel in the parish in which marriages may be solemnized, a register book of banns made of durable materials and marked in the manner directed by section fifty-four of this Act for the register book of marriages, and all banns shall be published from the said register book of banns by the officiating clergyman, and not from loose papers,

and after each publication the entry in the register book shall be signed by the officiating clergyman, or by some person under his direction.

(4) Any reference in the last foregoing subsection to a parochial church council shall, in relation to an authorised chapel in an extra-parochial place, be construed as a reference to the chapel warden or other officer exercising analogous duties in the chapel or, if there is no such officer, such person as may be appointed in that behalf by the bishop of the diocese.

8 Notice to clergyman before publication of banns.

No clergyman shall be obliged to publish banns of matrimony unless the persons to be married, at least seven days before the date on which they wish the banns to be published for the first time, deliver or cause to be delivered to him a notice in writing, dated on the day on which it is so delivered, stating the christian name and surname and the place of residence of each of them, and the period during which each of them has resided at his or her place of residence.

9 Persons by whom banns may be published.

(1) Subject to the provisions of this section and of section fourteen of this Act, it shall not be lawful for any person other than a clergyman to publish banns of matrimony.

(2) Where on any Sunday in any church or other building in which banns of matrimony may be published a clergyman does not officiate at the service at which it is usual in that church or building to publish banns, the banns may be published—

> (a) by a clergyman at some other service at which banns of matrimony may be published; or

> (b) by a layman during the course of a public reading authorised by the bishop of the diocese of a portion or portions of the service of morning or evening prayer, the public reading being at the hour when the service at which it is usual to publish banns is commonly held or at such other hour as the bishop may authorise:

> Provided that banns shall not be published by a layman unless the incumbent or minister in charge of the said church or building, or some other clergyman nominated in that behalf by the bishop, has made or authorised to be made the requisite entry in the register book of banns of the said church or building.

(3) Where a layman publishes banns of matrimony by virtue of this section the layman shall sign the register book of banns provided under section seven of this Act and for that purpose shall be deemed to be the officiating clergyman within the meaning of that section.

10 Publication of banns commenced in one church and completed in another.

(1) Where the publication of banns of matrimony has been duly commenced in any church, the publication may be completed in the same church or in any other church which, by virtue of the Union of Benefices Measure, 1923, or the New Parishes Measure, 1943, has at the time of the completion taken the place of the first-mentioned

church for the purpose of publication of banns of matrimony either generally or in relation to the parties to the intended marriage.

(2) Where the publication of banns of matrimony has been duly commenced in any building which by virtue of a reorganisation scheme under the Reorganisation Areas Measure, 1944, ceases to be a parish church or, as the case may be, ceases to be licensed for marriages, the publication may be completed in such other building, being either a parish church or a building licensed for marriages, as may be directed by the bishop of the diocese to take the place of the first-mentioned building for the purposes of the publication of banns.

11 Certificates of publication of banns.

(1) Where a marriage is intended to be solemnized after the publication of banns of matrimony and the persons to be married do not reside in the same parish or other ecclesiastical district, a clergyman shall not solemnize the marriage in the parish or district in which one of those persons resides unless there is produced to him a certificate that the banns have been published in accordance with the provisions of this Part of this Act in the parish or other ecclesiastical district in which the other person resides.

(2) Where a marriage is intended to be solemnized in a church or chapel of a parish or other ecclesiastical district in which neither of the persons to be married resides, after the publication of banns therein by virtue of subsection (4) of section six of this Act, a clergyman shall not solemnize the marriage unless there is produced to him—

> (a) if the persons to be married reside in the same parish or other ecclesiastical district, a certificate that the banns have been published in accordance with the provisions of this Part of this Act in that parish or district; or

> (b) if the persons to be married do not reside in the same parish or other ecclesiastical district, certificates that the banns have been published as aforesaid in each parish or district in which one of them resides.

(3) Where banns are published by virtue of subsection (3) of section six of this Act in a parish or chapelry adjoining the parish or extra-parochial place in which the banns would otherwise be required to be published, a certificate that the banns have been published in that parish or chapelry shall have the like force and effect as a certificate that banns have been published in a parish in which one of the persons to be married resides.

(4) Any certificate required under this section shall be signed by the incumbent or minister in charge of the building in which the banns were published or by a clergyman nominated in that behalf by the bishop of the diocese.

12 Solemnization of marriage after publication of banns.

(1) Subject to the provisions of this Part of this Act, where banns of matrimony have been published, the marriage shall be solemnized in the church or chapel or, as the case may be, one of the churches or chapels in which the banns have been published.

(2) Where a marriage is not solemnized within three months after the completion of the publication of the banns, that publication shall be void and no clergyman shall solemnize the marriage on the authority thereof.

13 Publication of banns in Scotland, Northern Ireland or Republic of Ireland.

Where a marriage is intended to be solemnized in England, after the publication of banns of matrimony, between parties of whom one is residing in England and the other is residing in Scotland, Northern Ireland or the Republic of Ireland, then, if banns have been published or proclaimed in any church of the parish or place in which that other party is residing according to the law or custom there prevailing, a certificate given in accordance with that law or custom that the banns have been so published or proclaimed shall as respects that party be sufficient for the purposes of section eleven of this Act, and the marriage shall not be void by reason only that the banns have not been published in the manner required for the publication of banns in England.

14 Publication of banns on board His Majesty's ships.

(1) Where a marriage is intended to be solemnized in England, after the publication of banns of matrimony, between parties of whom one is residing in England and the other is an officer, seaman or marine borne on the books of one of His Majesty's ships at sea, the banns may be published on three successive Sundays during morning service on board that ship by the chaplain, or, if there is no chaplain, by the captain or other officer commanding the ship, and, where banns have been so published, the person who published them shall, unless the banns have been forbidden on any of the grounds on which banns may be forbidden, give a certificate of publication.

(2) A certificate issued under this section shall be in such form as may be prescribed by the Admiralty and shall, as respects the party who is an officer, seaman or marine as aforesaid, be sufficient for the purposes of section eleven of this Act, and all provisions of this Act (including penal provisions) relating to the publication of banns and certificates thereof and all rules required by section seven of this Act to be observed shall apply in the case of banns published under this section subject to such adaptations therein as may be made by His Majesty by Order in Council.

Source: *Marriage Act 1949. 1949 c. 76 (Regnal. 12_13_and_14_Geo_6) Part II. Available at http://www.legislation.gov.uk/ukpga/Geo6/12-13-14/76/part/II/crossheading/marriage-by-banns.*

MATIS HUNTING TRIALS, BRAZIL

The Matis is a semi-nomadic tribe in the Vale do Javari Indigenous Park, an area of 32,000 square miles in the far west of Brazil close to the country's borders with Peru and Columbia. Hunting is an essential part of the Matis way of life and so it follows that to become a true adult member of his tribe a Matis male must pass the Matis hunting trials initiation process. All Matis men must undergo this rite of passage several times throughout their lives to ensure their hunting skills remain viable. The trials consist of several stages and have been likened to torture by non-Matis people who have witnessed the event.

The Matis used to live in five different villages but many members died of diseases contracted on first contact with Brazilian outsiders during the 1970s and there are now only two Matis villages both of which lie along the banks of the River

Itui: Aurelio, which has around 160 inhabitants, and Beija Flor, which is home to about 130 Matis people. At first the Matis did not understand that it was Western diseases that decimated their villages after contact was made with outsiders. Rather, they thought that they had brought disaster upon themselves by their own belief system. Traditionally, the Matis understand the world through taste, which they divide into two types: *bata xo* (sweet) and *chimu* (sour things that have great power). If the balance between bata xo and chimu is upset then the Matis fear that a state of imbalance called *xo* is created, leading to disaster. As a result of their mistaken belief that their traditions had caused disaster, the Matis lost sight of some of their old ways and abandoned many of their traditional ceremonies and practices. These included those rituals that involve bitter substances such as a frog poison called *kampo*, ingesting *tatxi* (a bitter drink made from plant roots), and astringent poces leaves, which smart in the manner of giant stinging nettles leaving a vivid red rash where they touch the skin. The first of these, kampo, is an integral element of the Matis hunting trials. However over time the Matis have come to understand that it was not their beliefs that caused illness within their tribe, and so they have rekindled their traditional rituals, no longer fearing that they will cause widespread destruction and harm to their kinsfolk.

Matis villages lack a defined shape but tend to cluster around a longhouse, that is, an imposing triangular structure set on top of a hill that serves as the geographic center of the village and the cultural heart of village life. The longhouse is usually about 20 feet high and covered in woven thatch. The edifice tends to be decorated with the mandibles of animals that the tribe has hunted in the rainforest and it is in and around the longhouse that many Matis rituals occur. The longhouse is where the 11-foot-long blowpipes with which the Matis hunt are stored. The longhouse is also where poison is applied to the blowpipes. Blowpipes are very important to the Matis and the tribesmen are expert at using the weapons to hunt animals living in the rainforest canopy such as adult spider monkeys (the tribe keeps the young as pets). Hunting proficiency is considered a major asset for a Matis male and will gain him the respect of his elders and the admiration of the village women—a Matis hunter compliments a woman by bringing her freshly killed meat.

To become a hunter a Matis male must go through a precise multi-stage initiation rite. To start the trials, the Matis male has bitter poison poured into his eyes. This results in both extreme pain and temporary blindness but the Matis believe this discomfort enhances the male's other senses, making him a superior hunter. Next the male is whipped on his torso with lengthy rattan sticks. The rattan whip curls around the body as it is applied to the flesh leaving long red welts on the skin. Though unpleasant, this part of the trial is not particularly painful, unlike the third stage, which employs kampo frog poison to an excruciating effect. Kampo is extracted from the monkey frog (*Phyllomedusa bicolor*) by stretching the frog over a fire and scraping toxic excretions from its skin before releasing the creature back into the rainforest. Despite kampo's lethal properties, the poison is employed in the Matis hunting trials as a both purgative and curative. Matis tribal shamans have long used kampo to treat pain, illness, and other disorders because compounds in the frogs' slime hold anesthetic and tranquilizing properties. Scientists also believe that isolated peptides from the slime could be used to treat hypertension and strokes. Similarly, the Matis believe that exposing a male to kampo will make him a fitter, stronger hunter. For the final part of his trials several areas of the male's skin are burned (typically on the arm), the resulting blisters are burst, and a layer of skin removed in order to form an open wound. The kampo is combined with an older tribesman's saliva not only to symbolically pass the elder's wisdom to the initiate but also to activate the poison. The resultant mixture is placed upon the initiate's wound, often using a wooden needle. This allows the poison to enter the initiate's bloodstream directly and the effect is often immediate. The body responds by creating dizziness, a rapid pulse, the need to vomit violently, and an explosive emptying of the bowels. If a male proves resistant to frog poison he is considered to be strong and a second dose of poison is applied to another part of his body. Once the male has vomited and evacuated his bowels the poison is wiped from his skin and the immediate effects of the poison stop. Delayed consequences of the frog poison application include listlessness followed by a sense of euphoria and invincibility that last from 24 hours to several days. Thus the would-be Matis hunter is willing to undergo the frog poison trial as he believes the rite will make him a better hunter equipped with sharper senses and greater stamina. Some hunters also believe that kampo will dispel *panema*, a kind of magical power that can infect a person, animal, or thing and becomes manifest during certain events and is resident in a hunter until it is cured. A hunter only discovers he is affected by panema after a series of unfortunate occurrences while hunting.

It is important that Matis males go through this initiation process in order to prove their strength and to experience equality as adult members of society. That the Matis hunting trials are vital to the tribe's cultural identity is evinced by the fact that the ritual was revived while other Matis customs were not as they were not considered important enough to need restoring. Over time, the Matis have regained the cultural confidence that was dented by the waves of killer illness that led to the deaths of so many of their kinsfolk. As a result of this newly regained confidence, tribal traditionalists, particularly elders, tend to want old traditions to be both retained and reinvigorated, including the Matis hunting trials. However other members of the tribe, usually younger members, are greatly influenced by the ways of modern Brazil having experienced schooling and general contact with the world beyond their villages. These younger non-traditionalists want the Matis to foster closer ties with mainstream Brazilian society so it will be interesting to see for how much longer the Matis hunting trials continue to be practiced.

Another Matis custom involving hunters is the *txawa tanek*, or peccary dance. The Matis are often mistakenly thought by outsiders to decorate themselves in such a way as to resemble jaguars. Indeed, many outsiders, to the irritation of Matis members, refer to the tribe as the Jaguar People. Many Matis rituals, including the txawa tanek, do, however, see tribe members take on the look of animals. This custom takes place the day before a hunt and sees participants paint themselves red using *urucum* (annatto juice) and then dance in a line before entering the longhouse. Those taking part in the ritual dance imitate the guttural sounds of an Amazonian forest pig called the *txawa* or collared peccary and the dance leader bangs together two txawa skulls. The ritual is performed to attract peccaries to the hunters during the next day's hunt. Another ritual in which Matis men imitate an animal is *mapwa tanek*, or the capybara ritual, during which the men cover their bodies with clay and hop around imitating the capybara, the world's largest rodent. As capybaras are notoriously destructive the ritual often becomes overly boisterous and Matis women become the subject of unwanted rowdy attention. Other rituals see hunters climb a pole located in the longhouse and mimic a bird or animal in order to amuse the rest of the tribe.

The Matis *mariwin* ritual sees hunters emerge from the rainforest as the physical personification of their spiritual ancestors. The ritual is in decline but those who perform the ritual take it very seriously. During the ritual a clay horn is used to summon two tribe members to the longhouse where their bodies are painted black or yellow and they are dressed in ornate red clay masks and green ferns. They are also given whips with which to hit their children in order to stop them being naughty or lazy—the Matis never chastise their children so this is the only occasion on which corporal punishment takes place. The disguised tribe members also whip Matis hunters who wish to increase their individual level of xo, and pregnant women wanting to strengthen their fetus.

In 2007, English writer, explorer, and indigenous rights advocate Bruce Parry spent time with the Matis for the BBC ethnographic documentary series "Tribe." Parry both observed and participated in the tribe's many rituals, including the four-stage hunting trials, during which Parry experienced the unpleasant effects of kampo, which he reported as being less disagreeable than the feeling of poces leaves applied to the skin.

See also: Bullet Ant Initiation; Cow Jumping; Forehead-Cutting Initiation; Initiation by Semen Transferal; Land Diving; Log Riding; Maasai Warrior Initiation; Ritual Tattooing; *Sharo*: Public Flogging

Further Reading

BBC. "Matis." BBC: Tribe. October 29, 2014. Accessed December 14, 2014, at http://www.bbc.co.uk/tribe/tribes/matis/.
BBC. "Tribe: Matis." Season 3. DVD, 2007.
Coleman, Leo, ed. *Food: Ethnographic Encounters*. London: Berg, 2011.
Galvan, Javier A., ed. *They Do What? A Cultural Encyclopedia of Extraordinary and Exotic Customs from around the World*. Santa Barbara, CA: ABC-CLIO, 2014.
Khan, Abdul Qayyum Mushtaq, Amanda Morato do Canto, Bruna Minatovicz, and Ursula Romero. "Toxins Present in the Brazilian Fauna and Flora with Potential Medical Importance." Accessed December 14, 2014, at http://braziliantoxins.blogspot.co.uk.
Prada, Paulo. "Poisonous Tree Frog Could Bring Wealth to Tribe in Brazilian Amazon," *New York Times*, May 30, 2006. Accessed December 14, 2014, at http://www.nytimes.com/2006/05/30/business/worldbusiness/30frogs.html?pagewanted=all&_r=0.

MAYPOLES, EUROPE

A maypole is an extremely tall, decorated wooden pole erected as a part of folk festivals around which a maypole dance is performed. Maypoles are most often erected on May Day (May 1) and are found throughout Europe, especially England, Eastern Europe, and Scandinavia. Pagan groups refer to May Day festivals by the Celtic name Beltane. May Day and in particular the act of erecting maypoles are both redolent of fertility, flirtation, and the return to the primal instinct to procreate.

May Day is a modern spring festival but it has its roots in ancient European fertility rites with the maypole a kind of giant phallus that impregnated the earth after seed had been sown. May Day festivities began in pre-Christian times as rituals intended to ensure bountiful harvests. The festivals celebrated the battle between winter and summer that summer was sure to win. The spirit of the vegetation was believed to inhabit the maypoles that were a feature of the May Day celebrations for the maypoles were traditionally hewn from the branches of trees that were in bud, thereby symbolizing the potential for new life that existed within the maypoles. The maypoles were traditionally carried from house to house before being erected in a village square. Over the years, May Day festivities began to include special dances that were performed around maypoles in a tradition of celebration.

In some English villages it is traditional for May Day to be celebrated by young men and women who dance on their village green around a maypole. To make the maypole, unmarried men cut down a tall tree, remove its branches, and tie colored ribbons to the top. Villagers then hold on to the ends of the ribbons and then dance around the maypole. Originally, English maypoles were decorated with garlands of flowers and leaves. This type of maypole was known as a ribbon-less maypole and dancers would simply dance around the maypoles in circles in time with music that was typically played on a pipe, tabor, and fiddle. Over time, decorative ribbons began to be attached to the top of maypoles and dancers would

---

Beltane

Beltane is the English-language name for the ancient May Day festival held on May 1 or sometime equidistant between the spring equinox and the summer solstice. Beltane was celebrated traditionally throughout Ireland, Scotland, the Isle of Man, and other parts of the United Kingdom and Europe. Beltane is one of the four Gaelic seasonal festivals together with Samhain, Imbolc, and Lughnasadh. Traditionally, Beltane marked the start of summer when cattle were moved to summer grasslands with rituals enacted to safeguard the cattle, crops, and people as well as to encourage their growth. In the 20th century, Celtic neo-pagans and Wiccans have observed Beltane as a religious occasion. In the Southern Hemisphere neo-pagans sometimes celebrate Beltane in November.

wind in and out of each other in different directions around the maypole. Each dancer would hold a ribbon resulting in complex patterns of colored ribbons being formed. (*See* Plate 17.) When dancing around a maypole, the ribbons are gradually wound around the pole or plaited together meaning that the dancers then reverse the pattern of the dance to untangle the ribbons. Usually about 10 dancers will dance around a maypole often led by Morris dancers (i.e., English folk dancers) playing traditional English folk music on fiddles, pipes, tabors, accordions, and concertinas.

Often a procession takes place prior to the dancing. A young woman that has been appointed May Queen for the day normally leads the procession. The May Queen, who is normally chosen because she is considered the prettiest girl in her village, wears a crown of leaves and flowers and she is occasionally accompanied by a May King, that is, a man who dresses in green to symbolize the fact that May Day is a springtime festival redolent of fertility. In some parts of England, the May Queen and May King are referred to as the May Bride and May Groom thereby highlighting the original emphasis of May Day on fertility and sexual flirtation. The earliest written references to maypoles in England occur in a 14th-century poem called "Chance of the Dice." There is very little evidence that maypoles are traditional in other parts of the United Kingdom such as Wales or Scotland. From the 15th century, however, references to maypoles appear frequently in the parish records of English villages. During the 17th century, the strict Protestants known as the Puritans were outraged at what they considered the sexual immorality and licentiousness that typically accompanied the drinking and dancing associated with May Day celebrations involving maypoles, leading to Parliament banning the erecting of maypoles in 1644. However when King Charles II was restored to the English throne a few years later, people all over England erected celebratory maypoles as a sign of loyalty to the king. The popularity of maypoles surged again during the Victorian era when maypoles were considered a bucolic delight. It should be noted however that Victorians tended to ignore the significant pagan fertility aspects both of May Day and maypoles instead preferring to see dancing around the maypole as a game for children.

In the Czech Republic, May Day has been a major celebration for centuries. On this day it is customary for Czech people to kiss their true love under a blooming cherry tree or birch tree. Moreover, according to Czech legend any girl that does not receive a kiss will wither and die within the year. Czech villages hold dances to celebrate May Day and erect maypoles. On the eve of May 1, single Czech men go into the forests to cut down a tall tree from which they remove all the lower branches. The tree's trunk is then decorated with garlands, scarves, ribbons, and flowers, and the tree is erected as a maypole in the village square. Once erected, some of the men that felled the tree stand guard over the maypole until dawn on May Day. Meanwhile, the rest of the men travel covertly to neighboring villages and attempt to snatch their maypoles. This is kind of a competition as the men hope to steal as many village maypoles as possible. Then on the first Sunday of

May, villagers that did not allow their maypole to be taken travel around the village visiting the homes of unmarried women who are then given small gifts. In the evening, everybody celebrates the coming of summer by dancing, eating, and generally having fun. Similarly, in Germany, it is traditional for young unmarried men to fell a fir tree on the eve of May Day. Once the tree has been felled the men remove the branches and decorate the trunk before setting the tree up in the village square as a maypole. Men then guard the tree overnight to prevent men from neighboring villages from stealing the maypole. If the men from another village do manage to steal the maypole then those that stole the maypole will require a ransom of a good meal and a barrel of beer to ensure the maypole's safe return.

In Sweden, maypoles decorated with leaves and flowers are associated with Midsummer celebrations, which according to a decision by the Swedish Parliament in 1952 must be celebrated on a weekend between June 20 and 26. Maypoles are a fairly recent addition to Swedish Midsummer traditions having traveled to Sweden in the late Middle Ages from Germany. Since spring starts later in Sweden than it does in Germany, it originally proved difficult to find the leaves with which to decorate maypoles on May 1, so the erecting of maypoles was delayed until Midsummer. The Swedish tradition of dancing around the maypole at Midsummer is also very old though the dances have changed over time. Today, official Midsummer festivals that take place in Sweden normally include exhibitions of folk dancing by dancers wearing traditional costumes, as well as ring dances, maypoles dances, and games. Most particularly Swedish Midsummer celebrations include *Små grodorna*, meaning The Little Frogs, a dancing game in which everyone hops around the maypole while singing about little frogs. The frog dance is also performed at Christmas when people of all ages hop like frogs around the Christmas tree.

Romance is another major facet of Midsummer in Sweden for according to Swedish tradition any unmarried girl who picks seven or sometimes nine species of flowers on her way home from dancing around the maypole and places them under her pillow at Midsummer will dream of her future husband. Moreover, Swedish folklore tells that Midsummer's Eve is a magical time for romance though during this night romantic relationships are also tested because under the influence of alcohol, people make alcohol-fuelled revelations that lead both to weddings and divorces. Indeed, Midsummer is a popular day for weddings and christenings to occur in Sweden. It is also commonly believed in Sweden that around nine months after Midsummer night many baby cradles will rock, as it is understood that much sexual activity takes place on Midsummer night leading to Midsummer babies.

The sexual symbolism of the maypole is highlighted in the classic British folk horror film *The Wicker Man* (1973). When a policeman arrives on the remote Scottish island of Summerisle in time for the islanders' May Day celebrations he comes across children performing a maypole dance and learns that the children are taught the phallic nature of the maypole from a young age.

See also: *Andrzejki*: St. Andrew's Eve; Cerne Abbas Giant (Volume 1); Dyngus Day; Jumping Over the Broom; Looking for Fern Blossoms; May Crowning Ritual (Volume 1); Monstrous Punishments for Naughty Children (Volume 1); Obando Fertility Dance (Volume 1); Phallus Festivals (Volume 1); *Schuhplattler* and *Ländler*

Further Reading

BBC. "May Day History and Folklore." BBC News: UK. April 30, 1998. Accessed November 20, 2015, at http://news.bbc.co.uk/1/hi/special_report/86133.stm.

Brockman, Norbert C. *Encyclopedia of Sacred Places, Volume 1*. Second edition. Santa Barbara, CA: ABC-CLIO, 2011.

Jones, Alison. *Larousse Dictionary of World Folklore*. Edinburgh, UK: Larousse, 1996.

Kábelová, Andrea. "May 1st—Day for Love." Czech Republic, April 26, 2011. Accessed November 20, 2015, at http://www.czech.cz/en/103913-may-1st-day-for-love.

Real Scandinavia. "Midsummer in Sweden: Origins and Traditions." Accessed November 20, 2015, at http://realscandinavia.com/midsummer-in-sweden-origins-and-traditions/.

Simpson, Jacqueline, and Steve Roud. *Oxford Dictionary of English Folklore*. Oxford, UK: Oxford University Press, 2000.

Stradling, Rod. "All about Maypole Dancing." Accessed November 23, 2015, at http://www.maypoledance.com.

Swedish Institute. "Midsummer." Sweden, June 11, 2015. Accessed November 20, 2015, at https://sweden.se/culture-traditions/midsummer/.

MEHNDI, INTERNATIONAL

Mehndi, the Sanskrit word for myrtle that was appropriated into Hindi to mean the henna plant (*Lawsonia inermis*), is the term used to describe reddish colored henna designs painted on the skin, particularly the hands and feet. Mehndi is a near-obligatory part of Muslim, Hindu, and Sephardic Jewish wedding celebrations in India, Pakistan, North Africa, the Middle East, and Europe as well as places where migrants from these areas have settled such as the United Kingdom, the United States, and Canada. However mehndi is most closely associated with Indian weddings for mehndi is an essential decoration for brides, and sometimes grooms, from the Indian subcontinent, as well as their wedding guests who may be painted at pre-wedding parties. Mehndi designs are not permanent and so are akin to temporary tattoos that can be visible for a number of weeks. However as well as being a form of skin decoration mehndi is also intended to confer blessings, grace, and good luck as a kind of amulet worn upon the skin. Daubing the skin with henna is also a traditional homeopathic remedy in North Africa and India where the plant is applied to heal burns, boils, sore throats, and fungal infections among other health issues. The plant is also used in cosmetics especially as a hair dye used to turn hair a reddish color.

To use henna, dried henna leaves are crushed to a fine powder and then made into a paste. There are very many names for mehndi because there are so many Asian dialects. Other names and alternate spellings for mehndi include *mehendi*, *mehedi*, and *mendi* as well as the Sanskrit word *mendika*.

Painting designs on to the skin using henna is an ancient art form passed down through oral transmission, usually with patterns and designs, from one generation of women to the next. Indeed the use of henna to mark the skin is thought to have a very long history for traces of henna have been found on the hands of ancient Egyptian mummies dating from over 5,000 years ago. The use of henna in India is also believed to stretch back in time, for cave paintings discovered at the UNESCO World Heritage site of Ajanta, 280 miles east of Mumbai, are thought by some people to have been painted using henna. Additionally, the Sanskrit text the *Navanitaka* dating from 200 BCE uses the word *madayantika*, which some scholars believe refers to henna. Indian tales also attest to mehndi's long history in India. For instance Hindu folklore tells that Parvati, the consort of the god Shiva, was said to paint herself with henna in order to win his affection thereby earning mehndi a reputation of being able to confer marital happiness and seductive allure to those who wear it. Henna has also been associated with Islam for a very long time. Indeed it is said that the prophet Mohammed used the plant to dye his beard. However the custom of Muslim women painting their bodies with mehndi only really became popular during the Mogul Era (1526–1858; also written Mughal) when many thousands of Hindus converted to Islam. Muslim brides are decorated with mehndi the night before their wedding at a special party called the henna night.

Another theory as to why mehndi is associated with marriage is that henna's red color is reminiscent of blood loss caused by the expected rupturing of a bride's hymen on her wedding night. In addition according to Indian tradition there is no formal coming of age for pubertal girls. Instead, an Indian female is only considered to become a sexually mature woman when she marries. Therefore mehndi is closely associated with the sexual initiation of females by their husbands and as such is included in the ancient Hindu text the *Kama Sutra*, part of which provides advice on sexual intercourse, as one of the 64 arts of women. Thus it can be said that the painting of mehndi is a transformational rite of passage for a bride.

To celebrate marriage, an Indian woman will have her hands and sometimes feet painted with mehndi. To do this the design is painted on by another woman, often a specially trained mehndi artist, sometimes at a mehndi parlor, and left to dry. The dried henna paste is then washed off, leaving a reddish stain. A folk belief found across the Indian subcontinent is that the deeper the shade of red left on the bride's skin by the henna, the stronger will be the love and bond between husband and wife.

The use of mehndi varies between cultures and geographical regions though it is nearly always prized for its symbolic associations with love and desire than for the beauty of the intricate designs. There are four types of mehndi designs, each linked to a geographical region: Middle Eastern, North African, Indian and Pakistani, and Southeast Asian. Middle Eastern mehndi designs tend to comprise floral patterns as do North African mehndi, though North African designs tend to be more geometric than do the Middle Eastern patterns. Indian and Pakistani mehndi tends to be very intricate and extravagant. Southeast Asian mehndi designs tend to combine Indian and Middle Eastern designs. Some of the most common mehndi patterns incorporate peacocks, lotus flowers, birds, leaves, and the sun. Hindu brides often have their groom's name incorporated into their wedding day mehndi design on the palms of their hands. According to tradition, if the groom is unable to find his name among the intricate pattern then he will always be dominated by his bride.

Mehndi also plays an important part during the time of Karva Chauth (also written as Karwa Chauth), an ancient Hindu festival during which married women fast from sunrise until moonrise while praying for their husband's longevity and prosperity. Karva Chauth is celebrated mainly in northern India in October and sees wives dress in their wedding clothes having been painted with mehndi. In the lead-up to Karva Chauth, markets in northern India become crowded with henna artists and wives also make appointments at beauty parlors to have their mehndi applied.

Married Indian women usually have mehndi applied on their hands, before performing any kind of ritual. Indeed once an Indian bride becomes a sexually active woman she will go on to use mehndi at various times throughout her life as a form of expression. Only if she is widowed will the woman stop using mehndi.

See also: Hindu Wedding Ceremony; Moroccan Weddings; Mummification (Volume 3); Muslim Wedding Ceremony; Ritual Tattooing; Virginity Testing; Vrindavan: The City of Widows (Volume 3)

Further Reading
Anakee Miczak, Marie. *Henna's Secret History: The History, Mystery & Folklore of Henna*. Lincoln, NE: iUniverse.com Inc., 2001
Indobase.com. "Beauty: What Is Henna." Accessed April 17, 2015, at http://beauty.indobase.com/mehendi/.
Roome, Loretta. *Mehndi: The Timeless Art of Henna Painting*. New York: St. Martin's Press, 1998.
Society for the Confluence of Festivals in India (SCFI). "Karwa Chauth." Accessed April 17, 2015, at http://www.karwachauth.com.

MENSTRUAL CUSTOMS, INTERNATIONAL

Menstruation is the monthly discharge of blood and tissue through the vagina that is experienced by human females that are neither pregnant nor menopausal. The word menstruation, which is commonly referred to as periods, derives from the Latin word *mensis* meaning month, which in turn is related to the Greek word for moon, *mene*. In many cultures around the world, females experiencing their monthly bleed are considered to possess sacred or magical powers, most probably because of the inherent association between blood as symbol of life and death and female fertility. Some peoples also view the red color of menstrual blood as sacred. For instance, in Polynesia the word *tapu* (or *tabu*) that derives from the words for to mark and menstruation is used to suggest wonder and esteem. Similarly the Dakotan (Sioux language) term *wakan* is used to refer to something that is wonderful and magical and is also applied to women experiencing their period. The blend of reverence and awe in which some peoples regard menstruating women has led to the evolution of several cultural customs that are focused on menstruation. Though many of these customs revolve around so-called menstrual taboos, some uphold menstruating women as powerful, creative, and dominant.

It is the tradition among the Kalash (also known as the Kalasha or the Nuristani), an indigenous people living in the Kalash Valley in Chitral, Pakistan, to isolate menstruating women in a menstrual hut known as a *bashali* (also written as *basali* or *bashleni*). The Kalash religion is polytheistic and the Kalash abide by their ancient traditions, including superstitions about menstruation and pregnancy. For this reason, when a Kalash woman menstruates she is secluded in the *bashali* that contains a shrine to Dezalik, the goddess of fertility that the Kalash believe protects women during childbirth. Only pregnant and menstruating women may enter the bashali. Kalash women consider their entering the bashali as a religious ritual intended to ensure the fertility and productivity of the world rather than as demeaning or unpleasant treatment. Unlike Nepalese women who may be resentful or fearful of being made to stay in a *goth* (a rudimentary hut made from mud, dung, and straw) for the duration of their monthly period, Kalash women are said to view the bashali as a holy place exclusively intended for women.

It is important to remember that Kalash women experience far fewer periods in their lives than women in the West because Kalash women tend not to use birth control and so are pregnant, and therefore not menstruating, far more often than Western women. For this reason, it is a rare for a Kalash woman to experience menstruation for one week every month—for Kalash women this only happens when they start to menstruate as young girls or as they approach the end of their childbearing years. While staying in the bashali, menstruating women do not touch the figure of Dezalik until they have completed their menstrual cycle and only then after they have washed themselves in a ritual manner. Menstruating Kalash women believe Dezalik is their protector and so throw walnuts, redolent of fertility, at an icon of the goddess while asking the goddess to ease the pain and discomfort of their bleeding by imploring, "Make it finish quickly."

Elsewhere in Asia, the Bauls living in Bengal, India, break with much of Indian tradition by celebrating menstrual blood. The Bauls are a religious group that have renounced Bengali society and believe in a unique mixture of Hinduism and Islam. The Bauls venerate bodily fluids and break with the Indian tradition of seeing menstrual blood as polluting by allowing sex between men and menstruating females and, perhaps most extremely, by drinking menstrual blood. The Bauls believe that drinking menstrual blood provides nutrition and nourishment and mix the blood with coconut milk, cow's milk, camphor, sugar, and palm juice. The Bauls also sing songs in celebration of menstrual blood as the Bauls consider menstrual blood to be the repository of reproductive seed. A Hindu menstruation celebration called *Manjal Neerattu Vizha* (Turmeric Bathing Ceremony) is held by Tamils in India as the final element of a Tamil girl's coming-of-age celebration. While men oversee most Hindu ceremonies women lead this joyous ceremony as it marks a girl's transition to womanhood. This coming-of-age ceremony begins with the start of the girl's first menstruation, which is marked by a time of ritual seclusion. During this seclusion the girl sits apart from other people on a wooden plank in the corner of a hut called a *kudisai*. The kudisai is made from the leaves of coconut palms and mango and neem trees and may be located inside or outside the girl's family home. The kudisai is equipped with everything the girl might need while she is secluded, including toiletries and clothes, and while secluded the girl is fed, bathed, and generally pampered by her female relatives. The girl is also told to rest. When the girl visits the bathroom she must carry neem leaves and something made from iron as these are believed to fend off malevolent spirits. Additionally, the girl must eat special foods on the 9th, 11th, and 13th day of her seclusion. During the girl's seclusion she is ordered not to look at birds on an empty stomach, not to venture out alone, and to avoid housework. The girl is also barred from entering the *pooja*, or prayer room, and she must not touch flowering plants lest the plants wilt or touch foods containing tamarind, salt, or rice. The girl is forbidden from doing these things because her menstrual blood is considered to be a powerful receptacle of *Shakti*, the dynamic cosmic energy that is the personification of sacred female creativity and fertility.

The end of the girl's seclusion is marked by a purification ritual known as *puniya-thanam* during which neighborhood women paint the girl's feet with a mixture of red ochre, yellow turmeric, and limestone. The final part of the menstrual coming-of-age ceremony is the *Manjal Neerattu Vizha*, a lavish communal feast to which all the community is invited, including men. At Manjal Neerattu Vizha, the girl is given gifts by her friends and relatives, particularly her maternal uncles, as well as new clothes. It is on the day of this ceremony that the girl receives her first sari, which she wears to the event. Moreover, as a reward for entering womanhood the girl's grandparents give her additional saris. Similar ceremonies are enacted as part of wedding festivities and to celebrate a pregnancy, and though this custom is falling out of fashion in some areas it is still very popular in small towns. Another southern Indian menstrual custom, *Goriyo*, or Monsoon Austerity Ritual, sees menstruating females eat only raw foods for two weeks in order to mark the transitioned from girlhood to womanhood. The custom also includes the *Kala Ritu* ceremony during which a girl's mother encourages her daughter to take a pledge of chastity until marriage. As part of this ceremony the mother teaches the girl about sexuality, morality, spirituality, and the social responsibility of being a woman. The mother also gives the girl her first sari, which is colored white to symbolize virginity.

Another menstruation celebration sees some Jewish mothers slap their daughters when the girls begin their first period. The history of this custom and the reasons behind it are not clear. Some Jewish scholars have suggested that as the mothers' slapping of the girls' faces brings blood to the girls' cheeks, the slap confers a blessing for the girls' fertility and well-being while also warning the girls to guard their virginity. A number of Jewish women have tried to establish women's circles to induct daughters into knowledge of menstruation, but efforts to establish such circles have largely failed, as many women are uncomfortable with the idea. Menstruation is not generally celebrated in Judaism, with women needing to visit the *mikveh* (ritual bath) 12 to 15 days after the start of their period.

In Africa, the San people living in Botswana, South Africa, Zambia, Zimbabwe, and Namibia consider menstruating women to be extremely powerful. For this reason, a girl's first period is considered a cause of celebration though San girls do not generally experience their first period until the age of about 19 years because they eat diets that are low in calories and fat. When a San girl does have her first period she is secluded in a menstrual hut and elder San women hold a party in honor of the girl having reached adulthood. At the party, the older women surround the menstrual hut housing the menstruating girl and perform the Eland Bull Dance around the hut. This dance sees the elder women mimic the bull's mating dance ritual while an older man bearing bull horns or sticks approaches the dancing women from behind and pretends to sniff at their exposed buttocks. The dancing women imitate an animal's mating pattern in order to signify that since the girl has experienced her first menstrual period she is now biologically mature, fertile, and ready to marry.

See also: Entering the *Bashali* (Volume 1); *Kumari* and *Deuki* (Volume 1); Menstrual Taboos; Purity Ball; Sunrise Ceremony; Urethral Subincision

Further Reading

Buckley, Thomas, and Alma Gottlieb. *Blood Magic: The Anthropology of Menstruation*. Berkeley: University of California Press, 1988.

Clarke, Richard. "Tamil Coming of Age—Manjal Neerattu Vizha." Living in the Embrace of Arunachala, March 17, 2009. Accessed September 1, 2015, at https://richardarunachala.wordpress.com/2009/03/17/tamil-coming-of-age-manjal-neerattu-vizha/.

Hanssen, Kristin. "Ingesting Menstrual Blood: Notions of Health and Bodily Fluids in Bengal," *Special Issue: Blood Mysteries: Beyond Menstruation as Pollution*, 41(4), Autumn 2002, 365–379.

Lewis-Williams, David J., and D. G. Pearce. *San Spirituality: Roots, Expression, and Social Consequences*. Walnut Creek, CA: AltaMira Press, 2004.

Maggi, Wynne. *Our Women Are Free: Gender and Ethnicity in the Hindukush*. Ann Arbor: University of Michigan, 2001.

Matthiessen, Maxie. "From Menstrual Huts to Drinking Blood. The Weird and Wacky World of Cultural Attitudes to Menstruation. Pt. 1." Ruby-Cup.com. April 17, 2013. Accessed August 6, 2015, at http://www.ruby-cup.com/blog/from-menstrual-huts-to-drinking-blood-the-weird-and-wacky-world-of-cultural-attitudes-to-menstruation-pt-1/.

Meyer, Melissa L. *Thicker Than Water: The Origins of Blood as Symbol and Ritual*. New York: Routledge, 2005.

Milgram, Goldie. "Ritual of Welcoming Bodily Change." RitualWell. Accessed August 6, 2015, at http://www.ritualwell.org/ritual/ritual-welcoming-bodily-change.

Tiwari, Maya. *Women's Power to Heal: Through Inner Medicine*. New York: Mother Om Media, 2011.

Wasserfall, Rahel R., ed. *Women and Water: Menstruation in Jewish Life and Law*. Hanover, NH: University Press of New England, 1999.

MENSTRUAL TABOOS, INTERNATIONAL

Menstruation is invested with great importance in many societies as it is often seen as the physical manifestation of a girl's transition to adulthood. As a time of great change, the process of menstruation is often regarded with a degree of fear and confusion. Additionally, there are many cultural taboos surrounding the topic of menstruation. Often this is because monthly periods are considered dirty or embarrassing with menstruating women seen as ritually unclean and as both polluted and polluting. Some anthropologists suggest that there are various categories of menstrual taboo including the fear that menstrual blood is dangerous to others, taboos that require menstruating women to be isolated, the prohibition of married women from having sex with their husbands, and the banning of menstruating women from preparing foods. However other academics believe that these various taboos stem from the same basic concept of the menstruating woman as unclean and therefore should be regarded as a single overarching menstrual taboo.

Several major religions traditionally see menstruation as unclean. Christianity, Judaism, Islam, and Hinduism all suggest that menstruating females are impure. Indeed both the Jewish Talmud and the Christian Bible describe menstruating women as ritually unclean and declare that any person that touches a menstruating woman will remain unclean until nightfall. Muslim females are not allowed to pray, fast, or perform other religious duties while menstruating because Islam sees blood as unclean. For this reason, Muslim wives are not permitted to have sexual intercourse with their husbands while they have their period. Hindu females are not allowed to take part in normal everyday duties while they are experiencing their period and can only resume normal life once they have been ritually purified. Indeed throughout India periods are generally seen as taboo with menstruating women forbidden to enter temples, prepare certain foods in kitchens lest the food decay, or to take baths.

There is a general air of silence around the issue of women's health in India and particularly around menstruation because Indian traditions see menstruating females as impure, unclean, and unhealthy. Some Indian people even consider menstruating women to be living under a curse for the duration of their period. Because menstruation is not discussed and girls are not generally educated about personal hygiene issues relating to menstruation, many Indian females suffer from urinary tract infections and skin disorders as a result of ignorance of menstrual hygiene. Furthermore, a 2003 study found that reusing absorbent cloths was associated with a two-and-a-half-times greater risk of serious cervical health problems compared to using clean cloths or sanitary towels; this suggests that the practice of reusing cloths may be linked to India's high level of cervical cancer. Indeed in 2010 it was estimated that only 12 percent of Indian females used sanitary towels. Instead, it is common in India for women to use pieces of cloth often recycled from sheets that are washed and reused time and again. Alternatively, very poor Indian women may use leaves, sawdust, or even sand to absorb their menstrual blood. The reluctance of Indian women to buy sanitary protection is partly due to economic reasons but mainly because women are too embarrassed to shop for sanitary products hence 75 percent of Indian women living in cities that do buy sanitary towels insist on the towels being wrapped in newspaper so that it is not apparent that they have bought the items. This same sense of embarrassment also commonly leads to girls leaving school when they start their periods.

At present, a number of non-governmental organizations (NGOs) are attempting to redress Indian's menstrual taboos. For example one NGO, Goonj, runs educational campaigns aimed at dispelling myths surrounding menstruation. Goonj also makes affordable sanitary towels from recycled saris that are then sold to women that cannot afford, or do not ordinarily have access to, sanitary products. Another educational initiative aimed at allaying Indian superstitions surrounding menstruation is Menstrupedia, an educational website that provides comic book guides to puberty, periods, and personal hygiene.

In rural areas of Nepal, the centuries-old tradition of *chaupadi* persists despite being banned in 2005. Chaupadi sees menstruating Hindu women made to live in a cramped mud-hut called a *goth*, in cattlesheds, and in outbuildings while they experience their period and is the result of the Hindu belief that the blood associated with menstruation (as well as childbirth) is impure. While living under the constraints of chaupadi, females may not walk near temples or enter houses and they have limited contact with other people with family members bringing them food. According to chaupadi tradition, women must also not use public water sources, attend public gatherings, or touch cattle. Some women are also banned from drinking milk in fear that the cow from which the milk came will stop producing milk in the future. Girls experiencing their period may also have to miss a week of schooling every month as they are not allowed to interact with boys at school and are embarrassed at displaying the visible evidence of their bleeding because they do not own any sanitary towels.

Apart from suffering ostracism, women living under chaupadi also have to contend with living in uncomfortable conditions for the sheds in which they stay are unheated, poorly ventilated, and liable to attack by wild animals. Menstruating females living under chaupadi are also in danger of dying from a lack of medical provision if they suffer complications as a result of their menstruation and there have been reports of women being raped while staying in chaupadi isolation. The tradition of chaupadi persists because villagers fear that communal ill fortune such as crop failures, water shortages, and animal attacks will occur if women do not adhere to the chaupadi tradition. After a number of females died while staying in chaupadi isolation, there is now a growing resentment against the chaupadi tradition. For instance, the authorities in the village of Bhageshwar declared the settlement a chaupadi-free zone in December 2012. However such bans seem to be mainly superficial when it is considered that the Nepal Supreme Court banned chaupadi in 2005. The outlawing of chaupadi by the Nepalese government has had a limited effect however for the ban does not extend to Nepal's western districts where around 90 percent of women in Achham district continue to practice chaupadi, according to health workers.

Another type of menstrual seclusion occurs among the Manchineri people living in Brazil, Peru, and Bolivia that perform a puberty ritual called *hapijihlu*, a reference to menstrual blood and also sometimes referred to as "when I was painted." During hapijihlu, various limitations are placed on a menstruating girl. The ritual begins when a girl begins her first menstrual period when she may be isolated by being separated from the rest of her community and indeed her family as she is confined to a hammock suspended close to the ceiling of her family home, sometimes in an out-of-the-way corner of the house. By being made to lie inert in her hammock high in the air, the girl becomes invisible to other people, except perhaps her mother or another elder female who are allowed to tend the girl. This part of the ritual is known as "my mother lifted me up" and is intended to demonstrate the girl's ability to regulate the physical processes of her body.

Elsewhere, the subject of menstruation is also taboo with menstruating females seen as a danger to men. For instance, New Zealand Māoris traditionally consider menstrual blood to be contaminated by dreaded *kahukahu*, a type of malign disease demons responsible for stillbirths and child ghosts that inhabit menstrual clots known as *paheke*. As menstruating women were believed to harbor malevolent kahukahu, a number of limitations were traditionally placed on Māori women experiencing their periods. For instance, according to Māori tradition a boy's growth will be stunted if he is stepped over by a menstruating woman. Similarly if a man possessing psychic powers sits on a seat previously sat on by a menstruating woman then he will lose his powers. For these reasons Māori tradition dictates that menstruating women should be isolated. Māori women traditionally use a kind of diaper or apron called a *marototo* as sanitary protection, within which ghosts of babies are said to reside until the marototo is placed among reeds at the end of the woman's bleeding. In some areas of New Zealand, it is customary for bloodied marototos to be buried so that the kahukahu can be rendered powerless and unable to attack the living. The marototo is offered to the gods and incantations called *karakia* intoned, thereby rendering the kahukahu harmless. According to Māori teachings, if a marototo remains above ground an animal may eat it or it might be flown over by a moth resulting in the disease demons entering the animal and attacking people. Similarly, if a marototo is thrown into a river, a fish may eat the marototo and become possessed.

Taboos surrounding menstruation also exist in the West. For example, the symbolism of several Western fairytales can be interpreted as alluding indirectly to menstruation. This is exemplified by Little Red Riding Hood's donning her scarlet cape and the blood resulting from Sleeping Beauty pricking her finger on a spindle as a teenager. Furthermore, in the United States and the United Kingdom blue liquid is usually substituted for the presence of blood in sanitary towel advertisements in order to show the absorptiveness properties of the products. In 2011, sanitary towel manufacturer Always broke with tradition by running an advertisement showing a sanitary towel with a red dot at its center. This was seen as a historic first for traditionally sanitary towel advertisements are loaded with symbolism and imagery. The seeming need for discretion when discussing periods in Western society has also resulted in a raft of euphemisms for menstruation ranging from "Aunt Flo," and "on the rag" to "surfing the crimson wave," as referred to in the 1995 film *Clueless*. Another film, *Carrie* (1976), based on the 1974 novel of the same name by Stephen King and remade in 2012, deals explicitly with menstrual taboos in its opening scenes that depict the titular character, who is ignorant of such matters, being pelted with sanitary products by her peers when she experiences her first period while showering after gym class.

Menstrual taboos are increasingly in the news. For example it was widely reported that when the U.K. parliament debated the removal of the so-called tampon tax (which in essence argues that tampons are a luxury product) in 2015, one woman member of Parliament (MP), Stella Creasy, apparently refused to speak to any male MP that used the euphemistic term sanitary products rather than say the word tampons. Additionally in recent years, a number of female athletes have taken steps to address the issue of menstrual taboos in public. For instance, in January 2015 British tennis player Heather Watson made the news internationally when she told a press conference that her loss at the Australian Open tennis championships was partly due to feeling dizzy and nauseated after starting her period. Meanwhile, Harvard University graduate Kiran Gandhi made international headlines when she ran the 2015 London Marathon without using sanitary products thereby allowing her menstrual flow to visibly stain her clothing. Gandhi claimed that she had decided to do so in order to show solidarity with women that do not have access to sanitary towels or tampons and also to try and erase taboos surrounding menstruation. Meanwhile in 2015, the social media website Instagram came under fire when the site's authorities told artist Rupi Kaur that a photograph of the artist violated its community guidelines by showing a small patch of menstrual blood that had leaked through the artist's trousers on to her bed cover. Kaur protested Instagram's decision, which led to the artwork being restored to the website. Instagram argued that the photograph had been removed in error.

Businesses based in the West have also come to realize that not all women around the world have access to sanitary products. In January 2014, the New York-based company THINX launched a special type of leak-resistant, antimicrobial underwear specifically designed to be both a back-up for tampons and to ultimately replace them entirely. The people behind THINX not only aim to remove the social awkwardness surrounding periods but also aim to help women in developing countries that do not have access to sanitary products. THINX works on a buy-one-give-one model, so that for each pair of THINX sold a donation is made to AFRIPads. This is a Ugandan social business that trains women to make and sell reusable, low-cost sanitary pads, which are subsequently sold at low prices to local women. THINX also claims that its underwear is environmentally friendly as it can help eliminate the estimated 12 billion pads and 7 million tampons included in landfill sites in the United States.

See also: Breast Ironing; Entering the *Bashali* (Volume 1); Fairytales (Volume 1); Female Genital Cutting; *Kumari* and *Deuki* (Volume 1); Menstrual Customs; Sunrise Ceremony; Training Bra; Urethral Subincision

Further Reading

Bhalla, Nita. "'Menstrupedia' Aims to Break Taboo over Periods in India," *Reuters*, April 10, 2014. Accessed August 4, 2015, at http://in.reuters.com/article/2014/04/10/india-women-menstrupedia-idINDEEA3908W20140410.

Bobel, Chris. *New Blood: Third-wave Feminism and the Politics of Menstruation*. New Brunswick, NJ: Rutgers University Press, 2010.

Buckley, Thomas, and Alma Gottlieb. *Blood Magic: The Anthropology of Menstruation*. Berkeley, CA: University of California Press, 1988.

Chitrakar, Navesh. "Banished Once a Month," Reuters: Photographer's Blog, March 5, 2014. Accessed August 4, 2015, at http://blogs.reuters.com/photographers-blog/2014/03/05/banished-once-a-month/.

Delaney, Janice, Mary Jane Lupton, and Emily Toth. *The Curse: A Cultural History of Menstruation*. Revised expanded edition. Champaign: University of Illinois Press, 1988.

Gebreyes, Rahel. "How Tennis Player Heather Watson Confronted the Taboo of Menstruation in Sports," *Huff Post Women*, January 26, 2015. Accessed August 9, 2015, at http://www.huffingtonpost.com/2015/01/26/heather-watson-menstruation-sports_n_6539144.html.

Guardian News and Media Limited. "Nepal's Chaupadi Tradition Banishes Menstruating Women—in Pictures," *The Guardian*, March 8, 2014. Accessed August 4, 2015, at http://www.theguardian.com/global-development/gallery/2014/mar/08/nepal-chaupadi-tradition-banishes-menstruating-women-in-pictures.

Jha, Rupa. "100 Women 2014: The Taboo of Menstruating in India." BBC News: World, October 27, 2014. Accessed August 4, 2015, at http://www.bbc.co.uk/news/world-asia-29727875.

Johnson, Emma. "Can These Panties Disrupt the $15 Billion Feminine Hygiene Market?" *Forbes*, May 28, 2015. Accessed November 5, 2015, at http://www.forbes.com/sites/emmajohnson/2015/05/28/can-these-panties-disrupt-a-15-billion-feminine-hygiene-market/.

Jones, Alison. *Larousse Dictionary of World Folklore*. Edinburgh, UK: Larousse, 1996.

Meyer, Melissa L. *Thicker Than Water: The Origins of Blood as Symbol and Ritual*. New York: Routledge, 2005.

National Library of New Zealand. "The Kahukahu." *Transactions and Proceedings of the Royal Society of New Zealand, 37*, 1904. Accessed August 4, 2015, at http://rsnz.natlib.govt.nz/volume/rsnz_37/rsnz_37_00_000330.html.

News Corp. "Kiran Gandhi Ran the London Marathon without a Tampon in a Bid to Break the Stigma Surrounding Women's Periods," *The Daily Telegraph*, August 8, 2015. Accessed August 9, 2015, at http://www.dailytelegraph.com.au/news/nsw/kiran-gandhi-ran-the-london-marathon-without-a-tampon-in-a-bid-to-break-the-stigma-surrounding-womens-periods/story-fni0cx12-1227475480183?utm_content=SocialFlow&utm_campaign=EditorialSF&utm_source=DailyTelegraph&utm_medium=Facebook.

Rustad, Harley. "Nepalese Menstruation Tradition Dies Hard," *The Globe and Mail*, April 30, 2013. Accessed August 4, 2015, at http://www.theglobeandmail.com/news/world/nepalese-menstruation-tradition-dies-hard/article11644844/.

Saul, Heather. "Menstruation-themed Photo Series Artist 'Censored by Instagram' Says Images Are to Demystify Taboos around Periods." *The Independent*. March 30, 2015. Accessed May 29, 2016, at http://www.independent.co.uk/arts-entertainment/art/menstruation-themed-photo-series-artist-censored-by-instagram-says-images-are-to-demystify-taboos-10144331.html.

Schultz, Colin. "How Taboos around Menstruation Are Hurting Women's Health." Smithsonian.com. March 6, 2014. Accessed August 4, 2015, at http://www.smithsonianmag.com/smart-news/how-taboos-around-menstruation-are-hurting-womens-health-180949992/?no-ist.

Virtanen, Pirjo Kristiina. *Indigenous Youth in Brazilian Amazonia: Changing Lived Worlds*. New York: Palgrave Macmillan, 2012.

Woods, Rose. "Bloody Awful: The 'Tampon Tax' and the 'M Word'," *Huffington Post*, November 5, 2015. Accessed November 5, 2015, at http://www.huffingtonpost.co.uk/rose-woods/tampon-tax_b_8461722.html.

MONEY DANCE, INTERNATIONAL

The money dance (also sometimes called the dollar dance or apron dance) is an event that occurs at some wedding receptions. During the money dance, male guests pay to dance for a short time with the bride or, occasionally, female guests will pay to dance with the groom. The specifics of the dance vary from place to place. The money that ensues from the money dance is usually put toward paying for the newlyweds' honeymoon or to help them set up home together.

Some people claim that the money dance originated in Poland at the start of the 20th century. In Poland, the money dance begins after the newlyweds have danced their first dance. The best man announces the start of the money dance and starts the dance by pinning money in note form to the bride's dress. Alternatively the bride may carry a purse into which guests place the money or she may don a special apron in to the pocket of which the money may be placed. A newly evolved version of the money dance in Poland sees the female guests pin money to the groom's lapel. In this instance the bridesmaids start the money dance by being the first to pin their money to the groom. In Poland, the money dance is known as *Pani Mloda* (Apron Dance). When all the guests have finished dancing with the bride or groom, the newlyweds then dance together and the groom throws his wallet into his new wife's apron or purse and grabs hold of his wife and her apron. The newlyweds then leave the reception venue together as husband and wife.

Elsewhere in Eastern Europe, the money dance is performed differently. For example, in Ukraine the bride removes her wedding veil and puts on an apron into which guests can put the requisite money. The Ukrainian money dance differs to that in Poland for in Ukraine the bride begins the dance by dancing first with her father and then the best man followed by the other male reception guests. In Hungary, the money dance takes place toward the end of the reception; the bride's father or the best man shouts out "The bride is for sale!" When this is exclaimed all the male guests wait in line to dance with the bride having first pinned money to her dress or placed it in one of her shoes or in the center of the reception venue. In Portugal, the money is also placed in the bride's shoe, which is either placed in the middle of the room or passed from guest to guest to receive their money.

The money dance is a very familiar element of Greek and Cypriot wedding receptions. In Greece, the money is pinned to both the bride and groom while in Cyprus the money is both fixed to the couple as they dance and also thrown over the newlyweds in a shower of notes. Meanwhile in former Yugoslav countries, money is not pinned to the bride at all but rather given to the best man. In nearby Albania, money is attached the bride and groom during a dance known as the Napoleon dance. This dance sees the money stuck to the groom's forehead and in the pockets of his jacket while the bride has money pushed into her hands and down her wedding gown. Relatives of the couple also shower them with money. Another version of the money dance occurs in Spain where guests in general give the bride money in order to dance with her. After the money dance, items of the bride and groom's clothing, especially the groom's tie and the bride's garter, are auctioned to raise money. These specific items of clothing are chosen as they are believed to be lucky.

Outside of Europe, the money dance occurs in the United States, the Philippines, Mexico, Turkmenistan, and Nigeria. At wedding receptions in Turkmenistan, money is thrown into the air by guests and then gathered up by children who proceed to give it to the newlyweds. Since the notes are usually low denomination, the money is more of a symbolic gesture than a way of giving the couple a sizeable amount of money. Instead, the action of throwing the money is intended to confer prosperity upon the newlyweds. In the Philippines, on the announcement of the money dance all the male guests lines up to pin money to the bride's dress and veil while all the female guests wait their turn to dance with the groom. During the first dance at Nigerian receptions relatives of the newlyweds and guests take turns to approach the bride and groom, and occasionally their mothers, and shower them with small-denomination notes as they dance. This tradition is known as spraying and although widespread throughout Nigeria, it is most common among people belonging to the Yoruba and Igbo groups, both in Nigeria itself and within Nigerian immigrant communities in other countries.

In Mexico and places with sizeable Latino populations, the money dance (*baile del dólar* in Spanish) is a new tradition that sees relatives of the newlyweds line up to dance with the couple all the while pinning money to their clothing. At some

Latino weddings it is also traditional for the groom to be held by the hands and feet and thrown up and down in the air by the groomsmen while his wife follows on behind. The bridesmaids meanwhile pick up the groom's shoes and socks as a sign that the bride will look after her husband. Latino wedding receptions also commonly feature a children's game called *A La Vibora De La Mar* (sea snake) during which the bride and groom stand on chairs set slightly apart from each other with the bride's veil acting as a bridge between the newlyweds. Everyone present at the reception then forms two lines and skips under the "bridge" until somebody is caught in the veil.

In the United States, the type of money dance performed depends on the ethnicity of the wedding parties. Some American wedding planners do not feel it is in good taste for guests to pay money for the groom's time but instead advocate that guests "pay" for the chance to dance with the groom using chewing gum or pretend money.

See also: Cajun Weddings; *Hora* and *Horah*; *Lindo*; *Schuhplattler* and *Ländler*

Further Reading

Blackwell, Carole. *Tradition and Society in Turkmenistan: Gender, Oral Culture and Song*. London: Routledge, 2001.

Herrera-Sobek, Maria. *Celebrating Latino Folklore: An Encyclopedia of Cultural Traditions*. Volume 1. Santa Barbara, CA: ABC-CLIO, LLC, 2012.

Lemieux, Diane. *Nigeria—Culture Smart!: The Essential Guide to Customs & Culture*. London: Kuperard, 2011.

Monger, George P. *Marriage Customs of the World: From Henna to Honeymoons*. Santa Barbara, CA: ABC-CLIO, 2004.

MOONIE WEDDINGS, INTERNATIONAL

Mass weddings are a feature of the Family Federation for Peace and Unification or Unification Church, often referred to as Moonies. These mass weddings tend to be held in Seoul, the capital city of South Korea, as well as in other large cities around the world, usually in vast venues such as sports stadia, and see tens of thousands of identically dressed couples marry simultaneously. In some instances the couples have not met each other before they wed as partners are usually chosen and arranged by church authorities. Alternatively, partners may meet a few days prior to a mass wedding or couples may be married before they join the church and decide to renew their vows as church members. The Unification Church refers to marriages as The Blessing. The church claims to have approximately 3 million members around the world though others dispute this claim and suggest the number is much smaller. The church is also controversial with critics claiming it is a personality cult.

Although Reverend Sun Myung Moon founded the Unification Church in 1954, the church did not begin holding mass weddings until 1982, after which time they were held every three years until 1995. To begin with only a few couples participated in Moonie weddings but the number of couples involved grew rapidly. Indeed in 1997 30,000 couples were wed en masse in Washington, DC. The most recent Moonie wedding occurred in Gapyeong, located 50 miles to the east of Seoul, during which 3,800 couples were married simultaneously in front of some 20,000 guests and other members of the church. According to the Unification Church, a further 12,000 church members took part in the wedding online. During the mass wedding Moon's wife, Hak Ja Han Moon, sprinkled couples with holy water as they were called on to a stage and then declared the couples to be married.

The church holds mass weddings reasoning that the weddings are part of a spiritual journey taken by believers that will eventually lead to world peace and spiritual completion. Because the Unification Church sees family disintegration as the cause of the world's biggest problems, the church feels that the institution of the family can be purified and blessed through mass marriage. Though some members of the church argue that there is an element of romance to Moonie weddings, they also assert that members should be able and willing to wed and care for anybody with whom they are paired in marriage. The church's teachings also stress that the most important aspect of marriage is the attitude that people bring to the union for, since no person is perfect, everybody that enters into marriage should try their hardest to make marriage successful. In the past, many couples were personally brought together by Moon, who disapproved of romantic love arguing that it led to sexually promiscuous relationships that in turn resulted in mismatched couples, unhappy relationships, and ultimately a failing global society. Moon tended to select cross-cultural couples with the intention of establishing a multicultural church. This trend continues today with the result that members that go through mass-marriage ceremonies often do not share a common language or culture. Nowadays, church authorities do not, however, necessarily bring couples together for in some instances matchmaking is performed by parents that are members of the church.

Members of the Unification Church that agree to be matched by church authorities must swear on oath that they will be virgins at the time of their marriage and once couples are married they must not consummate their marriage for at least 40 days after their wedding.

See also: Arranged Marriage and Forced Marriage; Yumi Sakugawa, "An Asian American Wedding," 2009

Further Reading

Chryssides, George D., and Margaret Z. Wilkins, eds. *A Reader in New Religious Movements: Readings in the Study of New Religious Movements*. London: The Continuum International Publishing Group, 2006.

Guardian News and Media Limited. "Moonies Hold Mass Wedding in South Korea," *The Guardian*, March 3, 2015. Accessed June 13, 2015, at http://www.theguardian.com/world/2015/mar/03/moonies-mass-wedding-south-korea-unification-church-hak-ja-han-sun-myung-moon.

Monger, George P. *Marriage Customs of the World: From Henna to Honeymoons*. Santa Barbara, CA: ABC-CLIO, 2004.

Sim, David. "Thousands of Couples Marry in Mass Wedding at 'Moonies' Church in South Korea [Photo report]," *International Business Times*, March 3, 2015. Accessed June 13, 2015, at http://www.ibtimes.co.uk/thousands-couples-marry-mass-wedding-moonies-church-south-korea-photo-report-1490223.

MOROCCAN WEDDINGS, MOROCCO

The North African country of Morocco has a rich cultural history and many active traditions. Among these are the country's many lavish and symbolic wedding traditions as well as pre-wedding customs. Moroccan weddings can last as long as seven days and are very expensive events.

Before a Moroccan wedding takes place, a lengthy courtship is held. It was once the tradition in Morocco for parents to arrange marriages. However today most Moroccans choose their own marriage partners though they do tend to ask their parents' permission before announcing any engagement. During a Moroccan betrothal the groom's family pays a dowry to their future daughter-in-law's family so that she can purchase household furniture and other items for her new marital home. In addition, the husband-to-be sends his betrothed jewelry made of gold, luxurious fabric, clothing, and perfume every Moroccan feast day. This can prove expensive as Moroccan courtships can last anywhere from six months to two years. Once a wedding date has been set, preparations begin in earnest. For example, five days before the wedding a mattress and blanket are taken to the bridal chamber.

A wedding-day custom sees the bride led to the bridal chamber and bathed in a special bath called a *hammam*, which is filled with skin-purifying milk. A female attendant called a *negaffa* oversees the bathing custom. The negaffa is usually an older married female friend or relative and it is her job to ensure that the bride is sufficiently beautified for her wedding day. While this ritual bathing is traditional, today the custom mostly takes place in rural areas of Morocco—in major cities the bath is generally omitted from wedding preparations.

After her bath, the bride is enveloped in an ornately decorated wedding kaftan that is usually white in color. In modern Morocco, the kaftans tend to be bought from shops, as off-the-rack gowns are generally cheaper than those crafted by hand and feature labor-intensive and therefore costly embellishments. These days, it is also quite difficult to find hand-made kaftans for sale. Once dressed in the kaftan the bride is given heavy jewelry to wear and has make-up applied, particularly thick dark kohl eyeliner. Next, the bride and her female attendants experience the *beberiska* ceremony in which it is customary for the women to have their hands and feet decorated with henna by a person employed solely for that purpose, though some modern Moroccan women eschew this custom as they feel it is outdated. The designs painted on the bride are much more elaborate than those applied to the other females and tend to feature geometric shapes and floral patterns intended as good luck charms to ensure fertility and to warn off evil spirits. Often the name of the groom is included in the designs. Usually a bride is excused from doing any household chores until the henna has faded, which, depending on how dark the stain is, can last between five days and two weeks. The beberiska ceremony is also the time when the married members of the bride's entourage give the bride a sex education lesson for traditionally the bride is a young virgin who is generally ignorant of such matters. Sometimes during the beberiska ceremony the bride is made to sit behind a curtain that symbolizes the imminent change in her life—in remote areas of Morocco the sitting-behind-a-curtain custom takes place the day before the wedding.

After all the pre-wedding customs have been completed, a feast is prepared with extra food readied in case unexpected guests arrive. In times past, the wedding parties would prepare the food but today it is usually prepared by outside caterers. Once the food is made the wedding festivities begin. At Moroccan weddings males and females celebrate at separate locations. At some time in the evening the groom leaves the men and makes his way to the bride accompanied by a group of his friends who sing, dance, and make a lot of noise, usually by banging drums and hooting car horns. The bride is hoisted into the air on a circular cushion or lifted onto a table by her wedding party while the groom is lifted onto the shoulders of his friends. (See Plate 18.) It used to be the case that the couple would then be transported to the bridal chamber where they would be expected to consummate their marriage. In times gone by once the newlyweds had had sex the sheets of the marital bed would be inspected for signs of blood confirming the bride's lost virginity. However this practice is generally seen as outdated and tends not to occur today. Also, at modern Moroccan weddings rather than immediately consummate the marriage, the couple and their attendant parties tend to unite and the bride changes into clothes that reflect her home region. After celebrating further the bride changes her outfit once more and the newlyweds leave the party and retire for some personal time either in the bridal chamber or, as occurs more recently, at a hotel.

The couple then travel to their new home, which the new wife would circle three times to signify that she has become the new keeper of the hearth. Throughout the week of the wedding, the newly married couple visit their friends and relatives and have guests round to their house so that they can show off their new home and the gifts they have received.

The music at Moroccan weddings takes the form of either modern music played on traditional instruments or traditional music of Andalusina, Arabian, or Berber origin. The Berbers, or Amazighs, are pre-Arab inhabitants of North Africa, an ethnicity indigenous to the area that lies west of the Nile Valley. There are many scattered Berber tribes living in countries including Morocco, Algeria, Tunisia, Mauritania, and Libya. As a result of colonization there are also a significant number of Berber communities in France. In Morocco, nearly one-third of the population is of Berber descent. While most Berbers are Muslim the Berber people maintain unique customs, one of which is the annual *Imilchil Moussem* or Berber

Marriage Festival, which is also known as the September Romance. The festival, which is a traditional event in the cultural calendar of the Aït Yaazza Berbers, is held in September at Imilchil, a location high in the Atlas Mountains. It is a unique event that draws around 30,000 participants, plus cattle and horses, from several Berber tribes, including the surrounding tribes the Aït Sokham and Aït Bouguemmaz. The festival also attracts many tourists.

The Berber marriage festival is thought to have begun when a young man named Isil (which means groom in the Berber language) fell in love with a young woman called Tislit (meaning bride) but the two were denied permission to marry as their families were at war. The lovers were consumed by sadness at not being allowed to wed and cried themselves to death, their tears forming a lake. Today, two lakes at Imilchil are named after the lovers—a mountain divides the lakes so that even in death the lovers remain apart. The families of Isil and Tislit are said to have been so distraught at the deaths of the youngsters that they vowed to forever more allow the young to choose their own spouses, hence the Imilchil marriage festival sees young people select their own partners. Another possible origin for the Berber marriage festival is that at some point in time Moroccan authorities declared that the Berbers must assemble once per year to register all Berber births, marriages, and deaths, which they did at the Imilchil festival. The growth of tourism in Morocco meant that the country's tourism chiefs encouraged the tradition to continue.

While the Imilchil Moussem takes the form of a grand marketplace where Berbers can trade items, it also acts as Morocco's biggest wedding fair. The Imilchil festival takes place near the tomb of a holy man, Sidi Mohammed Maghani, who in life used to bless marriages. The Berbers congregate and erect tents to sleep under. Women arrive at the festival wearing ceremonial clothing while men wear white clothing including white turbans. The couples dance and generally flirt. While some couples know each other before the festival, most do not and contrary to rumors few of the marriages are prearranged. Thus the festival provides young men and women with the chance to meet each other in public and decide whom to marry. The meetings are fast-paced, akin to Western speed dating, with the difference being that a successful interaction leads to marriage rather than a date. As well as the meetings being brief in duration the interactions are further complicated by the fact that often the women will remain covered so that prospective husbands cannot see what the potential brides look like. Men may, however, get clues about a woman's appearance from her family who try to guide the men and women into making good decisions. Once they have received a favorable gesture from a woman, a man may hold her hand—dropping the hand signals romantic rejection. Women are allowed to refuse a man's offer of marriage but if she wishes to accept a man's proposal then she will tell him that he has captured her liver as the Berbers consider the liver to be the organ of romance and well-being.

The festival lasts for three days and is a time of much eating, trading, and general celebration. During the festival, the families of those who wish to marry will settle legal and financial matters including how much the husband will have to pay to the bride's family. Toward the end of the festival, the marriage ceremonies begin, though some couples that become engaged at the festival travel home and wed in their own villages. Those who marry at the festival in communal marriages may do so as it is less expensive to be part of a big wedding than to pay for a private event. Thus some Berber parents like their children to marry at the festival to keep down costs.

Away from the Imilchil festival a Berber wedding, which lasts for three days, usually begins with the groom asking his parents permission to wed. If they agree, the grooms' parents meet with the bride's parents arrange the dowry. A government official oversees the writing of the marriage contract. The groom then starts accumulating the goods required by the dowry package. If the bride calls off the wedding she must return the goods. However if the couple divorces, the bride is allowed to keep the dowry items.

On the day of the wedding the dowry is brought to the bride's home where all the dowry items are verified against the marriage contract. Later the same day animals are killed to provide meat for the wedding feasts.

It is extremely important that the bride is a virgin when she marries, as it would bring great shame to her family if she were found to be unchaste. The next morning, everyone who has participated in the wedding has breakfast and then they return to their own homes, except the bride's mother who stays with her daughter until it is time for the her to go to her new husband's home. It is the Berber custom that all brides live with their husband's families. It is usual for the husband's family to control all aspects of the bride's life and quite often she will be subjected to physical and verbal abuse from both her husband and his family. A Berber husband is also allowed to take a second wife if he so chooses. Indeed it is legal for a Berber man to take up to four wives.

See also: Christian Wedding Ceremony; Jewish Wedding Customs; Moonie Weddings; Muslim Wedding Ceremony; Polygyny; *Shabka*; Virginity Testing

Further Reading

Becker, Cynthia. *Amazigh Arts in Morocco: Women Shaping Berber Identity*. Austin, TX: University of Texas Press, 2006.

Galvan, Javier A., ed. *They Do What? A Cultural Encyclopedia of Extraordinary and Exotic Customs from around the World*. Santa Barbara, CA: ABC-CLIO, 2014.

Magrini, Tullia, ed. *Music and Gender: Perspectives from the Mediterranean*. Chicago, IL: The University of Chicago Press, 2003.

Morroco.com. "Wedding Customs—Age-old Marriage Traditions." Accessed December 12, 2014, at http://www.morocco.com/culture/weddings-customs/.

Sadiqui, Fatima, ed. *Women and Knowledge in the Mediterranean*. Abingdon, UK: Routledge, 2013.

Travel Exploration.com. "Imilchil Marriage Festival." Explore Morocco. Accessed December 12, 2014, at http://www.travel-exploration.com/subpage.cfm/Imilchil_Marriage_Festival.

MUSLIM WEDDING CEREMONY, ISLAM

Muslim marriages are not considered to be a union of romantic soul mates but rather are social contracts that confer rights and obligations to both the husband and wife. In addition Muslim marriages are not considered a "to death do us part" arrangement as both the husband and wife may seek a divorce if either party breaks his or her marriage contract. This suggests that Islam views marriage in a realistic rather than romantic way. However Islam does consider marriage to be the ideal state in which Muslims should live. Most Muslim marriages are arranged by the parents of the bride and groom. Though arranged marriages are not requisite in Islam, it is usual for parents to organize marriages as this is seen as the best way of ensuring that children will be happy and settled.

There is a great deal of variation in the way in which Muslim weddings are conducted because many Muslims who marry come from widely differing cultures. For instance, the marriage between two European Muslims will differ from a Muslim marriage ceremony held in Africa or Indonesia. Also, for Muslims living in non-Islamic countries it may be necessary for the bride and groom to undergo two ceremonies with the first being a religious ceremony and the second a legally binding ceremony that makes the marriage legal according to the country in which the couple live. For instance, in the United Kingdom a Muslim couple may have a religious ceremony and also a ceremony at a registry office that confirms their marriage as legal. In the United Kingdom if the marriage is held in a mosque then the marriage contract documents are recorded with the mosque but also registered with the local government authorities in order to meet the civil obligations of the marriage. If this procedure is not followed then the marriage will not be recognized under British law and the legal rights of the spouse would be invalid. Muslim wedding ceremonies need not, however, take place in a mosque. If a mosque is chosen as a wedding venue then male and female guests may have to sit in separate rooms or in the same room but divided by a partition.

A Muslim wedding ceremony is a simple ceremony known as a *nikah* or *nica*. The bride need not be present at the nikah as long as she has given her consent to be married and sends two witnesses to oversee the drawing-up of the marriage agreement. For the nikah to be deemed proper the witnesses must be adults considered to be good Muslims of sound mind. The groom must also pay a dowry or marriage gift called a *mahr* to the bride's family for the nikah to be judged correct in the eyes of Islam.

At its simplest, a Muslim wedding ceremony consists of the offer of the bride in marriage and the acceptance of the proposition known as the *Al-Ijab wal-Qubul*. During this ceremony the bride's guardian in marriage, or *wali*, offers the bride to the groom saying words along the lines of "I give you my daughter/my ward in marriage in accordance to the Islamic Shari'ah in the presence of the witnesses here with the dowry agreed upon. And Allah is our best witness." The groom-to-be then accepts by replying "I accept marrying your daughter/ward, giving her name to myself in accordance with the Islamic Shari'ah in the presence of the witnesses here with the dowry agreed upon. And Allah is our best witness." On saying these words the wedding ceremony is considered complete.

However usually a nikah consists of readings taken from the Muslim holy book, the Qur'an, followed by both the husband and bride exchanging vows in front of witnesses. Though it is not necessary for a religious official to be present it is usual for an Imam to perform the ceremony and give a brief sermon blessing the marriage that is called a *Khutba-tun-Nikah*. This marriage sermon comprises three verses of the Qur'an, and is a way of blessing the marriage and praising Allah. The marriage ceremony ends with the saying of prayers for the bride and groom, as well as their families, the local Muslim community, and all Muslims in general.

Though Muslim marriage ceremonies vary widely, there are a number of common factors between marriages. For instance all Muslim marriages must be declared publicly and must never take place clandestinely. The public declaration of the marriage normally occurs during a lavish party called a *walimah* that is usually held specifically to allow couples to declare their marriage. Other marriage customs depend upon the prevailing culture of the country in which the couple resides rather than being dictated by the laws of Islam. For instance, in some cultures the bride and groom may sit on throne-like chairs placed on a platform facing their wedding guests. Other cultures may see the bride and groom given money or gifts. If a Muslim wedding happens in an Asian country or sees the marriage of two Asian Muslims (or Muslims with Asian heritage) living in the West, then the wedding may be preceded by at least one pre-wedding party as well as post-wedding celebrations. Part of the pre-wedding celebrations for Asian couples often include parties to which the bride- and groom-to-be invite their friends and family, akin to bachelor and bachelorette parties, with male guests kept in a separate room from the female guests, who often celebrate by having their hands and feet painted with henna. Such wedding celebrations tend to be large-scale, lavish, expensive affairs and result in the wedding lasting several days despite Islam stressing the need for moderation in all things.

Alternatively, a Muslim wedding may be celebrated quietly with only close relatives and friends present. Other Muslim weddings may feature the firing of guns, dancing, and fun in general.

See also: Arranged Marriage and Forced Marriage; *Hijab*; Hindu Wedding Ceremony; *Mehndi*; Moroccan Weddings; Polygyny; *Shabka*; Yumi Sakugawa, "An Asian American Wedding," 2009

Further Reading
Joseph, Suad, and Afsāna Nağmābādī, eds. *Encyclopedia of Women & Islamic Cultures: Family, Body, Sexuality and Health Volume 3*. Leiden, Netherlands: Brill, 2006.
Single Muslim. "The Muslim Marriage." Accessed April 16, 2015, at http://uk.singlemuslim.com/marriage_articles/marriage_ceremony.php.
Waris Maqsood, Ruqaiyyah. "Muslim Weddings." BBC: Religions, September 8, 2009. Accessed April 16, 2015, at http://www.bbc.co.uk/religion/religions/islam/ritesrituals/weddings_1.shtml.

N

NECK ELONGATION, THAILAND, MYANMAR, AND SOUTH AFRICA

Neck elongation is a type of voluntary body modification that is customary in several parts of the world and involves coils of brass placed around the necks of females in order to give the appearance of a stretched neck. This practice is customary in Thailand and Myanmar (formerly Burma) where the traditional concept of female beauty considers a very long neck to be attractive and highly prized. The results of neck elongation can be so extreme that the women that have undergone the process are sometimes referred to as giraffe women. It should be noted however that the term neck elongation is a little misleading as the neck does not actually elongate during the process of neck elongation. Rather the brass coils that are placed around the females' necks from shoulder to chin at a young age actually force the chin upward while simultaneously forcing the ribs and shoulders downward thereby creating the impression of an extremely long neck.

In Thailand and Myanmar, women belonging to the Padaung people and Kayan tribes are most closely associated with the custom of neck elongation. The practice of neck elongation in these areas of Asia is very old for legendary explorer Marco Polo became the first foreigner to document the custom in the 1300s. After the great political turmoil and establishment of the Burmese military dictatorship in 1962, minority ethnic groups including the Padaung and Kayan migrated to the border area between Burma and northern Thailand. In order to keep alive some of their traditions post-migration, Padaung and Kayan females preserved the custom of wearing neck coils while in exile. Today, the Thai government promotes the viewing of women that practice neck elongation as a tourist attraction in order to draw outsiders to villages on the Thailand-Myanmar border. Such active promotion has, however led to accusations that the government is exploiting both traditional cultural customs and the women that undergo the practice for financial gain turning an age-old custom into little more than a freak show. In 2008, the United Nations refugee agency (UNHCR) criticized the Thai government's treatment of the so-called giraffe women and suggested that tourists should stop visiting the border villages where the women live.

The reason for the neck elongation among the Padaung people is not fully known. One suggestion is that the practice began as a way to protect women from animals such as tigers that tend to grab prey by the neck, to ward off evil spirits, or as a way to display status and wealth. There may also be a folkloric reason behind the custom for according to Padaung mythology the Padaung were created when a long-necked dragon was impregnated by the wind. The people's tradition of neck elongation therefore ties in with their belief in their descent from the Dragon

Mother. An alternative theory is that the coils originated when Paduang men placed coils around the necks of Padaung women to prevent the women marrying other men with the thinking being that foreign raiders would find the women's elongated necks unattractive and so would not want to carry the women away.

According to tradition, only girls born on a Wednesday that has a full moon may wear the brass coils, which they start to wear before the onset of puberty. Recently however all girls have begun to undergo the practice with critics suggesting this is to attract more tourists. Females generally start wearing brass neck coils when they are around five years old, though there have also been reports of girls as young as two years old having coils placed around their necks with subsequent coils added when they reach 8, 13, and 15 years old. Again, this is said to be in order to attract tourists. The initial coils placed on the young girls are about half an inch wide and as the girls grow older the length of the neck coils increases gradually until the coils are able to go around the neck about 20 times. The neck coils weigh between 5 and 20 pounds, which is quite a heavy weight for a girl to carry 24 hours a day. A Padaung female usually sports at least two distinct coils with the lowest, widest coil wrapping around her shoulders and the upper coil encircling her neck. Once the girl reaches adulthood the coils around her neck are between 12 and 15 inches high.

Scientific analysis of the effects of neck elongation is limited. Researchers have reported that the wearing of heavy coils around the throat left wearers with squashed ribs and collarbones and high-pitched voices due to changed wrought on the larynx. It has also been suggested that wearing the coils causes the women to have such weak neck muscles that they are unable to hold up their heads. Indeed it has been asserted that some wearers have such weak necks that if their coils were to be removed their heads would flop around leading the women to suffocate. However the accuracy of such claims is dubious and even if women were to suffer from seriously weakened neck muscles the muscles would be able to be rehabilitated. Moreover older wearers are allowed to change their coils, a procedure that requires the assistance of several other women and takes many hours to complete, while elderly women and younger women that wish to protest against the custom's exploitation by the Thai government have been known to remove their coils. In such cases the women are said to take only a few days to recover normal neck strength.

Kayan women wear brass coils around their legs as well as their necks. However unlike neck rings, which cause irritation when first worn that quickly resolves itself, leg rings rub against the women's skin leading to discomfort and abrasions when worn for long periods. For this reason, women tend to wear pieces of cloth under the leg rings in order to protect the skin of their legs.

Neck elongation also occurs among the Ndebele tribe of South Africa. However unlike the neck elongation practiced in Thailand and Myanmar, the Ndebele wear coils made of both brass and copper. Ndebele girls begin to wear the neck rings when they marry at around the age of 15 years. The newly married women may also wear coils around their legs and waists. The married women's coils are usually made from metal rings decorated with smaller metal hoops as well as glass rings called *isigolwani*. If a Ndebele woman is married but not yet living with her husband in their own home then she will wear a smaller neck decoration called a *rholwani*, which is replaced by an isigolwani once the woman has moved in with her spouse. Other women may wear rings decorated with fabrics, grasses, and beads. The Ndebele neck rings originated as a symbol of a wife's loyalty to her husband and are only removed when the man dies. The Ndebele neck rings came to attention in the West in 2002 after Mattel, the makers of the Barbie doll, dressed a Princess of South Africa Barbie in neck rings.

See also: Breast Ironing; Hair Removal; *Pika* and *Nyora*; Ritual Tattooing; Scarification; *Thaipusam*: Extreme Ritual Flesh Modification; Tooth-Filing Ceremony; Training Bras

Further Reading

Galvan, Javier A., ed. *They Do What? A Cultural Encyclopedia of Extraordinary and Exotic Customs from around the World.* Santa Barbara: ABC-CLIO, 2014.

Harding, Andrew. "Burmese Women in Thai 'Human Zoo.'" BBC News, January 30, 2008. Accessed August 21, 2015, at http://news.bbc.co.uk/2/hi/asia-pacific/7215182.stm.

Huay Pu Keng. "Background and Culture." 2008. Accessed August 21, 2015, at http://www.huaypukeng.com/info_rings.htm.

Pitts-Taylor, Victoria. *Cultural Encyclopedia of the Body: Volume 1 and 2.* Westport, CT: Greenwood Press, 2008.

Sabatello, Maya. *Children's Bioethics: The International Biopolitical Discourse on Harmful Traditional Practices and the Right of the Child to Cultural Identity.* Leiden, Netherlands: Martinus Nijhoff Publishers, 2009.

NKUMBI, DEMOCRATIC REPUBLIC OF CONGO

Nkumbi is a grueling rite of passage experienced by boys belonging to the Pygmy peoples living in the Congo region of Africa, particularly the Mbuti (Efe) tribe of the Democratic Republic of Congo. The Mbuti maintain a joint ritual with nearby Bantu villagers. The reasons for the ritual are twofold for not only does the ritual prepare boys for the obligations and trials of adult life but also ensures a sense of continuity between past, present, and future and between the dead and the living. This is because the villagers think that only the initiated can join their ancestors who they consider to be a far-off tribe. Women and uninitiated boys are not allowed to view the ritual.

Nkumbi occurs every three years and is an initiation to adulthood during which Pygmy boys aged between about 9 and 12 years of age that habitually dwell in the forests move to the nearby village. Here the Pygmy boys live in close proximity to the village boys with whom they will attend a sort of forest circumcision school located some way from the village. The boys spend several months singing and dancing and learning to hunt and fish. During their time in the forest, elders whip the boys frequently in an attempt to instill toughness and the boys are kept quiet by having their mouths filled with leaves when they are not singing. The village boys lead the Pygmy boys into the forest where they are circumcised together. Boys that are circumcised together share a life-long bond called *kare*, or blood brotherhood, while any boy that tries to avoid the ritual is thought to be cursed and to bring the ire of his ancestors upon himself. As the boys view the nkumbi ritual as an extremely important event, they bear the pain and discomfort of the ritual as stoically as possible. Each batch of boys that have gone through nkumbi together belongs to a type of high-school age grade. Each group of boys acquires a name from a significant event that occurs during the group's initiation, so boys will, for example, say that they are a hurricane, if that event took place during their initiation with that name given to the group of boys to which they belong.

The nkumbi ritual begins with two days of dancing performed by the villagers and then the segregation of the boys at a special camp some distance from the village. Over the next few days the boys taking part in the ritual are ritually bathed and have their heads shaved ahead of their circumcision. The boys also undergo privations in regard to food and drink. For instance boys may be forbidden from touching bananas or standing in the rain. Boys may also be forbidden from using their hands when they eat and certain types of meat, salt, and pepper may be denied to the boys.

The next day the boys are painted with white clay from head to foot in order to symbolize the death of their childhood and they experience a series of ordeals such as being whipped with leaves, having to sit for hours with a rigid back, and singing the same song repetitively. When it comes to the circumcision, the Pygmy boys are circumcised first. This is seen as a way in which the Pygmy boys "may clean the knife" for the village boys and is but one of the ways in which the Pygmy boys are treated as inferior to the village boys. Boys are circumcised in pairs consisting of a superior village boy and a subordinate Pygmy boy. In the future though the boys will be linked through kare, they will not be linked as equals though they will be mutually obligated to each other. As well as circumcision, the boys may also undergo ritual scarification during which elders use two razor blades to make around 20 cuts in each boy's chest before rubbing mud into the wounds.

Pygmy fathers put their sons through nkumbi for purely pragmatic, economic reasons for the ritual confers on the Pygmy boys the same adult status as boys from the village and also means the Pygmy boys will be able to call on their blood brothers through invoking kare. Additionally, the close ties forged by the kare are financially beneficial as it means the Pygmies have access to resources and employment opportunities in the village that they would not have ordinarily. Also, since the boys go off to their forest school for months on end their families are spared the expense of providing their food that is, instead, borne by the villagers. Meanwhile the village elders permit the Pygmies to share in the custom as it provides villagers with a way to bring the Pygmies under their control. Moreover the village-dwellers believe that once the Pygmy boys have gone through nkumbi they become the subjects of the village spirits. Some village people believe this means that the Pygmy boys will be able to act as their slaves in the afterlife.

Once the boys have gone through nkumbi and the boys return to their families in the forest it becomes apparent that little has changed in the way the boys interact with their families. Indeed it is common for circumcised boys to sit on their mothers' laps to signify that they remain children. This is because in Pygmy society boys will not be considered men until they have become successful hunters even if they have been circumcised.

See also: *Brit Milah* (Volume 1); Bullet Ant Initiation; Cow Jumping; Dipo Womanhood Ceremony; Female Genital Cutting; Forehead-Cutting Initiation; Initiation by Semen Transferal; Land Diving; Log Riding; Matis Hunting Trials; *Sharo*: Public Flogging; *Sünnet;* Urethral Subincision; Xhosa Circumcision

Further Reading

Ben-Ari, Eyal. "Pygmies and Villagers, Ritual or Play? On the Place of Contrasting Modes of Metacommunication in Social Systems," *Symbolic Interaction,* 10(2), Fall 1987, 167–185.

Everyculture.com. "Efe and Mbuti." Countries and Their Cultures. Accessed June 16, 2015, at http://www.everyculture.com/wc/Brazil-to-Congo-Republic-of/Efe-and-Mbuti.html.

Grinker, Roy Richard, Stephen C. Lubkemann, and Christopher B. Steiner, eds. *Perspectives on Africa: A Reader in Culture, History and Representation.* Second edition. Malden, MA: Blackwell Publishing Ltd., 2010.

Kunin, Seth Daniel. *Religion: The Modern Theories.* Edinburgh, UK: Edinburgh University Press Ltd., 2005.

NYUMBA NTOBHU: TRADITIONAL SAME-SEX MARRIAGE, TANZANIA

Nyumba ntobhu is a traditional same-sex marriage system found in the Tarime district of the Mara region of western Tanzania in which two women live as husband and wife. In nyumba ntobhu, which translates as woman marrying woman, the two married women live together as husband and wife, bearing children in their union and generally doing all the things traditionally expected of a married couple except the two women do not have sex with each other. Nyumba ntobhu sees older women wed younger women so that the younger woman can produce children and help with housework. The women that enter into nyumba ntobhu also claim that the system helps them to deal with problems of domestic violence. Nyumba ntobhu is not akin to homosexual same-sex marriage as known in the West as romantic love is not a factor in the formation of nyumba ntobhu marriages. Instead, nyumba ntobhu marriages tend to be entered into for matters of inheritance and economics. Nyumba ntobhu can also take the form of polygamous marriage for the older woman may marry two younger women, both of whom bear children.

It is not known exactly why nyumba ntobhu became established as a cultural practice. Some people postulate that the system came about because of male violence against women. Also the system proposes an alternative family structure that is useful for older women who do not have male heirs to inherit their property or whose daughters have moved out of the village to live with their husbands. In this way, nyumba ntobhu provides security for elderly women, meaning that they do not have to live on their own and they have a companion to perform household chores, to help with farming, and to carry water. In return for the younger woman's hand in marriage, the older woman pays a bride price to the parents of the younger woman, often in the form of cattle.

When the same-sex couples involved in nyumba ntobhu wish to have children, they hire a man, known as a street man, and pay him to inseminate the younger female. The rented man enters into an agreement stating that he will not attempt to claim paternal rights to any children and the older woman of the couple becomes the guardian of the children resulting from the younger woman's pregnancy. The resulting children then assume the surname of the older woman. In return for inseminating the younger woman the man is paid in food or is given a goat. Alternatively, a relative of the older woman's former husband (the older wife may have married previously) may agree to father her children for no payment in order to ensure that the name of the older woman's previous husband lives on.

Occasionally the man that inseminated the younger woman may try to claim a child he has helped produce, but the same-sex couples can normally avoid this problem by choosing a man who is a stranger or who is known locally to be unreliable. Sometimes a wealthy woman that is unable to have children of her own will chose to marry a younger woman so that the younger woman can provide her with the children that she cannot herself produce. As it is quite usual for Tanzanian women to be banned from inheriting property, the nyumba ntobhu system is an option for infertile women. Thus the older women can claim the children born to the younger woman as the couple's own, thereby providing them with security in their old age. Nowadays, nyumba ntobhu is not the sole preserve of barren woman as some Tanzanian women are opting not to wed men for fear of suffering domestic violence, a belief that is backed up by Tanzanian Minister of Information and Culture Fenela Mukandara, who has asserted that domestic violence is particularly prevalent in the Mara region of the country. Moreover, the United Nations has stated that northern Mara has the highest rates of domestic violence against females in Tanzania with 60 percent of women reporting that they have suffered physical or emotional abuse.

The practice of nyumba ntobhu is not without its critics. For instance some villagers are against the practice, as they believe it has led to an increase in the spread of HIV as the younger women have sex with the street men in the hope of bearing children for their older wives. There are also reports of younger wives having unprotected sex with many men not necessarily in order to become pregnant, which also leads them vulnerable to sexually transmitted diseases. Village elders warn younger wives to be aware of their sexual health for if a younger wife does become ill this creates a greater financial burden for the older wife. Meanwhile international civil rights advocates have suggested that nyumba ntobhu discriminates against young women. Critics believe that because village elders decide which older women the young women shall marry this takes away the young women's rights to choose their own life partner. Critics also point out that young Tanzanian men are not able to marry the young women that they wish to wed because the young women are marrying the older females, a problem that is exacerbated by some older women choosing to have several wives. However those that advocate nyumba ntobhu argue that the alternative marriage system would lose its stronghold in the region if local men started to treat their wives in a respectful, non-violent manner.

See also: Arranged Marriage and Forced Marriage; *Lobola*; Polyandry

Further Reading

Bohela, Tulanana. "Why Some Tanzanian Women Are Marrying Women." BBC News: Africa, August 26, 2015. Accessed August 28, 2015, at http://www.bbc.com/news/world-africa-34059556.

Majani, Florence. "Tanzania Marriages of Convenience," *Mail & Guardian*, November 14, 2014. Accessed August 27, 2015, at http://mg.co.za/article/2014-11-13-tanzania-marriages-of-convenience.

Suleyman, Miguel. "Mara's Same-sex Marriage Baffles Western Researchers," *The Citizen*, August 31, 2013. Accessed August 28, 2015, at http://www.thecitizen.co.tz/News/Mara+s+same+sex+/-/1840392/1975156/-/vbkvkwz/-/index.html.

0

OMIAI: JAPANESE MATCHMAKING, JAPAN

Omiai, meaning to look at each other, is a form of blind date that occurs in Japan. Omiai began in the 12th century as a formal meeting with the objective of organizing a forced marriage. This type of marriage was the norm because in Japan at this time marriage was seen as a practical arrangement between families rather than as a romantic concept. Over time omiai changed from being a forced marriage to becoming an arranged marriage strongly influenced by a couple's parents. During the Fifteen Year War (1931–1945), around 69 percent of Japanese marriages were arranged through omiai. After World War II, however, this number dropped sharply as marriages based on romantic love started to be favored. This trend has continued and today only about 6 percent of marriages in Japan come about through the traditional omiai process of employing a matchmaker.

In the 1960s, omiai became a type of introduction that gave men the opportunity to see if they wished to accept the daughters being offered to them as wives by the girls' parents, usually through some form of semi-formal dinner date. Prior to this omiai dinner, both participants were thoroughly investigated by a professional matchmaker called a *nakodo*. The matchmaker also checked the couple's family history, schooling, and job prospects before arranging the meeting. It was tacitly understood that if a couple did not think they were compatible then they could back-out of an omiai without losing face, but it was desirable that a couple would like each other nonetheless.

Nowadays, the meaning of omiai has moved away from its traditional connotation. Today, omiai is more akin to a blind date set up by the friends, family, or acquaintances of two single individuals as a form of introduction that may or may not lead to romance. Often people will introduce two friends by going out as a large group then if the two singletons take a fancy to each other they will go out together on their own dates. Alternatively, in modern Japan a go-between can arrange an omiai meeting based on the compatibility of two individuals as well as their parents' input. These meetings usually take place in smart restaurants and it is traditional for the couple's parents to attend. The go-between chairs the meeting and helps move the couple's relationship along until they either wed or break up. This type of arrangement has its disadvantages, however, as it is neither an arranged marriage nor is it a romantic uniting of two individuals. Also both parents and the matchmaker will usually encourage the couple to marry quickly—couples normally take between three and six months to decide whether or not to marry under such circumstances.

Today, Japan has a National Matchmaking Association, *Zenkoku Nakodo Rengokai*, which provides one-to-one consultation to individuals looking for a marriage partner. The *Zenkoku Nakodo Rengokai* combines the role of the traditional nakodo with the concept of the modern matchmaking database to help clients meet each other. The matchmakers meet each client to go through lists of possible spouses and create shortlists from which the meetings will be scheduled that may eventually lead to *ren'ai kekkon*, or love marriages.

See also: Arranged Marriage and Forced Marriage; *San-san-kudo*; Shanghai Marriage Market; Yumi Sakugawa, "An Asian American Wedding," 2009

Further Reading

Clements, Jonathan. *Modern Japan: All That Matters*. London: John Murray Learning, 2014.

Ishimaru, Yasko. "Omiai." Accessed September 2, 2015, at http://faculty.tru.ca/jhu/Omiai.pdf.

May, Jennifer. "Matchmaking in Japan." Japan Visitor. Accessed September 2, 2015, at http://www.japanvisitor.com/japanese-culture/match-making.

P

PIKA AND *NYORA*, ZIMBABWE AND MOZAMBIQUE

The Ndau are an ethnic group living in the African nations of Zimbabwe and Mozambique. Ndau women undergo a series of beautification rituals as rites of passage from girlhood to womanhood, the most well-known of which is, perhaps, *pika*. Pika is a series of beauty marks, typically made using a pin, that are made on the cheeks, foreheads, and stomachs of girls when they reach puberty. It is a matter of personal choice for a Ndau female as to whether she undergoes pika marking but many Ndau believe that the marks lift a woman above the realms of everyday womanhood toward the extraordinary.

The pika marks show that the females have physically matured and can now be considered attractive by males. Indeed Ndau women often claim that pika are made both to attract men and for the benefit of men. Moreover without the pika markings a Ndau female will not be considered an adult Ndau woman for pika are seen as outward signs of the females' belonging to the Ndau tribe, and as signs of beauty and adulthood. Pika usually consist of three marks made on both cheeks, the stomach and the forehead though variations of pattern can be found. Some women (e.g., those living in Machaze in Mozambique) also have pika marks made on their legs as well as on their faces and stomachs.

The Ndau also practice scarification, or *nyora* (also called *kutema nyora*), which the Ndau believe makes women more beautiful and also more pleasing to men. The nyora marks are normally made by slicing the skin with a knife or razor blade and then applying clay or ash to the wounds so that keloids (lumpy scars) form on the skin. Nyora markings are normally made on the stomach, face, thighs, and chest. The decorative scar tissue that results from the scarification is also thought to improve sexual relations between the women that have been cut and their husbands as Ndau men enjoy the feel of the women's bumpy, scarred skin while Ndau women are said to enjoy having their scars stroked by their husbands. For this reason Ndau women feel it is necessary to undergo the scarring process so as not to displease their men. Indeed it has been known for an Ndau woman to be inspected by her fiancé's aunts on the day of her wedding to check that she has nyora markings. If a women is found to be without the markings she will be ordered to undergo cutting before she can be accepted as her husband's wife.

Both pika and nyora are considered rites of passage for Ndau women and there is a degree of rivalry between women in regards to their skin ornamentation. When Ndau women gather at the riverside to bath they will often assess the pika and nyora markings of other women. Those that do not display any markings are subject to derision and are likened to a barbell (i.e., a fish without scales).

There are also reports that the Ndau practice tooth filing though there is little documentation for this. Reports suggest however that the Ndau women file their upper incisors into sharp points. However this is not exclusive to the Ndau; another neighboring people, the Chopi, also undergo tooth filing.

See also: Breast Ironing; Dipo Womanhood Ceremony; Ear-Piercing Ceremonies; Female Genital Cutting; Forehead-Cutting Initiation; Ritual Tattooing; Scarification

Further Reading

MacGonagle, Elizabeth. *Crafting Identity in Zimbabwe and Mozambique.* Rochester, NY: University of Rochester Press, 2007.

MacGonagle, Elizabeth. "Living with a Tyrant: Ndau Memories and Identities in the Shadow of Ngungunyana," *The International Journal of African Historical Studies,* 41(1), 2008, 29–53.

Praise, T. P. "A Phenomenological Investigation into the Effects of Traditional Beliefs and Practices on Women and HIV & AIDS with Special Reference to Chiping District, Zimbabwe." PhD Dissertation. The University of Zimbabwe, June 2010. Accessed May 25, 2015, at http://www.google.co.uk/url?sa=t&rct=j&q=&esrc=s&source=web&cd=10&ved=0CFoQFjAJ&url=http%3A%2F%2Fwww.genderlinks.org.za%2Fattachment.php%3Faa_id%3D20142&ei=U1NjVcGgO4GwUdDcgKgO&usg=AFQjCNHnDCM78YaJl5yg__GyYYnUwYgRgQ&sig2=kEHBEJ2GhMLNhZ3C3wKsYA&bvm=bv.93990622,d.d24.

POLTERABEND, GERMANY

A *Polterabend* is an especially raucous, informal party held on the eve of a wedding in Germany. The word Polterabend translates as "noisy evening" though over recent years the event has started to be referred to as Rumbling Evening in some areas of Germany. Though the origins of Polterabend are unknown, the custom is a very long-held German tradition that also occurs in parts of Switzerland, Austria, Poland, Russia, and Denmark where Germany once had a significant cultural influence. Germanic Mennonites living in the United States also hold Polterabend parties. In Germany, Polterabend parties are held to mark the nuptials of both heterosexual and same-sex unions as well as the moving in together of co-habiting couples.

It is believed that the Polterabend tradition may have evolved from the pagan beliefs of Germanic tribes living in ancient times. These tribes believed that evil spirits and malign forces could be banished from weddings if guests made a great deal of noise by breaking dishes, cracking whips, and knocking pans together. Glass items, particularly mirrors, were never included in Polterabend festivities, as they were considered unlucky and capable of bringing ill fortune to a marriage. The ancient Germans believed that once such malign supernatural entities had been exorcised from the wedding they could not then go on to sabotage the newly wedded couple's married life. Also, as a noisy festive occasion the Polterabend doubled as a pre-wedding celebration.

Traditionally, the bride's family would host a lavish celebration on the eve of the wedding at which the bride's female relatives would present her with a myrtle wreath that they themselves had made or, occasionally, had bought especially for the celebration. The garland of myrtle then served as the bride's crown during the marriage service. The wreath also had a symbolic function as the wreath was mainly decorated with white embellishments that hinted that very soon the bride-to-be would put on her white wedding dress. Another custom that occurred during ancient Polterabend parties saw the bride touch the wine glass of every guest present at the event. The Polterabend also saw the presentation of small gifts to the soon-to-be married couple, though major gifts were held back and presented at the wedding itself. The later portion of the Polterabend saw friends of the bride perform songs and guests would play games and act in comedic plays. Such revelries created a lively atmosphere and the event would continue until midnight. After midnight the noisy events demanded by the occasion would take place.

Another aspect of the Polterabend took place earlier in the day when those who knew the engaged couple, usually members of their community or village, would compile a list of the couple's good and bad points. If a couple were deemed to have more attributes than failings then their marriage was approved by their acquaintances. This approval was signaled by those that compiled the list creating a great noise outside the homes of the bride-to-be and her fiancé on the stroke of midnight. Those that had gathered to create the din would throw around old crockery causing it to break and bang pans on the front doors of the couple's respective homes creating shards of pottery and other remains to accumulate. This would then be scattered along paths by the community members. Eventually the custom of scattering the pottery and other rubble evolved so that those who attended the Polterabend began to smash pots and dishes against the side of the house holding the party and dropping it from windows. The families of the engaged couple also began to leave open doors as they thought this encouraged evil to leave the event. To further encourage malign spirits to disappear some families also daubed holy water on the walls of the house as this was thought to rid a house of ghosts living within walls of the house.

In this way the Polterabend eventually morphed into a way for communities to wish engaged couples a long and happy life together and to rid the couple of any malign influences. Today, the Polterabend is also seen as a way of marking the couple's transition from youths to adults about to embark on a new chapter in their lives. This is further alluded to by the way in which the engaged couple have to clean up after the revelries the next day—their working together a sign of the cooperation they will need to demonstrate in order to be happily married. However the Polterabend is not just a way of looking to the couple's future for the guests that attend the Polterabend tend to be old school-friends of the couple.

Since the 19th century, most weddings in Germany have taken the form of civil ceremonies presided over by a registrar that may or may not be supplemented with a religious service the next day. Today, the Polterabend is usually held on the night of the civil ceremony, though some couple's prefer the event to take place a few days before the first marriage service. Modern Polterabend parties tend to persist into the early hours of the next morning, unlike the Polterabend parties of earlier times that would finish shortly after midnight. The guest-list for modern Polterabend parties usually consists of the couple's school friends and other pals. Though friends of the couple, these guests are not usually invited to a German couple's wedding as weddings are typically reserved for a couple's very closest relatives and friends rather than people that they used to attend school with. German couples often get married in their thirties and may not have been in everyday close contact with their school chums for some time. Thus the Polterabend offers these friends a chance to catch up with the couple and celebrate the couple's marriage in their presence. In the afternoon of the day on which the Polterabend is scheduled to occur, friends and neighbors dress the front door of the couple's home with flowers. According to tradition, the couple may not look at the decorated door before the Polterabend begins. Once the couple arrives at their home, guests bring forth the cracked and chipped crockery that they have set aside for use in the Polterabend. The couple then serves their guests food and alcoholic drinks, particularly cake and beer. Before the cake is served, guests and family members mill around sharing memories of the couple's early life, particularly stories that are comical and poke fun at the bride and groom. Once cake has been served to the guests the party's atmosphere becomes rowdier as guests start to break their pots, pans, and dishes in the traditional manner as well as cracking whips and generally generating a great deal of noise. The Polterabend continues into the early hours with guests drinking, singing and dancing, and showering the couple with good wishes for their future life together.

Over the years, Polterabend parties have become big business as hetero- and homosexual couples plus those couples that choose to live together rather than marry all now hold the parties. This is partly because Germany granted legal recognition to homosexual couples in 2001 and because in the past co-habiting was not socially acceptable and so was not celebrated.

The commercialization of the modern Polterabend means that today specialized Polterabend planners and venues exist. If a couple chooses to hold their Polterabend at a venue other than their home, then they can opt for a specialized venue that is designed in a traditional rustic style or at a hotel or hostel. Such venues are an attractive proposition for many couples as the venues take charge of all the party preparations, provide overnight accommodations, and allow guests to be as noisy as they like during the festivities.

Other countries have similar traditions to the Polterabend. For example, in Finland friends of the bride parade the bride through the streets of her home village or town dressed in outlandish costume on the eve of her wedding. As they parade the bride along the streets, the friends create much noise in order to draw the attention of passersby to the bride. Once they have seen the bride, passersby then give her money. Alternatively, a Finnish Polterabend may take the form of a mock Lucia celebration known as a Polter-Lucia. The Lucia festival takes place on December 13 each year and celebrates Saint Lucia, a figure associated with light, purity, and virginity. The Lucia festival has been a major Swedish festivity for over 400 years and involves young girls parading through streets holding candles while dressed in white and wearing a wreath of candles in their hair. For this mock Lucia parade, a Finnish bride-to-be is disguised as a drunken version of Saint Lucia, wearing a mass of broken candles and her teeth especially blackened for the occasion. The bride-to-be then makes a speech from a balcony and then is driven around the town's streets in a pedal boat known as a love boat that is transported on the back of a truck.

Meanwhile the German American communities living in the Appalachians, Missouri, and elsewhere perform a variation of the Polterabend, called a shivaree (or chivaree). Though most popular during the 19th and early 20th centuries, the custom still takes place very occasionally.

The name shivaree harks back to the *charivari* custom of medieval France. The charivari was a wedding custom during which newly married couples would be subjected to a great deal of noise, especially loud singing, ringing bells, and the banging together of pots and pans. The bed sheets of the bridal chamber would also be tied together or made dirty. Indeed the charivari was such a shameless and rowdy occasion that authorities eventually banned it. The custom did, however, persist in remote rural areas of France and was exported to French-speaking areas of Canada and to Louisiana where frontier-folk gave the custom a new lease of life. In Canada, particularly in Ontario, the name charivari evolved into chivaree, while in the United States the spelling shivaree became the norm.

Today, the charivari custom mainly continues through the pranks and mischief evident during bachelor and bachelorette parties as well as the shivaree. This is a noisy, mock serenading of a newly married couple within their home either on their wedding night or a few nights after the couple have married. The guests at the shivaree usually make noise by playing horns and kettles and banging spoons, shovels, and washtubs. The noise continues until the couple inside the house invites those making the noise into their home for food and drink.

See also: Bachelor and Spinster Balls; Blackening the Bride; Cajun Weddings; Jumping Over the Broom; Same-Sex Marriage; Wedding Cake; Wedding Dress and Wedding Ring

Further Reading

Epp, Melvin D. *The Petals of a Kansas Sunflower: A Mennonite Diaspora*. Eugene, OR: Resource Publications, 2012.

Galvan, Javier A., ed. *They Do What? A Cultural Encyclopedia of Extraordinary and Exotic Customs from around the World*. Santa Barbara, CA: ABC-CLIO, 2014.

The German Way. "German Weddings." The German Way: Expat Blog, October 7, 2013. Accessed November 30, 2015, at http://www.german-way.com/german-weddings/.

Jones, Alison. *Larousse Dictionary of World Folklore*. Edinburgh, UK: Larousse, 1996.

Monger, George P. *Marriage Customs of the World: From Henna to Honeymoons.* Expanded second edition. Santa Barbara, CA: ABC-CLIO, 2013.

Olson, Ted, and Anthony P. Cavender, eds. *A Tennessee Folklore Sampler: Selections from the Tennessee Folklore Society Bulletin (1935–2009).* Knoxville: The University of Tennessee Press, 2009.

POLYANDRY, INTERNATIONAL

Polyandry is the name given to an ancient form of plural marriage in which a woman has two or more husbands (or male lovers) at once. The word polyandry derives from the Greek *polys*, meaning many, and *aner*, which translates as man. Polyandry is an infrequently occurring practice but is most common within patriarchal societies that nonetheless display simple, non-bureaucratic structures, situated in areas where economic survival is uncertain and where the economies are also male-dominated. Thus polyandry occurs in some regions of India, particularly the Himachal Pradesh area, isolated regions of Tibet, parts of Sri Lanka, and among the Yanomamö people living in the Amazon rainforest and the Bari people of Venezuela.

Though polyandry is often frowned upon by societies, and may even be illegal in some countries, there are many instances of successful polyandrous marriages. The world's major religions have varying views of polyandry. The practice is forbidden in Christianity, Islam, and Judaism. Hinduism frowns upon polyandry but does not prohibit the custom possibly because an ancient tale of polyandry can be found in the ancient Hindu narrative work *Mahabharata* in which the princess Draupadi weds five Pandava brothers. Draupadi's hand in marriage is the prize for winning an archery contest that is won by one of the five brothers and since all five brothers are instructed to share the prize between them they all marry the princess. However even in religions that tolerate polyandry, the practice occurs rarely.

The tale of Draupadi and the Pandava brothers reflects that the most common form of polyandry is fraternal polyandry whereby a woman weds two or more brothers. This form of polyandry occurs in Himachal Pradesh in northern India as well as among the Toda people of southern India, and in Nepal and Tibet. In fraternal polyandry marriages when the eldest brother weds the woman, all the husband's brothers automatically become the woman's husbands too. However younger brothers are allowed to opt out of this arrangement if, for example, they find another woman to marry, enter religious orders, or move away from home in search of work. In the case of fraternal polyandry all the husbands live with the wife within one house and share her equally. No brother has exclusive sexual access to the wife. If children result from a fraternal polyandrous marriage in India, then the eldest brother is considered to be the father of all the children, irrespective of whether of not he is the biological father. Thus regardless of who his or her actual father is, a child born of a fraternal polyandrous marriage in northern India will call the eldest brother *pitaji*, meaning father, while the younger brothers will be called *chacha*, meaning uncle even if they known that one of their "uncles" is really their father. In contrast, in Tibet, society considers all the husbands to be the fathers of a woman's children. Similarly, the Bari people of Venezuela assign two living fathers to a single child. This has been found to increase a child's likelihood of surviving to the age of 15 years significantly, an effect known as the "father effect." The social recognition of two men as legitimate fathers of a single child is classed as informal polyandry for while the two men are not formally married to the same woman they co-habit with the child's mother and society views both men as the mother's legitimate mates, and, therefore, fathers to her child.

Sometimes fraternal polyandry occurs hand-in-hand with sororal polygyny whereby a woman's husband takes his wife's sister as another wife. This sort of marital union binds families closely together.

Another type of polyandry sees unrelated men marry the same woman. This form of marriage has been most closely documented in Sri Lanka and begins with a woman marrying a man in a monogamous union. The wife then marries for a second time, or more. The woman's first husband then becomes her main husband, which means that he is the husband with the most decision-making power and authority within the three-way relationship. The woman lives with her husbands in the same household unit and all her husbands are thought of as fathers of her children.

Other variations may also occur within polyandry. For instance, two men sharing one wife may invite a second woman, such as the wife's sister, to become part of their polyandrous marriage. In this way the union becomes simultaneously both polyandrous and polygynous (a man having more than one wife at a time). Polyandry can also occur on a temporary basis, for example if a woman's husband becomes disabled or is absent for a space of time and another man steps in to replace the husband for a short time. This may happen if a woman needs a man to act as head of the household for some reason or because the principal husband knows he will be absent for a time and needs a man to protect his wife, and, thus his financial interests. When this arrangement is made the substitute husband is expected to take on all the duties of the primary husband, including having marital sex with the wife. If the wife has a child by the substitute husband the principal husband is unworried as the substitute is a man of his own choosing. Once the woman's primary husband returns to health or comes back home, the household reverts to its former ways. This form of substitute polyandry has been recorded among Inuit communities.

Polyandrous relationships are entered into for a number of reasons. First, a polyandrous marriage brings several men and therefore incomes to a household. This is true in regions where men are the main breadwinners. Second, proponents of polyandry assert that such an arrangement brings stability to families, particularly in areas where there is a great disparity in the ratio of men to women. Such a sex ratio disparity may be the result of organized female migration or the infanticide of female children. Polyandry occurs in such instances as it reduces competition between males for available females to marry. Third, fraternal polyandry helps keep inherited assets within families—when one generation of brothers takes one wife between them the next generation of the family do the same. Thus it is not necessary to divide the inheritance as all the descendants live in the one house, sharing the same resources. This is an especially important consideration when inheritances take the form of herds of cattle or tracts of land in areas where herds are small and farming land is scarce because it means that already meager resources are not divided to the extent that they become worthless. Indeed recent research suggests that economic reasons are the overriding factor in the formation of polyandrous marriages thus such unions tend to persist within communities where land and cattle are so scarce that dividing these resources between households would render them into quantities so small that they become meaningless. For example, in the neighboring villages of Malang and Tholang, situated within the Lahaul Valley in the Himalayan region of India, where small farms are shaped on the edge of mountains, polyandry can be the deciding factor between life and death—dividing land among many sons would leave each son with too small an amount of land to produce sufficient amounts of food. The harsh mountain weather also means that the planting season is brief and can end abruptly so people living in this area must take every opportunity they can to maximize their ability to grow crops. Another suggested advantage of polyandry is that it reduces birth rates. Whereas, for instance, six brothers with a wife each would be able to produce dozens of children, polyandrous marriages rarely produces more than six children because one wife can only bear a finite number of offspring.

Those that enter into polyandrous relationships face several challenges. For instance, as power within the family structure typically rests with the primary husband within a non-fraternal polyandrous relationship, or with the eldest brother in a fraternal polyandrous marriage, all other husbands find themselves subordinate to the more senior husband with little chance to change their situation and gain their own autonomy unless they leave the marriage. Thus non-primary husbands may become resentful of their situation. This may be a particular problem if the secondary husbands are younger brothers as then sibling rivalries may also come to the fore. Another problematic aspect of polyandry is that while the ideal situation sees all the husbands share the wife equally in all ways, including sexually, this may not be the case in reality with the wife enjoying the company of one husband more than any of the others. The outcome of such favoritism is often familial tension. Another consequence of polyandry that occurs specifically in cases of fraternal polyandry where there is a great age gap between the eldest and youngest brothers. In such cases the youngest brother will have entered into a marriage instigated by the eldest brother who usually takes a wife of an appropriate age to be his wife. Consequently, the youngest brother then finds himself married to a wife that is several years too old for him. This may result in the wife and the youngest brother having a poor relationship marked by sexual frustration. Additionally if the eldest husband dies while the wife is still married to his other brothers, the wife will find herself in the strange position of being both a widow and a wife simultaneously.

Polyandry thrives where economic opportunity is scarce, meaning that people are willing to sacrifice individual, personal liberty for financial security. However in recent years instances of polyandry have decreased. One of the main reasons for this is that increased globalization means that even in the remotest areas of Tibet, Western ideals of romantic love between loving couples are becoming predominant. Other reasons for the decline of polyandry include increased sex education in tandem with greater awareness of women's rights and the growth of religions that prohibit polyandry.

See also: Arranged Marriage and Forced Marriage; Polygyny

Further Reading

Dreger, Alice. "When Taking Multiple Husbands Makes Sense," *The Atlantic*, February 1, 2013. Accessed February 12, 2015, at http://www.theatlantic.com/health/archive/2013/02/when-taking-multiple-husbands-makes-sense/272726/.

Galvan, Javier A., ed. *They Do What? A Cultural Encyclopedia of Extraordinary and Exotic Customs from around the World*. Santa Barbara, CA: ABC-CLIO, 2014.

Hewlett, Barry S., ed. *Father-Child Relations: Cultural and Biosocial Contexts*. New Brunswick, NJ: Transaction Publishers, 1992.

Polgreen, Lydia. "One Bride for 2 Brothers: A Custom Fades in India," *New York Times*, July 16, 2010. A accessed February 12, 2015, at http://www.nytimes.com/2010/07/17/world/asia/17polyandry.html?pagewanted=all.

POLYGYNY, INTERNATIONAL

Polygyny, from the Greek *poly* meaning many and *gyne*, wife or woman, is a system of plural marriage in which a man may take more than one wife. Polygyny differs from polygamy because polygamy is a broad term referring to that state of having more than one spouse rather than the custom of a man having more than one wife. Polygyny is widespread in Africa where the so-called polygyny belt stretches from Senegal to Tanzania. Polygyny also occurs in South America among indigenous groups such as the Amazonian Shipibo tribe. Many Muslim communities in Asia, the Middle East, and Europe (only in a few fundamentalist Balkan Muslim communities and Muslim states that were formerly Soviet states) permit polygyny under a variety of conditions and there is a long history of polygyny in Hinduism. Islam permits a man to have four wives as long as he believes that he can treat them all equally and fairly. This is set out in Chapter 4 verse 3 of the Islamic holy book the Qur'an. However polygyny is not permitted by Christian denominations and most Jewish societies do not permit polygyny either. It is often thought that members of The Church of Jesus Christ of Latter-day Saints (commonly referred to as Mormons) are permitted to practice polygyny but this is not the case for Mormons discontinued the custom at the end of the 19th century.

Indeed members that are found to be practicing any form of plural marriage today face excommunication.

There are many different reasons why polygyny is practiced though the most oft-cited reason for a man marrying many wives is that this provides a husband with a variety of sexual partners and, therefore, greater sexual gratification. Another reason for polygyny is that by having more than wife a man ensures that he always has a wife available to do his bidding whether sexually or in terms of keeping house or caring for children. This is important in cases where a wife dies, goes on a long-term visit to see her family, or abandons the husband for it means that the husband still has a wife to serve him. Some recent researchers have suggested that Western academics over-emphasize the sexual element of polygyny but it is nonetheless an aspect of that particular marriage system.

It has been suggested that one of the side-effects of polygyny is that the fertility of individual wives within polygyny decreases. This effect is well documented and is known in some circles as the polygyny-fertility hypothesis. Many academic studies have investigated this theory and suggest that polygyny limits the fertility of individual wives and the fertility of all of a man's wives through mechanisms such as sexual abstinence following the birth of babies and lengthy intervals between conceptions. This theory seems to be backed-up by academic research contrasting fertility rates among monogamous and polygynous societies. For example, research carried out in rural southern Jordan found that rates of fertility among wives in monogamous married couples was much higher than fertility rates among wives in polygynous relationships. It was also found that husbands would take new, younger wives when the fertility of his oldest wives began to decline.

The emphasis on the sexual gratification of the husband, the importance of his happiness, and the constant need to produce children within polygynous marriage has led some people to suggest that polygyny as a marriage system is concerned with the happiness of men rather than women and sits at odds with modern lifestyles, particularly in Westernized communities. Indeed in some African countries the increasing influence of the West on traditional ways of marriage has resulted in a decrease in polygyny. For example among Kikuyu women living in Kenya rates of polygyny have fallen as women reject the concept in favor of trying to arrange marriages based on Western, Christian ideals of romance and monogamy. There have been repeated calls to the United Nations to protect women from the subjugation that many consider inherent within polygyny. Those who oppose polygyny assert that the practice leads to arguing, envy, and emotional anxiety among wives, removes the individuality of women, and results in high divorce rates. Advocates of polygyny, however, argue that polygyny allows for the formation of intensely loyal support networks among wives, solidarity among a population's women in general, secure childcare arrangements, a reduction of incidents of adultery and divorce, and the opportunity for wives to have lengthy breaks from sexual intercourse and resultant pregnancies. For these reasons, even though several African countries have outlawed polygyny the practice is unlikely to become extinct. Indeed, even in countries where the marriage system is banned or is generally considered outdated polygyny still persists.

See also: Muslim Wedding Ceremony; Polyandry

Further Reading

Al-Islam.org. "The Concept of Polygamy and the Prophet's Marriages." Accessed October 7, 2015, at http://www.al-islam.org/articles/concept-polygamy-and-prophets-marriages-sayyid-muhammad-rizvi.

Bilaal, Philips, Abu Ameenah, and Jameelah Jones. *Polygamy in Islam*. Riyadh, Saudi Arabia: International Islamic Publishing House, 2005.

The Church of Jesus Christ of Latter-day Saints. "Do Mormons Practice Polygamy?" February 21, 2012. Accessed October 7, 2015, at https://www.mormon.org/faq/practice-of-polygamy.

Koktvedgaard Zeitzen, Miriam. *Polygamy: A Cross-Cultural Analysis*. Oxford, UK: Berg, 2008.

Rogers, Curtis. *Polygyny: The Ancient African Welfare System*. Bloomington, IN: Xlibris Corporation, 2013.

POVITICA, EASTERN EUROPE

Povitica, also known as *potica* (pronounced po-teet-sa), is an Eastern European sweet bread baked traditionally at Christmas, but that is also served at any other celebratory time of the year, especially weddings and anniversaries. Povitica is similar in texture to brioche as it is a sweet or savory yeast bread dough filled with a contrasting filling that, when sliced crosswise, reveals filigree swirls of alternating dough and filling. The filling for sweet povitica is often made from walnuts and honey though sweet povitica can also be made with poppy seed, cream cheese, or dried fruit fillings. Savory povitica are made using herbs such as tarragon. Povitica can be baked in a log shape, or shaped into a ring or a horseshoe before baking. Alternatively, povitica may be constructed in the manner of a jelly-roll and then spiraled into a ring-shaped baking tin.

The name povitica derives from the Slovenian word *poviti* meaning to wrap in. There is no one set recipe for povitica so each family has their own recipe. However the authentic Slovenian walnut potica recipe is said to be as follows: Grease a tin with butter or oil and then in a bowl mix together plain flour, yeast, egg yolks, tepid water, butter, salt, and sugar. Then in a separate bowl combine crushed walnuts, honey, sugar, milk, an egg, ground cinnamon, and either fruit brandy or rum. The dough should be prepared at room temperature but once the dough is made it is left in a warm place as this encourages the dough to rise. When the dough has risen a hole is made in the middle of the dough into which are stirred eggs, melted butter, and hand-hot milk. The dough is then beaten for 15 minutes so that bubbles appear in the dough and the dough starts to come away from the sides of the mixing bowl. The dough is then covered with a cloth and left to rise again. Meanwhile, the filling is made by combining the walnuts with hot sweetened milk, warm honey, and cinnamon. Eggs are mixed into the walnut-mixture once it is cool. Next, the dough is rolled out and then the filling is spread over the dough. The dough is then rolled up tightly and placed in the baking tin where it is left to rise and then brushed with egg prior to baking. The dough is then baked in the oven for one hour and then left to cool in its tin for 15 minutes before being turned out onto a board, sprinkled with confectioner's sugar, sliced, and served. Making povitica is therefore a lengthy process and so the baking of the bread tends to be reserved exclusively for special occasions.

See also: *Beschuit met Muisjes*, *Suikerboon*, and *Dragées* (Volume 1); Birthday Cakes (Volume 1); Groaning Cheese and Groaning Cake (Volume 1); *Halva* (Volume 3); *Koliva* (Volume 3); *Lindo*; Wedding Cake

Further Reading

IFeelSlovenia. "Walnut Potica." Accessed June 11, 2015, at http://www.slovenia.info/?recepti=8321&lng=2&redirected=1.

Patent, Greg. *A Baker's Odyssey: Celebrating Time-honored Recipes from America's Rich Immigrant Heritage*. Hoboken, NJ: John Wiley & Sons Inc., 2007.

Rolek, Barbara. "What Is Potica or Povitica?" About Food. Accessed June 11, 2015, at http://easteuropeanfood.about.com/od/products/a/strawberryhill.htm.

PURITY BALL, UNITED STATES

A purity ball, officially called a father-daughter purity ball, is a recently invented controversial formal dance with Christian religious overtones that sees the public affirmation of a girl's chastity before marriage. Purity balls are attended by fathers and their daughters, and sometimes mothers and uncles, and usually sees girls vow to remain sexually abstinent until marriage while their fathers promise to protect their daughters' purity. Purity balls have been likened to a cross between a marriage ceremony, a debutante ball, and a prom. Girls need not be teenagers to attend purity balls for some attendees have been as young as four years of age.

The first purity ball was held in Colorado Springs in 1998, the idea of Randy Wilson, the National Field Director for Church Ministries for an American conservative Christian advocacy group called the Family Research Council, and his stay-at-home wife Lisa, who have seven daughters. By the 2000s, purity balls had spread across the United States and today organizers of purity balls claim to be at the vanguard of a national movement within the United States with purity balls also held in 17 countries around the world. However it is not possible to know how many purity balls are held around the world, or even in the United States, as they take place at grass-roots level though purity ball advocates say that they sell hundreds of purity ball organizing kits each year. Purity ball kits include a manual costing around $100 (plus postage) that explains the purpose of the balls and how to organize an event, plus also available are DVDs of previous purity balls, digital templates to print tickets and the like, and purity ball jewelry. Those who attend purity balls and buy purity ball equipment tend to be evangelical Christians.

Purity balls follow a fairly standard structure though specifics vary. The Colorado Springs Purity Ball is an annual event held in a luxurious hotel. The event begins with a three-course dinner. After dinner, fathers and daughters congregate along the walls of a ballroom that is dominated by a large crucifix. Fathers then walk up to the cross carrying swords that they then form into a ceremonial arch through which fathers and daughters proceed to the cross. Once they are standing in front of the cross, fathers and daughters kneel and hymns are played. Sometimes fathers embrace their daughters as the pair prays. Next fathers sign a pledge promising that they will be a model of purity for their daughters, displaying a pattern of integrity that their daughters can follow throughout their lives and their daughters silently promise to lead chaste lives before God as symbolized by laying a white rose on the crucifix that is the ball's centerpiece. After the laying down of the rose the night's dancing begins with fathers dancing with their daughters. Sometime during the evening fathers and daughters pose for pictures and fathers may present the daughters with purity rings that the girls wear on their left hand.

Those who advocate purity balls assert that they are joyous events encouraging deeply affectionate relationships between fathers and daughters that will discourage girls from experiencing premarital sexual relations, which, proponents feel, result from girls finding romance with boys rather than caring deeply for their fathers. However critics of purity balls contend that the balls propagate antifeminist messages, limiting women's sexual freedom, and ignoring the fact that some daughters are lesbian, bisexual, or transgender. Critics also feel that purity balls spread the message that a woman's worth is defined by her virginity and emphasizes that she is a possession to be passed from her father to her husband. Indeed some commentators find it unsettling that, in essence, purity balls permit fathers to be in charge of a girl's sexuality and permitted to give away his daughter's virginity to the new man in her life, her husband. Further, critics also point out that purity balls demonstrate an absurd double standard for to attend purity balls girls dress up in adult women's clothing, usually by wearing spaghetti-strapped evening dresses and high heels, which both denote adult sexuality, and, in addition, purity balls fail to take into account teenage boys' burgeoning sexuality and their potential for premarital sex. However some organizers of purity balls do invite sons to watch events so that they can aspire to the same level of sexual purity. Indeed organizers of the purity balls also host manhood ceremonies. These take place when a boy reaches 12 years of age, the age at which Jesus began to question rabbis and discuss the Scriptures "in His Father's house." As part of the ceremony, sons are given purity rings as a symbol that the boys should follow a life righteous in mind, body, and soul and to ensure that the boys do not endanger young women's hearts by entering into impure relationships. In short, the ring is intended to remind boys to honor God always. During the ceremony boys are also given a sword symbolizing that they are now men and warriors of God. On a practical level, purity balls do not seem to prevent premarital sexual relations for studies in the United States focusing on abstinence-only education reveals a high level of disconnect between teenagers' intention to remain chaste and life practices. A five-year-long study comparing U.S. teenagers who had taken a purity pledge with those who had not found that those who had vowed to remain chaste broke their vows and also had just as many sexual partners as those who had not sworn themselves to stay virginal until marriage. However the study also found that those teenagers who took the virginity pledge were significantly less likely to use contraceptives than teenagers who had not made a promise. This has lead critics of purity balls to argue that virginity pledges and purity balls create an environment of sexual ignorance.

See also: Bachelor and Spinster Balls; Bed-Courtship; Filipino Debut; *Lobola*; Maidens' Garlands; Reed Dancing Chastity Ceremony; Virginity Testing

Further Reading

Anderson, Kristin J. *Modern Misogyny: Anti-Feminism in a Post-Feminist Era*. Oxford, UK: Oxford University Press, 2015.

Banerjee, Neela. "Dancing the Night Away, with a Higher Purpose," *New York Times*, May 19, 2008. Accessed January 2, 2015, at http://www.generationsoflight.com/html/news.html.

Generations of Light. "What about Boys." 2007. Accessed January 2, 2015, at http://generationsoflight.com/html/boys.html.

Generations of Light. "What Is a Purity Ball?" 2007. Accessed January 2, 2015, at http://generationsoflight.myicontrol.com.

Gibbs, Nancy. "The Pursuit of Teen Girl Purity," *Time*, July 17, 2008. Accessed January 2, 2015, at http://content.time.com/time/magazine/article/0,9171,1823930,00.html.

PurityBall.com. "Hosting Your Own Purity Ball." Accessed January 2, 2015, at http://www.purityball.com/host.html.

R

RAG WEEK, UNITED KINGDOM AND IRELAND

RAG Week is a tradition among university students in the United Kingdom. The name RAG Week stands for Raising and Giving Week and sees students undertake a number of activities in order to raise money for charity. Indeed it has been estimated that RAG Week activities raise between £6 million (about $8.8 million) and £9 million (just over $13 million) each year. University fundraising initiatives are governed by the National Student Fundraising Association (NaSFA).

RAG Week began in the 19th century, most probably by medical students. Traditionally, each university held its own RAG Week, which saw a number of fundraising activities take place over the course of seven days, as well as the production of so-called RAG Mags, comic and often crude booklets. However over the years RAG Week has changed to become a major annual fundraising event that can last throughout a university's whole academic year. While some smaller U.K. universities may hold a week of events that raise a few thousand pounds for charity, larger universities run RAG activities throughout the whole year that include international expeditions and large-scale events.

Each university may choose how the money that it raises is spent. This means that thousands of national and international charities benefit each year. For example, in 2011 Sheffield University raised £202,400 (about $295,908), 85 percent of which went to local charities. Sometimes the amounts raised by large U.K. universities' RAG activities are quite staggering. For instance, Loughborough University, which is home to one of the United Kingdom's largest RAG societies, raised a staggering £1,404,952.28 (about $2,054,040) in 2012, meaning that since RAG records began in 1980, Loughborough University has raised £12,077,657.12 (roughly $17,657,534) for charity in total.

Traditionally, RAG Week consists of a number of activities. At present, one of the most popular of these activities is called Jailbreak, which sees students travel as far away from their university as physically possible within 36 hours without spending any money on transport but rather relying on their powers of persuasion and the goodwill of strangers. This usually means that students have to hitchhike and cadge as many lifts as possible. Jailbreak raises money because the students are sponsored depending on the distance they manage to travel. It is considered a great achievement for Jailbreak students to reach Continental Europe, though two students from Durham University reached Sydney in Australia. The students had worked out the e-mail address of entrepreneur and owner of Virgin Airways, Sir Richard Branson, who was sufficiently impressed by the students' initiative to offer them return air tickets. Jailbreak is not just fun for it can raise huge amounts of money. For example, in 2011, Cambridge University RAG Jailbreak raised £40,000 (around $58,480) after 121 teams of students took part. Not all RAG Week activities necessitate international travel however. In fact some of the other most popular ways of raising money during RAG Week include students being sponsored to go on blind dates, on pub crawls, skydiving, mountain climbing, and simply hold parties. Fancy dress, being pushed around town in a shopping trolley, and sitting in baths of baked beans are other popular traditional money-earners. A recent RAG Week trend has seen students sponsored to have tattoos, often of their university mascot or crest.

There is a certain amount of competitiveness between universities to see which can raise the most funds for charity. This means that the many RAG Week committees around the United Kingdom tend to steal ideas from each other and students look for ever more ridiculous ways to earn money. This sometimes leads to complaints from people that are not involved in RAG Week. Those who are not in favor of RAG Week often complain that RAG activities promote drunkenness while some people dislike being pestered for money regardless of how good a cause the money will go to. RAG activities have also ended with arrests. For example in 2011, 30 students in Galway, Ireland, were arrested by police after people complained of damaged property, intimidation tactics, drunkenness, and disorderly behavior during National University of Ireland Galway's RAG Week. Organizers of RAG Weeks insist, however, that most RAG activities are not alcohol-fueled excuses for rowdiness and stress that student unions monitor events closely so there is little chance of events escalating out of control. Punishment is also severe for those who step out of line. Moreover, some universities no longer refer to their RAG Weeks as such in order to avoid negative connotations.

Similar to RAG Week is the Canadian tradition of Shinerama. This is Canada's largest post-secondary education charity fundraiser for it involves more than 35,000 students from over 60 university and college campuses raising money and awareness of the fatal genetic disease Cystic Fibrosis.

See also: *Russefeiring* and Schoolies Week

Further Reading

Gidda, Mirren. "RAG Awards: Students Honoured for Charity Fundraising," *The Guardian*, September 5, 2013. Accessed October 11, 2015, at http://www.theguardian.com/education/mortarboard/2013/sep/05/national-rag-awards.

McMaster Students Union Inc. "Shinerama." Accessed October 11, 2015, at https://www.msumcmaster.ca/services-directory/18-shinerama.

Orr, Gillian. "Bad Behaviour That's All in a Good Cause: Students Are Carrying on the RAG Tradition," *The Independent*, February 2, 2012. Accessed October 11, 2015, at http://www.independent.co.uk/news/education/higher/bad-behaviour-thats-all-in-a-good-cause-students-are-carrying-on-the-rag-tradition-6298083.html.

REED DANCING CHASTITY CEREMONY, KINGDOM OF SWAZILAND

The Reed Dancing Chastity Ceremony (called *umhlanga* in the Swazi language and *Umkhosi woMhlanga* by Zulus) is a rite of passage performed by Zulu females from five years old to their mid-twenties (known as maidens) who congregate voluntarily each August or September at the Ludzidzini Royal Compound in Lobamba, the royal and legislative capital of the Kingdom of Swaziland, commonly referred to as simply Swaziland. The ceremony takes the form of a lively eight-day-long festival that promotes respect for young women and female independence and stresses the importance of chastity, though in truth many Swazis say virginity is no longer strictly necessary for a maiden to take part in the ceremony. The festival begins with unmarried women cutting reeds that they then present to the royal known as *Indlovukazi*, or the Queen Mother, and then, finally, perform a dance. It is estimated that in 2012 some 30,000 females participated in the ceremony.

Swaziland is a landlocked country bordered by Mozambique and South Africa about the size of Connecticut. The country is geographically isolated and has developed a rich variety of customs and traditions. The Reed Dancing Chastity Ceremony was adopted in 1840 and evolved from both a custom of the neighboring Zulu-speaking Ndwandwe clan and the Swazi custom of *umcwasho*, a period of time when young women were not allowed to be touched by men. During the period of umcwasho women were given a large tassel to wear that symbolized their chastity and the women could only remove the tassel when they reached a marriageable age. If a maiden became pregnant before she married, her family had to pay a fine of money or a cow to the local chief. The period of sexual abstinence would end in a feast and then dancing. The most recent period of umcwasho began in 2001 when King Mswati III imposed a five-year long sex ban on the country's teenage girls asserting that if propositioned by a man, girls should throw their umcwasho tassels outside the man's house and his family would have to pay a fine of a cow. This period of umcwasho was an effort to reduce Swaziland's extremely high rates of HIV and AIDS that at the time saw 29 percent of Swazis between 15 and 19 years old HIV positive with the figure rising to 42 percent for pregnant women. The 2001 ban on sexual relations proved very unpopular and in urban areas most young women refused to wear the large umcwasho tassel. Rural Swazis did, however, abide by the rules of umcwasho for many community chiefs insisted girls wore the tassels to get a place at school. Ironically, in 2001, King Mswati III fined himself a cow for breaking the ban by taking a 17-year-old as his ninth wife. The marriage sparked protests outside the king's palace among people already angered by the fact that the king's daughters had not had to wear the umcwasho tassel.

The tradition of the Reed Dancing Chastity Ceremony developed to allow the king to find another wife. The Swaziland royal family appoints an official called the Captain of the Girls, or *induna*, from among the ranks of common women and it is the Captain's job to announce the date of the Reed Dancing Chastity Ceremony on local radio. The induna is usually an expert dancer and is made aware of all royal protocol. One of the king's daughters is also selected to act as a royal counterpart of the commoner induna. The Reed Dancing Chastity Ceremony held today echoes the custom of umcwasho as young girls cut reeds for the Indlovukazi that will be used to make walls and windbreaks needed at KwaNyokeni Palace in Nongoma (the former capital of KwaZulu) and at Ludzidzini Royal Compound. The strengthening of the royal residences against the elements highlights that the Reed Dancing Chastity Ceremony is a symbolic reinforcement of Swazi womanhood, for the festivities allow Swazi females to show solidarity with each other and with the Indlovukazi, who is both their queen and the guardian of their knowledge of traditional medicine.

On the first day of the ceremony the girls congregate at the village that is the home of the Indlovukazi, currently Ludzidzini. The maidens come from over 200 Zulu clans and are registered immediately on their arrival for security reasons. Men who have been appointed by their respective chiefs guard the girls who sleep in huts set up in the village. On the second day of the ceremony the maidens are divided into two groups: the younger group consists of girls up to 13 years old while the other group is made up of adolescents and women in their twenties. In the afternoon, the maidens go to the reed beds accompanied by their male protectors. The group of younger girls is transported by truck to the reed beds in Bhamsakhe that at 10 kilometers (6.3 miles) distance are the reeds nearest to the royal residence. The older group of girls travels to Ntondozi around 30 kilometers (18 miles) away. As it is usually dark by the time the girls arrive at the reed beds they stay overnight in government-approved accommodation before cutting reeds the next day. The maidens use long knives to cut between 10 and 20 reeds. Traditionally, maidens would cut grass that they would weave into a rope and on to which they would tie bunches of reeds. Nowadays, however, the girls usually put their cut reeds straight into carrier bags. Once they have finished collecting reeds the girls spend another night in the official accommodation. The next day the girls travel back to the Indlovukazi's village with each maiden carrying the reeds she has collected. The girls arrive back at nightfall signifying that they have journeyed over a large distance. The fifth day marks the end of the maidens' arduous work as they prepare for their dance. Costumes are made, consisting of beaded skirts that reveal their thighs, colorful sashes, anklets made from cocoons, and bead necklaces. The costume does not include a shirt or other top so the maidens dance with their breasts exposed. As the king's daughters also take part in the ritual dance, they wear a red feather headdress that distinguishes them from the other girls. The commoner maidens are also given the long knife to carry with which they cut the reed. The knife is symbolic of their virginity. Today Swaziland has rates of HIV infection running at 26 percent—the highest in the world—and the Swaziland authorities see the Reed Dancing ceremony as a national effort to promote the importance of girls maintaining their virginity until marriage and thereby try to combat rates of HIV and AIDS.

On the sixth day, the first dance is held from 3 p.m. to 5 p.m. As they dance the girls deposit their bunches of reeds outside the Indlovukazi's personal quarters and then continue dancing in the main arena. One of the king's daughters leads the girls in their dancing and in choosing a reed to hold during the ritual. According to Zulu mythology if an unchaste girl takes part in the dance her reed will break when she holds it, causing her great embarrassment, hence spectators wait with bated breath when the girls choose their reeds and there is much cheering when the girls' reeds remain intact.

Girls dance and sing in groups according to their chiefdoms with each group of girls singing different songs simultaneously. On the seventh day, which is the last day of dancing, the maidens dance in front of spectators made up of foreign dignitaries and tourists. The king is also present on this second day of dancing and comes down from his luxury box with a regiment of bare-chested men wearing patterned skirts, beaded sashes, and leopard-skin loincloths. The king, who practices polygyny (the current king has 15 wives) and his attendants make their way through the mass of bare-breasted girls all the while looking out for future royal wives and then return to the royal box. When the king has returned to the box, the maidens exclaim in the national language of Siswati, "This land is for the king and people must not distribute it without his consent." Swaziland is Africa's last absolute monarchy with about 60 percent of the land owned in some way by the king and with around 70 percent of the country's 1.2 million citizens living on land held in trust by the king, whose authority is supported and enforced by a network of local chiefs who have the power to evict their tenants without explanation. Lacking title deeds, Swazi peasant agriculturalists are often displaced to make way for royal family investments, and most Swazis are prevented from investing in basic farming infrastructure. According to the United Nations, this is one of the reasons that roughly two-thirds of Swazis are unable to meet their basic food requirements and poverty in the country runs at a rate of 43 percent. Such conditions mean that life expectancy at birth in Swaziland is just 54 years. Such is the king's power and influence that it is therefore wise for the maidens to pay tribute to their king. On the eighth and final day of the ceremony, the king orders the sacrifice of many cattle in honor of the girls. Once they have collected a piece of sacrificial meat, the maidens head back to their chiefdoms and the ceremony is declared over.

The Reed Dancing Chastity Ceremony is Swaziland's most public cultural tradition and is marketed to foreign tourists in an effort to cultivate an image of the country as a nostalgic throwback to pre-colonial Africa. Tourists who feel uneasy at seeing multitudes of bare-breasted females dancing for the entertainment of the king are informed that the girls attend the event voluntarily. However this is only true to an extent for although many of the girls do attend willingly, non-governmental organizations such as Women and Law in Southern Africa (WLSA), suggest that some communities levy fines on the parents of girls that are absent. Community leaders fine the parents mostly out of a desire to please the king, who in turn uses the Reed Dancing Chastity Ceremony for propaganda purposes hence the singing of songs in praise of the king. That said, when interviewed most girls who have taken part in the ceremony say that although the ritual is tiring it is an enjoyable and exciting time and a welcome change from a life of household chores and cooking. Interestingly, most girls who attend the event also think it is highly unlikely that they will become a royal bride and also would not want to marry the king as that would entail losing all contact with their families.

See also: Virginity Testing; Wodaabe Courtship Dance and Festival

Further Reading

Arnett, Jeffrey Jensen, ed. *International Encyclopedia of Adolescence: A–J, index, Volume 1*. New York: Routledge, 2007.

BBC. "Swazi King Drops Sex-ban Tassels." BBC News, August 23, 2005. Accessed December 28, 2014, at http://news.bbc.co.uk/1/hi/world/africa/4165432.stm.

Galvan, Javier A., ed. *They Do What? A Cultural Encyclopedia of Extraordinary and Exotic Customs from around the World*. Santa Barbara, CA: ABC-CLIO, 2014.

Rosen, Jonathan W. "Last Dance for the Playboy King of Swaziland?" *National Geographic News*, October 3, 2014. Accessed December 28, 2014, at http://news.nationalgeographic.com/news/2014/10/141003-swaziland-africa-king-mswati-reed-dance/.

Roy, Christian. *Traditional Festivals: A Multicultural Encyclopedia, Volume 1*. Santa Barbara, CA: ABC-CLIO, 2005.

RITUAL TATTOOING, INTERNATIONAL

Ritual tattooing, by which is meant the act of giving or receiving tattoos that have some special significance rather than solely acting as body adornment, may occur for several reasons. In many cultures the most common reason for ritual tattooing is that the tattooing is part of an individual's rite of passage to adulthood and may or may not broadcast an individual's marriageability. However ritual tattoos may also be given as a way to ward off evil or disease, to mark certain accomplishments, or simply to act as an outward signal that a person belongs to a social class, rank, tribe, or community including military divisions and fraternities. There is a long history of ritual tattooing among peoples living in Polynesia, Micronesia, Melanesia, and Asia. In the United States, members of the non-denominational Church of Body Modification may also acquire tattoos as part of their search for spiritual fulfillment.

The word tattoo is thought to have originated from the Polynesian word *tatau*, meaning both to mark and workmanlike, or correct. This etymology reflects that there is a long history of ritual tattooing in Polynesia, the region of the world that includes New Zealand, Hawaii, Easter Island, and various South Pacific nations including Samoa, Tonga, Tuvalu, and Fiji. In recent years, there has been a surge of interest in traditional ritual tattooing among young people in Samoa and elsewhere in Polynesia. In Samoa, it is customary for young men and women to receive ritual tattoos in order to show their social rank and family heritage. The history of tattooing in Samoa stretches back over 2,000 years though according to Samoan oral tradition it was two Fijian women that introduced the practice to Samoa. Prior to 1830 when Christian missionaries arrived in Samoa, all Samoan males were tattooed between the ages of 14 and 18 years. Males were tattooed at this age because this was when males were deemed to have stopped growing which was important for if a male continued to grow once he was tattooed his tattoo would stretch and become deformed. Missionaries disapproved of the ritual tattooing and persuaded islanders to only tattoo the sons of chiefs with tattoos serving as a permanent mark of their dedication to their culture and their ability to withstand pain. In modern-day Samoa, tattoos signify status, community, and power and it is a matter of pride for a Samoan to receive tattoos. Samoan tattoo artists are known as *tafuga* and use pigment made from mixing sugar water with burned candlenut soot to make their designs. Samoan males receive traditional tattoos called *pe'a* with their first tattoo inked when they start puberty. These tattoos are especially painful to receive as they are administered using a tool consisting of a short length of bamboo with a piece of tortoiseshell tied at right angles to one end that in turn has a bone comb attached. The tafuga uses a small hammer to tap the tool thereby inserting the pigment under the skin. The tattooing process can take weeks, even months, to complete and it may be necessary for the person being tattooed to have periods of recuperation between tattooing sessions.

Today, while Samoan tattoos still include traditional elements such as geometric lines, over the years the tattoos have evolved to include freehand symbols including the *kava* bowl signifying hospitality and emblems taken from nature such as seashells, birds, and centipedes. (*See* Plate 19.) For a Samoan male to receive a pe'a is still considered an achievement, for a tattoo can extend from mid-back to the knees including very sensitive body parts. Indeed there are various types of pe'a design that are specific to certain parts of the body. For instance a *va'a* (canoe) stretches across the mid-back, a *tasele* covers the perineum, a *tafumiti* appears on the scrotum, and *tafito* is specific to the penis. Any man that displays a complete a pe'a tattoo is respected for his courage and endurance. Contrastingly, men that are not tattooed are commonly referred to as *telefua* or *telenoa*, meaning naked, while men that display an unfinished tattoo because they have not been able to withstand the pain of receiving a whole design, or cannot afford to pay a tattooist for a large tattoo, are referred to as *pe'a mutu* (mark of shame).

Samoan women also receive a tattoo called a *malu* to mark their attainment of adulthood. Malu designs are less elaborate than pe'a designs and since they extend only from the thighs to the knees these tattoos are rarely visible except during traditional *siva* dances.

Elsewhere in Polynesia, New Zealand Māoris are famous for their facial tattoos called *moko* that reflect the traditional Māori belief that the head is the most sacred part of the body. Māoris also display tattoos on their thighs and buttocks. Māori tattoos do not tend to include geometric shapes, animals, or names but rather feature curved and spiraling designs. One example of this type of tattoo is the *raperape*, a double spiral tattooed on the buttocks of Māori warriors.

Māoris perform ritual tattooing as the marks reveal which clan an individual belongs to, their social rank, and their personal achievements. In addition, moko tattoos have long been considered a mark of adulthood. Once a young adult male Māori has his first moko tattoo he then goes on to receive additional tattoos at other life stages. Though painful, Māori men do not mind receiving extra tattoos as they believe that they make them more attractive to women. Tattoos are not the exclusive preserve of Māori men, however, for Māori women also display tattoos including moko facial tattoos on their lips and chin as well as occasionally tattoos on their necks and backs. Female Māori tattoos are not as heavy as male moko however.

Māoris developed their tattooing tradition in the 1500s when they would use an *uhi* chisel fashioned from bird bones in conjunction with a small mallet to carve facial skin. Using these tools produced grooves that were then filled with black ink by a tattoo artist known as a *tahunga-ta-moko*. The pigment used by the tahunga-ta-moko was made from soot, tree ash, and dead caterpillars and was stored in an ornate receptacle called an *oko*, which was treated as a family heirloom. Once a Māori man had received his extensive moko tattoos he would rest with medicinal karaka tree leaves across his face to help his scars to heal. Also, because freshly carved skin was liable to infection any man that had unhealed moko was forbidden to have sex or eat solid food. Men suffered the pain and inconvenience of the moko, however, because they recognized that the tattoos signified their bravery and resolve. Māori tattooing methods have changed little over the years except that toward the end of the 19th century Māori tattoo artists switched to using needles rather than chisels, a move that made the tattooing procedure quicker and resulted in faster healing and smoother markings. Despite the modernization of moko methods, the tattoos fell out of popularity during the early 20th century. This resulted in a period during which moko went into decline but during the 1990s there was a major revival of traditional Māori culture including tattooing. Part of the reason for the renewal of interest in traditional Māori ways was that New Zealand museums began providing information on how moko could reveal family ancestry and tribal lineage. Once the cultural significance of moko became common knowledge, there was an upsurge in the number of young Māoris receiving tattoos, not just on their faces but also on their torsos, shoulder, and arms. There was also a significant increase in the number of women training to become moko tattooists, a role traditionally reserved for men. In fact the revival of interest in Māori culture means that moko tattoos have found favor with non-Māoris too. For example, in 2013 pop star Rihanna opted to sport a Māori tattoo on her right hand. Though Rihanna received her tattoo through the traditional chiseling method, many Māoris were dismayed to see such a well-known non-Māori display a traditional tattoo. Many Māoris disapprove of non-Māoris adopting Māori tattoo conventions as they believe that such tattoos should be displayed exclusively by Māoris in order to signify tribal affiliations. Māoris opposed to non-Māoris carrying Māori tattoos feel affronted that outsiders have appropriated their cultural heritage and rendered the designs a fashion trend bereft of cultural understanding. Contrastingly, some moko artists have welcomed the interest in traditional tattooing as it means there is more work for moko tattooists though they have had to adopt modern tattooing methods such as using sterile equipment and electric tools. As a compromise between traditional moko and Māori-esque designs desired by non-Māoris, a compromise tattoo called *kirituhi* (drawn skin) has evolved that resemble traditional Māori tattoos but that do not refer to any element of Māori culture or symbolism.

In Papua New Guinea, a nation populated by many different tribes, tattooing is traditionally associated with peoples living in the southwest of the country. In the past it was usual for women belonging to these tribes to have their entire faces and bodies tattooed with black geometric patterns. According to tradition the women would receive their first tattoo, on their hands, at five years old and then receive further tattoos at each important life stage—the tattoos would start at the hands and then work up the arms and across the body culminating in tattoos on the breasts and stomach that signified that the women had attained adulthood and were ready to marry. In general, women were tattooed by other women who used a mixture of charcoal and water that was applied to the skin using a lemon branch into which several thorns were inserted. This thorny stick instrument, called a *gini*, was tapped with another stick to apply the ink under the females' skin. This ritual tattooing practice became virtually extinct during the mid-20th century. However women living in Papua New Guinea's Oto Province still receive tattoos via the traditional gini method when they are 18 years of age to indicate that they are ready to wed. The women are tattooed by other women with each generation taught how to apply the body adornments. Whereas it was once customary for women in this region to be tattooed over their entire body, nowadays it is normally just their face that is marked. Nonetheless these facial tattoos are large-scale and can take over a week to complete. While the tattoos are being applied the woman being tattooed lives in seclusion with the tattooist so that others do not see her until her tattoos are complete and her scabs have healed. Another Papua New Guinean tribe, the Motuan, also draws tattoos onto tribeswomen during celebrations though this tribe uses pens to mark the skin.

In Myanmar (formerly Burma), although ritual tattooing has fallen out of favor ritual tattoos can still be seen on the skin of senior citizens as well as on younger tribespeople that are attempting to restore the tradition. For example, the Karen people, of whom there are around 7 million living in Myanmar, employ tattoos as amulets against disease. The Karen believes that illness originates in the stomach and so tattoo their bellies to ward off sickness. Traditionally, these tattoos feature complex designs employing many magical symbols and though the Karen now follow the Christian faith many members of the tribe, particularly older members, continue to employ protective tattoos. Another Myanmar tribe, the Shan, traditionally tattoo trousers on males when they reach puberty to signify to women that they were of marriageable age. The men would have their buttocks, genitals, thighs, and torso tattooed during a process that was so painful that men would smoke opium to reduce the pain. Though this practice is dying out, trouser tattoos are still visible on elderly Shan men. The trouser tattoos were always made using blue-black ink obtained from soot but the Shan also display red tattoos that act as medicinal amulets against disease. These protective tattoos are normally created by doctors or monks using either traditional tools topped with a Buddhist icon whose power is thought to transfer to the person wielding the implement or modern electric devices.

As in Myanmar, in Taiwan certain old and young tribespeople display ritual tattoos. For example, elderly members of the Atayal people display ritual tattoos, as do some younger tattoo revivalists. The Ayatal are one of some 14 Taiwanese aboriginal groups and are the second largest with a population of around 90,000 people. Facial tattooing is a traditional element of Ayatal culture and this led to the tribe being called the Wangtsifan (with *wang* meaning king) by the Japanese when they occupied Taiwan during the years 1895–1945. The Japanese used this term because the Ayatal would tattoo the word wang across their faces. The Ayatal also employed ritual tattooing during rites of passage to adulthood. For instance, the Ayatal, who like many other Southeast Asian tribes once practiced head-hunting, would give a male warrior a tattoo once he had collected an enemy's head for the first time. Ayatal women would also receive tattoos when they had learned to weave their own ceremonial clothes. That an Ayatal woman was able to weave her own clothes was an important accomplishment as it proved that she would be able to make clothes for her husband and children and was, therefore, ready for marriage. Consequently, in terms of marriageability it was important that both Ayatal men and women should be able to display tattoos—for an Ayatal man tattoos showed his skill as a warrior and for a woman they signified her ability to care for a family. Both male and female Ayatal would also receive tattoos as a distinct kinship mark that would allow their spirit to be recognized in the afterlife by other members of their kinship clan. Without such a mark the Ayatal individual would be unrecognizable to his or her fellow clan people and be doomed to loneliness in the next world.

Though the Japanese outlawed Ayatal tattooing in the 1930s due to its association with head-hunting, the practice is no longer prohibited. In recent years, a number of young Ayatal have revived the tattooing tradition albeit using modern tattooing techniques and equipment, and many elderly Ayatal still display their marks.

See also: Breast Ironing; Ear-Piercing Ceremonies; Forehead-Cutting Initiation; Human Tooth Sharpening; Neck Elongation; Scarification; *Thaipusam*: Extreme Ritual Flesh Modification; Tooth-Filing Ceremony

Further Reading

DeMello, Margo. *Inked: Tattoos and Body Art Around the World*. Santa Barbara, CA: ABC-CLIO, 2014.

Friedman; Anna Felicity. *World Atlas of Tattoo*. London: Quintessence Editions Ltd., 2015.

Galvan, Javier A., ed. *They Do What? A Cultural Encyclopedia of Extraordinary and Exotic Customs from around the World*. Santa Barbara, CA: ABC-CLIO, 2014.
National Park Service U.S. Department of the Interior. "Samoan Art in the Tatau (Tattoo)." Accessed September 24, 2015, at http://www.nps.gov/npsa/learn/education/classrooms/samoan-art-in-the-tatau.htm.
Neluis, Thomas, Myrna L. Armstrong, Cathy Young, Alden E. Roberts, LaMicha Hogan, and Katherine Rinard. "Prevalence and Implications of Genital Tattoos: A Site Not Forgotten," *British Journal of Medical Practitioners*, 7(4), December 2014, a732. Accessed May 30, 2016, at http://bjmp.org/files/2014-7-4/bjmp-2014-7-4-a732.pdf.
The Pitt Rivers Museum. "Burmese Tattooing." Pitt Rivers Virtual Collections: Body Art. Accessed September 25, 2015, at http://web.prm.ox.ac.uk/bodyarts/index.php/permanent-body-arts/tattooing/172-burmese-tattooing.html.
Polynesian Cultural Center. "Samoa: Samoan Tattoos." Accessed September 25, 2015, at http://www.polynesia.com/polynesian_culture/samoa/samoantattoos.html#.VgUzQDqvvR0.
Theobald, Donna. "Samoan Tattoo Patterns." Love to Know: Beauty & Fashion. Accessed September 25, 2015, at http://tattoos.lovetoknow.com/samoan-tattoo-patterns.

RUMSPRINGA, UNITED STATES AND CANADA

Rumspringa, also written as *Rumschpringe* or *Rumshpringa*, is a term coined by the Pennsylvania German Amish that roughly translates as running around. Some Amish use the word to describe a time of adolescence, exploration, and learning in the lives of young members of their community. The Amish are a Christian sect that follows the basic teachings of the Christian faith and emphasizes adult baptism, community, pacifism, a simple life kept distant from popular culture, and the separation of the church from the state. However there is no official set of rules by which the Amish must live and all Amish communities vary. Therefore it is difficult (and wrong to an extent) to generalize about "the Amish" as one homogenous group.

The Amish sect originated in Switzerland, Austria, and Germany as part of the Anabaptist movement in 1525. In 1693, the Amish established their own branch of Anabaptism in Switzerland and eastern France under the leadership of their founder Jakob Ammann—all Amish communities are derived from this group. During the 18th century, the Amish left Europe and settled in North America in order to escape religious persecution and today there are around 300,000 Amish living in 30 states, in the U.S., especially Pennsylvania, as well as in the Canadian province of Ontario. Over half the Amish population is aged under 18 years.

Wherever the Amish settle they establish their own distinct agrarian communities. The Amish are famous for shunning most modern technology, so-called "English" fashions and prevailing contemporary attitudes as they feel that the influence of the modern world will distract them from the simple set of unwritten rules that God has established for them, which they call *Ordnung*. This is the reason that the Amish do not own televisions, computers, radios, or similarly modern devices, nor do they wear clothes that feature zippers, buttons, or snaps. Instead, the Amish ride in horse-drawn buggies and depending on which branch of the sect they belong to may also refrain from smoking and drinking. Federal law allows the

Amish to educate their children in small schoolhouses and they may remove their children from school at the age of 14 years.

The Amish do not baptize their members at birth as they believe it is up to each individual to decide whether they wish to belong to the church. Instead of being baptized as a baby, the Amish take a baptismal vow as an adult to follow the Ordnung lifestyle. At some time between the ages of roughly 16 and 22 years, young Amish adults must promise, before both God and their community, that they will be accountable to the church for the remainder of their lives, understanding that if they break their vow by wavering from the Ordnung way of life or straying from the church in some other way, they will suffer the opprobrium of their community and risk excommunication. It is a common misconception that Amish youths who refuse to join the Amish church will be shunned by their community for the rest of their lives—those who reject baptism are allowed to interact with family and community because they have not broken any religious vows. Only baptized Amish who later renounce the church face exclusion. The Amish do not punish those who leave the church prior to baptism.

The time between childhood and the moment when an Amish youth takes his or her baptismal vow is called Rumspringa. To most Amish people, Rumspringa equates to a period of adolescence during which youths can defy parental values and question the norms of their community while still living in the parental home. Indeed most Amish youths live with their parents during Rumspringa and join youth groups that crisscross their region, often but not always with adult chaperones, as they embark on contact with the non-Amish world. These youth groups often have 100 to 200 members and have names redolent of adventure and freedom such as The Drifters, The Shotguns, or The Bluebirds. However for some Amish people, Rumspringa represents a time when they can experience the modern, so-called "English" lifestyle free from the control of elders and, potentially, opt to leave their Amish community and live in the outside world.

As they are yet to be baptized, Amish youngsters have not taken vows to live by their church's way of life and so some Amish do use Rumspringa to explore other cultures and lifestyles. Traditionally, Amish youths are not subject to parental control on weekends and typically spend their time hiking, picnicking, playing various sports, or participating in "singings"—when several dozen Amish teenagers congregate at a home and sing for several hours followed by talking and eating. Singings are attended by both singles and couples and after a singing a boy may ask a girl on a first date by asking to drive her home in his buggy. If a relationship develops, dating couples will spend evenings at the girl's home and attend community social events. Because Amish marriages are not arranged, individuals may date several people before selecting a spouse. However both members of the couple must be baptized before they can marry.

During Rumspringa it is traditional for youths to enjoy activities including dating, swimming, ice-skating, playing volleyball, enjoying picnics, and participating in barn dances. However young Amish people may also opt to experience racier activity during Rumspringa such as wearing "English" fashions, going to the cinema, driving a car, and buying a television while also making friends outside the Amish community. In the most extreme cases, youths may travel beyond their communities to participate in activities, or even visit nightclubs and bars, or rent buildings for parties. Youths that choose this more rebellious behavior also tend to attend all-night parties featuring Amish bands that play electric instruments, dance, drink beer, smoke, and occasionally take recreational drugs. There have even been cases of this behavior leading to Amish youths who have experienced Rumspringa taking on the role of drug dealers within their communities. This has led rural law enforcement agencies to educate Amish elders about drugs such as cocaine, marijuana, and methamphetamine so that they in turn can teach their communities about the dangers of substance abuse, how to identify a pot farm and meth lab, and the legal consequences of producing, owning, using, and dealing drugs. A more frequent issue that arises from Rumspringa is alcohol abuse and drunk-driving as there have been several instances of Amish youths being arrested for driving buggies and cars while under the influence of alcohol. Amish elders frown upon such behavior and encourage authorities to punish the youths as severely as possible, especially if the behavior causes harm to others.

Unsurprisingly, Rumspringa behavior causes parents anxiety, as they do not know which lifestyle their child will decide to choose in the long run. Further, to this an Amish youth may take on part-time work to earn money during Rumspringa thereby coming into contact with non-Amish. This adds to the consternation felt by Amish parents during their child's Rumspringa as they do not know the type of people with whom their child is mixing and they fear the influence of these outsiders on their child. That said, an increasing number of Amish adults are mixing with the "English" as they take jobs as carpenters, furniture makers, and factory workers that necessitates mixing with outsiders.

As well as discovering the outside world, Rumspringa also sees Amish youths learn about themselves both physically and emotionally. It is not customary for Amish children to receive sex education at school and their daily life is gender segregated. During Rumspringa it is not unheard of for Amish youths to experience unprotected sexual activity, particularly after having drunk alcohol or taken drugs. The youths' lack of sex education sometimes results in cases of sexually transmitted diseases and unplanned pregnancies—occasionally weddings are arranged hurriedly because an unmarried Amish girl is expecting a baby. However the Amish strongly disagree with sexual relations before marriage and notwithstanding whether their partner was Amish or "English" such sexual activity places Amish girls in danger of punishment and even shunning. If a member of the Amish church breaks with church rules and refuses to confess to his or her transgression he or she faces excommunication. Taking their cue from several biblical passages, the Amish practice shunning, or *meidung*. How shunning is performed varies between Amish groups but it can take the form of refusing to eat ritual meals at a table with an excommunicated former member of their group, or generally refusing to interact with him or her socially. The Amish do not do this out of vindictiveness however. Rather, they hope to prompt the ex-member into confessing his or her sin. The degree to which parents shun their wayward children varies depending on the strictness of the group to which the parents belong. However shunned children rarely live in their parent's home though they are sometimes allowed to return to their community for weddings, funerals, and other public events.

Rumspringa also sees some Amish discover their true sexual orientation. Amish youth who discover that they are homosexual, bisexual, or transgender face a very difficult decision for if they come out as gay, lesbian, bisexual, or transgender they fear they will be shunned and so will have to leave behind both their family and church for the Amish religion is resistant to increasingly tolerant contemporary attitudes to LGBT rights and same-sex relationships. However if an Amish youth decides to stay in his or her community, the youth knows that he or she will have to remain "in the closet," conforming to the Amish way of life by marrying, having children, and following the social norms prescribed by Ordnung.

Despite the temptations of the non-Amish world, between 80 and 90 percent of Amish youth stay with their church and take their baptismal vows after experiencing Rumspringa. It has been suggested that the percentage is so high because Rumspringa impresses upon young Amish men and women that joining the church is a matter of free will and not something that is forced upon them. Also, it seems that the non-Amish lifestyle holds little appeal for Amish youngsters as a significant proportion of those who experience Rumspringa report that they felt a sense of emptiness in the "English" world. However others have argued that the youngsters' ties to their family and friends, plus economic concerns, prove too strong for the young to turn their back on their community. Those who do not take their baptismal vows tend to either drift away from their communities gradually or leave to escape abuse within their family or enter higher education. Most people who do leave the Amish church remain religious in some way and struggle to balance their inherent Amish sensibilities with "English" life.

See also: Baptism and Christening (Volume 1); Bed-Courtship; Courtship Whistling; Gap Year; Walkabout

Further Reading

Corporation for Public Broadcasting. "General Article: Top Ten FAQ?" PBS: American Experience. Accessed December 18, 2014, at http://www.pbs.org/wgbh/americanexperience/features/general-article/amish-faq/.

Galvan, Javier A., ed. *They Do What? A Cultural Encyclopedia of Extraordinary and Exotic Customs from around the World.* Santa Barbara, CA: ABC-CLIO, 2014.

LGBTAmish.com. "Home." Accessed December 17, 2014, at http://www.lgbtamish.com.

Stevick, Richard, A. *Growing Up Amish: The Teenage Years.* Baltimore, MA: The Johns Hopkins University Press, 2007.

WelcometoLancasterCounty.com. "Rumspringa." Accessed December 18, 2014, at http://www.welcome-to-lancaster-county.com/rumspringa.html.

RUSSEFEIRING, NORWAY, AND SCHOOLIES WEEK, AUSTRALIA

Russefeiring, often referred to by the abbreviated name of *russ*, is an unofficial annual rite of passage to adulthood for teenagers living in Norway. Russefeiring takes the form of three weeks of consecutive high-school graduation parties held before the summer examination period from April 26 to May 17, thus coinciding with Norwegian Constitution Day. During russefeiring teenagers wear color-coordinated overalls, participate in parades, and decorate their cars. However russefeiring parties are often fueled by alcohol and involve skinny-dipping, sexual experimentation, and flirting with law enforcement officers much to the disgrace of older Norwegians. The extremely boisterous nature of russefeiring is highlighted by the fact that the celebration is sometimes referred to by the name *truekersfylla* meaning "three-week binge."

The name russefeiring is usually thought to derive from two root words: russ, meaning graduating student, and feiring, which translates as celebration. However other etymology has been suggested. For instance some argue that the name may come from the Latin word *deprositurus*, which means taking off the horns and therefore recalls Norway's Viking past. The early history of russefeiring is not known though the general consensus among historians is that the tradition dates back to the 18th century when young Norwegians wishing to go to university in the Danish capital Copenhagen had to pass an entrance examination. After passing the exam, the Norwegian students were officially said to have graduated from high school. Russefeiring in its present form dates back to 1905 when graduating high-school students were presented with red caps to signify their change of status from adolescent to adult. Every Norwegian school had its own Russ committee consisting of elected pupils that helped to organize events. Elected pupils would be given titles such as Russ President, who was responsible for developing, printing, and managing a newspaper advertising the russ events that were to take place over the ensuing three weeks. Some of the russ information published included an official *knot* list detailing activities students hope to accomplish. Today students also create spoof Facebook sites on which members can log tongue-in-cheek statements about their hopes for their future after graduating from high school.

Perhaps the most eye-catching elements of russefeiring are the wearing of colorful overalls and the presentation of caps to mark the culmination of the three-week celebration. Students that participate in russefeiring are supposed to wear overalls in the color that signifies their area of study. For instance red, the most popular color, denotes general studies including math, history, and English, while blue signifies students who took economics and business administration, and black represents students who studied vocational studies such as computing and carpentry. Additionally, green overalls denote students who studied agriculture and white signifies students that studied medicine or sports. White can also denote students that do not drink alcohol for religious reasons. One particular quirk of the russefeiring overalls is that students are not supposed to remove the overalls except when sleeping, not even for washing.

Another well-known russefeiring custom sees graduating students create fake business cards called *russekort* that feature ridiculous information rather than real details, plus jokes. The cards are in no way to be taken seriously and are made purely for fun. Students hand out the cards to passing strangers and the cards always prove strangely entertaining to young children. Indeed young children look forward to russefeiring each year as they try to collect as many fake business cards as possible with the child that collects the most cards considered lucky by their friends. As well as wearing brightly colored overalls and making fake business cards, Norwegians enjoying russefeiring also buy vehicles that they then decorate. This particular element of russefeiring dates back to the 1950s when students would paint their cars either blue or red—the colors of the Norwegian flag along with white—so that the cars could enter into parades held to mark Norwegian Constitution Day, the National Day of Norway that is also a national holiday held annually on May 17. Over time, cars were replaced by vans and minibuses that students could afford by pooling their money together. Today students paint vans the same color as their overalls and decorate them with complex patterns as these help differentiate same colored vehicles from one another. Those who buy buses must choose a theme to follow when decorating their vehicle. The students then fix loud-speaker systems to the bus as well as special lighting systems. All this decorating comes at a high price for each student can expect to pay $6,000 on making their vehicle look russ-worthy. Indeed one bus can cost almost $400,000. In order to offset some of the cost, students approach businesses for sponsorship or donations toward their vehicles. Companies comply with sponsorship requests as having their names on the side of russ vehicles equates to a form of mobile advertising. At the end of the period of russefeiring, prizes are awarded to the owners of russ vehicles with prize categories including Most Creative Russebuss and Most Creative Russebuss Name. The modifications made to the russ vehicles means that in essence the vehicles become mobile party venues resulting in behavior of which many older Norwegians disapprove. The most contentious aspect of russefeiring is that nowadays students use the tradition as an excuse to drink huge quantities of alcohol. The legal drinking age in Norway is 18 years. This, combined with the fact that most Norwegians graduate from high school at 19 years of age, means that there is no legal measure to stop students from drinking heavily in celebration of leaving school. The high level of intoxication during russefeiring results in many road traffic accidents as students drive while under the influence of alcohol. Indeed so many accidents have been caused by drink-fueled drivers celebrating russefeiring that a regulation has been passed demanding that each russefeiring vehicle must have a designated driver who will not consume alcohol. As well as the alcohol-fueled road traffic accidents a great many Norwegian students also develop alcohol poisoning during russefeiring. However as Norwegian youngsters see heavy alcohol consumption as a matter of pride and as a group bonding experience symbolic of a lack of individual identity, it is unlikely that students enjoying russefeiring will stop their rowdy antics.

Further russefeiring controversy is caused by the fact that russefeiring caps feature russefeiring knots tied to their back—in this case the word knots refers to a series of mischievous tricks devised by the Russ committee that must be witnessed by one other person for the practitioner to win a prize. These pranks are controversial as they often include actions that are at best morally questionable or anti-social and at worst illegal. Some knot pranks are extremely mundane such as spending the night in a tree, for which students receive a stick as a reward; talking to a lamp-post for 10 minutes; wearing bread as shoes for a day; or eating a beef burger in two mouthfuls, thereby winning the burger wrapper as a prize. However the pranks itemized on the knot list become increasingly more daring. For example, downing a bottle of wine in less than 20 minutes earns a student a wine cork; if they drink 24 bottles of beer in 12 hours they earn a beer bottle cap. Other pranks in recent years have seen students run naked down high streets, enter into scuffles with police, or engage in sexual behavior such as having sex 17 times between May 1 and May 17 or having sex in a forest. It is not unknown for accusations of rapes to occur during russefeiring.

The three-week russefeiring period ends on the morning of May 17 when students are presented with their russ caps. In the afternoon the newly graduated students take part in a parade to celebrate Norwegian Constitution Day and then return home to study for their exams. It may seem strange to some that Norwegian students indulge in full-on partying just before taking final exams that determine whether or not they will graduate from high school. However any student who fails his or her exams has the consolation that they can re-sit the exams the next year and participate in russefeiring for a second time.

A similar custom to russefeiring occurs in Australia where so-called Schoolies or Schoolies Week (called Leaver's Week in Western Australia) sees those who have just graduated from high school indulge in week of summer parties in late November and early December. Many Australians consider Schoolies Week a cultural rite of passage, as it bridges the transition from school pupil to adult. This sense of rite of passage is marked by the most enduring Schoolies Week custom that sees school leavers run down to a beach and dive into the ocean. This dive into open water symbolizes that the students' schooling is finished forever.

After graduating from high school, young people emerge into the adult world, making their own life choices. Like russefeiring, Schoolies Week is a controversial celebration to mark the end of schooling and has been described by the Australian media as a holiday from hell involving teenage sex, drugs, alcohol, violence, and arrests, characterized by sexual assault, binging on illegal substances, and even death. It should be noted, however, that the Australian media was rebuked by government officials for describing Schoolies Week in such terms as it was felt this painted a picture of Australian youths as drunken, aggressive youths. The fact remains, however, that Schoolies Week is notorious for very high rates of binge drinking among school leavers though the number of school leavers binge drinking fell dramatically between 2000 and 2005, according to government statistics. This decline was probably due to the fact that teetotalism started to be seen as cool and responsible behavior.

Schoolies Week is also a major tourism event within Australia. The school-leaving celebration was first held at Broadbeach on Australia's Gold Coast in the 1970s. Today Schoolies Week celebrations are concentrated on the Gold Coast location of Surfers Paradise. Schoolies Week tends to center on Gold Coast locations because the Gold Coast has a reputation for controversial, sexual liberalism beginning with notorious so-called "pyjama parties" in the 1950s during which teenagers danced with each other while wearing sleepwear, the wearing of tiny bikinis in the 1960s, and later topless bathing. Such is the rowdy reputation of Schoolies Week on the Gold Coast that some tourists are deterred from going to the area during the summer. Since 1995 the Gold Coast City Council and Queensland State Government have provided organized entertainment for Schoolies Week revelers to try to calm down events and minimize loutish behavior. Since the early 1990s, other Queensland destinations have also become associated with the occasion, including Mooloolaba on the Sunshine Coast, and other Queensland locales such as Airlie Beach on the Whitsunday Coast and Magnetic Island.

Outside of Queensland, Schoolies week destinations include Byron Bay, Coffs Harbor, and Port Macquarie, while in the state of Victoria destinations include Lorne and Torquay. In South Australia, the only Schoolies Week destination is Victor Harbor though this is the second largest Schoolies Week destination in Australia. Outside of Australia Schoolies Week is rapidly becoming popular in Bali, Fiji, and Vanuatu.

See also: Inter-Railing; RAG Week; *Rumspringa*; Twenty-First Birthday Traditions

Further Reading

Galvan, Javier A., ed. *They Do What? A Cultural Encyclopedia of Extraordinary and Exotic Customs from around the World*. Santa Barbara, CA: ABC-CLIO, 2014.

Kelly, Peter, Jenny Advocat, Lyn Harrison, and Christopher Hickey, eds., *Smashed!: The Many Meanings of Intoxication and Drunkenness*. Clayton, Australia: Monash University Publishing, 2011.

Klatt, Morgan. "Russefeiring." Living in Oslo. Accessed January 4, 2015, at http://morganklatt.blogspot.co.uk/2012/04/russefeiring.html.

Mostar.me. "Russ Knots." Accessed January 4, 2015, at http://mostar.me/wp-content/uploads/2012/11/RussK.pdf.

Prideaux, Bruce, Gianna Moscardo, and Eric Laws, eds. *Managing Tourism and Hospitality Services: Theory and International Applications*. Oxfordshire, UK: CAB International, 2006.

S

SAME-SEX MARRIAGE, INTERNATIONAL

Same-sex marriage (also referred to as gay marriage, marriage for gays and lesbians, equal marriage, civil unions, or civil partnerships) is the marriage between two people of the same sex that love each other in a romantic way. Same-sex marriage may be achieved either through a secular civil ceremony or through a wedding in a religious setting.

The first law allowing marriage between people of the same sex was enacted in 2001 in the Netherlands. Many other countries have since legalized same-sex marriage including Argentina, Belgium, Brazil, Canada, Denmark, Finland, France, Iceland, Ireland, Luxembourg, Mexico (in certain jurisdictions), New Zealand, Norway, Portugal, Slovenia, South Africa, Spain, Sweden, Uruguay, United Kingdom (in England, Scotland, and Wales), and the United States and its territories. In May 2015, Ireland became the first country in the world to introduce same-sex marriage via a popular vote. More than 62 percent of people that voted did so in favor of legalizing same-sex marriage. This came some 22 years after Ireland decriminalized homosexual acts. The parliament in Greenland (an autonomous territory belonging to Denmark) also unanimously approved same-sex marriage and adoption in May 2015.

Though same-sex marriage may seem a very 21st-century concern, formal religious ceremonies in which two people of the same sex who love each other were wedded together for life can be found worldwide throughout history. For example, same-sex unions were known in ancient Greece and ancient Rome. The acceptance of same-sex relationships in ancient Rome is evident in the fact that the Roman Emperor Hadrian had matching marble statues made of himself and his lover Antinous.

Meanwhile, throughout the Ming dynasty period females living in the Chinese province of Fujian could bind themselves in contracts to younger females through elaborate ceremonies, as could males. Similar arrangements existed in ancient European history as well. Native American peoples such as the Sac and Fox nations revered shamans known as Two-Spirit (formerly known as *berdache*). The term Two-Spirit is applied to intersex or androgynous people, who in the past, were commonly married to members of the same sex. For instance, androgynous or effeminate men would be married to masculine men, while masculine females were given feminine women as wives. Rather than focusing on the homosexuality of Two-Spirit people, however, many Native Americans instead emphasized their spirituality. According to traditional Native American beliefs, a person's basic character is a reflection of their inner spirit. Because every living thing is considered to originate from the spirit world, androgynous and transgender people are felt to be doubly blessed as they are viewed as having the spirit of a man as well as the spirit of a woman. Also as they are seen as having two spirits they are believed to be more spiritually remarkable than a masculine male or feminine female. Traditionally, Two-Spirit people helped care for children and the elderly and often served as adoptive parents for abandoned children. During the 20th century, however, homophobia increased among many Native Americans as a result of the European Christian influence upon Native Americans. This homophobia meant that the respect and admiration with which Native American communities traditionally regarded Two-Spirit peoples was greatly reduced. Christian missionaries, government officials, and tribal elders often forced Two-Spirit individuals to conform to fit prevailing gender roles. Moreover the imposition of European American marriage laws on Native Americans meant that Two-Spirit same-sex marriages were no longer considered legal. The renewal of Native American cultural pride that has occurred since the 1960s, coupled with the rise of gay and lesbian rights movements, has resulted in a revival of respect for Two-Spirit people among Native Americans.

Across Europe, from the classical era through the end of the Middle Ages royalty, aristocrats, soldiers, and others would enter into formal unions of sworn brotherhood through rituals that allowed men to express their regard for one another. In Renaissance Italy, although it was socially acceptable for same-sex lovers to live together it was illegal. For example in 1497, an apothecary was banished from Florence for living with another man as husband and wife because the couple had broken the law by swearing upon a Bible to be faithful to each other while standing in front of an altar. The fact that even those officials that punished the pair considered them to be married highlighted the contradiction between the general population's view of same-sex marriage and the view taken of such unions by the law. In the Christian West, same-sex marriage, however, was largely the preserve of women. Some time after 1600, Dutch scholars Rudolf Dekker and Lotte van de Pol recorded instances of so-called female husbands living in England, Germany, and the Netherlands. Moreover in the early 1730s, two women decided to move from a village just north of London, England, to east London in order to escape blackmailers and to live together as husband and wife. The women ran a pub, with one of the two women dressing as a man and calling herself James. The pair became successful publicans and pillars of their community as everybody presumed that they were legally married.

By the beginning of the 21st century, same-sex marriage had become increasingly accepted. For instance, the Pew Research Center carried out a poll in 2001 that found that Americans were against same-sex marriage by a 57 percent to 35 percent margin. By 2015, however, support for same-sex marriage had increased so that 55 percent of Americans supported same-sex marriage while 39 percent opposed the idea. Despite this growing acceptance, organizations such as the

National Organization for Marriage (NOM) continue to oppose same-sex marriage arguing that marriage should be the union of one man and one woman. Same-sex marriage is a contentious issue for many people who look at the subject from a political or religious viewpoint.

As a result of this contentiousness, debates continue over whether people in same-sex relationships should be allowed to marry and if so what the status of partners should be. Same-sex marriage can provide same-sex partners with comparable status to those in mixed-sex marriages with regards to state benefits and taxes paid to the governments for services. Same-sex marriage also gives same-sex partners legal protections in matters such as inheritance and hospital visitations.

People opposed to same-sex marriages often argue against such marriages from a religious standpoint. For instance, same-sex marriage is not allowed in most Muslim countries. Indeed in many Muslim nations same-sex relationships (let alone same-sex marriage) are viewed as sinful and may see participants punished—sometimes by being put to death. The Catholic Church is also opposed to same-sex marriage on the grounds that marriage is the conduit through which the grace of God flows to a couple as well as the children that they produce while they are married. The Catholic Church also views marriage as a sacrament that is important both religiously and socially. Many conservative Catholics argue that the Bible compares the relationship between a husband and wife to that between Christ and the Church. Since the Catholic Church sees marriage as a holy sacrament it feels, therefore, that marriage must be treated with respect and defended from any change that might cause it harm.

One of the main arguments put forward by opponents of same-sex marriage is that the main purpose of the institution of marriage is to produce children and that since gay men and lesbians either cannot or may not produce offspring they should not be permitted to wed. Critics of this argument point out, however, that many same-sex couples do have children while some mixed-sex marriages do not produce children yet are still legal. It should be noted that some Catholics are distressed by mixed-sex couples that choose not to have children on the grounds that these couples are guilty of profoundly disturbing the essence of the sexual act, the main purpose of which is to bring forth children. With regards to the rearing of children within a same-sex marriage, opponents of same-sex marriage argue that same-sex marriages undermine the right of a child to be raised by both of their biological parents. Conversely, many advocates of same-sex marriage contend that the financial, psychological, and physical well-being of children is increased by allowing same-sex marriage for they point to evidence that children benefit from being raised by two parents within a lawful union.

Another primary objection to same-sex marriage raised by critics is that same-sex marriage damages the institution of marriage in general. This argument is sometimes termed the slippery slope argument as critics of same-sex marriage suggest that by allowing two men or two women to marry each other the state paves the way for other non-traditional marriages—for example for a man to marry a dog or a woman to marry a cat. Also, say critics, same-sex marriage might lead to unions in which, for example, two men marry three women.

See also: *Hijra*; Initiation by Semen Transferal; Jumping Over the Broom; *Nyumba Ntobhu*: Traditional Same-Sex Marriage; Same-Sex Civil Partnership Ceremony Text, United Kingdom

Further Reading

Catholic Answers. "Gay Marriage." Documents. Accessed November 23, 2015, at http://www.catholic.com/documents/gay-marriage.

Dabhoiwala, Faramerz. "The Secret History of Same-sex Marriage," *The Guardian*, January 23, 2015. Accessed November 22, 2015, at http://www.theguardian.com/books/2015/jan/23/-sp-secret-history-same-sex-marriage.

Heaphy, Brian, Carol Smart, and Anna Einarsdottir. *Same Sex Marriages: New Generations, New Relationships*. Basingstoke, UK: Palgrave Macmillan, 2013.

McDonald, Henry. "Ireland Becomes First Country to Legalise Gay Marriage by Popular Vote," *The Guardian*, May 23, 2015. Accessed November 23, 2015, at http://www.theguardian.com/world/2015/may/23/gay-marriage-ireland-yes-vote.

Monger, George P. *Marriage Customs of the World: From Henna to Honeymoons*. Santa Barbara, CA: ABC-CLIO, 2004.

National Organization for Marriage. "Our Work." Accessed November 22, 2015, at https://nationformarriage.org/main/ourwork.

Newton, David E. *Gay and Lesbian Rights: A Reference Handbook*. Second edition. Santa Barbara, CA: ABC-CLIO, 2009.

Newton, David E. *Same Sex Marriage: A Reference Handbook*. Santa Barbara, CA: ABC-CLIO, 2010.

Pew Research Center. "Gay Marriage around the World." Accessed November 22, 2015, at http://www.pewforum.org/2015/06/26/gay-marriage-around-the-world-2013/.

Rocke, Michael. *Forbidden Friendships: Homosexuality and Male Culture in Renaissance Florence*. Oxford, UK: Oxford University Press, 1996.

Spilsbury, Louise. *Same-Sex Marriage*. New York: The Rosen Publishing Group, 2010.

Vicinus, Martha. "'They Wonder to Which Sex I Belong': The Historical Roots of the Modern Lesbian Identity," in Henry Abelove, Michèle Aina Barale, and David M. Halperin, eds., *The Lesbian and Gay Studies Reader*, 432–452. New York: Routledge, 1993.

William, Walter L. "The 'Two-Spirit' People of Indigenous North Americans," *The Guardian*, October 11, 2010. Accessed November 23, 2015, at http://www.theguardian.com/music/2010/oct/11/two-spirit-people-north-america.

Related Primary Document: Same-Sex Civil Partnership Ceremony Text, United Kingdom

Same-sex marriage is the marriage between two people of the same sex that love each other in a romantic way. In some areas of the world, such as the United Kingdom, a same-sex marriage is sometimes referred to as a civil partnership. Same-sex marriage

may take the form of a secular civil ceremony or a wedding in a religious setting. In the United Kingdom the words spoken by the person officiating the ceremony may take the form of the 2012 script template, below, known as The Lordship that notes the legality of the couple's loving union. When writing a script for their ceremony a same-sex couple wishing to marry in the London borough of Haringey must ensure all words in italics feature in their ceremony and the ceremony must follow in the order described below. The ceremony must not include any religious content and must fit within a maximum 40-minute timeframe. The Superintendent Registrar or a Deputy Registrar must approve all same-sex marriage scripts at least seven working days before the ceremony.

The Lordship

Good Morning / Afternoon ladies and gentleman, my name is ENTER NAME, welcome to ENTER NAME OF VENUE for the Civil Partnership Ceremony of………… and…………..

This place in which we are now met has been duly sanctioned according to law for the registration of Civil Partnerships. If any person present knows of any lawful impediment to this partnership they should declare it now.

Today marks the beginning of the rest of ………and…………. lives together.

By entering into a Civil Partnership today the bond between this couple will grow stronger day by day, month by month and year after year.

These two people will build upon the love and commitment they have already shown to one another. Love that has brought us all here for this celebration today.

COUPLE STAND

OPTION FOR COUPLE TO READ A FEW WORDS TO ONE ANOTHER

………………..and……………….today is a moment in history for both of you.

In the presence of your witnesses, friends and family the words that you say today complete the foundations for a long and happy future together for both of you. You both bring with you happy memories from the past and the future is set for you to have many more special times together.

COUPLE STAND

……………..and……………. the words that you are both about to say declare your love and commitment to one another.

PARTNER 1

I promise that I will be there for you ENTER PARTNER 2 NAME each and every day

In good times and bad I will be by your side

I will be your guardian, your partner and support you on our lifelong journey together.

PARTNER 2

I promise that I will be there for you ENTER PARTNER 1 NAME each and every day

In good times and bad I will be by your side. I will be your guardian, your partner and support you on our lifelong journey together.

ALL STAND

WITH RINGS START HERE

Ladies and gentlemen ……….and………….have brought rings with them today.

The full circle of the rings symbolises the complete love between two people.

……………..and……………….. will now exchange rings and say the words that will formally declare them both civil partners in law.

PARTNER 1

I give you this ring as a symbol of my love and commitment to you

I will wear it with pride at all times each and every day

PARTNER 2

I give you this ring as a symbol of my love and commitment to you

I will wear it with pride at all times each and every day

WITHOUT RINGS START HERE

PARTNER 1

I promise to be open and truthful with you and

No distance or obstacle will get in our way

With love from the deepest of my heart

I …………….. take you …………….. to be my civil partner in law.

PARTNER 2

I promise to be open and truthful with you and

No distance or obstacle will get in our way

With love from the deepest of my heart

I…………….. take you …………….. to be my civil partner in law.

Ladies and gentlemen the couple are about to sign the schedule that will make them legal civil partners.

………………..and……………….. please read back to me together the following words before you sign your schedule today.

I declare that I know not of any legal reason why we may not register as each others partner. I understand that on signing this document we will be forming a civil partnership with each other.

...................and......................you have both demonstrated your lifelong commitment to one another today.

In the presence of your friends, family and witnesses it gives me great pleasure in declaring that you are now both civil partners to one another.

Congratulations,

ROUND OF APPLAUSE

Source: *Haringey Civil Partnership Scripts March 2012. Haringey Council Services. Available at http://www.haringey.gov.uk/sites/haringeygovuk/files/civil_partnership_scripts-2.pdf.*

SAN-SAN-KUDO, JAPAN

San-san-kudo, meaning three-three-nine times and also written as san san kudo or sansan-kudo, is one of Japan's oldest wedding customs. As such, san-san-kudo is a binding ceremony involving the ritualized drinking of the rice wine *sake* and is considered by some to be the most important element of a Shinto wedding, often taking place in Shinto temples. A san-san-kudo ceremony can also be an element of Western-style weddings or Japanese Buddhist weddings, but in this case the san-san-kudo ceremony takes place at the reception and is not the actual wedding ceremony. Traditionally, however, the san-san-kudo ceremony is the only formal, requisite part of a Shinto marriage ceremony. Unlike many wedding celebrations, the san-san-kudo ceremony is a somber affair that lasts around 40 minutes and is usually recorded for posterity.

The san-san-kudo tradition began in the 1600s and is a ceremony rich in symbolism and meaning. The ceremony is presided over by the future bride and groom and both parents of each—if the couple met through a matchmaker then the matchmaker may also be invited to the ceremony. For the ceremony, three ceremonial sake cups called *sakazuiki*, each of which is slightly bigger than the other, are stacked one on top of the other in ascending order with the largest cup at the bottom of the stack. The cups are placed on a plain wooden table and then filled with the rice wine poured from a sake pot. Each person present then takes three sips of sake from the three cups. The groom takes the top cup and then cups are swapped amongst the drinkers. The initial three sips symbolize the three couples present—the betrothed couple, the groom's parents and the bride's parents. The second three sips represent the three human weaknesses of passion, hatred, and ignorance. The number three is important to the ceremony because three is not divisible by two and is therefore regarded as a lucky number at Japanese festivities, especially during nuptial events. The *ku* element of the word kudo refers to the number nine, which is considered a lucky number in Japanese culture, while the end part of the word—*do*—means deliverance from the three human faults. Drinking the sake slowly in small sips and swapping the cups is a highly symbolic act representing the patience that must exist between a husband and wife and symbolizes the perseverance needed to make a marriage successful.

Apart from the ritualistic drinking of sake another important part of the san-san-kudo custom is the forming of a special rosary. The rosary features 21 beads that symbolize the bride and groom, both sets of the couple's parents, and the Buddha all strung along one length, thereby representing the joining of the two families. As well as the drinking of sake and the fashioning of the rosary, the two families also honor each other by proffering flowers, toasting each other, and writing a letter that expresses their thankfulness and love for each other now that they will be united. Another highlight of the event is the making of gold origami cranes. In Japanese custom, the crane is representative of endurance and success and so to mark the san-san-kudo ceremony 1,001 paper cranes are folded to confer good luck, permanency, loyalty, and harmony to the upcoming marriage. Sometimes a san-san-kudo ceremony also sees couples offer twigs from the sacred tree of the Shinto gods, *Sakaki*.

On the day of the san-san-kudo ceremony the bride-to-be wears two different outfits. The first is a white kimono called a *shiro*, which the bride wears during the actual ceremony. Later, for the post-ceremony reception, the bride changes into an elaborate brocade kimono called a *uchikake* kimono. Traditionally, the bride wears her hair tied in a bun accessorized with colorful *kanzashi* decorations as well as a white wedding hook known as the *tsuno kakushi*. This is worn to conceal the two golden horns at the front of the tsuno kakushi that symbolize the bride's deference to her husband. To complete her outfit, the bride carries a very small purse called a *hakoseko*, a little sheathed sword called a *kaiken*, and a fan that is worn attached to the bride's obi belt, which symbolizes the bride's happiness and future well-being.

At the reception many different food courses are served, though never multiples of four courses as the Japanese word for the number four sounds very similar to the word for death. In keeping with the heavy symbolism of the san-san-kudo ceremony, the foods served at the reception tend to be symbolic. For instance lobster is often served as the shellfish is red when cooked and red is the Japanese color of good luck while clams are also popular on account that their hinged shell represents the union of two individual entities just as marriage will unite the bride and groom and their families.

Though the san-san-kudo ceremony is normally associated with weddings in Japan, the ceremony can also be used to forge a deep and lasting bond between two unrelated people. To this end, the ceremony is sometimes enacted to deepen the ties between new geishas (i.e., female entertainers who perform and converse with male customers) and those that have been in the role for longer. For instance, in the Japanese city of Kyoto the san-san-kudo ceremony is used as an initiation ceremony for new geishas and sees the new geisha exchange cups of sake with her sister geishas. The Japanese term *en musubi*, which refers to the tying together of fates, is used to describe the san-san-kudo ceremony when it is performed to bond together geishas and the same term is applied to marriages in Japan.

See also: Coming of Age Day; Log Riding; *Omiai*

Further Reading
Beau-coup Favors Inc. "Japanese Wedding Traditions and Customs." Accessed April 18, 2015, at http://www.beau-coup.com/japanese-wedding-traditions.htm.
Dalby, Liza. *Geisha*. Updated edition. Berkeley: University of California Press, 2008.
Japanese Style Inc. "Japanese Wedding Traditions: San San Kudo." Japanese Style. Accessed April 18, 2015, at http://www.japanesestyle.com/archive/partywedding/japanese-wedding-traditions-san-san-kudo.
Nakamaki, Hirochika. *Japanese Religions at Home and Abroad: Anthropological Perspectives*. Abingdon, UK: Routledge, 2003.
Thomas, G. M. *Extremes: Contradictions in Contemporary Japan: A Modern Journey across Japan*. E-version. London: Kaichan Europe, 2013

SCARIFICATION, AFRICA AND PAPUA NEW GUINEA

Scarification is the deliberate scarring of the flesh. This can be done for several reasons—as a form of body art, to show that an individual has reached adulthood, or to signal that the scarred person is ready to marry. Additionally, scarification can indicate that a person is protected by the gods, that he or she is a hunter or a parent, or that a person is able to endure suffering. Scarification can also reveal to which tribe or cultural group an individual belongs. Scarification mostly occurs in West Africa and in Papua New Guinea. Scarification was a widespread Aboriginal custom in Australia but nowadays is confined to people living in areas of Arnhem Land in the Northern Territory. There, young men and women, usually around the age of 16 or 17 years, receive cuts on their chests, shoulders, and stomachs.

There is a very long history of scarification in Africa. Rock paintings depicting the process that are between 7,000 and 10,000 years old have been located in the Sahara Desert. During the 18th and 19th centuries, when the Transatlantic slave trade saw millions of Africans captured and sent to the Americas as slaves, tribes would mark the faces of their children in order to indicate to which tribe or family a child belonged if the child was forced into slavery and later needed identifying.

Usually scarification begins during adolescence as part of a child's rite of passage to adulthood. However some groups, such as Benin's Bétamarribé people, scar their children. Bétamarribé children have their faces, legs, chests, stomachs, backs, and shoulders scarred to reveal their social status. When Bétamarribé children stop taking milk from their mothers, usually at around two years of age, they receive their first scars in the form of a delicate pattern of lines that covers their face. The scars are made by an *odouti*, or traveling scarmaster/mistress, who decides which pattern a child should receive. The odouti determines the correct pattern by throwing shells called *cowries* into a bucket of water. The pattern that the shells create in the water informs the odouti as to which of their repertoire of scars they should make on the child. The scarring takes place outdoors, often in the shade of a tree so that the child can lie on a bed of leaves. The odouti makes the scars using a small, sharp tool called a *teponte* that he or she uses to create rows of little cuts into the skin in intricate patterns. The process takes about 30 minutes to complete, which is less time than it takes to scar a teenager or adult. When the pattern of scars is complete, the cuts are cleaned and treated with skin-nourishing shea butter. The odouti also spits into the cuts as the saliva, like the shea butter, is thought to repel evil spirits that may have been attracted by the scent of the child's blood. After this the cuts are left to heal over, resulting in scars.

Scarification takes place without any anesthetic and is a painful, bloody procedure. Children are permitted to scream, cry, and curse the odouti while their parents look on. Some members of the Bétamarribé find watching the scarification of children so distressing that they do not allow their own children to receive the ritual scars. However there are many reasons Bétamarribé parents do allow their child to experience scarification. At the most basic level, scarification shows that a child belongs to their tribe. If a Bétamarribé child dies before it receives the ritual marks then he or she would not be considered to be Bétamarribé by ancestral spirits and the child would not be allowed to be buried in the village graveyard. Scarification also honors ancestors and offers the child divine protection. The Bétamarribé, like other African tribes that perform scarification, particularly the Baule and Senofo of Côte d'Ivoire and the Bafia of Cameroon, feel that scarification makes an individual human. These tribes also think that scars make people look beautiful as the decorations distinguish scarred skin from the unmarked natural skin of other species. If a tribesperson does not display scarring then they will find it difficult to attract a spouse. The Baule and Senofo both favor a pattern of lines that radiate outward from the mouth as these markings are supposed to protect their children from evil spirits and harm in general. The Baule also think that some scars protect against enchantment and disease as long as a small amount of poison is injected into the scar. This is known as a *kanga* mark.

When adolescents or adults undergo the scarification process they must bear the pain stoically in order to show that they are resilient and can stand the discomfort. At adolescence, Bétamarribé boys undergo an initiation ritual during which scars are made on their chests and stomachs in order to show that they have attained adulthood. Boys belonging to the Dinka tribe of South Sudan receive a pattern of horizontal marks across their foreheads to show that they have reached adulthood.

Adolescent Bétamarribé girls also receive scars on their stomachs as well as their lower backs and buttocks. The scars reveal that the girl is an adult, old enough to marry. When she marries, the girls receives further scars on her shoulder blades and when she becomes pregnant for the first time the girl undergoes further scarification. The Ga'anda people of northeastern Nigeria carry out scarification on their daughters when the girls are aged around five years old. The ritual scarring, called *hleeta*, sees the girl scarred on her stomach, buttocks, chest, back, forehead, legs, and arms. The ritual takes place over six stages held at two-year increments. Hleeta is part of the process of arranged marriage that takes place when the ritual scarification is completed. The scars are also supposed to show that adulthood can only be achieved through pain. Contrastingly, the Ga'anda do not scar their sons. Instead Ga'anda boys experience their own three-month long initiation ritual, *sapta*, during which time they are whipped and experience psychological torments. Meanwhile among the Nuba of southern Sudan, girls undergo scarification to signify important life-events such as menstruation and the birth of their first child. The scars received by a Nuba woman usually run from her breasts to her navel, plus marks on her arms, back, legs, and neck. Nuba men also undergo scarification on their arms and torsos to signify that they have achieved manhood.

In addition to wanting to signify that a community member has become an adult, some African tribes perform scarification as a beautification process. For example, the Barabaig of Tanzania cut the faces of boys in such a way as to emphasize the contours of their faces. These cuts are very deep, resulting in scarring to the skull. Similarly, the Tiv people of Nigeria scar their faces with long, straight lines along their cheekbones in order to highlight their attractive bone structure. The Tiv's scarification is purely decorative and men also receive cuts to their arms, legs, and backs. The scars are made in geometric patterns and to simulate animal markings.

In the Sepik region of Papua New Guinea, boys belonging to the Chambri tribe undergo scarification as a part of their initiation rite into manhood, a rite that can take place at any age but usually between the ages of 11 and 30. Chambri scarification is intended to create scars that represent crocodile scales as well as to test the boys' self-restraint and strength. The crocodile is a highly important spiritual and symbolic animal in Papua New Guinea, and the Chambri believe that they are descended from crocodiles for their folklore tells the story of crocodiles that migrated from the Sepik River onto land and eventually become humans. The Sepik River runs parallel with Chambri Lake close to where the Chambri tribe lives spread over three villages—Indingai, Killimbit, and Wombum. Some boys and young men from Palembei village in east Sepik also take part in the ritual.

In recognition of this ancestral connection the scars resulting from the initiation ceremony symbolize the teeth marks of the crocodile that has "swallowed" the initiate during the ritual. The scars inflicted on the young men consist of hundreds of deep cuts in cascading patterns down their backs, arms, chest, and buttocks to give their skin the look and feel of a crocodile's body.

The scarring procedure is extremely painful and the young men must display discipline, focus, and dedication. It is not unknown for initiates to die during the procedure and knowing this some initiates are understandably fearful before the procedure starts. To begin the ceremony an initiate goes to his uncle in a special building called the spirit house where he stays for six weeks before the rite takes place. On the day of the ceremony the initiate is held down while tribal leaders make hundreds of slices 2 centimeters (about 0.7 inches) long into the boy's skin using a piece of bamboo. The process takes place without the use of anesthetics and the only pain relief that boys receive is a medicinal plant that the boys chew. The young man must remain stoic during the scarification to demonstrate that he has enough strength to be considered a man. Once the cuts have been made, the boy lies near a fire so that smoke can blow on his open wounds and clay and tree oil are pushed into the cuts. This sculpts the scars so that they stay raised above the surface of the skin when healed. When the scarification process is over the newly scarred boy is adorned with tribal jewelry and a headdress to signify that he has become a man.

In the Solomon Islands, the ritual scarification of boys and girls, *segesege*, takes place to mark their transition from childhood to adulthood—girls also undergo full-body tattooing. Today, however, it is young children who experience segesege, rather than adolescents. This is probably because it is easier to persuade a child to undergo the process than it is to get a teenager to agree to be cut. Parents of children who undergo segesege see their social status rise while their children's markings mean that they are regarded as particularly beautiful by other parents.

See also: Female Genital Cutting; Forehead-Cutting Initiation; *Pika* and *Nyora*; Ritual Tattooing

Further Reading

Brooks, Katherine. "This Is the Last Generation of Scarification in Africa," *Huffpost Arts & Culture*, September 23, 2014. Accessed December 27, 2014, at http://www.huffingtonpost.com/2014/09/23/scarification_n_5850882.html.

Cheer, Louise. "Agonising Rites of the Crocmen: Boys Are Cut So That the Scars Look Like Crocodile Scales in Tribal Initiation into Manhood," *Daily Mail*, August 12, 2014. Accessed December 27, 2014, at http://www.dailymail.co.uk/news/article-2722740/The-ancient-initiation-ritual-scars-boys-look-like-crocodiles.html.

DeMello, Margo. *Encyclopedia of Body Adornment*. Westport, CT: Greenwood Publishing Group Inc., 2007.

DeMello, Margo. *Faces around the World: A Cultural Encyclopedia of the Human Face*. Santa Barbara, CA: ABC-CLIO, 2012.

Galvan, Javier A., ed. *They Do What? A Cultural Encyclopedia of Extraordinary and Exotic Customs from around the World*. Santa Barbara, CA: ABC-CLIO, 2014.

Guynup, Sharon. "Scarification: Ancient Body Art Leaving New Marks." National Geographic Channel, 2004. Accessed December 27, 2014, at http://news.nationalgeographic.com/news/2004/07/0728_040728_tvtabooscars.html.

National Geographic Society. "Crocodile Scars." 2014. Accessed December 27, 2014, at http://video.nationalgeographic.com/video/newguinea-crocscars-pp.

News Limited. "Crocodile Scarification Is an Ancient Initiation Practised by the Chambri Tribe of Papua New Guinea." News.com.au, August 13, 2014. Accessed December 27, 2014, at http://www.news.com.au/travel/world-travel/crocodile-scarification-is-an-ancient-initiation-practised-by-the-chambri-tribe-of-papua-new-guinea/story-e6frfqai-1227021565106.

SCHUHPLATTLER AND LÄNDLER, GERMANY AND AUSTRIA

In the human world, dance has been ritualized and standardized as a way to celebrate joy, express devotion, and also to attract others. Over time dance has evolved as a way to demonstrate physical fitness, mental capability, and potential fertility. Each step, bend, spin, tap, throw, gesture, and movement conveys a different meaning. Achieving coordinated dance necessitates the possession of energy, flexibility, balance, muscularity, and spatial awareness and dance ability reveals levels of physical fitness, stamina, and the brain's power of motor control. In addition certain sets of movements in dance, and indeed some dances, are provocative and downright flirtatious.

Schuhplattler, meaning shoe-slapping or slap-dancing, is a folk courtship dance performed by males that is popular in the Alpine regions of Germany and Austria as well as in the Tyrol region that spreads across Austria and Italy. In the Tyrol, the dance is often accompanied by yodeling. Schuhplattler is also performed in the United Kingdom and the United States in areas where people with German heritage have settled, such as Anaheim, California. The name Schuhplattler is thought to have its origins in the fact that during the dance performers strike the soles of their shoes (*schuhe*) with their hands held flat (*platt*). Performing the Schuhplattler is referred to as *plattling*. There are around 150 different forms of Schuhplattler, demonstrating many regional variations.

As Schuhplattler is a folk dance it is difficult to determine its exact history, though dance historians think it was invented by hunters, farmers, and woodsmen who sought to imitate a male bird, the *Auerhahn*, or native Bavarian black grouse, that spins in a circle while flapping its wings and kicking its feet as a mating display. The poem *Ruodlieb,* written by a Bavarian monk living just south of Munich in 1050, details a dance very similar to an early form of Schuhplattler. When the Empress Consort of Russia, Alexandra Feodorovna (born Princess Charlotte of Prussia), visited a spa in nearby Wildbad Kreuth in 1838 locals performed a dance very like the Schuhplattler in her honor. The dance was performed to the folk tune *Laendler* and saw boys improvise moves including leaps, stomps, and stamps while girls rotated in time with the music beside the boys. At the time this improvised form of Schuhplattler was known as Bavarian dancing. By the mid-19th century, the Schuhplattler had become increasingly standardized. Though there are very many variations of Schuhplattler in general the dance is characterized by boys jumping up and down and slapping the soles of their shoes and various parts of their bodies (usually their thighs, buttocks, knees, and cheeks) percussively in order to create highly complicated syncopated rhythms in an exhausting display. Dancers also may slap other dancers as well as the leather shorts (*lederhosen*) that are traditionally worn by boys dancing the Schuhplattler in an attempt to create more noise. Meanwhile, girls twirl in circles slowly and coyly in the center of the dancing boys. These boisterous movements derive from ancient animal dances and mimic the mating Auerhahn. Two basic versions of the Schuhplattler developed over time. One version saw two men who imitate amorous strutting birds as they fight aiming to impress the female of the species. The second version of the Schuhplattler was intended for a male/female couple. In this version, the girl plays the role of the demure hen, simultaneously encouraging and resisting the male's sexual advances. Though a dance for couples, this version of the Schuhplattler did not see the pair touch until near the end of the dance when the male eventually managed to impress the female with his dancing abilities. Once the female had been won over the couple would move on to dance the final part of the Schuhplattler when they would dance together in the waltz-like *Ländler*. A group version of Schuhplattler also began to be performed as so-called group plattling with an exhibition of group plattling performed in 1858 in Upper Bavaria to honor a visit by King Max II. Young men from Ramsau who created increasingly complicated routines developed the group version of Schuhplattler further. Indeed the routines were so complex that the boys started to learn them without the presence of girls who might prove a distraction and soon the boys went a step further by foregoing the female element totally during both rehearsals and performances. This all-male version of group Schuhplattler quickly proved popular and members of the Schuhplattler Society of Miesbach, established in 1866 in Miesbach south of Munich, near Germany's border with Austria, were soon seen as the main practitioners of this form of the dance. The next important milestone in the history of Schuhplattler came in 1883 when Joseph Vogl founded the Club for Preservation of Folk Costume in the Leizach Valley in nearby Bayrischzell. Since then the club has regulated all aspects of Schuhplattler and developed the folk costumes that are associated with the dance today.

During the early 20th century the German youth movement *Wandervogel* took up the Schuhplattler as they traveled around Germany performing folk dances and songs and playing folk music on guitars. Eventually the Wandervogel were suppressed by the Nazis who supplanted the group with the Hitler Youth and claimed the Schuhplattler as an exemplar of German culture for the purposes of pro-Nazi propaganda.

Over time, the final section of the Schuhplattler, the Ländler, developed into its own dance, a slow-step waltz, in which the male would place his hands on the woman's waist while the woman placed her hands on the man's shoulders. Yodeling or singing and the playing of traditional folk instruments often accompanied the dance inspiring couples to perform swinging movements, jumps, and lifts. Indeed the climax of the dance saw the man lift the woman forcefully into the air before bringing her gently back down to the ground to signal the end of the dance. Dance historians assert that this climactic leap evolved from ancient fertility rituals intended to bring about a bountiful harvest. It is thought that the height that the woman's skirt reached when she was thrown into air revealed the height that corn crops would reach thus men strived to throw the woman as high into the air as possible.

Both the Schuhplattler and Ländler have both met with outrage from moralists who considered the dances indecent since they caused dancers to display limbs and come into close physical contact. Claims of immorality on the part of the dancers led to the dances being banned several times. Even as late as 1760 attempts were made in Germany to outlaw the Ländler, though in 1765 the writer Goethe recorded that in order to enter German high society it was necessary to know how to dance the Ländler. The acceptance of German folk dances during this period was partly due to the fashion for folk dances in England.

During the 20th century German folk dances were seen as propagating Germanic stereotypes and as somewhat comical as they involved leather-clad dancers slapping their own and each other's thighs. However academics such as Dr. Alexandra Kolb argue that after the displacement of people from Germany and Austria to the United Kingdom and the United States during the era of the Third Reich dances such as the Schuhplattler and the Ländler were performed as way of uniting communities. While part of the purpose of performing Schuhplattler and Ländler today is to preserve folk traditions, this fondness for the past does not preclude the development of new forms of the dance. This is reflected by the fact that there is now a Schuhplattler club for gay dancers. The *Schwuhplattler* group, founded in Bavaria in 1997, performs an all-male group version of the Schuhplattler called the *reinen Burschenplattler* as well as other German folk dances including the *Mühlrad* (Mill Wheel), *Steckentanz* (Stick Dance), and the *Bandltanz* (May Pole Dance). In recognition of the Schwuhplattler commitment to upholding local cultural traditions, the club has been awarded official recognition as a charitable organization, and is often asked to perform upon request of the Cultural Office of the Bavarian Capital of Munich.

See also: *Hora* and *Horah*; Maypoles; Obando Fertility Dance (Volume 1); Purity Ball; Wodaabe Courtship Dance and Festival

Further Reading

Bröcker, Marianne. "Folk Dance Revival in Germany," Folk Music Revival in Europe, *The World of Music*, 38(3), 1996, 21–36.

d'Schwuhplattler. "About Us." Accessed January 2, 2015, at http://www.schwuhplattler.de/wersanmir.en.html.

d'Schwuhplattler. "History." Accessed January 2, 2015, at http://www.schwuhplattler.de/geschichte.en.html.

Knowles, Mark A. *The Wicked Waltz and Other Scandalous Dances: Outrage at Couple Dancing in the 19th and Early 20th Centuries*. Jefferson, NC: McFarland & Company, Inc., 2009.

Middlesex University. "Dance Research Wins Prestigious Gertrude Lippincott Award." Middlesex University London. October 23, 2014. Accessed January 2, 2015, at http://www.mdx.ac.uk/news/2014/10/dance-research-wins-prestigious-gertrude-lippincott-award.

Nonverbal World. "Human Courtship and Dance." Accessed January 2, 2015, at http://www.nonverbal-world.com/2011/04/courtship-and-dance.html.

Rosenberg, Joseph. *German: How to Speak and Write It*. New York: Dover Publications, 1962.

Scheff, Helene, Marty Sprague, and Susan McGreevy-Nichols. *Exploring Dance Forms and Styles: A Guide to Concert, World, Social, and Historical Dance*. Champaign, IL: Human Kinetics. 2010.

SECULAR CONFIRMATION, EUROPE

Secular confirmation, also known as secular coming of age, civic confirmation, or humanist confirmation, is a voluntary coming-of-age ceremony for teenagers arranged by a secular organization that is akin to a Christian confirmation. Such ceremonies are popular in Scandinavia—for instance, in Norway around 15 percent of young people opt to undergo secular confirmation—and in Germany. Participants meet weekly for the duration of a year to learn about subjects such as national history, ecology, morality and ethics, and world affairs. The period of learning culminates in a ceremony that celebrates the youngsters' learning and marks the start of their adult lives. Norwegian teens living outside of the country can also experience a secular confirmation for classes can also be taken as a correspondence class by e-mail.

The concept of the secular confirmation as seen in Iceland, Norway, Denmark, and Germany developed from the 19th-century humanist and ethical movements that deliberately resisted organized religions, especially religions linked to the state. For centuries, the Lutheran state churches of Scandinavia held confirmation ceremonies. In Norway, these were compulsory by law until 1912 and saw youngsters questioned by the clergy to see whether they comprehended and agreed with the church's teachings. If they did not then students were not allowed to marry, to dress as adults, or to find adult employment.

When Scandinavia modernized, Scandinavian people began to enjoy religious freedom and those that did not believe in any form of religion decided to institute a new form of coming-of-age celebration that was not connected to religion. The first Scandinavian civil confirmation was held in Copenhagen, the capital of Denmark, in 1915 and was organized by the Association Against Church Confirmation. This later changed its name to The Association for Civil Confirmation. Meanwhile, in Norway academics and labor leaders established the Association for Civil Confirmation in 1950 and the first Norwegian civil confirmation ceremony, held the following year, featured just 34 youngsters. In 1956, members from the Association for Civil Confirmation helped establish the Norwegian Humanist Association, Human-Etisk Forbund (HEF), which assumed responsibility for civil confirmations in Norway. Today, the annual secular confirmation ceremonies held at City Hall are a great tradition in Oslo, the Norwegian capital. There are 12 Oslo ceremonies each year taking place over five successive weekends. The ceremonies see 1,000 youngsters walk in procession down the great staircase at City Hall, the venue of the Nobel Peace Prize ceremony, watched by their upstanding friends and families. Once the teenagers have proceeded down the staircase they receive their diplomas for having completed their confirmation studies.

In Germany, teenagers that wish to experience a ceremony akin to a Christian confirmation but are of no religion opt for a ceremony called *Jugendweihe*, meaning youth consecration. Jugendweihe began in the 19th century as an alternative to Christian confirmation and soon became established as an accepted rite of passage for teenagers aged 13 and 14 who were not religious but wished to mark their passage to adulthood. The tradition of Jugendweihe survived the era of the Weimar Republic and was then adopted by the Nazis. After World War II, the ceremony was adopted by the East German politburo and was used by the state to generate social uniformity and conformity. Though Jugendweihe was not obligatory in Communist East Germany, the ceremony became so ingrained in society that anyone that did not undergo the ceremony was regarded as an anomaly. The tradition of Jugendweihe continues in modern, unified Germany as a way of marking children's transition to adulthood. Today, German children participate in nine months of events that aim to educate the teenagers by broadening their horizons and making them consider morals and ethics as well as subjects such as multiculturalism, culture, and history. There are nonetheless critics of Jugendweihe. For example, some people that grew up in East Germany claim that the concept of Jugendweihe in modern Germany is dishonest since many modern young Germans are ignorant of the connection between Jugendweihe and Communist East Germany.

In Finland, 14- and 15-year-olds can participate in Prometheus Camps. These are politically neutral, non-religious coming-of-age camps organized by the Prometheus Camp Association of Finland, also known as Protu. The first Prometheus Camp was organized by the Finnish Philosophy and Life Stance Teachers' Coalition in 1989 with the Prometheus Camp Association established in 1990 to organize the camps. Today, there are several Prometheus Camps throughout Finland all of which run during the summer months and are staffed by volunteers most of whom are under 20 years of age. Camp fees, membership dues, and a small subsidy from the Finnish Ministry of Education finance the camps.

At a Prometheus Camp, teenagers are taught about a range of topics that are important to young people including drug use, sex and sexuality, and the environment from a neutral standpoint free from any political, religious, or ideological prejudice. Teenagers do not go to lessons at the camps but rather engage in debates, group work, dramas, and games with the intention of learning about ethics and life issues. As well as learning, those attending Prometheus Camps also go hiking, cycling, and sailing. The weeklong camp culminates with a Prometheus Ceremony to which the teenagers' families and friends are invited. During the ceremony the teenagers perform a play about the week and are given a Prometheus diploma, a Prometheus medallion, and a crown of leaves. Similar confirmation camps are held in Sweden and are organized by *Humanisterna,* the Swedish Humanist Association.

There are three main reasons why teenagers wish to undergo secular confirmation. Firstly, secular confirmation classes and camps allow teenagers to meet other youngsters from different backgrounds, who attend different schools and come from various social classes. Many Scandinavians and Germans feel that in this way secular confirmation strengthens social cohesion and nurtures a feeling of community. The second reason that teenagers opt to undergo secular confirmation is that the confirmation ethics classes require students to research subjects and youngsters report that this gives them a valuable insight into the world thereby helping to foster tolerance for other people and instilling in teenagers a need to be committed to a cause. Thirdly, secular confirmation classes introduce students to voluntary work. For example, in Germany some 60,000 teenagers enter into voluntary work each year in preparation for their secular confirmation. In this way, secular confirmation engenders a sense of social commitment and encourages a desire to maintain civil society.

See also: Coming of Age Day; *Gwallye*; Same-Sex Marriage; Secular Confirmation; Nordic Napping (Volume 1)

Further Reading

Human-Etisk Forbund. "Humanist Confirmation in Norway—A Rite of Passage Has Come of Age." The Norwegian Humanist Association. November 15, 2012. Accessed August 12, 2015, at http://www.human.no/Servicemeny/English/?index=10.

Liu, Eric. "What Scandinavia Can Teach U.S. Teens about Coming of Age," *The Atlantic*, March 11, 2014. Accessed August 12, 2015, at http://www.theatlantic.com/politics/archive/2014/03/what-scandinavia-can-teach-us-teens-about-coming-of-age/284360/.

Miller, Kalle. "Prometheus Camps as an Alternative to the Finnish Confirmation Camps." ENGA14 Finnish Institutions Research Paper. Fall 2013. Accessed August 12, 2015, at https://www15.uta.fi/FAST/FIN/A14PAPS/km-prom.html.

Sange.fi. "About Prometheus Camps." Accessed August 12, 2015, at http://sange.fi/protu/english/aboutus.html.

Schweitzer, Friedrich. "Confirmation Work in Europe, Religious Identity, National Heritage and Civil Society: Insights From an International Empirical and Comparative Study in Seven Countries," in Francis-Vincent Anthony, ed., *Religious Identity and National Heritage: Empirical-Theological Perspectives*, 227–343. Leiden, Netherlands: Koninklijke Brill NV, 2012.

Walker, Tamsin. "A Secular Rite of Passage."·DW, March 12, 2005. Accessed August 12, 2015, at http://www.dw.com/en/a-secular-rite-of-passage/a-1516020.

SHABKA, ISLAM AND COPTIC CHRISTIANITY

Shabka is a set of jewelry that is part of the *Mahr*, or compulsory Islamic marriage payment, and it can also be included in the financial arrangements made prior to the marriage of Coptic Christians living in North Africa. Shabka sets are particularly associated with Egypt and Qatar. Shabka is also important to Palestinian Muslims living in the West Bank region of the Middle East who view shabka as both the true expression of a groom's affection for this bride and a way of announcing an engagement. Indeed it has been claimed that to Palestinian Muslims shabka is as essential to a marriage as a marriage certificate. Shabka may be presented to a bride at the same time as the bride and groom officially sign the marriage contract and the religious ceremony, *katb il kitab*, takes place, or during an engagement party or just before the couple consummates their marriage.

Family is a very important institution in Egypt as it is regarded as the foundation of social cohesion and the basis for raising children. In Egypt, parents are responsible for child rearing and in return children are expected to care for their parents as they get older. Marriage is then held in great regard as it represents a legitimate mechanism for creating families and ensuring the continuance of Egyptian society. As marriage is considered such a central aspect of Egyptian life, weddings are treated as prestigious events. Though in Egypt men and women are generally permitted to choose their own marriage partners, marriage in Egypt is nonetheless a form of socioeconomic contract between families that transforms the role of individuals in society and in the eyes of the law.

In recent years, the costs of Egyptian weddings have risen considerably. This is mainly due to the rising prices of items required for marriages to take place and of the numerous ceremonies associated with Egyptian weddings. Egyptian marriages consist of several stages, one of which sees the groom pay a monetary dowry to the bride's family in order to help buy her a trousseau called *gihaz* that consists of brand-new electrical goods, particularly televisions and refrigerators, and home furnishings. The groom and his family must pay for two-thirds of the cost of the marriage though recently women have increasingly contributed to costs, as they are now more likely to have jobs. That said, the majority of all Egyptian wedding costs are the responsibility of the groom and his family. An additional cost that the groom and his family must bear is the cost of the shabka, which in Egypt has a dual meaning. On the one hand, shabka can refer to the gift of gold and diamonds that the groom gives to his bride at the wedding. However the term can also mean an engagement party and commitment ceremony that "ties" the bride and groom to the marriage. As a wedding gift the price a groom pays for shabka reveals both the regard in which the groom holds his bride-to-be and the state of his finances. That the groom is willing to pay the expense of shabka also signals that the groom takes his approaching wedding very seriously.

The cost of shabka varies greatly in Egypt. Low- and middle-income families tend to buy shabka made of gold while the Egyptian upper classes and wealthy families will buy shabka featuring diamonds. The cost of gold shabka is around $120–$350 and comprises one or more bracelets and a wedding ring made of 21-carat gold. Coptic Christians in Egypt also include shabka in their engagements. Indeed the value of the shabka is written into the engagement contract.

Most Egyptians view shabka as indicative of social status and therefore it plays an important part in allowing a newlywed couple to establish their place in the social hierarchy of their relatives and friends. For this reason, it is customary for the bride's family to display the shabka during the wedding ceremony so that guests can see how greatly the groom values his new wife. The showing of the shabka usually sees the bride's mother or sister carry the jewelry on a silver platter covered in flowers as they walk among the wedding guests. This allows the guests to take a close-up look at the shabka. However the women carrying the shabka ensure that guests do not touch the jewelry. This display ends when the groom is presented with the shabka by the bride's mother or sister and presents it in turn to his bride in front of the guests. The groom then helps his bride put on the jewelry.

In Qatar, a traditional shabka is made of gold, usually around 22 carats, and is quite delicate. The traditional shabka comprises a round, gold head-piece with gold chains descending from it called a *taasa*, a number of gold bangles called *asaawir*, either a heavy golden chain known as a *salsala* or a gold necklace called an *aqd*, plus *shaghaabaat*, which are gold earrings, and also, finally, two gold bracelets attached to gold rings by gold chains, *al-kaff*. However traditional shabka sets have fallen out of fashion in recent times, particularly in Qatar, where modern shabka sets consist of a bangle, ring, necklace, earrings, and an expensive watch.

In Qatar, few people buy the traditional shabka now. In Qatar, these can only be found in the gold market or at the market called *Souq Al-Waagif*, which specializes in traditional Qatari artifacts. Instead of traditional shabka, most Qataris buy the *shabka* sets from either the gold market or from designer jewelry stores. In Qatar, it is usual for women to choose the shabka set though the groom, or his family, will pay for it. In Qatar, shabka sets typically cost from 5,000 Qatari riyals (about $1,374) to 100,000 Qatari riyals (roughly $27,472). If a family wishes to display their wealth then they will buy the bride two to four different shabka sets.

As a result of the expense of holding a wedding in Egypt, partly because of the cost of shabka, an increasing number of young Egyptians are entering into *urfi* marriages—unregistered marriages that are usually kept from public knowledge. However many Egyptian families are happy to bear the cost of the jewelry as they see it as a form of saving for the newlyweds' future. As Egyptians consider marriage as a state that lasts until death, they understand that couples may endure periods of financial hardship or when extra finances are needed, for example when paying for a child's education or marriage. Since the value of gold usually increases more than it decreases, buying and storing gold in the form of shabka means a couple have a hoard of gold ready for when they most need it. Shabka also performs a decorative purpose as brides wear their shabka when invited to such major social functions as weddings. In this instance, wearing her shabka allows a woman to show off her social and financial standing and wearing the jewels proves she has not had to sell-off her jewelry to meet economic difficulties. If a family does have to sell the shabka it is considered a major sacrifice by the wife's family as it means she has had to help her husband in supporting the family financially. This means that most husbands see the selling of their wife's shabka as a last resort and they tend to greatly value their wife's sacrifice as they understand that selling her shabka represents a significant loss on the wife's part. However some families view the selling of the shabka as the correct way for a wife to assist financially during difficult times. Indeed wives do not always lose out when they sell their shabka as it is traditional for a husband to promise to buy his wife a better shabka when the couple's financial fortunes improve.

See also: *Lobola*; Moroccan Weddings; Muslim Wedding Ceremony

Further Reading

Adelaal, Yousra. "Qatar Culture: Shabka Shop." *Qatar Visitor*. 2015. Accessed January 7, 2015, at http://www.qatarvisitor.com/culture/shabka-shop.

Galvan, Javier A., ed. *They Do What? A Cultural Encyclopedia of Extraordinary and Exotic Customs from around the World*. Santa Barbara, CA: ABC-CLIO, 2014.

Hogan, Elena, N. "Jewels of the Occupation: Gold Wedding Jewelry in the West Bank," *Journal of Palestine Studies*, 39(4), summer 2010, 43–49.

Inhorn, Marcia C. *Infertility and Patriarchy: The Cultural Politics of Gender and Family Life in Egypt*. Philadelphia: University of Pennsylvania Press, 1996.

SHANGHAI MARRIAGE MARKET, CHINA

The Shanghai Marriage Market (*rénmín Gāngyuán xiāngqīn jiāo*, which means "People's Park blind date corner") is a weekly marriage market in which parents, grandparents, uncles, and aunts of unmarried adults flock to People's Park in Shanghai, China, every Saturday and Sunday from noon to 5 p.m. Similar marriage markets also occur in other major cities including Beijing and Shenzhen.

Going to the market is a traditional weekend pastime for older members of Shanghai's population. Exactly how the unmarried youngsters feel about the marriage market is not known. However as many parents keep secret the fact that they are advertising their children for marriage—parents do not need the consent of their children to post their details—it is probable that most would not welcome the intervention of their parents in matters of the heart.

The main aim of those attending the marriage market is to find a suitable marital partner for a young person of marriageable age, though some older people also go to the market to find a mate for themselves. The market, which gets very busy at weekends, is divided into two sections—the free zone and the amateur matchmaking zone. The free zone is where parents go to find a match for their children and also to list their children as looking for a partner. Details of unmarried youngsters are written on pieces of paper in the form of pamphlet biographies that are stuck to umbrellas acting as mini market stalls that line the park's paths, or alternatively, they are tied to lengths of string tied to trees or bushes, or simply laid on the floor. Older people then scan the pamphlets for good matches for their children or sit behind their child's pamphlet until another parent shows interest in their child.

The paper pamphlets act as mini biographies of the young unmarried people and include details such as the person's birthday and Chinese Zodiac sign, aspects of their physical appearance such as their height and weight, what hobbies the person enjoys plus practical issues such as their job and their monthly income. The market also features a so-called overseas corner for parents who have children living outside China. Indeed distance is no obstacle to parental matchmaking with a documented case of a mother advertising her 36-year-old daughter who was working as an accountant in Toronto, Canada. The market's second zone is where professional and amateur matchmakers head to find matches for their clients. Many animated discussion break out through the course of the weekend as relatives of the unmarried youngsters broker marriage deals, extolling the virtues of their marriage candidate while wondering if the prospective brides and grooms on offer are really as advertised.

Exactly when the Shanghai Marriage Market began is open to conjecture. Some historians say it started in 1996 as a low-tech way for parents to advertise their unmarried children while others assert that the market started in 2004 or 2005. Parents advertised their children's education and employment history in the hope of matching their child with another suitably qualified singleton. Chinese parents felt the need to take their children's dating into their own hands because their single children were too busy to look for love and were also socially awkward with the opposite sex because China's former one-child policy means that most Chinese children born during the 1980s do not have siblings and so are not used to meeting and talking to members of the opposite sex. The country's former one-child policy also means that there is a discrepancy between male and female populations with almost three times as many women looking for spouses than there are men looking for wives. Another reason for the establishment of the marriage market is that in China, a land that emphasizes the importance of continuing family lines, there is great social pressure on children to marry before they reach 30 years of age. Indeed some parents are so worried that they employ professional marriage matchmakers to assist in the search for a partner for their child. Matchmakers do not charge male clients a fee but as China has a surfeit of unwed females women must pay a fee of around $500. The professional matchmakers also discriminate against their female clients in that men born after 1970 may sign-up with a matchmaker but women must be under 33 years of age. When questioned about this discrimination, matchmakers point out that there is a shortage of suitable, unmarried, urban men while there is a glut of single women. This is because men tend to marry "down," that is, marry younger or less educated women. The resulting surplus of unwed females, especially those over 30 years old, are known in China as *shengnü* (meaning leftover women).

However despite wanting their children to marry, Shanghai parents are not so desperate that they are not picky about choosing a good match for their child. Parents often exaggerate their child's achievements, earnings, and good looks resulting in children going without dates. It has been claimed that Shanghai's Marriage Market harks back to an era when Chinese parents arranged the marriages for their children. This is reflected in the fact that at the market parents usually meet each other before a couple starts dating, as is the tradition in China. That being said, China is rapidly modernizing resulting in traditions being discarded.

Shanghai also hosts an annual love and marriage expo to help young people find mates. This event attracts 18,000 lovelorn singletons.

See also: Arranged Marriage and Forced Marriage; Moroccan Weddings; One-Child Policy (Volume 1); Single's Day and Black Day; Visiting-Girls Courtship Tradition; Yumi Sakugawa, "An Asian American Wedding," 2009

Further Reading

Bones, Alicia. "Shanghai Marriage Market." Atlas Obscura. Accessed January 2, 2015, at http://www.atlasobscura.com/places/shanghai-marriage-market.

China Highlights. "The Shanghai Marriage Market—An Engrossing Experience!" Accessed January 2, 2015, at http://www.chinahighlights.com/shanghai/article-shanghai-marriage-market.htm.

Davis, Deborah S., and Sara L. Friedman, eds. *Wives, Husbands, and Lovers: Marriage and Sexuality in Hong Kong, Taiwan and Urban China*. Stanford, CA: Stanford University Press, 2014.

Hunt, Katie. "Glut of Women at Shanghai's Marriage Market." CNN World: On China, November 3, 2013. Accessed January 2, 2015, at http://www.cnn.com/2013/11/03/world/asia/shanghai-marriage-market/.

SHARO: PUBLIC FLOGGING, NIGERIA AND BENIN

Sharo is an initiation into manhood practiced by the Fulani (also called the Fulbe or Fula) people of Nigeria and Benin that sees males around 15 years old flogged in public as a test of bravery. As well as being a rite of passage to adulthood the flogging is seen by some Fulani as a precursor to marriage while others see the flogging as a competitive sporting event contested by clans. Fulani society is based around rituals and ceremonies of which sharo is undoubtedly the most important. Sharo can be held in honor of a dignitary such as a chief, to celebrate a marriage, to mark the naming ceremony of a famous sharo exponent's first child, or as a community event. Normally, such public flogging events last for one week and take place twice per year—once during the dry season at corn harvesting time and again during the Islamic festival of *Id-el-kabir*. However sharo may also be enacted during the festival of *Sallah* (or *Sallan* in Hausa) that falls at the end of the Muslim holy period of Ramadan. Sharo may also be practiced at a weekly market. Sharo is an important tradition for all Fulani males but the most ardent practitioners of the flogging are the Jafun Fulani tribes of Nigeria.

The build up to sharo sees all the local Fulani people (both male and female) gather in the market square along with other clans that may travel many miles for the occasion. As sharo is a special event everybody wears their finest clothes and there is a general atmosphere of excitement and expectation. Music is played, crowds dance, and entertainers walk among the people performing magic tricks. Next, all the women present start to perform a well-choreographed dance and the boys that are about to be flogged are brought into the square together with their seconds. The seconds are other males that are willing to act as substitutes should any of the boys decide not to be flogged. By acting as substitutes, these males will save face on the part of both the unwilling boy and his clan. The boys that are about to be flogged are also accompanied by their family and friends and are eyed with interest by local unmarried girls who are eager to see which boys are willing to test their bravery by withstanding the flogging, though often a boy that is willing to be flogged will do so as he realizes that his show of bravado will allow him to woo a girl he already has his heart set on. The single girls consider it very important that a boy shows steadfastness in the face of pain as the stoicism is thought to demonstrate the boy's ability to protect a wife and children.

Before sharo starts, any boy that is to go through the pain of public flogging is given pain-reducing drugs or undergoes spells and enchantments that will help him withstand the trial. The boy will also be dressed in lucky amulets said to possess protective powers that will help him through his painful ordeal. Next, men acting with mock-fierceness clear the ground that is to be used as the flogging arena. Then the first boy to be flogged is brought forward and strikes a defiant, macho, bare-chested pose. At the same time the music that has been entertaining the gathered spectators swells and quickens in pace to signal the event will start soon. The boy then crosses one of his legs over the other and lifts one arm into the air while holding a staff or mirror. The boy uses the mirror to watch the girl he wishes to wed as a reminder of why he is undergoing the flogging and also to check that his face remains composed during the flogging. This is important for if the boy reveals the pain that he feels as he is flogged he may not be allowed to marry the girl of his choosing. Boys must also endure the pain without flinching or crying so as to prove that they possess the bravery, strength of spirit, and stoicism expected of an adult Fulani man. Next, another bare-chested boy is brought forward. This boy holds a strong, flexible cane measuring about half an inch thick. The boy holding the cane aims at the first boy with great deliberation so as to hit a particularly tender point on the other boy's rib area. The blows from the cane are heavy enough to draw blood yet the boy being hit must declare his desire to receive harder, more painful blows and the boy wielding the cane is scrutinized by the onlookers that have formed a ring around the flogging arena to make sure he is not shirking from his duty of delivering painful hits. Meanwhile, the boy being hit must not arch his body away from the cane as it hits his body. The boy must also avoid crying out in pain, grimacing, or showing any form of emotion other than bravery in the face of pain lest he be labeled a coward by the rest of his community. Indeed it is almost requisite for they boy being hit to taunt the boy administering the cane that his blows are not hard enough. The boy carrying out the flogging must also sneer and goad the boy being hit so as to increase the air of menace surrounding the flogging.

It is expected that any boy being flogged will be able to endure the continual blows from the cane until the end of the ceremony. Once the ritual concludes the now-man is congratulated by his family and friends and given gifts. The single girls that have watched the ordeal with an eye to marriage also congratulate the man. At the end of the ritual, the man's wounds are covered with herbal pastes that are said to quicken the healing though even once healed the wounds will leave scarring. Men have also been known to be left with broken ribs after undergoing sharo. The man will not mind the resultant scars however. Indeed the man will show the scars with great pride as they serve to demonstrate his bravery, masculinity, and worthiness to marry. If the man had been unable to endure his flogging he would have lost the respect of all watching women and would not be allowed to woo the girl he desired as a wife.

The man that has been flogged returns to the scene of his flogging about five days later when the position of the flogged and flogger are reversed. This time the man that was flogged will flog the boy that caned him thereby making the flogger a man, but also to exact a type of revenge. Indeed in recent years a darker element has entered the sharo cultural tradition as the flogging has been used to exact revenge. In this case, a victim of crime will hit the wrong-doer with a stick that has been soaked in urine that makes the blows from the cane both extra stinging and potentially highly infectious. As a result of this vengeance-fueled sharo, authorities in northern Nigeria have sought to put an end to the tradition. However the Fulani consider the tradition to be an essential part of their culture and will not countenance its abolition.

In Benin, sharo differs in that it is a contest between two boys from different clans that each give and receive three blows from a flexible tree branch. The boys and their fathers specially select the stick to be used on the basis that it looks as though it will deliver painful blows. Before the flogging starts the boys' fathers may also sharpen the stick to make sure that it will inflict as much pain as possible. During Benin sharo one boy will strike his opponent three times and then roles are reversed so that the boy that was flogged becomes the flogger. The boys know that they must not give any sign of the pain that they feel as they are flogged as their clans-people that have gather as spectators will decide which of them is the winner based on which of the two boys has shown the least discomfort during their flogging. The winner is rewarded by having white talc powder daubed on his skin and coins placed on his forehead. The victory also means that the victor is considered a man rather than a boy.

See also: Bullet Ant Initiation; Cow Jumping; Forehead-Cutting Initiation; Log Riding; Maasai Warrior Initiation; Matis Hunting Trials; Ritual Tattooing; Scarification; *Thaipusam*: Extreme Ritual Flesh Modification; Xhosa Circumcision

Further Reading

Galvan, Javier A., ed. *They Do What? A Cultural Encyclopedia of Extraordinary and Exotic Customs from around the World*. Santa Barbara, CA: ABC-CLIO, 2014.

National Geographic Society. "Fulani Initiation Rites," *National Geographic*. Accessed June 30, 2015, at http://video.nationalgeographic.com/video/benin_fulaniinitiation?source=relatedvide.

Ndukwe, Pat I. *The Heritage Library of African Peoples: Fulani*. New York: The Rosen Publishing Group Inc., 1996.

Okehie-Offoha, Marcellina U., and Matthew N. O. Sadiku, eds. *Ethnic and Cultural Diversity in Nigeria*. Trenton, NJ: Africa World Press Inc., 1996.

SHINBYU, BUDDHISM

Shinbyu, sometimes written as *shin-byu* or spelled *shinpyu*, is the Burmese name for an obligatory period of initiation in the life of Theravada Buddhist males. Theravada Buddhism is a branch of the Buddhist religion that is dominant in Myanmar (formerly Burma), Thailand, Laos, Sri Lanka, and Cambodia and also practiced in China, Vietnam, and Bangladesh as well as in countries in which Theravada Buddhist people have settled, including the United States. Shinbyu is a rite of passage for Theravada Buddhist males younger than 20 years old—boys as young as 4 years old may undergo shinbyu if they are able to pronounce the Theravada Buddhist scriptures known as the *Pali* correctly, though most boys experience shinbyu between the ages of 9 and 12 years. Any male that does not experience this ritual will not be considered a good Buddhist for the shinbyu ritual marks the *samanera*, or first step to ordination to become a Buddhist priest. Buddhist parents, therefore, consider their son's shinbyu as a rite of passage to manhood that will influence the rest of the boy's life. In Myanmar, the country with which shinbyu is most associated, it is considered the duty of all parents to let their son experience shinbyu. Therefore sons join a Buddhist monastic community called *sangha* where they become immersed in the teachings of Buddhism and study the *Dhamma*, the cosmic laws of Buddhism, for a period of the boy's choosing that may last for as short a time as a week to the rest of the boy's life. Parents consider it a great honor for their son to experience shinbyu as they believe it will bring about good karma for their family. Thus the shinbyu ceremony is afforded much pomp and pageantry.

According to Theravada Buddhist tradition, the first Shinbyu ceremony took place over 2,500 years ago when the Buddha allowed his only son to become a novice monk. Today, shinbyu ceremonies usually take place when schools are shut for the summer holidays and the occasion is accompanied by much fanfare with feasts held for the novices' relatives and guests, including their sponsors. While many shinbyu ceremonies are small-scale and feature only one or two boys, shinbyu ceremonies held en masse also take place for which up to 1,000 wealthy sponsors fund the initiation of boys who have for some reason been unable to have their own shinbyu ceremony.

For the ceremony, boys dress in spectacular clothing, princely attire that is intended to remind onlookers that the Buddha's son was himself a priest. The elaborately dressed boys ride horses, or in cars if the ceremony is occurring in a major city, in procession shaded from the sun by golden parasols. (*See* Plate 20.) The boys are accompanied by their parents and relatives, while the boys' sisters and other local women dressed in silk carry the boys' sets of yellow monastic robes, as well as offerings and ornate wooden boxes containing *paan* (areca nuts wrapped in betel leaves) and lotus blossoms. The whole procession is accompanied by a troupe of dancers and musicians playing folk tunes and the procession makes its way to the local spirit house or *nat*, where prayers are said. When a shinbyu procession is in progress, nobody in a village may cook or light a fire. Once the devotions are over the procession moves on to a pagoda where everyone pays homage to the Buddha. Next the boys return to their homes where they change out of their ornate robes and rest until they visit the local monastery at some time before evening. At the monastery the boys' relatives watch as the monks shave the boys' heads, and sometimes their eyebrows, using a sharp blade in a ritual called *hsan cha* during which boys are not permitted to cry. This ritualistic shaving is intended as a sign that the boys are willing to renounce their vanity and live a simple life free from material considerations. It is tradition that the boys' hair should not fall to the floor but rather must be caught in a white cloth that is then presented to the boys' family. Next the boys ask the chief monk to allow them to become novices, or *ko-yin*. In return, the monk conducts a ceremony to grant the boys request and the boys put on their yellow robes to show that they are transformed. The boys then chant the Ten Precepts, rules by which Buddhist monks live that include vowing not kill, steal, lie, or indulge sexually; to refrain from dancing or singing; and to abstain from sleeping in a big bed. New novices usually stay at the monastery for at least a week, looked after by the monks whose daily routines the boys follow.

If the shinbyu ceremony is taking place in the West where Buddhist temples and monasteries are rare then the ceremony may take place in a private home that has been decorated plainly in line with the Buddhists ideals of the renunciation of worldly goods, is single-sex, and does not have food cooked after midday. A monk from Myanmar will preside over the ritual but the ceremony, including the head shaving, donning of monastic robes, and chanting of the Ten Precepts, will be watched over by the boy's close relatives only. When shinbyu takes place in a family home the shinbyu period usually lasts for only a matter of weeks. However during this time conventional familial hierarchies are transformed with parents expected to obey their son, who in turn becomes distant from his parents, as they are *daga-jee*, or laypeople.

See also: Ear-Piercing Ceremony; Secular Confirmation

Further Reading

Lee, Jonathan H. X., and Kathleen M. Nadeau, eds. *Encyclopedia of Asian American Folklore and Folklife*. Volume 3. Santa Barbara, CA: ABC-CLIO, 2011.

Maung, Lwin. "Rahula, the First Samanera in this Sasana." NOVICEHOOD: Initiation of Novicehood in Myanmar (Shinpyu Ceremony in Burma). December 8, 1999. Accessed May 3, 2015, at http://www.myanmarnet.net/nibbana/initiate.htm.

Mingalapar.com. "Shinbyu: Rite of Passage from Boy to Manhood." Accessed May 3, 2015, at http://mingalapar.com/shinbyu-rite-of-passage-from-boy-to-manhood/.

Ministry of Hotels and Tourism, Union of Myanmar. "Traditions & Lifestyles: Shinbyu." Fascinating Myanmar. Accessed May 3, 2015, at http://fascinatingmyanmar.info/traditionsandlifestyle/activitiesandlifestyles/shin_byu.html.

SIKH WEDDING CEREMONY, SIKHISM

Sikhism is the main religion of northern India and places great store upon marriage. Sikhism sees marriage not simply as the joining of two loving people or the uniting of two families but as the bonding of two souls. This is because according to Sikh thinking the aim of life is to merge the individual soul, or *atma*, to God, Parmatma, a merger that is facilitated by marriage as the married couple strives to achieve their union with God. Adults Sikhs may wed once they are fully able to take on the responsibilities of marriage. For this reason, child marriage is forbidden within Sikhism. Sikh marriages may be arranged but equally Sikh adults may meet each other and decide to marry though they should seek the approval of their elders. In India, religious advice suggests that a Sikh couple should marry free from worry about their prospective spouse's caste—India's system of social class categorization. Sikh weddings are lively, colorful occasions known for their festive, happy atmosphere.

Any Sikh considered *Amritdhari*—a man or woman that has undergone traditional Amrit initiation (akin to baptism) and practices the recommended Sikh code of daily life—may perform a Sikh marriage ceremony. The officiating person explains to the couple the duties of married life according to the traditional teachings and outlines the mutual obligations of being husband and wife. The formal Sikh betrothal ceremony is called a *shagan* and is held at either the groom's family home or at a *gurdwara*, or Sikh temple. The ceremony sees the groom's family exchange gifts such as sweets and money with the bride's family and a formal agreement to the impending marriage is made. The betrothed couple may also exchange rings. Unlike Muslim or Hindu marriage, Sikh tradition forbids the giving of dowries as a Sikh father is expected to present only his daughter during the marriage agreement. Therefore no dowry agreement is made during a Sikh betrothal.

Wedding formalities begin three days before the wedding day, which may take place on any day that is acceptable to both families—unlike Hindus, Sikhs do not hold with superstitions about auspicious days and horoscopes. The first wedding ritual takes place during the three-day build up to the wedding day with the *akhand paath*, the three-day-long reading of the Sikh holy book the Sri Guru Granth Sahib. While the akhand paath is ongoing, the bride and groom experience the *myah* ritual. This ritual sees the couple's families massage the hands, feet, and faces of the bride and groom with oil, tamarind powder, and flour every morning and night. Then on the eve of the wedding, both the bride and groom have *mehndi* applied to their hands and feet. Another popular pre-wedding custom held on the eve of the ceremony is the *Sangeet*, during which the bride and groom's friends and family sing and feast. In cities, the Sangeet takes the form of an evening party that continues until the early hours of the next day.

Once the bride has been decorated with mehndi and *sangeet* she undergoes the *chooda* (or *choora*) ceremony during which she is dressed in 21 red and cream ivory bangles that the bride wears throughout her wedding and for 40 days after the wedding day. During the ceremony the bride's maternal aunt and uncle attach ornaments called *kalira* to the bangles. The kalira make it impossible for the bride to perform any household chores for the 40 days of marriage during which she wears her bangles. This means that the bride has 40 days in which to settle into married life before having to start doing housework.

Sikh weddings normally take place in the morning and are finished by midday. The morning of the wedding includes the *gharoli* ceremony that takes place at the groom's residence. This ceremony sees the groom's sister-in-law and other relatives travel to the well in the gurdwara where they fill an earthen pot called a *gharoli* with water. This water is then used to wash the bridegroom. Meanwhile, the bride undergoes the *kuvaar doti* (or *kuwaar dhoti*) ceremony during which the groom's father gives the bride a dress called a *kuvaar doti*. *Kuvaar* translates as maiden, so the kuvaar doti ceremony marks the last time that the bride will dress as a maiden. The bride is also anointed with a paste of turmeric and sandalwood and then bathes. After her bath the bride puts on her the kuvaar doti. Then, sometimes before the wedding ceremony begins, the bride undergoes the *nath* ritual, during which her uncle fits her with a nose ring. Meanwhile the groom is dressed in an outfit that conforms to the five essential elements of Sikh attire known as the five Ks: *kesh*, uncut hair coiled under a turban; *kangha*, a wooden comb symbolizing order in life; *kara*, a bracelet made of steel; *kachera* (or *kaccha*), which are white shorts worn under clothes in order to maintain chastity; and a *kirpan*, a short sword that reminds Sikhs to fight for truthfulness while defending the defenseless. As part of his preparations, the groom's sisters drape his turban with a *sehra*, a shiny mantilla. Once he is properly attired the groom mounts a lavishly decorated horse called a *ghodi*. A nephew of the groom known as a *sarbala* accompanies the groom throughout the ceremony. The groom and his party then set out for the temple where the ceremony will be held.

Next, hymns are sung at the gurdwara that is the wedding venue before the bride and groom arrive. Then, as the groom, his family, and the bride's family arrive hymns are sung specifically to welcome them. When both families and the groom have arrived a gift exchanging ceremony called *milni* or *milnee* occurs to symbolize that they accept each other through marriage. The gift exchange is accompanied by hymns sung from the Sri Guru Granth Sahib. Once the gift exchange has concluded the wedding ceremony, or *anand karaj* (ceremony of bliss or blissful union) takes place. The ceremony starts with the *kirtan* during which religious singers called *ragis* sing hymns all the while watched by the bride and groom who sit with their guests as the ragis perform. Next, the bride and groom are invited to sit in front of a copy of the Sri Guru Granth Sahib. Alternatively, the groom will sit in front of the holy book and the bride's mother and a friend will lead the bride to him. Either way the bride will end up sitting on the groom's left-hand side in front of the Sri Guru Granth Sahib. The person presiding over the ceremony then delivers a short speech on the importance of marriage from a religious perspective and outlines the duties of marriage.

After the homily, the bride and groom and their parents stand for prayers that ask God to bless the couple's marriage. Next, the most significant part of the wedding ceremony takes place—the *palaa* ritual. During this ritual a pink or yellow shawl symbolizing physical connection through spiritual union is folded lengthways. Then, one end of the shawl is placed over the groom's shoulder and into his hands by the bride's father while the other end is presented to the bride who takes hold of the fabric while the ragis perform a prayer called the *shabad palai*. Next, the couple stands while four prayers known as the *laavan*, meaning the breakaway, are performed by the ragis and by the person overseeing the ceremony. The prayers performed at this stage of the wedding refer to a breakaway because the bride is breaking away from her family. The first of the four prayers is spoken and then sung as the bride and groom walk clockwise around the Sri Guru Granth Sahib. The couple is joined together by the palaa shawl as they walk with the groom leading the bride. The couple finishes their walk around the holy book as the ragis finish singing their prayer. The couple then bows to the book and stands, or sits, waiting for the next prayer to begin. Each time a prayer is performed the couple walk around the Sri Guru Granth Sahib.

Once the four lavaan prayers have been performed, wedding guests shower the bride and groom with petals. The person officiating the ceremony then ends the ceremony by declaring the couple husband and wife. To mark their union, the couple feed each other fruit as a first act of marriage. Meanwhile, a song of bliss is sung and the guests are given blessed food called *gurupahad* or the blessed sweet pudding, *karah pasad*.

The final part of the wedding celebrations is the *doli*, the name for the palanquin that symbolizes the bride's send-off from her family. Prior to her leaving for her new home, the bride performs traditional cooking and serves rice to her family as part of the doli ceremony. The bride will also throw uncooked rice at her relatives before being led out of her old home by her male relatives and then sat in the palanquin by her father. This is the signal for the bride's relatives to bid her farewell. This can prove to be a very emotional time. On reaching the groom's house the bride is greeted by her mother-in-law who stands at door to receive her new family member. A kind of wedding reception called the *phera* or *phere pauna* is held at the couple's new home on the evening of the bride's arrival. The reception is normally hosted by the groom's parents and acts as a formal introduction of the newlyweds to their extended family and society in general. The next morning, the couple visits the bride's family home where they are blessed by the bride's relatives and receive gifts. The couple then sets out on their honeymoon.

See also: Hindu Wedding Ceremony; *Mehndi*; Muslim Wedding Ceremony; Sikh Death Customs (Volume 3)

Further Reading

Iloveindia.com. "Sikh Wedding Rituals." Accessed August 22, 2015, at http://weddings.iloveindia.com/indian-weddings/sikh-wedding.html.

MatrimonialsIndia.com. "Customs and Traditions—Sikh Wedding." Accessed August 22, 2015, at http://www.matrimonialsindia.com/help/sikh.php.

Monger, George P. *Marriage Customs of the World: From Henna to Honeymoons*. Santa Barbara, CA: ABC-CLIO, 2004.

Singh, Gurmukh. "Sikh weddings: Anand Karaj." BBC: Religions, October 1, 2009. Accessed August 22, 2015, at http://www.bbc.co.uk/religion/religions/sikhism/ritesrituals/weddings.shtml.

SINGLES' DAY, CHINA, AND BLACK DAY, SOUTH KOREA

Singles' Day is an extremely popular annual Chinese event that sees singletons celebrate their single status. The day is sometimes described as the Anti-Valentine's Day. Singles' Day is held on November 11 for when written numerically the date becomes 11/11, for the four number 1s are said to resemble bare sticks which is significant since in China *guanggun*, meaning bare stick, is the term used to refer to someone that is unmarried.

It is not known for sure just when Single's Day was invented though it most probably began as a series of events held at Chinese universities such as at Nanjing. However it is well documented that in 2009 the online retailer Tmall.com, part of the Alibaba.com online retailer, adopted the day and turned it into an online shopping extravaganza marked by all-day half-price sales run by the Tmall and Tabao online shops. Indeed today Single's Day is perhaps most notable for being the world's largest online shopping event as young urban consumers celebrate the date by buying gifts online. Bachelors and bachelorettes also mark the day by hosting parties and singing karaoke. However it is the sheer volume of online shopping that really marks Single's Day. In 2012, 213 million Chinese shoppers logged on to the Alibaba website looking for bargains resulting in the sales for Tmall and Taobao reaching a high of $3.1billion. This represented a 367-percent increase from the year before. Then, in 2014, Alibaba's Singles Day sales hit a record of $9.3 billion in gross merchandise value, which was a 60 percent increase from the $5.8 billion of 2013. Part of the reason for the increase in sales is that Alibaba has endeavored to connect Chinese online shoppers to foreign brands and sellers. This can be seen in the fact that in 2014 more than 200 retailers from over 20 countries participated in the event with Chinese shoppers finding overseas deals not just though Alibaba's own e-commerce sites such as Tmall and Taobao but also through foreign retailers' own websites and then paying with Alipay, the online payment provider that provides a secure payment option and international shipping for Chinese shoppers buying online.

A day for singles is also held in Korea. However this is not a celebration of being single, as is suggested by the name of the day, Black Day. Black Day is held annually on April 14 and is an unofficial holiday that sees singles wear black clothing and eat black bean paste noodles called *Jjajangmyeon* as they gather together and share tales of heartbreak. Black Day falls after both Valentine's Day and White Day on March 14. In South Korean, on Valentine's Day, women present the men that

> ## Solo Weddings
>
> In 2014, a Japanese travel agency, Cerca Travel, began offering customers a two-day solo wedding package costing ¥300,000 (about $2,819) that enables single women to experience being a bride. The package allows women to choose a wedding kimono or dress, accessories, a bridal bouquet, a hairstyle, and special make-up before travelling to Kyoto for a photo shoot to record the look. Women may hire a decorative man to pose with her in the photos. Organizers say the concept of solo marriages is aimed at singletons that want to have photographs of themselves as brides while they are still young and attractive, though married women may also avail themselves of the package if they so wish.

they love with chocolates, and then on White Day men return the compliment. This combination of Valentine's Day and White Day also occurs in Japan, which adopted the Western Valentine's tradition and added its own cultural influences. However Japan does not have a Black Day, which is specifically for people that did not receive gifts on either Valentine's Day or White Day. Like Singles' Day, Black Day is a major retail opportunity that has recently seen matchmaking services and cinema ticket businesses target those marking the day by setting up events such as speed-dating nights.

As an alternative to Black Day, South Korea celebrates around 13 holidays devoted to the subject of love. These include the self-explanatory Kiss Day on June 14, Green Day on August 14 during which loving couples dress in green and walk in forests drinking inexpensive Korean alcohol called *soju* from a green bottle, and Hug Day on December 14 that sees couples spend the day hugging.

See also: Looking for Fern Blossoms; Shanghai Marriage Market; St. Catherine's Day; St. Dwynwen's Day

Further Reading

Chen, Liyan. "Happy Singles Day! China's Anti-Valentine's Festival Is the World's Biggest E-Commerce Holiday," *Forbes*, November 10, 2014. Accessed June 1, 2015, at http://www.forbes.com/sites/liyanchen/2014/11/10/happy-singles-day-chinas-anti-valentines-festival-is-the-worlds-biggest-e-commerce-holiday/.

Christiansen, Bryan, ed. *Handbook of Research on Effective Marketing in Contemporary Globalism*. Hershey, PA: Business Science Reference, 2014.

Robins-Early, Nick. "Alone on Valentine's Day? South Korea Has a Holiday Just for You," *The World Post*, February 13, 2015. Accessed June 1, 2015, at http://www.huffingtonpost.com/2015/02/13/korea-black-day_n_6672380.html.

Smith, K. Annabelle. "Korea's Black Day: When Sad, Single People Get Together and Eat Black Food." Smithsonian.com, February 13, 2013. Accessed June 1, 2015, at http://www.smithsonianmag.com/arts-culture/koreas-black-day-when-sad-single-people-get-together-and-eat-black-food-16537918/?no-ist.

SISTERS' MEAL FESTIVAL, CHINA

The Sisters' Meal Festival or Eating Sisters' Rice Festival, known as *Jia Liang* in the Miao language, is the most well-known festival of the Miao people, a Chinese ethnic group also known as the Hmong. The festival is both a courtship festival and a celebration of spring and is held in the southwestern province of Guizhou on the 15th and 16th days of the third lunar month. The festival is particularly enjoyed in the counties of Taijiang and Jianhe that are situated on the banks of the Qingshui River. The festival is sometimes described as the world's oldest St. Valentine's Day, despite the fact that the festival lasts for more than one day. The Miao name for the festival, Jia Liang, derives from *Jia* meaning meal and *Liang*, which is the name of a fragrant shrub known to ward off mosquitoes and that colors food an appetizing yellow color.

The Sisters' Meal Festival is very old and reflects the earliest marriage customs of ancient China. There are several theories as to how the festival came into being. According to one legend, up to 80 beautiful, unmarried girls living in this remote area of China decided to hold a festival on the 15th day of the second month of spring in order to advertise their existence to the outside world and hopefully find husbands. Meanwhile, another legend tells that unmarried girls hated the idea of being separated from their families after marriage to such an extent that the festival was arranged to allow girls to stay with their families while looking for husbands. Another legend suggests that the mothers of unmarried girls organized the festival so that their daughters did not have to marry their own cousins out of a shortage of available single men.

Whichever legend is correct, the Sisters' Meal Festival originated as a way for young men from neighboring villages to woo young women who could then reciprocate (or not) the men's attentions by presenting them with so-called sister's rice. The young men would come to the village and romance the women they wished to pursue by singling out their intended and serenading them. In return for their romantic overtures, the women would give the men a drink of rice wine and parcels of rice that had been dyed red and then tied in their sister's handkerchief that were decorated with a variety of symbols. This tradition continues today as does a specific code that accompanies the giving of the rice. This code revolves around the items that accompany the rice for if a man receives a rice parcel together with one chopstick then this shows that the woman does not wish to pursue a relationship with the man that serenaded her. Similarly if a man receives a piece of garlic or a red chili in his rice parcel then he has received an outright refusal of his advances. However if a man is given two chopsticks with his rice parcel this is the equivalent of the woman professing her love for him and consenting to his courtship. Alternatively, if a man receives a rice parcel containing pine needles then this is an indication that he should present the girl with threads and silks and that she will wait for him to return to her with these items.

In the run-up to the festival Miao girls collect wild flowers and leaves from mountain locations that they then use to produce the natural colors with which to dye the glutinous rice that they cook in their family homes. Today the rice is dyed blue, pink, yellow, and white, in order to symbolize spring, summer, autumn, and winter respectively, as well as red. In honor of the festive occasion the Miao girls don their finest traditional clothing along with elaborate heavy silver necklaces and very large silver headpieces. In Miao culture, the larger and more ornate the jewelry worn by a girl the more beautiful the girl is considered. Also the silver color of the jewelry and headpieces is significant as the Miao consider silver a symbol of purity and chastity. When the young men begin to arrive for the festival they identify which of the unmarried girls they wish to marry and start to sing to her. The girls then give the boys a rice parcel inside of which is the item that symbolizes whether or not they reciprocate the man's affections. If a man is unlucky enough to receive a chili or garlic he will not become angry as he understands that he can still be friends with the girl he likes.

On the second day of the festival successful romantic pairings are celebrated with activities such as horse racing, bullfighting, and *lusheng* folk music played on traditional wind instruments.

See also: Chinese Coming-of-Age Ceremonies; Hmong Names; Visiting-Girls Courtship Tradition

Further Reading

China Highlights. "Sisters' Meals Festival." Accessed July 21, 2015, at http://www.china highlights.com/festivals/sisters-meals-festival.htm.

ChinaTourGuide.com. "Sisters' Meal Festival of the Miao." Accessed July 21, 2015, at http://www.chinatourguide.com/guizhou/Sisters_Meal_Festival.html.

Xing, Li. *Festivals of China's Ethnic Minorities*. Beijing, China: China Intercontinental Press, 2006.

SOCK GARLAND, GERMANY, AND SOCK DANCE, CANADA

Germany is home to many birthday traditions, some of which are heart-warming (e.g., the *Geburtstagskränze* ring of birthday candles), and some of which are ambiguous in nature in that they are not really unpleasant but they do present a certain degree of unkindness. For instance when an unmarried man living in Germany celebrates his 25th birthday it is traditional to give him a *Sockenkrantz*, or sock garland. The garland is strung outside the man's home and around his property as a path leading to a birthday party. As the man follows the sock garland, he finds alcoholic drinks spaced at intervals every few feet along the length of the garland and the man must drink the beverages as he works his way toward his party. The reason that the bachelor must follow a trail of socks comes from the fact that in Germany the term *alte Socke*, meaning "an old sock," is a pejorative expression used to describe a confirmed bachelor. Unmarried women turning 25 years of age and living in Germany face a similar tradition. In this case 25-year-old spinsters must follow a trail of cigarette packets or, if they do not smoke, a garland of other similarly sized boxes. This is because the German expression to describe an unmarried woman is *eine alte Schachtel*, which translates as "an old box" and is a derogatory expression akin to calling a single woman an "old maid."

The association between the longtime unmarried and socks also exists in French-speaking areas of northeastern Ontario, Canada. Here, a time-honored, good-natured tradition mocks or teasingly punishes older brothers or sisters whose younger sibling marries before they do. The Ontario sock tradition occurs on the day of the younger sibling's wedding, during the dance that follows the wedding meal. Members of the wedding party call the older sibling to the center of the dance floor and then instruct the older sibling to remove his or her shoes to enact the tradition. The younger sibling, or another member of the family, then puts on the elder sibling's feet a pair of colorful, striped, highly embellished knee-high socks that have been made by a family member especially for the occasion. The older sibling is then told to dance to a piece of music with a strong beat, unaccompanied in the middle of the dance floor, all the while cheered on by all the wedding guests who also tease the older sibling and sometimes throw money at him or her (sometimes the older sibling makes several hundred dollars from performing the sock dance). The guests may also spin the sibling around in order to make the sibling dizzy. At the end of the dance, the unmarried sibling removes the ceremonial socks to signal that the ritual is over. The sibling usually keeps the socks as a souvenir. If there is more than one older sibling then the siblings dance together and if an older sibling has several younger siblings all of whom marry before he or she does then the older sibling may have to perform the sock dance many times. Though the tradition is lighthearted, it is more or less mandatory with any sibling that refuses to take part suffering mockery, jeering, and practical jokes. In contrast, in southwestern Ontario it is traditional for older siblings to dance in a pig trough as punishment for being unmarried while their younger sibling is wed. This tradition, known as *Pointe-aux-Roches* used to see siblings dance in a washbasin or on an upturned wooden bench. Nowadays, however, a clean pig trough is used. The trough is either made or bought by the sibling's family especially for the occasion.

In New Brunswick, while spinsters would dance in a pig trough, older unmarried male siblings would be made to eat from the trough. Today, in New Brunswick, particularly in the southeastern area of the province, single older siblings must dance around a pig trough that has been filled with alcohol. The alcohol used is usually a mixture of beer and spirits and the older sibling must drink the highly alcoholic concoction for the tradition to be fulfilled.

It is thought that the sock dance and the trough dance hark back to the age-old fundamental rule found in many cultures that older siblings should marry before their younger brothers and sisters. When this unwritten rule is broken by a younger sibling marrying first, these dances allow the community to comment on the flouting of their cultural rules. In times past, society would prevent the rule break by simply delaying the wedding of the younger sibling. Today, however, older siblings are punished by having to carry out a humiliating task in public ritual—dancing in public wearing ridiculous socks. By dancing in this way, the older sibling atones for his or her "crime" of not being married and is forgiven by the community.

Socks are also a feature of Danish weddings for in Denmark after the married couple's first dance male wedding guests surround the groom and gradually close in on him closing the circle. Once the groom is encircled, the male guests lift the groom into the air and use a pair of scissors to cut the groom's socks. According to Danish tradition, cutting the socks that the groom wears on his wedding day will stop the man from committing adultery in the future.

See also: Birthday Candles (Volume 1); Birthday Humiliations for Singletons; Birthday Torments (Volume 1); Cajun Weddings; Face in Birthday Cake; Party Games (Volume 1); *Piñata* (Volume 1); Twenty-First Birthday Traditions

Further Reading

Bauer, Ingrid. "Birthday Customs in Germany." German.About.com. Accessed February 6, 2015, at http://german.about.com/od/holidaysfolkcustoms/a/Birthday-Customs-In-Germany.htm.

Gomez, Henar. "Germany: 25 and Unmarried." Wanderwings. August 29, 2013. Accessed February 6, 2015, at http://www.wanderwings.com/2013/08/germany-25-and-unmarried.html.

Peper Harow. "Sock Traditions around the World." November 21, 2014. Accessed February 6, 2015, at http://www.luxurymenssocks.com/blog/recent/sock-traditions-around-the-world.html.

Pichette, Jean-Pierre. "Dance of the Unwed Older Sibling," *Encyclopedia of French Cultural Heritage in North America*. Accessed February 6, 2015, at http://www.ameriquefrancaise.org/en/article-395/dance_of_the_unwed_older_sibling.html.

ST. CATHERINE'S DAY, FRANCE

A very old French custom sees single women wear outlandish hats every November 25 in honor of Saint Catherine, the patron saint of milliners and couturiers. In France, unmarried women over 25 years old are known as Catherinettes, though this term is somewhat dated. Similarly, St. Catherine's Day hat wearing has gradually fallen out of fashion, first because French society became less religious and second because it became less important for women to marry early. However St. Catherine's Day hat wearing still takes place either ironically or as a long-observed family tradition.

Saint Catherine was born Catherine of Alexandria in Egypt in the fourth century CE and according to Christian legend she was executed after refusing the advances of the Roman Emperor Maxentius. As a result of her martyrdom, Catherine was made the patron saint of unmarried females and so in order to honor Catherine on her saint's day, girls in France wear hats. The custom became popular among working class females employed in the Parisian fashion industry during the 19th century. During the 1920s and 1930s St. Catherine's Day festivities reached their

> ### La Fête du Muguet
>
> Every year on May 1 France celebrates the *Fête du Muguet*, or Festival of Lily-of-the-Valley when people give the flowers to their loved ones. The tradition began on May 1, 1561, when French King Charles IX was given a bouquet of lily-of-the-valley as a symbol of good fortune for the coming year. The king then instituted an annual custom of giving bouquets of lily-of-the-valley to the ladies of his court on May 1. Around 1900, it became usual for French men to present bouquets of lily-of-the-valley to their sweethearts as a symbol their affection. Today the flowers are also presented as tokens of affection between close friends and relatives.

peak of popularity as seamstresses' assistants used the occasion to escape their harsh working conditions and parade the streets wearing their millinery creations. The women's employers frowned upon the parade as it was generally seen as a way of warding off celibacy and therefore carried overtly sexual connotations.

On St. Catherine's Day, the oldest unmarried female in a community dons a traditional French starched cap while the community's other females wear paper bonnets. It is also traditional on this day for unmarried females to pray to Saint Catherine for a husband and crown a statue of the saint with a hat. In addition Catherinettes send each other postcards.

The hats worn by the Catherinettes are made by their friends and are traditionally colored either yellow, denoting faith, or green, representing wisdom, and are supposed to be worn all day long in the manner of a crown. In the evening of St. Catherine's Day Catherinettes are treated to a meal, ball, or party by their friends. Once a female marries she stops taking part in the St. Catherine's Day celebrations.

The French have a saying that if a female is under 25 and single she will pray: "*Donnez-moi, Seigneur, un mari de bon lieu! Qu'il soit doux, opulent, libéral et agréable!*" which translates as "Lord, give me a well-situated husband. Let him be gentle, rich, generous, and pleasant!" but that if she is still single after the age of 25 the woman will pray thus: "*Seigneur, un qui soit supportable, ou qui, parmi le monde, au moins puisse passer!*" meaning, "Lord, one who's bearable, or who can at least pass as bearable in the world!" Then, if the woman is still unmarried at the age of 30 she is likely to pray, "*Un tel qu'il te plaira Seigneur, je m'en contente!*" which is a desperate plea meaning, "Send whatever you want, Lord; I'll take it!" The English also call upon Saint Catherine to protect them from spinsterhood with the old saying: "Saint Catherine, Saint Catherine, O lend me thine aid, And grant that I never may die an old maid."

A statue by Julien Lorieux dedicated to the St. Catherine's Day hat-wearing custom can be found in Montholon Square in Paris.

See also: Bachelor and Spinster Balls; Birthday Humiliations for Singletons; Maidens' Garlands; Single's Day and Black Day; Virginity Testing

Further Reading

Fabulously French. "Happy St. Catherine's Day." Accessed November 23, 2014, at http://fabulouslyfrench.blogspot.co.uk/2013/11/happy-st-catherines-day.html.

Invisible Paris. "Les Catherinettes de la Sainte Catherine." Accessed November 23, 2014, at http://parisisinvisible.blogspot.co.uk/2010/11/les-catherinettes-de-la-sainte.html.

Levi, Giovanni, and Schmitt, Jean Claude, eds. *A History of Young People in the West: Stormy Evolution to Modern Times*. Volume 2. Cambridge, MA: Harvard University Press, 1997.

ST. DWYNWEN'S DAY, WALES

Every January 25, people in Wales celebrate St. Dwynwen's Day, the day commemorating Saint Dwynwen, the Welsh patron saint of lovers. Though the Vatican no longer recognizes Saint Dwynwen as a saint officially, Saint Dwynwen remains extremely popular in her native Wales, particularly in the county of Anglesey where she lived. St. Dwynwen's Day is virtually unknown outside of Wales, where celebratory dinners, events, and fixtures celebrating the saint are held each January and it is traditional on this day for a man to present his lover with a lovespoon.

According to folklore, Dwynwen was the fairest daughter of the Welsh king Brychan Brycheiniog. According to the most popular version of Saint Dwynwen's tale, one day Dwynwen met a prince, Maelon Dafodrill, and the pair fell in love. However according to various versions of the tale Dwynwen could not allow herself to love Maelon as either unbeknownst to Dwynwen her father had arranged for her to marry another, or, according to another variant, Dwynwen had vowed to become a nun. Either way, once Dwynwen realized her love for Maelon would come to naught she is said to have prayed to God begging that he would allow her to forget Maelon. Soon after, an angel visited Dwynwen in her sleep and presented the distraught maiden with a potion to expunge her memory of Maelon, who was subsequently transformed into a block of ice. God also gave Dwynwen three wishes. Dwynwen's first wish was that Maelon be thawed and her second wish was that God fulfill the hopes of true lovers. For her third wish, Dwynwen asked that she should never wed. God met all Dwynwen's wishes and to show her gratitude to God she devoted her life to him, establishing a convent on the island of Llandwyn (meaning the enclosure of Dwynwen) that lies off the coast of Anglesey. According to legend, the first nuns to live here were Saint Dwynwen, her sister, and other broken-hearted women.

The remains of Saint Dwynwen's convent are still visible today as is a well that is said to have belonged to Saint Dwynwen and that became a place of pilgrimage for lovers after her death in 465 CE. According to legend, the well is inhabited by sacred fish (or eels) that can predict if lovers will be faithful to each other and if the well's waters boil in the presence of lovers it is said that the couple will be happy and lucky. Married women also visit the well, sprinkling the water with breadcrumbs covered with a handkerchief. It is said that if the fish visibly disturb the water swimming under the handkerchief then the woman's husband is faithful.

> ### Opposition to Valentine's Day
>
> In February 2016, the president of Pakistan Mamnoon Hussain condemned Valentine's Day as alien to Pakistani culture and a facet of Western life that was contrary to Islam. Meanwhile, in a town in the northwest of Pakistan, shops were banned from selling anything related to Valentine's Day on the grounds that the day of love results in immorality. In neighboring India, Valentine's Day is opposed by some conservative Hindus who claim the day is alien to India's national culture while some Indian Muslims argue the day infringes on traditions like arranged marriage.

Owners of sick pets are also known to visit the well in the hope that their beloved animal companions will be healed.

Recently, the popularity of St. Dwynwen's Day has increased greatly. This is possibly as a result of the Welsh independence movement that has seen Wales gain its own parliament. The influence of Welsh nationalism on St. Dwynwen's Day is evinced by the Welsh Language Board's decision to print bilingual Welsh/English-language St. Dwynwen's Day cards in 2003. However another more romantic reason for the growing interest in St. Dwynwen's Day is that the Welsh wish to say *dwi'n dy garu di* ("I love you") three weeks before those celebrating St. Valentine's Day.

See also: Leap Year Proposal; Lovespoons; St. Catherine's Day

Further Reading

Historic UK. "St. Dwynwen's Day." Accessed May 31, 2015, at http://www.historic-uk.com/HistoryUK/HistoryofWales/St-Dwynwens-Day/.
Lloyd Evans, Dyfed. *Welsh Legends and Folk-tales*. Kindle edition, 2012.
Monger, George P. *Marriage Customs of the World: From Henna to Honeymoons*. Santa Barbara, CA: ABC-CLIO, 2004.
Welsh Government. "St. Dwynwen's Day." Wales Cymru. Accessed May 31, 2015, at http://www.visitwales.com/explore/traditions-history/st-dwynwens-day.

SÜNNET, TURKEY

Sünnet is the Islamic male circumcision custom practiced in Turkey. The word sünnet is Arabic in origin and translates as "busy path" for the ritual of circumcision is seen by adherents as a step on the path to God and also refers to the path of good and evil that humans must encounter in life. Circumcision is considered the most important child-related custom in Anatolia, the Asian region of Turkey, and is therefore the most oft-performed religious ritual practiced in the area. Indeed parents are under enormous social pressure to have their son circumcised as no objection to the ritual is allowed. If a boy is not circumcised then he will face great social stigma and humiliation. There is no specific age at which sünnet must occur though the ritual marks the transition of a male from boy to man. A boy who is to be circumcised is known as *Sünnet Çocuğu*, meaning Child of Circumcision.

Sünnet performs several functions in Turkish society. For instance, a lavish circumcision ceremony allows families to unite and means the family is considered respectable. Also, Anatolian parents see it as their duty to see that their son is circumcised and so feel glad when sünnet is performed. Sünnet is considered so important to Turkish society that wealthy families will often pay for the sünnet ceremony of poor boys and orphans to take place alongside the ceremonies of their own sons. Sometimes charities also pay for sünnet ceremonies to take place.

In Turkey, boys are usually circumcised when they are six or seven years old—though it is traditional for sünnet to take place when boys are an odd-numbered age—and certainly before they reach puberty. Recently, it has become the fashion in major cities for boys to be circumcised at birth while still in hospital so that the boy does not have to undergo the scary, painful procedure at a later age. However this changes the nature of sünnet for the ceremony is traditionally a rite of passage to manhood rather than a birth ritual.

Sünnet tends to take place in spring, summer, and autumn, particularly on weekends, though it was once traditional for sünnet to occur on Thursdays because Fridays were a day of rest. Families start to prepare for sünnet two months before the ceremony takes place, depending on the boy's age and the family's financial circumstances. The family chooses a date for the ritual to occur on and around 10 days before that date the family announces that ceremony will take place. An announcement of a sünnet ceremony is usually made by sending out invitations for guests to attend the ritual or by sending messengers to spread the news. In traditional communities it is important that everybody is invited to the ceremony.

The boy who is to be circumcised will be prepared by his family for the event anywhere from a few months to a few days before the ceremony takes place—the more traditional his community the longer the period of preparation the boy will experience. This preparation period is a time of mixed emotions for the boy as he experiences a mix of exciting moments and begins to fear the coming of the operation. Part of a boy's preparation for his sünnet ceremony is his special circumcision outfit, part of which is a light-blue colored hat that has the word *Maşallah* (meaning Wonderful, may God avert the evil eye) embroidered on the front and a piece of bridal tinsel hung from the back. Wealthy families may also dress their son in jewelry for the occasion while in villages a boy's circumcision outfit also features a cloth called a *çevre* and a large napkin called a *yağlık*, both of which hang around the boy's neck and shoulders.

A few days before the ceremony, or even on the day itself, the boy that is to be circumcised parades or rides on horseback or in a car around his village or town with his friends and everyone is informed that the boy is parading because the time of his sünnet ceremony is approaching. The boy's parade around his community demonstrates the love and protectiveness that the community feels toward the boy.

On the day of the ceremony guests congregate and chant *Mevlit*, a long poem written by Süleyman Çelebi praising the life of the Prophet Muhammed that is also said as a prayer sung as a hymn on important occasions. The guests then feast and await the arrival of the newly circumcised boy. Meanwhile, the boy is brought into the circumcision hall just before noon and does not dismount from his horse or exit his car until he receives money from his father. Once the father has given the boy the money the sünnet ceremony begins. The sünnet ceremony sees the removal of the boy's foreskin. To facilitate this procedure the boy sits on the lap of either a relative or his *kirve*, a man equivalent to a Christian godfather who usually pays for the sünnet ceremony to be held. The boy is forced to open his legs while the person on whom the boy is sitting pins his arms by his side. Meanwhile, everyone present proclaims encouraging words stressing the importance of sünnet in making the boy a man. Before and during the ceremony the words "*Allahu ekber*" ("God is the greatest") are said as is "*oldu da bitti maşallah, iyi olur inşallah*" meaning "It has happened at once, May God preserve him; it will grow better, by God's will." The man who performs the circumcision procedure is known as a *sünnetçi* (circumciser), *abdal* (wiseman), or *kızılbaş abdal* (scarlet-head wiseman). Increasingly, a government-authorized health professional called a *fenni sünnetçi* (scientific circumciser) performs circumcision operations in hospitals or clinics.

The freshly circumcised boy is then clothed in a long loose dress and placed gently upon a highly decorated bed prepared in one corner of his home, where he can rest and recuperate from the circumcision procedure. Sometimes the boy is placed on the bed in such a way as to display his bloody underwear.

After lunch, guests gather at the boy's bedside, note his stained clothing, and say "everything remained in the past, you will gain your health soon." The guests then give the boy gifts to mark the importance of sünnet and the boy's transition to manhood. Traditional gifts include clothing, gold, and, money and, depending on a person's relationship with the boy, a gold coin called a *Cumhuriyet Altını* may be presented. After the presentation of the gifts, entertainment begins and continues often until late in the evening.

See also: *Brit Milah* (Volume 1); Female Genital Cutting; Urethral Subincision; Xhosa Circumcision

Further Reading

Hart, Kimberly. *And Then We Work for God: Rural Sunni Islam in Western Turkey*. Stanford, CA: Stanford University Press, 2013.

Jernigan, Meg. "What Do You Do at a Turkish Sunnet Festival?" *USA Today*. Accessed January 3, 2015, at http://traveltips.usatoday.com/turkish-sunnet-festival-100369.html.

Mymerhaba. "Circumcision (Sünnet)." Accessed January 3, 2015, at http://www.mymerhaba.com/Circumcision-(Sünnet)-in-Turkey-121.html.

Turkish Cultural Foundation. "Circumcision." Lifestyles. Accessed January 3, 2015, at http://www.turkishculture.org/lifestyles/ceremonies/circumcision/tradition-of-circumcision-541.htm?type=1.

SUNRISE CEREMONY, APACHE, UNITED STATES

The Apache Sunrise Ceremony, or *na'ii'ees* or *na ih es*, meaning "preparing her" or "getting her ready," is one of the most well-known North American Indian puberty rites. The ceremony is experienced by Apache girls soon after their first menstruation and is timed so that the last day of the ceremony coincides with the full moon. The ceremony is commonly referred to as the Sunrise Dance by Western Apaches. The specifics of the ceremony vary between tribes, but always consist of several arduous highly symbolic rituals that traditionally last for four days and four nights. The Sunrise Ceremony celebrates the female in terms of the Apache's Creation stories, recognizing that the female's ability to give birth means that she can create life. The ceremony also symbolizes the Apache's belief that within the female resides all the supreme energy forces of life. Through the multitude of sacred ceremonies, dances, songs, feasting, and re-enactments that are a feature of the Sunrise Ceremony, girls become infused with physical and spiritual power and come to understand their role as Apache women. It is thought that around one-third of Apache females experience a Sunrise Ceremony. Some of these ceremonies last only one to two days rather than the traditional four days because of the costs involved in holding the ceremony and some ceremonies are held jointly to offset expense.

The White Mountain Apaches of Arizona and the Fort Apache Indian Reservation, also in Arizona, sponsor about 20 Sunrise Ceremonies every year, most of which take place on weekdays during spring and summer. Outsiders may attend public ceremonies involving several girls on the Fort Apache Indian Reservation and the Mescalero Reservation in New Mexico, where several girl take part in ceremonies held as part of the tribe's July 4 celebrations. Sunrise Ceremonies are important to tribal life as they bring people together, strengthen emotional bonds, and intensify the Apaches' ties to their spiritual and cultural heritage.

A Sunrise Ceremony sees a girl become invested with supernatural, sacred virtues through both her physical maturation and her participation in the numerous rituals that bond her to the main supernatural female entity of the Apaches, Esdzanadehe, known in English as White Painted Woman. Indeed for the duration of the Sunrise Ceremony a girl is so closely identified with White Painted Woman that she is known by that name rather than her own.

White Painted Woman is the mother of the Creator and according to some Apache myths, slept with the Sun producing a son, Killer-of-Enemies (also known as Slayer-of-Monsters), who would go on to become an Apache cultural hero. Killer-of-Enemies triumphed over Owl Man Giant who was terrorizing the people. When Killer-of-Enemies returned from the fight, White Painted Woman shouted her delight at the victory, a cry that is echoed during the Sunrise Ceremony. White Painted Woman established the Sunrise Ceremony as a coming-of-age rite for all females born of her people that instructs females and guides them in the ways of womanhood. Also, when she became elderly White Painted Woman walked toward the east where she met her younger self and subsequently merged with the younger version becoming young again. In this way, White Painted Woman was reborn signaling that she persists from generation to generation, a concept symbolized by the repeated holding of the Sunrise Ceremony. As the spiritual representation of the universal cycle of life as well as the annual rebirth of the earth, White Painted Woman is a Mother-Earth figure symbolizing fertility and fruitfulness. The Apaches believe that White Painted Woman is the essence of life from whom they were created and who provided their people with teachings and commanded girls to dress in her image and to perform puberty rituals.

The Sunrise Ceremony has taken place since time immemorial. However the ceremony was made illegal in the early 1900s, when the U.S. government banned Native American spiritual practices and rituals. As a result of this ban, the ceremony was practiced less often, and those ceremonies that did take place were performed secretly. It was not until 1978, when the American Indian Religious Freedom Act was passed, that the Sunrise Ceremony was conducted openly on most reservations. However today costs and time constraints mean that the Sunrise Ceremony does not always occur in its traditional manner. As a single ceremony costs around $10,000 to hold—it is expensive to perform. In order to offset some of the costs some families of girls beginning puberty in the same year may sponsor joint Sunrise Ceremonies, in which several newly menstruating girls celebrate together. A ceremony also takes up a significant amount of time—not just the days of the ceremony but also days of pre-ceremony preparation and post-ceremony recovery too. Indeed a Sunrise Ceremony actually lasts much longer than the four days and nights of the ceremony itself for from the time a girl experiences her first period she starts to participate in rituals and ritualized gift-giving occurs for up to two years after the four-day ceremony is held. Therefore, in actuality the Sunrise Ceremony in its entirety can last up to three years. Thus, some girls celebrate their Sunrise Ceremony for only one or two days, rather than the traditional four days and nights.

A Sunrise Ceremony serves many purposes on a personal, spiritual, and communal level and is often regarded as one of the most important events an Apache female can experience. For instance, by drawing on various myths of White Painted Woman, a girl relates deeply to her cultural and religious heritage. In her connection to White Painted Woman the girl harnesses an inner strength and overcomes any dark forces in her nature. The girl's transformation into White Painted Woman is thought to empower her and imbue her with the qualities associated with the supernatural figure. Through the process of the ceremony a girl also learns to acknowledge her own spirituality, her sacredness as a woman, and her ability to do good. Indeed some girls also discover their ability to heal during the ceremony. A girl that goes through a Sunrise Ceremony also discovers what it means to be a woman, first through coming to terms with physical changes brought about by puberty, such as menstruation, and being educated in matters of sexuality. A girl also learns how she has developed physical strength and fortitude. In order to endure the four days of dancing and running that are a feature of a Sunrise Ceremony a girl must undergo demanding physical training. The arduous nature of the dancing and running means that this physical element of the Sunrise Ceremony is often regarded as a sacred ordeal that strengthens a girl both bodily and emotionally. This is particularly true if the running and dancing take place during inclement weather. Additionally, many Apache females say that experiencing the Sunrise Ceremony greatly increases their self-confidence and that when the ceremony ends they feel as though they have left behind their childhood. Another important aspect of the Sunrise Ceremony is that it teaches girls how to act as an Apache woman. This includes the need to work hard, to please others, and to present herself at all times with dignity and a pleasant demeanor even when she is tired or not feeling her best. To this end, during the Sunrise Ceremony a girl must be stoic as her temperament during the rituals is thought to reveal the disposition she will display in later life.

A Sunrise Ceremony typically involves at least six months of intensive preparation and teaching. Much of this preparation entails creating the girl's highly symbolic white buckskin dress (costing around $1,000), building a lodge, and locating bee pollen, eagle feathers, and ochre—obligatory religious objects that are needed for the Sunrise Ceremony to occur. An abalone shell, the symbol of White Painted Woman, is also required, as this will be plaited into the girl's hair on her forehead. Meanwhile, the girl's family engages in a great deal of food preparation, as throughout the ceremony they must provide food and gifts to everyone taking part in the ceremony as well as spectators.

Once an Apache girl starts to menstruate for the first time she tells all her female relatives and her mother, or head of the family, who then initiates the holding of the Sunrise Ceremony by selecting the important figures that will lead the girl through the various ritual stages of the ceremony, most especially her godmother and the medicine man. The girl's godmother is carefully selected by the girl's family for the godmother is the girl's primary attendant during her Sunrise Ceremony and will go on to enjoy an especially close bond with the girl once the ceremony is completed. The godmother accompanies the girl as she performs the various ritual stages necessitated by her ceremony, including the many hours of dancing (both day and night) including the highly significant Sunrise Dance, and running—the girl runs to all four directions, north, east, south, and west, as this represents the four stages of life and the four seasons. The girl runs toward the east at sunrise. The godmother must also massage the girl during a ceremony known as The Massaging. This is an important element of the Sunrise Ceremony as it sees the re-enactment of White Painted Woman's myth during which the girl's body is massaged by her godmother to symbolize that the Sunrise Ceremony is molding the girl into the form of White Painted Woman. The girl should be massaged within four days of her first period so if a godmother has not been chosen by this time an interim godmother may perform the massage. The massage also transmits the wisdom of the elder woman to the girl and is also thought to shape the girl into a beautiful, strong adult. The godmother also provides the girl with emotional support throughout the ordeal and prepares food and drink. As the role of godmother is so physically and emotionally draining families strive to choose a strong, fit, and steadfast woman as godmother. When choosing the godmother the girl's family visits the chosen woman's home at sunrise and places the feather of an eagle on her foot. The family also offers her a prayer stone and gifts such as a sacred turquoise stone and asks her to act as godmother to the girl. A family may ask up to four women to be the godmother and acceptance of the offer is signaled by a woman removing the feather from her foot. When a woman accepts the role of godmother the girl's family gives her more gifts, food, and money, the amount of which varies depending on the family's wealth.

Another female relative of the girl, usually an older sister, is also active in the ceremony, acting as a companion dancer to keep the girl's energy and spirits high. Only the companion and the godmother may touch the girl once her cheek has been daubed with bee pollen. This is because the girl becomes sacred from the moment the ritual smearing of the pollen, a sacred symbol of fertility, occurs, its presence transforming the girl into White Painted Woman. Similarly, for the duration of the Sunrise Ceremony the girl cannot drink except for water through a straw. This is because if a cup touches her lips it is feared she may grow whiskers. Likewise the girl may not scratch an itch except with a special scratching stick as this might cause scarring.

Another important figure within the Sunrise Ceremony is that of the medicine man. The medicine man is selected by the girl's family in a manner similar to that employed to choose the godmother. The medicine man is important as he presides over much of the ceremony, leading the ceremony's many songs and incantations and paying the singers and musicians that perform during the ceremony. The medicine man also places an eagle feather in the girl's hair (symbolic of guidance and strength) and presents her with her buckskin dress during a ritual called The Dressing Ceremony. The medicine man conducts prayers and 32 songs within a ceremonial tepee that faces east. Each pole of the tepee represents both a day of Creation and the four cardinal directions—north, east, south, and west. Within the tepee the medicine man tells the story of Creation through sacred song and asks the Creator to bless the girl and her family. The actions of the medicine man are guided by the position of the stars and constellations particularly the Big Dipper. The medicine man is accompanied by the masked *Gans*, or Crown Dancers, who dance their Crown Dance with the girl. This dance lasts all night long and takes place inside the tepee.

Another element of the Sunrise Ceremony, The Painting Ceremony, involves the girl's skin being covered with a holy mixture of clay, pollen, and cornmeal that she must not remove for the duration of the ceremony. (*See* Plate 21.) After The Painting Ceremony, the Crown Dancers perform once more and then the girl is allowed to rest for the remainder of the day. On the last day of the ceremony, the girl blesses her people and performs acts of healing on people who desire her healing abilities. The girl is then undressed by her godmother and receives gifts. The Sunrise Ceremony is then said to be over.

Many other North America Indian peoples also celebrate a girl's transition to adulthood through ritual and ceremony. For instance the Navajo *kinaalda*, which also honors White Painted Woman in the form of Changing Woman, is very similar to the Sunrise Ceremony. According to the Navajo myth, Changing Woman was the daughter of First Man and First Woman. The couple devised a puberty ceremony for their daughter that involved running toward the rising sun four times. For this reason, the kinaalda begins on the fourth night after a girl starts her first period and sees a girl run toward the east, singing and praying, on each day of the ceremony. This ritual transforms the girl into the Changing Woman and allows her to receive the blessing of her people and gifts. However the kinaalda differs from the Sunrise Ceremony for at the start of the ceremony the girl washes her hair in bubbles from a yucca root and ties her hair back for the four-day duration of the ritual. For the first three days, the girl spends most of her time readying corn husks and grinding more than 100 pounds of corn and wheat in order to make a giant cornmeal cake, which is then heated in a fire pit in the ground. For the duration of the ritual the girl must stay awake at night, sitting with a straight back and her legs straight out in front of her. This is particularly important during the night on which prolonged prayers are said. The following morning, the girl runs toward the dawn once more and then blesses the cornmeal cake, which has been cooking all night in the fire pit. The girl then offers the first piece of the cornmeal cake to the Sun, and serves the rest of the cake to her people. In this way not only does the Navajo girl give to her community but she also receives back from her community blessings, acceptance, and love for throughout the ceremony the girl is the subject of many prayers that she enjoy a long, healthy, and prosperous life.

Meanwhile the Jicarilla Apache puberty ceremony, *keesta*, sees a girl accompanied throughout her ritual by a male companion as well as an older woman who passes on to the girl her wisdom. Keesta celebrates the role of women within Jicarilla society as well as the belief that men and women are equally important in society, unable to exist without each other. During the ceremony the girl is taught about life in general and together with the male companion is taught to embrace her sexuality, which it is stressed, is essential to the renewal of life. The girl is also taught that through prayer she will be able to manage all aspects of her life, particularly the pain of childbirth. To symbolize that the girl is expected to create life she is given symbolic gifts such as a blanket, which as a woman the girl will be able to use to wrap around her children.

See also: Apache Baby Ceremonies (Volume 1); Cradleboards (Volume 1); Entering the *Bashali* (Volume 1); Menstrual Customs

Further Reading
Brivium. "Apache Sunrise Ceremony." Religious Forums, May 3, 2006. Accessed February 6, 2015, at https://www.religiousforums.com/threads/apache-sunrise-ceremony.31789/.
Mails, Thomas E. *Secret Native American Pathways: A Guide to Inner Peace*. Second edition. San Francisco, CA: Council Oak Books, 2003.

Markstrom, Carol A. *Empowerment of North American Indian Girls: Ritual Expressions at Puberty*. Lincoln: University of Nebraska Press, 2008.

Navajo People, Culture & History. "Kinaalda—Celebrating Maturity of Girls among the Navajo." Navajo People, Culture & History, December 16, 2010. Accessed February 4, 2015, at http://navajopeople.org/blog/kinaalda-celebrating-maturity-of-girls-among-the-navajo/.

Sharp, Jay W. "Profile of an Apache Woman." DesertUSA.com. Accessed February 4, 2015, at http://www.desertusa.com/desert-people/apache-women.html.

Tiller, Veronica E. Velarde. *Culture and Customs of the Apache Indians*. Santa Barbara, CA: ABC-CLIO, 2011.

Wagner, Dennis. "An Apache Dance into Womanhood." AZCentral.com. October 5, 2014. Accessed February 6, 2015, at http://www.azcentral.com/story/news/local/arizona/2014/10/05/apache-dance-sunrise-ceremony-womanhood/16616029/.

Yupanqui, Tika. "Apache Female Puberty Sunrise Ceremony." Becoming Woman, January 15, 2001. Accessed February 4, 2015, at http://www.webwinds.com/yupanqui/apachesunrise.htm.

THAIPUSAM: EXTREME RITUAL FLESH MODIFICATION, HINDUISM

Thaipusam is an annual three-day Hindu festival and test of faith held in honor of the god Lord Muruga during which mainly Tamil followers of the religion voluntarily demonstrate their penitence by undergoing eye-watering acts of body piercing and carrying heavy objects. The festival is celebrated on the eve of the full moon each January or February in countries including India, Sri Lanka, Myanmar, Malaysia, Singapore, and Indonesia. Tamils living in South Africa, Trinidad and Tobago, Fiji, Mauritius, Reunion, Guadeloupe, and Canada also hold Thaipusam festivals. However the largest Thaipusam festival is held in Kuala Lumpur in Malaysia, concluding in the Batu Caves just outside the city. The caves are one of the most significant shrines to Lord Muruga to be found outside of India and see the convergence of some 1.3 million people. Those that take part in the Thaipusam festivities are mainly men aged over 18 years, their families and spectators including tourists. However not all countries welcome the Thaipusam celebration for it is heavily regulated in Singapore and outlawed in India, though a version does take place at the Periyanayaki Amman Temple in Pelani, though this does not include flesh piercing. Part of the reason for laws governing Thaipusam is that during the 1970s and 1980s some participants placed themselves in extreme danger by wearing shoes made from nails and blades or threaded knives into their arms. However it is the sight of seeing such acts of extreme flesh modification that draws tourists to view the Thaipusam festivals.

The name Thaipusam derives from the word *Thai*, which is the name of the 10th month of the Hindu calendar, correlating with the period running from the end of January to the end of February, and *Pusam*, which is the name of a star that travels through the sky during this period. The Thaipusam festival honors Lord Muruga, who is esteemed by all Hindus and is famed for using a magical lance to slay his enemy, the monstrous Soorapadman. Further to this, the god is revered by Hindus living in the southeast Indian state of Tamil Nadu to such a degree that Lord Muruga is sometimes referred to as the God of the Tamils. This evinced by the fact that the various names by which Lord Muruga is known—Swaminathan, Subramanian, and Kartikeya—are popular names among Tamils. Lord Muruga is the god of self-discipline, self-denial, and freedom from physicality through death so to honor the god and the lance with which he killed his enemies, participants in Thaipusam undergo forms of extreme body modification including the piercing of their tongues, foreheads, and cheeks, and having hooks threaded through their skin—sometimes with offerings weighing up to 220 pounds attached to the hooks which increases the strain on the body. Participants also carry elaborate frames weighing between 20 and 40 pounds called *kavadis* through streets and climb extremely high staircases at the top of which they leave offerings to Lord Muruga such as fruit, coconuts, and incense. In Malaysia, penitents haul heavy weights attached to their backs via hooks up 272 steps in order to complete their penance.

Preparations for Thaipusam, which begin several months in advance, see participants and their families abstain from eating meat, drinking alcohol, having sex, smoking, and watching television. Participants also practice saying prayers, dancing, and chanting in the run-up to the festival as this is thought to prepare the participants for their ordeal both mentally and spiritually. Participants that elect to carry a kavadi usually do so in order to attain particular aims such as curing a relative of illness, which they believe can only be achieved through penitence. The size of the kavadi carried by the penitents is determined by the seriousness of the penitent's prayer. Kavadi carriers may decorate their kavadi however they wish though most choose to enhance their burden with peacock feathers as these recall the peacock ridden by Lord Muruga. An icon of Lord Muruga is transported ahead of the kavadi carriers who are accompanied by their families and other participants carrying pots of milk. On the day of the piercings, priests prepare those that want to be pierced. During the festival the dancing, chanting, and singing sends participants into a trance that dulls the pain they feel when they are pierced. Participants, who have holy ash daubed on their foreheads, believe that the spirit of Lord Muruga enters their body during the festival and that this is why they do not bleed when they are pierced. Similarly, the piercings rarely leave any scarring—this is due to the application of a medicinal salve, *vibhuti*, on the pierced flesh.

The chants and dancing performed by the kavadi carriers puts them into an ecstatic trance-like state that medical research has found does produce an increased level of endorphins that alleviates the pain felt by the piercings. Indeed participants will not be pierced until they have entered the necessary trance and those participants that do claim to feel pain as they are pierced assert that after the first two or three hooks are inserted they become unaware of their pain though they can still hear their flesh ripping. The point on the body that is to be pierced is first covered in vibhuti, which is composed of cow dung (cows are sacred to Hindus), milk, ash, spices, and butter. Once the skin has been covered in the vibhuti, it is pierced with a small lance or large pin that remains sticking through the skin for the duration of the penitent's participation in the event. (*See* Plate 22.) Trained priests also push numerous metal hooks through the epidermis of participants. The hooks go through the skin and attach to strips of material that in turn connect to either heavy weights or the planks that are part of the kavadi. Once they have been pierced participants start to perform a trance-dance composed of whirling movements and then begin to proceed along a predetermined route that tends to end with participants delivering offerings to a shrine of Lord Muruga. Once they have left their offerings those that have been pierced emerge from their trance, the metal is removed from their skin and they feel elated that they have managed to withstand the sacrifice of their flesh in order to prove their faith and please Lord Muruga.

See also: Breast Ironing; Ear-Piercing Ceremony; Female Genital Cutting; Forehead-Cutting Initiation; Human Tooth Sharpening; Ritual Tattooing; Scarification; Tooth-Filing Ceremony

Further Reading

Galvan, Javier A., ed. *They Do What? A Cultural Encyclopedia of Extraordinary and Exotic Customs from around the World.* Santa Barbara: ABC-CLIO, 2014.

National Geographic Society. "Thaipusam." *National Geographic.* Accessed May 1, 2015, at http://video.nationalgeographic.com/video/malaysia-thaipusam-pp.

Vooght, Clare. "Stripped to the Waist with a Skewered Tongue and Hooks Embedded in His Back: The Only White Man to Join Malaysia's Spectacular Thaipusam Festival." *Daily Mail*, February 4, 2015. Accessed May 1, 2015, at http://www.dailymail.co.uk/travel/travel_news/article-2938125/Australian-tourist-joins-Malaysian-locals-tongue-cheek-pierced-Hindu-Thaipusam-ceremony-following-48-day-fast.html.

TOOTH-FILING CEREMONY, INDONESIA

The tooth-filing ceremony is one of the most unusual Hindu customs to occur on the Indonesian island of Bali, a land with a rich cultural history of traditions and rituals. These ceremonies are known as *mapandes* in the High Balinese language and as *matatah* in the Common Balinese tongue and is the last of the group of rituals that Balinese parents have performed on behalf of their child that are known as *tingkah dadi janma*, meaning the way of becoming a human being. The tooth-filing ceremony is extremely important as a religious and social ritual as it marks the rite of passage for pre-pubescent boys whose voice begins to break and for girls who experience their first menstrual cycle. Tooth-filing ceremonies take place in villages as well as urban areas as the island's capital Denpasar throughout the months of July and August.

The tooth-filing ceremony is a very important custom for the whole family as parents would never consider allowing a child to reach adulthood without his or her teeth being filed, and a Balinese Hindu's teeth most definitely must be filed before they wed. Whole families take part in tooth-filing ceremonies, wearing clothing colored white and yellow, the colors that traditionally denote holiness. For the ceremony boys where ornate clothing while girls wear clothes made from embellished fabrics, plus jewelry and a golden headpiece resembling a tiara. Tooth-filing ceremonies can be expensive to hold so in order to reduce costs the recent trend is for group ceremonies to be held.

Archeological evidence suggests the history of the tooth-filing ceremony dates back at least 2,000 years. However the first Hindus arrived on Bali in the fourth century CE thus it follows that tooth-filing ceremonies were not originally

Hindu. Today, however, on Bali the ceremony is almost exclusively practiced by Hindus.

The aim of a tooth-filing ceremony is to file down a child's six molar teeth so that they resemble flat molars. On a superficial level tooth filing may seem a purely aesthetic procedure, particularly since the Balinese consider pointy teeth to be ugly. However the tooth-filing ceremony actually has a deep-rooted religious significance since Hindus consider canine teeth to be symbolic of symbol of lust, avarice, wrath, drunkenness, confusion, and envy. Therefore a tooth-filing ceremony aims to rid the individual of these invisible evil tendencies rendering the body more physically and spiritually beautiful as well as symbolizing the rite of passage from childhood to adulthood. The teeth are ground down to help remove the six specific forces of evil: *loba* (greed), *kama* (lust), *moha* (confusion), *mada* (insobriety), *matzarya* (envy), and *krodha* (wrath). The lower canines are usually left alone. However it is a common Balinese belief that people will be denied entry to heaven if their teeth are not sufficiently filed down as they might be mistaken for wild, fanged creatures rather than as humans.

Preparations for the tooth-filing ceremony start that day before the ritual takes place. Parents decorate the ceremony venue with flowers and fruit and hang up banners announcing the event. Parents also make ready the food that will be eaten during the feat accompanying the ceremony. Meanwhile, a Brahmin, or priest, sanctifies the instruments he will use to grind down the teeth. The boy or girl who will undergo the tooth-filing ceremony is not allowed to leave his or her house as they must stay indoors and meditate on the importance of the ceremony he or she will experience shortly. Another reason the children must stay indoors is that people fear they are particularly vulnerable to attack by supernatural forces at this time. The night before the ceremony the parents decide how many people will surround their child when their teeth are filed. Traditionally, two, four, or six people may be present in order to confer good luck on the child. Groups of uneven numbers are thought to bring bad luck and endanger the child's chance of a good marriage.

Tooth-filing ceremonies are usually held between 4 a.m. and 6 a.m., before the sun rises, and are accompanied by religious songs. The ceremony is performed by a Brahmin of a higher caste who has been taught to act as a dentist (*Sangging*) in order to enact the tooth-filing rite. The Sangging uses basic tools to conduct his work. These tend to include a file, a small hammer, and a carver that have been purified with holy water prior to the ceremony by a lay priest. In addition, the child's family provides items such as a mirror, a piece of sugar cane, and some young coconut. To begin the ceremony, the fearful child is brought into the venue and made to lie down on a flat platform made of bamboo that is especially erected for the occasion. This part of the ceremony usually features background music that is played to try and pacify the frightened child. The child's family then surrounds the bamboo bed, offering emotional support, and trying to allay the child's fears. The first stage of the ceremony sees the Sangging place a small piece of sugar cane in the child's mouth, between the upper and lower sets of teeth, in order to prevent the mouth from shutting. The Sangging then starts to grind and file the teeth—this is a painful experience for the child as he or she is not given any anesthetic prior to the procedure. All the while the watching family must remain in perfect silence. The only person permitted to speak is the priest who chats to the child to try and distract the boy or girl from the unpleasant sensation of his or her teeth being deliberately eroded. The Sangging aims to file the upper canine teeth flat enough to create a continual line of even top teeth. Once the upper teeth form this even line the Sangging allows the child to see his or her newly shaped teeth in a mirror bought specially for the occasion. The child is allowed to suggest a few minor alterations to the end result. Occasionally parents inspect the Sangging's dentistry to make sure the teeth have been filed correctly and may request further filing. An individual's tooth-filing ceremony takes around 10 minutes to complete. During the ceremony the child must not shout out in pain or complain in any way as the uncomplaining endurance of pain is expected of anyone going through the rite of passage. When the priest has finished the child is viewed as spiritually stronger and is bidden to make a private prayer of thanksgiving in an isolated location. Though the tooth-filing ceremony is very painful, the child is glad to experience the procedure as they understands that they are now considered an adult by society and will assimilated into wider society. To celebrate their child's entry into adulthood the parents invite friends and family to a ritual feast usually centered on a buffet featuring spiced meats, rice, fruit, and cake.

The cost of a child's ceremonial clothing and the ritual meal can be very high. Thus tooth-filing ceremonies have started to reveal the inequality of income among the Balinese as well as divisions of social class. Rich families often use their influence to hold ostentatious feasts showcasing lavish outside catering and live bands. Wealthy families also tend to add to the cost of the ceremony by placing announcements in the society pages of Bali's newspapers. At the opposite end of the social scale poor families use tooth-filing ceremonies as a means to unite families and guide their child to adulthood rather than as a way to raise the social cachet of families or individual children. Poorer families cannot afford extravagant fripperies and so they focus on the tooth-filing ceremony as a religious observance rather than as a social event. Such is the disparity of income on Bali that in order to make sure that the tooth-filing ceremony continues to be held modifications have been made to the way the ritual takes place. These amendments include group ceremonies that allow the poorest families to share the cost of the ritual. Another way for poor families to offset the cost of the tooth-filing ceremony is to combine the ritual with some other occasion, such as a wedding or cremation. Further, in order to allow children from all levels of Balinese society to participate in a tooth-filing ceremony there are three levels of tooth-filing ritual. The first level, *nista*, is the most basic. Next comes, *madya*, which is a ceremony on a medium scale and finally there is the most lavish form of the ceremony, *utama*. All three levels are viewed as appropriate to fulfilling the religious requirements of the tooth-filing ceremony as prescribed by Balinese Hinduism.

In the Philippines, the Dumagat tribe practice a form of voluntary tooth modification in which they saw through the top six incisors and canines so that the teeth form a line running parallel with the gums. Often the teeth are then dyed black. There is no religious or magical element to this tooth-sawing procedure, which occurs in late adolescence for purely aesthetic reasons.

See also: Forehead-Cutting Initiation; Human Tooth Sharpening; Menstrual Taboos; Menstruation Customs; Scarification; Training Bra

Further Reading
Galvan, Javier A., ed. *They Do What? A Cultural Encyclopedia of Extraordinary and Exotic Customs from around the World.* Santa Barbara, CA: ABC-CLIO, 2014.
Headland, Thomas N. "Teeth Mutilation among the Casigurian Dumagat," *Philippine Quarterly of Culture and Society,* 5(1-2), March–June 1977, 54–64.
Indo.com. "July—the Season for Balinese Tooth Filing Ceremonies." Bali & Indonesia on the Net. Accessed January 4, 2015, at http://www.indo.com/indonesia/news74.html.

TRAINING BRAS, UNITED STATES, EUROPE, AND AUSTRALASIA

Training bras, also known as trainer bras or bralettes, are undergarments designed for girls in the early stages of puberty to wear in order to allow them to become accustomed to wearing bras later in life. Training bras tend to be made of lightweight, stretchy material and take the form of a pullover garment featuring narrow straps and an elastic band that holds the bra in place. Alternatively, training bras may make up part of a camisole. Training bras conceal a girl's nipples and breast buds (small swellings around the nipple that signal the onset of pubertal changes) but tend not to be underwired and so do not offer support for developing breasts. In Western cultures, a girl's first training bra is often viewed as a rite of passage as she enters womanhood. That said several designers and shops have created training bras for much younger girls. For instance, in 2006 Target began stocking bras aimed at three- and four-year-olds while Australian retailer Big W stocked a padded bra designed for eight- to ten-year-olds. The manufacture of bras aimed at such young girls has led to accusations that retailers use training bras to financially exploit the so-called tween market of pre- and early adolescent girls.

The history of the training bra is fairly short. At the turn of the 20th century, a girl aged 12 or 13 was expected to wear a one-piece "waist," that is, a camisole that did not have cups or darts in front. As the girl's breasts developed she would wear different styles of the same garment, which featured increasing levels of construction such as stitching, tucks, and boning. These design features were intended to support and shape her breasts and accentuate the narrowness of her waist. The bra itself had yet to be invented so the camisole did not have cups so the bosom was worn low and flat. Without the uplift created by cups there was also no cleavage.

If a girl's parents were sufficiently wealthy, a girl could simply wear adult bras in increasing sizes as her breasts grew. Training bras were first marketed in the United States in the 1920s. However this was an era when many females made their own clothes, including their underwear and girls tended to wear an undershirt until they were sufficiently physically developed to fit an adult bra. Advertisements for training bras were viewed with longing by girls who could not afford to buy their own undergarments and could not persuade their parents to pay for what were usually viewed as frivolous, unnecessary, and expensive clothing—in the 1930s, a training bra in the Sears Roebuck catalog cost 25 cents for two. In the years between World War I and World War II home economics teachers endeavored to teach girls how to make their own training bras but this ultimately proved unsuccessful, particularly when the mass-production of training bars began in the 1950s. Interest in training bras increased at this time for it was generally agreed that they were important from a physiological and psychological standpoint. It has also been argued that the transition from homemade to mass-produced training bras was vitally important to how adolescent girls came to consider their breasts. Mass-produced bras encouraged girls to cultivate their own ideas of taste and style without the direct input of their mothers, who, traditionally, made the clothes worn by their daughters and governed what they wore. Buying training bras from a shop also made girls consider how they felt about their bodies. Unlike homemade clothes that could be fitted to the person who intended to wear it, off-the-peg clothes came in standard sizes. Therefore individuals had to fit into clothes that were manufactured from a pattern that represented what makers considered the norm with sizes starting at an AAA cup.

If clothes failed to fit, especially clothes intended for such an intimate body part as the bosom, then girls tended to perceive that there was something amiss with their bodies. Thus mass-produced bras available in standard cup sizes increased the self-consciousness young women felt about their developing breasts. Indeed it has been noted that around the time training bras began to be mass-produced, letters started appearing in magazines from girls worried that their figures did not live up to the full-breasted ideal propagated by curvy film stars of the era such as Marilyn Monroe and Jayne Mansfield. Magazines aimed at young women also started carrying adverts for training bras alongside promotions for acne treatments.

Apart from the men involved with manufacturing the garments, training bras were an all-female domain. Girls would compare breast sizes and judge which of their school friends was, or was not, wearing a bra while changing in school locker rooms, and mothers would help their daughters achieve a desirable figure by providing them with a training bra. In 1952, American physician Frank H. Crowell endorsed training bras as a way of supporting the breast and advocated that girls should wear training bras to prevent their breasts form sagging and stretching blood vessels as well as to improve blood circulation with the intention that this would allow girls to breastfeed successfully in later life. Crowell also opined training bras would prevent unattractive drooping of the breasts and suggested mothers should check their daughters' breasts regularly to see that they were developing properly. By this, Crowell meant that mothers should check their daughters' figures every three months to see that their breasts were positioned correctly. One way of charting the adolescent bust line was to make a girl stand sideways in a dimly lit room against a wall covered with white paper. The mother would then shine a bright light on her daughter and have her position her bosom in a provocative way and trace the silhouette on to the paper thereby sketching the outline of her daughter's bust.

In the 1950s America saw doctors and entrepreneurs promote a general philosophy of junior figure control of which training bras were part. Companies including Warners, Maidenform, Formfit, Belle Mode, and Perfect Form promoted the idea that girls needed both training bras and lightweight girdles to prepare their figures for adulthood and ensure that they developed in a desirable way. The 1950s were also a time when new fabrics were being invented. New materials including nylon and two-way fabrics allowed bras to provide support for breast tissue and led the way for a post-war renaissance of the undergarment industry as both mothers and now daughters clamored to buy foundation garments that would uplift their busts and hold in their stomachs. Training bras, along with sanitary pads and acne cream, meant that teenage girls were a rich source of income for manufacturers.

Training bras are often at the center of controversy. Some feminist academics disapprove of training bras as they feel that the garments prove no function other than to construct a form a gendered body discipline for young women that both creates and exploits the body image issues experienced by many teenage girls. Others argue that training bras eroticize young girls by turning their breasts into lingerie-clad sexual objects. Such controversy has not prevented many stores, designers, and celebrities from creating ranges of training bras. These include the Pink line by lingerie giant Victoria's Secret, well known for its sexy underwear and lavish catwalk shows featuring scantily clad supermodels. An online petition against the line, which features lacey push-up bralettes, garnered 19,000 signatures. Victoria's Secret countered criticism that the Pink line was too overtly sexual for pubertal youngsters by arguing that their Pink line is aimed at college-aged women and not at adolescent girls. That said, recent Victoria's Secret runway shows have featured teen heartthrobs such as Justin Beiber in 2012, so it could be argued that the company may well appeal to young teenagers.

In the United Kingdom, tough guidelines have been drawn up by the British Retail Consortium aimed at curbing the sale of underwear that many consider as too suggestive for young girls, such as training bras emblazoned with slogans including "Future Porn Star." British stores Marks & Spencer, Next, and Sainsbury's, among others, have signed up to abide with the voluntary guidelines that state training bras must be designed to provide comfort, support, and modesty and not to enhance the bust. Therefore training bras sold by these shops must not feature underwiring or padding.

See also: Breast Ironing; Child Beauty Pageants (Volume 1); Menstruation Customs

Further Reading

Brunberg, Joan Jacobs. *The Body Project: An Intimate History of American Girls*. New York: Vintage, 1997.

Cole, Annabel. "How Victoria's Secret Is Trying to Turn Your Teenage Daughter into a Sex Object." *Mail Online*. April 24, 2013. Accessed December 10, 2014, at http://www.dailymail.co.uk/fe-mail/article-2314367/How-Victorias-Secret-trying-turn-teenage-daughter-sex-object.html.

Shipman, Tim. "High Street Shops to Ban Padded Bras and 'Sexually Suggestive' Clothes for Young Girls." *Mail Online*. June 4, 2011. Accessed December 10, 2014, at http://www.dailymail.co.uk/news/article-1394123/High-street-shops-ban-clothes-sexualise-little-girls.html#ixzz1e38AdIwb.

Smith, Merril D., ed. *Cultural Encyclopedia of the Breast*. Lanham, MA: Rowman & Littlefield, 2014.

The Sydney Morning Herald. "Sexy, Sassy, Still in Primary School," *Sydney Morning Herald*, December 23, 2006. Accessed December 10, 2014, at http://www.smh.com.au/news/national/sexy-sassy-still-in-primary-school/2006/12/22/1166290740883.html?page=fullpage#contentSwap3.

Younger, Shannon. "Goodbye Training Bras, Hello Lingerie: Retailers Target Tween Girls." Chicago Now. March 4, 2013. Accessed December 10, 2014, at http://www.chicagonow.com/tween-us/2013/03/girls-training-bras-lingerie-retailers-target-tween/.

TROBRIAND RITUALIZED SEX AND COMMITMENT, PAPUA NEW GUINEA

The Trobriand Islands, currently known as the Kiriwina Islands, are an archipelago of coral atolls belonging to Papua New Guinea. The island is famed for its annual two-month-long yam festival as well as for a local custom that has earned the islands the nickname the Islands of Love. This soubriquet is, however, somewhat misleading for the nickname developed because during the yam festival it is traditional for island women to be permitted by the village chief to capture men and force them to fulfill the women's sexual desires. The men do not have a choice in the matter and for this reason women will claim to *rep*, or rape, the men. When once all women were allowed to assault men, today only unmarried women are permitted to ambush men during the yam festival. Foreigners rarely witness this behavior however and most reports of male rapes by island women are anecdotal.

The rationale behind the forced sexual intercourse is that it causes the islands' yam crops to grow more abundantly. Interestingly, however, while islanders see a correlation between the fecundity of nature and sex between humans the people of the Trobriand Islands do not traditionally feel that there is any link between sex and conception. Indeed people living on the Trobriand Islands believe that there is no physical connection between a father and child and that the mother is the sole progenitor of any offspring with children conceived when a child's spirit enters the female's head and travels down to her womb on a wave of blood. Islanders assert that sexual intercourse merely facilitates the entry of the child's spirit into its mother.

In order to act out their sexual desires during the yam festival the women hide in the bushes and waylay men that walk past. Any man is considered fair game with the only rule being that the women can only ambush men that are not from their own tribe or village. Some men are even sexually assaulted twice. The men of the Trobriand Islands know that they are in danger of being assaulted but most claim that once they have gotten over the shock of being targeted they actually enjoy the rough treatment. The only downside, according to island men, is that if they are unable to perform sexually when they have been ambushed island women are permitted to urinate over them and bite off their eyebrows and eyelashes. For a man to have his face marked in this way leaves him open to a great deal of ridicule from fellow islanders who understand that the reason for his loss of facial features is that he was unable to sexually fulfill the women. The yam festival is considered a perilous time for men to journey out alone so men tend to travel in groups in case they are ambushed and assaulted.

On the Trobriand Islands pre-adolescent children are encouraged to engage in erotic games with each other and act out sexualized adult behavior from the age of seven or eight years. Indeed islanders see such behavior as an essential rite of passage to adulthood. Premarital sex is considered acceptable in Trobriand society and islanders usually become sexually active as young adolescents, usually between the ages of 11 and 13 years. To signal sexual attraction, girls will scratch, hit, and whip boys that they like in order to leave marks on the boys' skin. The boys take great pride in showing off their bruises as the markings demonstrate that girls have found them attractive. The bruises are also considered a sign of manliness and that the boys are reaching manhood.

The parents of young Trobriand girls are expected to teach their daughters how to be seductive and to this end teach the girls alluring dances and other skills considered necessary to attract males. The girls, who do not wear anything on their top halves, also wear skirts made from banana leaves and jewelry fashioned from seashells that are thought to make girls more attractive in the eyes of island boys. In addition, girls also learn magic spells that are passed down from one generation to the next and that are supposed to enable the females to enchant males. Teenage girls are taught specific rituals to go with each of the spells.

Both adolescent boys and girls change sexual partners frequently. However over time adolescents forge natural bonds with preferred sexual partners and gradually come to reject the advances of others. As there is no traditional marriage ceremony on the Trobriand Islands this is considered a type of formal commitment. If a couple wishes to announce their commitment to one another they will sleep together and wake up to watch the sunrise together. The couple will then state their intentions while standing in the garden of one of their parents. The girl's mother then brings the couple cooked yams and once the couple start to eat the yams they are considered formally "married." The couple then lives together in either the house belonging to the young man's father or that belonging to his maternal uncle. Meanwhile, the relatives of the young girl are responsible for keeping the couple stocked with yams. It is important to note that on the Trobriand Islands yams are not merely vegetables but symbols of wealth that are given between families to cement familial bonds. For one year after the formal declaration of commitment the couple will eat yams together and then, after a year, begin to eat yams separately. Alternatively, a couple can demonstrate their commitment to each other by staying with each other for a period of weeks. If the girl accepts a gift from the boy then she will move into his home where she will spend every waking moment in his company. Word will then spread through the community that she is committed to the boy. If, however, in the long run a match turns out to be unhappy then the formal commitment may be dissolved.

All Trobrianders belong to one of four clans and there are, therefore, strict rules pertaining to incest and intermarriage that state that islanders must practice exogamy, that is, marry someone from outside their own clan. Also islanders may not marry their siblings or matrilineal relatives of the same generation. The fear of incest is woven into Trobriand culture through myths that tell of a brother and sister that committed suicide having slept with each other. Fathers are expected to be especially wary of sleeping with their daughters although father-daughter incest is at the heart of many Trobriand fables that tell of a father overcome with lust on seeing his beautiful girl.

The sex lives of the Trobrianders was well documented by famous anthropologist Bronislaw Malinowski in his 1927 book *Sex and Repression in Savage Society* and his 1929 work *The Sexual Life of Savages in North-Western Melanesia: An Ethnographic Account of Courtship, Marriage and Family Life among the Natives of the Trobriand Islands, British New Guinea*. Malinowski's study was groundbreaking in that he wrote his work having lived with the islanders for two years. Malinowski stressed that what to early 20th-century Westerners seemed to be the islanders' uncontrolled sexuality was in fact premarital sex that followed well-established rules and demonstrated sexual desire filtered through systems of kinship.

In 1906, the Trobriand Islands came under control of Australia, leading to the islands being settled by Christian missionaries from Europe. The missionaries tried to instill in the islanders the need for monogamy and sexual abstinence. However other European settlers went about establishing brothels on the islands. The establishing of brothels eventually led to a rise in cases of sexually transmitted diseases in the 1980s and 1990s that was blamed on the islanders themselves, who were painted as sexually promiscuous and immoral. Another consequence of the Trobrianders' open sexuality is that the islands have attracted sex tourists, particularly sex tourists interested in pedophilic interactions with children. Pedophiles are especially drawn to the Trobriand Islands because they think they have a lower risk of catching sexually transmitted diseases such as HIV/AIDS from the islands' children. However as a consequence of sex tourism on the Trobriand Islands in the 1990s, the islands—like Papua New Guinea itself—became the epicenter of AIDS in the Pacific region and the Trobriand Islands briefly became known as the Islands of Risk rather than the Islands of Love. Today, however, young Trobrianders are given sex education and taught about safe sex and contraception with the aim of curbing rates of HIV infection.

See also: Bachelor and Spinster Balls; Bed-Courtship; *Devadasi* System (Volume 1); Initiation by Semen Transferal; *Kumari* and *Deuki* (Volume 1); Looking for Fern Blossoms; Purity Balls; *Russefeiring* and Schoolies Week

Further Reading

Bolin, Anne, and Patricia Whelehan. *Human Sexuality: Biological, Psychological, and Cultural Perspectives*. New York: Routledge, 2009.

Farrell, Nicole S. "Where Women Ambush Men," *Trinidad Express*, July 21, 2012. Accessed April 30, 2015, at http://www.trinidadexpress.com/woman-magazine/Where_Women_Ambush_Men-163265806.html.

Galvan, Javier A., ed. *They Do What? A Cultural Encyclopedia of Extraordinary and Exotic Customs from around the World*. Santa Barbara, CA: ABC-CLIO, 2014.

Malinowski, Bronislaw. *Sex and Repression in Savage Society*. London: Taylor & Francis e-library, 2003.

Meyer, Melissa L. *Thicker Than Water: The Origins of Blood as Symbol and Ritual*. New York: Routledge, 2005.

Robbins, Richard. *Cengage Advantage Books: Cultural Anthropology: A Problem-Based Approach*. Sixth edition. Belmont, CA: Wadsworth Cengage Publishing, 2013.

TWENTY-FIRST BIRTHDAY TRADITIONS, INTERNATIONAL

Certain birthdays—a person's 21st birthday, for example—are considered landmark occasions for they confer on the individual greater rights, privileges, and responsibilities. In many cultures around the world, a person's 21st birthday is seen as proof of his or her coming of age and ultimate achievement of adulthood.

That reaching a 21st birthday is a sign of maturity is signaled by the old tradition of giving a 21-year-old the so-called key of the door. This is a long-held tradition in the United Kingdom, Australia, and elsewhere and demonstrates that the person turning 21 is now suitably adult and responsible enough to have his or her own front-door key. In the United Kingdom, it is tradition on a person's 21st birthday for he or she to be given a key—either an actual front-door key or an over-sized mock key—while someone sings the words, "I've got the key of the door, never been 21 before."

In New Zealand, 21 years was the legal age of majority until 1970, meaning that only when a person reached 21 years of age did they become an independent adult free from parental authority in the eyes of the law. Recently the age of majority has changed to 20 years but many New Zealanders still regard 21 as the age at which an individual reaches adulthood. As such, New Zealand families often hold lavish parties when a person reaches 21 years old. Since the 1930s, the British influence over New Zealand has meant that the traditional key of the door has featured largely at these parties with ornate keys given as gifts and birthday cakes shaped like keys presented to the person turning 21. Occasionally, an oversized gold colored key is signed by all the party guests and then presented to the person celebrating his or her birthday as a memento of the occasion. In 2006, Māori families adapted this tradition for they began to carve keys or lintels (*pare*) that they would give as treasured 21st-birthday souvenirs. Alternatively, a Māori male may be given a *taiaha* (a traditional weapon) rather than a pare when he turns 21 years of age. A less sophisticated New Zealand 21st-birthday tradition sees the birthday celebrant drink a yard-glass of beer. This is a very tall glass holding about 1.4 liters (around 2.5 pints) of ale that is often spiked with stronger alcohol.

The 21st birthday is the occasion of men's coming of age in the Philippines. In the Philippines, coming of age is known as the Debut or Cotillion and this happens at 18 years for women and 21 years for men. However this shares little in terms of lavishness with the West's concept of a debutante's social coming out or cotillion, for Filipino men tend to celebrate their 21st birthdays in a very low-key manner, if at all.

See also: Birthdays (Volume 1); Chinese Coming-of-Age Ceremonies; Coming of Age Day; *Gwallye*

Further Reading

Danico, Mary Yu, ed. *Asian American Society: An Encyclopedia*. Thousand Oaks, CA: SAGE Publications, 2014.

Jones, Alison. *Larousse Dictionary of World Folklore*. Edinburgh, UK: Larousse, 1996.

Rajendra, Vijeya, and Sundran Rajendra. *Cultures of the World: Australia*. Tarrytown, NY: Marshall Cavendish Benchmark, 1990.

Swarbrick, Nancy. "Birthdays and Wedding Anniversaries—Birthday Rituals." Te Ara—the Encyclopedia of New Zealand. Accessed October 11, 2015, at http://www.teara.govt.nz/en/birthdays-and-wedding-anniversaries/page-2.

U

URETHRAL SUBINCISION, AUSTRALIA, AFRICA, AND SOUTH AMERICA

Subincision of the urethra, also known as penile subincision, is an invasive form of male genital cutting that involves slitting along the underside of the penis to the urethra. Subincision is usually performed as part of a male's transition from adolescence to manhood. The practice is most closely associated with Aboriginal Australians (who refer to subincision colloquially as "whistle cock"), but it also takes place in Africa, South America, and Polynesia. In Australia, subincision is mostly practiced by Aboriginal communities living in the country's central desert regions whose religious beliefs tend to focus upon fertility, life, and birth. Aborigines living on the coast and in the north and south of the country do not tend to perform genital modification. Among Aborigines subincision is often associated with the mother of fertility, Kunapipi (the origin of all human life), or Gadjeri, who confers fertility to both males and females. This reflects the widely held theory that subincision is performed in an attempt to give female fertility to males. Psychoanalysts have suggested that subincision is an attempt to mimic female genitalia by constructing a male vagina with the blood that accompanies a subincision procedure an attempt to replicate menstruation.

The Aboriginal Australian practice of subincision is connected to their belief in Dreamtime, a mythical time of creation also known as The Dreaming or Creation Period. In Aboriginal mythology, the Dreamtime was a time when the empty landscape was crossed by totemic beings and instilled with the spirits of animals, plants, and places. According to Aboriginal belief each animal, plant, and place created by the Dreamtime has a tale attached to it that is disseminated via oral tradition and ritual practices. Through these Dreamtime myths and stories, the Aborigines learn that the universe is not centered on humans but rather on nature. Thus Aborigines believe that they are part of the land and connected in various ways to the various elements that make up the landscape. Belief in Dreamtime influences all aspects of Aboriginal life including traditions, customs, and ritualized events such as births, marriages, and deaths. Aborigines believe that subincision has existed among their people since the time of their creation, though few Aboriginal myths make mention of the practice. However while myths about the custom are scarce the procedures and rites associated with subincision are prevalent in Aboriginal cosmology. The rites surrounding subincision are usually attributed to a local totemic spirit though these are often shared between Aboriginal tribes that live adjacent to each other. For instance, the Aranda community regard the southern Tjilpa cat-men as responsible for instructing their people about the rituals necessary for subincision and ordeal by fire, while they believe the Lakabara hawk-men brought them the ritual of circumcision.

In most Aboriginal populations subincision is a rite of passage performed to mark a boy's transition to adulthood and is associated with maturity, the ability to withstand pain, and the capability to act as a responsible member of a community. The ritual starts when a group of men from the community dress themselves as ancestral spirits and take the initiate away from his mother. The boy is then taken to a sacred site that only males may enter. Here the initiate undergoes a sequence of ritualized testing that lasts several weeks but varies in specifics of ordeals, duration, and arrangement. However these ordeals often include circumcision, drinking blood, and body adornment. The initiate also receives teachings that older male members of the community think will kelp the initiate transform into a mature man. This includes the learning of a sacred language that the boy must learn in order to be able to pass it on to future generations. The weeks of sequestration also includes the performance of mythological tales. The rituals experienced by a boy belonging to the Yiwara include having an incisor tooth extracted and then used to pierce his septum. The initiate then watches as the other men enact through song and dance the story of totemic kangaroos. Finally the boy is made to lie on his back across a "table" made of men who are on their hands and knees and undergoes subincision at the hands of an older man wielding a sharp stone flute. While this is taking place male spectators re-open their subincisions. Other methods of subincision have also been documented. For example, sometimes subincision is self-inflicted and it has been known for two young men to stand waist-high in a river and perform the procedure on each other either one at a time or simultaneously

The series of ordeals and education usually lasts several weeks and completion of this period is marked by the subincision. The subincision procedure is equivalent to a urethrotomy as performed in Western medicine usually to help ease urethral constriction and involves slicing open the underside of the penis using a sharp implement such as a pointed rock. The subincision is made by first creating a cut about one inch long on the underside of the penis and then slicing through the corpus spongiosum (a mass of erectile tissue that lies along the bottom of the penis) to the urethra. The cut runs the length of the underside of the penis from the meatus (the urethral opening) on the glans of the penis to the scrotum.

Subincision can cause several medical problems, most due to the relocation of the urethral opening. One of the main challenges for a man who has undergone subincision is the need to crouch when urinating as after subincision urine is ejected through the subincision on the underside of the penis. Subincision also impedes the ability to deliver semen during sexual intercourse as the opening of the urethra is now located close to the scrotum—for this reason, some anthropologists suggest that subincision originated as a primitive form of birth control. Subincised men usually get around this problem by squeezing together the two halves of the penis during ejaculation in order to enhance the chances of reproduction occurring. Another medical issue associated with subincision of the urethra is the increased risk of sexually transmitted diseases and infections because of the exposure of the urethra.

While psychoanalysts have suggested that subincision is an attempt by males to replicate female genitalia and menstrual bleeding and is, therefore, an acknowledgement of female fertility and the female's ability to create life, others theorize that subincision and related blood-letting is an attempt to forge stronger bonds of kinship and homosocial relationships among male members of Aboriginal communities. The scars of subincision are also thought to act as a badge of honor symbolizing the subincised male's physical bravery. Other academic research on the subject of subincision suggests that the procedure reflects the eroticized nature of the Aborigines and that this form of genital alteration is intended to widen the erect penis thereby increasing the sexual satisfaction of the subincised man's partner. Indeed it has been reported that a woman who has experienced a *burra* (Aboriginal subincised penis) will subsequently refuse to have sex with a non-subincised man as she fears she will never know such sexual satisfaction again. Research also proposes that subincision is an attempt to fashion the human penis into a resemblance of the naturally bifurcated penis of the kangaroo, an animal notorious for sustained procreation. Indeed the Walbiri people, among others, have a special feeling of kinship with kangaroos. A recurrent motif of Walbiri myth is that kangaroos instructed them in the art of subincision and gave the Walbiri people the sharp stone knife, *gandi*, with which to create many burra that would make their penises look like the forked penis of the kangaroo and would therefore allow Walbiri men to fan their urine on the ground like the kangaroo and possess the sexual stamina of the animal. Kangaroos were also said to have told the Walbiri men how to draw blood by inserting sticks into their subincisions. The Walbiri maintain that a law passed to them through dream ordered all males to be subincised during initiation to adulthood as this would allow the men to please women sexually, to urinate quickly by spraying urine on the ground, and promote hygiene and eradicate odor. However despite the large amount of academic research into subincision some critics argue that it is pointless to speculate on the subject as Aboriginal cosmology offers no explanation as to why or how the procedure should be performed thereby nullifying all interpretations.

Since 1960, there has been a significant decrease in the number of Aborigines undergoing subincision of the urethra. In 2010, the Royal Australasian College of Physicians advised parents in Australia and New Zealand not to allow their children to be circumcised except for therapeutic reasons. This advice greatly affected the willingness of parents to let their sons be circumcised or undergo the related procedure of subincision. This, together with the fact that today most young Aborigine men are urbanized and consider themselves distant from traditional Aboriginal beliefs, means that subincision is experienced by fewer and fewer males. However any male who does undergo the process is held in great esteem by his peers.

Away from Australia, in Fiji subincision is performed to release pathogenic evil spirits while in Papua New Guinea men of the Wogeo tribe practiced the custom on themselves to emulate the blood-letting experienced by Woego women during menstruation. It has also been reported that boys between 7 and 10 years of age, and therefore before having reach biological puberty, belonging to the Samburu tribe in Kenya, have performed subincision on themselves, years before they are circumcised, for no apparent ritual reason but rather to relieve their feelings of boredom and loneliness while herding cattle. It has also been suggested that the Samburu perform self-subincision in order to need to squat during urination like a female. However this theory lacks solidity as neighboring tribes who do not practice subincision also squat to urinate. A more accepted theory is that the Samburu recognize that subincision leads to greater sexual sensitivity.

Tribes inhabiting the Amazon basin in South America perform subincision for the purely practical reason of removing a parasitic fish, *cetopsis candiru*, a member of the catfish family. The cetopsis candiru is especially feared because it feeds by attaching itself to a person or animal with its mouth and violently bites and pushes until it is completely inside its host and begins feeding voraciously. The mythology of many Amazonian tribes tell of a fish that swims up the urine stream of unwary men who are so uncouth as to urinate in the great Amazon. Attacks by parasitic fish do have a footing in reality for the cetopsis candiru are attracted by the smell of chemicals in urine and swim toward it, swimming up the urine stream to the penis and lodging in the urethra (women swimming in the river have also suffered the fish entering their urethras). Attacks by cetopsis candiru have been likened to a painful, bizarre sexual assault as a man looks down and sees the fish half-absorbed by their own body. Though often thought of as urban myths, attacks by cetopsis candiru that have ended in hospitalization have been documented in medical journals. One particularly well-documented case from 1997 saw a Brazilian man stand in the Amazon to urinate with the result that a 5.26-inch-long cetopsis candiru swam into his urethra where it died from lack of oxygen and had to be removed under anesthetic. Indeed when cetopsis candiru travel up to the urethra they must be removed or an excruciating and sometimes deadly infection can occur, hence some Amazonian males practice subincision to rid themselves of the parasitic fish.

See also: *Brit Milah* (Volume 1); Female Genital Cutting; High-Platform Exposure of the Corpse (Volume 3); Maasai Warrior Initiation; Menstruation Customs; *Nkumbi*; *Sünnet*; Xhosa Circumcision

Further Reading

Bass Fishing Gurus. "Candiru Fresh Water Monster." Accessed December 28, 2014, at http://www.bassfishing-gurus.com/fresh-water-monster-candiru-asu.php.

Favazza, Armando R. *Bodies under Siege: Self-mutilation, Nonsuicidal Self-injury, and Body Modification in Culture and Psychiatry*. Third edition. Baltimore, MD: The Johns Hopkins University Press, 2011.

Galvan, Javier A., ed. *They Do What? A Cultural Encyclopedia of Extraordinary and Exotic Customs from around the World*. Santa Barbara, CA: ABC-CLIO, 2014.

Lobdell, John E. "Considerations on Ritual Subincision Practices," *The Journal of Sex Research,* 11(1), February 1975, 16–24.

Meyer, Melissa L. *Thicker Than Water: The Origins of Blood as Symbol and Ritual.* New York: Routledge, 2005.

Montagu, Ashley. *Coming into Being among the Australian Aborigines: A Study of The Procreative Beliefs of the Native Tribes of Australia.* Abingdon, UK: Routledge, 1974.

Wade, Jeremy. *River Monsters.* London: Orion Books, 2011.

Womack, Mari. *The Anthropology of Health and Healing.* Plymouth, UK: AltaMira Press, 2010.

V

VINOK, UKRAINE

A *vinok* (plural *vinky*), sometimes referred to as a Ukrainian wreath, is a highly symbolic floral garland worn on the head by girls and unmarried women living in Ukraine. (*See* Plate 23.) The word *vinok* means wreath in Ukrainian. The vinok symbolizes the female principle, feminine wisdom, sagacity, grace, and beauty. However the vinok is not just an accessory for the garland is regarded as a tool imbued with mystical power able to convey feelings and emotions. In pre-Christian times, the vinok was also commonly believed to protect females from both evil spirits and the evil eye. Girls start to wear vinky woven by their mothers when they are around three years old. However the flowers and colors included in the wreaths change depending on the occasion on which the wreath worn and the specific symbolic or medicinal reason for wearing the wreath. The vinok is also a symbol of marriage, hence the ancient Ukrainian word for marriage is *vinchannia*, meaning having had wreaths placed on the head, which derives from the word vinok. Today vinky are still used during traditional Ukrainian wedding ceremonies for wreaths of myrtle or periwinkle are placed on the head of the bride and groom once they have said their marriage vows.

Vinky are also used in love divination and have influenced Ukrainian idioms. For example, a popular expression denoting a girl's lost virginity is "She lost her wreath." This is a notable event for a woman to lose her virginity before she marries is taboo in Ukraine as women are expected to be virgins on their wedding night.

There is a very long tradition of vinok-wearing in Ukraine. It has been suggested that in prehistoric times people belonging to a solar cult wore vinky. For this reason vinky are worn on *Ivana Kupala,* an ancient pagan nighttime festival held annually in Ukraine over two nights starting on July 6. Ivana Kupala corresponds to Midsummer's Night and the celebrations begin with the lighting of a fire-pit over which revelers must jump. Indeed revelers who are in love with each must jump over the fire while holding hands and, according to tradition, a girl who is in love should wear a vinok while jumping as this will ensure the vinok's magical properties are invoked. Also during Ivana Kupala young women place their vinky, which are especially made from daisies and wheat, on a body of water with a candle floating inside of the floral ring. It is believed that the way in which a vinok floats down the river or lake foretells whom a woman will wed. Further, if a vinok does not float along on the water but rather remains stationary it is thought that its owner will never marry. Moreover, tradition suggests that if the vinok sinks then the woman will soon die. Similarly, if the candle is extinguished then some other misfortune will befall the wreath's owner. Young local men watch this ritual and dive into the water to retrieve the wreath of the girl he loves.

Today, knowledge of how to construct vinky and which flowers to include in the wreaths is passed down from generation to generation and harks back to Ukrainian flower lore and folk medicine. Traditionally, vinky should be made from real flowers though nowadays it is acceptable to make vinky from fabric blossoms too. The shape of vinky also vary with wreaths made as full or half garlands or consisting of a single flower. Some vinky also contain ribbons and veils. Currently, it is very trendy for Ukrainian brides to wear a vinok on their wedding day as this chimes with the upsurge in interest in ethnic arts and crafts and traditional national dress, and with feelings of nationalism in general. The upsurge of interest in vinky has in turn led to a surge in work for traditional craftswomen and artists.

When real flowers are used in a vinok the blooms are often selected because they are thought to be imbued with some particular property or represent a specific sentiment. For instance, strawflowers, also known as the everlasting flower, are included as they represent well-being and maintain their color and shape when dried meaning that a vinok may be preserved without losing its prettiness. Similarly myrtle is a delicate yet evergreen plant and so symbolizes eternal life. Flowers symbolic of femininity that are often added to vinky include cherry blossom and apple blossom, which are also symbolic of love, happiness, fertility, and knowledge. Other plants that might be added to vinky include species of cranberry, which are thought to symbolize beauty and loyalty, and lovage, which is considered to be aphrodisiac and also represents fidelity, as do cornflowers. Roses, peonies, and hollyhocks symbolize devotion as well as romantic love and hopefulness. Plants associated with sexual purity that are included in vinky include daisies, marigolds, and chamomile. Hops included in a vinok represent compassion while the red poppy, a culturally important flower in Ukraine, symbolizes sorrow.

The color of the ribbons added to vinky is also highly symbolic. For instance, brown or rust colored ribbons are considered the colors of nature and so represent fruitfulness and generosity while blue ribbons symbolize the skies, life-giving water, air, well-being, and openness. Light yellow ribbons represent the sun, youthfulness, and family, with deep yellow or golden ribbons suggesting spirituality and sagacity. Green ribbons are associated with newness, prosperity, and optimism and are particularly used at Christmas, Easter, and Epiphany. Similarly, white ribbons represent birth, chastity, and jubilation. Other colored ribbons included in vinky include violet for knowledge, loyalty, honesty, and endurance; and pinkish hues such as raspberry pink redolent of trustworthiness and munificence and rose pink for plenty, victory, and joy. Red, meanwhile, is considered a magical color representative of love, desire, Christianity, and piety. Some vinky include ribbons of many colors in order to symbolize many different sentiments, usually familial happiness, harmony, and love. When this is the case the ribbons are attached to the vinok in the following order: in the center of the vinok is the rust colored ribbon, to the left and the right of this are tied two light yellow ribbons, then two light green and dark green ribbons, then two light blue and dark blue ribbons. On the outside of these are attached on one side one deep yellow ribbon and on the other side a violet ribbon, then comes a raspberry pink ribbon and a rose pink ribbon. White ribbons are then placed on both sides. The white ribbon on the left-hand side of the vinok is embroidered with an image of the sun while the white ribbon on the right-hand side is embroidered with a depiction of the moon. An unembroidered white ribbon may be included to remember a deceased friend or relative. In addition, if the wearer of the vinok has light blue ribbons woven into her hair it means that she is calling for the help and sympathy of others. This is particularly true of orphaned girls.

See also: Birth Trees (Volume 1); Bulgarian Weddings; Funeral Plants (Volume 3); *Lazarovden*; Looking for Fern Blossoms; St. Catherine's Day; Traditional Mourning Colors (Volume 3); Wearing Flowers to Honor War Dead (Volume 3); Wedding Dress; Yew Trees (Volume 3)

Further Reading

Life with a Ukrainian Wife. "A Wreath from Ukraine: Old Traditions and Modern Twists." May 2010. Accessed April 30, 2015, at http://www.ukrainianmatchmaker.net/2010/05/bridal-wreath-from-ukraine-old.html.

Paszczak Tracz, Orysia. "The Things We Do . . ." *The Ukrainian Weekly, LXVII*(31), August 1, 1999. Accessed May 2, 2015, at http://www.ukrweekly.com/old/archive/1999/319917.shtml.

UkrainianCalgary. "Flowers, Family, Future—The Vinok." August 13, 2012. Accessed April 30, 2015, at http://ukrainiancalgary.blogspot.co.uk/2012/08/flowers-family-future-vinok.html.

Worldwide News Ukraine. "Ivana Kupala Holiday Signifies Solstice." July 9, 2012. Accessed May 2, 2015, at http://wnu-ukraine.com/news/culture-lifestyle/?id=1886.

VIRGINITY TESTING, INTERNATIONAL

Virginity testing is the practice of determining whether an individual has experienced sexual intercourse. The practice is usually aimed at females and occurs in many countries, especially in Asia, the Middle East, and Africa, where a woman's sexual purity is highly prized and virginity testing is considered a way to curb woman's premarital sexual activity. Virginity testing has also been known to occur in Spain in recent times. The practice of virginity testing is highly controversial and is considered an infringement of women's human rights by many, even if the women who undergo the testing do so willingly. This is the opinion of the United Nations World Health Organization (WHO), which has recommended the practice be stopped on the grounds that it is discriminatory against women, degrading, and unscientific. Critics also assert that virginity testing is often unhygienic and can spread disease.

Virginity testing is performed is different ways around the world. Usually the vagina is examined to see whether or not the girl's hymen, the thin membrane of skin that may stretch across part of the vaginal opening, is intact. An opening in the hymen allows the menstrual flow to pass out of the body. The absence of a hymen is thought by some to indicate a female is not a virgin as they assume the membrane is torn during sexual intercourse. However while most girls are born with a hymen some are born without it and the membrane may also have been ruptured by playing sports, riding horses, or torn by the insertion of tampons.

The most common form of virginity testing is the so-called two-finger test (TFT). During this test a doctor inserts fingers into a woman to conduct a forensic examination to determine her degree of vaginal laxity. The doctor then delivers a medical opinion on whether the woman has experienced habitual sexual intercourse. This invasive test is required by courts in some Indian states—including those in Delhi and Mumbai—during rape cases and, according to local reports, the Indian Medical Association endorses the test. However in 2014, the Indian Health Ministry issued a new procedure for dealing with female rape victims clarifying that health workers tending and inspecting rape survivors should not conduct the TFT. However, this protocol has yet to be instigated nationwide. The TFT is also part of the mandatory health examinations administered to female law officers in Indonesia. Women who apply to be police officers in Indonesia have been subjected to virginity testing since at least 1965. This is because in 1965 the police force was placed under the command of the Indonesian military, which has long conducted virginity testing on female recruits. Married women are not eligible to become police officers and while failing the virginity test does not disqualify a female police applicant, she may accrue fewer points than if her hymen were intact.

Traditionalists in several Africa countries encourage virginity testing, usually by the TFT method. In Swaziland virginity testing is widespread as it is thought to discourage sexual activity leading to high rates of HIV, while in rural South Africa it is estimated that tens of thousands of girls are brought together each month to undergo tests. Indeed in July 2004, at the Nomkhubulwane fertility festival approximately 3,000 young girls underwent ritual virginity testing. In Kwa Zulu Natal, South Africa mass virginity testing called *ukuhlowa kwezintombe* takes place in public. Around 85 girls aged between 5 and 22 years of age are tested in groups of 10 at a time, each accompanied by their mothers. The girls are made to lie down on grass mats placed on the floor of soccer pitches and are examined by so-called virginity testers who probe the girl's external genitalia with gloved hands looking for signs of vaginal abuse and sexually transmitted diseases. That virginity testing is often unhygienic and disease spreading is highlighted here, as the testers' gloves are not changed between girls. However in Africa virginity testing is not limited to females for Zulu boys are also tested. Zulu boys are checked for a hard foreskin that is thought to denote sexual purity and the boys are also made to urinate on a piece of wire strung about three feet off the ground between two trees without using their hands. If a boy urinates in a straight line he is declared a virgin but if the boy produces a shower of urine he is considered impure. Boys are also told to urinate in sand for the urine of a virgin is thought to make a straight hole in the sand.

Elsewhere virginity testing is performed not as an anti-HIV measure but to determine so-called moral crimes. According to the group Human Rights Watch, in Afghanistan authorities routinely subject females accused of such "moral crimes" as running away from home, *zina* (consensual premarital sex), and attempted zina, to virginity testing. Women accused of these crimes are often fleeing domestic violence or forced marriage yet if intercepted by authorities the woman can expect to undergo virginity testing several times either because of bureaucratic policies or mistakes, or because she is subsequently charged with additional crimes such as robbery and assault for which testing is also imposed. The results of the virginity tests may carry great weight with judges and are thought to have contributed to many wrongful convictions. In Afghanistan female rape victims often do not report the offense or seek assistance, as they fear they will be accused of zina, which authorities believe can be corroborated through virginity testing.

Another common method of checking for a woman's virginity is the so-called "handkerchief test" for brides. This test relies on the widespread myth that a female virgin will bleed when her hymen ruptures on the occasion of her first sexual intercourse. Thus it follows that if a woman does not bleed then she is not a virgin and so a bride that does not bleed on her wedding night will be suspected on having had premarital sex. In Sri Lanka, newlywed couples are given a cloth to spread across their bed on their wedding night on which they must consummate their marriage. The groom's mother and other female relatives then inspect this cloth for bloodstains that they believe will "prove" the bride's freshly broken hymen. A similar practice occurs within gypsy communities in Spain. In 2005, famous gypsy flamenco dancer Juan Manuel Fernandez Montoya known as "Farruquito" (the Little Pharaoh) submitted his teenage bride, Rosario Alcantara, to the "test of the handkerchief" when they married at the Christ of the Gipsies church in Seville, Spain. Once the newlyweds arrived at their reception, the bride underwent the test that would "prove" her virginity. The traditional Spanish gypsy custom sees women guests extract blood from the bride's hymen on a white handkerchief. If the handkerchief is removed from the bride stained with the so-called "three roses" of a virgin's blood, the bride is declared a virgin and fit to wed. In this case, Alcantara was judged to have produced "four roses" of blood, which, according to tradition, meant the congregation could shower the cloth with sugared almonds. Images of the bloodied handkerchief were subsequently broadcast on all the major television stations in Spain, attracting much outcry from Spanish women's groups.

In a November 2014 WHO handbook it was recommended that healthcare workers should never use virginity tests on women subjected to intimate partner violence or sexual violence. The handbook stresses the need to respect for women's rights and comfort, and makes clear that any physical examination must be conducted only when informed consent has been given. The handbook concludes that virginity tests, including the TFT, have no scientific validity and are degrading and invasive. It also asserts that the Convention on the Elimination of All Forms of Discrimination against Women and other human rights treaties forbid discrimination against women and that virginity testing constitutes discrimination against women for such procedures deny women their rights on a basis of equality with men.

See also: Arranged Marriage and Forced Marriage; *Chokha Thavani Viddhi*: Devipujak Purification Trial; Female Genital Cutting; *Lobola*; Moroccan Weddings; Reed Dancing Chastity Ceremony; *Vinok*

Further Reading

Cochrane, Joe. "'Virginity Test' Stokes Indonesia Debate," *New York Times*, December 11, 2014. Accessed January 6, 2015, at http://www.nytimes.com/2014/12/12/world/asia/for-police-career-in-indonesia-some-women-must-first-pass-virginity-test.html.

Grinker, Roy Richard, Stephen C. Lubkemann, and Christopher B. Steiner, eds. *Perspectives on Africa: A Reader in Culture, History and Representation*. Second edition. Chichester, UK: John Wiley & Sons, 2010.

Human Rights Watch. "UN: WHO Condemns 'Virginity Tests.'" Human Rights Watch, December 2, 2014. Accessed January 6, 2015, at http://www.hrw.org/news/2014/12/01/un-who-condemns-virginity-tests.

Kleinman, R. L., and P. Senanayake, eds. *Family Planning: Meeting Challenges, Promoting Choices*. Carnforth, UK: Parthenon Publishing Group Ltd., 1993.

McNeil Jr., Donald G. "Rape: Rights Group Calls Test to Determine Sexual Activity a 'Second Assault' in India," *New York Times*, September 13, 2010. Accessed January 6, 2015, at http://www.nytimes.com/2010/09/14/health/14glob.html?scp=1&sq=rape%20test&st=cse&_r=0.

Sexuality Information and Education Council of the United States. "Virginity Testing: Increasing Health Risks and Violating Human Rights in the Name of HIV-Prevention." Accessed January 6, 2015, at http://www.siecus.org/index.cfm?fuseaction=Feature.showFeature&featureID=1199.

Wilkinson, Isambard. "Outrage at Virginity Test for Flamenco Star's Bride," *The Telegraph*, 2005, September 28. Accessed January 6, 2015, at http://www.telegraph.co.uk/news/worldnews/europe/spain/1499437/Outrage-at-virginity-test-for-flamenco-stars-bride.html.

Woolf, Lind M. "Virginity Testing." Women and Global Human Rights. Accessed January 6, 2015, at http://www2.webster.edu/~woolflm/virginitytest.html.

VISION QUEST, NATIVE AMERICAN

Vision quest, also sometimes referred to as a vision fast, is an age-old rite of passage to adulthood, self-knowledge, and spiritual understanding practiced by many Native Americans tribes. Some Native American tribes consider a vision quest as the single initiation needed for an individual to become an adult while for other Native Americans, such as the Lakota, a vision quest, which they call *Hanblecheyapi* (or *hanbleceya*, meaning crying out for a vision) is one of several steps necessary to attain adulthood. Vision quests have been likened to the Christian rite of confirmation as both rituals see those undergoing the rite assume responsibility for their own spiritual path. Indeed some people that have experienced a vision quest go on to become healers having received their power through prayer.

Though boys traditionally experience vision quests, today females and adults also undergo the experience, as do some non-Native Americans. Vision quests are significant experiences because they leave those that have experienced them with knowledge and skills that can benefit their community as a whole. Traditionally, a vision quest sees a young male reach puberty and then leave his tribe for a few days during which time he fasts while connecting with his spiritual guardian. The guardian spirit often appears in animal or bird form and is a vision that will guide the initiate throughout their existence. An individual may undertake several vision quests throughout his or her life as he or she searches for understanding and spiritual guidance, but traditionally the first of these quests for enlightenment takes place during the teenage years.

The origin of the vision quest is not particularly mystical despite the spiritual nature of the ritual for historically a boy would embark on a vision quest in order to determine whether he should become a scout, hunter, warrior, or medicine man. The vision quest provided a way for boys to discover their true calling by communing with spirit guides. When a boy embarks on a vision quest he will meet with a holy man in order to learn the appropriate way to conduct his ritual. When a Lakotan boy wishes to begin a vision quest, he will take a pipe filled a blend of tobacco called to *kinnikinnick* to the medicine man. The boy and the medicine man then smoke the pipe together thereby cementing their relationship in the presence of the Great Spirit, Wakan Tanka. Next the boy undergoes a vapor bath in a sweat lodge, a kind of ceremonial sauna built by a medicine man for the purpose of holding purification and healing rituals. By partaking of the ritual steam bath the boy becomes purified physically, mentally, emotionally, and spiritually. Finally, the boy leaves his people to journey to an area of wilderness at higher altitude. Vision quests normally take place within a circle measuring 10 feet in diameter that is located in a remote natural setting, often in an area considered sacred. The location of the vision quest is sometimes prepared before the initiate arrives to

---

Wysoccan Rite of Manhood

In times past, Quebec's Algonquin Indian tribe conducted an initiation rite for adolescent boys that saw boys taken to a secluded area and often caged. The boys would then consume *wysoccan*, an extremely strong hallucinogen. This ritual was intended to erase the boys' childhood memories thereby enabling them to become men. However the resultant severe memory loss meant some boys forgot their own identities, did not recognize their families and sometimes lost the ability to speak. If any initiated boy did remember his previous life, he was made to consume wysoccan again.

begin his quest. For example, in the Lakotan tradition the spot will be cleared of all vegetation and creatures by the vision seeker's assistants who then place five poles made from willow into holes that are sprinkled with kinnikinnick. The holes mark the boundary of the vision quest location and indicate the north, east, south, and west. In the center of these poles is a central pole against which the initiate may rest if he becomes tired, all the while still facing the east. The initiate then arrives on horseback with the medicine man who then gives the initiate a filled pipe that is said to ward off danger.

The boy spends a maximum of four days in contemplation and humbleness as signaled by the wearing of his hair loose. During this time the boy stands or sits facing the sun or the morning star, both of which are believed by Native Americans to be imbued with supernatural powers, for a period of 24 hours. During these 24 hours the boy must not move and may forgo sleep as he prays that he will receive a vision, all the while becoming increasingly aware of his environment. The vision that the initiate seeks is not merely a visual image seen by the eye but an all-encompassing experience during which all the initiate's senses become heightened to the utmost degree by the appearance of sacred, spiritual beings within the area in which the vision quest is occurring. It is not unusual for vision seekers to experience fear while on a vision quest, not just because they experience heightened sensation, but because they come to realize that they are alone and defenseless in the wilderness. However the initiates do not flee or seek help when they feel scared, for they understand that they must endure fear in order to gain spiritual insight and that through suffering they can demonstrate their worthiness to receive visions and be classed as an adult.

Modern thinking suggests that people undergoing vision quests experience visions because the seclusion and loneliness of the vision quest removes the initiate from his or her everyday normal routine thereby leaving him or her to return to nature and reconnect with his or her soul. Also, the fasting and sleep deprivation that are major elements of the vision quest ritual interferes with the individual's usual psychological condition leading to a state of altered consciousness. Some academics also believe that the physical suffering and element of self-sacrifice necessitated by the vision quest ritual opens a pathway to the spiritual realm that allows the individual to commune with his or her spirit and receive visions imbued with sacred knowledge.

Native American shamans, both male and female, also undertake vision quests in order to gain knowledge and insight for personal and professional reasons as well as to use for the benefit for their community as a whole. Novice shamans undergo vision quests as part of their training too. This is true not just of Native American shamans— in Nepal it is traditional for novice shamans to experience a similar process to the vision quest. Traditionally, Nepalese shamans are blindfolded and left overnight on precarious platforms known as *da suwa* (life trees) that are located high above the treetops. Here the shamans experience beneficial visions on their way to becoming qualified shamans.

See also: *Isanaklesh Gotal*; Matis Hunting Trials; Secular Confirmation; *Shinbyu*; Sunrise Ceremony

Further Reading

Garrett, Michael, and J. T. Garrett. *Native American Faith in America.* New York: Facts on File Inc., 2003.

Martínez, David. "The Soul of the Indian: Lakota Philosophy and the Vision Quest," *Wicazo Sa Review,* 19(2,Colonization/Decolonization, n I,) Autumn 2004, 79–104.

Pratt, Christina. *An Encyclopedia of Shamanism Volume 2 N–Z.* New York: The Rosen Publishing Group Inc., 2007.

VISITING-GIRLS COURTSHIP TRADITION, CHINA

The visiting-girls courtship tradition (or *gantuozong* in phonetic Chinese) is an ancient custom belonging to one of China's smallest ethnic groups, the Dai people. The Dai, which consists of three separate though very similar factions called the Han Dai, the Flower Belt Dai, and the Jinuo Dai, make up around eight percent of the population in the Yunnan Province in the southwest of the country. All three Dai groups celebrate the visiting-girls courtship ritual that sees single young men and women meet up to determine whether they have romantic feelings for each other. The courtship custom always takes place following the harvest season when the Dai, who are predominantly farmers, are not so busy as earlier in the year. It is very rare for Dai boys and girls to interact socially apart from during the visiting-girls courtship and formal dating or romance is taboo in some Dai villages. Thus the visiting-girl's courtship tradition is very important to the young members of the Dai community.

The ritual begins with all the houses in a village extinguishing their lights and bonfires are lit. Eligible girls, usually 15 or 16 years old, sit around the fires and gently turn their own individual spinning wheel. Young men draped in red blankets approach the girls quietly from behind. The young men then "visit" the girls by walking amongst them playing guitars or other musical instruments. As the boys walk around the girls they evaluate their looks. If a boy finds a girl physically attractive, he will walk closer to her at a slow pace and serenade her. A traditional courting song may be as follows:

> The spring breeze re-awakens the sleeping grass,
> On the mountain slopes bloom all kinds of flowers.
> My dear, you are the most exquisite flower,
> Nobody can help admiring you.
> The first time this young man sees you,
> His loving eyes forget how to blink.
> He goes to the mountain slopes to fetch firewood,
> Raises the chopper but forgets to cut.
> His legs forget to step forward,
> Though they are made to walk.

> This young man wants to become a bee,
> That flies among beautiful flowers.
> Yet he dares not go on,
> He hovers in the air,
> For fear that other bees have already been there.

(See Curriculum Corporation, p. 113, in Further Reading, below.)

If the girl reciprocates the boy's interest she will produce a small stool from beneath her long skirt and beckon the boy to sit down. This is the only part of the ritual in which the girl has a direct choice in her courtship for she is not permitted to initiate a courtship lest she seem too overtly sexual. If a girl fancies a boy who is not interested in her then the girl must turn away any prospective suitors and hope that the boy she is attracted to eventually notices her. If a boy does choose a girl who fancies him then he will sit on the stool produced by the girl. As soon as he sits down, he wraps the girls in his blanket. Before this point the boy and girl do not speak to each other. Now, however, the couple enters into a deep conversation about love and discusses plans for the future. This conversation does not however constitute a marriage contract for having spoken the couple may find they are not suited to each other. If this happens then the courtship ends immediately. In cases where a girl fails to become engaged after participating in the visiting-girls custom, she will most likely be forced to take part in the ritual again or she may be allowed to look for a husband among men who have not taken part in the ritual.

If the couple do like each other then the pair then begins a courtship that, usually, centers on the boy visiting the girl's parental home—girls always remain living with their parents until they marry. The girl's parents chaperone the newly acquainted couple and the rest of the community also keeps a close eye on the pair. The boy continues to visit his chosen love in the hope that the two will get to know each other and the visits continue for as long as the boy remains interested in the girl (it is very rarely the case that a girl will reject a suitor). During the visits the boy will present the girl with many gifts such as hair combs and the courtship is considered to be ongoing for as long as the girl accepts the presents. After a number of visits it is thought that the couple will have gotten to know each other and determined whether or not they are compatible. The couple may not get to know each other physically however for there are many restrictions about what a couple may do before they are married. For instance, the pair may not be alone together let alone hold hands or kiss. The visiting-girls custom demands that there not be sex before marriage and the couple must not interact physically until the actual wedding ceremony takes place.

After a number of visits, the boy will feel able to ask the girl's parents for her hand in marriage and preparations for the marriage will begin. In some villages a boy must not speak directly to his beloved's parents but rather he must approach a formal matchmaker who acts as intermediary by proposing on his behalf. A boy can also propose by removing a girl's hair comb or scarf. If the girl accepts a boy's proposal then it is traditional for her to act aghast, shouting and making a show of resistance. If the girl does not ask for the return of her hair accessory then it is assumed that she has accepted the boy's proposal. In contrast, if the girl does demand that the boy give back her hair adornment then she signals her rejection of the boy's proposal and the courtship must begin again.

A couple's wedding date is decided by their parents and the ceremony usually takes place in the girl's parents' home. It is customary for the betrothed couple to visit a Buddhist temple on the day of the wedding and then return to the girl's parents' house. On their way home the couple, accompanied by friends and relatives, explode firecrackers and all the people in their village seek to be the first to see the couple return from the temple. While the couple is at the temple a small round table is prepared in the girl's parents' home. The table is draped with red or white fabric and banana leaves. At the center of the table are two small bags shaped liked circular cones wrapped in banana leaves that contain a roasted hen and a chicken, while the table also holds a glass of wine, salt, glutinous rice, and a ball of white thread. The wedding begins as soon as the couple enters the house. The eldest male present sits in front of the table and officiates the ceremony. Other relatives and friends then sit down in order of importance. The bride and groom kneel in front of the eldest male and as he makes a congratulatory speech as relatives and friends stretch out their right hands on to the table. When the presiding male has finished speaking, the couple is deemed to be married and they place a handful of glutinous rice into wine. They then remove the rice and offer it as a sacrifice to the cooked poultry and the package of salt. The rice is then replaced on the table. This ritual is repeated three times. Next, the eldest male takes a long thread from the ball of thread set on the table and binds it around the couple's shoulders from left to right. He then ties the other end to the table while giving the couple his blessing. Next, the eldest male uses another white thread to tie the wrists of the boy and girl separately. When all this is done the oldest onlookers take the white threads and bind the newlyweds as a way of expressing their best wishes.

To mark the wedding, both the bride and groom must present a banquet of fine food and wine during which their parents and the village elders sit on the floor at a small table while the couple's other relatives and their friends sit in a courtyard. Everyone then sings and dances in celebration well into the early hours. After the wedding, it is usual for the newlyweds to live in the bride's parents' home for three years before moving to their own home.

Another ancient Dai courting custom is *Dui Bao*. *Dui* means to throw and *bao* translates as pouch or bag and refers to an embroidered triangular pouch with colorful yarn tassels at its corners. Young Dai men and women use the colorful bags to signal romantic intentions for the Dui Bao tradition sees the youths line up facing each other, throwing the pouches back and forth. If couples wish to get to know each other better they continue to throw the bags between them while stepping closer together with each throw of the bag.

See also: Bed-Courtship; Courtship Whistling; Looking for Fern Blossoms; Lovespoons; Moroccan Weddings; Shanghai Marriage Market; Wodaabe Courtship Dance and Festival

Further Reading

An, Chunyang, and Bohua Liu, eds. *Where the Dai People Live.* Beijing, China: Foreign Languages Press, 1985.

Curriculum Corporation. *Access Asia: Secondary Teaching and Learning Units.* Melbourne, Australia: Curriculum Corporation, 1998.

Galvan, Javier A., ed. *They Do What? A Cultural Encyclopedia of Extraordinary and Exotic Customs from around the World.* Santa Barbara, CA: ABC-CLIO, 2014.

Han, Carolyn. *The Demon King and Other Festival Folktales of China.* Honolulu: University of Hawai'i Press, 1995.

W

WALKABOUT, AUSTRALIA

Walkabout is the term used by non-Aborigines for the rite of passage experienced by Aboriginal Australian boys 13 years of age. The practice sees the boys live in the wild for six months by retracing the extremely long walks that they believe were taken by their ancestors. The aim of Walkabout is to make the boys sufficiently mature to survive independently. To non-Aborigines the routes taken by the youngster during Walkabout may seem like random wandering but they are in fact based on tribal understandings and demonstrate the intimate knowledge of the landscape possessed by Aboriginal Australians as well as their understanding of tribal history and the places considered sacred by their people. Some anthropologists consider Walkabout a form of pilgrimage, as the practice is in essence a ritualized transcendent expedition.

It is thought that indigenous peoples have inhabited Australia for around 60,000 years. Today, there are around 600 various Aboriginal Australian groups speaking some 250 languages. These various groups do, however, share a single version of their origins and prehistory and engage in a rich oral culture. At the heart of this oral tradition lie spiritual values based on a belief in Dreamtime, a mythical time of creation that is sometimes referred to as The Dreaming or Creation Period. Aborigines see all aspects of life as part of a complex network of inter-relationships that can be traced back to their ancestors' connection to the surrounding environment. For Aboriginal Australians, all aspects of human existence are interwoven in a mythic structure and connected to the creative force of Dreamtime. Moreover, Aborigines believe that as their ancestors wandered the land they left tracks across the landscape that in time became the features visible against the backdrop of the Outback.

According to Aboriginal beliefs, when Dreamtime concluded these ancestors morphed into the landscape becoming mountains and hills. Thus for many thousands of years Aboriginal Australians have lived lives inextricably linked to the land, which they believe to be a living entity. For this reason an important element of Walkabout is to repeat these ancestral trails. Anthropologists refer to these ancestral routes, which crisscross Australia, as songlines or dreaming tracks. The name songlines comes from the fact that Aborigines tend to sing songs as they walk the routes. In practical terms the songlines are essential to youngsters undertaking Walkabout as the lines connect watering holes, landmarks, and sources of food. Traditionally, those undertaking Walkabout are sustained by foraging for wild foods. For this reason, it is important that those people on Walkabout know how to identify and harvest traditional Aboriginal foods such as bush tomatoes,

Illawarra plum (also known as Daalgaal or Gidneywallum), quandongs (a Vitamin C-rich fruit that tastes similar to a peach or rhubarb), lilli pillies (native Australian berries), muntari berries, wattle seeds, Kakadu plums, and bunya bunya nuts (pinecone seeds that taste similar to cobnuts).

Aboriginal Australians consider themselves to custodians of the land with spiritual and environmental responsibilities. By taking part in Walkabout, young Aboriginal Australian men come to understand all aspects of their landscape thereby connecting with their ancestors. By going on a Walkabout, Australian Aborigines heighten their cultural and spiritual connection with both the land and their forebears. Once an Aborigine returns from his Walkabout he feels a sense of completeness both within himself and the world in general.

Non-Aboriginal popular culture first really became aware of the Walkabout tradition in 1934 when a magazine called *Walkabout* was printed that featured writing about culture, science, and travel. Then in the 1950s the Australian Broadcasting Corporation aired a 10-program television series called *Australian Walkabout*, which celebrated the Australian Outback. However perhaps the most famous depiction of the Aboriginal tradition came about in 1971 when Nicholas Roeg's film *Walkabout* garnered international praise. *Walkabout* stars Aboriginal actor David Gulpilil and tells the story of two young non-Aboriginal children who, lost in the Outback, survive thanks to the skills they learn from Gulpilil's character that comes across the non-Aboriginal children while he is on his Walkabout. As the film shows Gulpilil's character to be at total oneness with the landscape he is presented as symbolic of nature and tradition. Gulpilil reprised his *Walkabout* role in the 2008 Baz Luhrmann film, *Australia*, starring Nicole Kidman and Hugh Jackman. In *Australia,* Gulpilil's character leads his grandson into the Outback so that the youngster can learn the ways of his ancestors. As Walkabout is recognized as an exclusively Australian concept, in 2008 Tourism Australia launched an advertising campaign to capitalize on the international momentum of Luhrmann's *Australia* that stressed the opportunity of losing oneself in the Australian Outback via Walkabout as a way to leave behind the pressures of everyday life.

Today, Aborigines still perform Walkabout but no longer travel solely by foot. Instead, the most modern forms of Walkabout sees Aborigines use cars, boats, and light aircraft to cross the country and visit important sights in Australia. This does not, however, mean that individuals undertaking Walkabout do not appreciate the interconnectedness of living things nor that the epic journey has lost its spiritual element. Walkabout is still understood to be an extremely powerful and important Aboriginal rite. The contemporary form of Walkabout remains true to the concept's history as a celebration of Aboriginal ancestral heritage, though today to go on a Walkabout is as much about escaping from the pressures of modern life and to reconnect with the inner self and nature as it is to learn how to exist in the Outback.

See also: Bachelor and Spinster Balls; *Hajj*; Inter-Railing; *Kumbh Mela*

Further Reading

Davidson, Linda Kay, and David Martin Gitlitz. *Pilgrimage: From the Ganges to Graceland: An Encyclopedia, Volume 1*. Santa Barbara, CA: ABC-CLIO, 2002.

Inchaustegui, Juan Matias, and Miguel Martin Perez. *Walkabout, The Aboriginal Rite of Passage*, September 2013. Accessed November 14, 2015, at https://juanmatiasblog forenglish.files.wordpress.com/2013/09/juan-matias-and-miguel-walkabout-final-template.pdf.

Mills, Jean, and Richard Mills, eds. *Childhood Studies: A Reader in Perspectives of Childhood*. London: Routledge, 2000.

Tiedgen, Nicole. "Walkabout." Tourism Australia. Accessed November 14, 2015, at http://www.tourism.australia.com/story-ideas/story-ideas-aboriginal-australia-1757.aspx.

WEDDING ANNIVERSARIES, INTERNATIONAL

Wedding anniversaries are yearly commemorations of the date on which a married couple wed. As such, wedding anniversaries can be considered minor rites of passage. Despite the fact that wedding anniversaries are in essence personal celebrations, certain wedding anniversaries, especially 25th, 50th, 60th, and 70th wedding anniversaries, tend to be considered particularly important celebrations that are attended by members of a couple's extended family and friends. In general, however, if a wedding anniversary is not a milestone anniversary then it will be a fairly low-key celebration that sees the married couple go out to dinner in a restaurant and exchange cards and gifts—it is quite usual for a husband to buy his wife flowers too.

Traditionally each wedding anniversary is associated with a different material gift. Though these gifts vary widely from country to country the most commonly observed wedding anniversary gifts by year seem to be as follows:

Year—Gift:
1st—Cotton or Paper
2nd—Paper or Cotton
3rd—Leather
4th—Fruit
5th—Wood
6th—Iron or Sugar
7th—Wool or Copper
8th—Bronze or Salt
9th—Copper or Pottery
10th—Tin
11th—Steel
12th—Silk
13th—Lace
14th—Ivory
15th—Crystal
20th—China
25th—Silver

30th—Pearl
35th—Coral
40th—Ruby
45th—Sapphire
50th—Gold
55th—Emerald
60th—Diamond
70th—Platinum

As a result of the association between certain wedding anniversaries with a particular gift, some wedding anniversaries are known by an adjective. For instance, a 25th wedding anniversary is referred to as a silver wedding anniversary (or silver anniversary or silver wedding) while a 50th wedding anniversary is known as a golden wedding anniversary (or golden anniversary or golden wedding). In general, the longer a marriage exists the greater the wedding anniversary gifts increase in value.

The history of wedding anniversaries probably dates back to Medieval Germany where husbands would crown their wives with silver or gold wreaths to mark their 25th and 50th years of married life. Other wedding anniversary gifts probably developed from more commercial origins during the 19th and 20th century hence today a modern list of alternative wedding anniversary gifts has also entered public consciousness. This list is more commercial with, for example, clocks given for first wedding anniversaries, household appliances for fourth wedding anniversaries, furniture given on 17th wedding anniversaries, and improved real estate presented on 42nd wedding anniversaries. The modern list of anniversary gifts also reflects longer life expectancies as the list includes gift ideas up to and including the 100th year of marriage, when a 10-carat diamond should be presented.

Additionally, in the United Kingdom and Commonwealth realms, couples that celebrate their 60th, 65th, 70th, and every-year-after wedding anniversaries may be sent a personalized message by Queen Elizabeth II. Similarly, Roman Catholics may apply to the Vatican for a Papal Blessing Parchment on their 10th, 25th, 40th, 50th, and 60th wedding anniversaries.

See also: Birthdays (Volume 1); Birthstones (Volume 1)

Further Reading

Chicago Public Library. "Wedding Anniversaries." *Chicago Public Library Archive*. Accessed October 12, 2015, at http://web.archive.org/web/20071128062709/http://www.chipublib.org/008subject/005genref/giswedding.html.

Debretts.com. "British Anniversaries." *Debretts.com: Rites of Passage*. Accessed October 12, 2015, at http://www.debretts.com/british-etiquette/rites-passage/wedding-anniversaries/british-anniversaries.

Jones, Alison. *Larousse Dictionary of World Folklore*. Edinburgh, UK: Larousse, 1996.

Monger, George P. *Marriage Customs of the World: From Henna to Honeymoons*. Santa Barbara, CA: ABC-CLIO, 2004.

The Royal Household. "Queen and Anniversary Messages." The Official Website of The British Monarchy. Accessed October 12, 2015, at http://www.royal.gov.uk/HMTheQueen/Queenandanniversarymessages/Anniversarymessages.aspx.
Vatican. "Information about Applying for Papal Blessing Parchments." Office of Papal Charities. Accessed October 12, 2015, at http://www.vatican.va/roman_curia/institutions_connected/elem_apost/documents/rc_elemosineria_doc_20130218_benedizioni_en.html.
Watts, Linda S. *Encyclopedia of American Folklore*. New York: Facts on File, Inc., 2007.

WEDDING CAKES, INTERNATIONAL

The cutting of a newly married couple's wedding cake is the highlight of many Western wedding receptions. Often in the West a wedding cake is made from sponge cake or fruitcake that is covered in marzipan and then frosting. Newlyweds normally cut into their wedding cake in a ceremonial fashion and are often photographed doing so.

The traditional multi-tiered wedding cake as known in the West today is often thought to be an English invention that was created by the 19th-century English baking industry to resemble a church steeple located in London, the capital of England. In the earliest days of the English wedding cakes there existed several different types of cake, each intended for different classes of wedding. For instance so-called two-guinea bride-cakes were made for the poorer classes while expensive, lavishly decorated cakes were baked for those that could afford them. It was only during the latter part of the 19th century that the term wedding cake was used to describe such cakes, replacing the earlier term bride-cake.

Cakes and breads baked especially to celebrate a marriage have, however, existed for a long time. In Elizabethan times, it was customary for many small spiced buns to be made to celebrate nuptials and in a poem by Thomas Campion (1575–1620) there is a reference to a bridal cake, which at that time may well have referred to a type of matrimonial spiced bun. The concept of one large cake being baked to mark the occasion of a wedding began to evolve around 1660 when French chefs were brought to England by British King Charles II. The French chefs took the tradition of making individual small buns to serve at a wedding and decided to envelop each bun in a hard sugar crust. Each sugarcoated bun was then decorated with toys and figurines before being broken into pieces and scattered over the bride's head.

Today, there are a wide variety of wedding cakes around the world. One of the most eye-catching is the traditional French *croquembouche* (sometimes written as *croque-en-bouche*) that is also served in parts of Belgium. The name croquembouche derives from the French phrase *croque en bouche,* meaning crack in mouth. This is apt as croquembouche is a tall, conical structure of mini, cream-filled choux pastry buns, akin to profiteroles, that is widest at the base and enveloped in hard, spun toffee-like sugar. (*See* Plate 24.) When making a croquembouche the baker will wait until the toffee is cool before decorating it with *dragées* (sugared almonds) and, occasionally, French *macarons*—pastel colored confections made from egg whites, powdered sugar, and ground almonds. On top of the croquembouche are set figurines of the bride and groom.

Similar to a croquembouche is the Icelandic wedding cake known as *kransakaka* and the *kransekage* that is the traditional wedding cake of Denmark. Both kransakaka and the kransekage are types of wreath cake that consist of almond pastry ring cakes of decreasing size placed one on top of the other to form a tapering cone of cake. Each ring cake is typically decorated with white frosting and the cake as a whole is filled with sweets and chocolates. Throughout Scandinavia, wreath cakes are also served at other important festive occasions such as birthdays, baptisms, and at Christmas. Sometimes in Norway, wedding receptions do not feature a wedding cake as such but rather include a traditional *brudlaupskling* (sometimes called *Bryllupskake*), a fancy bread topped with cream cheese and fruit syrup that is folded over and then cut into squares.

A highly decorative, large round bread called *korovai* is served at Ukrainian wedding receptions. Korovai is considered a sacred part of the wedding process because it is decorated with designs intended to invoke eternal love and unity. Korovai is made over several days starting at the bride or groom's house on the Friday or Saturday before the wedding. People from both families take part in the ritual as making the korvai is considered a demonstration of unity between the two families. It is usual for married women to make korovai, though the marriage should be the women's first. Widows are not allowed to help make the korovai as a Ukrainian superstition holds that that the marital circumstances of the women that make the bread will be passed on to the newly wedded couple. The baking of korovai is highly ritualistic. For instance, the women that make the dough bind it using a specially embroidered towel and wash their hands in holy water. When the dough is ready to bake, one of the women makes the sign of the cross on top of the shovel used to place the bread in the oven and also makes the sign of the cross over the oven and over the bread. The women then say a silent prayer before placing the korovai delicately in the oven. The appearance that the bread takes on when it emerges from the oven is considered extremely important. Ideally, the bread should not display any cracks on its top and or sides as cracks are thought to mean the upcoming marriage will end in divorce. Many Ukrainian people also believe that it is unlucky for a korovai to come out of the oven twisted. Once the bread is ready it travels to the church with the soon-to-be married couple where it is blessed. During the marriage ceremony the korovai stays close to the altar before being taken to the wedding reception where it is placed in a location where all the guests can see it.

Another conical Scandinavian wedding cake is the *spettekaka* (meaning spit or skewer cake) that is traditionally served at weddings in Skåne county located in southern Sweden. A spettekaka takes the form of a two- to three-foot-tall conical meringue that is made by drizzling meringue mix consisting of eggs, potato flour, and sugar over a cone-shaped spit that rotates over a low heat. In this way a number of fine, lacy meringue layers are formed that dry out and become crisp. The meringue has a very distinctive taste similar to spun sugar. Once the lacy layers are crisp they are then decorated with frosting before being cut into rectangles. The baking of spettekaka in Sweden dates back to the 17th century when it was traditional for two spettekaka to be made for each wedding—one to stand on the bridal table and one to be broken over the bride's head. This is not, however, necessarily the case today. The first published recipe for spettekaka appeared in a cookbook in 1733 and today the European Union has awarded spettekaka Protected Geographical Indication status. A similar spit cake is the Hungarian *kürtőskalács*, which is popular in Hungarian-speaking parts of Romania and is a staple of Transylvanian wedding receptions. The name kürtőskalács derives from the Hungarian for stovepipe, which is apt since the cake is made in a tall, slim cylinder shape.

Another tall wedding confection cooked on a rotating spit is the *sakotis* (meaning branched) that is served at weddings in Lithuania. Sakotis is made from a cookie-type pastry dough formed into a spiky Christmas tree shape and baked until it is a yellow color. The tree-shaped pastry is then decorated with fresh flowers and herbs that protrude from the top of the "tree," chocolate or jelly. Sakotis is also served at Christmas, birthday, and baptismal celebrations. In Polish, sakotis is referred to as *sekacz* or *senkacz,* while in German it is called *baumkuchen* (tree cake). A baumkuchen type cake called *baamkuch* is traditionally served at weddings in Luxembourg.

As Europeans settled in the United States, they brought with them their traditional wedding cakes. By the 1890s, this mass immigration meant that two kinds of wedding cake were customarily served at American weddings: the pound cake and the plum cake. Pound cakes were so-called because they tended to consist of one-pound quantities of butter, sugar, flour, and currants though when served at weddings pound cakes were usually referred to as bride-cakes. Once baked the pound cakes were then covered with frosting. The heavier plum cake, which was then called black cake and featured thick, hard icing, was associated with the groom. Over the course of the 20th century the black cake was increasingly made as a white cake and often more than one was made so that the cakes could be stacked one on top of the other. Often slices of the black cake were given to bridesmaids to eat with a glass of wine before the wedding party headed to the church for the marriage service. In Virginia, it is traditional for both a bride cake and a black cake to be made, stacked together with the black cake on top and then the newlyweds cut into both cakes with the bride giving a slice of her cake to the groom and the groom offering a slice of his cake to his new wife. A commonly enacted American wedding cake tradition sees newlyweds cut their wedding cake together and then the bride will push a slice of the cake into her husband's face. In Bermuda, two cakes are commonly baked for weddings. The larger of the two cakes is occasionally referred to as a bride's cake and takes the form of a multi-tiered fruitcake covered with silver leaf. The smaller cake, which is called the groom's cake, is a pound cake enrobed in gold leaf. The traditional topper for a Bermudan wedding cake is a living tree sapling that the newlyweds plant together as a sign of their growing love for each other.

In China, it is usual for a collection of pastries known as bridal cakes to be served at wedding receptions. The number of bridal cakes served depends on how many people attend the wedding but an even number of cakes is always served to emphasize the importance of coupledom. Chinese bridal cakes often feature pastry made from eggs, lotus seeds, or mung beans. In the past after Chinese families met at their betrothal meeting to discuss a possible marriage, both families would send their friends and family so-called Double Happiness cakes or dragon and phoenix cakes together with the wedding invitations. These cakes are baked with a dragon and phoenix pattern imprinted on the surface and are usually filled with pastes made from lotus seed, red beans, or green beans. The cakes are also customarily presented to the bride's family by the relatives of the groom as part of the proposal gift. The bride's relatives then offer some of the cakes in honor of their ancestors while sending the remainder of the cakes to their friends and other relatives together with invitations to the wedding. In modern China, it is increasingly common for dragon and phoenix cakes to be served to guests to guests at the wedding instead. Elsewhere in Asia, in Indonesia a huge, multi-layered cake called a *kek lapis* dating back to the Dutch colonization of Indonesia is served at weddings. This cake is normally made from layers of vanilla and chocolate sponge flavored with cinnamon and nutmeg. In South Korea, the traditional wedding cake, *tteok*, is so well loved that there is a national Tteok Museum in the country's capital city, Seoul. Tteok is thought to be around 2,000 years old and there are a number of varieties of the cake. The type of tteok served at Korean weddings normally features a rice flour cake that has been steamed and filled with a variety of different fruits and nuts or a paste made from red beans or mung beans.

In Japan, it is sometimes the case that an elaborate artificial cake is created as the centerpiece of the wedding reception. These mock cakes are normally made from rubber and wax and include a slot through which newlyweds can simulate the cutting of the cake. However while the newlyweds cut a fake cake their guests are fed a plain sheet cake. German-style *baumkuchen* is also frequently served at Japanese wedding receptions having been introduced to Japan by a German man, Karl Juchheim, who was interred in Okinawa during World War I. Today baumkuchen are often given as return presents for Japanese wedding guests because when a baumkuchen is sliced the slice is typically ring-shaped.

See also: *Beschuit met Muisjes, Suikerboon,* and *Dragées* (Volume 1); Birthday Cakes (Volume 1); British Wedding Traditions; Bulgarian Weddings; Face in Birthday Cake; *La Soupe*

Further Reading
Charsley, Simon R. *Wedding Cakes and Cultural History*. London: Routledge, 1992.
ChinaBridal.com. "Complete Guide to Chinese Wedding." Accessed December 2, 2015, at http://www.chinabridal.com/etiquette/guide.htm.
Cyrwus, Oksana. "Wedding Bread—Korovai," Ukraine Marriage Guide. Accessed December 2, 2015, at https://ukrainemarriageguide.com/?item=korovai.

Doyle, Sarah. "A World Tour of Wedding Cake Traditions." The Knot. Accessed December 2, 2015, at https://www.theknot.com/content/a-world-tour-of-wedding-cake-traditions.
Juchheim Co., Ltd. "Baumkuchen." Juchheim Group. Accessed December 2, 2015, at http://www.juchheim.co.jp/english/policy/p_baumkuchen/.
Lee, Robyn. "Snapshots from Sweden: Spettekaka from Fricks Spettkaksbageri." Serious Eats, June 13, 2011. Accessed December 2, 2015, at http://sweets.seriouseats.com/2011/06/snapshots-from-sweden-spettekaka-from-fricks-spettkaksbageri-billinge.html.
Monger, George P. *Marriage Customs of the World: From Henna to Honeymoons.* Santa Barbara, CA: ABC-CLIO, 2004.
Oleson Moore, Jessie. "Wedding Cake Wednesday: Traditional Wedding Sweets from around the World," Craftsy, January 15, 2014. Accessed December 2, 2015, at http://www.craftsy.com/blog/2014/01/traditional-wedding-cakes-from-around-the-world/.

WEDDING DRESS AND WEDDING RING, INTERNATIONAL

A wedding dress (sometimes referred to as a wedding gown) is the outfit worn by a bride during her wedding ceremony. The color, style, and ceremonial significance of the dress depend on the culture of the wedding participants. In the West, brides often wear a white wedding dress, while in the East brides often choose a red gown as red is considered an auspicious color. In other areas of the world, it is usual for a bride to wear her country's national dress while in some places the bride will wear her dowry or heavy jewelry in order to display her wealth.

The attire chosen by a bride is often a result of fashion and folklore meaning that dresses vary hugely around the world. For instance in Norway brides wear traditional national dress called a *bunad* (meaning clothing) that is presented to her for her confirmation. (*See* Plate 25.) Each region of Norway has its own particular style of bunad but it typically consists of a long woolen skirt, a linen shirt, an apron, waistcoat, cap, and shawl as well as a leather belt on to which many silver brooches are pinned. These items are all heavily embroidered as is the matching purse that is also part of the bunad outfit. Traditionally, bunads represented the concept of family and the home. As the bunad is worn for celebrations and special occasions—especially baptisms, confirmations, balls, and Norwegian Constitution Day—it is possible to see people walking to and from church wearing the outfit during the Norwegian wedding season (May–June). To signal that a Norwegian woman is wearing her bunad to get married she wears a golden crown, headdress, or elaborate jewelry on her head and she may also wear a veil if it is part of her region's bunad. The bride may also carry a small copy of the Bible in her purse. Once the woman is married she will wear a silver belt around her bunad and to signal that she is now a figure of authority she may add a silver key to her belt. Similar to Norway it is also traditional for Moroccan brides to wear a crown. For example brides belonging to the Fassi group (people from Fez) wear a dress made from gold brocade fabric together with a crown and pearl headdress. The Fassi bride is then carried in a procession with only her face visible.

It is, however, the white wedding dress that is most commonly associated with weddings, not just in the West but also in Japan and Korea where women belonging to the Unification Church wear Western-style white gowns for their mass wedding. British royal Queen Victoria began the trend for brides to wear white wedding dresses when she wore a white dress for her wedding to Prince Albert of Saxe-Coburg and Gotha in 1840. Prior to Queen Victoria's wedding, British women had married in whatever color was considered fashionable and flattering, particularly red. Moreover, at this time white was considered the color of mourning so for the queen to wear white to her wedding was very unusual. The queen's outfit was in itself groundbreaking as she broke with tradition by designing her dress herself and eschewing fancy jewelry, crown, and velvet robes in favor of a wreath of orange blossoms. Queen Victoria was not the first royal to wear white for her wedding, as a number had previously, including Mary, Queen of Scots in 1558. However it was Queen Victoria who is widely credited with creating the trend. A few years after Queen Victoria's wedding it was commonly understood that white was the most fitting color for a bride's dress as the color was emblematic of purity and girlish innocence. Today only around 5 percent of wedding dresses worn by brides in the West are not white. In Japan, when a bride opts to wear traditional wedding attire she will wear white under her traditional red and gold robes—red and gold being the traditional Japanese colors of celebrations and happiness. In Colombia, brides wear white dresses augmented with touches of gold. Here the dress is also used in a form of divination for all bachelors present at the wedding place a shoe under the brides dress and then the groom picks one of the shoes thereby indicating which of the bachelors will wed next.

Brides belonging to the Russian Orthodox Church also wear white, as do Buddhist bridegrooms. A growing number of Chinese brides are also opting for a white Western-style gown although many others still wear the traditional Chinese wedding color of red. Sometimes a Chinese bride will wear both a white dress and a red dress at different points of her wedding ceremony thereby combining Western and Eastern traditions.

As well as a white dress, it is also traditional in the United Kingdom, United States, Brazil, Australia, and New Zealand to wear "something old, something new, something borrowed, something blue." These items are small tokens of good luck that the bride wears or carries on her wedding day and are rarely obvious to anyone but the bride herself and her closest family and friends. The tradition originated from a Victorian rhyme with something old representing permanency, something new looking to the future, something borrowed symbolizing happiness, and something blue (often a garter worn on the bride's thigh) representing love and faithfulness. Another superstition surrounding the wedding dress is that it is unlucky for the groom to see his bride's dress before the wedding, especially if the bride is wearing the dress.

In the West, many brides consider choosing their wedding dress as a rite of passage and place great emphasis upon having their friends and family present as they try on wedding dresses in the hunt for the perfect gown. The drama inherent in choosing the right wedding dress has led to a number of reality television shows focused on the trials and travails of shopping for wedding dresses, including "Say Yes to the Dress" (and the related show "Say Yes to the Dress: Atlanta") and "I Found the Gown." Though these shows are produced in the United States, they are aired internationally. Indeed in the United Kingdom, the television channel TLC often devotes it entire Friday night schedule to showing only these programs—leading the channel to dub its Friday schedule as "Friday Bride-day." The channel also frequently devotes entire Saturday morning–afternoon schedules to showing hours of back-to-back episodes of "Say Yes to the Dress." From watching "Say Yes to the Dress" it is possible to conclude that the tradition of the groom not seeing his bride's dress before the wedding seems to be on the wane as a number of brides now bring their fiancé with them to see the trying on of dresses. Changing styles of wedding dress are also apparent with styles such as the mermaid and fit-and-flare vying for popularity with the traditional fairytale princess-type gown. Dresses featuring see-through lace corsets and plunging necklines also seem to be in vogue, thereby suggesting that the fashion for brides to look virginal on their wedding day is falling out of fashion.

Another very traditional item of wedding attire is the wedding ring (also known as a wedding band), which is usually placed on the couple being married during their marriage ceremony. The purpose of a wedding ring, which is often but not always made of metal, is to indicate that the wearer is married. The ring is normally worn at the base of the right of left ring finger, though this depends on prevailing local customs. Traditionally, only wives wore wedding rings, but at some point during the 20th century it became accepted for both the husband and wife to wear a wedding ring.

Wedding type rings were first used in ceremonies that took place in ancient Greece and ancient Rome, when the rings formed part of a dowry and were part of the formal betrothal process. Indeed these earliest rings were not viewed as ornamental but were important for their intrinsic physical value. The concept of a ring as a pledge evolved from an ancient Roman custom with the ritual of the giving of the ring to the bride viewed as a pledge of faithfulness during the *sponsalia* (engagement ceremony), which occurred before the bride went to live at the groom's home. The exchange of rings, which is part of virtually all modern Western marriage ceremonies, originates from the wedding rituals of early Christian Europe, for the late Roman custom of using a ring as a pledge continued in the earliest days of Christianity in Europe. Wedding ceremonies during which rings were exchanged and consecration ceremonies that saw bishops "married" to the Church kept the Roman concept of the ring as a pledge of loyalty. The earliest ceremonies involving an exchange of wedding rings can be found in liturgical books used in Europe during the Middle Ages, though in truth these ceremonies marked the period of betrothal rather than a marriage. Betrothal ceremonies varied throughout Europe, but a few elements such as the giving of rings as a betrothal "payment," alongside 13 gold or silver coins recurred all through the region. The payment of 13 coins, known as *arrhae* in the Latin West, or earnest money, represented the bride's share of her husband's wealth that she was entitled to keep in the event of her husband's death. The proportion of the husband's wealth to which the bride was entitled was called her dower, from which the term dowager, meaning a wealthy widow, evolved. By the 12th century, the giving of rings during the betrothal ceremony was standard practice in most of Europe. Over the years the giving of the rings at betrothals became a personal rather than ecclesiastical issue. In response, churches throughout Europe combined the betrothal ceremony and the marriage ritual into one rite, although in some areas of Europe distinct betrothal and wedding ceremonies still took place with a ring employed as a pledge of loyalty during the betrothal.

Over the years, however, the betrothal and wedding ceremonies morphed into a single rite throughout Europe to the end that a betrothal as a distinct ceremony rarely occurs today. The merging of the two ceremonies means that today wedding rings are often a single set of rings, though the custom of giving a separate engagement ring still continues in some places. In Sweden it is customary for a third ring to be given to a bride to commemorate her first baby and entrance into motherhood.

There are many types of traditional wedding rings. During the 16th and 17th centuries rings known as gimmel rings were popular in England, Germany, and elsewhere. The name gimmel derives from the Latin *gemellus*, meaning twin, for a gimmel ring typically features two interlocking hoops. Traditionally, a couple would each receive one of these hoops during their betrothal ceremony. The separated hoops were then reunited at the wedding ceremony as a way for to demonstrate that the bride and groom both consented to the marriage. Similar rings formed from more than two hoops are usually referred to as puzzle rings. As puzzle rings feature three links they meant that a third person could witness a couple's betrothal vows all the while holding on to the third link of the ring until the marriage ceremony took place. Some gimmel rings featured a *fede*, that is, the motif of two clasped hands joined together that symbolizes the joining of the bride and groom's hands during the marriage ceremony. The symbol of the fede is still commonly found on rings today.

The name fede come from the Italian *mani in fede* (hands in trust) and has given its name to a type of ring featuring clasped hands that symbolize the connection between husband and wife. The motif of the fede has been in existence since Roman times, but is particularly associated with Ireland where it is known as the *Claddagh* motif (with a heart and crown) or the *Fenian Claddagh* (without a crown). The Irish Claddagh ring is so called because it originated in Claddagh, Galway, and has been worn there constantly through the ages. What sets the Claddagh ring apart from other fede rings is the heart motif in the center of the ring and the crown set above the heart. The Claddagh ring has been popular in Ireland and elsewhere since the 17th century and is still a popular style of ring worn today as a sign of love and loyalty.

See also: British Wedding Traditions; Bulgarian Weddings; Christian Wedding Ceremony; First Communion (Volume 1); *Mehndi*; Moonie Weddings; Moroccan Weddings; *Shabka*; *Vinok*; Tear Catchers and Mourning Jewelry (Volume 3); Warding Off the Evil Eye (Volume 1)

Further Reading

Begley, Sarah. "The White Dress That Changed Wedding History Forever." *Time*, February 10, 2015. Accessed November 24, 2015, at http://time.com/3698249/white-weddings/.

Bronner, Simon J., ed. *Encyclopedia of American Folklife*. Volumes 1–4. London: Routledge, 2015.

Fedorak, Shirley A. *Pop Culture: The Culture of Everyday Life*. Toronto, Canada: University of Toronto Press Incorporated, 2009.

Foley, Michael P., with Alexander E. Lessard, Angela Lessard, and Alexandra Foley. *Wedding Rites: The Complete Guide to Traditional Vows, Music, Ceremonies, Blessings, and Interfaith Services*. Grand Rapids, MI: William B. Eerdmans Publishing Company, 2008.

Irish Claddagh Rings. "Fede Rings." Accessed November 24, 2015, at http://www.irishclad daghrings.com/information/fede_rings.htm.

Juliet and Oliver. "Where Do Wedding Rings Come From?" Juliet & Oliver: Official Blog, March 9, 2015. Accessed November 24, 2015, at http://www.julietoliver.com/blog/where-do-wedding-rings-come-from/.

Monger, George P. *Marriage Customs of the World: From Henna to Honeymoons*. Santa Barbara, CA: ABC-CLIO, 2004.

My Little Norway. "Bunad—Norwegian Traditional Costumes." Accessed November 24, 2015, at http://mylittlenorway.com/2009/05/bunad-norwegian-traditional-costumes/.

Quinn, George. "The Claddagh Ring," *The Mantle*, no. 13, 1970, 9–13. Accessed November 24, 2015, at http://places.galwaylibrary.ie/history/chapter267.html.

Trustees of the British Museum. "Fede Ring / Gimmel-ring." The British Museum: Collection Online. Accessed November 24, 2015, at http://www.britishmuseum.org/research/collection_online/collection_object_details.aspx?objectId=79510&partId=1.

Related Primary Document: Yumi Sakugawa, "An Asian American Wedding," 2009

Historically a number of anti-miscegenation laws have governed marriage between whites and non-whites in the United States. These laws originated with rules drawn up in Virginia and Maryland at the start of the colonial period. In 1880 laws were established that forbade marriage between whites and Negroes, mulattos, and Mongolians. Then, in 1922 the passing of the Cable Act meant that an American woman could lose her citizenship if she married a man that was alien and ineligible for American citizenship, by which was meant an Asian man. After World War II, however, anti-miscegenation laws faced increasing opposition, culminating in a 1967 legal case known as Loving v. Virginia, which saw the Supreme Court rule unanimously that anti-miscegenation laws violated the 14th Amendment. The 14th Amendment addresses several aspects of citizenship and the rights of citizens, including the right of citizens to enjoy equal protection of the laws. The amendment came into being in response to issues related to former slaves following the end of the American Civil War. At the same time opposition to mixed-race marriages began to lessen within ethnic communities most likely as a result of the growing civil rights movement. In the wake of such social change interracial marriages became increasingly common, and since the 1980s the number of white Americans marrying Asians has risen to the extent that some sociologists now refer to an Asian American pan-ethnic identity.

The following piece looks at some of the consequences of interethnic relationships.

The ceremony took place in the banquet hall of a fancy Vietnamese restaurant, where a Christian priest led the wedding vows. The reception afterward took place in the adjacent dining area, where Vietnamese soup, seafood and fried rice were served one course at a time. During the dinner, family and friends stood up to give their heartfelt wishes to the newly married couple in Vietnamese and English. At one point, the bride changed out of her white wedding gown and into an elaborate ao dai with a matching khan dong headdress in red and gold. This was the dress she wore when she and the groom walked over to each table to thank them for their attendance. As this was my first time attending the wedding of a person my age, simply imagining the meticulous planning that went into the wedding was overwhelming. Which family pays for what part of the wedding? Who decides what orchid centerpiece decorates which table? How do people know how big the wedding cake has to be and how big the individual slices have to be so that each guest gets a piece? There are additional cultural issues to address when you are involved in an Asian American wedding. Should the ceremony be conducted in English, the mother tongue, or both? Should the guests bring envelopes of money (the Asian way), open a gift registry (the American way), or leave it to the guests to decide for themselves? Wearing the traditional ethnic dress to the ceremony: yea or nay? Things get even more complicated when the bride and the groom are of different ethnicities. Earlier this year, I met a Japanese woman who married a Jewish man when she moved to America. She took Jewish conversion classes before the wedding, had a small ceremony in Los Angeles, and then went out of the country for several weeks to have a reception for her family in Japan and another for the groom's family in Israel. Where is the wedding planner who specializes in organizing the cultural and geographical logistics of a multi-racial wedding? After all, many of the long-term couples in my circle of friends are of mixed-race, which means that should a wedding occur in the future, they would have their own unique set of cultural challenges to confront when they plan their own respective weddings. Such as my other Vietnamese American friend, who may one day marry her boyfriend who is one-quarter Chinese and three-quarters white. Or my Hindu friend who dreads telling her parents that her Taiwanese Hapa boyfriend does not fit into her parents' mold of an ideal husband who is of the family's geographical region, language, caste, and nationality. Or my Muslim Cham friend who has yet to tell her parents about her Caucasian boyfriend of eight years for fear of disappointing them that she will probably not continue the shrinking lineage of the once-great Champa kingdom of Southeast Asia. In the latter cases, these couples need a great wedding planner who is good at planning multi-racial weddings and diffusing multi-racial family drama. At the ceremony I attended, the bride and the groom had a sand-mixing ritual before they exchanged their wedding vows. The bride held a glass flask filled with red sand, and the groom held a glass flask filled with gold sand. Together, they poured their respective glasses into a larger glass vase that now contained both the red and the gold sand. As the priest explained to the guests, the multicolored sand symbolized the union of their once-separate lives combining inseparably to create completely new patterns that would have never existed. This ritual was a symbol of their own union, but the mixing of multi-colored sand may as well be a symbol for the institution of Asian American marriages, and the entire Asian American community as a whole. We are creating new patterns simply by living and breathing here. Two completely different cultures are combining by the second to create a completely new way of thought that would have been unheard of a decade ago. Every day, cultural traditions are broken, tinkered with or reimagined. We have the freedom to create these new patterns for ourselves.

Source: *Reprinted with permission from Pacific Citizen, www.pacificcitizen.org.*

WEDDING MARCH AND BRIDAL CHORUS, INTERNATIONAL

In many countries it is traditional for so-called wedding marches to be played on an organ to mark the start and finish of a Christian wedding ceremony, most often as the bride walks down the aisle of the church toward her groom and then as the newly married couple walk back down the aisle to exit the church. Two of the most popular wedding marches are the wedding recessional from the suite of incidental music to *Ein Sommernachtstraum* (*A Midsummer Night's Dream*, 1842) by Felix Mendelssohn (1809–1847) and *Bridal Chorus* (or *Treulich geführt* in German) by Richard Wagner (1813–1883), commonly referred to as "Here Comes the Bride."

Mendelssohn's piece is technically a wedding march due to it brisk pace and joyful feel, though musical authorities also class the tune as a recessional as it is often played after the wedding ceremony has taken place. Mendelssohn's "Wedding March" is heard several times throughout *Ein Sommernachtstraum*, but appears first between Acts 4 and 5. The piece became popular as a wedding tune as a result of British royal, Princess Victoria (daughter of Queen Victoria) choosing the piece for the occasion of her marriage to Prince Frederick William of Prussia in 1858. Queen Victoria was an admirer of Mendelssohn's music and the composer often played for the queen when he visited Britain. The fact that Mendelssohn's "Wedding March" was originally written to accompany a secular comedy fantasy about romantic confusion and lustful, mythical beings makes it, perhaps, an odd choice to complement Christian weddings. Indeed some Christian churches, such as the Chapel of St. Thomas Aquinas at the University of St. Thomas in Minnesota, do not allow the tune to be played, arguing that it is a secular piece of music from a play that hinges on magical enchantment and pokes fun at the concept of romantic attachment.

Mendelssohn's tune is frequently paired with the "Bridal Chorus" from Wagner's opera's *Lohengrin*, which tells the German mythological tale of Lohengrin, a knight of the Holy Grail who is guided by a swan to rescue a princess, Elsa, that he later marries. However the story does not have a happy ending as Lohengrin has to return to the castle of the Grail and Elsa dies of a broken heart. Despite this

> **The Association of Richard Wagner with Nazism**
>
> Adolf Hitler admired Richard Wagner's music for he felt Wagner's operas embodied his own vision of a heroic Germany. There is, however, much discussion about the degree to which Wagner's work may have influenced Nazi thinking though the Nazis did employ elements of Wagner's work that they felt were useful propaganda. The association of Wagner with anti-Semitism and Nazism means that the performance of Wagner's music is sometimes highly controversial. Indeed Wagner's operas have never been performed in the modern State of Israel and the rare public instrumental performances of Wagner's operas in Israel have provoked outcry.

unhappy ending, many millions of brides and grooms have walked down the aisles to Wagner's "Bridal Chorus" over the years, the piano-vocal score of *Lohengrin* being published in 1851 and also been played at the marriage ceremony of Princess Victoria and Prince Frederick William in 1858. As a result of the royal couple's choice of music Wagner's "Bridal Chorus" continues to be a wedding standard throughout the world more than a century later.

In Wagner's opera *Lohengrin* the "Bridal Chorus" is accompanied by words and sung by Elsa's ladies-in-waiting after Lohengrin and Elsa marry. The lyrics reveal that the tune is not concerned with the religious or spiritual aspects of marriage but, rather, is focused on the act of consummating the marriage. The song is sung by the ladies-in-waiting as a comment on the fact that the newly married Elsa is on her way to join her husband in the bedchamber. This is suggested by the lyrics. For instance the song begins "*Treulich geführt ziehet dahin, wo euch der Segen der Liebe bewahr'!*", which translates as "Faithfully guided, draw near to where the blessing of love shall preserve you!" thereby hinting at carnal pleasures to come while later on the ladies-in-waiting sing "*Streiter der Tugend, bleibe daheim! Zierde der Jugend, bleibe daheim! Rauschen des Festes seid nun entronnen, Wonne des Herzens sei euch gewonnen!*" meaning "Champion of virtue, remain here! Jewel of youth, remain here! Flee now the splendors of the wedding feast, may the delights of the heart be yours!" which obviously alludes to the act of consummation.

The "Bridal Chorus" acquired the alternative title "Here Comes the Bride" when it was used as music to accompany a silent film of the same name in 1915, a title created by prolific film writer Shannon Fife. Fife's evocative title instantly became synonymous with Wagner's tune and very quickly lyricists invented new, less sexual, words to accompany the "Bridal Chorus" that referred to Fife's film title. These lyrics included lines such as "Here comes the bride, friends by her side" or the equally trite "Here comes the bride, all dressed in white."

Like Mendelssohn's "Wedding March," some churches do not allow Wagner's "Bridal Chorus" to be played during weddings. This is usually because of the lyrics' sexual content that focuses on the act of consummation rather than the sanctity of marriage. Another reason is that Wagner is often considered to have been anti-Semitic and so some churches do not welcome his music. A third, more light-hearted reason, is that a well-known parody of Wagner's "Bridal Chorus" exists. The parodied lyrics of this version are as follow: "Here comes the bride, all fat and wide/See how she wobbles, from side to side/Here comes the groom, thin as a broom/And here comes the usher, the old toilet flusher!" Though much loved by children and those with a childish sense of humor, these lyrics are frowned upon by some churches for although they would not be sung by wedding guests they are nonetheless often foremost in the minds of guests when the "Bridal Chorus" is played at weddings. For this reason stricter churches ban the song on the grounds that these alternative lyrics do not sit well with the sacred nature of marriage.

See also: British Wedding Traditions; Cajun Weddings; Christian Wedding Ceremony; Horseshoes; Royal Weddings; Wedding Cake; Wedding Dress and Wedding Ring

Further Reading

Alsop, Marin. "Marin Alsop's Guide to Mendelssohn's 'A Midsummer Night's Dream.'" NPR Music, May 24, 2014. Accessed February 8, 2015, at http://www.npr.org/blogs/deceptivecadence/2014/05/23/315246245/marin-alsops-guide-to-mendelssohns-a-midsummer-nights-dream.

Beauman, Francesca. *How to Wear White: A Pocketbook for the Bride-to-Be.* London: Bloomsbury Publishing, 2013.

Cryer, Max. *Common Phrases: And the Amazing Stories behind Them.* New York: Skyhorse Publishing, 2010.

LyricsTranslate.com. "The Bridal Chorus/The Wedding March." Accessed February 8, 2015, at http://lyricstranslate.com/en/treulich-gefuehrt-bridal-chorusthe-wedding-march-bridal-chorusthe-wedding-march.html.

Studwell, William E. *The National and Religious Song Reader: Patriotic, Traditional, and Sacred Songs from around the World.* Binghamton, NY: The Haworth Press Inc., 1996.

University of St. Thomas. "UST Wedding Music Guidelines." Accessed February 8, 2015, at https://www.stthomas.edu/media/campusministry/pdf/MusicGuidelines6-25-13.pdf.

WHITE COAT CEREMONY AND PINNING CEREMONY, INTERNATIONAL

A white coat ceremony is a recently invented rite of passage for first-year medical students that welcomes the students into the medical profession. During the ceremony first years are presented with white coats emblematic of authority and excellence in clinical care by alumni of their course. A white coat ceremony takes place at the start of the first year of medical school before students have taken any lectures or classes. Students' friends and families, who are invited to attend the ceremony by the medical faculty, watch as the first-years take up the mantle of the medical profession. White coat ceremonies are most common in the United States but also take place in Europe and Israel.

The first white coat ceremony was held at Columbia University in 1993. A white coat ceremony is an opportunity to instill in medical students the need for compassion, dedication, and accountability. During the ceremony students are also congratulated on the achievement of being selected to enter medical school and are reminded of the commitments of medical students, namely that they are responsible for becoming, and staying, proficient in the science of medicine and the skills of the medical practitioner, as well as their obligations of being a caring medic. To reinforce these duties, an eminent doctor often gives a brief lecture welcoming the new student medics and emphasizing the importance of doctors marrying humanity with scientific medical practice.

White coat ceremonies differ but usually guests congregate in the medical faculty's auditorium and stand up when the medical students enter the room in a line. When the students have all progressed into the auditorium everyone sits and listens to the talk by the eminent medical professional. Next, the robing ceremony takes place during which all the medical students are presented with their white coat, either by senior members of the faculty staff or alumni, as their name is read out aloud. As the students receive their coats they are congratulated by the staff and alumni and cheered by their friends and family. Next, the students stand up and, encouraged by the senior medical staff, make various professional commitments to study hard, train thoroughly, put their patients' interest ahead of their own, and value the opinions of their colleagues. New students also swear to be compassionate, to encourage their fellow students, to abide by their university's rules, and to always be worthy of the honor of being a medic. After the oaths are complete, the students leave the auditorium and enjoy a reception with their friends and families.

A pinning ceremony is a meaningful ceremony dedicating newly qualified nurses to the nursing profession. Before a pinning ceremony new nurses choose the person to whom they would like to dedicate their pin, including a teacher, a friend, or a relative. Then during the pinning ceremony the person chosen by the new nurse accompanies the nurse on to the stage where a member of the nursing faculty gives the selected person a pin to attach to the nurse's clothes. The pin symbolizes that the new nurse is accepted by her peers. Next, candles are lit in honor of Florence Nightingale, the founder of modern nursing practices, and the new nurses vow to abide by her ideals of nursing. The nurses then recite the International Council of Nurses Pledge.

The pinning ceremony originated during the 12th century when the Knights Hospitaller, a monastic religious and military order also known as the Order of Saint John, tended to wounded Christian pilgrims during the Crusades (i.e., military campaigns of the Middle Ages). When people were initiated into the Knights Hospitaller, they were inducted into the society they went through a ceremony during which each new knight was given a Maltese cross to wear on their arms. In the 1860s, Florence Nightingale was presented with the Red Cross of St. George for her nursing of injured men during the Crimean War. However Nightingale wished to reward the nurses that had worked alongside her and so presented a medal of excellence to her best nursing graduates. By 1916, it became the norm in the United States for nursing schools to present all new nurses with a pin at a ceremony to mark their graduation. Graduates wore the pin so that they could be identified as nurses and as evidence of their education. Today, the pinning ceremony is an emotional occasion that symbolizes the completion of nursing students' education and their acceptance by their peers.

See also: *Baccalauréat* and *Matura*

Further Reading

Brosnan, Caragh, and Bryan S. Turner, eds. *Handbook of the Sociology of Medical Education.* Abingdon, UK: Routledge, 2009.

Georgetown University. "White Coat Ceremony Marks Official Start of Medical School." Accessed May 11, 2015, at http://www.georgetown.edu/news/white-coat-ceremony-2014.html.

Gillon, Raanan. "White Coat Ceremonies for New Medical Students," *Western Journal of Medicine, 173*(3), September 2000, 206–207. Accessed May 11, 2015, at http://www.ncbi.nlm.nih.gov/pmc/articles/PMC1071071/.

Oermann, Marilyn H., and Kathleen T. Heinrich, eds. *Annual Review of Nursing Education, Volume 4, 2006.* New York: Springer Publishing Company Inc., 2006.

Pfeffer, Jennifer. "Nursing Pinning Ceremony: A Rite-of-Passage for Graduates." Rasmussen College, December 5, 2012. Accessed May 11, 2015, at http://www.rasmussen.edu/degrees/nursing/blog/nursing-pinning-ceremony-rite-of-passage-for-graduates/.

WODAABE COURTSHIP DANCE AND FESTIVAL, AFRICA

The annual Wodaabe courtship dance and festival is a matchmaking event belonging to the Wodaabe tribe (also known as the Peulh Bororos), a small pastoral population belonging to the Fulani group that lives in Africa's Sahel desert. The most famous Wodaabe festival takes place in In-Gall, a town in Niger. Courtship events held here attract members of other nomadic tribes, not just from the Wodaabe tribe, meaning that crowds in excess of more than 50,000 can amass to celebrate the festival.

The event is unusual as it sees men dance in order to impress young women spectators and win their romantic attentions. The festivities are known as *Gerewol* in the Wodaabe language, meaning "to line up." This name is apt for once the men have danced before the women they line up and wait to be judged by the females in much the same way as a Western beauty pageant. The women select whom they consider to be the most physically attractive dancer from another clan and either spend a few nights with him or suggest marriage. The Wodaabe have an unusual way of marriage for both men and women may be married to two people simultaneously. Tribe members normally arrange a first marriage (*koogal*) to a man of the same lineage to the female when the female is a baby. This first marriage is arranged at a festival called *Worso*, where members of the same clan meet to arrange marriages and celebrate the birth of babies. It is at the Wodaabe festival of Gerewol that a woman's second marriage (*teegal*), a love match, is established with the festival allowing a woman to choose a second husband from a different clan.

The Wodaabe festival takes place on a date that coincides with both the end of the fasting necessary for Ramadan and the end of the rainy season, usually in September or October. The event is usually held in a marketplace where tribal meetings and other social gatherings occur. However the location of the festival is kept secret and told to a select few people a couple of days before it takes place. Preparations for the festivities take a many months to complete, including song and dance rehearsals for the men taking part, buying clothes, and readying make-up and jewelry. In preparation for the festival Wodaabe, men paint their faces with tribal markings using red ochre, or white or pale yellow clay; paint their lips with black lipstick made from charred bones of the cattle egret; shave their hairline to make their faces appear longer; and braid their hair. (See Plate 26.) Wodaabe men are used to dancing from a young age and take care of their bodies, often spending more time on beautifying themselves than Wodaabe women. Indeed members of the Wodaabe tribe place great cultural value on vanity and consider personal grooming and physical beauty to be extremely important. The Wodaabe ideal of beauty is that a man should be tall and slim with a long face, wide eyes, thin lips, light-colored skin, white teeth, and an aquiline nose. Good manners, affability, and stamina are also considered essential for a Wodaabe man to be attractive to women.

On the day of the festival, the dancers (*sukaabes*) don handmade, indigo colored skirts, necklaces made of cowry shells, and turbans into which ostrich feathers are inserted. These are considered very sexy items as cowry shells are thought to look like female genitalia and vertical ostrich feathers symbolize the penis.

The festival features many activities including singing, hypnosis, and camel racing. There are also several types of dances of which the most important is the *Yaake*. When performing the dances the men form a line, standing shoulder to shoulder in front of the watching women. To attract the women's attention the men first perform the energetic *raume* dance by standing tall on their tip-toes and making expressive moves imitative of an egret, the bird which the Wodaabe associate with expressivity. As they dance, the men also sing by vibrating their black-painted lips, mimicking the egret whose bones have been used to paint their lips. The men also grin profusely to show off the whiteness of their teeth. During the raume men from different clans dance together in a circle counter-clockwise.

The festival of dance lasts for seven days. At the conclusion of the seventh day, the men line up in order to be judged. Three girls considered the most beautiful by tribal elders choose the year's best performer. These girls are usually of a high social rank and are sometimes the daughters of former winners. To make their judgments the girls walk very slowly up and down the line of dancing men with their heads bowed. When they have chosen a winner, the girls walk toward the winning dancer and gently tap him on the shoulder to indicate their preference. The winner may be taken as a lover by a judge and he will be celebrated for years to come. Other participants may also enter into flirtatious activity as no shame is attached to setting aside marriage vows for the duration of Gerewol and it is quite permissible for sexual flings to take place.

During the festival participants eat as little as possible and drink performance-enhancing libations made from tea bark. The tea bark has a hallucinogenic effect and it has been known for dancers to fall into a trance while performing. This has led some critics of the festival to argue that the courtship dance is dangerous and is run by evil forces. Although most of the Wodaabe are Muslim, the men taking part in the festival use magic potions, spells, and sorcery to make themselves as beautiful as possible, to improve their dancing, and to see harm come to their competitors all in the hope of attracting a woman.

The men aim to attract a woman from a different clan and enter into a love marriage with her. Therefore during the festival the men and women flirt and if a women takes a fancy to a man she will show her affection by following him to a bush. If this occurs the man must be polite and employ florid language to seduce the woman. The man must be wary however for if he rushes his overtures the woman may run away from him. The new couple may spend several nights together, sleeping on the man's mat in the bushes. If they think they are compatible, the couple marries. Before they wed, however, the woman must introduce the man to her parents who arrange a bride price with the prospective groom in exchange for their daughter. This dowry-like contract usually sees the woman swapped for a gift of cattle and water bottles filled with milk. Once this is arranged the man introduces his bride-to-be to his clan. If a woman is already in a second marriage and wants to wed again the man can still take her to meet his clan but this is a dangerous situation for the husband may try to win back his wife. In Wodaabe culture it is considered acceptable to attract and steal another's wife but it is a humiliation for a man to lose his wife to another man. The couple are deemed married when an animal is sacrificed to mark their union.

Many factors threaten the future of the Wodaabe festival of courtship and dance, including drought, war, and the insurgence of al-Qaeda in North Africa. Droughts mean that there is a lack of water for both people and animals, leading young men and women to abandon traditional ways of life choosing to settle in cities rather than continue to struggle as pastoralist nomads. However in urban areas people tend to hold Gerewol bi-annually in an attempt to safeguard nomadic traditions in the face of increased marginalization of tribal groups and urbanization in general.

The courtship dances performed at Gerewol are also performed by troops of Wodaabe dancers at hotels as tourist entertainment. However when performed for tourists the dances are not truly part of the Gerewol tradition as they do not end in courtship or marriage and are merely a form of employment.

See also: Bachelor and Spinster Balls; Bed-Courtship; Child Beauty Pageants (Volume 1); Death Dance (Volume 3); *Lobola*; Looking for Fern Blossoms; Obando Fertility Dance (Volume 1); *Pika* and *Nyora*; Polygyny; Sunrise Ceremony

Further Reading

Allan, Timothy. "Gerewol." Accessed December 20, 2014, at http://humanplanet.com/timothyallen/2011/01/gerewol_wodaabe_niger_bbc-human-planet-deserts/.

Bovin, Mette. *Nomads Who Cultivate Beauty: Wodaabe Dances and Visual Arts in Niger*. Uppsala, Sweden: Nordiska Afrikainstitutet, 2001.

Galvan, Javier A., ed. *They Do What? A Cultural Encyclopedia of Extraordinary and Exotic Customs from around the World*. Santa Barbara, CA: ABC-CLIO, 2014.

Lane, Megan. "The Male Beauty Contest Judged by Women." BBC News: Africa. January 20, 2011. Accessed December 20, 2014, at http://www.bbc.co.uk/news/world-africa-12215138.

Monger, George P. *Marriage Customs of the World: An Encyclopedia of Dating Customs and Wedding Traditions*. Expanded second edition. Santa Barbara, CA: ABC-CLIO, 2013.

X

XHOSA CIRCUMCISION, SOUTH AFRICA

Every year, many thousands of males belonging to the Xhosa (also called the ama-Xhosa) people of South Africa undergo a rite of passage to manhood involving ritual circumcision. Participants in the ritual range in age from boys as young as six to men in their mid-twenties though the average age for males to undergo the ritual is 18 years. This circumcision, which is part of a secretive ritual sometimes referred to as *ulwaluko* or *ukwalasu*, is highly controversial and often results in males being maimed, having to undergo amputations, or even dying. Indeed such is the crude nature of Xhosa circumcision that the practice has been described as male genital mutilation. Xhosa circumcision is part of a three-week-long initiation period that takes place during the December school-holidays.

As Xhosa circumcision is a sacred ritual, males that have undergone the ritual do not tend to talk about their experiences as any male that does reveal the specifics of the ritual risks being ostracized by society and called *impipi*, meaning traitor. Xhosa males often feel that they have no alternative but to undergo the initiation and attendant circumcision as they believe that society will consider them as unmanly and that no woman will marry then if they have not experienced the ritual. Further, uncircumcised Xhosa men risk being shunned by their peers and being beaten by circumcised men who disapprove of the uncircumcised male's refusing to conform to Xhosa tradition.

To begin their passage to manhood initiates, known as *abakhwetha*, that have been put forward for circumcision by their parents and have agreed to circumcision leave their villages and are taken into the bush by tribal elders. Here, the males spend time living in huts, learning survival tactics and about the concept of *ubuntu*, or selflessness. The males then enter so-called circumcision schools where they coat themselves in white clay, as a symbol of newness and innocence, and are educated about the practicalities of becoming a Xhosa man such as how to wrestle and use a stick to fight. Initiates also undergo other rituals that are intended to transform them into fully adult men. The exact nature of these rituals is mysterious because the rites take place in secret but it is known that they include being subjected to exposure to cold winter weather. These rituals often leave the initiates sleep deprived, dehydrated, and starving. Then one day during their initiation the males are huddled in blankets and undergo their circumcision to the rhythmic beating of drums. The circumcision operation is usually performed outdoors by a specialist circumciser called an *ingcibi*, who has usually been circumcised himself and uses a double-edged spear to slice away foreskin. Some males are circumcised in local hospitals but this can lead to their rejection by other males. Indeed in

1993, Xhosa males that had been circumcised by an ingcibi killed tribesmen that had undergone the procedure in hospital.

Once the operation has been performed the freshly circumcised men undergo a period of isolation before returning to their villages where they are now considered *amakrwala*, or new adults. To celebrate their new status the men are given new possessions including clothes, drink *umqombothi*, a fermented mixture of crushed mealie malt (corn malt), sorghum, and water, and allowed to eat *incum*, the brisket of beef or ox that is considered the best part of the animal to eat and is, therefore, reserved for circumcised men. Meanwhile the men's boyhood possessions and clothes are burned to symbolize that they have left behind their childhood.

The dangers of Xhosa circumcision are manifold and it has been estimated that of Xhosa boys admitted to hospital as a result of undergoing circumcision 9 percent have died (mostly from septic shock), 52 percent lost the skin from their penile shaft, 14 percent suffered from infected lesions, 10 percent lost the glans of their penis, and 5 percent lost their penis either through gangrene or because their penis was so damaged that it had to be amputated. These figures do not include males that did not seek hospital treatment so the actual number of men left injured or ill through Xhosa circumcision is open to conjecture. It is, however, known that in 2013, 31 initiates died in Mpumalanga Province alone, while in East Province 500 males died during Xhosa circumcision during the period 2006 to 2014 with 83 males dying in 2013.

In 2012, Xhosa circumcision hit the headlines when a boy called Asanda broke the code of secrecy that surrounds Xhosa circumcision and went public about his circumcision. Asanda revealed that a folk surgeon who used the same spear to circumcise dozens of boys had circumcised him and a bandage had been applied around his penis so tightly that the blood supply to the organ was inhibited. This led to Asanda's penis becoming gangrenous and needing hospital treatment. After Xhosa circumcision penises that become infected with dry gangrene ultimately fall away from the body naturally, but penises suffering from wet gangrene occasionally have to be amputated to prevent the infection from spreading. Many Xhosa males that lose their penises as a result of their circumcision believe their penises will regrow as this is what they are told by folk medicine practitioners such as traditional nurses. However in actuality loss of the penis can result in males suffering from psychological issues, physical problems such as recurring infections as well as practical problems such as needing a catheter to urinate and being unable to have penetrative sexual intercourse. Many Xhosa males have also been infected with HIV as a result of undergoing their circumcision because of the tradition of using one spear to circumcise many initiates.

In 2014, the Congress of Traditional Leaders of South Africa, which promotes traditional South African customs and values, blamed untrained opportunists seeking to make money from initiates' families for the large number of males suffering as a result of their circumcision. To try to combat this problem the congress announced a new initiative that would see the state unite with medical professionals in an effort to teach villagers about safe and hygienic circumcision practices such as using a sterilized scalpel to remove skin.

See also: *Brit Milah* (Volume 1); Female Genital Cutting; *Sünnet*; Urethral Subincision

Further Reading

Denniston, George C., Frederick Mansfield Hodges, and Marilyn Fayre Milos, eds. *Male and Female Circumcision: Medical, Legal and Ethical Considerations in Pediatric Practice.* New York: Kluwer Academic/Plenum Publishers, 1999.

Kirsch, Beverley, and Silvia Skorge. *Clicking with Xhosa: A Xhosa Phrasebook.* New edition. Claremont, South Africa: David Philip Publisher, 2005.

Maykuth, Andrew. "Manhood, at What Cost? Ritual Circumcision Is a Rite of Passage in South Africa's Xhosa Tribe. Its Modern Legacy Includes Death and Maiming." Philly.com. Accessed May 11, 2015, at http://articles.philly.com/2000-02-01/living/25576756_1_circumcision-traditional-surgeon-xhosa.

NYP Holdings Inc. "Botched Circumcision Becoming Health Crisis in South Africa," *New York Post*, June 4, 2014. Accessed May 11, 2015, at http://nypost.com/2014/06/04/botched-circumcisions-becoming-health-crisis-in-south-africa/.

Z

ZOU HUN: MOSUO WALKING MARRIAGES, CHINA

The Mosuo people (sometimes called the Moso or Na) living in southwestern China are famous for their matrilineal culture in which women do not marry and fathers are not expected to support their children. Indeed the Mosuo do not have any word equivalent to the English words "husband" or "father." The region in which the 40,000 strong Mosuo population lives is called the Kingdom of Women by the Chinese because Mosuo women make the majority of important decisions, are in charge of household finances, own land and property, and have full rights to their children. During the 1960s and 1970s, China's Communist rulers tried to make the Mosuo abandon their traditions and adopt lifelong monogamy. However in recent years China has relaxed its stance somewhat meaning that the Mosuo have retained their marriage customs. Another reason that the Mosuo have been able to keep their traditions alive is that until recently their remote Himalayan location near Tibet has been kept fairly isolated with few transport links to the rest of China. Consequently, the Mosuo have, for the most part, been able to maintain their way of life.

When Mosuo children are around 12 to 14 years of age, they experience a coming-of-age ceremony. Before this ceremony, Mosuo children of both sexes dress in the same way but once the children reach the appropriate age, girls receive a skirt during a skirt ceremony and boys are given trousers in a so-called trouser ceremony. Once a Mosuo female has undergone a coming-of-age ceremony she is given her own bedroom, called a flower chamber, and once she has experienced puberty she is allowed to invite male partners for so-called walking marriages, or *zou hun*. This night visiting is also sometimes called *tisese*, meaning "goes back and forth." These marriages are referred to as walking marriages because the men involved walk to the house of their female partner at night where they stay before returning to their own home the next morning. During the day the women's male partners, known as *axias*, fish, rear animals, and care for their families before going to visit their woman at night.

The Mosuo tend to live in extended families consisting of many generations. Indeed it is not unusual for a household to comprise great grandparents, grandparents, parents, children, grandchildren, aunts, uncles, nieces, and nephews all living together. In general all the people within a household live within communal quarters that do not include private bedrooms or living quarters except for the flower chambers given to females that have had a coming-of-age ceremony.

A popular misconception is that Mosuo women are sexually promiscuous, changing sexual partners whenever they desire. However while Mosuo women are permitted to change partners as often as they feel like it, and it would be unusual for a woman to keep with the same sexual partner for her entire life, Mosuo women tend to enter into long-term relationships with men from their tribe that anthropologists refer to as serial monogamy. Mosuo relationships are based on affection, romance, and sexual desire but even though these pairings are long-term, a Mosuo man never lives with the Mosuo woman with whom he is in a relationship nor does the woman stay with the man. Instead, the man remains with his extended family for whom he is responsible while the woman stays with her family. The couple never shares property and if children result from the relationship the man is not responsible for them. Moreover, it is not uncommon for Mosuo children to be ignorant of their father's identity. If a man does want to be included in his children's lives then he must visit the mother's family and give them gifts while stating his desire to be involved in the lives of his offspring. If the mother's family decides to include the man, he will be given an official title within the family but he will not be considered part of the family. Moreover, the children will be raised solely by the mother's family and will assume her family name.

Despite their lack of involvement in the lives of their children, Mosuo men are responsible for looking after all the children born to the females within his own extended family—for example, the children born to his sisters, nieces, and aunts. Similarly, sisters will raise each other's children collectively. For this reason, Mosuo children consider their extended family to be their aunts and uncles because all members of the extended family help and nurture the children. Though this family structure may differ from the image of the family popular in the West, it is, in fact, a very stable family model. Divorce never occurs within Mosuo communities because there are no marriages, issues of child custody never arise, property does not have to be divided, and if a mother dies her children are cared for by her extended family. Another benefit to Mosuo system is that since neither male nor female children ever leave home families do not prefer one gender over the other though each generation of women within a family must produce at least one daughter to create the correct gender mix of children. As a consequence of this, gender imbalance does not tend to occur within Mosuo families. In fact, if a family does become imbalanced in terms of gender the family may adopt children of the appropriate gender from another family or two families may swap children to correct a gender imbalance.

One downside of the Mosuo system is that in recent years outsiders have been attracted to Mosuo society as they see Mosuo women as sexually unrestrained. The Chinese government has begun to promote the Mosuo to Chinese tourists and has even installed a tollbooth charging entry to Mosuo land via a new main road. This marketing of the Mosuo to outsiders has resulted in sex tourists being lured to Mosuo areas as they are under the misapprehension that Mosuo women offer sex at night to strangers for free. Moreover prostitutes imported from elsewhere in China and from Thailand, but wearing traditional Mosuo clothing, have been installed in newly built hotels, casinos, and bars in the main Mosuo village of Luoshui. To this end, there is now a red-light district centered on Lake Lugu, along the shores of which many Mosuo villages are established.

See also: Bed-Courtship; Chinese Coming-of-Age Ceremonies; *Nyumba Ntobhu*: Traditional Same-Sex Marriage; Polyandry; Visiting-Girls Courtship Tradition

Further Reading

Garrison, Marsha, and Elizabeth S. Scott, eds. *Marriage at the Crossroads: Law, Policy, and the Brave New World of Twenty-First-Century Families*. New York: Cambridge University Press, 2012.

HREF. "In China, Mosuo Women Rule." ABC News, May 19, 2002. Accessed September 26, 2015, at http://abcnews.go.com/WNT/story?id=130332.

Lugu Lake Mosuo Cultural Development Association. "Walking Marriages." Lugu Lake Mosuo Cultural Development Association. 2006. Accessed September 26, 2015, at http://www.mosuoproject.org/walking.htm.

Shaitly, Shahesta. "Is China's Mosuo Tribe the World's Last Matriarchy?" *The Guardian*, December 19, 2010. Accessed September 26, 2015, at http://www.theguardian.com/lifeandstyle/2010/dec/19/china-mosuo-tribe-matriarchy.

Selected Bibliography for Volume 2

Alexander, Marc. *The Sutton Companion to British Folklore, Myths & Legends*. Stroud, UK: Sutton Publishing Limited, 2002.
Anders Silverman, Deborah. *Polish-American Folklore*. Urbana: University of Illinois Press, 2000.
Austin, Daniel, and Hilary Bradt. *Madagascar*. Eleventh edition. Chalfont St. Peter, UK: Bradt Travel Guides Ltd., 2014.
Bayor, Ronald H., ed. *Multicultural America: An Encyclopedia of the Newest Americans*. Volume 4. Santa Barbara, CA: Greenwood, 2011.
Bhalla, Prem P. *Hindu Rites, Rituals, Customs and Traditions*. New Delhi, India: Hindoology Books, 2009.
Bolin, Anne, and Patricia Whelehan. *Human Sexuality: Biological, Psychological, and Cultural Perspectives*. New York: Routledge, 2009.
Brockman, Norbert C. *Encyclopedia of Sacred Places, Volume 1*. Second edition. Santa Barbara, CA: ABC-CLIO, 2011.
Bronner, Simon J., ed. *Encyclopedia of American Folklife*. Volumes 1–4. London: Routledge, 2015.
Buckley, Thomas, and Alma Gottlieb. *Blood Magic: The Anthropology of Menstruation*. Berkeley: University of California Press, 1988.
Crawford, Suzanne J., and Dennis F. Kelley, eds. *American Indian Religious Traditions: An Encyclopedia*. Santa Barbara, CA: ABC-CLIO, 2005.
Davidson, Linda Kay, and David Martin Gitlitz. *Pilgrimage: From the Ganges to Graceland: An Encyclopedia, Volume 1*. Santa Barbara, CA: ABC-CLIO, 2002.
Delaney, Janice, Mary Jane Lupton, and Emily Toth. *The Curse: A Cultural History of Menstruation*. Revised expanded edition. Champaign: University of Illinois Press, 1988.
DeMello, Margo. *Encyclopedia of Body Adornment*. Westport, CT: Greenwood Publishing Group Inc., 2007.
DeMello, Margo. *Faces around the World: A Cultural Encyclopedia of the Human Face*. Santa Barbara, CA: ABC-CLIO, 2012.
Denniston, George C., Frederick Mansfield Hodges, and Marilyn Fayre Milos, eds. *Male and Female Circumcision: Medical, Legal and Ethical Considerations in Pediatric Practice*. New York: Kluwer Academic/Plenum Publishers, 1999.
Fedorak, Shirley A. *Pop Culture: The Culture of Everyday Life*. Toronto, Canada: University of Toronto Press Incorporated, 2009.
Galvan, Javier A., ed. *They Do What? A Cultural Encyclopedia of Extraordinary and Exotic Customs from around the World*. Santa Barbara, CA: ABC-CLIO, 2014.
Herdt, Gilbert. *The Sambia: Ritual, Sexuality, and Change in Papua New Guinea*. Second edition. Belmont, CA: Wadsworth Cengage Learning, 2006.
Herdt, Gilbert H., ed. *Ritualized Homosexuality in Melanesia*. Berkeley: University of California Press, 1984.
Herdt, Gilbert H., ed. *Rituals of Manhood: Male Initiation in Papua New Guinea*. New Brunswick, NJ: Transaction Publishers, 1998.

Herrera-Sobek, Maria. *Celebrating Latino Folklore: An Encyclopedia of Cultural Traditions*. Volume 1. Santa Barbara, CA: ABC-CLIO, 2012.

Herzig, Rebecca M. *Plucked: A History of Hair Removal*. New York: New York University Press, 2015.

Idler, Ellen L., ed. *Religion as a Social Determinant of Public Health*. Oxford, UK: Oxford University Press, 2014.

Isaacs, Ronald H. *Rites of Passage: A Guide to the Jewish Life Cycle*. Hoboken, NJ: KTAV Publishing House Inc., 1992.

Jones, Alison. *Larousse Dictionary of World Folklore*. Edinburgh, UK: Larousse, 1996.

Joseph, Suad, and Afsāna Nağmābādī, eds. *Encyclopedia of Women & Islamic Cultures: Family, Body, Sexuality and Health Volume 3*. Leiden, Netherlands: Brill, 2006.

Lancy, David F. *The Anthropology of Childhood: Cherubs, Chattel, Changelings*. Second edition. Cambridge, UK: Cambridge University Press, 2015.

Lee, Jonathan H. X., and Kathleen M. Nadeau, eds. *Encyclopedia of Asian American Folklore and Folklife, Volume 1*. Santa Barbara, CA: ABC-CLIO, 2011.

MacDermott, Mercia. *Bulgarian Folk Customs*. London: Jessica Kingsley Publishers Ltd., 1998.

Maggi, Wynne. *Our Women Are Free: Gender and Ethnicity in the Hindukush*. Ann Arbor: University of Michigan, 2001.

Markstrom, Carol A. *Empowerment of North American Indian Girls: Ritual Expressions at Puberty*. Lincoln: University of Nebraska Press, 2008.

Melton, J. Gordon. *Religious Celebrations: An Encyclopedia of Holidays, Festivals, Solemn Observances, and Spiritual Commemorations*. Volume 1. Santa Barbara, CA: ABC-CLIO, 2011.

Meyer, Melissa L. *Thicker Than Water: The Origins of Blood as Symbol and Ritual*. New York: Routledge, 2005.

Mitchell, Claudia A., and Jacqueline Reid-Walsh. *Girl Culture: An Encyclopedia*. Volume 1. Westport, CT: Greenwood Press, 2007.

Monger, George P. *Marriage Customs of the World: From Henna to Honeymoons*. Santa Barbara, CA: ABC-CLIO, 2004.

Newton, David E. *Gay and Lesbian Rights: A Reference Handbook*. Second edition. Santa Barbara, CA: ABC-CLIO, 2009.

Newton, David E. *Same-Sex Marriage: A Reference Handbook*. Santa Barbara, CA: ABC-CLIO, 2010.

Nolt, Steven M., and Thomas J. Meyers. *Plain Diversity: Amish Cultures and Identities*. Baltimore, MA: The Johns Hopkins University Press, 2007.

Peters, F. E. *The Hajj: The Muslim Pilgrimage to Mecca and the Holy Places*. Princeton, NJ: Princeton University Press, 1994.

Pitts-Taylor, Victoria. *Cultural Encyclopedia of the Body: Volume 1 and 2*. Westport, CT: Greenwood Press, 2008.

Plutschow, Herbert E. *Matsuri: The Festivals of Japan*. Richmond, UK: Japan Library, 1996.

Reinier, Jacqueline S., and Priscilla Ferguson Clement, eds. *Boyhood in America: An Encyclopedia, Volume 1: A–K*. Santa Barbara, CA: ABC-CLIO, 2001.

Roy, Christina. *Traditional Festivals: A Multicultural Encyclopedia, Volume 2*. Santa Barbara, CA: ABC-CLIO, 2005.

Shell-Duncan, Bettina, and Ylva Hernlund, eds. *Female "Circumcision" in Africa: Culture, Controversy, and Change*. Boulder, CO: Lynne Rienner Publishers, 2002.

Sherrow, Victoria. *Encyclopedia of Hair: A Cultural History*. Westport, CT: Greenwood Press, 2006.

Sherrow, Victoria. *For Appearance' Sake: The Historical Encyclopedia of Good Looks, Beauty, and Grooming*. Westport, CT: The Oryx Press, 2001.

Shoup, John A., ed. *Ethnic Groups of Africa and the Middle East: An Encyclopedia*. Santa Barbara, CA: ABC-CLIO, 2011.

Simpson, Jacqueline, and Steve Roud. *Oxford Dictionary of English Folklore*. Oxford, UK: Oxford University Press, 2000.

Smith, Merril D., ed. *Cultural Encyclopedia of the Breast*. Lanham, MA: Rowman & Littlefield, 2014.

Studwell, William E. *The National and Religious Song Reader: Patriotic, Traditional, and Sacred Songs from Around the World*. Binghamton, NY: The Haworth Press Inc., 1996.

Tiller, Veronica E. Velarde. *Culture and Customs of the Apache Indians*. Santa Barbara, CA: ABC-CLIO, 2011.

Watts, Linda S. *Encyclopedia of American Folklore*. New York: Facts on File, Inc., 2007.

Comprehensive Index

The volume in which each entry appears is indicated in **bold**.

Abadinto (baby-naming ceremony), **1**:1
"Abide With Me" (hymn), **3**:1–3, 97
Aboriginal traditions. *See* Australians, Aboriginal
Abortion, **3**:180–182, 310; forced, **1**:256–258
Achambi ceremony, **1**:131
Acrostic jewelry, **3**:287
Adhaan, **1**:234
Adoption, baby showers for, **1**:24
Advent calendars, **1**:349–350
Afghani celebrations and practices: betrothal, **2**:1–3; burqa wearing, **2**:130; forced marriage, **2**:8; *halva*, **3**:113, 115; *Khwahish khwari*, **2**:1; *Labsgriftan*, **2**:1; *Shirin-i-grifgan*, **2**:1–2; *takht e khina*, **2**:2; virginity testing, **2**:357. *See also* Central Asian practices; South Asian celebrations and practices
African American traditions: folk medicine, **1**:30–31; jazz funerals, **3**:127–129; jumping over the broom, **2**:163–165; mistletoe, **1**:219; potty training, **1**:286
African celebrations and practices; arranged marriage, **2**:5, 7; breast ironing, **2**:30–32; cairns, **3**:23; christening gowns, **1**:94; cutting the umbilical cord, **1**:112–113; eating human placenta, **1**:123; female genital cutting, **2**:89–94; food taboos during pregnancy, **1**:146; forehead-cutting initiation rite, **2**:98–101; kangaroo care, **1**:183; lip plugs, **2**:191–195; menstrual customs, **2**:227; mourning color, **3**:305; polygyny, **2**:261; potty training, **1**:286; scarification, **2**:293–296; Tomb of the Unknown Soldier, **3**:295; urethral subincision, **2**:350; virginity testing, **2**:355–358; Wodaabe courtship dance and festival, **2**:383–386; *Yankan Gishiri*, **1**:362–363; *Zur-zur* (*zur zur; zurzur*), **1**:362–363. *See also* North African celebrations and practices; Sub-Saharan Africa; West African celebrations and practices

Afro-Brazilian traditions, **1**:345
Afterbirth. *See* Placenta
Agatharchides of Chidus, **2**:90
Aghoris sect, **3**:77
Aguman Sanduk Festival, **1**:105
Akan tribal groups, **1**:1
Akka goddess customs, **1**:4–7
Alaskan celebrations and practices, **1**:9
Albanian celebrations and practices: *Matura Shtetërore*, **2**:15; Napoleon dance, **2**:234; parental leave, **1**:266. *See also* Albanian funeral customs; Eastern European celebrations and practices
Albanian funeral customs, **3**:3–4; funeral cakes, **3**:93; graveyard traditions, **3**:3–4; "wailing funeral," **3**:3–4; washing the corpse, **3**:3
Alcohol consumption, **2**:16–17, 29, 63, 65, 97, 106, 181–182, 282–283, 316, **3**:313
Algerian celebrations and traditions: hamsa hand symbol, **1**:345. *See also* North African celebrations and practices
Algonquin tribe, **2**:359
Alimony, **2**:1
Alkaline hydrolysis, **3**:5–6, 104

All Hallow's Day, **3**:6, 109–110
All Hallows' Eve, **3**:263
All Saints' Day, **3**:6–8, 59, 263–264. *See also* Feast of All Saints
All Souls' Day, **3**:6–10, 59, 110, 263–265
All Souls' Day cakes, **3**:265
All Souls' Eve, **3**:264
Allerheiligenstriezel, **3**:265–266
Alnwick Castle, **3**:96
Alphorn music, **3**:238
Amajursuk, **1**:79
Ameen ceremony, **1**:47–48
American Indian Religious Freedom Act, **2**:327
American Society for Psychoprophylaxis in Obstetrics (ASOP), **1**:201
Amish practices: baptism, **2**:278; bed-courtship, **2**:23–26; *Rumspringa*, **2**:24, 277–280
Ampe, **1**:149–150
Amphidromia (Running Round) ritual, **1**:23
Amphiphontes, **1**:37
Amrit shanchar, **2**:70
Amulets, protective, **1**:195, 218, 344, 345, **2**:308, **3**:96
Anabaptists, **2**:25
Anal sex, **2**:149
Anatolia, **2**:323–325
Ancestor worship, **3**:20, 77, 91, 126, 181–182, 244
Ancient Babylonia, **3**:7
Ancient Egypt, **1**:22–23, 39, **2**:112, **3**:74; mummification, **3**:185–187
Ancient Greece, **1**:22, 34–35, 37, **2**:285, 375, **3**:7, 96
Ancient Rome, **1**:44, 230, **2**:285, 375, **3**:7, 96, 302
Andrzejki (St. Andrew's Eve), **2**:3–5
Ang pleen **1**:229
Anga people, **3**:187
Anglican Church, **1**:27, 95, 98–99, 142, 231, **2**:185, **3**:275; hymns, **3**:1–3. *See also* Church of England
Animism, **2**:90
Ankou, **3**:10–11
Antambahoaka people, **1**:133, 298–300
Antenatal care. *See* Prenatal care

Antenatal classes, **1**:74
Anthony of Padua (saint), **1**:99
Anti-Social Behaviour, Crime and Policing Act, **2**:8
Anti-Valentine's Day, **2**:315
Anzac Day, **3**:152, 236–237, 317
Aokigahara Forest (Japan), **3**:278–279
Apache ceremonies: baby ceremonies, **1**:7–9; Sunrise Ceremony, **2**:326–331
Apollo (Greek god), **2**:21
Apostle spoons, **1**:313–314
Appalachian traditions: birthday customs, **1**:41; shivaree/chivaree, **2**:257
Apple howling, **2**:44
Aqeeqah (*Aqiqa*) ritual, **1**:235
Aquamation, **3**:5–6
Argentinian celebrations and practices, **3**:247; government-approved baby names, **1**:153; same-sex marriage, **2**:285; *San La Muerte*, **3**:246–249. *See also* South American celebrations and practices
Argile, **1**:71
Arlington National Cemetery, **3**:24–26, 55–56, 178, 237, 273, 294
Armenia: Assyrian populations in, **2**:10; mourning color, **3**:304
Armistice Day, **3**:223
Arranged marriage, **2**:5–7, 10, 37–38, 136, 159, 237, 241, 251–252, 295, 312
Artemis (Greek goddess) **1**:34, 37, 217
Arvel (arvil) cake, **3**:92
Asamoutalik, **1**:79
Asante tribe, **1**:151
Ascension Day, **1**:140
Ashanti people, **3**:90
Ashes fireworks, **3**:268
Asian celebrations and practices: Buddhism, **3**:18; cairns, **3**:23; cremation, **3**:42; eating human placenta, **1**:123; female genital cutting, **2**:89; food taboos during pregnancy, **1**:146; grave rental, **3**:102; kangaroo care, **1**:183; ritual tattooing, **2**:272; teething remedies, **1**:329; Tomb of the Unknown Soldier, **3**:295; virginity testing,

2:355–358. *See also* Central Asian practices; Chinese celebrations and practices; Japanese celebrations and practices; Korean celebrations and practices; South Asian celebrations and practices; South Korean celebrations and practices; Southeast Asian celebrations and practices

Assisted suicide, **3**:11–15

Association for Civil Confirmation, **2**:300

Association for International Co-operation (*Gesellschaft fur Technische Zusammenarbeit*, GTZ), **2**:30

Assyrian betrothal and weddings, **2**:9–14

Astrological signs, **1**:42, 44–45, 233, 354

Astronomy, Babylonian, **1**:45

Atayal people, **2**:276

Atiq ceremony, **1**:9–11

Attachment parenting, **1**:250

Australasian celebrations and practices: birthday bumps, **1**:40; christening gowns, **1**:94; hair removal, **2**:112; mourning color, **3**:302; nursery rhymes, **1**:250; Tomb of the Unknown Soldier, **3**:295; training bras, **2**:338–341. *See also* Asian celebrations and practices; Australian celebrations and practices; New Zealand celebrations and practices

Australia, Hmong immigrants in, **2**:137

Australian celebrations and practices: "Abide With Me," **3**:1–3; alkaline hydrolysis, **3**:5–6; Anzac Day, **3**:152, 236–237, 317; Australian War Memorial, **3**:295–296; bachelor and spinster balls (B and S balls/B&S's), **2**:16–19; birthday cakes, **1**:35; birthday celebrations, **1**:35; breastfeeding, **1**:56; Buddhist death practices, **3**:21; cardboard box bed scheme, **1**:74; childhood vaccinations, **1**:85; cremation, **3**:42; embalming, **3**:73; Gap year, **2**:103; Girl Guides, **1**:152; Goth subculture, **3**:101–102; high-platform exposure of the corpse, **3**:115–118; jury duty, **2**:168; *koliva*, **3**:135; Leaver's Week, **2**:283; lotus birthing, **1**:201; missing man formation, **3**:179; mistletoe, **1**:219; mummification, **3**:185; parental leave, **1**:266, 269–270; Parental Leave Guide, **1**:269–270; Passion plays, **3**:208; pensions, **3**:228, 230; Pregnancy and Infant Loss Remembrance Day, **3**:216–218; Remembrance Day, **3**:223–224; riderless horse, **3**:236–237; Schoolies Week, **2**:283–284; space burial, **3**:267; spontaneous shrines, **3**:269; Steiner schools, **1**:318, 320; twenty-first birthday, **2**:344; urethral subincision, **2**:347–349; wake, **3**:313; walkabout, **2**:365–367; wedding dresses, **2**:374; Zoroastrianism, **3**:338. *See also* Australasian celebrations and practices; Australians, Aboriginal

Australian War Memorial, **3**:295–296

Australians, Aboriginal, **1**:42, 355–356, **2**:293, 347–351, 365–367, **3**:115–118, 230

Austrian celebrations and practices: All Souls' Day, **3**:8; anti-Santa Claus movement **1**:297–298; Klawbauf, **1**:222–223; *Kürbisfest*, **3**:111–112; *Martinstag*, **3**:111; ossuaries, **3**:201; parental leave, **1**:266; Passion plays, **3**:208; pensions, **3**:230; *Polterabend*, **2**:254; *Reifeprüfung*, **2**:15; *Schuhplattler* and *Ländler*, **2**:297–299; soul cakes, **3**:263–265; spontaneous shrines, **3**:269; University of the Third Age, **3**:307; *Vatertag*, **1**:140

Autumn Festival (Diwali), **2**:73–75

Aztec practices, **1**:283, **2**:112, 177, **3**:58, 250, 256

Baba Dochia, **1**:16

Baba Marta (Grandmother March), **1**:13–17

Baba Umer Durga shrine, **1**:127

Baba Yaga, **1**:223

Babies: *achambi* ceremony for, **1**:131; and the Blidworth Cradle Rocking Ceremony, **1**:51–52; as mini-gods,

1:253; beds for, **1**:72–75; birth year of (Chinese Zodiac), **1**:310–311; on cradleboards, **1**:109–111; ear-piercing, **1**:177, 307; feeding rituals, **1**:178–179; first and ritual baths, **1**:3, 42, 92, 178; first food, **1**:176, 259–260, 275–276; first haircut, **1**:177, 227, 232–233; Hindu rituals for, **1**:175–177; 100th day celebration, **1**:92; keeping from contact with the ground, **1**:253–254; learning to walk, **1**:93; leaving home for the first time, **1**:324; predicting gender of, **1**:5–6, 20–21, 187, 348–349; premature, **1**:183–184, 194; protection against evil spirits, **1**:78–79, 91–92, 114; quilts given to, **1**:178; salting, **1**:64–65; seventh day celebration, **1**:305–307; sleeping with parents, **1**:74–75; spitting on, **1**:316–317; sprinkling cake on, **1**:317; stolen by fairies, **1**:77–80; supernatural harm to **1**:79; swaddling, **1**:195, 320–322; unbaptized, **1**:77, 78, **3**:313; unregistered, **1**:256; vaccinations for, **1**:85–87, 320. *See also* Abortion; Baby ceremonies; Baby naming practices; Children; Cutting the umbilical cord; Stillbirth
Babinden, **1**:105
Baby ceremonies: Apache, **1**:7–9; Atiq, **1**:9–11; Hindu, **1**:175–177; pagan, **1**:24–25; Sikh, **1**:311–313
Baby hammocks, **1**:300–301
Baby Jumping Festival (*El Salto del Colacho*), **1**:126–128
Baby naming practices: Abadinto, **1**:1; Akan, **1**:1–4; Atiq, **1**:9–11; *brit milah*, **1**:60–61; Chinese, **1**:90; Ghanaian, **1**:150; government-approved names, **1**:153–157; Hopi, **1**:177–180; Korean, **1**:188; Latvian, **1**:204; Muslim, **1**:234–235; Sikh, **1**:311–313; Thai, **1**:141–142; Wiccan name chant, **1**:354; Wik-Mungkan (Wik-Mungknh), **1**:355–356. *See also* Naming rituals
Baby racing, **1**:21–22
Baby showers, **1**:22–24, 175, 90
Baby throwing, in India, **1**:127
Babylonian astronomy, **1**:45
Baccalauréat (le bac), **2**:15–16
Bachelor and spinster balls (B and S balls/B&S's), **2**:16–19
Bachelor parties, **2**:38, 257
Bachelorette parties, **2**:38, 257
Bafia tribe, **2**:294
Bahaya people, **1**:113
Bajang, **1**:79
Bal de noce (wedding dance), **2**:47–48
Balangandā (amulet), **1**:345
Bali: Barong dance, **1**:206; lotus birthing, **1**:210; *ngaben (pelebon)*, **3**:193–196; *Nyabutan* ceremony, **1**:253; Schoolies Week, **2**:284; tooth-filing ceremony, **2**:335–337
Bangladesh: cutting the umbilical cord, **1**:113; forced marriage, **2**:8; *halva*, **3**:114. *See also* South Asian celebrations and practices
Bantu people, **2**:245
Baoji, **2**:50
Baptism and Christening: of adults, **1**:28; Amish, **2**:278; in Baptist churches, **1**:27–29; in the Bulgarian Orthodox Church, **1**:65–66; Christian, **1**:25–29; *el bolo*, **1**:125–126; in Ghana, **1**:1–4; gifts for, **1**:313–314; by immersion, **1**:26–29; of infants, **1**:25–26, 28; by pouring, **1**:26, 27; Roman Catholic, **1**:27; special biscuits for, **1**:31–32; by sprinkling, **1**:26–27; symbolic, **2**:79–80. *See also* Christening gowns
Baptist churches, **1**:26, 27–29, **2**:60, 185
Bar mitzvah, **1**:42, 281–282, **2**:19–21
Bara people, **3**:51
Barabaig people, **2**:295
Barakat Bundle scheme, **1**:74
Barbados, **3**:231
Bari people, **2**:258, 259
Barong dance, **1**:206
Baskania, **1**:345
Bat mitzvah, **2**:19–21

Bathing: of brides, **2**:160, 237, 313; of the groom, **2**:313; for purification, **1**:246–247; in the River Ganges, **1**:233, **2**:173–175; ritual, **1**:49, **2**:134, 160, 226, 227. *See also* Washing
Baule tribe, **2**:294
Bauls (Bengali, India), **2**:225–226
Bavaria, soul cakes, **3**:265
Baznayeh Assyrians, **2**:12
Beachy Head (England), **3**:278
Bealltainn (Beltane), **1**:293, **2**:219
Bean throwing, **1**:308–309
Beards, **2**:21–23
Beauty pageants for children, **1**:80–83
Bed dances, **2**:53–54
Bed-courtship, **2**:23–26
Bedwetting remedies, **1**:29–31
Beer Dance, **2**:54
Bees and death, **3**:12–13
Beinhaus (Bone House), **3**:201
Belarus, parental leave, **1**:266. *See also* Eastern European celebrations and practices
Belgian celebrations and practices: Armistice Day, **3**:225; assisted suicide, **3**:12; *Martinstag*, **3**:111; mourning color, **3**:304; parental leave, **1**:266; pensions, **3**:230; same-sex marriage, **2**:285; spontaneous shrines, **3**:269; *suikerboon*, **1**:32; wedding cakes, **2**:369
Beltane, **1**:293, **2**:219
Bemba people, **2**:52–55
Benedict XV (pope), **3**:8
Benevolent societies, **3**:128
Benin: breast ironing, **2**:30; burial customs, **3**:128; cutting the umbilical cord, **1**:113; female ritual servitude (*trokosi*), **1**:330–333; scarification, **2**:293–294; *Sharo*, **2**:307, 309. *See also* West Africa
Bera út, **1**:214
Berber people, **2**:238
Berlin ironwork jewelry, **3**:287
Bermuda, **2**:371, **3**:231
Beschuit met Muisjes, **1**:31–32
Beshik Toi, in Kyrgyzstan, **1**:194–195
Bétamarribé people, **2**:293–294

Betrothal: Afghani, **2**:1–3; Assyrian, **2**:9–14; in Ethopia, **2**:67; lengthy engagements, **2**:94–95
Betsileo people, **3**:85
Bible, **1**:26, 28, 45–46, 52, 83, 96, 98, 115, 144, 244–245, 281, **2**:22, 91, 93–294, **3**:7
Biddies, **1**:16
Bildungsroman, **1**:135–136
Birth control, **1**:256–258
Birth customs: in the *bashali*, **1**:129–30; in Bulgaria, **1**:63–67; in China, **1**:89–93; confinement after, **1**:226; drink for women after, **1**:208–209; epidural injections, **1**:202; Korean, **1**:186–189; in Kyrgyzstan, **1**:193–194; Lamaze technique, **1**:201–202; in Latvia, **1**:203–204; lotus birthing, **1**:210–213; male re-enactment of birth, **1**:105; mock birthing, **1**:19; Muslim, **1**:234–235; preparation for childbirth, **1**:201–203, **1**:289–290; recovery after childbirth, **1**:290; in Tibet, **1**:323–324; water birth, **1**:346–348. *See also* Churching of Women
Birth trees, **1**:33–34
Birthday candles, **1**:37–38
Birthday celebrations, **1**:42–44; birthday beats, **1**:40; birthday cakes, **1**:34–36, **2**:85; cards, **1**:38–40; first birthday, **1**:92–93, 291; foods for, **1**:34–36; games, **1**:273–274; in Ghana, **1**:149–151; "Happy Birthday" song, **1**:171–173, **1**:263; humiliations for singletons, **2**:26–28; message from the Queen, **3**:171–173; milestones associated with, **1**:43; of notable figures, **1**:43; piñata, **1**:283, 284; *Sockenkrantz*, **2**:318–319; torments, **1**:40–41; twenty-first birthday, **2**:344–345; Vietnam, **3**:288–289
Birthday Parade, **1**:43
Birthday torments, for unmarried persons, **2**:26–28
Birthing blood, **1**:25
Birthing fluids, **1**:69
Birthing pools, **1**:347. *See also* Water births

Birthstones, **1**:44–46
Biscuits, for babies and/or baptism, **1**:31–32
Bismallah ceremony, **1**:47–48
Bizane ts'al (cradleboard ceremony), **1**:7–8
Black Caribs, **1**:106
Black Day, **2**:315–316
Blackening the Bride, **2**:28–30
Blang (Bulang) people, **2**:50
The Blessing (Unification Church weddings), **2**:235
Blessings: for bride and groom, **2**:12, 13, 40; of a child in the womb, **1**:99; given by *devadasis*, **1**:116; of Dinka and Nuer boys, **2**:99; of gifts, **2**:40; in a handfasting ceremony, **2**:121–124; of a marriage, **2**:59–60, **2**:242; pagan baby welcomings, **1**:24–25; with sacred cattail pollen, **2**:157; at Sikh wedding, **2**:313–314; Wiccan, **1**:354; of women after childbirth, **1**:98–100
Blessingway ceremony, **1**:48–51
Blidworth Cradle Rocking Ceremony (England), **1**:51–52
Blind man's buff/bluff, **1**:273
Blood drinking, **2**:205
Blooding, **1**:53–54
Bloodletting ritual, **2**:149
Blue Peter (television program), **1**:54
Blue Peter Badge, **1**:54–55
Body hair removal, **2**:110, 111–113
Body mutilation, **2**:30, **3**:90–91
Bolivian practices, **3**:247; burial of dissected llama fetuses in house foundations, **1**:69; menstrual taboos, **2**:230; pensions, **3**:231. *See also* South American celebrations and practices
Bon Festival, **3**:7
Bonbonniere, **1**:32
Bone houses (ossuaries), **3**:200–203
Bonnet Rippers (Amish Romance Novels), **2**:24
Books, for children, **1**:73, **1**:87–89, **1**:198–201
Borneo: couvade, **1**:104; mother roasting, **1**:228

Bosnia and Herzegovina: *Matura*, **2**:15; parental leave, **1**:266. *See also* Eastern European celebrations and practices; Yugoslav countries
Box, as funeral plant, **3**:95
Boy Scouts Association of the United Kingdom, **1**:302. *See also* Scouts and Scouting
Boy Scouts of America, **1**:303–304. *See also* Scouts and Scouting
Boys: clothing for first communion, **1**:143; feminization of, **2**:149–150; firstborn, **1**:280–283; *pidyon haben* ceremony, **1**:280–283. *See also* Babies; Boys' coming-of-age ceremonies; Children; Circumcision
Boys' coming-of-age ceremonies: Brazil, **2**:41–43; bullet ant initiation, **2**:41–43; China, **2**:51; forehead-cutting initiation rite, **2**:98–101; *Gempuku*, **2**:61; *Gwallye*, **2**:105–106; land diving, **2**:184; Maasai traditions, **2**:205–208; Nkumbi, **2**:245–247; scarification ritual, **2**:294, 295; *Sharo*, **2**:307–309; *shinbyu*, **2**:83, 310–312; *Sünnet*, **2**:323–325; *upanayana*, **1**:337; urethral subincision, **2**:347–351; vision quest, **2**:358–361; *wysoccan* rite of manhood, **2**:359
Bradley method, **1**:202–203
Brazilian practices, **3**:247; All Souls' Day, **3**:9; bullet ant initiation, **2**:41–43; charms against the evil eye, **1**:345; couvade, **1**:104; eating the ashes of the dead, **3**:67–70; endocannibalism, **3**:76–77; fertility symbol, **1**:346; *Festa de debutantes*, **2**:185; jury duty, **2**:165; lip plugs, **2**:192; Matis hunting trials, **2**:215–219; menstrual taboos, **2**:230; mourning color, **3**:302; national mourning, **3**:192; Passion plays, **3**:208; pulling of earlobes on birthdays, **1**:41; same-sex marriage, **2**:285; wedding dresses, **2**:374. *See also* South American celebrations and practices
Brazilian wax, **2**:112–113

Breast ironing, **2**:32–32
Breastfeeding, **1**:55–59, 105, 130, 181, 202, 209, 267, 321; benefits of, **1**:55–56; encouragement of, **1**:73, 75, 306–307; human-animal, **1**:57–58; laws allowing public, **1**:56; long-term, **1**:56–57; and shared nursing, **1**:57; supernatural creatures interfering with, **1**:79; women advised against eating calabash chalk, **1**:71
Breton mythology, **3**:10–11
Bride-price, **2**:1, 11, 100, 117, 195–197, 248, 385
Brides: adorning with henna, **2**:2–3; blackening, **1**:78, **2**:28–20; blessed by *devadasis*, **1**:116; carrying over the threshold, **2**:36; gifts given to, **2**:2, 11, 37–39; gifts of jewelry for, **2**:37, 134, 302–305; giving away, **2**:34; jewelry worn by, **2**:312–313; kidnapping of, **2**:51; removal of body hair, **2**:112; ritual bathing of, **2**:160, 237, 313; throwing the bridal bouquet, **2**:34–35; washing and dressing, **2**:11; wedding superstitions, **2**:33–34
Bris shalom, **1**:62
Brit banot ceremony, **1**:62
Brit milah (*bris milah.bris*), **1**:59–63
Brit shalom, **1**:62
British celebrations and practices: horseshoes, **2**:142; jury duty, **2**:165, 167, 168, 170–171; missing man formation, **3**:177–178; national mourning, **3**:191; official birthday celebrations, **1**:43; Passion plays, **3**:206; Punkie Night, **3**:112; Remembrance Sunday, **3**:152; sin eating, **3**:92. *See also* British wedding traditions; English celebrations and practices; United Kingdom celebrations and practices
British wedding traditions, **2**:32–37; carrying the bride over the threshold, **2**:36; giving away the bride, **2**:34; honeymoon, **2**:36; superstitions, **2**:32–33; throwing rice, **2**:34; throwing the bridal bouquet, **2**:34–35; wedding locations, **2**:32
Brunei, **1**:181
Brunsviger, **1**:35
Bubonic plague, **1**:252, **3**:42, 83–84, 207, 248
Buddhist celebrations and practices **1**:43; attitudes toward death, **3**:18–21; cremation, **3**:42; funeral rites, **3**:123; *Mizuko kuyo*, **3**:180–183; *shinbyu*, **2**:83, 310–312; sky burial, **3**:260; *Ullambana*, **3**:330; *Yulanpen* Festival, **3**:329
Bulgarian celebrations and practices, **1**:63–67; Baba Marta, **1**:13–17; *Babinden*, **1**:17–19, 105; cremation, **3**:103; Enyovden, **2**:177; horo dance, **2**:140; *koliva*, **3**:135; *Ladouvane*, **2**:182–183; *Lazarovden*, **2**:186–188; *Matura*, **2**:15; mock weddings, **1**:19; Monument to the Unknown Soldier, **3**:294; national mourning, **3**:192; pregnancy superstitions, **1**:63; Saturday of Souls, **3**:251–253; spitting on babies, **1**:316; St. Sylvester's Day, **2**:183. *See also* Bulgarian Orthodox Church; Bulgarian weddings; Eastern European celebrations and practices
Bulgarian Orthodox Church, **1**:65–66
Bulgarian weddings, **2**:37–41; arranged marriages, **2**:37–38; engagement, **2**:37–38; *Galena*, **2**:40; parties before, **2**:38; reception, **2**:39
Bullet ant initiation, **2**:41–43
Bull-jumping ceremony, **2**:66
Bullying, **1**:41
Bundling, **2**:24–25
Burakha (marriage service), **2**:12
Burial rituals. *See* Funeral practices
Burial societies, **3**:70
Burkina Faso, **2**:92. *See also* West African celebrations and practices
Burma. *See* Myanmar
Burning the Ashen Faggot, **2**:43–44
Burning the Clavie, **2**:44–45
Burumu (body painting), **2**:154
Burying biscuits, **3**:93
Burying the Box, **3**:95

Cairns, **3**:23–24, 262
Cajun weddings, **2**:47–49; *bal de noce* (wedding dance), **2**:47–48; *charivari*, **2**:48; dancing with broom or mop, **2**:47; food, **2**:48; reception, **2**:48
Caking Night, **3**:264
Calabar stone, **1**:71
Calabash chalk, **1**:71–72
Caldecott Medal, **1**:88
Callatiae tribe, **3**:77
Cambodian practices: Hmong names, **2**:136; mother roasting, **1**:229; treatment of the placenta, **1**:69. *See also* Southeast Asian celebrations and practices
CAME Women and Girl's Development Organisation (Cawogido), **2**:30
Cameos, **3**:287
Cameroon, **2**:30–31, 294
Canada, Assyrian populations in, **2**:10
Canadian celebrations and practices, **1**:9, 10; baby racing, **1**:21; *Baccalauréat* (*le bac*), **2**:15–16; bedwetting cures, **1**:30; birthday beats and digs in, **1**:40; birthday bumps, **1**:40; boxes for babies **1**:74; breastfeeding, **1**:56; changeling beliefs, **1**:79; childhood vaccinations, **1**:85; eating calabash chalk, **1**:71; embalming, **3**:73; Gap year, **2**:103; Girl Guides, **1**:152; jury duty, **2**:168; *Mehndi*, **2**:222; mortuary totem poles, **3**:183–185; National War Memorial, **3**:296; noses greased with butter for birthdays, **1**:41; pantomime, **1**:261; parental leave, **1**:266, 267; Passion plays, **3**:208; Pregnancy and Infant Loss Remembrance Day, **3**:216–218; *Pysanka*, **3**:66; Remembrance Day, **3**:223; *Rumspringa*, **2**:277–280; same-sex marriage, **2**:285; Shinerama, **2**:268; sock dances, **2**:319–320; space burial, **3**:267; *Waldkindergärten*, **1**:341; water births, **1**:347; Zoroastrianism, **3**:338. *See also* North American celebrations and practices
Canary Islands, **3**:185, 186
Candlemas, **1**:51, 98, **3**:9

Candles: Advent, **1**:349–350; as baptism gift, **1**:29; birthday, **1**:37–38; on birthday cakes, **1**:34, 37, 38, 42, 171; blessing of, **1**:51, **3**:9; in the Blessingway ceremony, **1**:50, 51; in the Blidworth cradle rocking ceremony, **1**:51; in the *brit banot* ceremony, **1**:62; in the *brit milah* ceremony, **1**:60; candle-leaping, **1**:252; in the Christingle service, **1**:95–97; on Christmas trees, **1**:38; in the Churching of Women service, **1**:99; around a corpse, **1**:37; in the *Klausjagen* procession, **1**:296; in midwife folklore, **1**:64; penis-shaped, **1**:278–279; for Pregnancy and Infant Loss Remembrance Day, **3**:217; for *Quccija*, **1**:291; used for sacred severance, **1**:113; for the saining rite, **1**:294; in the *Sebou* ceremony, **1**:306–307; for Slava, **1**:242, 243; soul candle, **3**:105; in the Wiccaning ceremony, **1**:354; for *Zaduszki* (*dzień zaduszny*), **3**:333. *See also* Candlemas
Canopic jars, **3**:186
Caparisoned horse (Cap horse), **3**:236
Cardboard box beds, **1**:72–75
Caribbean: *La Quinceañera*, **2**:177–180; Nine-Nights, **3**:196–198
Carnet de Santé Maternité, **1**:238
Carrera Día del Padre, **1**:139
Castration ceremony, **2**:132
Catholic Church: on assisted suicide, **3**:14; on cremation, **3**:42; Greek, **3**:251; missionaries in North America, **1**:283–284; objection to plastination, **3**:214–215; opinion of jazz funerals, **3**:128; opinion of mummification, **3**:185; opposition to alkaline hydrolysis, **3**:6; opposition to *Famadihana*, **3**:86. *See also* Folk Catholicism
Catholic Church celebrations and practices, **1**:37, 45, 98–99; All Souls' Day, **3**:6–10; color symbolism, **3**:305; combining with indigenous beliefs, **3**:246–247; crucifixion rituals, **3**:47–50; *Dia de los Muertos*, **3**:60; first communion, **1**:142–144;

funerals, **3**:36–37; *La Quinceañera*, **2**:177–180, 187; Martinstag, **3**:111; May crowning ritual, **1**:217–218; Name days, **1**:241; Passion plays, **3**:206–209; prayers at Filipino debut, **2**:96; Saint Nicholas, **1**:294–298; wedding anniversaries, **2**:368; wedding ceremony, **2**:58–59. *See also* Christian Church celebrations and practices; Eastern Orthodox Church celebrations and practices; Greek Orthodox Church celebrations and practices
Celestis Inc., **3**:267
Celtic Reconstructionist Paganism, **1**:293
Celtic traditions, **3**:109–110; handfasting, **2**:32; New Year, **3**:112; Passion plays, **3**:206
Cemeteries: Arlington National, **3**:24–26, 55–56, 178, 237, 273, 294; blessing of, **3**:8; bonfires in, **3**:333; burial ceremonies in, **3**:20, 337; Caterpillar Valley, **3**:296; Chinese, **3**:33–34; Cimetière du Père Lachaise, **3**:298; in France, **3**:296; in Greece, **3**:103; taking Easter eggs to, **3**:66; in England, **3**:102; Highgate Cemetery, **3**:298–299; Isola di San Michele (San Michele Island), **3**:121–122; in Japan, **3**:104, 181; Merry Cemetery, **3**:299; in Poland, **3**:333–334; procession to, **3**:3, 54, 127–128; vertical, **3**:104; visits on All Souls' Day, **3**:9; Yew trees in, **3**:327–328. *See also* Ossuaries; Remembrance Sunday; Tombstone Tourism
Central Africa. *See* Cameroon; Central African Republic; Chad; Democratic Republic of Congo
Central African Republic, **2**:192. *See also* African celebrations and practices; Sub-Saharan African celebrations and practices
Central American practices: belief in the evil eye, **1**:343; the umbilical cord, **1**:113; kangaroo care, **1**:183; water births, **1**:346. *See also* Guatemalan practices; Mexican celebrations and practices

Central Asian practices: arranged marriage, **2**:5; forced marriage, **2**:8; *halva*, **3**:113. *See also* Afghani celebrations and practices; Asian celebrations and practices; Kyrgyzstan; Mongolia; Uzbekistan
Central Europe, *Pysanka*, **3**:66
Ceremony of the Christmas Cheese, **3**:28–29
Cerne Abbas Giant, **1**:75–77
Chachapoya people, **3**:186
Chad, **2**:30, 192–193. *See also* African celebrations and practices; Sub-Saharan African celebrations and practices
Chambri tribe, **2**:295–296
Changeling beliefs, **1**:77–80
Changing of the Guard Ceremony, **3**:24–26
Charades, **1**:274
Charing Cross, **3**:72–73
Charitable giving, **2**:267–268
Charivari, **2**:48
Chelsea pensioners, **3**:26–29
Cheppewa tribe, **1**:119
Chesapeake Bay Bridge (Maryland), **3**:278
Chevra Kadisha, (Holy Society), **3**:130
Child beauty pageants, **1**:80–83
Child, Early and Forced Marriage (CEFM), **2**:9, 136. *See also* Forced marriage
Childermas (Feast of the Holy Innocents), **1**:83–84, 245
Childhood vaccinations, **1**:85–87
Child-rearing, slow parenting, **1**:314–315
Children: All Souls' Day traditions involving, **3**:8; and the blooding ritual, **1**:53; books for, **1**:73, 87–89, 198–201; and breastfeeding, **1**:55–59; celebration of one-year milestone, **1**:141; development of, **1**:106; exploitation of, **1**:80, 82; exposure to heavy metals, **1**:71; in Finland, **1**:72; First Steps celebration, **1**:66–67; goddess protector of, **1**:5; Jesus's regard for, **1**:28; Muslim, **1**:47; names of, **1**:42; napping in cold temperatures, **1**:249–250; sexualization of, **1**:82–83; washing of, **1**:18. *See also* Babies; Boys; Girls

Children's Act (Nepal), **1**:192
Children's Day (Japan), **1**:184–186
Children's Day Olympics, **1**:184
Children's Laureate, **1**:87–89
Children's Peace Monument, **1**:185
Chile, **3**:185. *See also* South American celebrations and practices
Chinchorro mummies, **3**:185–186
Chinese celebrations and practices: baby racing, **1**:21, 22; birthday celebrations, **1**:36; Buddhist practices, **3**:18, 20; government-approved baby names, **1**:153, 155; hair removal, **2**:112; Hungry Ghost Festival, **3**:7; Long-Horn Miao minority group, **2**:138; *Moon-Yuet*, **1**:226–228; New Year messages, **1**:39; one-child policy, **1**:256–258; origin of the piñata, **1**:283; potty training, **1**:286, 287; *Qingming* Festival, **3**:219–222; same-sex marriage, **2**:285; Shanghai Marriage Market, **2**:305–307; *Shengziao*, **1**:310–311; Singles' Day, **2**:315–316; Sisters' Meal Festival, **2**:317–218; treatment of the placenta, **1**:68; Universities for the Ages, **3**:307–308; *Yu Lan Jie*, **3**:329–332; *Zui yuezi*, **1**:361–362. *See also* Asian celebrations and practices; Chinese coming-of-age ceremonies; Chinese pregnancy and birth rituals
Chinese coming-of-age ceremonies, **2**:49–52; *baoji*, **2**:50; Dong ceremony, **2**:51; Guan Li, **2**:49–50; Ji Li, **2**:49–50; Puni ceremony, **2**:50–51; Yi ceremony, **2**:51
Chinese funeral customs, **3**:29–34, 305; cemeteries, **3**:33–34; funeral strippers, **3**:30; grave rental, **3**:103–104; mourning color, **3**:304, 305; mummification, **3**:185, 186; sky burials, **3**:259–263; space burial, **3**:267; wakes, **3**:32–33, 313
Chinese lunar calendar, **1**:20
Chinese philosophy, **1**:310–311
Chinese pregnancy and birth rituals, **1**:20–21, **1**:89–93; 100th day celebration, **1**:92; baby hammocks (*yao lan*), **1**:300; baby naming, **1**:91; birth announcements, **1**:91; childbirth conventions, **1**:90–91; eating human placenta, **1**:123; bath, **1**:92; first birthday, **1**:92–93; learning to walk, **1**:93; pregnancy taboos, **1**:89–90, 145–146; *Zuo yuezi*, **1**:92. *See also* Chinese celebrations and practices
Chinese wedding customs: arranged marriage, **2**:5, 7; kidnapping of the bride, **2**:51; Visiting-girls courtship tradition, **2**:360–364; walking marriages, **2**:391–393; wedding cakes, **2**:371–372; wedding dresses, **2**:374
Chinese Zodiac signs, **1**:310–311, **2**:30
Chiribaya people, **3**:186
Chisungu, **2**:52–55
Chivaree/Chivari, **2**:257
Chokha thavani viddhi (purification ritual), **2**:55–56
Chola temples, **1**:117
Chopi people, **2**:254
Christening. *See* Baptism and Christening
Christening gowns, **1**:26, 93–95
Christian celebrations and practices, **1**:83–84; baptism and christening, **1**:25–29; birthstones, **1**:44; christening gown, **1**:93–95; color symbolism, **3**:305; Churching of Women, **1**:98–100; confirmation, **1**:42; Easter eggs, **3**:65–67; female genital cutting, **2**:90; first communion, **1**:142–144; hymns, **3**:1–3; menstruation as unclean, **2**:228; Mothering Sunday, **1**:230–232; Passion plays, **3**:206–209; Protestant, **1**:27; purity ball, **2**:264–268; saining, **1**:294; Saint Nicholas, **1**:294–298; Stations of the Cross, **3**:275–277. *See also* Catholic Church celebrations and practices; Christian churches; Christian funeral practices; Christian weddings; Eastern Orthodox Church celebrations and practices; Greek Orthodox Church celebrations and practices; Lutheran Church; Orthodox Church celebrations and practices; Pentecostal Church;

Protestant Church celebrations and practices; Russian Orthodox Church celebrations and practices
Christian churches: Coptic, **2**:302; Episcopal, **2**:60; evangelical, **2**:265; Free Wesleyan, **3**:300–301; in Ghana, **3**:87–88; Methodist, **1**:27, **2**:60, **3**:275, 300; Moravian, **1**:95; Mormon, **1**:303, **2**:161–162; objection to Dipo rite by, **2**:73; opposition to *Famadihana*, **3**:86; Pentecostal, **1**:26–27; Presbyterian, **1**:27, **2**:60; saints associated with death, **3**:247; view of beards by, **2**:22. *See also* Anglican Church; Church of England
Christian funeral practices, **3**:35–37; for Wiccans, **3**:319
Christian missionaries, **2**:343
Christian weddings, **2**:58–61; Catholic ceremony, **2**:59–60; marriage banns, **2**:210–215; Protestant ceremony, **2**:60–61; wedding music, **2**:379–381; wedding rings, **2**:375–376
Christingle, **1**:95–98
Christmas Cheese, Ceremony of, **3**:28–29
Christmas celebrations: Americanization of, **1**:297; Christmas carols, **1**:245; Christmas Eve traditions, **2**:44; Christmas stockings, **1**:294; Christmas trees, **1**:38; commercialization of, **1**:297; and the Nativity play, **1**:244–246; piñatas, **1**:284
Chrysanthemums, as funeral plants, **3**:95
Chudakarm/Chudakarna, **1**:232
Chupa (*huppah*), **2**:160–161
Church of Body Modification, **2**:272
Church of England, **1**:26–27, 76, 231, **2**:60, **3**:164, 293; on assisted suicide, **3**:13; marriage banns, **2**:210–211. *See also* Anglican Church
Church of Jesus Christ of Latter-day Saints (Mormons), **1**:303, **2**:261–262
Churching of Women, **1**:98–103
Cimetière du Père Lachaise, **3**:298
Circumcision, **1**:59–63, 298–300, **2**:149, 245–247; criticism of, **1**:61–62; of girls, **2**:206; Maasai, **2**:206; Muslim, **1**:234, 235–237; *Sünnet*, **2**:323–325; Xhosa, **2**:387–389. *See also* Female genital cutting; Male genital cutting
City of Widows, **3**:309–311
Civic confirmation, **2**:300–302
Claddagh ring, **2**:376
Clava Cairns, **3**:23
Clean-birth kits, **1**:74
Clear Bright Festival, **3**:219
Cleveland Lyke-Wake Dirge, **3**:158
Clitoral excision, **2**:91. *See also* Female genital cutting
Clypping the Church, **1**:230
Cold Food Festival, **3**:219, 221
Columbaria, **3**:104
Comanche tribe, **3**:305
Coming-of-age ceremonies: Brazil, **2**:41–43; China, **2**:49–52; Coming of Age Day (*Seijin no Hi*), **2**:61–64; *Gwallye*, **2**:105–106; Mosuo ceremony, **2**:391; secular confirmation, **2**:300–302. *See also* Boys' coming-of-age ceremonies; Chinese coming-of-age ceremonies; Girls' coming-of-age ceremonies
Commedia dell'arte, **1**:261–262
Condemned prisoner's last meal, **3**:37–40
Condolences, **3**:40–41
Confirmation: Christian, **1**:42; secular, **2**:300–302
Convention on the Elimination of All Forms of Discrimination Against Women, **2**:8, 358
Convention on the Rights of the Child, **2**:8, 31
Coptic Christianity, **2**:302
Cornflowers, for remembrance, **3**:317
Corpus Christi Festival, **1**:126–127
Cot death, **1**:321
Côte d'Ivoire, **2**:30, 294. *See also* West African celebrations and practices
Courtship whistling, **2**:64–66
Couvade, **1**:104–107
Covering the belly button, **1**:108–109
Cow jumping, **2**:66–68
Cradleboard, **1**:109–111, 119
Cradleboard ceremony, **1**:7–8
Cradlesongs, **1**:213–215
Crants/Crantses, **3**:161

Cremation, 3:41–44, 68–69; in Asia, 3:104; in Greece, 3:103; Hindu, 3:118–119; in Indonesia, 3:193–195; in Japan, 3:124–125; liquid, 3:5–6; in Papua New Guinea, 3:162; in the Sikh tradition, 3:257–258; and space burial, 3:267–268; by Zoroastrians, 3:338

Creutzfeldt-Jakob disease (CJD), 3:77

Croatian celebrations and practices: danse macabre, 3:52; *Lindo*, 2:190–191; *Matura*, 2:15; *Mirila*, 3:175–177; parental leave, 1:266; *Sokacko Kolo*, 2:194; Summer Festival, 2:194. *See also* Eastern European celebrations and practices; Yugoslav countries

Croning ceremonies, 3:44–46

Cross-dressing, 1:19, 263

Crucifixion rituals, 3:47–50

Crying-baby sumo competition, 1:111–112

Cuba: *La Quinceañera*, 2:185–188; national mourning, 3:192

Cult of Dionysus, 1:279

Cult of the Dead, 3:105

Cumberland Sound Inuit, 1:10

Cutting the umbilical cord traditions, 1:112–114, 130, 210–213

Cyprus, 2:234, 3:230, 231

Cyriac's Mead, 1:77

Czech Republic: Andrzejki, 2:3; anti-Santa Claus movement 1:297–298; Cert, 1:222–223; *Majáles*, 2:208–209; *Matura*, 2:15; May Day, 2:220–221; mourning color, 3:302; *Oblévačka*, 2:79; ossuaries, 3:201–202; parental leave 1:266; soul cakes, 3:264; spontaneous shrines, 3:269; University of the Third Age, 3:307. *See also* Eastern European celebrations and practices

Dahomean tribe, 3:128

Dakota people, 3:305

Dala (Dalecarlian) horse, 1:115–116

Dalit caste, 1:118

Dallas Ethiopian Community Edir, 3:70

Dancing: *Abang*, 2:88; in the cow-jumping ceremony, 2:67; Death Dance, 3:51–52; Dinki-Mini, 3:197; *Ekombi* (wedding dance), 2:88; fertility dance, 1:255–256; at Filipino debut, 2:96; *hora* (horah), 1:19, 2:20, 40, 139–140; in Indonesia 1:204–207; *Kunima*, 3:197; at *La Quinceañera*, 2:179; in *Lazarovden*, 2:187; *Lindo*, 2:190–191; around the Maypole, 2:219–220; Morris dancers, 2:220; peccary dance, 2:217–218; puberty dance, 2:72; *Schuhplattler* and *Ländler*, 2:297–299; *Sokacko Kolo*, 2:194; at wedding celebrations, 2:13, 35, 47–48. *See also* Death Dance; Money Dance

Dandelions, and bedwetting, 1:31

Dani people, 3:90–91

Danish celebrations and practices: birthday customs, 1:35, 2:26–28; cutting the groom's socks, 2:320; danse macabre, 3:52; Girl Guides, 1:152; government-approved baby names, 1:153; *kagemand* and *kagekone*, 1:35; *kanelmø* (cinnamon maid), 2:26; *kanelsvend* (cinnamon man), 2:26; Nordic napping, 1:249; *pebermø* (pepper maid), 2:26; *pebersvend* (pepper man), 2:26; *Polterabend*, 2:254; same-sex marriage, 2:285; secular confirmation, 2:300; *slå kitten af tønden*, 1:285. *See also* Scandinavian celebrations and practices

Danse macabre, 3:52

Daruma Doll, 1:185

Dastaar Bandi (Dastar Bandi), 2:69

Daughters of Eve, 2:93

Dawn Songs, 2:154

Day of Delivery Assistance, 1:17

Day of Flowers, 2:184

Day of the Commemoration of All the Faithful Departed, 3:6–7. *See also* All Souls' Day

Days of the week, 1:220–221

Death: Buddhist attitudes toward, 3:18; Christian saints associated with, 3:247; personification of, 3:10–11; symbolic depictions of, 3:168–170. *See also* Death rituals; Funeral practices

Death Dance, **3**:51–52
Death divination, **3**:328
Death rituals: Albanian, **3**:3–4; Buddhist, **3**:18–21; Catholic, **3**:6–10; Chinese, **3**:29–34; Delaware Indian, **3**:53–56, 305; The Great Passing, **3**:105–107; Muslim, **3**:188–190. *See also* Death rituals; Funeral practices; Lakota death rituals
Death with Dignity Act (Oregon), **3**:13–14
Debut (Philippines), **2**:95–97, **2**:345
Debutante balls, **2**:96
Dekate (Tehtn Day), **1**:23
Delaware Indian death rituals, **3**:54–56, 305
Democratic Republic of Congo: funeral insurance schemes, **3**:71; *Nkumbi*, **2**:245–247; tooth sharpening, **2**:143. *See also* African celebrations and practices
Den to (baby-naming ceremony), **1**:1–4
Denmark. *See* Danish celebrations and practices
Denville Hall and Brinsworth House, **3**:56–57
Depilation, **2**:111–113
Descansos, **3**:269
Desert Flower (Dirie), **2**:93
Deuki, **1**:192–193
Devadasi system, **1**:116–119
Devi (Hindu goddess) **1**:189
Devipujak purification trial, **2**:55–56
Dewaqthad idha, **2**:10
Dezalik (fertility goddess) **1**:129–130
Dia de los Muertos, **3**:52, 58–61, 169
Diana, Princess of Wales, **1**:199, **3**:40–41, 174, 270
Dias de la Muerte, **3**:249
Dignitas, **3**:13
Diné. *See* Navajo ceremonies
Dinka tribe, **2**:98, 142–143, 294
Dipo Womanhood Ceremony, **2**:71–73
Dirie, Waris, **2**:93
Divination: with candle wax, **3**:334; folk, **1**:348–349. *See also* Death divination; Love divination
Divorce, **1**:48, 58, **2**:1, 160, 189, 221, 241, 262, 370, 392; handparting, **2**:127–128

Diwali, **2**:73–74; celebrated by Barack Obama, **2**:76–77
DIY funerals, **3**:210–211
Djibouti, **2**:89, 91, 93. *See also* Sub-Saharan African celebrations and practices
Dogon tribe, **2**:143
Doll Festival (*Hina Matsuri*), **1**:184, 185
Domestic violence, **2**:247–248
Dominican Republic, Nine-Nights, **3**:196–198
Dong people, **2**:51
Donkey party, **1**:274
Doom Metal, **3**:62–63
Doot coekjes, **3**:93
Dowry and dowries, **2**:1, 40, 117, 136, 159–160, 240–242, 303, 312, 373, 375
Dragées, **1**:32
Dream catchers, **1**:119–122
Dreamtime, **2**:347–348, 365, **3**:116–117
Druid practices, **1**:219, **2**:32, **3**:109, 328
Dumagat tribe, **2**:338
Dunmow Flitch Trials, **2**:78–79
Dunstan (saint), **2**:141
Dwynwen (saint), **2**:322
Dyngus Day, (*Śmigus-Dyngus*), **2**:79–81
Dzień zaduszny (*Zaduszki*), **3**:333–335
Dzinto (baby-naming ceremony), **1**:1

Ear piercing, **1**:177, 307, **2**:83–84
Earth's Prayer (Navajo), **1**:49
Easter egg trees, **3**:67
Easter eggs, **3**:65–67, 334
Easter Island, **2**:272
Easter Monday, **2**:79
Easter pageants, **3**:206
Easter traditions: Bulgarian, **2**:40; crucifixion reenactment, Philippines, **3**:47–50; Greek Orthodox, **1**:17
Eastern Catholic Church, **3**:135
Eastern European celebrations and practices: arranged marriage, **2**:5; looking for fern blossoms, **2**:199–201; *Povitica*, **2**:263–264; *Pysanka*, **3**:66–67, 334; *Śmigus-Dyngus* (Dyngus Day), **2**:79–81. *See also* Albanian celebrations and practices; Belarus; Bosnia and Herzegovina; Bulgarian celebrations and practices;

Croatian celebrations and practices; Czech Republic; Hungary; Kosovo; Latvian celebrations and practices; Lithuanian celebrations and practices; Macedonia; Moldova; Montenegro; Polish celebrations and practices; Romanian celebrations and practices; Russian celebrations and practices; Serbian celebrations and practices; Slovakian celebrations and practices; Slovenian celebrations and practices; Ukrainian celebrations and practices; Yugoslav countries

Eastern Orthodox Church celebrations and practices, **1**:26, 27, 65–66, **3**:7, 135–136, 192, 251, 252; Easter eggs, **3**:65–66; Saturday of Souls, **3**:251–252. *See also* Greek Orthodox Church celebrations and practices; Orthodox Church celebrations and practices; Russian Orthodox Church celebrations and practices

Eating Sisters' Rice Festival, **2**:317–318

Eating the ashes of the dead, **3**:67–70

Ecuadorean practices: cutting the umbilical cord, **1**:113; shrunken heads, **3**:255–257. *See also* South American celebrations and practices

Edir (eddir, iddir), **3**:70–72

Education: admission to university, **2**:57–58; in Amish communities, **2**:24, 277–278; *Baccalauréat* and *Matura*, **2**:15–16; choosing Options, **2**:56–58; Gap year, **2**:103–104; Hindu *upanayana* ceremony, **1**:337; *Majáles* festival, **2**:208–209; Steiner schools, **1**:318–320; University of the Third Age (U3A), **3**:307–308

Efe tribe, **2**:143, 245

Efik tribe (Nigeria), **2**:86

Eggs, **1**:144–145, 149. *See also* Easter eggs

Egyptian celebrations and practices: burying the placenta, **1**:235; female genital cutting, **2**:89–90, 93; mourning color, **3**:302, 304; *Sebou*, **1**:305–307; *shabka*, **2**:302–303; water births, **1**:346. *See also* Ancient Egypt; Middle Eastern celebrations and practices; North African celebrations and practices

Eid Al-Adha, **2**:115–116

Eileithyia (goddess of childbirth), **1**:23

Ein Risz in der Maurer (*A Break in the Wall*), **2**:25

El bolo, **1**:125–126

El Salto del Colacho (The Devil's Jump), **1**:126–128

Elderling ceremonies, **3**:44–46

Eleanor Crosses, **3**:72–73

Elimination communication, **1**:286

Elizabeth II (queen of England), **3**:171–172, 295

Embalming, **3**:73–76

Empire State Building (New York City), **3**:278

Endocannibalism, **3**:67, 76–77

Enfant changé, **1**:77

Engagement. *See* Betrothal

English celebrations and practices: *Ankou*, **3**:10–11; bedwetting cures, **1**:29–30; belief in the evil eye, **1**:343; Blidworth Cradle Rocking Ceremony, **1**:51–52; Burning the Ashen Faggot, **2**:43–44; burying biscuits, **3**:93; Cerne Abbas Giant, **1**:75–77; Chelsea pensioners, **3**:26–29; Childermas, **1**:84; choosing Options, **2**:56–58; danse macabre, **3**:52; Denville Hall and Brinsworth House, **3**:56–57; Dunmow Flitch Trials, **2**:78–79; Eleanor crosses, **3**:72–73; Eyam Plague Sunday Service, **3**:83–84; funeral plants, **3**:95; Goth subculture, **3**:99–101; Grasmere Rushbearing ceremony, **1**:164–166; grave rental, **3**:102; Highgate Cemetery, **3**:298–299; Kissing Friday, **2**:80; Ladybird Books, **1**:198–201; Little Edith's Treat, **1**:207–208; "Lyke-wake Dirge," **3**:158–160; Maidens' Garlands, **3**:161–162; marriage banns, **2**:210; Maypoles, **2**:220; minute's silence, **3**:174–175; "Monday's Child," **1**:220–221;

Mothering Sunday, **1**:230–232; passing bells, **3**:205–206; Royal Wootton Bassett, **3**:239–241; same-sex marriage, **2**:285; Scroggling the Holly, **1**:304–305; soul cakes, **3**:263; souling, **3**:9; Tomb of the Unknown Warrior, **3**:293–295; war memorials, **3**:293–296; wassailing (apple howling), **2**:44; wedding cakes, **2**:369; wedding traditions, **2**:32; witch balls, **1**:356; yew trees, **3**:327–328. *See also* British celebrations and practices; British wedding traditions; United Kingdom celebrations and practices

Engozi, **3**:71

Entering the *Bashali* (Pakistan), **1**: 128–132

Enyovden, **2**:182

Epilation, **2**:111–113

Epiphany, **2**:44

Episcopal Church, **2**:60. *See also* Anglican Church; Church of England

Episiotomy, **1**:187

Eritrea, **2**:89, 92, 93. *See also* Sub-Saharan African celebrations and practices

Estonia, **3**:230

Ethiopia: betrothal, **2**:67; cow jumping, **2**:66–68; *edir*, **3**:70–71; lip plugs, **2**:193–194. *See also* African celebrations and practices

Etoro tribe, **2**:149

Etruscan culture, **1**:345

Eucharist: for the dying, **3**:105; at funeral services, **3**:37; in a wedding ceremony, **2**:59, 61. *See also* Holy Communion

Eukonkanto (wife-carrying), **2**:35

Eulogies, **3**:80–83

European celebrations and practices: *Baccalauréat (le bac)*, **2**:15–16; belief in the evil eye, **1**:343; biscuits for baptisms, **1**:31–33; cairns, **3**:23; christening gowns, **1**:94; Easter eggs, **3**:65–66; eating human placenta, **1**:123; funeral plants, **3**:94–96; government-approved baby names, **1**:154; grave rental, **3**:102; interrailing, **2**:147–148; kangaroo care, **1**:183; *Matura (Mature, Matur, Maturita, Maturità, Maturität, Mamypa)*, **2**:15–16; Maypole, **2**:219–222; mourning color, **3**:302, 304–305; Nordic napping, **1**:249–250; ossuaries, **3**:200–203; pensions, **3**:228; secular confirmation, **2**:300–302; soul cakes and soul breads, **3**:263–266; spontaneous shrines, **3**:269; Steiner schools, **1**:318; *tand-fé*, **1**:326; Tomb of the Unknown Soldier, **3**:295; training bras, **2**:338–341; water births, **1**:347; yew trees, **3**:327–329. *See also individual European countries by name*

Euthanasia, **3**:11–12

Evans, Thom, **2**:23

Evergreen herbs, as funeral plants, **3**:96

Evil eye and evil spirits (devils): amulets/charms against, **1**:14, 344–345, **2**:324; protection against, **1**:306, 316, 318, 324, 356–357; **2**:191, 294, **3**:33, 305; warding off, **1**:235, 305, 306–309, 318, 342–346, 356, **2**:12, 39, 237, 243, 254; release of, 349

Excarnation, **3**:259–262, 339–340

Exhumation, **3**:102–105, 121, 202

Exogamy, **2**:343

Extreme ritual flesh modification, **2**:333–335

Eyam Plague Sunday Service, **3**:83–84

Face in birthday cake, **2**:85

Fady, **1**:33

Fairies; on Mount Velebit, **3**:176; protection from, **1**:78; stealing human babies, **1**:77–80

Fairy bread, **1**:35

Fairy Day, **1**:304

Fairy Investigation Society (FIS), **1**:78

Fairytales, **1**:134–138, 262; alluding to menstruation, **2**:230–231. *See also Weihnachtsmärchen*

Famadihana, **3**:85–87

Family and Medical Leave Act (U.S.), **1**:265
Family Federation for Peace and Unification, **2**:235
Family planning. *See* Birth control
Fantasy coffins, **3**:87–90
Fassi people, **2**:373
Fat Buddha (Hotei), **1**:214
Fat Tuesday, **3**:66
Father Christmas, **1**:296–297, 304–305. *See also* Saint Nicholas; Santa Claus
Father's Day, **1**:138–140
Fathers: bonding with children, **1**:75; preparation for childbirth, **1**:104; traditions involving, **1**:350–351
Fattening room seclusion, **2**:86–89, 153–155
Fave dei Morti, **3**:265
Feast of All Saints, **3**:109. *See also* All Saints' Day
Feast of Corpus Christi, **1**:126–127
Feast of Saint Joseph, **1**:139
Feast of the Banners, **1**:184
Feast of the Holy Innocents, **1**:83–84, 245
Feast of the Presentation, **1**:98
Feast of the Willow Branches, **2**:188
Fellatio, **2**:149–152
Female circumcision. *See* Female genital cutting (FGC)
Female genital cutting (FGC), **2**:8–9, 86–87, 89–94
Female Genital Mutilation. *See* Female genital cutting (FGC)
Female impersonators, **1**:263
Feminism and feminists, **1**:5, 23, **2**:189–190, 196
Fertility: celebration of, **1**:13; deities associated with, **1**:5–6, 34–35, **2**:225; government control over, **1**:256–258; promotion of, **1**:18, **2**:237; rituals, **1**:19, 256–257; symbols of, **1**:14, 75–76, **1**:218–219, 346, **2**:200
Festival of Lights. *See* Diwali
Festival of Lily-of-the-Valley, **2**:321
Festival of Remembrance (British Legion), **3**:2. *See also* Remembrance Day
Fetish-wear, **3**:100
FGM National Clinical Group, **2**:93

Fidanzamenti, **2**:94–95
Fidanzati in casa, **2**:94–95
Figa (amulet), **1**:345
Fiji: birth trees, **1**:33; ritual tattooing, **2**:272–273; Schoolies Week, **2**:284; urethral subincision, **2**:349
Filahta, **1**:345
Filipino debut (Filipino Cotillion), **2**:95–97, **2**:345
Final fireworks, **3**:268
Finger amputation, **3**:90–91
Finnish celebrations and practices: birthday celebrations, **1**:35; cardboard box beds, **1**:72–75; changeling beliefs, **1**:79; Girl Guides, **1**:152; leap year proposals, **2**:189; Nordic napping, **1**:249; parental leave, **1**:266; pensions, **3**:230; *Polterabend*, **2**:256–257; Prometheus Camps, **2**:301; same-sex marriage, **2**:285; universal minimum pension, **3**:231; wife-carrying (*eukonkanto*), **2**:35. *See also* Saami people; Scandinavian celebrations and practices
Fire-Hair Shaving ceremony, **1**:140–142
First communion, **1**:142–144. *See also* Holy Communion
First Nation people, **3**:117, 183–185
First Steps celebration, **1**:66–67
Firstborn males, **1**:280–283
Fistulas, **1**:362
Fitampoha, **3**:86, 243–245
Flanders Fields Memorial Poppy, **3**:315
Flanders Passion plays, **3**:206
Flower garlands, **3**:161
Folk art, Dala horses, **1**:115–116
Folk Catholicism, **3**:49, 269
Folk divination, **1**:348–349
Folk medicine, **1**:124, 130–131
Folk narratives. *See* Fairytales; Folktales
Folk saints, **3**:246–250
Folklore: monsters, **1**:221–226; Ozark and Appalachian, **1**:356–357; pagan, **1**:126; Roma, **2**:44; Saint Nicholas, **1**:294
Folktales, and nursery rhymes, **1**:252
Food and Agriculture Organization of the United Nations (FAO), **1**:146

Food taboos in pregnancy, **1**:86, 89–90, 144–147, 187
Forced marriage, **2**:7–9, 136
Forced Marriage Unit (FMU), **2**:8
Fore people, **3**:77–78
Forehead-cutting initiation, **2**:98–101
Founder's Day (Chelsea pensioners), **3**:28
France: government-approved baby names, **1**:153, 155; Hmong immigrants in, **2**:137
French celebrations and practices: *Ankou*, **3**:10–11; *Baccalauréat (le bac)*, **2**:15–16; baptism customs, **1**:32; birth commemorations, **1**:32; *Carnet de Santé Maternité*, **1**:238; Cimetière du Père Lachaise, **3**:298; danse macabre, **3**:52; jury duty, **2**:165; *La Soupe*, **2**:181–182; La Tombe Du Soldate Inconnu, **3**:294, 295; *Le Bal des Débutantes*, **2**:97; Memorial Days, **3**:225; minute's silence, **3**:174–175; mistletoe, **1**:219; mourning color, **3**:304; national mourning, **3**:192; nursery rhymes, **1**:251; parental leave, **1**:266; Passion plays, **3**:206; St. Catherine's Day, **2**:320–322; same-sex marriage, **2**:285; space burial, **3**:267; spontaneous shrines, **3**:269; sugared almonds, **1**:32; swaddling, **1**:321; tooth mouse, **1**:326; *Universite du Troisieme Age*, **3**:307; water births, **1**:347; wedding customs, **1**:32; yew trees, **3**:327
Frau Perchta, **1**:223
Free Wesleyan Church, **3**:300–301
French Guiana, **2**:185. *See also* South American celebrations and practices
Fulani (Fulbe, Fula) tribe, **2**:307, **2**:383–386
Full moon, **1**:37
Fundoshi, **2**:110
Funeral cakes, **3**:92–93
Funeral candy, **3**:93–94
Funeral Doom, **3**:62–63
Funeral monuments, *Mirila*, **3**:175–177
Funeral music and songs, **3**:97–98, 127–129
Funeral plants, **3**:94–96, 328

Funeral practices: Aboriginal, **3**:116–117; candles around the corpse, **1**:37; Christian, **3**:155; DIY funerals, **3**:210–211; *Famadihana*, **3**:85–87; fantasy coffins, **3**:87–90; green burials, **3**:104, 320; high-platform exposure of the corpse, **3**:115–118; Netherlands, **3**:323; pauper's funeral, **3**:209–211; personalized hearses, **3**:211–213; ritual feasts, **3**:53–55; Romanian, **3**:237–239; snuff, **3**:92; state funerals, **3**:271–275; Tongan, **3**:300–302; Voodoo, **3**:336–337; Wiccan, **3**:318–322; involving yew trees, **3**:327–328; Zoroastran, **3**:338–341. *See also* Death rituals; Japanese funeral customs; Jewish funeral customs
Funeral processions, **3**:273; riderless horse, **3**:236–237; Royal Wootton Bassett, **3**:239–241
Funerary sculpture, **3**:163–164

Ga people, **1**:149, **3**:87–88
Ga'anda people, **2**:100, 294–295
Gaelic festivals, **2**:219
Galena, **2**:40
Gambia, **2**:92. *See also* Sub-Saharan African celebrations and practices; West African celebrations and practices
Gamelan music, **1**:204–206, **3**:195
Gap year, **2**:103–104
Garifuna people, **1**:106–107
Gautama Buddha, **1**:210
GAVI (Global Alliance for Vaccines and Immunisation), **1**:86 –87
Gay marriage. *See* Same-sex marriage
GCSE subjects (General Certificate of Secondary Education), **2**:56–58
Geishas, **2**:292–293
Gempuku, **2**:61
Gender issues: gender equality, **1**:33–34; gender segregation, **2**:279; *hijra* population, **2**:131–133; short-term gender transformation, **1**:106
General Certificate of Secondary Education (GCSE), choosing options, **2**:56–58
Geophagia, **1**:71

George Washington Bridge (New York/New Jersey), 3:278
German celebrations and practices: Advent calendars, 1:349–350; All Souls' Day, 3:8–9, 265; assisted suicide, 3:13; *bar mitzvah*, 2:21; birthday customs, 2:26–28; breastfeeding, 1:56; candle superstitions, 1:37; changeling beliefs, 1:77; danse macabre, 3:52; Easter egg trees (*Osterbrunnen*), 3:67; eating human placenta, 1:124; Frau Perchta, 1:223; glass blowing, 1:357; government-approved baby names, 1:153, 154, 155; grave reuse, 3:103; jury duty, 2:165; *Kinderfest*, 1:36–37, 42, 273; *klinken putzen*, 2:27; Krampus, 1:221–223; Liberation Day, 3:225; love divination, 2:3; *Martinstag*, 3:111; May Day, 2:221; Memorial to the Fallen of the War, 3:295; Memorial to the Victims of Fascism and Militarism, 3:295; mistletoe, 1:219; *Mutterpass*, 1:237–238; nursery rhymes, 1:251; parental leave, 1:66; Passion plays, 3:206–208; plastination, 3:213–216; *Polterabend*, 2:254–258; Round Birthdays, 1:43; Saint Nicholas, 1:297; *Schuhplattler* and *Ländler*, 2:297–299; secular confirmation, 2:300–301; silver spoon, 1:313; sock garlands, 2:318–319; soul cakes, 3:263–264; space burial, 3:267; spontaneous shrines, 3:269; Steiner schools, 1:318; swaddling, 1:321; University of the Third Age, 3:307; *Vatertag*, 1:139–140; *Volkstrauertag* (People's Day of Mourning), 3:225; *Waldkindergärten*, 1:341–342; *Weihnachtsmärchen*, 1:349–350; witch balls, 1:356
German Federation of Nature and Forest Kindergartens (BVNW), 1:341
Germany: Hmong immigrants in, 2:137; retirement and pensions, 3:228–229
Gesellschaft fur Technische Zusammenarbeit (GTZ), 2:30

Ghanaian practices: baby-naming ceremony 1:1–4; birthday traditions, 1:149–151; Dipo Womanhood Ceremony, 2:71–73; fantasy coffins, 3:87–90; female ritual servitude (*trokosi*), 1:330–333. *See also* West African celebrations and practices
Ghost marriages, 3:221–222
Ghosts: Chinese, 3:329–332; Jewish, 3:132
Girl Guides movement, 1:151–153, 303. *See also* Scouts and Scouting
Girl Scouts of the United States of America, 1:152. *See also* Scouts and Scouting
Girl Summit, 2:8
Girls: circumcision of, 2:206 (*see also* Female genital cutting); clothing for first communion, 1:143; given in marriage to a deity, 1:116–119; offered to Hindu temple, 1:192–193; and ritual servitude, 1:330–333; serving as incarnation of goddess Devi, 1:189–190. *See also* Babies; Children; Girls' coming-of-age ceremonies
Girls' coming-of-age ceremonies, 2:269; *ameen* ceremony, 1:47–48; *Brit banot* ceremony, 1:62; Chinese, 2:51; Dipo Womanhood Ceremony, 2:71–73; Filipino debut, 2:95–97; *gryerye*, 2:106; *Iria* ceremony, 2:153–155; *Isanaklesh Gotal*, 2:155–159; *La Quinceañera*, 2:177–180; *Lazarovden*, 2:186–188; Maasai traditions, 2:205, 2:206; *Mehndi*, 2:223; menstrual customs, 2:226–227; *Mogi*, 2:61–62; *nahtwin*, 2:83; *Pika* and *Nora*, 2:253–254; scarification ritual, 2:294–295; Sunrise Ceremony, 2:326–331; Tamil celebration, 2:226; training bras, 2:338–341; vision quest, 2:359; Zambia, 2:52–55. *See also* Coming-of-age ceremonies
Goddesses: Aztec, 3:58; of childbearing and children, 1:5–6, 23, 90; Devi (Hindu), 1:189–190; earth, 1:69, 194, 203, 2:71; Earth Mother, 1:8, 2:155; of fertility, 1:117, 129–130, 2:225; of fertility, childbirth and

water, **1**:4–7; of love, **1**:6, **2**:182; of luck/fate, **1**:203–204; of menstruation, **1**:6; of pregnancy, **1**:4–7
Godparents, **1**:26, 66, 125, 204, **2**:178
Gokarna Aunsi, **1**:139
The Golden Bough, **1**:218
Golden Gate Bridge (San Francisco), **3**:278–279
Golden Week (Japan), **1**:184
Gongua ba Buniwae (the Care), **1**:106
Good Friday, **3**:275. *See also* Holy Week
Goth subculture, **3**:99–102, 297; bands, **3**:99–100; cinema, **3**:101; fashion, **3**:100; magazines, **3**:100–101
Government-approved baby names, **1**:153–157
Grasmere Rushbearing, **1**:164–166
Grave rental, **3**:102–105, 121
The Great Passing, **3**:105–107
Greek celebrations and practices: almonds at spinsters' funerals, **3**:162; Childermas, **1**:84; cremation, **3**:103; *filahta*, **1**:345; grave rental, **3**:102; *koliva*, **3**:135–136; leap year marriage, **2**:189; love divination, **2**:3; March celebration, **1**:16–17; money dance, **2**:234; mourning color, **3**:302; parental leave, **1**:266; pensions, **3**:230; soul cake, **3**:93. *See also* Ancient Greece; Greek Orthodox Church celebrations and practices
Greek Orthodox Church celebrations and practices: charms against the evil eye, **1**:345; Churching of Women script, **1**:100–103; Easter, **1**:17; *koliva*, **3**:135; Name days, **1**:241; opposition to cremation, **3**:42, 103. *See also* Eastern Orthodox Church celebrations and practices
Greek-Catholic churches, **3**:251
Green burial customs, **3**:104, 320
Green Day, **2**:316
Greenland, **1**:9, 10, **2**:285
Grenada, Nine-Nights, **3**:196–198
Gretna Green, **2**:104–105, 210
Groaning Cake (Kimbly), **1**:166–169
Groaning Cheese, **1**:166–167

Grooms: blackening, **2**:28; carrying the bride over the threshold, **2**:36; creeling, **2**:29; gifts given to, **2**:13, 37–38; Jewish ceremony for, **2**:159–160; ritual bathing of, **2**:11, 213
Groom's cakes, **2**:48
Grýla, **1**:223
Guanches, **3**:186
Guanyin (Buddhist deity), **1**:90
Guaraní Indians, **3**:247
Guatemalan practices: covering the belly button, **1**:108; *Tuj* or *Temascal*, **1**:333–335; worry dolls, **1**:357–358. *See also* Central American practices
Guinea, **2**:30. *See also* West African celebrations and practices
Guinea Bissau, **3**:71. *See also* Sub-Saharan African celebrations and practices; West African celebrations and practices
Gulab Jamun, **1**:36
Guyana, Nine-Nights, **3**:196–198
Gwallye, **2**:105–106
Gyerye ceremony, **2**:106
Gypsies. *See* Roma celebrations and practices

Hadaka Matsuri (naked festival), **2**:109–110
Haida Gwaii, **3**:184
Haida tribe, **3**:183–185
Hair cutting: ceremonial **1**:9, 195; on *Hajj*, **2**:116
Hair removal, **2**:111–113
Hair shaving, **1**:338, **2**:207, 116
Hair-pinning ceremony (Ji Li), **2**:49–50
Hairwork, **3**:287
Haiti: Nine-Nights, **3**:196–198; zombies and voodoo death traditions, **3**:335–338
Hajj (pilgrimage), **2**:113–116
Hallowe'en (Halloween), **3**:109–111, 328, 334
Halva (halawa, halvah, halava, halwa), **3**:113–115
Hamar people, **2**:66
Hammaspeikko (Tooth Troll), **1**:325
hampas-palayak, **1**:285

Hamsa hand symbol, **1**:344–345
Handfasting, **2**:32, 117–119; ceremony, **2**:119–126
Handkerchief test, **2**:357
Handparting, **2**:127–128
Hanselling, **1**:351
Hanshi Festival, **3**:219, 221
Hanuman (monkey god), **1**:117
"Happy Birthday" Song, **1**:171–173, 263
Hatsu Miyamairi, **1**:174
Haulage of the Midwife (*Vlechugane*), **1**:19
Hausa people, **1**:362–363
Hawai'i, **1**:67–68, **2**:272
Haworth Traders Christmas Committee, **1**:304
Head shaving ritual, **2**:116, 207
Healthcare, for pregnant women, **1**:72, 73, 237–238. *See also* Indigenous medicine
Hearses, personalized, **3**:211–213
Henna, **1**:51, **2**:2–3, 222–224, 237–238, 242, 312
Herbal remedies, **1**:30, 90, 181, 229, 307
Herodotus, **2**:90
Herrick, Robert, **2**:44
Hesono-o, **1**:173–175
Hesperides (Herrick), **2**:44
Highgate Cemetery, **3**:298–299
High-platform exposure of the corpse, **3**:115–118
Hijab, **2**:128–130; poppy-print, **3**:316
Hijra population, **2**:131–133
Himalayas, **3**:23. *See also* Tibetan practices
Hindu celebrations and practices: arranged marriage, **2**:6; baby rituals, **1**:175–177; birthstones, **1**:44–45; British weddings, **2**:32; cremation, **3**:42; *devadasi*, **1**:116–119; Diwali, **2**:73–75, 77; extreme ritual flesh modification, **2**:333–335; forced marriage, **2**:8; *halva*, **3**:114; and the *hijra* population, **2**:131–133; Karva Chauth (Karwa Chauth), **2**:224; *Kumbh Mela*, **2**:173–175; lotus birthing, **1**:210–211; *Makar Sankranthi*, **3**:114; Mangalore Dasara, **3**:311; *Manjal Neerattu Vizha* (Turmeric Bathing Ceremony), **2**:226; menstruation as unclean, **2**:228; Mundan ceremony, **1**:232–234; *ngaben* (*pelebon*), **3**:193–196; *Pasni*, **1**:275–276; polygyny, **2**:261; tooth-filing ceremony, **2**:335–338; *Upanayana* (Sacred thread ritual), **1**:337–339; Vrindavan, **3**:309–311; wedding ceremonies, **2**:133–136
Hindu death customs, **3**:118–120; mourning, **3**:119; post-death rituals, **3**:118; riverside cremation, **3**:119
Hitler Youth, **2**:298
HIV/AIDS, **2**:31, 92, 132, 248, 269–270, 343–344, **3**:71
Hmong people, **2**:317–318; names, **2**:136–139; treatment of the placenta, **1**:67
Hogmanay, **1**:293
Hogueras festival, **1**:128
Holi (springtime festival), **2**:75–76
Holiva, **3**:333
Holland. *See* Netherlands
Holly Queen and Princesses, **1**:304–305
Holy Communion, **1**:32; first, **1**:142–144; in a wedding ceremony, **2**:59, 61. *See also* Eucharist
Holy Mosque (Mecca), **2**:116
Holy Week, **3**:47–50. *See also* Good Friday; Palm Sunday
Homosexual communities, **2**:8, **3**:250. *See also* LGBT issues
Homosexuality, ritualized, **2**:148
Hong Kong: grave rental, **3**:104; jury duty, **2**:167; *Qingming* Festival, **3**:219–221. *See also* Asian celebrations and practices
Hopi traditions: *Katsina* (*katchina*, *kachina*) dolls, **1**:179, 358–359; naming rites, **1**:177–180
Hop-tu-Naa, **3**:112
Hora (horah) dance, **1**:19, **2**:20, 40, 139–140
Horseshoes, as good luck charm, **2**:141–142
Hotei, **1**:214
Hounen Matsuri, **1**:277
Huitzilopochtli (Aztec god of war) **1**:283
Human rights, **2**:30
Humanist confirmation, **2**:300–302

Hungarian celebrations and practices:
All Souls' Day, **3**:8, 265; birthday customs, **1**:41; eating human placenta, **1**:123; funeral plants, **3**:95; Krampusz, **1**:222–223; *Martinstag*, **3**:111; *Matura*, **2**:15; mourning color, **3**:305; national mourning, **3**:192; parental leave, **1**:266; spontaneous shrines, **3**:269; *Vizbevető*, **2**:79; wedding cakes, **2**:371. *See also* Eastern European celebrations and practices

Hunger Safety Net Programme, **3**:231

Hungry Ghost Festival, **3**:7, 329–332

Hyakunichimairi (*Hyaku niche mairi*), **1**:259

Iban people of Borneo, **2**:144

Ibani tribe, **1**:68, 69

Ibo tribe, **2**:142

Icelandic celebrations and practices: *Eddas*, **1**:326; government-approved baby names, **1**:153, 154–155, 157–164; *Grýla*, **1**:223; lullabies, **1**:214; parental leave, **1**:265; same-sex marriage, **2**:285; secular confirmation, **2**:300; wedding cake, **2**:370

Ifaluk Island, **1**:287

Igbo tribe, **1**:68, **2**:234

Imbolc, **2**:219

Imilchil Moussem (Berber Marriage Festival), **2**:238–240

Incan practices, **3**:186, 256

Incubus, **1**:79

Indian celebrations and practices: arranged marriage, **2**:5–7; baby hammocks, **1**:301; baby-throwing, **1**:127; belief in the evil eye, **1**:343; birthday traditions, **1**:36, 40, 41; boxes for babies, **1**:74; Buddhist practices, **3**:18, 20; cremation, **3**:41; *devadasi* system, **1**:116–119; Devipujak purification trial, **2**:55–56; Diwali, **2**:73–75; endocannibalism, **3**:77; food taboos during pregnancy, **1**:146; forced marriage, **2**:8; hair removal, **2**:112; *halva*, **3**:113–114; *hijra* population, **2**:131–133; Kali Pooja, **2**:74–75; Karva Chauth, **2**:224; *Mehndi*, **2**:222, 223; menstrual taboos, **2**:228–229; mourning color, **3**:304; navjote ceremonies, **1**:247–248; *ngaben*, **3**:195–196; polyandry, **2**:258, 260; potty training, **1**:286; *sati* (*suttee*), **3**:43; Sikh death customs, **3**:257; Sikh wedding ceremonies, **2**:312–315; space burial, **3**:267; state funerals, **3**:273; teething remedies, **1**:329; virginity testing, **2**:356; Vrindavan (City of Widows), **3**:309–311; Zoroastran funerals, **3**:338–341. *See also* South Asian celebrations and practices

Indian Arts and Crafts Act (1990), **1**:120

Indigenous medicine, **1**:181

Indonesian celebrations and practices: birth trees, **1**:33; birthday celebrations, **1**:36; cutting the umbilical cord, **1**:113; eating human placenta, **1**:123; food taboos during pregnancy, **1**:145; headhunters, **3**:256; *Jamu* medicine and massage, **1**:181–182; *Legong*, **1**:204–207; living with the dead, **3**:155–158; Muslim dress for women, **2**:130; *ngaben* (*pelebon*), **3**:193–195; *Nyabutan* ceremony, **1**:253–254; tooth sharpening, **2**:143; tooth-filing ceremony, **2**:335–338; wedding cakes, **2**:372. *See also* Southeast Asian celebrations and practices

Indra Jatta Festival, **1**:190–191

Infant mortality: in China, **1**:226; in Egypt, **1**:306; in Finland, **1**:72; in Ghana, **1**:2; in Kyrgyzstan, **1**:195; in Texas, **1**:75; in Tibet, **1**:323

Infibulation, **2**:91. *See also* Female genital cutting

Initiation ceremonies: bullet ant initiation, **2**:41–43; cow jumping, **2**:66–68; forehead-cutting, **2**:98–101; for *hijra*, **2**:132; ritual, **1**:53; by semen transferal, **2**:148–152. *See also* Boys' coming-of-age ceremonies; Chinese coming-of-age ceremonies; Coming-of-age ceremonies; Girls' coming-of-age ceremonies

Institute for Plastination (IfP), **3**:213
International Association of Universities of the Third Age (IAUTA), **3**:307
International Child Protection Day, **1**:22
International Cremation Federation (ICF), **3**:41
International Day of Zero Tolerance for Female Genital Mutilation, **2**:93
International Needs Ghana (ING), **1**:332
International Wave of Light, **3**:217
Interrailing, **2**:147–148
Inuit people, **1**:9–11, **1**:79
Iran: Assyrian betrothal and weddings, **2**:9–14; *halva*, **3**:113, 115; mourning color, **3**:302; national mourning, **3**:191; Zoroastrianism, **3**:338. *See also* Middle Eastern celebrations and practices; Persia
Iraq: Assyrian betrothal and weddings, **2**:9–14; *Halawat tamr*, **3**:114–115. *See also* Middle Eastern celebrations and practices
Iria ceremony, **2**:153–155
Irish celebrations and practices: Beltane, **2**:219; birthday customs, **1**:40; changeling beliefs, **1**:77; funeral snuff, **3**:92; Girl Guides, **1**:152; Lisdoonvarna Matchmaking Festival, **2**:16–17; RAG Week, **2**:267–268; Saint Brigid and the Biddies, **1**:16; same-sex marriage, **2**:285; spontaneous shrines, **3**:269; sprinkling cake, **1**:317–318; wakes, **3**:313; yew trees, **3**:327
Isanaklesh (Mescalero Apache Earth Mother Goddess), **1**:8, **2**:155
Isanaklesh Gotal (The Feast), **2**:155–159
Isbister Chambered Cairn, **3**:262
ISIL (Islamic State), **3**:192
Isla de las Munecas, **3**:61
Islamic celebrations and practices: *Adhaan*, **1**:234; *ameen* ceremony, **1**:47–48; *aqeeqah (aqiqa)* ritual, **1**:235; baby naming, **1**:234–235; beards, **2**:22; betrothal and marriage, **2**:1; birth rites, **1**:234–235; *bismallah* ceremony, **1**:47–48; British weddings, **2**:32; burying the placenta, **1**:235; circumcision, **1**:234, 235–237; death rituals, **3**:188–190; female genital cutting, **2**:90; forced marriage, **2**:7–8; hair removal, **2**:112; *Hajj*, **2**:113–116; head shaving, **1**:234; *Hijab*, **2**:128–130; and the *hijra* population, **2**:131–133; *Id-el-kabir*, **2**:307; menstruation customs, **2**:228; opposition to cremation, **3**:44; polygyny, **2**:261; prayer for babies, **1**:194; ritual ear-piercing, **2**:83–84; *shabka*, **2**:302–305; *tahneek* ritual **1**:234; *taweez*, **1**:234; *Umrah*, **2**:113; wedding ceremonies, **2**:40, 222, 241–242
Islamic State (ISIL), **3**:192
Islamophobia, **3**:316
Island of the Dolls, **3**:61
Isle of Man: Beltane, **2**:219; Hop-tu-Naa, **3**:112
Isola di San Michele (San Michele Island), **3**:121–122
Israel: birthday child on a chair, **1**:40; food taboos during pregnancy, **1**:145. *See also* Middle Eastern celebrations and practices
Italy: birthday customs, **1**:41; birthstones, **1**:44; *danse macabre*, **3**:52; Father's Day, **1**:139; *Fave dei Morti*, **3**:265; *Fidanzamenti* and *Fidanzati in casa*, **2**:94–95; Isola di San Michele (San Michele Island), **3**:121–122; La Befana, **1**:223; *mano fico*, **1**:346; Marantega (tooth witch), **1**:326; *Matura*, **2**:15; mourning color, **3**:302; mummification, **3**:185; Nativity play, **1**:245; ossuaries, **3**:201; *Pan dei Morti*, **3**:265; parental leave, **1**:266; Passion plays, **3**:206; pensions, **3**:230; soul cakes, **3**:263–264; Tomb of the Unknown Soldier, **3**:294
Ivana Kupala, **2**:353
Ivy, **3**:328
Iztapalapa Passion play, **3**:208–209

Jack o'lanterns, **3**:110, 112
Jailbreak, **2**:267
Jainism, **3**:245–246; Diwali, **2**:73–74, 76–77

Jamaica: Nine-Nights, **3**:196–198; pantomime, **1**:261; treatment of the placenta, **1**:69
Jamu medicine and massage, **1**:181–182
Jāṇi Day, **2**:200
Japanese celebrations and practices: baby naming ceremony, **1**:259; baby racing, **1**:22; Bon Festival, **3**:7; Buddhist practices, **3**:18, 20; crying-baby sumo competition, **1**:111–112; cutting the umbilical cord, **1**:113; government-approved baby names, **1**:153, 155; *Hadaka Matsuri* (naked festival), **2**:109–110; *Hatsu Miyamairi*, **1**:174; *Hesono-o* (wrapping umbilical cord as keepsake), **1**:173–175; *Hyakunichimairi* (*Hyaku niche mairi*), **1**:259; *Kanchu Misogi*, **2**:110–111; *Koshikijima no Toshidon*, **1**:225; log riding, **2**:197–199; lullabies, **1**:214; mistletoe, **1**:219; *Namahage*, **1**:223–224; *Okuizome*, **1**:259–260; *Omiai*, **2**:251–252; *Omiya-mairi*, **1**:174; *Onbashira* festival, **2**:197–199; *Oshichiya Meimeishiki*, **1**:259; *Ososo Matsuri* (Vagina Festival), **1**:279; parental leave, **1**:266, 267; pensions, **3**:228, 230–231; phallus festivals, **1**:277–280; ritual tattooing, **2**:276; *San-san-kudo* (*san san kudo*; *sansan-kudo*), **2**:291–293; *Seijin no Hi* (Coming of Age Day), **2**:61–64; *Setsubun*, **1**:307–309; shrine outing, **1**:259; teething remedies, **1**:329; universities for older students, **3**:308; Valentine's Day, **2**:316; *Waldkindergärten*, **1**:341; wedding cakes, **2**:372; wedding dresses, **2**:374; *Yamadashi*, **2**:198. See also Asian celebrations and practices; Japanese funeral customs
Japanese funeral customs, **3**:123–127; arrangement of the corpse, **3**:123–124; cremation **3**:125; fetus memorial service, **3**:180–183; funeral plants, **3**:95; grave rental, **3**:104; memorial observances, **3**:126; mourning clothes, **3**:303–304; mourning colors, **3**:303–304; mummification, **3**:185; Obon, **3**:126–127; procession to location of the funeral, **3**:124; space burial, **3**:267; *Toro Nagashi*, **3**:127; wake, **3**:124–125, 313
Japanese matchmaking, **2**:251–252
Jazz funeral, **3**:127–129
Jerusalem and the Via Dolorosa, **3**:275–276
Jewelry: as gifts for brides, **2**:37, 134, 302–305; mourning, **3**:286–288; ritual wedding and betrothal gifts, **2**:1–2; worn by brides, **2**:312–313
Jewish celebrations and practices: bar mitzvah, **2**:19–21; bat mitzvah, **2**:19–21; beards, **2**:22; birth trees, **1**:33; birthstones, **1**:44, **1**:46; *brit banot*, **1**:62; *brit milah*, **1**:59–63; *brit shalom* (*bris shalom*), **1**:62; British weddings, **2**:32; female genital cutting, **2**:90; forced marriage, **2**:8; *hora* dance, **2**:138–140; menstrual customs, **2**:226–228; *Pidyon haben* (Redemption of the first-born), **1**:280–283; *Pidyon habit* ceremony (Redemption of the firstborn daughter), **1**:282; wedding customs, **2**:159–162, 222. See also Jewish funeral customs
Jewish funeral customs, **3**:129–133; burial, **3**:130–131; dying, **3**:130; mourning, **3**:131; objection to plastination, **3**:214; opposition to cremation, **3**:44; Shiva, **3**:132
Jewish ghosts, **3**:132
Jia Liang (Sisters' Meal Festival), **2**:317–318
Jicarilla Apache tribe, **2**:330
Jivaroan tribes, **3**:255, 256–357
John XXIII (pope), **3**:185
John Paul II (pope), **3**:192, 276
Jolly Roger, **3**:170
Joninės, **2**:200
Jordan, **2**:262. See also Middle Eastern celebrations and practices
Jugendweihe, **2**:300–301
Juks-akka (childbirth goddess), **1**:5
Jumping over the broom, **2**:163–165
Jury duty, **2**:165–171

Kachina. See *Katsina*
Kagekone, **1**:35
Kagemand, **1**:35
Kaiapo (Kayapo) tribe, **2**:190
Kalash (Kalasha or Nuristani) people, **1**:128, **2**:225
Kalash religion, **1**:128–129
Kali (Hindu goddess), **2**:74
Kali Pooja, **2**:74–75
Kami-dana (god-shelf), **1**:214
Kanamara Matsuri (Festival of the Steel Phallus), **1**:278–279
Kanchu Misogi, **2**:110–111
Kanelmø (cinnamon maid), **2**:26
Kanelsvend (cinnamon man), **2**:26
Kangaroo care, **1**:183–184
Karan people, **2**:275–276
Kare-Kare community, **1**:362
Kashiwa mochi, **1**:185
Katarzynki (St. Catherine's Day), **2**:3–4, 320–322
Katarzynki gingerbread, **2**:4
Katsina (*katchina, kachina*) dolls, **1**:179, 358–359
Kayan people, **2**:243, 244
Keesta, **2**:330
Kenya, **1**:316, **2**:93, **3**:231. See also African celebrations and practices
Keraki tribe, **2**:149
Ketubah, **2**:160
Khandoba (god of farming and herding), **1**:117
Kheyapta-d khitna, **2**:11
Khitan, **1**:235. See also Circumcision
Khoya, **1**:36
Khwahish khwari, **2**:1
Khwan ceremony, **1**:140–142
Kickapoo Indian tribe, **2**:64–66
Kikuyu people, **2**:262
Kimbly, **1**:166
Kimono rental, **2**:62
Kinaalda, **2**:330
Kinderfest, **1**:37, 42, 273
Kingdom of Swaziland, **2**:269–272
Kiriwina Islands, **2**:341–344
Kiss Day, **2**:316
Kissing Friday, **2**:80
Kite flying, **3**:221

Kiv people, **2**:142
Klama puberty dance, **2**:72–73
Klausjagen, **1**:296
Klinken putzen, **2**:27
Kodomo Noi Hi (Japan), **1**:184–186
Kola Peninsula, **1**:4
Koliva (*kolyva, kollyva, kollyba*), **3**:135–138
Konaki sumo (Crying Sumo), **1**:111–112
Korean celebrations and practices: baby naming, **1**:188; childbirth customs, **1**:186–189; mourning color, **3**:302; placenta in folk medicine, **1**:124; pregnancy customs, **1**:186–187. See also Asian celebrations and practices; South Korean celebrations and practices
Koroonduk, **1**:195
Korowai tribe, **3**:78
Koshikijima no Toshidon, **1**:225
Kosovo, **2**:15. See also Eastern European celebrations and practices; Yugoslav countries
Kotobuki Bako, **1**:173–174
Krada, **1**:150
Krahonowska-Malkowska, Olga, **1**:152
Krampus **1**:221–223, 298
Krampusnacht, **1**:222
Krobo people, **2**:71–73
Krustaba, **1**:204
Kulemba, **2**:100
Kumari and *Deuki,* **1**:189–193
Kumbh Mela, **2**:173–175
Kunstmärchen, **1**:135
Kuru, **3**:77
Kusti ritual, **1**:246–248
Kutema nyora, **2**:253
Kyrgyzstan, **1**:193–196, **3**:231. See also Central Asian practices

L'Ankou, **3**:10–11
La Befana, **1**:21:23
La Calavera Catrina, **3**:58
La Cincuentañera, **2**:180
La Craie, **1**:71
La cuarentena, **1**:197–198
La Fête du Muguet, **2**:321
La fiesta de quince años see *La Quinceañera*
La Quinceañera, **2**:96, 177–180

La Soupe, **2**:180–181
Labsgriftan, **2**:1
Lachrymatory bottles, **3**:286
Ladouvane, **2**:182–183
Ladybird Books, **1**:198–201
Laetare Sunday, **1**:230
Laima (Latvian goddess of luck/fate), **1**:203–204
Lakota death rituals, **3**:139–152; give-away, **3**:141; memorial ceremony, **3**:140–141; Native American Grave Protection and Repatriation Act, **3**:142–152; spirit-keeping ceremony, **3**:139; spirit-releasing ceremony, **3**:139–140
Lakota tribe, **1**:120, **2**:358–359
Lamaze technique, **1**:201–202
Land diving competitions (*Gol, Nanggol, Nagol, N'gol*), **2**:183–186
Ländler, **2**:298–299
Langsuir, **1**:79
Lanie wosku (pouring wax), **2**:4
Lanimer Day, Scotland, **1**:353
Lany poniedzalek (Wet Monday), **2**:79
Laos: Hmong names, **2**:136; mother roasting, **1**:228–229; tooth dyeing, **2**:144. *See also* Southeast Asian celebrations and practices
Las Posadas, **1**:284
Last meal of condemned prisoner, **3**:37–40
"The Last Post," **3**:152–155
Latin American celebrations and practices: anti-Santa Claus movement, **1**:297–298; christening gowns, **1**:94; covering the belly button, **1**:108–109; danse macabre, **3**:52; *Dia de los Muertos*, **3**:52, 58–61; *La cuarentena*, **1**:197–198; *La Quinceañera*, **2**:177–180; *Las Posadas*, **1**:284; Name Days, **1**:241. *See also* Central American celebrations and practices; Mexico
Latvian celebrations and practices: birth traditions, **1**:203–204; birthday customs, **1**:40; childhood vaccinations in, **1**:85; Ligo, or Jāņi Day, **2**:200; parental leave, **1**:266; universal minimum pension,
3:231. *See also* Eastern European celebrations and practices
Laughing Buddha (Hotei), **1**:214
Lazarovden, **2**:186–188
Le Bal des Débutantes, **2**:97
Leap Year Proposal, **2**:189–190
Leaver's Week, **2**:283
Legong, **1**:204–207
Les Relevailles, **1**:98
LGBT issues, **2**:8, 280, **3**:250
Liechtenstein, *Matura*, **2**:15
Ligo, **2**:200
Lilacs, **3**:95
Lilies, **3**:94–95
Lily-of-the-Valley, **3**:95
Lindo, **2**:190–191
Linga (Philippine deity), **1**:256
Lip plugs, **2**:191–195
Liquid cremation, **3**:5–6
Lisdoonvarna Matchmaking Festival, **2**:16–17
Lithuanian celebrations and practices: baby racing, **1**:21–22; birthday customs, **1**:40; government-approved baby names, **1**:153, 155; Joninės, **2**:200; parental leave, **1**:266. *See also* Eastern European celebrations and practices
Little Edith's Treat, **1**:207–208
Living with the Dead, **3**:155–158
Llama fetuses, dissected, **1**:69
Lobola, **2**:195–197
Lockets, **3**:287
Log riding, **2**:197–199
Lohusa Şerbeti, **1**:208–210
Lolita look, **3**:100
Lone Charger, **3**:236
Long-Horn Miao minority group, **2**:138
Longoria, Eva, **2**:112
Looking for fern blossoms, **2**:199–201
Lotus birthing, **1**:210–213
Love divination, **1**:167, **2**:3–5, 44, 177–178, 353, **3**:110, 112
Lovespoons, **2**:201–203
Lucia celebrations, **2**:256–257
Lughnasadh, **2**:219
Luk Thep dolls, **1**:358
Lullabies, **1**:213–215

Lutheran Church, **1**:27, 349, **2**:60, 185, 300, **3**:275. *See also* Christian celebrations and practices
Luxembourg: parental leave, **1**:266; same-sex marriage, **2**:285; spontaneous shrines, **3**:269
"Lyke-wake Dirge," **3**:158–160

Maasai traditions, **1**:316; blood drinking, **2**:205; Maasai warrior initiation, **2**:205–208
Mabele, **1**:71
Macau, *Qingming* Festival, **3**:219
Macedonia, **2**:15, 140. *See also* Eastern European celebrations and practices; Yugoslav countries
Madagascar, **1**:133; death dance, **3**:51; *Famadihana*, **3**:85–87; Sakalava royal death traditions and *Fitampoha*, **3**:243–245; Sambatra mass circumcision festival **1**:298–300
Madder-akka (Mother Goddess), **1**:5
Madrasah school, **1**:47
Madrinas, **2**:178. *See also* Godparents
Magnetoscope, **1**:348
Mahandeo (Kalash deity), **1**:129
Maidens' Garlands, **3**:161–162
Majáles festival, **2**:208–209
Makar Sankranthi, **3**:114
Make-shift memorials. *See* Spontaneous shrines
Makonde people, **2**:143
Malagan ceremonies, **3**:162–164
Malagasy ethnic group, **3**:85
Malawi, **2**:192, **3**:51. *See also* African celebrations and practices
Malaysian celebrations and practices: belief in demons, **1**:79; birth trees, **1**:33; breastfeeding, **1**:56; ear-piercing ceremonies in, **2**:83–84; food taboos during pregnancy, **1**:145; government-approved baby names, **1**:153; indigenous medicine in, **1**:181; *moon-yuet*, **1**:227; mother roasting, **1**:228; Muslim dress for women, **2**:130; Remembrance Day, **3**:223; *sarung buaian*, **1**:300–301; tooth sharpening, **2**:143; treatment of the placenta in, **1**:67. *See also* Southeast Asian celebrations and practices
Male genital cutting, **2**:347–351. *See also* Circumcision
Mali, tooth sharpening, **2**:143. *See also* West Africa
Malta, *Quccija* (*il-Quccija*), **1**:291–292
Mangalore Dasara, **3**:311
Mani-Mala: A Treatise on Gems, **1**:44
Manjal Neerattu Vizha (Turmeric Bathing Ceremony), **2**:226
Mano cornuta, **1**:344
Mano fico, **1**:346
Māori people, **1**:69–70, **2**:230, 273–274, 345; mourning ritual, **3**:281–283. *See also* New Zealand celebrations and practices
Mara (Latvian earth goddess), **1**:203
Marantega, **1**:326
Marawtungwni ceremony, **1**:180
March celebrations, **1**:16
Märchen. *See* Fairytales
Mardi Gras, **3**:66
Marriage Act (Britain), **2**:32, 211–215
Marriage banns, **2**:210–215
Marriages: arranged, **2**:5–9, 10, 37–38, 94, 100, 136, 159, 237, 241, 251–252, 295, 312; exogamous, **2**:343; forced, **2**:5–9, 136; Ghost, **3**:221–222; handfasting, **2**:117–118; leap year, **2**:189–190; mixed (Catholic and non-Catholic), **2**:58–59; multi-racial, **2**:378–379; polyandrous, **2**:258–261; polygamous, **2**:240, 247; polygynous, **2**:261–263; same-sex, **2**:117, 119, 247–249, 256, 285–291; as union of families, **2**:10; *urfi* (unregistered), **2**:304. *See also* Wedding traditions and customs
Martenitsi, **1**:13–16
Martini, **3**:111
Martinique, zombies, **3**:335
Martinsmas, **3**:111
Martinstag, **3**:111
Martisor (Romania), **1**:16
Massacre of the Innocents, **1**:83–84, 245
Massage, *jamu*, **1**:181

Matchmakers: and arranged marriages, **2**:5; Irish, **2**:17; Japanese, **2**:251–252, 291; Jewish, **2**:159; *nayan*, **2**:6–7, 159; in the Shanghai Marriage Market, **2**:305–306
Maternity boxes, **1**:72–75
Maternity Grants Act (Finland), **1**:72
Maternity leave, **1**:266–268. *See also* Parental leave
Matetha-d dhamanta, **2**:10
Matis hunting trials, **2**:215–219
Matronales Feriae, **1**:230
Matronalia, **1**:230
Matura (*Mature, Matur, Maturita, Maturità, Maturität, Mamypa*), **2**:15–16
Matura Shtetërore, **2**:15
Maundy Money, **3**:164–167
Mauritius, **3**:231
May Day celebrations, **1**:76, 217–218, **2**:209; Maypoles, **2**:219–222
May Queen, **2**:220
Mayan traditions, **2**:177, **3**:256; hair removal, **2**:112; midwives, **1**:112; therapeutic steam bath (*Tuj or temascal*), **1**:333–335; worry dolls, **1**:357–358
Maypoles, **2**:219–222
Mbuti (Efe) tribe, **2**:143, 245
Mecca, pilgrimage to, **2**:113–116
Medical students, white coat ceremony, **2**:381–382
Mehinako tribe, couvade, **1**:104
Mehndi, **2**:222–224, 312. *See also* Henna
Melanesia, **1**:104, **2**:272
Memento Mori, **3**:167–171; jewelry, **3**:286
Memorial feasts, **3**:4–5, 7
Memorial to the Fallen of the War (Germany), **3**:295
Memorial to the Victims of Fascism and Militarism (Germany), **3**:295
Menabe Sakalava, **3**:86
Mende people, **1**:113
Menin Gate Memorial to the Missing, **3**:153–154
Mennonites, **2**:254
Menstrual customs, **2**:224–228; African, **2**:227; of the Bauls, **2**:225–226; Hindu, **2**:226; Jewish, **2**:226–227; in Pakistan **2**:225; in Polynesia, **2**:224–225

Menstrual taboos, **2**:228–233
Menstruation, **1**:14, **2**:52–54; access to sanitary products, **2**:231–232; celebration of, **2**:225–226; goddess of, **1**:6; seclusion during, **1**:129, **2**:225–226, 229–230; as unclean, **2**:228. *See also* Menstrual customs; Menstrual taboos
Mentawai tribe, **2**:142, 143
Mere-Ama (water goddess), **1**:6–7
Merina people, **3**:85
Merry Cemetery, **3**:105, 299
Mescalero Apache, *Isanaklesh Gotal* (The Feast), **2**:155–159
Mesmerism, **1**:348
Mesoamerican practices, **3**:185–186
Message from the Queen, **3**:171–173
Methodist Church, **1**:27, **2**:60, **3**:275, 300
Metrosexual look, **2**:22–23
Mexican celebrations and practices: birthday customs, **2**:85; courtship whistling, **2**:64–66; cutting the umbilical cord, **1**:112; *Dia de los Muertos*, **3**:52; Father's Day, **1**:139; food taboos during pregnancy, **1**:145–146; money dance, **2**:234–235; mourning color, **3**:302; Passion plays, **3**:208–209; pensions, **3**:231; *piñata*, **1**:283–286; placenta as folk medicine, **1**:124; same-sex marriage, **2**:285; Santa Muerte, **3**:246, 249–250; spontaneous shrines, **3**:269. *See also* Central American celebrations and practices; Latin American celebrations and practices
Miao people, **2**:317–318. *See also* Hmong people
Mice, as bedwetting cure, **1**:29
Micronesia, **2**:272
Mictlan (Aztec god), **3**:58
Mictlancihuatl (Aztec goddess), **3**:58
Middle Eastern celebrations and practices: female genital cutting, **2**:89–94; forced marriage, **2**:8; hair removal, **2**:112; *halva*, **3**:113–115; *Mehndi*, **2**:222, 223; Muslim modes of dress for women, **2**:128–130; Tomb of the Unknown Soldier, **3**:295; virginity testing, **2**:355–358. *See also* Egyptian

celebrations and practices; Iran; Iraq; Israel; Jordan; Palestine; Qatar; Saudi Arabia; Syria; Turkish celebrations and practices
Midsummer celebrations, **2**:182, 221
Midwives, **1**:5, 131; Aboriginal, **1**:355; Bulgarian, **1**:17–19, 63–64; celebration of, **1**:17–19; Guatemalan, **1**:334; kidnapped by fairies, **1**:77; in Kyrgyzstan, **1**:194; Mayan, **1**:112; Mexican, **1**:112; Southeast Asian, **1**:229; treatment of umbilical cord by, **1**:112, 114; Zulu, **1**:112
Mieszko I (Poland), **2**:80
Milk names (*ru ming*), **1**:91
Minghun (ghost marriages), **3**:221–222
Ministry for the Promotion of Women and Family (Cameroon), **2**:31
Minute's silence, **3**:173–175, 224
Mirila, **3**:175–177
Miscarriage, **3**:180, 216
Missing man formation, **3**:177–180; in motorsports, **3**:179–180
Missouri, shivaree/chivaree, **2**:257
Mistletoe, **1**:218–220
Mithras cult, **1**:42
Mizuko kuyo, **3**:180–183
Moccasin ceremony, **1**:8
MoD Lyneham, **3**:239
Mogi, **2**:61–62
Mohel, **1**:60
Moldova, **1**:16, 266, **3**:231. *See also* Eastern European celebrations and practices
Moment of silence. *See* Minute's silence
"Monday's Child," **1**:220–221
Money dance, **2**:233–235
Mongolia, **1**:266, **3**:24. *See also* Central Asian practices
Monstrous punishments for naughty children, **1**:221–226
Montenegro, **2**:15. *See also* Eastern European celebrations and practices; Yugoslav countries
Montjoie, **3**:73
Moon burial, **3**:267–268
Moonie weddings, **2**:235–237
Moon-Yuet (Full Moon), **1**:226–228
Moravian Church, **1**:95

Mormons (Church of Jesus Christ of Latter-day Saints), **1**:303, **2**:161–162
Morning sickness remedy, **1**:71
Moro reflex, **1**:321
Moroccan celebrations and practices, **2**:237–240; eating human placenta, **1**:123; government-approved baby names, **1**:153, 155; wedding dresses, **2**:373. *See also* North African celebrations and practices
Mortuary totem poles, **3**:183–185
Moses (biblical), **1**:62
Mosquito netting, **1**:74
Mosuo people, **2**:391–393
Mother Goose songs and rhymes, **1**:250
Mother Nature, **1**:13
Mother roasting, **1**:228–230
Mother's Day, **1**:138
Mothering Sunday, **1**:230–232
Mothers. *See* Women
Mounukyia, **1**:37
Mourning jewelry, **3**:286–288
Mourning rituals, Māori, **3**:281–283
Mozambique, *Pika* and *Nora*, **2**:253
Mrtva pocivala, **3**:177
Mummification, **3**:185–188; of heads, **3**:256
Mummy brown, **3**:188
Mundan ceremony, **1**:232–234
Mundana, **1**:232
Mursi tribe, **2**:193–194
Music: Alphorn, **3**:238; Dawn Songs, **2**:154; doom metal and funeral doom, **3**:62–63; for funerals, **3**:1–3, 97; in the *Isanaklesh Gotal* ritual, **2**:156–158; Punk Rock, **3**:99; for weddings, **2**:379–381
Muslim celebrations and practices. *See* Islamic celebrations and practices.
Mutterpass, **1**:237–238
My Home Library scheme, **1**:88
Myanmar (Burma): Buddhist death practices, **3**:20; ear-piercing ceremonies, **2**:83; Hmong names, **2**:136; mother roasting, **1**:228; neck elongation, **2**:243–244; ritual tattooing, **2**:275. *See also* Southeast Asian celebrations and practices

Naam karan naming ceremony **1**:311–313
Nachisungu, **2**:52–53
Naga sadhus, **2**:174
Nagashi-bina, **1**:185
Nahtwin, **2**:83
Nakisumo (Sumo of Tears), **1**:111
Namahage, **1**:223
Namahage Sedo Festival, **1**:224
Name days, **1**:241
Naming rituals: adult names, **2**:106; "ox names," **2**:100. *See also* Baby naming practices
Nana Kloweki (earth goddess), **2**:71
Naozot ceremony, **1**:246
Napoleon dance, **2**:234
National Matchmaking Association (Japan), **2**:251
National Mills Day (Netherlands), **3**:324
National mourning, **3**:191–183, 324
National Organization for Marriage (NOM), **2**:287
National Senior Olympics Games, **3**:254
National Service of Remembrance, **3**:223–224
National Tooth Fairy Day, **1**:325
National War Memorial (Canada), **3**:296
National War Memorial (New Zealand), **3**:296
Native American celebrations and practices: cradleboard, **1**:109–111; Death Dance, **3**:51; Dream catchers, **1**:119–122; eating human placenta, **1**:123; hair removal by, **2**:112; herbal remedies, **1**:30; Hopi naming rites, **1**:177–180; menstrual customs, **2**:225; mourning color, **3**:305; preserving the umbilical cord, **1**:174; same-sex marriage, **2**:285–286; scalping, **3**:256; vision quest, **2**:358–361. *See also* Apache ceremonies; Hopi traditions; Navajo traditions
Native American Grave Protection and Repatriation Act, **3**:142–152
Native Americans: Cheppewa tribe, **1**:119; Delaware Indians, **3**:53–56, 305; Ojibwa people, **1**:119–120
Native Hawaiian Religion, **1**:68
Nativity play, **1**:244–246

Navajo traditions: Blessingway, **1**:48–51; *kinaalda,* **2**:330
Navjote ceremony, **1**:246–249
Nazar boncugu, **1**:344
Nazca people, **3**:186
Nazism, **2**:380, **3**:171
Ndau people, **2**:253–254
Ndebele tribe, **2**:244–245
Ndwandewe clan, **2**:269
Neck elongation, **2**:243–245
Neo-pagan practices, **3**:111; croning ceremonies, **3**:44–46; handfasting, **2**:117–119; jumping over the broom, **2**:163–165. *See also* Pagan celebrations and practices; Wiccan funerals
Nepal: cremation, **3**:41; Father's Day, **1**:139; *halva,* **3**:114; killing of royal family, **1**:191; *Kumari* and *Deuki,* **1**:189–193; menstrual customs and taboos, **2**:225, 229–230; Pasni weaning ceremony, **1**:275–277; treatment of the placenta in **1**:67; vision quest, **2**:360. *See also* South Asian celebrations and practices
Netherlands celebrations and practices: anti-Santa Claus movement, **1**:297–298; assisted suicide, **3**:12; Assyrian populations in, **2**:10; *beschuit met muisjes,* **1**:31–32; cremation, **3**:42; Gap year, **2**:103; lovespoons, **2**:202; *Martinstag,* **3**:111; mourning color, **3**:304; National Mills Day, **3**:324; national mourning, **3**:324; parental leave, **1**:266; Passion plays, **3**:208; pensions, **3**:231; Remembrance of the Dead Day, **3**:225; Saint Nicholas, **1**:295–296; same-sex marriage, **2**:285; silver spoon, **1**:313; space burial, **3**:267; spontaneous shrines, **3**:269; *suikerboon,* **1**:32; University of the Third Age, **3**:307; windmills, **3**:323–325
Netsilingmiut people, **1**:79
Network of Aunties Association, **2**:31
New Brunswick, **1**:41
New Ireland, **3**:162–163
New Order Amish, **2**:25
New Year cards, **1**:39

New Year traditions, **2**:44–45
New Zealand celebrations and practices: "Abide With Me," **3**:1–3; Anzac Day, **3**:152, 236–237, 317; birth trees, **1**:33, 35; Gap year, **2**:103; Girl Guides, **1**:152; government-approved baby names, **1**:153, 155; jury duty, **2**:168; menstrual taboos, **2**:230; National War Memorial, **3**:296; parental leave, **1**:266, 267; pensions, **3**:228, 231–234; Remembrance Day, **3**:223; riderless horse, **3**:236–237; ritual tattooing, **2**:272, 273–274; same-sex marriage, **2**:285; Steiner schools, **1**:318, 320; *Tangihanga*, **3**:281–283; treatment of the placenta, **1**:69–70; twenty-first birthday, **2**:344–345; University of the Third Age, **3**:307; wake, **3**:313; wedding dresses, **2**:374. *See also* Māori people
Newbery Medal, **1**:88
Newfoundland, **1**:41
Ngaben, **3**:193–196
Ngilai, **1**:79
Niagara Falls, **3**:279
Nicholas (saint). *See* Saint Nicholas
Niger: arranged marriage, **2**:7; Wodaabe courtship dance and festival, **2**:383–386. *See also* African celebrations and practices; West African celebrations and practices
Nigerian celebrations and practices: breast ironing, **2**:30; burial customs, **3**:128; cutting the umbilical cord, **1**:113; eating calabash chalk, **1**:71; fattening room seclusion, **2**:86–89; female genital cutting, **2**:93; migration to Nigeria, **1**:1; money dance, **2**:234; *Sallah*, **2**:30; scarification, **2**:294–295; *Sharo*, **2**:307–309; treatment of the placenta in, **1**:68–69; *Yankan gishiri*, **1**:362; *Zur-zur*, **1**:362. *See also* African celebrations and practices; West African celebrations and practices
Nikolaustag, **1**:222
Nine-Nights, **3**:196–198

Nirwaan (*nirvana*) ceremony, **2**:132
Nkumbi, **2**:245–247
Nomkhubulwane fertility festival, **2**:356
Nora, **2**:253
Nordic napping, **1**:249–250
Norse myths, **1**:135
North African celebrations and practices: *Mehndi*, **2**:222, 223; *shabka*, **2**:302. *See also* Algerian celebrations and practices; Egyptian celebrations and practices; Moroccan celebrations and practices; Sudan
North America, First Nation groups in, **3**:117
North American celebrations and practices: "Abide With Me," **3**:1–3; Groaning Cheese and Groaning Cake, **1**:166–169; hair removal, **2**:112; *halva*, **3**:113; horseshoes, **2**:142; lotus birthing, **1**:210; mourning color, **3**:302; nursery rhymes, **1**:250; Santa Claus, **1**:296; teething remedies, **1**:328–329; Tomb of the Unknown Soldier, **3**:295. *See also* Canadian celebrations and practices; United States celebrations and practices
Northern Ireland: choosing Options, **2**:56–58; political assassinations, **3**:269; Remembrance Day, **3**:223; wedding traditions, **2**:32
Norwegian celebrations and practices: Girl Guides, **1**:152; jury duty, **2**:165; parental leave, **1**:265; retirement and pensions, **3**:229; *Russefeiring*, **2**:281–283; same-sex marriage, **2**:285; secular confirmation, **2**:300; wedding customs, **2**:370, 2:373; wedding spoons, **2**:202. *See also* Saami people; Scandinavian celebrations and practices
Nose buttering, **1**:41
Nova Scotia, **1**:41
Nuba tribe, **2**:295
Nuer tribe, **2**:98
Nuliayuq (Inuit spirit of the sea), **1**:11
Nursery rhymes, **1**:250–253
Nurses, pinning ceremony, **2**:382–383
Nwaotam (placenta-related festival), **1**:69

Nyabutan ceremony, **1**:253–254
Nyakyusa tribe, **3**:51
Nyumba Ntobhu, **2**:247–249
Nzu, **1**:71

Oak trees, **3**:328
Obama, Barack, **2**:76–77
Obando fertility dance, **1**:255–256
Oberammergau Passion Play, **3**:207–208
Oberon's Palace (Herrick), **1**:325
Obituaries, **3**:199–200
Oblievačka (Oblévačka), **2**:79
Obon (Bon), **3**:126–127
Oceania, Tomb of the Unknown Soldier, **3**:295
Odd Fellows (Oddfellows) society, **3**:96, 128
Oie Houney, **3**:112
Ojibwa people, **1**:119–120
Okuizome, **1**:259–260
Old Order Amish, **2**:25
Ombliguera, **1**:108
Omiai, **2**:251–252
Omiya-mairi, **1**:174
Onabasulu tribe, **2**:149
Onbashira festival, **2**:197–199
One-child policy, **1**:256–258
Onge people, **1**:57–58
Operation Mercy India (OM), **1**:118
Origami cranes, **1**:185
Orkney Islands, **1**:293, **2**:28, **3**:261
Orthodox Catholic Church, **3**:66
Orthodox Church celebrations and practices: funeral practices, **3**:107; Name days, **1**:241; Saturday of Souls, **3**:251–253. See also Eastern Orthodox Church celebrations and practices; Greek Orthodox Church celebrations and practices; Russian Orthodox Church celebrations and practices
Oshichiya Meimeishiki, **1**:259
Ososo Matsuri (Vagina Festival), **1**:279
Ossuaries, **3**:103, 200–203
Oto, **1**:149
Our Lady of Salambao, **1**:256–257
Overtoun Bridge (Scotland), **3**:279–280
Ovoo (cairn), **3**:24

Pachamama (earth goddess), **1**:69
Pacific Northwest, lip plugs, **2**:191
Padaung people, **2**:243
Padmasambhava, **1**:210
Padrinos, **1**:125, **2**:178. See also Godparents
Pagan celebrations and practices: baby welcoming, **1**:24–25; croning ceremonies, **3**:44–46; elderling ceremonies, **3**:44–46; jumping over the broom, **2**:163–165; Saging ceremonies, **3**:46; saining, **1**:293–294. See also Neo-pagan practices; Wiccan funerals
Pakistan: burqa wearing, **2**:130; entering the *Bashali*, **1**:128–132; forced marriage, **2**:8; *halva*, **3**:115; *Mehndi*, **2**:222, 223; menstrual customs, **2**:225; Zoroastrianism, **3**:338. See also South Asian celebrations and practices
Palaa ritual, **2**:314
Palestine, **1**:235, **2**:302. See also Middle Eastern celebrations and practices
Palm Sunday, **2**:188
Pan American Health Organization (PAHO), **1**:86
Pan dei Morti, **3**:265
Pancake Day, **3**:66
Pang-sai, **1**:323–324
Panikhida, **3**:252
Pan-Indian Movement **1**:120
Pantomime, **1**:261–265
Panuda, **1**:65
Pão de Deus, **3**:264–365
Paoli Amish, **2**:25
Papua New Guinea: couvade, **1**:104, 106; cutting the umbilical cord, **1**:113; endocannibalism, **3**:76–77; finger amputation, **3**:90–91; initiation by semen transferal, **2**:148–152; *Malagan* ceremonies, **3**:162–164; mummification, **3**:185, 187; ritual tattooing, **2**:275; ritualized sex, **2**:341–344; scarification, **2**:293–296; urethral subincision, **2**:349–350
Paraguay, **3**:247
Parental leave, **1**:265–267
Paris, *Le Bal des Débutantes*, **2**:97

Parsley, 3:96
Party games, 1:273–275
Paschal (saint), 1:256
Paschal eggs. *See* Easter eggs
Pasni weaning ceremony, 1:275–277
Passing bells, 3:205–206
Passion plays, 3:206–209
Paternal/Paternity leave, 1:267, 270–272. *See also* Parental leave
Pauper's funeral, 3:209–211
Peace Memorial Park, 1:185
Peace Pledge Union, 3:316
Pebermø (pepper maid), 2:26
Pebersvend (pepper man), 2:26
Pelebon, 3:193–196
Penda idols, 1:13–14
Penile subincision, 2:347–351
Penis. *See* Phallus
The Penis Festival, 1:277–278
Pennsylvania Dutch practices, 3:93; bed-courtship, 2:24–25
Pensions and Retirement, 3:228–236
Pentecostal church, 1:26, 27
Persia, 1:42. *See also* Iran
Personalized hearses, 3:211–213
Peruvian practices: menstrual taboos, 2:230; mummification, 3:185; shrunken heads, 3:255–257. *See also* South American celebrations and practices
Peterson, Frederick, 2:64
Phallus: broomstick as, 2:163–164; Cerne Abbas Giant, 1:75–76; used in chisungu ceremony, 2:53; Maypole as, 2:221
Phallus festivals, 1:277–280; Clean (or Dirty) Monday (Tyrnavos, Greece), 1:279–280; *Kanamara Matsuri* (Festival of the Steel Phallus), 1:278–279; The Penis Festival (Tagata Jinja), 1:277–278
Philippine celebrations and practices: Aguman Sanduk Festival, 1:105; breastfeeding, 1:56; crucifixion rituals, 3:47–50; Filipino debut/Cotillion, 2:95–97; *hampas-palayak* or *pukpok palayok*, 1:285; money dance, 2:234; mother roasting, 1:228; Obando fertility dance, 1:256–257; Passion plays, 3:208; piñatas, 1:285; tooth-filing, 2:338; twenty-first birthday, 2:345. *See also* Southeast Asian celebrations and practices
Physician Assisted Suicide (PAS), 3:11
Pidyon haben (Redemption of the firstborn), 1:280–283
Pidyon habit ceremony (Redemption of the firstborn daughter), 1:282
Pika, 2:253
Pilgrimage, 2:173–175
Piñata, 1:274, 283–286
Pinning ceremony, 2:382–383
Pin-the-tail-on-the-donkey, 1:274
Pirts (*Pirtiņa*), 1:204
Pisanki, 3:66–67, 334
Pius X (pope), 1:143
Pius XII (pope), 1:201
Pizho idols, 1:13–14
Placenta: burying of, 1:25, 67–70, 235; eating, 1:123–125; in folk medicine, 1:124
Placentophagy, 1:123–125
Plastination, 3:213–216
Pogacha, 1:65
Poison garden, 3:96
Polish celebrations and practices: All Souls' Day, 3:8, 265; *Andrzejki* (St. Andrew's Eve), 2:3–5; birthstones, 1:44; Easter eggs (*pysanka*), 3:66; first communion, 1:144; government-approved baby names, 1:153, 155; Hallowe'en, 3:334; *Katarzynki* gingerbread, 2:4; *Lanie wosku* (pouring wax), 2:4; *Matura*, 2:15–16; Nordic napping, 1:250; *Pani Mloda* (money dance), 2:233; pensions, 3:230; *Polterabend*, 2:254; *Śmigus-Dyngus* (Dyngus Day), 2:79–81; spring celebration in, 1:16; *Talerzyki*, 2:4; *Zaduszki* (*dzień zaduszny*), 3:333–335. *See also* Eastern European celebrations and practices
Polterabend, 2:254–258
Polter-Lucia celebration, 2:257

Polyandry, **2**:258–261
Polygyny, **2**:259, 261–263
Polygyny-fertility hypothesis, **2**:262
Polynesia: menstrual customs, **2**:224–225; ritual tattooing, **2**:272–273; urethral subincision, **2**:347, 349
Poppies: black, against imperialism of warfare, **3**:317; purple, for animals killed in warfare, **3**:317; red, as symbol of remembrance, **3**:314–318; white, as symbol of peace, **3**:316
Poppy Appeal, **3**:314–316
Poppy Day, **3**:223
Poppy etiquette, **3**:315–316
Portugal: Father's Day, **1**:139; Girl Guides, **1**:152; government-approved baby names, **1**:153; money dance, **2**:234; mourning color, **3**:302; ossuaries, **3**:201–202; *Pão de Deus*, **3**:264–365; pensions, **3**:230; same-sex marriage, **2**:285; *Santora* cake, **3**:264; soul cakes, **3**:263
Post-traumatic stress disorder, **2**:31
Poto, **1**:71
Potty training, **1**:286–288
Povitica, **2**:263–264
Prayers: for baby's gender, **1**:187; at baptisms, **1**:29; in *bismallah* ceremony, **1**:47; in Blessingway ceremony, **1**:49; for the dead, **3**:7; in *Dia de los Muertos* celebrations, **3**:59; for the dying, **3**:105; at Filipino debut, **2**:96; at funeral services, **3**:273; Hindu, **1**:175–177, 275–276; Hindu death rituals, **3**:118; Islamic, **1**:194, **3**:189; Jewish, **3**:130, 132; at a Jewish wedding, **2**:161; during labor and childbirth, **1**:211; for a new baby, **1**:234, 312; for the new mother and baby, **1**:209; at *pidyon haben* ceremony, **1**:282; by pregnant women, **1**:312; in *Quinceañera* mass, **2**:186; to San La Muerte, **3**:247; at Setsubun, **1**:308; Sikh, **2**:70; at Sikh wedding, **2**:313–314; on the Stations of the Cross, **3**:275–277; to the sun, **1**:179; in *upanayana* ritual, **1**:338; at weddings, **2**:13, 59–60; in Zoroastrianism, **1**:246–248
Pre's Rock, **3**:270
Pregnancy and Infant Loss Remembrance Day, **3**:216–218
Pregnancy yoga, **1**:289–290
Pregnant women: Blessingway ceremony for, **1**:50–51; classes for, **1**:74; eating calabash chalk, **1**:71; food for, **1**:166–169; food taboos, **1**:71, 89–90; 144–147; in Malaysia, **1**:79; targeted by trows, **1**:78. *See also* Women
Prehistoric Burial Cairns of Balnuaran of Clava, **3**:23
Prenatal care, **1**:72, 73, 237–238
Pre-Raphaelite Brotherhood (PRB), **1**:136, 137
Presbyterian church, **1**:27, **2**:60
Prince Edward Island, **1**:41
Prinsessornas Kokbok, **1**:35
Prinsesstårta, **1**:35
Prophet's Mosque (Medina), **2**:116
Prostitution, **1**:116–118, 193, 278, **2**:392–393, **3**:249, 310
Protestant Church celebrations and practices, **3**:35–36; funeral cakes, **3**:92; objection to plastination, **3**:214; wedding ceremonies, **2**:60–61. *See also* Christian celebrations and practices; Christian churches
Psychoprophylaxis, **1**:201
Public flogging, **2**:307–309
Puerto Rico, **1**:40–1
pukpok palayok, **1**:285
Pumi (Primi) people, **2**:50–51
Punk rock, **3**:99
Punkie Night, **3**:112
Pure Brightness Festival, **3**:219
Puritans, **2**:25
Purity ball, **2**:264–266
Pussy willows, **3**:253; spanking with, **2**:80, 81
Putting on Moccasins, **1**:8
Pygmy people, **2**:245
Pysanka, **3**:66–67, 334

Qatar, **2**:304. *See also* Middle Eastern celebrations and practices
Qinghai-Tibetan Plateau, **3**:259–260
Qingming Festival, **3**:219–222, 329
Qiqiqtamiut Inuit, **1**:10
Quarter Days, **1**:293
Quccija (il-Quccija), **1**:291–292
Quebec, **1**:40. *See also* Canada
Queen Charlotte Islands, **3**:184
Quinceañera, **2**:96, 185–188
Qur'an, **2**:128–129, 242, 261

Radonitsa, **3**:253
RAF Lyneham, **3**:239
RAG Week (Raising and Giving Week), **2**:267–268
Reagan, Ronald, eulogy on the *Challenger*, **3**:81–83
Reed Dancing Chastity Ceremony, **2**:269–272
Reifeprüfung, **2**:15
Religious holidays, birthdays of religious figures, **1**:43
Religious milestones, **1**:42. *See also* Baptism and Christening; Confirmation; First Communion; Holy Communion
Remembrance Day, **3**:152, 174, 223–226, 296, 314–315
Remembrance Sunday, **3**:2, 152, 174, 223–227, 314, 316; Early Day Motion, **3**:226–227
Renaming procedures, **1**:11
Reproduction, government control over, **1**:256–258
Requiem mass, **3**:8
Reschtach, **2**:28–30
Reseau National des Associations de Tantines (RENATA), **2**:31
Resomation, **3**:5–6
Retirement and Pensions, **3**:228–236, 308
Retirement homes: Denville Hall and Brinsworth House, **3**:56–57; Royal Hospital Chelsea, **3**:26–29
Riderless horse, **3**:236–237
Rite for the Blessing of a Child in the Womb, **1**:99
Rites of passage. *See* Boys' coming-of-age ceremonies; Chinese coming-of-age ceremonies; Coming-of-age ceremonies; Girls' coming-of-age ceremonies
Ritual body mutilation, finger amputation, **3**:90–91
Ritual sacrifice, **1**:235, **2**:72, 99, 115
Ritual servitude, female, **1**:116–118, 331. *See also Devadasi* system; *Kumari* and *Deuki*
Ritual tattooing, **2**:272–277
Ritualized homosexuality (RHS), **2**:148
Ritzenthaler, Robert, **2**:64
River Ganges, **1**:233
Roma celebrations and practices: arranged marriages, **2**:37–38; forced marriage, **2**:8; jumping over the broom, **2**:163–165; virginity testing, **2**:357
Roma folklore, **2**:44
Roman Catholic Church. *See* Catholic Church; Catholic Church celebrations and practices
Romanian celebrations and practices: eating the ashes of the dead, **3**:69; funeral traditions, **3**:237–239; The Great Passing, **3**:105–107; *koliva*, **3**:135; love divination, **2**:3; *martisor* (March celebration), **1**:16; Merry Cemetery, **3**:299; parental leave, **1**:266; *Pysanka*, **3**:66; spitting on babies, **1**:316. *See also* Eastern European celebrations and practices
Rosemary, **3**:96, 317
Round Birthdays, **1**:43
Roy, Sandip, **2**:76–77
Royal Air Force (RAF), **3**:178
Royal British Legion, **3**:314–316
Royal Hospital Chelsea, **3**:26–29
Royal Maundy Service, **3**:164–167
Royal Wootton Bassett, England, **3**:239–241
Rumspringa, **2**:24, 277–280
Running Round (*Amphidromia*) ritual, **1**:23
Rushbearing ceremonies, **1**:164–166
Russefeiring, **2**:281–283
Russia, Assyrian populations in, **2**:10
Russian celebrations and practices: Baba Yaga, **1**:223; birthstones, **1**:44, 46; love divination, **2**:3; mourning color, **3**:302; national mourning, **3**:192; *Polterabend*, **2**:254; *Pysanka*, **3**:66; Saint Nicholas, **1**:294; space burial,

3:267; water births, **1**:347. *See also* Eastern European celebrations and practices; Eastern Orthodox Church celebrations and practices; Russian Orthodox Church celebrations and practices; Soviet Union

Russian Orthodox Church: name days, **1**:241; opposition to cremation, **3**:44; *Radonitsa*, **3**:253; wedding dresses, **2**:374

Saami people (Sami, Samer, or Lapps), **1**:4–7
Sacred ceremonies, **1**:37
Sacred severance, **1**:113
Sadhus, **2**:174
Saging ceremonies, **3**:46
Saining, **1**:293–294
Saint Aidan, **1**:165
Saint Apollonia, **1**:326
Saint Brigid, **2**:189
Saint Catherine of Alexandria, **2**:320–321
Saint Claire, **1**:256
Saint Francis of Assisi, **1**:245
Saint Jerome, **1**:45
Saint John the Baptist, **1**:26, **2**:200
Saint Martin of Tours, **3**:111
Saint Nicholas, **1**:294–298. *See also* Father Christmas; Santa Claus
Saint Odilo of Cluny, **3**:7
Saint Oswald, **1**:165
Saint Oswald's Day, **1**:165
Saint Oswald's Hand, **1**:165
Saint Patrick, **2**:189
Saint Walpurga's feast day, **1**:217
Saint Wilfrid, **3**:278
Saints: feast days of, **1**:241; folk, **3**:246–250
Sakalava royal death traditions, **3**:243–245
Sake, **1**:224, **2**:63, 291–292
Sallekhanā, **3**:245–246
Salting the baby, **1**:64–65
Sambatra mass circumcision festival, **1**:298–300
Sambia tribe, **2**:148, 149–152
Samburu tribe, **2**:350
Same-sex marriage, **2**:285–291
Samhain, **2**:219, **3**:109–111
Samoan practices: hair removal, **2**:112; ritual tattooing, **2**:272–273
San La Muerte (Saint Death), **3**:246–249
San Pascualito, **3**:248
San Pedro Cutud Lenten Rites, **3**:48–49
San-san-kudo (*san san kudo; sansan-kudo*), **2**:291–293
Santa Claus, **1**:296. *See also* Father Christmas; Saint Nicholas
Santa Muerte, **3**:246, 249–250
Sar-akka (childbirth goddess), **1**:5–6
Sarung buaian, **1**:300–301
Sateré-Mawé tribe, **2**:41–43
Sati (*suttee*), **3**:43
Saturday of Souls, **3**:135, 251–253
Saudi Arabia, **1**:56. *See also* Middle Eastern celebrations and practices
Scalping, **3**:256
Scandinavian celebrations and practices: cairns, **3**:24; changeling beliefs, **1**:77; kangaroo care, **1**:183; nursery rhymes, **1**:250, 251; parental leave, **1**:265; protection from fairies, **1**:78; secular confirmation, **2**:300; trolls, **1**:78; University of the Third Age, **3**:307; wedding cakes, **2**:370. *See also* Danish celebrations and practices; Finnish celebrations and practices; Norwegian celebrations and practices; Saami people; Swedish celebrations and practices
Scarification, **2**:98–101, 253, 293–296
Schmidt Sting Pain Index, **2**:41–42
Schoolies Week, **2**:283–284
Schuhplattler, **2**:297–299
Schwuhplattler Group, **2**:299
Scottish celebrations and practices: belief in the evil eye, **1**:343; Beltane, **2**:219; blackening the bride, **2**:28–30; Burning the Clavie, **2**:44–45; cairns, **3**:23; changeling beliefs, **1**:78; christening gown, **1**:95; Gretna Green, **2**:104–105, 210; handfasting, **2**:117–118; hanselling, **1**:351; Lady Haig Poppy Factory, **3**:315; Lanimer Day, **1**:353; Nordic napping, **1**:250; passing bells, **3**:205–206; saining, **1**:293–294; same-sex marriage, **2**:285; silver spoon, **1**:351; wedding traditions, **2**:32; wetting the baby's head, **1**:351; Whuppity Scoorie, **1**:351–353; yew trees, **3**:328

Scouts and Scouting, **1**:152–153, 302–304
Scriptural Way of the Cross, **3**:276
Scroggleve, **1**:304
Scroggling the Holly, **1**:304–305
Sebou, **1**:305–307
Secular coming of age, **2**:300–302
Secular confirmation, **2**:300–302
Sedreh-pushi (*Sedreh-pooshi*), **1**:246
Seelënnacht, **3**:9
Seijin no Hi (Coming of Age Day), **2**:61–64
Seijin-shiki, **2**:61
Semen practices, **2**:148
Senegal, **2**:93. *See also* West Africa
Senior Sporting Events, **3**:254–255
Senofo tribe, **2**:294
Sentimental jewelry, **3**:288
September 11 attacks, **3**:2, 174, 270
September Romance, **2**:239
Serbian celebrations and practices: *koliva*, **3**:135; Saturday of Souls, **3**:251–253. *See also* Eastern European celebrations and practices; Yugoslav countries
Serbian Orthodox traditions, Slava, **1**:242
Servia, *Matura*, **2**:15
Setsubun (Children's bean-throwing festival), **1**:307–309
Sex taboos, **2**:53
Sexual intercourse: after childbirth, **1**:104–106, 197, 361; on the Cerne Abbas Giant, **1**:76; with a *deuki*, **1**:192; with a *devadasi*, **1**:117–18; with an incubus, **1**:79, 222; in marriage, **1**:175; while menstruating, **2**:228; in Moonie weddings, **2**:236; during pregnancy, **1**:90; ritualized, **2**:341–344; with a succubus, **1**:79; with a *trokosi*, **1**:331–332
Sexually transmitted disease (STD), **1**:118, 278, 363, **2**:248, 349. *See also* HIV/AIDS
Shabka, **2**:302–305
Shalaluo (skirt-changing ceremony), **2**:51
Shanghai Marriage Market, **2**:305–307
Shared nursing, **1**:57. *See also* Breastfeeding
Sharo, **2**:307–309
Shashu, **1**:69

Shengxiao (Chinese Zodiac), **1**:310–311
Shinbyu (*shin-byu; shinpyu*), **2**:83, 310–311
Shinerama, **2**:268
Shinto traditions: deities, **1**:214; funeral rites, **3**:123; *Kanchu Misogi*, **2**:110–111; *Onbashira* festival, **2**:197–199; *Ososo Matsuri*, **1**:279; thanksgiving ritual, **1**:174
Shipibo tribe, **2**:261
Shirin-i-grifgan, **2**:1–2
Shiva, **3**:132
Shivaree/chivaree, **2**:257
Shona people, **2**:195
Shortbread, pinned to christening gowns, **1**:94
Shoutao, **1**:36
Shrines, spontaneous, **3**:269–271
Shrove Tuesday, **3**:66
Shrovetide, **1**:293
Shrunken heads, **3**:255–257
Siad, Fatima, **2**:93
Siberia, **1**:310. *See also* Russian celebrations and practices
Sicily, *Fidanzamenti* and *Fidanzati in casa*, **2**:94–95
Sierra Leone, **1**:113, 145. *See also* West African celebrations and practices
Sikh celebrations and practices: *Amrit shanchar*, **2**:70; baby rites and *naam karan* naming ceremony, **1**:311–313; beards, **2**:22; British weddings, **2**:32; cremation, **3**:42; *Dastaar Bandi* (*Dastar Bandi*), **2**:69; death customs, **3**:257–259; Diwali, **2**:73–74, 77; Five Ks, **2**:69–70, **3**:258; forced marriage, **2**:8; wedding ceremonies, **2**:312–315; women wearing turbans, **2**:69
Silver Spoon, **1**:313–314, 351
Simnel cake, **1**:231
Simplicity parenting, **1**:314–315
Sin eating, **3**:92
Singapore; indigenous medicine, **1**:181; jury duty, **2**:167; missing man formation, **3**:179; Remembrance Day, **3**:223. *See also* Southeast Asian celebrations and practices
Singings, **2**:278

Singles' Day, **2**:315–316
Sinterklaas, **1**:296
Sisters' Meal Festival, **2**:317–318
Skirt-changing ceremony (*shalaluo*), **2**:51
Sky burials, **3**:259–263
Slå kitten af tønden, **1**:285
Slava, **1**:242
Slava cake, **1**:242
Slovakian calendar, **1**:241
Slovakian celebrations and practices: love divination, **2**:3; *Matura*, **2**:15; mourning color, **3**:302; *Oblievačka*, **2**:79; spontaneous shrines, **3**:269. See also Eastern European celebrations and practices
Slovenian celebrations and practices: childhood vaccinations, **1**:85–86; danse macabre, **3**:52; *Matura*, **2**:15; *mrtva pocivala*, **3**:177; parental leave, **1**:266; Parkelj, **1**:222–223; same-sex marriage, **2**:285; University of the Third Age, **3**:307. See also Eastern European celebrations and practices; Yugoslav countries
Slow parenting movement, **1**:314–315
Śmigus-Dyngus (Dyngus Day), **2**:79–81
Soccer games, **3**:2
Social Cash Transfer Programme, **3**:231
Sock dances, **2**:319–320
Sock garlands, **2**:318–319
Sockenkrantz, **2**:318–319
Sokacs, **2**:191
Solomon Islands, **1**:33, **2**:296
Somalia, **2**:89, 91. See also Sub-Saharan African celebrations and practices
Song, in the *Isanaklesh Gotal* ritual, **2**:156–158
Sor Sai Karchey, **1**:229
Soul bells, **3**:205
Soul cakes and soul breads, **3**:263–266
Souling, **3**:263–264
Soulmas Day, **3**:6
South African celebrations and practices: boxes for babies, **1**:74; breast ironing, **2**:30; breastfeeding, **1**:56; cutting the umbilical cord, **1**:112; Girl Guides, **1**:152; jury duty, **2**:167; neck elongation, **2**:244–245; same-sex marriage, **2**:285; space burial, **3**:267; virginity testing, **2**:356; Xhosa circumcision, **2**:387–389
South American celebrations and practices: All Souls' Day, **3**:9; belief in the evil eye, **1**:343; eating human placenta, **1**:123; hair removal, **2**:112; kangaroo care, **1**:183; lip plugs, **2**:191–195; polygyny, **2**:261; potty training, **1**:286; *San La Muerte*, **3**:246–249; Tomb of the Unknown Soldier, **3**:295; University of the Third Age, **3**:307; urethral subincision, **2**:350. See also Argentinian celebrations and practices; Bolivian practices; Brazilian practices; Ecuadorean practices; French Guiana; Peruvian practices; Uruguay; Venezuela
South Asian celebrations and practices: belief in the evil eye, **1**:343–344; forced marriage, **2**:8. See also Afghani celebrations and practices; Asian celebrations and practices; Bangladesh; Indian celebrations and practices; Nepal; Pakistan; Sri Lanka
South Korean celebrations and practices: Black Day, **2**:315–316; *Gwallye*, **2**:105–106; Moonie weddings, **2**:235; *Waldkindergärten*, **1**:341; wedding cakes, **2**:372. See also Asian celebrations and practices; Korean celebrations and practices
South Pacific, **1**:46
Southeast Asian celebrations and practices, **3**:85; *Mehndi*, **2**:224; mother roasting, **1**:228–230; potty training, **1**:286. See also Asian celebrations and practices; Cambodian practices; Indonesian celebrations and practices; Laos; Malaysian celebrations and practices; Myanmar; Philippine celebrations and practices; Singapore; Thailand; Vietnam
Southern Africa, *Lobola*, **2**:195–197
Soviet Union, **1**:201. See also Russian celebrations and practices

Space burial, **3**:267–268
Spanish celebrations and practices: *Dia de los Muertos*, **3**:52; *El Salto del Colacho*, **1**:126–128; Father's Day, **1**:139; government-approved baby names, **1**:153; grave rental, **3**:102; mourning color, **3**:302, 304; ossuaries, **3**:201; Passion plays, **3**:206, 208; parental leave, **1**:66; pensions, **3**:230; Perez Mouse (Ratón Perez), **1**:326; same-sex marriage, **2**:285
Spitting on babies, **1**:316–317
Spontaneous shrines, **3**:269–271
Spring celebrations, **1**:16, 307–309; *Tết Nguyên đan*, **3**:288–292
Spring cleaning rituals, **1**:13
Sprinkling cake, **1**:317–318
Sprinklings (second baby showers), **1**:23
Sri Guru Granth Sahib, **1**:311–312, **2**:313–314, **3**:258–259
Sri Lanka: Buddhist practices, **3**:18, 20; Passion plays, **3**:208; polyandry, **2**:258, 259; virginity testing, **2**:357. *See also* South Asian celebrations and practices
Sri Santeswar temple, **1**:127
St. Andrew's Eve (*Andrzejki*), **2**:3–5
St. Basil's Day, **3**:136
St. Brigid's Day, **1**:16
St. Catherine's Day (*Katarzynki*), **2**:3–4, 320–322
St. Dwynwen's Day, **2**:322–323
St. John's Day, **2**:200
St. Lazarus's Day, **2**:186
St. Martin's Day, **3**:111
St. Mary of the Purification church, **1**:51–52
St. Mary's church in Hanwell, **1**:96
St. Nicholas Day, **1**:222
St. Sylvester's Day, **2**:183
St. Theodore Saturday **3**:136
St. Theodore's Day (*Todorovden*), **2**:40
State funerals, **3**:271–275
Stations of the Cross, **3**:275–277
Statutory Maternity Pay (SMP), **1**:267
Steam baths, **1**:228–229, **1**:333
Steampunk, **3**:100
Steiner schools, **1**:318–320
Steiner Waldorf Schools Fellowship (SWSF), **1**:318

Sterilization, forced, **1**:256, 257
Stillbirth, **3**:180, 216, 313
Stiller Tag (Silent Day), **3**:225
Student Zone, **2**:209
Sub-Saharan African celebrations and practices: fattening room seclusion, **2**:89; *Yankan Gishiri*, **1**:362–363; *Zur-zur* (*zur zur; zurzur*), **1**:362–363. *See also* Central African Republic; Chad; Djibouti; Eritrea; Gambia; Guinea-Bissau; Somalia; Sudan; Zimbabwe
Succubus, **1**:79
Sudan: burying the placenta, **1**:235; female genital cutting, **2**:89, 91; lip plugs, **2**:191; scarification, **2**:294–295. *See also* North African celebrations and practices; Sub-Saharan African celebrations and practices
Sudden infant death syndrome (SIDS), **3**:216
Sudreh, **1**:246, 248
Suicide landmarks, **3**:278–280
Suikerboon, **1**:32
Sukusendal, **1**:78
Sumatra, **2**:142
Summer National Senior Games, **3**:254
Summer solstice, **2**:199–201
Sun God offerings, **1**:254
Sünnet, **2**:323–325
Sunrise Ceremony, **2**:326–331
Sunset Service, **3**:240
Suriname, **3**:231
Surrogacy, baby showers for, **1**:24
Swaddling, **1**:320–322
Swaziland, **2**:269–272, 356, **3**:231
Sweden, Assyrian populations in, **2**:10
Swedish celebrations and practices, **1**:4; birthday cakes, **1**:35; Dala horse, **1**:115–116; funeral cakes, **3**:92; funeral candies, **3**:93; government-approved baby names, **1**:153, **1**:155; lullabies, **1**:215; *Martinstag*, **3**:111; Maypoles, **2**:221; Nordic napping, **1**:249; parental leave, **1**:265; pensions, **3**:229; royal family, **1**:35; same-sex marriage, **2**:285; wedding cakes, **2**:370–371. *See also* Scandinavian celebrations and practices

Swiss celebrations and practices: assisted suicide, **3**:12–13; birth trees, **1**:33; danse macabre, **3**:52; *Klausjagen*, **1**:296; *Martinstag*, **3**:111; *Matura*, **2**:15; parental leave, **1**:266; *Polterabend*, **2**:254
Sympathetic pregnancy, **1**:104
Syrian celebrations and practices: Assyrian betrothal and weddings, **2**:9–14; Childermas, **1**:84; forced marriage, **2**:8; *halva*, **3**:115. *See also* Middle Eastern celebrations and practices

Taapu, **1**:109
Tahara, **1**:235. *See also* Circumcision
Tahneek ritual, **1**:234
Taishen (God of the Pregnant Womb), **1**:90
Taiwan: baby racing, **1**:21; breastfeeding, **1**:56; pregnancy and birth rituals, **1**:89–93; *Qingming* Festival, **3**:219; ritual tattooing, **2**:276; space burial, **3**:267. *See also* Asian celebrations and practices
Takht e khina, **2**:2
Talerzyki, **2**:4
Talmud, **2**:21
Tama the Cat, **3**:123
Tana Toraja people, **3**:155–157
Tangihanga, **3**:281–283
Tango no Sekkui (Feast of the Banners), **1**:184
Tantrics, **2**:55–56
Tanzania, **1**:46, **3**:71; death dance, **3**:51; female genital cutting, **2**:93; food taboos during pregnancy, **1**:145; lip plugs, **2**:193; *Nyumba Ntobhu*, **2**:247–249; scarification, **2**:295; spitting on babies, **1**:316; tooth sharpening, **2**:143. *See also* Maasai traditions
Taoism, **3**:329; *Zhongyuan* Festival, **3**:329
"Taps," **3**:152–155
Tattoing, ritual, **2**:272–277
Tawaf, **2**:114–115
Tawba people, **2**:100
Taweez, **1**:234
Taxidermy, **3**:283–285
Tear bottles, **3**:286
Tear catchers, **3**:286

Teething remedies, **1**:327–330
Teknonymy, **2**:138
Templar effigies (Temple Church), **3**:298
Temple Church (London), **3**:298
Tết Nguyên đan, **3**:288–292
Thailand: Buddhist practices, **3**:18, 20; Fire-hair shaving and Khwan ceremonies, **1**:140–142; Hmong names, **2**:136; *Luk Thep* dolls, **1**:358; mother roasting, **1**:228; mourning color, **3**:302; neck elongation, **2**:243–244; treatment of the placenta in, **1**:69, 124. *See also* Southeast Asian celebrations and practices
Thaipusam, **2**:333–335
Thanksgiving of Women after Childbirth, **1**:98, 100
Theravada Buddhism, **2**:310–312, **3**:18. *See also* Buddhism
Threading, **2**:112
Thula Baba Box, **1**:74
Thyme, **3**:96
Tiananmen Square protests, **3**:220
Tibetan Buddhism, **3**:18. *See also* Buddhism
Tibetan practices: Buddhist death practices, **3**:19–20; polyandry, **2**:258, 259; sky burials, **3**:259–263. *See also* Tibetan pregnancy and birth customs
Tibetan pregnancy and birth customs, **1**:323–324; one month leaving home, **1**:324; *pang-sai*, **1**:323–324; *tshe dbang* ceremony, **1**:323
Tikinagan, **1**:109
Tipos'asna, **1**:178
Tiv people, **2**:295
Tlingit tribe, **3**:183–185
Tobasichine (Child of Water), **1**:8
Toda people, **2**:258
Todorovden (St. Theodore's Day), **2**:40
Togo: breast ironing, **2**:30; female ritual servitude (*trokosi*), **1**:330–333. *See also* West African celebrations and practices
Toilet training. *See* Potty training
Tolling the Devil's Knell, **3**:205
Tomb of the Eagles, **3**:262
Tomb of the Unknown Soldier (Tomb of the Unknowns), **3**:24–26, 292–297
Tomb Sweeping Day, **3**:219–220

Tombstone tourism, 3:297–300
Tongan practices: funerals, 3:300–302; mourning color, 3:302; ritual tattooing, 2:272
Tooth dyeing, 2:143–144
Tooth fairy and tooth mouse, 1:324–327
Tooth sharpening, 2:142–143
Tooth Troll (*Hammaspeikko*), 1:325
Tooth-filing ceremony, 2:254, 335–338
Torah, 1:59–62, 281–282, 2:19–20
Totem poles, mortuary, 3:183–185
Totems, 3:117
Totenkopf, 3:170–171
Tourta, 1:65
Tower Hill Memorial, 3:296
Traditional Chinese Medicine (TCM), 1:89, 145–146
Traditional mourning colors, 3:302–306
Training bras (trainer bras, bralettes), 2:338–341
Trick or treating, 3:110
Trinidad, Nine-Nights, 3:196–198
Trobriand Islands, 2:112, 341–344
Trokosi (female ritual servitude), 1:330–333
Trolls, 1:78, 223, 293, 325
Trooping the Colour, 1:43
Trough dance, 2:319
Trows, 1:78, 293. *See also* Trolls
Ts'aal, 1:109
Tsach, 1:109
Tshe dbang (long life) ceremony, 1:323
Tsimshian tribe, 3:184
Tsue shen, 1:90
Tuareg people 2:7
Tuatha de Danann (People of the Goddess Danu), 1:77
Tuj (temascal), 1:333–335
Tumpeng, 1:36
Turkish celebrations and practices: Assyrian betrothal and weddings, 2:9–14; evil eye beads, 1:344; hair removal, 2:112; *halva*, 3:113; *Lohusa Şerbeti*, 1:208–210; Saint Nicholas, 1:294; spitting on babies, 1:316; *Sünnet*, 2:323–325; treatment of the placenta, 1:70. *See also* Middle Eastern celebrations and practices
Turkmenistan, money dance, 2:234

Turning of the Bones, 3:85–87
Tuvalu, ritual tattooing, 2:272
Twelfth Night, 2:44
Twenty-first birthday celebrations, 2:344–345
Two-finger test (TFT), 2:356

Uganda: *engozi*, 3:71; female genital cutting, 2:93; Senior Citizen Grant, 3:231
Ukrainian celebrations and practices: *koliva*, 3:135; love divination, 2:3; money dance, 2:234; parental leave, 1:266; *Pysanka*, 3:66–67, 334; *Śmigus-Dyngus* (Dyngus Day), 2:79–81; treatment of the placenta, 1:70; Ukrainian wreath, 2:353–355; *vinok*, 2:353–355; wedding cakes, 2:370. *See also* Eastern European celebrations and practices
Ukrainian diaspora, 2:15
Ukrainian Orthodox Church, 1:241
Uks-akka (childbirth goddess), 1:5–6
Ukuingishya abanacisungu, 2:53
Ullambana, 3:330
Umbilical cord: burial of, 1:69–70; traditions for cutting, 1:112–114, 130, 210–213; wrapping as keepsake, 1:173–175
Umbilical non-severance, 1:210
Umcwasho, 2:269
Umhlanga, 2:269
Umkhosi woMhlanga, 2:269
Umrah, 2:113
Unguentaria, 3:286
Unification Church, 2:235, 374
United Kingdom celebrations and practices: "Abide With Me," 3:1–3; alkaline hydrolysis, 3:5–6; bees and death, 3:12–13; Beltane, 2:219; birthday traditions, 1:40; blooding, 1:53–54; Blue Peter Badge, 1:54–55; breast ironing, 2:30; breastfeeding, 1:56; candles on birthday cakes, 1:38; cardboard box bed scheme, 1:74; child beauty pageants, 1:80; Children's Laureate, 1:87–89; choosing

Options, 2:56–58; christening customs, 1:32; Christingle, 1:95–96; cremation, 3:42, 44; cutting the umbilical cord, 1:113; eating calabash chalk, 1:71; embalming, 3:73; Father Christmas, 1:296–297; female genital cutting, 2:90; forced marriage, 2:8; funeral songs, 3:97; Gap year, 2:103; Girl Guides, 1:152–153; Groaning Cheese and Groaning Cake, 1:166–169; jazz funerals, 3:127–129; jumping over the broom, 2:163–165; jury duty, 2:165, 167, 168, 170–171; kangaroo care, 1:183; lotus birthing, 1:210; marriage banns, 2:210 –215; Maternity Leave Guide, 1:267–268; Maundy Money, 3:164–167; *Mehndi*, 2:222; menstrual taboos, 2:231; message from the Queen, 3:171–173; Mothering Sunday, 1:230–232; mourning customs, 3:303; Muslim weddings, 2:241; Name Day celebrations, 1:241; nativity plays, 1:245; Nordic napping, 1:250; nursery rhymes, 1:250; pantomime, 1:251–265; parental leave, 1:266; Passion plays, 3:208; Paternity Leave Guide, 1:270–272; pauper's funeral, 3:209–211; pensions, 3:228–230, 234–236; personalized hearses, 3:211–213; Pregnancy and Infant Loss Remembrance Day, 3:216–218; Protestant wedding ceremonies, 2:60; RAG Week, 2:267–268; Remembrance Day, 3:223–226; Remembrance Sunday, 3:152; same-sex marriage, 2:285, 288–291; Scouting movement, 1:152–153, 302–304; silver spoon, 1:313–314; souling, 3:263–264; space burial, 3:267; spontaneous shrines, 3:269; state funerals, 3:272–273; Steiner schools, 1:318, 320; teething superstitions and remedies, 1:327–328; tooth fairy, 1:325; twenty-first birthday, 2:344; University of the Third Age, 3:307; wakes, 3:313; *Waldkindergärten*, 1:341; water births, 1:347; wearing of poppies, 3:314–316; wedding anniversaries, 2:368; wedding customs, 1:32, 2:32–37; wedding dresses, 2:374; wedding ring test, 1:348–349; Wiccan funerals, 3:318; witch balls, 1:357; Zoroastrianism, 3:338. *See also* British celebrations and practices; English celebrations and practices; Irish celebrations and practices; Scottish celebrations and practices; Welsh celebrations and practices

United Nations, on breast ironing, 2:30

United Nations Children's Fund (UNICEF), 1:85, 86, 183, 192, 2:8

United Nations' Convention on the Elimination of All Forms of Discrimination Against Women, 2:8

United Nations' Convention on the Rights of the Child, 2:8

United Nations' Development Fund for Women (UNIFEM), 1:332

United States: Assyrian populations in, 2:10; Hmong immigrants in, 2:137; Polish communities in, 2:80–81

United States celebrations and practices: alkaline hydrolysis, 3:5–6; assisted suicide, 3:12–14; baby racing, 1:21, 22; *Baccalauréat (le bac)*, 2:15–16; bedwetting cures, 1:29–30; birthday customs, 1:40; breastfeeding, 1:56; Buddhist death practices, 3:21; cairns, 3:23; cardboard box bed scheme, 1:74; Changing of the Guard ceremony, 3:24–26; child beauty pageants, 1:80; childhood vaccinations, 1:85; christening gowns, 1:94; condemned prisoner's last meal, 3:37–40; cutting the umbilical cord, 1:113; *Dia de los Muertos*, 3:58–61; eating calabash chalk, 1:71; eating human placenta, 1:123; embalming, 3:73–76; Father's Day, 1:138–139; Girl Guides, 1:152; government-approved baby names, 1:153, 155;

Hindu celebrations, **2**:75; jazz funerals, **3**:127–129; jumping over the broom, **2**:163–165; jury duty, **2**:168, 169–170; kangaroo care, **1**:183; *koliva*, **3**:135; *La Quinceañera*, **2**:177–180; marriage banns, **2**:210; *Mehndi*, **2**:222; Memorial Poppy, **3**:315; menstrual taboos, **2**:231; minute's silence, **3**:174; missing man formation, **3**:178–180; money dance, **2**:234; pantomime, **1**:261; parental leave, **1**:265; Passion plays, **3**:208; Pregnancy and Infant Loss Remembrance Day, **3**:216–218; Protestant wedding ceremonies, **2**:60; purity ball, **2**:264–268; riderless horse, **3**:236–237; ritual tattooing, **2**:272; *Rumspringa*, **2**:277–280; same-sex marriage, **2**:285; Santa Muerte, **3**:246, 249–250; shivaree/chivaree, **2**:257; *Śmigus-Dyngus* (Dyngus Day), **2**:79–81; space burial, **3**:267; spontaneous shrines, **3**:269; state funerals, **3**:273–274; Steiner schools, **1**:320; Sunrise Ceremony, **2**:326–331; swaddling, **1**:321; *Tết Nguyên đan*, **3**:290; tooth fairy, **1**:325–326; training bras, **2**:338–341; Veterans Day, **3**:224; wakes, **3**:313; *Waldkindergärten*, **1**:341; water births, **1**:347; wedding cakes, **2**:371; wedding dresses, **2**:374–375; Wiccan practices, **1**:354, **3**:318; witch balls, **1**:356; Zoroastrianism, **3**:338. *See also* Amish practices; Cajun weddings; North American celebrations and practices

United States Centers for Disease Control and Prevention (CDC), **1**:86

United States Senior Games, **3**:254

Universal minimum pensions, **3**:231

University of the Third Age (U3A), **3**:307–308

Upanayana (Sacred thread ritual), **1**:337–339

Urethral subincision, **2**:347–351

Uruguay, **2**:285, **3**:247. *See also* South American celebrations and practices

Utah, *Holi* celebration in, **2**:75

Uzglavnica, **3**:176

Vaccinations, **1**:85–87, 320

Vado Mori, **3**:52

Vagina festival, **1**:279

Vaginal cutting, **1**:362–363

Valentine's Day, **2**:315–316, 323

Valentines cards, **1**:39

Vanitas, **3**:167–171

Vanuatu: exposure of the corpse, **3**:116; initiation by semen transferal, **2**:148–152; land diving competitions (*Gol, Nanggol, Nagol, N'gol*), **2**:183–186

Vatertag, **1**:139–140

Venezuela: eating the ashes of the dead, **3**:67–70; polyandry, **2**:258, 259. *See also* South American celebrations and practices

Vesak (Wesak), **1**:43

Veterans Day, **3**:224

Via Dolorosa, **3**:275–277

Victorian Era practices: baby showers, **1**:23; birthday parties, **1**:273; christening gowns, **1**:94; Christmas celebrations, **1**:297, 304–305; *dragées*, **1**:32; fairytales, **1**:135; Kissing Friday, **2**:80; lovespoons, **2**:202; mourning customs, **3**:302–303; national mourning, **3**:191; obituaries, **3**:199; pauper's funeral, **3**:209–210; wedding ring test, **1**:348; wedding superstitions originating in, **2**:33; writing of condolences, **3**:40–41

Victoriana, **3**:100

Vietnamese celebrations and practices: *Giao Thea*, **3**:290–291; Hmong names, **2**:136; mother roasting, **1**:228; New Year celebration, **3**:288; placenta in folk medicine, **1**:124; Tan Nien, **3**:291–292; *Tết Nguyên đan*, **3**:288–292; tooth sharpening, **2**:143. *See also* Southeast Asian celebrations and practices

Vigils, **3**:105–106

Vinok (Ukrainian wreath), **2**:353–355
Virgin Mary, **1**:45, 51, 64, 98–99, 203, 217–218, 242, 244, 251, 314, 326, 344, **2**:43, 178, **3**:9, 161, 207, 208
Virgin of Guadalupe, **2**:186
Virginity testing, **2**:72, 355–358; handkerchief test, **2**:357; two-finger test (TFT), **2**:356
Virgins' Crowns, **3**:161
Virgins' Garlands, **3**:161
Vision quest (vision fast), **2**:358–361
Visiting-girls courtship tradition, **2**:360–364
Vizbevető, **2**:79
Vlechugane (Haulage of the Midwife), **1**:19
Volkstrauertag (People's Day of Mourning), **3**:225
Voodoo death traditions, **3**:335–338
Vrindavan, **3**:309–311
Vrubnitsa, **2**:184

Wagner, Richard, **2**:380
"Wailing funeral," **3**:3–4
Wakes, **3**:31–32, 36, 54, 92, 106, 124–125, 139, 158–159, 196–197, 238, 261, 300, 313–314, 337
Walbiri people, **2**:249
Waldkindergärten, **1**:341–342
Waldorf schools, **1**:8, 318
Walkabout, **2**:365–367
Walking marriages, **2**:391–393
Walpurgisnacht (Walpurgis Night), **1**:217
Wandervogel, **2**:298
War dead, wearing flowers to honor, **3**:314–318
Wari people, **3**:78–79
Washing: of bride and groom, **2**:28; of the corpse, **3**:189, 258; of relics, **3**:243–244; ritual, **2**:72. *See also* Bathing
Wassailing, **2**:44
Water birth, **1**:346–348
Water children, **3**:181
Water: used for Amrit Sanchar, **2**:70; used for baptism, **1**:26–29; symbolism of, **3**:181
Waxing, **2**:112
Weaning, **1**:275–277

Wearing flowers to honor war dead, **3**:314–318
Weather balloons, ashes inside, **3**:268
Wechselbalg, **1**:77
Wedding anniversaries, **1**:32, **2**:367–369
Wedding cakes, **1**:317, **2**:35–36, 48, 369–373
Wedding dresses (wedding gowns), **2**:373–375
Wedding march and Bridal Chorus, **2**:379–381
Wedding receptions, **2**:35; Bulgarian, **2**:39; Jewish, **2**:162
Wedding ring test, **1**:348–349
Wedding rings, **2**:12, 39, 60, 94, 123–124, 375–376
Wedding traditions and customs: Afghani, **2**:1–3; Assyrian, **2**:9–14; besom weddings, **2**:163; blackening, **2**:28; bride-price, **2**:195–197; British, **2**:32–37; Bulgarian, **2**:37–41, 182–183; Cajun, **2**:47–49; chimneysweeps, **2**:33; Chinese, **2**:51; Christian, **2**:58–61; cutting the groom's socks, **2**:320; food, **2**:2, 263–264; French, **2**:180–181; German, **2**:254–258; Hindu, **2**:133–136, 222; horseshoes, **2**:142; Japanese, **2**:291–293; Jewish, **2**:159–162, 222; Latino, **2**:234–235; *Mehndi*, **2**:222; mock weddings, **1**:18–19; Moonie weddings, **2**:235–237; Moroccan, **2**:237–240; Muslim, **2**:40, 222, 241–242; music, **2**:379–381; piñatas, **1**:284; popular locations, **2**:104–105; Saami, **1**:6–7; Sikh, **2**:312–315; Sisters' Meal Festival, **2**:317–318; solo weddings, **2**:316; superstitions, **2**:374; Trobriand Islands, **2**:342–344. *See also* Marriages; Wedding cakes; Wedding receptions; Wedding rings
Wee Bell Ceremony, **1**:352
Weihnachtsmärchen, **1**:261, 349–350
Welsh celebrations and practices: birth trees, **1**:34; burying biscuits, **3**:93; choosing Options, **2**:56–58; forced

marriage, **2**:8; funeral plants, **3**:96; handfasting, **2**:117–118; lovespoons, **2**:201–203; pauper's funerals, **3**:211; same-sex marriage, **2**:285; souling, **3**:264; St. Dwynwen's Day, **2**:322–323; wedding traditions, **2**:32; yew trees, **3**:327

West African practices, **1**:1, 71. *See also* Africa; Benin, Burkina Faso; Côte d'Ivoire; Gambia; Ghana; Guinea; Guinea Bissau; Mali; Niger; Nigeria; Senegal; Sierra Leone; Togo

Western Europe, **2**:112. *See also* European celebrations and practices; *individual Western European countries by name*

Wet Monday (*lany poniedzalek*), **2**:79

Wetting the baby's head, **1**:350–351

Whistling, as courtship communication, **2**:64–66

Whitby Goth Weekend (WGW), **3**:101

Whitby jet, **3**:286–287

White coat ceremony, **2**:381–382

White Day, **2**:315–316

White Poppy Appeal, **3**:316

Whuppity Scoorie, **1**:351–353

Wiccan celebrations and practices: British weddings, **2**:32; croning ceremonies, **3**:44–46; handfasting, **2**:117–118; handparting, **2**:127–128; Wiccaning, **1**:353–355. *See also* Wiccan funerals

Wiccan funerals, **3**:318–322; *Book of Shadows*, **3**:318–319; for an elderly woman, **3**:321–322; graveside, **3**:319–320

Wife carrying, competitive, **2**:35

Wigs made from ancestors' hair, **2**:138

Wik-Mungkan (Wik-Mungknh) naming ceremony, **1**:355–356

Windmills, **3**:323–325

Witch balls, **1**:344, 356–357

Witchcraft, **1**:5, 293, **2**:12

Wodaabe courtship dance and festival, **2**:383–386

Wogeo tribe, **2**:349–350

Women: blessing after childbirth, **1**:98–100; bodily functions of, **1**:6; breast ironing as crime against, **2**:30; celebration of mothers, **1**:306; as Chelsea pensioners, **3**:28; forehead scars, **2**:99, 100; hair removal, **2**:111–113; head covering, **2**:128–130; henna night for, **2**:2; Muslim dress practices, **2**:128–130; ordination of, **3**:311; postpartum confinement, **1**:65, 188, 229, 334, 361–362; postpartum recovery, **1**:197–198, 228–230; pre-delivery confinement, **1**:166; rights of, **2**:261, **3**:310; rituals after childbirth, **1**:130–131, 165; seclusion of during menstruation and pregnancy, **1**:129, **2**:225–226, 229–230; at the *shirin-i-griftan*, **2**:2; subjugation of, **2**:262; violence against, **2**:66, 247–248; wearing Sikh turbans, **2**:69; widows, **3**:309–311. *See also* Breastfeeding; Menstrual customs; Menstrual taboos; Menstruation; Pregnant women

Women and Law in Southern Africa (WLSA), **2**:271

Women's rights, **2**:261, **3**:310

World Association of Girl Guides and Girl Scouts (WAGGGS), **1**:151, 302

World Food Programme, **1**:146

World Health Organization (WHO), **1**:55–56, 85, 86, 183, 275, **2**:91, 355, 357

World Masters Games, **3**:254

World Organization of the Scout Movement (WOSM), **1**:302. *See also* Scouts and Scouting

World Veterans Games, **3**:254

Worry dolls, **1**:357–358

Wrapping umbilical cord as keepsake (*Hesono-o*), **1**:173–175

Wuwsimtungwni ceremony, **1**:180

Wysoccan rite of manhood, **2**:359

Xhosa people, **3**:90; circumcision, **2**:387–389

Yam festival, **2**:341–342

Yamadashi, **2**:198

Yang phai, **1**:229

Yankan Gishiri, **1**:362–363

Yanomamö people, **2**:258

Yanomani people, **3**:67–69
Yellamma (fertility), **1**:117
Yemen, **2**:90
Yentas, **2**:159
Yew trees, **3**:327–329
Yoga, pregnancy, **1**:289–290
Yoruba tribe, **1**:68–69, 113, **2**:234, **3**:128
Yorubaland, ritual servitude in, **1**:331
Young British Artists (YBAs), **3**:169–170
Yu char kuei, **1**:93
Yu Lan Jie, **3**:329–332
Yugoslav countries, **2**:234. *See also* Bosnia and Herzegovina; Croatian celebrations and practices; Eastern European celebrations and practices; Kosovo; Macedonia; Montenegro; Serbian celebrations and practices; Slovenia
Yulanpen Festival, **3**:329
Yule logs, **2**:45
Yuletide traditions, **1**:293. *See also* Christmas celebrations

Zaduszki (dzień zaduszny), **3**:333–335
Zaire. *See* Democratic Republic of Congo
Zambian celebrations and practices: *Chisungu*, **2**:52–55; cutting the umbilical cord, **1**:112–113; *Nachisungu*, **2**:52–53; Social Cash Transfer Programme, **3**:231; *ukuingishya abanacisungu*, **2**:53
Zen Buddhism, **3**:18. *See also* Buddhism
Zenkoku Nakodo Rengokai, **2**:251–252
Zhongyuan Festival, **3**:329
Zhuazhou, **1**:93
Zimbabwe: *Pika* and *Nora*, **2**:253. *See also* Sub-Saharan African celebrations and practices
Zionism, **1**:62
Zo'e people, **2**:192
Zodiac constellations and signs, **1**:42, 44–45, 354; Chinese, **1**:233, 310–311, **2**:30
Zombie apocalypse, **3**:336
Zombies, **3**:335–338
Zoroastran practices: funerals, **3**:338–341; initiation, **1**:246–249
Zou hun, **2**:391–393
Zulu clans: midwives, **1**:112; Reed Dancing Chastity Ceremony, **2**:269–271; virginity testing, **2**:356–357
Zuo yuezi (sitting the month) **1**:92, 226, 361–362
Zur-zur (zur zur; zurzur), **1**:362–363

About the Author

Victoria Williams, PhD, is an independent writer and researcher living in London. She is author of ABC-CLIO's *Weird Sports and Wacky Games around the World: From Buzkashi to Zorbing* and has written on a variety of subjects, including Hollywood film (for ABC-CLIO's *Movies in American History: An Encyclopedia*), human sacrifice, and Mesoamerican mythology (for ABC-CLIO's *Conflict in the Early Americas*), British folk customs (for ABC-CLIO's *They Do What? A Cultural Encyclopedia of Extraordinary and Exotic Customs from around the World*), and other topics. Williams wrote her doctoral thesis (King's College, London) on European fairy tales in 19th-century British art and literature and on film, with special reference to the Brothers Grimm.